## SELECTED PHYSICAL QUANTITIES AND MEASUREMENT UNITS

| Physical quantity | Quantity symbol | Measurement unit | Unit symbol | Unit dimensions |
|---|---|---|---|---|
| | | *Fundamental Units* | | |
| length | $l$ | meter | m | m |
| mass | $m$ | kilogram | kg | kg |
| time | $t$ | second | s | s |
| electric charge | $Q$ | coulomb | c | c |
| temperature | $T$ | degree Kelvin | °K | °K |
| luminous intensity | $I$ | candle | cd | cd |
| | | | | |
| | | *Derived Units* | | |
| acceleration | $a$ | meter per second per second | m/s$^2$ | m/s$^2$ |
| area | $A$ | square meter | m$^2$ | m$^2$ |
| capacitance | $C$ | farad | f | c$^2$ s$^2$/kg m$^2$ |
| density | $D$ | kilogram per cubic meter | kg/m$^3$ | kg/m$^3$ |
| electric current | $I$ | ampere | a | c/s |
| electric field intensity | $\mathscr{E}$ | newton per coulomb | n/c | kg m/c s$^2$ |
| electric resistance | $R$ | ohm | $\Omega$ | kg m$^2$/c$^2$ s |
| emf | $E$ | volt | v | kg m$^2$/c s$^2$ |
| energy | $E$ | joule | j | kg m$^2$/s$^2$ |
| force | $F$ | newton | n | kg m/s$^2$ |
| frequency | $f$ | hertz | hz | s$^{-1}$ |
| heat | $Q$ | joule | j | kg m$^2$/s$^2$ |
| illumination | $E$ | lumen per square meter | lm/m$^2$ | cd/m$^2$ |
| inductance | $L$ | henry | h | kg m$^2$/c$^2$ |
| luminous flux | $\Phi$ | lumen | lm | cd |
| magnetic flux | $\Phi$ | weber | wb | kg m$^2$/c s |
| magnetic flux density | $B$ | weber per square meter | wb/m$^2$ | kg/c s |
| potential difference | $V$ | volt | v | kg m$^2$/c s$^2$ |
| power | $P$ | watt | w | kg m$^2$/s$^3$ |
| pressure | $p$ | newton per square meter | n/m$^2$ | kg/m s$^2$ |
| velocity | $v$ | meter per second | m/s | m/s |
| volume | $V$ | cubic meter | m$^3$ | m$^3$ |
| work | $W$ | joule | j | kg m$^2$/s$^2$ |

# The Holt Modern Physics Program

**WILLIAMS** · **TRINKLEIN** · **METCALFE**

**Modern Physics** (Student Text)
**Modern Physics** (Teacher's Edition)
**Laboratory Experiments in Physics**
**Exercises and Experiments in Physics**
**Tests in Physics** (duplicating masters)

JOHN E. WILLIAMS
FREDERICK E. TRINKLEIN
H. CLARK METCALFE

# modern physics

HOLT, RINEHART AND WINSTON, PUBLISHERS
New York • Toronto • London • Sydney

**JOHN E. WILLIAMS,** 2947 Java Road, Costa Mesa, California 92626; formerly physics and chemistry teacher at Newport Harbor High School, Newport Beach, California; and Head of the Science Department, Broad Ripple High School, Indianapolis, Indiana.

**FREDERICK E. TRINKLEIN,** 131 Brookville Road, Brookville, New York 11545; Dean of Faculty and physics teacher, Long Island Lutheran High School, Brookville, New York; and Adjunct Professor, Physical Science Department, Nassau Community College, Garden City, New York.

**H. CLARK METCALFE,** P. O. Box V2, Wickenburg, Arizona 85358; formerly chemistry teacher at Winchester-Thurston School, Pittsburgh, Pennsylvania; and Head of the Science Department, Wilkinsburg Senior High School, Wilkinsburg, Pennsylvania.

*Editorial Development*   William N. Moore, Roland J. Cormier, Pamela Hirschfeld
*Editorial Processing*   Margaret M. Byrne, Richard D. Sime
*Art, Production, and Photo Resources*   Vivian Fenster, Fred C. Pusterla, Robin Swenson
*Product Manager*   John W. M. Cooke
*Advisory Board*   John Taggart, Maurice E. Fey, Norman Hughes, David J. Miller, John W. Griffiths, William L. Paul
*Consultant*   John Matejowsky
*Researchers*   Pamela Floch, Gerard LaVan

The cover design of MODERN PHYSICS 1980 is a photograph of an experimental magnetic bubble lattice device, courtesy of the International Business Machines Corporation, Research Division. A detailed explanation appears on page 682.

Picture credits appear on page 680.

ISBN: 0-03-048726-9

4  039  9 8 7

# Preface

MODERN PHYSICS 1980 is the latest revision of a physics textbook first published in 1922. The many editions of MODERN PHYSICS have served more teachers and students than any other introductory physics text published in the United States. As with previous revisions, the aim of this edition is to increase its effectiveness with a changing population of teachers and students.

The basic concepts of physics are presented in a logical sequence believed to be the most productive for beginning students. Every effort has been made to present these concepts with such directness and simplicity that each student will achieve maximum comprehension. The organization of the text and the thoroughly understandable prose are designed to meet the requirements of today's physics students.

MODERN PHYSICS 1980 strikes a realistic balance between theory and practical application. College requirements are fully met. At the same time, the wide variety of topics gives teachers great flexibility in selecting appropriate subjects for students with varied interests and abilities.

The authors believe that an effective presentation of physics must be based on a rigorous treatment of mechanics. Thus, these fundamental concepts are developed early in the book. The introductory chapter has been revised to speak more directly to students. Measurement and problem-solving techniques are presented in the second chapter. Because mathematics is the language of physics, an adequate preparation in algebra and geometry is an essential prerequisite. The elementary trigonometry necessary for some problem solving is presented in the text where required.

The kinematics and dynamics chapters have been retained as reorganized and rewritten in the 1976 edition. The presentation of force and the actions of balanced and unbalanced forces follow the description of motion. Thus, the student has the advantage of having studied Newton's laws of motion before dealing with the topic of unbalanced forces.

The chapters on thermal effects, heat, and work have been reorganized to make the sequence of topics more effective. Similarly, the chapters on alternating currents, electronic devices, and high-energy physics have been extensively reorganized and rewritten. A serious effort has been made throughout the text to lower the functional vocabulary and to improve readability.

The International System of Units (SI) is used throughout MODERN PHYSICS, with minor exceptions where modifications are deemed appropriate for beginning students. The techniques of dimensional analysis are emphasized in all quantitative work. Furthermore, the derivation of each measurement concept is traced back to fundamental units. Such careful attention to the dimensional character of measurements throughout the book helps to unify the whole structure of physics.

A single-column format, adopted in the 1972 edition of MODERN PHYSICS, has been retained in this revision. Wide margins allow for flexible treatment of both textual and illustrative materials. *Marginal notes* are strategically placed throughout the text to reinforce important concepts, to provide supplementary information, and to assist students in developing productive study techniques. New terms, definitions, and principles are printed in *italic* and **boldface** type for emphasis and rapid review. Example problems with step-by-step solutions are used to illustrate important quantitative relationships and to ensure student comprehension of pertinent concepts.

Chapters generally are divided into major subdivisions. Question and problem sets are placed at the end of each subdivision to provide a liberal number and variety of exercises at frequent intervals throughout the book. The questions and problems are graded and differentiated as Group A and Group B. The A sets are constructed as essential drill exercises for *all* students. Vector analysis problems in these sets are limited to right triangles. The B sets are more difficult and challenging, and they provide for individual and group differences. Vector analysis problems in these sets include non-right triangles, which require more sophisticated solutions. Numbered sections within each chapter are identified by both chapter and section numbers for easy reference. For example, Section 4 of Chapter 10 is designated by the number 10.4, and it is referred to in other parts of the text as Section 10.4. Each chapter concludes with a Summary, which is a brief review of the major concepts presented in the chapter.

Color has been used wherever it aids understanding and has functional value. Three-dimensional effects are used in diagrams where pertinent. An eight-page, full-color insert of photographs and line drawings has been included between pages 332 and 333. Six Photo Essays appear in this edition. These essays provide supplementary information on relevant applications and frontiers of physics in a pictorial mode.

A *Mathematics Refresher* section precedes the Appendixes. This section briefly reviews the mathematical skills required for successful problem solving. *Appendix A* lists important equations presented in the sequence in which they appear in the text. *Appendix B* includes twenty-four tables of useful data, including a table of trigonometric functions and a table of logarithms. A *Glossary* of technical terms follows Appendix B.

The authors are especially indebted to Dr. Roger W. Clapp, Jr., Associate Professor of Physics, University of South Florida, Tampa; and Dr. F. Glenn Liming, Curriculum Head for Solar Energy, Southwestern Technical Institute, Sylva, NC, who critically reviewed the 1976 edition of MODERN PHYSICS. Their many valuable suggestions and criticisms were greatly appreciated. The authors also wish to express their gratitude for the valuable suggestions and comments provided by Mr. Dean M. Hurd, physics teacher at Canyon High School, Saugus, California, who prepared the *Teacher's Edition* Commentary for this edition of MODERN PHYSICS.

John E. Williams,
Frederick E. Trinklein,
H. Clark Metcalfe

# Contents

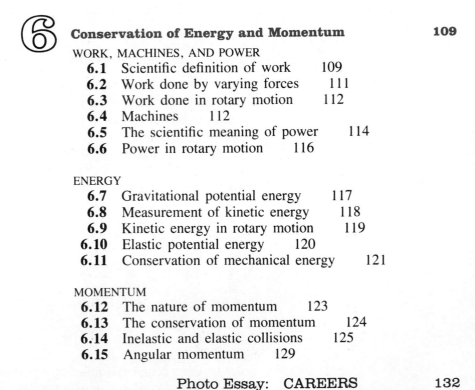

## 11    Sound Waves         231

## 12    The Nature of Light         258

## 15 Diffraction and Polarization                    334

## 16 Electrostatics                    354

## 17 Direct-Current Circuits 381

## 18 Heating and Chemical Effects 418

## 19 Magnetic Effects 433

## 20   Electromagnetic Induction                    457

## 21   Alternating-Current Circuits                 489

**22**

**23**

# 1

# Physics:
# The Science of Energy

## SCIENCE IN TODAY'S WORLD

Modern civilization would be impossible without large quantities of energy. Since 1940 energy usage in the United States has increased more than 400% while the accompanying population increase has been only about 75%. Thus the use of energy by each person in the United States has increased at a very fast rate.

Until recently, the world's energy demands were met almost entirely through the use of fossil fuels: wood, coal, petroleum,

### 1.1 The energy problem

| | Water | Wood | Oil and gas | Coal | Nuclear |
|---|---|---|---|---|---|
| 1976 | 0.781 | | 13.9 | 3.45 | 0.504 |
| 1970 | 0.680 | | 13.0 | 3.20 | 0.050 |
| 1960 | 0.428 | | 8.26 | 2.55 | |
| 1950 | 0.353 | 0.277 | 4.79 | 3.15 | |
| 1940 | 0.227 | 0.332 | 2.57 | 3.15 | |

**Figure 1-1** Energy production in the United States. The graph shows, in calories x $10^{15}$, the changing amounts of energy that have been obtained from various fuels since 1940.

and natural gas. Since these are limited in quantity, however, other sources must be found. Nuclear and solar energy are two alternate sources, and neither of them is limited. It has been calculated, for instance, that the energy demands of the whole world could be met by converting the solar energy falling on a 125-mile square plot of ground near the equator. At the present time, however, nuclear and solar energy make up only a small fraction of the total energy used. See the graph of energy usage shown in Figure 1-1. As our knowledge and means of converting these ample energy supplies into usable forms increase, we shall be better able to keep pace with rising energy needs. However, it will take more than just the efforts of science to solve the energy problem. Fuel conservation by all segments of the population must accompany new scientific advances.

*To prevent the interruption of solar energy at night time and during cloudy weather, huge solar satellites have been proposed.*

*The energy shortage and other world problems can be solved only if people in all specialties work together on them.*

## 1.2 Science and technology

Finding new energy sources falls into the realm of science. Developing and utilizing these discoveries are matters of technology. Briefly stated, *science* is the search for relationships that explain and predict the behavior of the observable universe. *Technology* is the application of these relationships to our needs and goals.

The complementary work of scientists and technologists is also referred to, respectively, as *research* and *development*. Both government and private industry allocate large sums of money to support the research and development activities of scientists and engineers. Without such support, there would be little improvement in the processes, products, and services that are derived from these activities.

A good example of the cooperative effort between science and technology is the miniaturized computer. At the heart of this amazing device is a tiny chip, such as the one shown in Figure 1-2, that contains thousands of transistors. This tiny chip has the calculating capacity of a vacuum tube computer that, twenty-five years ago, would have needed the space of an entire room.

One application of the miniaturized computer is the supermarket electronic checkout. This system reads and records the names and prices of items labeled with the Universal Product Code (UPC). This code, a series of black lines underscored by numbers, is read by a laser beam scanner and the coded information is relayed to the store's computer. This coded information is processed by the computer, which then displays the product's name and price and provides an itemized receipt. While it is recording each purchase, the computer is also checking the store's inventory for reordering purposes.

Computer-assisted instruction demonstrates the application of computers in the field of education. Individualized instruction in any subject is available to the student. The student retrieves the

**Figure 1-2** Magnified view of a modern computer chip containing hundreds of transistors. Here the chip is shown in comparison to the size of a paper clip.

*A system called PLATO (Programmed Logic for Automatic Teaching Operations) allows the student to ''converse'' with a computer by means of a typewriter and a TV screen.*

stored information and then converses with the computer by means of a typewriter or television screen.

In banks computers already handle most of the thirty-five billion checks Americans write each year. In hospitals computers are used to analyze the medical histories and symptoms of patients as well as to detect and monitor their ailments. A computer program can order prescriptions and alert nurses to administer them at the right time and in the right dosage. A major medical advance is the use of the computer to assemble thousands of X rays of any part of the body into a single, two-dimensional view as shown in Figure 1-3.

In the home computer devices may someday be as commonplace as the kitchen sink. When mass production and new technology bring the cost within reach of most budgets, routine chores of all kinds can be handled quickly and accurately by the computer chip. In cars computers can automatically apply the brakes, determine gas mileage, and check the oil and tire pressure; a miniradar can warn the driver of impending collisions.

Many applications of computers still await discovery. Today's high school students, who have grown up in our highly technological society, can meet this challenge as they become the engineers and scientists of the future.

**Figure 1-3** Computerized axial tomography. Cross-sectional views of the head and chest cavity are obtained from the computer assembly of tens of thousands of X-ray readings.

## 1.3 Scientific laws and theories

In science *a law (or principle) is a statement that describes a natural phenomenon.* Unlike laws that *restrict* behavior (i.e., traffic laws), scientific laws *describe* behavior. For example, Jacques Charles (1746–1823) observed, under certain controlled conditions, a relationship between the temperature and the volume of most gases. This regular behavior of gases, which you will study in greater detail in Chapter 8, is now known as Charles' law. A scientific law may be stated in words. However, in physics a law is usually expressed by a mathematical equation relating the natural phenomenon to the various factors that cause it.

*"Principle" sounds less absolute than "law."*

*A **theory** is a reasonable explanation of a series of observed phenomena.* A theory often involves an imaginary *model* that helps scientists picture the way an observed phenomenon could be produced. A good example of this is our modern atomic theory, which you will study in Chapters 7, 23, 24, and 25. Another example is the kinetic molecular theory. In this theory gases are pictured as being made up of many small particles called molecules that are in constant motion (kinetic). You will study the kinetic molecular theory in Chapter 7.

*A scientific law describes a natural phenomenon. A theory is a reasonable explanation of a series of phenomena.*

A useful theory, in addition to explaining past observations, serves to predict behavior that has not as yet been observed. After a theory has been publicized, scientists design experiments to test the theory. For example, if matter is composed of small particles called atoms, it should behave in a certain way. If observations confirm the scientists' predictions, the theory is supported. If observations do not confirm the predictions, the scientists must search further. There may be a fault in the experiment, or the theory may have to be revised or rejected.

## 1.4 Scientific hypotheses

Albert Einstein (1879–1955) was one of the greatest theoretical scientists of all time. Theoretical scientists work mostly with ideas. They use the results of other scientists' observations to develop their theories. Einstein's theories and predictions changed the course of modern science. Once he was asked to explain the way in which a scientist works. "If you want to know the essence of scientific method," he said, "don't listen to what a scientist may tell you. Watch what he does."

Science is a way of doing things, a way that involves imagination and creative thinking as well as collecting information and performing experiments. Facts (observations, principles, laws, and theories) by themselves are not science, but science deals with facts. The mathematician Jules Henri Poincaré (1854–1912) said: "Science is built with facts just as a house is built with bricks, but a collection of facts cannot be called a science any more than a pile of bricks can be called a house."

Most scientists start an investigation by finding out what other scientists have learned about the problem. After the known facts have been gathered, the scientist comes to the part of the investigation that requires considerable imagination. Possible solutions to the problem are formulated. These possible solutions are called **hypotheses**.

*A hypothesis is a possible solution to a problem.*

For example, at the time of Johannes Kepler (1571–1630), most scientists believed that the planets move in circular orbits. But the observed movements of the planets could not be satisfactorily explained by circular orbits. So Kepler formulated other hypotheses to explain planetary motion. The one that best fit the observations was: All the planets have elliptic orbits.

In a way, any hypothesis is a leap into the unknown. It extends

**Figure 1-4** ORMAK, a fusion research device, is operated at the Department of Energy's National Laboratory at Oak Ridge, Tennessee. ORMAK uses a magnetic system to contain the fusion plasma. The ability to fuse certain atoms could provide a future source of energy that is safe, economical, and almost limitless.

the scientist's thinking beyond the known facts. The scientist plans experiments, calculations, and observations to test hypotheses. For without hypotheses, further investigation lacks purpose and direction. In the case of Kepler, he continued his observations and calculations over a period of ten years after the announcement of his hypothesis about elliptic orbits. Eventually he was able to relate, in the form of an equation, the time required for one orbit of a planet with its distance from the sun.

When hypotheses are confirmed, they are incorporated into theories or laws. Thus Kepler's hypotheses have become parts of what are now known as Kepler's laws of planetary motion.

The scientist's laboratory is any place where an investigation can be conducted. To the astronomer the starry skies are a laboratory. The biologist may do experimental work in a swamp or an ocean. The physicist and chemist are often surrounded by a maze of apparatus housed in buildings designed specifically for their purposes, as you see in Figure 1-4.

## 1.5 Certainty in science

In a sense, there is no such thing as absolute truth in science. The validity of a scientific conclusion is always limited by the method of observation and, to a certain extent, by the person who made it. If a nurse took a patient's temperature with a thermometer that read 1° too high, the physicians might reach an incorrect conclusion about the condition of the patient. Scientists should keep in mind that the validity of their findings is limited by the precision of the apparatus used. Furthermore, not all limits are apparent to the experimenter. Galileo once tried to use lanterns to measure the speed of light between two distant points. It turned out that the time required to uncover and cover the lanterns was greater than the time required for light to travel the distance between them. His results were inconclusive.

*Do you think it is frustrating to deal with scientific uncertainties?*

This problem makes it doubly important to keep an open mind about the validity of scientific principles, theories, or hypotheses. A single crucial experiment can disprove any of them; but no amount of experimentation can ever prove any one of them absolutely. When a scientist is unwilling to question a statement in science, no matter how well established it is, that scientist has lost a very important attribute of a successful researcher. For this reason the famous physicist Niels Bohr (1885–1962) told his classes: "Every sentence I utter must be understood not as an affirmation but as a question."

The methods of science have been so successful in answering questions about the universe and in making life more pleasant and productive that it has been proposed that all areas of study make use of the methods that scientists have found successful. This proposal suggests that the attitudes necessary for successful work in science could bear fruit in other areas as well. Among these attitudes are imagination, a thirst for knowledge and understanding, a regard for data and their meaning, the demand for proof, a respect for logical thinking, patience in reaching conclusions, and the willingness to work with new ideas.

# questions

GROUP A

1. What are the disadvantages of using fossil fuels as energy sources?

2. List as many present and future applications of computers as you can. Compile a class list for the bulletin board and check it periodically to see whether any future applications become present ones during the school year.

3. What is meant by a theory?

4. (a) Define the term "laboratory." (b) How does your school's physics laboratory fit this definition?

5. Distinguish between science and technology.

GROUP B

6. List areas and decisions in your life that cannot be dealt with according to scientific methods. See if your classmates agree with your list.

7. Bring a UPC-marked item to class and compare it with those of your classmates for similarities and differences. Offer some explanations on the meaning of the lines and numbers.

8. Edison once said: "Genius is 1% inspiration and 99% perspiration." Explain this remark in terms of the work of scientists and technologists.

9. How does the work of Kepler illustrate the scientific method?

10. How does a hypothesis become part of a law?

11. Define the term "truth" as it relates to science.

12. Name the Nobel prize winners in physics for the past five years and list the contribution for which each of them received the prize.

# THE CONTENT OF PHYSICS

The best way to gain a concept of matter is to work with it and to describe its various forms. A description is not a definition in the real sense of the word, but it helps to bring an abstract idea down to familiar terms.

Matter can be described in terms of its measurable properties. In describing a person, you might refer to height, weight, eye color, hair color, etc. Similarly, all matter possesses properties. And just as a person can be identified by listing various characteristics, so a specimen of matter can be singled out by listing its properties.

The number of properties that can be measured for specimens of matter is very large. Entire handbooks of chemistry and physics are devoted to listings of the properties of various kinds of matter.

In the study of physics it is important to recognize the fact that unless a property can be measured and compared with some kind of standard it is of limited use to the scientist. Without measurement there can be no science.

## 1.6 Matter

*Words cannot fully describe a concept.*

A basic property of matter is its *mass*. **Mass can be defined as a measure of the quantity of matter in an object.** Mass measurements are based on the standard kilogram mass, which is kept in a special vault by the International Bureau of Standards in Sèvres, France (near Paris). Duplicates of this standard, such as the one shown in Figure 1-5, are stored in various places around the world, including the National Bureau of Standards near Washington, D.C.

But how does one determine the mass of an object? Is a comparison of size with the standard mass sufficient? Two objects may have the same apparent size, yet one may contain more hollow spaces, and thus less matter. Even if no holes can be seen, an object might simply have more matter within a space of the same size. A piece of brass and a piece of gold may have the same size and appearance, but they differ in mass.

## 1.7 Mass

**Figure 1-5** The United States duplicate of the standard kilogram mass is kept at the National Bureau of Standards near Washington, D.C.

We have just seen that size is of no value in determining the mass of an object. But scientists have found another property of matter that can be used—namely, the inertia of an object. *Inertia is the property of matter that opposes any change in its state of motion.* Inertia shows itself when objects are standing still as well as when they are moving. A baseball resting on the ground will not start moving by itself. A baseball in flight will keep moving unless something stops it. This does not mean that there are two kinds of inertia—a stationary kind and a moving kind; the same property of matter is merely showing itself in different circumstances.

## 1.8 Inertia

*Mass: the amount of matter in an object.*
*Inertia: a property of matter that resists a change in its state of motion.*

**Figure 1-6** An inertia balance, as viewed from above. When this instrument is set in horizontal motion (right), the period of vibration can be used to compare the magnitudes of masses attached to it.

The inertia of matter can be used to measure mass with a device called an inertia balance, shown in Figure 1-6. One end of the balance is clamped to a table. The pan on the other end can be made to vibrate horizontally. The number of times this device vibrates in a second of time depends upon the length and stiffness of the two supporting metal blades and upon the total mass of the pan and any objects placed on it. Since the blades vibrate horizontally, the action of the inertia balance is entirely independent of gravity, which acts vertically. The more massive the pan and its contents, the slower will be the changes in their motion and the longer will be the time they will take to go through a complete vibration. The time required for a single vibration is called the *period*.

*Period and time are reciprocals.*

Unknown masses can be measured by comparing their periods with the periods of objects having known masses. First, several of the known objects are used and their periods are plotted as functions of their masses, as shown in Figure 1-7. Then the period of an unknown object is measured and its mass is read from the graph.

The graph in Figure 1-7 is not a straight line. But by careful analysis of the data the relationship can be expressed by the following equation:

**Figure 1-7** Graph of inertia balance data. If the period of an object is measured, this graph can be used to find the mass of the object fastened to the pan.

$$\frac{m_1}{m_2} = \frac{T_1{}^2}{T_2{}^2}$$

in which $m_1$ and $m_2$ are two masses (*including* the mass of the pan in each case) and $T_1$ and $T_2$ are their respective periods.

Masses can also be compared using either a spring balance or a platform balance, as shown in Figure 1-8. For comparing masses, these devices depend upon the pull of the earth's gravity. The stretch of a spring depends upon the amount of pull on the spring. The greater the pull, the greater is the amount of stretch. Since the pull of gravity is greater on a large mass than it is on a small mass, the spring in a spring balance stretches farther for a

**Figure 1-8**  A spring balance (left) and a platform balance (right). Both instruments are used to compare masses.

large mass than it does for a small mass. The amount of stretch for standard masses can be marked on a scale. The stretch for an unknown mass can then be compared with the stretch produced by the standard mass.

In the case of a platform balance, a uniform beam is balanced at its center on a sharp blade. The blade acts as a pivot. If a mass is added to either side of the beam, the beam tips. Platforms of equal masses are placed on the beam at equal distances from the pivot. If an unknown mass is placed on one platform (usually the left one), known masses can be added to the other platform until the beam again balances. At that point, the known and the unknown masses are equal.

Now that we have discussed two important properties of matter, we can use these properties to define matter. *Matter is anything that has the properties of mass and inertia.*

## 1.9 Mass density

A property of matter that is closely related to mass is *mass density*. *Mass density* refers to the amount of matter in a given amount of space and is defined as the *mass per unit volume of a substance*. Thus if a substance has a mass of 45 g and occupies a space of 15 cm³, its mass density is 3.0 g/cm³. The mathematical equation is:

$$mass\ density = \frac{mass}{volume}$$

*Volume: quantity of space occupied by a substance, measured in cubic units of length.*

In giving the mass density of a substance, it is important to include the units (kilograms per cubic meter, grams per cubic centimeter, or some other unit of mass per unit of volume) in order that it may be compared with other values of mass densities. Mass density is an important quantity in describing or determining the substance of which an object is composed.

Mass density is a property that varies with the environment. The mass density of a gas increases when the gas is placed under pressure and decreases when the pressure is reduced. Such quantities as pressure and temperature, which describe the environment of an object, are called *conditions*. Very often a measurable property of an object will change if the conditions are changed.

*Some stars have mass densities of thousands of kilograms per cubic centimeter!*

## 1.10 Energy

There is a story that, when he was young, James Watt (1736–1819) became interested in steam power by watching water boil in a teakettle over a fire. When he plugged the spout of the kettle, the lid rose. Perhaps this observation eventually led Watt to the improvements of steam engines for which he is famous. In any case, this observation is a good example of how energy is related to work.

We say that work is done when a weight is lifted against the pull of the earth's gravity. Later we will define work more carefully; for now this common use of the word will be adequate. We do work when we lift the lid of a teakettle. When we plug the spout, the steam lifts the lid. Here, the work is done by the steam. So we reason that the steam in the kettle had the *capacity* for doing work before it lifted the lid. The steam had *energy*. **Energy is a quantity that has the capacity for doing work,** if the conditions are right. Since energy can often be transformed into mechanical work, the units we use for measuring energy are the same as the units of work.

*Energy is the capacity for doing work.*

Energy is sometimes quite noticeable because we have sense organs that are able to detect its presence in various forms. Our eyes respond to visible light. Our ears detect sound energy. Special nerves are sensitive to temperature, an indication of heat energy. Other nerves respond to electric energy.

Scientists have discovered forms of energy in addition to those that can be detected by our sense organs. Special detecting and measuring instruments had to be developed to change these forms of energy into something that we can sense. For example, we cannot directly sense X rays, a form of energy similar to visible light. But X rays can affect a piece of photographic film. Under visible light, we can look at a piece of exposed and developed X-ray film and tell where the X rays have affected the film. As another example, we cannot directly sense small amounts of infrared radiation, an invisible form of energy similar to light. (We can feel large amounts of infrared radiation as heat.) However, a special thermometer exposed to infrared radiation registers an increase in temperature. We can study the behavior of the thermometer and say there is the presence of invisible radiation. By means of devices such as these, scientists have extended the range and sensitivity of the human senses. Among the forms of energy that fall into this "extrasensory" category that humans cannot directly detect are chemical energy, gravitational energy, nuclear energy, and forms of energy similar to light, such as X rays and infrared rays.

Energy is a concept that unifies physics. More specifically, it is the concern of physicists to follow and measure the transformation of energy, for the forms of energy are mutually interchangeable. For example, consider the energy you expend when you walk. Traced backward, it came from the food you ate. The food got its energy from nutrients in the ground and radiations from the sun. The sun got its energy from nuclear reactions in its interior, etc. Tracing your walking energy forward, the friction and motion of your feet on the ground heat the ground slightly. This heat radiates into space and helps to evaporate water from the earth, making rain possible, etc.

## 1.11 Potential energy

Two important forms of energy that an object may have are its energy of position and its energy of motion. Energy of position is *potential energy*. Energy of motion is *kinetic energy*. A book resting on a desk top, as in Figure 1-9, acquired potential energy when someone did the work of lifting it to the desk top. The book has potential energy, or energy of position, while it is on the desk top. If the book is pushed off the desk top, it falls to the floor. While it is falling, it may strike some other object to which it gives some of its energy. This is kinetic energy, or energy of motion. When the book is stopped by the floor, the rest of its kinetic energy is transformed into other forms of energy, such as sound and heat.

In a way, the floor is an arbitrary zero level for our example. If a hole were cut in the floor under the book, the book would continue to fall and be able to do more work when its motion is stopped. For each problem in gravitational potential energy, an arbitrary zero level must be specified.

An object may also have potential energy that is not connected with gravitation in any way. For example, a compressed spring gets its energy from the push that is exerted on it to get it into a compressed position. This energy is called elastic potential energy. Elastic potential energy is not as easy to compute as the gravitational variety, since one must be familiar with the transformations of various forms of energy. Some of these forms of energy, especially those concerning the interior of the atom, can take the problem to the very frontiers of modern physics.

**Figure 1-9** An example of gravitational potential energy. The amount of energy of the books depends upon the zero level chosen for the experiment.

## 1.12 Kinetic energy

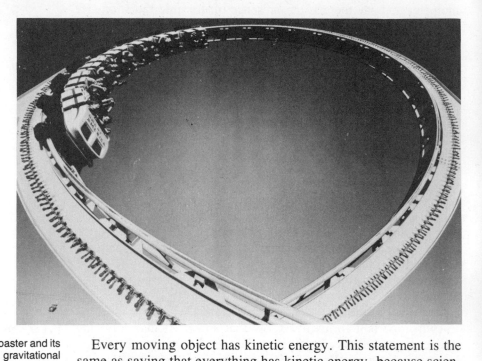

**Figure 1-10** As the roller coaster and its occupants descend, their gravitational potential energy changes into kinetic energy.

Every moving object has kinetic energy. This statement is the same as saying that everything has kinetic energy, because scientists believe that everything in the universe is moving in some way or other. Since the description of the motion of an object depends on another object in the universe designated as being "motionless," it is necessary to choose an arbitrary zero level or, in this case, an arbitrary stationary point. In ordinary, earthbound physics the surface of the earth is considered stationary. An object resting on the earth's surface is said to have zero kinetic energy even though the object rotates and revolves with the earth.

As Figure 1-10 shows, there is a constant interplay between potential energy and kinetic energy in physics. Consider the swinging of a mass at the end of a string. When the mass is at the top of its swing, it is momentarily stationary. At that point the energy of the mass is gravitational potential (except for internal energy). As the mass begins its downward swing, some of the gravitational potential energy changes into kinetic energy. At the bottom of the swing, which we will consider as the zero level for gravitational potential energy, the kinetic energy of the mass is at a maximum because it is moving at its maximum speed. As the mass swings up the other side of its arc, the energy interchange is reversed. The total amount of energy is always the same—it is merely changing from one kind to another. This discussion demonstrates the *law of conservation of energy*—the total amount of energy of all kinds in a given situation is a constant.

*Potential energy is energy due to the position of a mass. Kinetic energy is energy due to the motion of a mass.*

*Potential energy and kinetic energy are interchangeable. The total amount of energy in a situation remains constant.*

The conservation of energy was demonstrated in a striking way by the classical experiments with heat energy conducted by Count Rumford (1753–1814) and James Prescott Joule (1818–1889) in the early part of the nineteenth century. At that time most scientists thought of heat as a special kind of "fluid" called *caloric,* which was able to flow in and out of objects without affecting their weights. Count Rumford became interested in the caloric theory while supervising the boring of brass cylinders for the construction of cannon barrels. Figure 1-11 shows a model of Rumford's apparatus. During the boring process the brass cylinders became so hot that water placed on them could be brought to a boil. According to the caloric theory, the brass contained a specific amount of caloric. This caloric was being loosened from the brass as the metal was broken down into chips by the boring process. Count Rumford questioned this explanation since the amount of heat produced seemed limitless. As long as the horses provided the work to turn the boring tool, more heat developed. Rumford also demonstrated that if the boring tools were dull and no metal were ground to chips loosening caloric, caloric continued to pour out. In fact, the metal heated up even more. Rumford concluded that the heat produced was a result of the work done on the cannon barrel by the horses; it was not the result of a substance, caloric, present in the brass. He devised a simple experiment to prove his point, which became a landmark in the eventual rejection of the caloric theory.

Joule continued the investigation of heat by establishing the exact relationship between heat and mechanical energy. He found that the amount of heat produced is determined by the amount of mechanical work done. This relationship will be discussed more fully in Chapter 9. The equivalence between heat and mechanical energy provided strong evidence that heat must be a form of energy. It also supported the theory that the total amount of energy remains constant when it is transformed from one kind to another.

## 1.13 Conservation of energy

*An account of this experiment in Count Rumford's own words can be found on page 167 in* Great Experiments in Physics *by Shamos.*

**Figure 1-11** A model of Count Rumford's cannon-boring experiment. The cannon barrel was rotated against a stationary boring tool by a team of horses. Directly in front of the cannon is a small cubic container for the water used in the heat experiments.

### 1.14 Relationship between matter and energy

So far we have been discussing matter and energy as though they were two entirely different entities. Usually the two are inseparably related. All matter contains some kind of energy. Ordinarily, the idea of energy is associated with some substance such as a hot gas or an electrified object. In some cases it is necessary to associate energy with the empty space surrounding an electrified object.

In 1905 Einstein expressed the relationship between mass and energy with the following equation:

$$E = mc^2$$

*Einstein's mass-energy equation led to the development of nuclear power.*

in which $E$ stands for units of energy (work units), $m$ stands for mass, and $c$ for the speed of light. Einstein (Figure 1-12) developed this formula entirely from theoretical considerations, and there was no way of verifying it in the laboratory at the time. Recent experiments, however, have shown that such a relationship does exist.

Einstein's formula states that mass and energy are directly proportional to each other. When one increases, the other increases; when one decreases, so does the other. The equation may also be interpreted to mean that a given amount of mass is equivalent to a certain amount of energy.

A simple example will serve to illustrate the relationship between mass and energy. When you throw a ball, you are imparting energy to it. Energy is transferred from you to the ball. The mass-energy equation says that since $c$ is constant, the increase in energy $E$ will be accompanied by an increase in mass $m$. That is, while the ball is moving, its mass will be greater than it was while the ball was at rest. Both the energy and the mass of the ball have increased. The extra energy and mass of the ball came from you.

When an object is at rest with respect to the observer and the observer's measuring instruments, the mass of the object is said to be the *rest mass*. When the object is moving, its mass increases. This new mass, which increases rapidly as the object approaches

**Figure 1-12** Albert Einstein developed the equation that shows the relationship between matter and energy.

the speed of light, is called the *relativistic mass* because it is in keeping with Einstein's *theory of relativity*. In the mass-energy equation, *m* is the relativistic mass. Table 1-1 shows the relationship between the speed of an object and its relativistic mass.

Actually, what Einstein's equation means is that matter is a form of energy and the two terms emphasize different aspects of the same quantity. This is one of the most important concepts of contemporary physics.

It should not be assumed, however, that Einstein's mass-energy equation is a proof of the conservation of matter and energy. The equation has value even if the matter and energy of the universe were constantly changing. The conservation laws rest on repeated laboratory measurements that show that mass and energy are not lost in chemical and physical changes. Some scientists think that the law of conservation may not hold for large energies and masses in outer space, but this hypothesis has not been verified. The deviations predicted by these scientists are too small for direct measurement with present instruments.

The relationship between matter and energy will become evident in the study of physics in still another way. We usually think of light energy in terms of waves and of matter in terms of particles. Actually, there are times when light acts as though it has granular properties. In other words, there are aspects of light that can be explained only by assuming that it is made up of discrete particles. Similarly, particles of matter exhibit wave properties. This wave-particle duality of nature is a key as well as a puzzle in physics, and scientists admit that they are far from a complete understanding of it. Perhaps you will play a role in unlocking this fundamental secret of nature.

Table 1-1

| RELATIVISTIC MASS | |
| --- | --- |
| Speed of object (% of speed of light) | Relativistic mass (compared to rest mass) |
| 0 | 1.00 |
| 25 | 1.03 |
| 50 | 1.15 |
| 75 | 1.51 |
| 80 | 1.67 |
| 85 | 1.88 |
| 90 | 2.30 |
| 95 | 3.16 |
| 99 | 7.07 |
| 99.9 | 22.4 |

*Everything is a form of energy!*

## 1.15 Subdivisions of physics

The study of the physical universe is called *physical science*. *Chemistry* is a physical science. It deals with the composition of matter and reactions among various forms of matter. *Physics* is also a physical science. It is concerned with the relationship between matter and energy. The ultimate goal of physics is to explain processes and particles in terms of simple interactions and simple particles.

Since both chemistry and physics deal with matter, these two sciences overlap to some extent. But a distinguishing consideration in the study of physics is always the idea of energy: what it is, what form it takes, how it affects matter and how matter affects it, and how it can be changed from one form to another.

The study of physics can be subdivided in a number of ways. The sequence of topics followed in this book is one that has been used for many years because of its logical progression and because it leads from concepts that were developed many years ago to those at the very frontiers of physics.

*Classifying a concept is not as important as understanding it.*

The chapters in your text fall into four major categories: mechanics and heat, waves, electricity, and nuclear physics. The first category includes the study of motion, forces, work, power, and certain aspects of heat. These topics, and the ways in which they involve the transfer of energy, are considered in Chapters 3 through 9. (Chapter 2 describes measurement and problem solving, which are essential to the entire subject of physics.)

Waves are considered in Chapters 10 through 15. Sound energy and light energy are transmitted as waves. The nature of waves as a mechanism for energy transfer and the characteristics of sound and light comprise the subject matter of this section of your text.

Electricity involves a form of energy that is increasingly important to our way of life. In Chapters 16 through 22, the ways of generating and transmitting this vital commodity are explained. This section of the text also contains an introduction to the study of electronics, which is the basis for radio, television, and computers.

In the last three chapters of the book, the principles of nuclear and particle physics are introduced. It is here that the physicist tries to get to the very heart of the composition of matter and of the energy forms that bind the building blocks of the universe together. With topics ranging from "atom smashers" to the most distant star systems, this part of the course is usually called modern physics. The authors hope that as you reach this final section of the course, you will have caught the excitement of physics, a subject in which topics as well as possibilities are truly unlimited.

# summary

The world's growing population requires ever-larger amounts of energy. By discovering and developing new energy sources, science and technology can help to meet this need. Science and technology may be considered to be research and development. The miniaturized computer and its many applications are good examples of the impact of science and technology on our way of life. Even so, many applications of computers still await discovery.

Scientific laws, theories, and hypotheses are steps in the search for truth in the physical universe. A hypothesis is a possible solution to a scientific problem. Confirmed hypotheses become laws or theories, but even these are never absolutely certain.

Physics deals with matter and its properties. Among these properties are mass (the measure of the quantity of matter), inertia (the resistance of matter to change in its state of motion), and mass density (mass per unit volume). The environment of a sample of matter is called a condition. Physics further deals with the various types of energy and their transformations. Energy is the capacity for doing work. Potential energy is energy of position. Gravitational energy and elastic energy are forms of potential energy. Kinetic energy is energy of motion. Potential and kinetic energy are readily interchanged. However, the law of conservation of energy states that energy may be changed from one form to another without loss. The experiments of Count Rumford and James Prescott Joule verified this law.

Einstein's relativity equation, $E = mc^2$, states that energy and mass are directly proportional to each other and that they are interchangeable. Mass can thus be considered to be a form of energy.

Physics is a physical science. Its four main subdivisions are mechanics and heat, wave motion, electricity, and nuclear and particle physics. The last of these is also referred to as modern physics.

# questions

GROUP A

1. How does the mass of an object on the earth compare with the mass of the same object on the moon?
2. Distinguish between mass and mass density.
3. (a) Distinguish between properties and conditions. (b) Give examples of each.
4. When you drive an automobile, (a) what are the sources of energy? (b) How is the energy transformed?
5. Classify the following as having mainly potential or mainly kinetic energy: (a) gasoline, (b) water behind a dam, (c) a moving car, (d) a rocket in free flight, (e) gunpowder.
6. What limits the amount of heat energy that can be produced by the boring of a cannon barrel?
7. State the law of conservation of energy.
8. Give two meanings of the equation, $F = mc^2$
9. What is meant by the wave-particle duality of nature?
10. Briefly define the subdivisions of physics.

GROUP B

11. How can Figure 1-7 be used to find the mass of the balance pan used in the experiment?
12. Redraw Figure 1-7 using values of $T^2$ instead of $T$. What is the shape of the resulting graph?
13. Could a platform balance be used in a rocket that is in free flight? Explain.
14. Why are work and energy measured in the same units?
15. State a fact to support the caloric theory.
16. Why does it become increasingly difficult to increase the speed of an object as it approaches the speed of light?
17. In general, objects expand when heated. (a) How does this phenomenon show that heat is a form of energy? (b) Modify your explanation to fit objects that contract upon being heated?
10. On the basis of Count Rumford's observations and conclusions about heat, can you suggest how his experimentation led to the development by Joule of the mechanical equivalent of heat?

# energy

A viable alternative to the burning of fossil fuels is the woodburning stove. This cast iron stove heats an area of 370 m³ with about 13,500 kcal of heat for 14 hours.

Bottom left: Surface mining operation. Coal promises to be a significant clean-energy source when methods of refining remove the sulfur in it.

Bottom right: Secondary recovery, a new method of increasing the amount of oil recovered from a reservoir, involves injecting water or gas into the reservoir.

nergy, the unifying concept of physics, is a necessity of life. As such, the sources, conversion, and production of energy are major concerns of modern society. Presently, energy sources range from the direct utilization of the sun's radiant energy to the nuclear transformation of matter achieved in fission and fusion reactions. Heat stored in the earth since its formation and the liberation of the sun's energy locked up millions of years ago in fossil fuels are other examples of energy sources. The power of wind and of moving water can be harnessed to provide additional sources of energy. New frontiers of energy production are refuse recycling and ocean thermal energy conversion. The ultimate goal is the safe, economical, efficient, and widescale distribution of energy.

*Top right: Windmills have long been a source of power. In locations where it blows steadily enough, wind is a dependable energy source.*

*Bottom right: The design of this windmill improves its efficiency because wind from any direction turns the windmill.*

*Top left: The energy of falling water can produce electric power. This turbine, at the TVA's Cumberland plant, produces 1,300,000 kw of power.*

*Bottom left: Dams create a source of water for hydroelectric power. This dam of unique design is located in Yugoslavia.*

*Left: Solar energy shows great potential for the future. The 576 collector field panels gather the sun's energy and provide the heating and cooling for this Atlanta, GA, school.*

*Below: Solar radiation stored by the oceans could provide energy. In this artist's concept, turbine-generators will be turned by ammonia or propane vapor. The large thermal gradient between surface and deep-water temperatures could produce $1.6 \times 10^8$ watts of power.*

*Left: A solar heated home. Panels of water-filled drums, left, absorb the sun's energy. Solar water heater, right, circulates antifreeze. Windmill pumps water.*

*Bottom left: This resource recovery and energy production plant effectively utilizes solid waste to produce electrical power and reusable metal.*

*Bottom right: The recycling of biomass such as cornstalks can produce alcohol fuels that may be an alternative to gasoline.*

*Right: The Stanford Linear Accelerator in Palo Alto, CA, can accelerate electrons to 40 Gev as they travel along the 5-km path. The impact of these electrons on the target material produces nuclear transformations for the purpose of nuclear energy research.*

*Below. Heat from within the earth's crust causes groundwater to become hot enough to produce steam. When released through wells drilled to a depth of more than 2.5 km, the steam runs generators to produce electricity.*

# 2 Measurement and Problem Solving

## UNITS OF MEASUREMENT

### 2.1 Physical quantities and units

**Figure 2-1** Many countries already use the metric system. Its use in this stadium is part of the U.S. conversion program.

Over the centuries many different systems of measurement have been in use throughout the world, but the one that is best suited to modern measurements is the *metric system*. Developed in France near the end of the eighteenth century, the metric system uses a decimal basis that makes it as convenient to measure physical quantities as to make change with pennies, dimes, and dollars. In 1866 Congress made the metric system legal for use in the United States. Almost all the other countries of the world have adopted it as their official system of measurement, as Figure 2-1 illustrates. The Metric Conversion Act of 1975 specifies that "the policy of the United States shall be to coordinate and plan the increasing use of the metric system . . . and establish a United States Metric Board to coordinate the voluntary conversion." No target date for the conversion was set by this law.

In using a system of measurement, it is important to distinguish between *physical quantities* and *units of measurement*. Physical quantities are aspects of the universe. They can be measured with any desired units of measurement. For example, *length* is a physical quantity; the metric unit that is used to measure length is the *meter*.

Within each system there are a few fundamental units. All other units of measurement are then derived from these basic units. For example, since length and time are such important physical quantities, some natural length and time period could be chosen as fundamental units. A unit based on a natural phenomenon is called a *conceptual unit*.

Another way to establish fundamental units is to choose arbi-

22

trary values for them. For example, a certain quantity of matter can be selected as a unit of mass. A unit established in this way is called a *standard unit*. The disadvantage of the standard unit is that the arbitrary standard must be carefully preserved so that it can be used to keep the system accurate. If it is lost, the entire system is endangered. A conceptual unit, on the other hand, can be reestablished at any time.

Three physical quantities—*mass, length,* and *time*—are fundamental to the expression of other physical quantities of mechanics. Thus we refer to them as fundamental quantities. There are seven fundamental physical quantities. The units with which these quantities are measured are established by international agreements.

The definitions of other physical quantities provide their values in terms of the fundamental quantities that can be measured. For example, velocity can be defined in terms of length and time. To express a velocity, it is only necessary to know how to measure length and time. Similarly, momentum can be defined as the product of a mass and its velocity. To express momentum as a physical quantity, it is only necessary to know how to measure mass and velocity. Measuring these quantities is the same as measuring mass, length, and time.

When studying heat, it will be necessary to introduce a unit for *temperature*, another fundamental physical quantity. Later, during our study of light, we will introduce a fifth fundamental unit for measuring *luminous intensity*. Another fundamental unit we will use is the one for the measurement of *electric charge*. A seventh measures *molecular quantity*. The units for these seven fundamental physical quantities provide the basis from which the units for the other physical quantities can be derived.

Since the exchange of scientific information is now worldwide, international committees have been set up to standardize the names and symbols for physical quantities. In 1960 an International System of Units (abbreviated SI for Système Internationale) was adopted by the 11th General Conference of Weights and Measures. The quantities, units, and symbols on the inside front cover of this book and in Appendix B are based on the International System of Units. It is not necessary to memorize these words and symbols at this time, but you should become accustomed to their use as they are introduced in this and later chapters. The prefixes used in the metric system are shown in Table 2-1.

In the United States the government agency that deals with standards of measurement is the National Bureau of Standards. It is a goal of the National Bureau of Standards, and its counterparts in other countries, to establish reproducible standard units. This has now been accomplished for all of the fundamental units except the unit of mass.

*Units are used to measure quantities. A conceptual unit is based on a natural phenomenon. A standard unit has an arbitrary value.*

*The seven fundamental physical quantities are length, mass, time, temperature, luminous intensity, electric charge, and molecular quantity.*

Table 2-1

| METRIC SYSTEM PREFIXES | | |
| --- | --- | --- |
| Prefix | Symbol | Factor |
| tera (*tair*-ah) | T | $10^{12}$ |
| giga (*jig*-ah) | G | $10^{9}$ |
| mega | M | $10^{6}$ |
| kilo | k | $10^{3}$ |
| hecto | h | $10^{2}$ |
| deka | da | $10^{1}$ |
| deci | d | $10^{-1}$ |
| centi | c | $10^{-2}$ |
| milli | m | $10^{-3}$ |
| micro | $\mu$ | $10^{-6}$ |
| nano (*nan*-oh) | n | $10^{-9}$ |
| pico (*pea*-koh) | p | $10^{-12}$ |
| femto (*fem*-toh) | f | $10^{-15}$ |
| atto (*at*-oh) | a | $10^{-18}$ |

## 2.2 Length, mass, time

The International System of Units is also called the MKS system. This is because three of its fundamental units are the meter, the kilogram, and the second, measuring the three fundamental quantities length, mass, and time, respectively.

The MKS standard of length is the *meter* (m), which is based on a reproducible laboratory experiment. When an electric discharge is maintained in a sample of the gas krypton-86, as Figure 2-2 shows, the gas glows with a characteristic color similar to that of neon. This color, produced by the atoms of krypton, consists of several different wavelengths of light. One wavelength is an orange-red light. *The standard of length is based on the wavelength of the orange-red light emitted by krypton-86 atoms.*

**1 meter (m) = 1,650,763.73 wavelengths in a vacuum of orange-red light of krypton-86**

The number of wavelengths of light in a given distance can be counted by the use of an instrument known as an optical interferometer. This instrument is accurate to about two parts in one billion, or about one meter of uncertainty in measuring the distance between the earth and the moon. Scientists are already at work on an even more accurate standard. One way of providing such a meter of the future is to use a laser beam. Accuracy of better than one part in a trillion is theoretically possible with this device.

The metric units for the measurement of area and volume are derived from the meter, as Figure 2-3 indicates. A rectangular floor 3 meters long and 2 meters wide has an area of 6 square meters. Similarly, a rectangular tank 2 meters long, 1 meter wide, and 3 meters deep has a volume of 6 cubic meters.

*The liter* (L) *is a special name for a cubic decimeter* (1000 cm³). Since one milliliter (1 mL) is 1/1000th of a liter, it is equivalent to one cubic centimeter (1 cm³). In liquid measurements it is helpful to remember that it takes about 15 to 20 drops of water (depending on the shape of the dropper) to make one milliliter.

The MKS standard of mass is the *kilogram* (kg). It is defined as the mass of a certain cylinder designated as one kilogram. This standard is kept in Sèvres, France. Copies are located in other capitals of the world. The gram (g) is 1/1000th kilogram. One milliliter of water has a mass of approximately one gram. A United States nickel coin has a mass of about 5 g. A metric ton contains 1000 kg or 1,000,000 g.

It is interesting to note that mass units can be compared with each other and with the standard mass and contain a possible error of only a few parts in a billion. This difference corresponds to the mass of the ink in a single comma when compared to the mass of the ink in an entire book.

Scientists also use another mass unit suitable for comparing the masses of different atoms. This unit is needed in work with

**Figure 2-2** The standard of length. Emissions from this lamp containing the gas krypton-86 are used to obtain a very precise value for the standard meter.

**Figure 2-3** Relationship among metric units of length, volume, and mass.

10 cm

10 cm

10 cm

1 cm³

1 liter contains 1000 cubic centimeters or 1 kg of water at 4°C

chemical and nuclear reactions. It is called an *atomic mass unit*. The atomic mass unit is defined as 1/12th of the mass of an atom of carbon-12, the most abundant form of the element carbon. This unit can be related to the standard kilogram. You will work with atomic mass units in Chapters 7, 23, and 24.

The mass of an object should not be confused with its *weight*. Weight is the gravitational force between the earth and an object. Weight varies at different locations around the earth, but the mass of an object does not depend on its position.

The unit of force in the MKS system is the *newton* (n). In New York City a force of 9.803 n must be exerted to support a mass of one kilogram. For other locations in the United States, forces ranging from about 9.79 n to 9.82 n are needed to support one kilogram. The relationship 9.80 n per kilogram is a useful approximation. In most countries that use the metric system, the weights of people and objects are commonly described in kilograms instead of newtons. This use of units is not consistent with the International System of Units but is likely to continue.

The above differences in the value of the newton may give the impression that the newton is only loosely or approximately defined. That is not the case. A complete description of how the newton is determined will be given in Chapter 3. It will then become clear why the support of a given mass may require the exertion of different forces at different locations.

The unit of time is the *second* (s) (Figure 2-4). The standard second is based on the vibrations of cesium atoms. Radio waves of a certain frequency can cause cesium atoms to vibrate. Sensitive instruments can control the radio transmitter to keep it in step with these vibrations. Outside influences, such as changes in gravity, do not affect these vibrations. Therefore the vibrations of these atoms are used in a *cesium clock*. In 1964 this clock was adopted to provide the international standard of time.

**Figure 2-4** A bullet cutting through a playing card. Split-second timing was required to take this photograph.

**1 second (s) = 9,192,631,770 vibrations
of cesium-133 atoms**

*The meter, kilogram, and second are three of the seven fundamental units.*

# questions

GROUP A

1. (a) Distinguish between a conceptual unit and a standard unit in physics. (b) Give an example of each.

2. (a) List the fundamental physical quantities. (b) List several derived quantities.

3. (a) What is the present standard of length? (b) What units are derived from it?

4. What is the relationship between a cubic centimeter and a milliliter?

5. Distinguish between mass and weight.

6. Define the present standard of time.

GROUP B

7. What is the connection between the metric system and the SI?

8. How is the standard of mass related to the standard of length?

9. What is the present status of American plans to switch to the metric system? Consult the *Reader's Guide to Periodical Literature* in the library in order to obtain the latest information on this question.

10. Can you think of a relationship between the second and the meter?

# problems

GROUP A

1. How many mm are there in (a) 2 cm? (b) 3 m? (c) 5 km?

2. Compute the number of mL in (a) 3 liters (b) 20 liters.

3. Find the number of liters in 10 m³.

4. How many g are there in (a) 0.7 kg? (b) 8 kg?

5. Express your height in meters and your mass in kilograms.

6. The top of a square table is 85 cm on one edge. What is its area?

7. A container is 0.80 m long, 25 cm wide, and 95 mm deep. What is the volume of the tank in liters?

8. A nuclear device is rated as having the explosive power of five gigatons of TNT. To how many kilograms of TNT is this explosive power equivalent?

GROUP B

9. A cubic container holds 1.00 kg of water. (a) What is the volume of the container in liters? (b) in m³? (c) What is the length of one side in meters?

10. The mass of 1.00 cm³ of sea water is 1.04 g. What is the mass of one liter of sea water?

11. A cable has a mass of 4.52 g per centimeter. What is the mass of 15 km of the cable?

12. Compute the number of seconds in a year of 365.24 days.

# MAKING AND RECORDING MEASUREMENTS

## 2.3 Accuracy and precision

**Figure 2-5** The accuracy of measurement depends upon the instrument used and the care with which the reading is made.

The measurement of a physical quantity is always subject to some degree of uncertainty. There are several reasons for this: the limitations inherent in the construction of the measuring instrument or device, the conditions under which the measurement is made, and the different ways in which the person uses or reads the instrument, as you can see in Figure 2-5. Consequently, in reporting the measurements made during a scientific experiment, it is necessary to indicate the degree of uncertainty so far as it is known.

One way to express the uncertainty of a measurement is in terms of *accuracy*. **Accuracy** *refers to the closeness of a measurement to the accepted value for a specific physical quantity*. It is expressed as either an *absolute* or a *relative error*. *Absolute error* is the actual difference between the measured value and the accepted value. The equation for absolute error is

$$E_a = |O - A|$$

where $E_a$ is the absolute error, $O$ is the observed (measured) value, and $A$ is the accepted value. (The vertical bars mean that only the absolute value is used, regardless of sign.)

*Relative error* is expressed as a percentage, and is often called the percentage error. It is calculated as follows:

$$E_r = \frac{E_a}{A} \times 100\%$$

*Accuracy is expressed as absolute error or relative error.*

where $E_r$ is the relative error, $E_a$ the absolute error, and $A$ the accepted value.

In common usage accuracy and *precision* are frequently synonymous terms. But in science it is important to make a distinction between them. You should learn to use them correctly and consistently. In contrast with accuracy, **precision** *is the agreement among several measurements that have been made in the same way.* It tells how reproducible the measurements are and is expressed in terms of *deviation.* Figure 2-6 should help you to distinguish between accuracy and precision as used in science. As in the case of accuracy, deviations in precision can be given as absolute or relative (percentage). *Absolute deviation* is the difference between a single measured value and the average of several measurements made in the same way, or

$$D_a = |O - M|$$

where $D_a$ is the absolute deviation, $O$ is the observed or measured value, and $M$ is the mean or average of several readings.

*Relative deviation* is the percentage average deviation of a set of measurements and is calculated as follows:

$$D_r = \frac{D_a \text{ (average)}}{M} \times 100\%$$

where $D_r$ is the relative deviation, $D_a$ (average) is the average absolute deviation of a set of measurements, and $M$ is the mean or average of the set of readings.

The precision of your laboratory measurements will be governed by the instruments at your disposal. In a measuring instrument the degree of precision obtainable is called the *tolerance* of the device. Any figure for the tolerance of an instrument indicates only the limitations of the instrument. The instrument maker assumes that the instrument is used properly and that human errors are held to a minimum. The usual platform balance, for example, has a tolerance of 0.1 gram. Some modern research instruments, such as the precision balance shown in Figure 2-7, are almost unbelievably precise.

A third way of indicating the precision of a measurement is by means of *significant figures.* **Significant figures** *are those digits in a number that are known with certainty plus the first digit that is uncertain.* For example, if the length of a laboratory table was measured with a meter stick graduated in millimeters and found to be 1623.5 millimeters, the measurement has five significant figures. The 5 is the uncertain digit. It was an estimation of the value between two millimeter marks on the meter stick.

In working with significant figures, you can usually assume to know the last digit of a number, the uncertain digit, to within 1. For instance, when the value for $\pi$ is given as 3.14 you can assume that the true value lies between 3.13 and 3.15.

The following rules will help you to understand how significant figures are used in physics problems. Even these rules do not

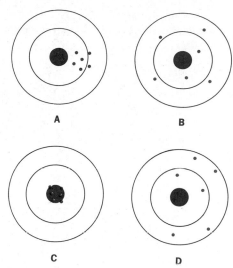

**Figure 2-6** Distinction between accuracy and precision. Six shots were fired at each target. In A, the precision is good, but the accuracy is poor. In B, the average accuracy is good, but the precision is poor. In C, both the accuracy and precision are good. In D, both the average accuracy and the precision are poor.

**Figure 2-7** A precision balance. With this instrument, differences of $10^{-8}$ kilogram can be measured.

*Precision can be expressed as absolute or relative deviation, tolerance, or by significant figures.*

cover all possible cases, however. Common sense will usually show how a specific case should be handled.

1. All nonzero digits are significant: 112.6°C has four significant figures.

2. All zeros between two nonzero digits are significant: 108.005 m has six significant figures.

3. Zeros to the right of a nonzero digit, but to the left of an understood decimal point, are not significant unless specifically indicated to be significant. In this book the rightmost such zero which is significant is indicated by a *bar* placed above it: 109,000 km contains *three* significant figures; 109,0$\overline{0}$0 km contains *five* significant figures.

4. All zeros to the right of a decimal point but to the left of a nonzero digit are not significant: 0.000647 kg has three significant figures. The single zero usually placed to the left of the decimal point in such an expression merely serves to call attention to the decimal point and is never significant.

5. All zeros to the right of a decimal point and following a nonzero digit are significant: both 0.07080 cm and 20.00 cm have four significant figures.

Further examples of these rules are given in Table 2-2.

6. Rule for addition and subtraction. Remember that the rightmost significant figure in a measurement is uncertain. The rightmost significant figure in a sum or difference will be determined by the leftmost place at which a doubtful figure occurs in any of the measurements being added or subtracted. The following example illustrates this rule.

Table 2-2

| SIGNIFICANT FIGURES | | |
|---|---|---|
| Two significant figures | Three significant figures | Four significant figures |
| 2300 | 5420 | 1521 |
| 4$\overline{0}$00 | 60$\overline{0}$0 | 504$\overline{0}$ |
| 5.2 | 73.0 | 4.050 |
| 0.16 | 0.915 | 0.3780 |
| 0.0078 | 0.0467 | 0.01520 |

13.05 cm
309.2 cm — leftmost place of doubtful figure in measurements being added
3.785 cm
326.035 cm — rightmost significant figure in the answer

The answer should therefore be recorded as 326.0 cm.

7. Rule for multiplication and division. In multiplication and division remember that when a doubtful figure is multiplied or divided by a number, the answer is likewise doubtful. Therefore the product or quotient should not have more significant figures than the least precise factor. The following example will illustrate the rule for multiplication.

3.54 cm × 4.8 cm × 0.5421 cm = 9.2113632 cm³

**least precise factor**                                          **rightmost significant figure in the answer**

Consequently, the answer should be recorded as 9.2 cm³. When more than one operation is involved in a calculation, the result may be rounded off to one figure more than the correct number of significant figures *after each operation*.

8. Rule for rounding. If the first digit to be dropped in rounding off is 4 or less, the preceding digit is not changed; if it is 6 or more, the preceding digit is raised by 1. If the digits to be dropped in rounding off are a 5 followed by digits other than zeros, the preceding digit is raised by 1. If the digits to be dropped in rounding off are a 5 followed by zeros (or if the digit is exactly 5), the preceding digit is not changed if it is even; but if it is odd, it is raised by 1.

*Significant figures should be used throughout the course.*

| EXAMPLE | *Divide 8937.50 cm² by 13$\overline{0}$ cm.* |
|---|---|
| SOLUTION | Only three significant figures are required for the answer, so the quotient of 68.750 is rounded off to 68.8 cm because the fourth figure is a 5 followed by a zero and the 5 is preceded by an odd digit. |

Many students doubt that an answer with two significant figures can be more acceptable than one with eight. This doubt may result from working with pure-number problems. These pure numbers do not represent measurements of physical quantities. Each digit in such a computation involving pure numbers is of equal importance, and the last digit of a pure number is not an estimation. However, in the computation shown above, remember that the last digit of each number is uncertain and that the quotient of a certain digit divided by an uncertain digit is uncertain. Working through such a division, circling all the uncertain digits at each step, is good practice and a convincing exercise.

---

## 2.4 Scientific notation

Scientists frequently deal with very large and very small numbers. The velocity of light in air is about 300,000,000 meters per second. The mass of the earth is about 6,000,000,000,000,-000,000,000,000 kilograms. The rest mass of an electron is 0.000,000,000,000,000,000,000,000,000,000,910,953,4 kilogram. These numbers are inconvenient to write and difficult to read. Through the use of the mathematical laws of exponents, however, it is possible to express these numbers in a much simpler way. *Using powers of ten in writing a number is called scientific notation.* Such numbers have the form

$$\mathbf{M} \times \mathbf{10^n}$$

where **M** is a number having a single nonzero digit to the left of the decimal point and **n** is a positive or negative exponent. To write a number in scientific notation:

1. Determine **M** by shifting the decimal point in the original number to the left or to the right until only one nonzero digit is to the left of it. Retain only significant figures in **M**.

2. Determine **n** by counting the number of places the decimal point has been shifted; if it has been moved to the left, **n** is positive; if to the right, **n** is negative.

*Scientific notation is sometimes called exponential notation. Can you explain why?*

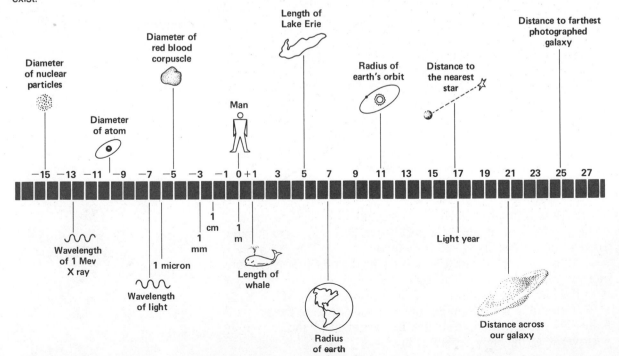

**Figure 2-8** The distance to this galaxy in the constellation Pisces is an order of magnitude somewhere between the distance across our own galaxy and the distance to the farthest photographed galaxy.

**Figure 2-9** Orders of magnitude of length within the universe in meters. The numbers above the scale are powers of ten. The earth is about halfway between the smallest and largest objects known to exist.

By following these rules, we see that the velocity of light can be written as $3 \times 10^8$ m/s, the mass of the earth as $6 \times 10^{24}$ kg, and the mass of the electron as $9.109534 \times 10^{-31}$ kg.

It is often helpful to know the magnitude of a number in terms of its powers of ten. In this form it can be compared quickly with other numbers. An approximation to the nearest power of ten of a number is called its *order of magnitude* (Figure 2-8). The order of magnitude of the velocity of light in m/s is $10^8$. The order of magnitude of the mass of the earth in kg is $10^{25}$, since its mass is nearer to $10^{25}$ kg than it is to $10^{24}$ kg. Similarly, the order of magnitude of the mass of the electron in kg is $10^{-30}$. Orders of magnitude of length of a number of objects in the universe are shown in Figure 2-9.

Diameter of nuclear particles

Diameter of atom

Diameter of red blood corpuscle

Man

Length of Lake Erie

Radius of earth's orbit

Distance to the nearest star

Distance to farthest photographed galaxy

−15  −13  −11  −9  −7  −5  −3  −1  0 +1  3  5  7  9  11  13  15  17  19  21  23  25  27

1 cm

1 mm

1 micron

Wavelength of 1 Mev X ray

Wavelength of light

1 m

Length of whale

Radius of earth

Light year

Distance across our galaxy

# SOLVING PROBLEMS

Scientists usually use the term "data" to refer to the numbers, units, and other information recorded when measurements are made. Much of your homework in physics will involve solving problems in which the necessary data are already provided for you. The problems at the ends of the chapters in this book are like that. Your objective is to use the data properly in order to find the quantity required.

The first step in solving a problem of this kind is to list carefully all the data provided. Be sure to include the correct symbol and unit for each physical quantity. If the symbol is not given in the problem, look it up inside the front cover of this book or in Appendix B, Table 3. Record these symbols correctly at the start. As you continue working the problem, be sure you use only these symbols. Also check to make sure that you have copied the right numbers of significant figures in each case.

In the laboratory most of the data needed must be obtained by direct measurement. In some experiments you will be told what to measure, what instruments to use, and even how many significant figures to use. But in other experiments you must make these decisions for yourself.

In recording and interpreting data in physics, you will use mathematical skills that you have acquired in previous courses. The Mathematics Refresher, following Chapter 25, contains a summary of information and skills from arithmetic, elementary algebra, plane geometry, and trigonometry that is useful in the study of physics. At this time you should review the information contained there and try some of the sample problems. Study carefully any topic with which you are not familiar.

*The Mathematics Refresher is a handy reference. Consult it frequently.*

The purpose of a scientific experiment is to discover relationships that may exist among the quantities measured. The experimenter controls the conditions of the experiment in order to obtain the most accurate measurements. Uncontrolled conditions might make the measurements so confusing that relationships would not be discovered. As an example, suppose you wished to discover any relationships that might exist between the mass of a homogeneous substance (the same throughout) and its volume. You measure the volumes of several samples of different substances and determine the mass of each. Since temperature affects the volume of most substances, you control this condition by taking all of your measurements at the same temperature, such as 20°C. Your data for three substances, with the volume measured in $cm^3$ at 20°C and the mass measured in grams, might look like Table 2-3.

Now you look for mathematical relationships among these numbers. As the volume of each substance increases, the mass also increases. But this statement is very general. You are looking

**Figure 2-10** Graph of three direct proportions. Straight lines are typical of these relationships.

Table 2-3

| | Mass | | | | Mass | | |
|---|---|---|---|---|---|---|---|
| VOLUME-MASS RELATIONSHIPS AT 20°C | | | | | | | |
| Volume (cm³) | aluminum (g) | water (g) | maple wood (g) | Volume (cm³) | aluminum (g) | water (g) | maple wood (g) |
| 1̄0 | 27 | 1̄0 | 6 | 6̄0 | 162 | 6̄0 | 36 |
| 2̄0 | 54 | 2̄0 | 12 | 7̄0 | 189 | 7̄0 | 42 |
| 3̄0 | 81 | 3̄0 | 18 | 8̄0 | 216 | 8̄0 | 48 |
| 4̄0 | 108 | 4̄0 | 24 | 9̄0 | 243 | 9̄0 | 54 |
| 5̄0 | 135 | 5̄0 | 30 | 10̄0 | 270 | 10̄0 | 60 |

for a specific equation. Sometimes, plotting the data on a graph reveals the equation that expresses the relationship among the measurements.

As you see, Figure 2-10 is a graph of the data in Table 2-3. The zero point is the origin of the graph. The horizontal line through the origin is called the X axis. On it are measured distances from the origin, or abscissas, equivalent to the various volumes. For convenience, use one small space to represent 1̄0 cm³. The vertical line through the origin is called the Y axis. On it are measured distances from the origin, or ordinates, equivalent to the various masses. Use one small space to represent 1̄0 g.

When the data for aluminum, water, and maple wood are plotted on the graph, the data for each substance can be connected by a straight line. The mathematical relationship between the mass and the volume is called a *direct proportion*. The symbol that means "is proportional to" is ∝. Hence the relationship between mass and volume is expressed mathematically as

$$mass\ (m) \propto volume\ (V)$$

*Plotting data that are **directly proportional** always results in the graph of a straight line.*

To illustrate another kind of graph, let us plot the data given in Table 2-4, which shows the time required to make a trip of 10̄0 kilometers at various speeds. A line drawn through the plotted points, as shown in Figure 2-11, is a *hyperbola*. Furthermore, the product of the speed and time is constant. *Two quantities whose product is a constant are in **inverse proportion**.*

A proportion can be changed into an equation by introducing a constant. In the volume-mass relationship the constant for each substance can be calculated from the data in Table 2-3. (For example, if each measurement in the volume column is multiplied by 2.7, the measured mass of aluminum results.) The equation for this relationship is $m = DV$ where $D$ is a constant. Solving the equation for $D$,

$$D = \frac{m}{V}$$

Table 2-4

| SPEED-TIME RELATIONSHIPS | |
|---|---|
| Speedometer reading (km/hr) | Time for 100-km trip (hr) |
| 20.0 | 5.00 |
| 30.0 | 3.33 |
| 40.0 | 2.50 |
| 50.0 | 2.00 |
| 60.0 | 1.67 |
| 70.0 | 1.43 |
| 80.0 | 1.25 |
| 90.0 | 1.11 |
| 100.0 | 1.00 |

This constant, $D$, *the ratio of the mass of a homogeneous substance to its volume, is called the* **mass density** of the substance. With this equation you can find any one of the three physical quantities ($D$, $m$, or $V$) provided the measurements for the other two are given. (Mass density is given in g/cm³ rather than kg/m³ because the latter would involve more cumbersome numbers. This deviation from the MKS system is used in other places in this book when the deviation helps to simplify the calculations.)

A carefully drawn graph provides you with another helpful tool. You can use it to estimate values between the plotted points (interpolation) and beyond the measurements made in the experiment (extrapolation).

Estimation of answers is not limited to interpolation and extrapolation. When you solve a problem in physics, you should make an intelligent guess about the answer before doing the actual computation. Such a "check for reasonableness" will frequently disclose major errors in arithmetic or algebra. After expending effort in recording and interpreting data, this final check is well worthwhile.

*The use of the centimeter, gram, and second as basic units is called the CGS system.*

**Figure 2-11** Graph of an inverse proportion. The curve is a hyperbola.

Physical quantities such as length, area, volume, mass, density, and time can be expressed in terms of magnitude alone as single numbers with suitable units. For instance, the length of a table can be completely described as 1.5 m. The mass of a steel block is completely described as 54 kg. *Quantities, such as these, that can be expressed completely by single numbers with appropriate units are called* **scalar quantities,** *or simply,* **scalars.** ("Scalar" is derived from the Latin word "scala," which means "ladder" or "steps" and implies magnitude.) Additional examples of scalars in physics are energy and temperature.

Other physical quantities, such as force, velocity, acceleration, electric field strength, and magnetic induction, cannot be completely described in terms of magnitude alone. In addition to magnitude these quantities always have a specific direction. *Quantities that require magnitude and direction for their description, and whose behavior can be described by certain mathematical rules, are called* **vector quantities.** *They can be represented by* **vectors.** ("Vector" is derived from a Latin word meaning "carrier," which implies displacement.) The ability to work with vectors is an important mathematical skill that is necessary in solving problems that deal with vector quantities.

A vector is usually represented by an arrow. The length of the arrow represents the magnitude of the vector, and the direction of the arrow shows the direction of the vector.

As an illustration, velocity is a vector quantity. The term velocity is used when both speed and direction are used to describe an object's motion. For example, imagine a plane flying

## 2.6 Vectors

*Scalar quantities have magnitude only.*

*Vector quantities have direction as well as magnitude.*

**Figure 2-12** Vector representation of a plane flying north with a velocity of 120 km/hr. Each mark on the arrow represents 10 km/hr.

north in quiet air at a speed of 120 km/hr (kilometers per hour). An arrow **ON** can be drawn to represent the plane's velocity. This is shown in Figure 2-12. The arrow starts at the plane's present position **O** and points to the north. (In vector diagrams, north is toward the top of the page, east is toward the right, south is toward the bottom and west is toward the left.) This arrow shows the plane's direction. The length of the arrow is directly proportional to the plane's speed.

Arrows representing vectors can be combined. The combination of two or more vectors is called the *resultant*. Many experiments have confirmed that the combination of vectors accurately represents the behavior of the objects.

As an example of the combination of two vectors acting in the same direction, suppose an airplane flies through still air with a velocity of 485 km/hr eastward. There is a tail wind with a velocity of 28 km/hr eastward. What is the resultant velocity of the airplane? Since the plane is flying in moving air, the plane's velocity with respect to the ground is the vector sum of its velocity in still air and the wind's velocity. Therefore 485 km/hr eastward + 28 km/hr eastward = 513 km/hr eastward, the resultant velocity of the airplane with respect to the ground. It has the same direction as the velocities that were combined. The vector solution of this problem is shown in Figure 2-13.

Now let us take another case. The airplane flies eastward, but the wind is a head wind having a velocity of 28 km/hr westward. What is the resultant velocity of the airplane? Again, the magnitude of the resultant is the algebraic sum of the magnitudes of the components. The head wind in the opposite direction can be taken into account by considering it as a negative velocity (with respect to the plane's eastward velocity, which we took as positive). In this case the resultant has the direction of the greater velocity. Therefore 485 km/hr eastward + 28 km/hr westward = 457 km/hr eastward. The vector solution of this problem is shown in Figure 2-14.

In a third case the airplane still flies eastward with a velocity of 485 km/hr. But now the wind has a velocity of 42.0 km/hr

**Figure 2-13** The magnitude of the resultant of two velocities in the same direction is the sum of the magnitudes of the component velocities. The resultant has the same direction as the component velocities.

Velocity of airplane in still air                    Resultant velocity of airplane

Velocity of tail wind

**Figure 2-14** The magnitude of the resultant of two velocities in opposite directions is the algebraic sum of the magnitudes of the component velocities. The resultant has the same direction as the greater velocity.

Velocity of airplane in still air                    Resultant velocity of airplane

Velocity of head wind

Velocity of airplane in still air 485 km/hr eastward

Resultant velocity of airplane 487 km/hr 4.9° south of east

Wind velocity 42.0 km/hr southward

**Figure 2-15** The resultant of two veloci-ties acting at an angle to each other is the diagonal of the parallelogram constructed by using the component velocity vectors as sides. The resultant velocity vector is the geometric sum of the component ve-locity vectors.

southward. What is the resultant velocity of the airplane? In Fig-ure 2-15 **OE** is the vector that represents the velocity of the air-plane, 485 km/hr east. The vector **OS** represents the velocity of the wind, 42.0 km/hr south. To find the resultant velocity, we construct the parallelogram of velocities, **OERS**. The diagonal of this parallelogram, **OR**, is the resultant velocity. When we compute its magnitude, we find it to be 487 km/hr. Its direction is 4.9° south of east. (To understand this calculation, a review of the Mathematics Refresher, 13. Triangles, will be helpful.) The parallelogram method can also be used when vectors are at angles other than right angles, as in Figure 2-16.

*Vectors acting at the same point but not in a straight line can be added by the parallelogram method.*

Vector B

Resultant

Vector A

**Figure 2-16** The parallelogram method can be used to find the resultant of two vectors even though they are not per-pendicular.

Vectors may also be added by placing arrows end to end as shown in Figure 2-17. This method is particularly helpful when it is necessary to find the resultant of three or more vectors that start from the same point. If the parallelogram method is used, it would be necessary to find the resultant of two of the vectors first, use this resultant with a third vector to find a second re-sultant, and continue this way until all the vectors have been applied. The final resultant then is the required answer. The pro-cedures shown in Figure 2-17 are really a shortcut for the paral-lelogram method. In using this method, it does not matter in what sequence the arrows are drawn.

**Figure 2-17** Vector addition. The order in which the vectors are added does not affect the magnitude and direction of the resultant.

The problems in this text range from those that are quite simple and involve only a single computation to those that re-quire several derivations and a number of separate mathemat-ical steps. In general, problems of the first type will be found in Group A at the ends of the chapters. Several examples of this type are given within the chapters themselves. Problems of greater difficulty involving several steps are included in Group B, and examples of these are shown in detail within the chapters.

## 2.7 Problem solving

36                                                                                                  CHAPTER 2

The method used to solve physics problems consists of a number of logical steps. These steps are described below and they are illustrated in examples given throughout this book.

1. Read the problem carefully and make sure that you know what is being asked and understand all the terms and symbols that are used in the problem. Write down all given data.

2. Write down the symbol for the physical quantity or quantities called for in the problem, together with the appropriate units.

*In this book the abbreviations for quantities are always italicized. The abbreviations for units are not.*

3. Write down the equation relating the known and unknown quantities of the problem. This is called the *basic equation*. In this step you will have to draw upon your understanding of the physical principles involved in the problem. It is helpful to draw a sketch of the problem and to label it with the given data.

4. Solve the basic equation for the unknown quantity in the problem, expressing this quantity in terms of those given in the problem. This is called the *working equation*.

5. Substitute the given data into the working equation. Be sure to use the proper units and carefully check the significant figures in this step.

6. Perform the indicated mathematical operations with the units alone to make sure that the answer will be in the units called for in the problem. This process is called *dimensional analysis*.

7. Estimate the order of magnitude of the answer.

8. Perform the indicated mathematical operations with the numbers. Be sure to observe the rules of significant figures.

9. Review the entire solution and compare the answer with your estimate.

Solving a problem in physics is not merely a matter of "plugging" a set of numbers into the appropriate equations. Understanding the basic principles of the problem is much more important than "getting the right answer."

## EXAMPLE

*A rectangular metal block is 2.63 cm long, 2.15 cm wide, and 1.52 cm thick. The mass of the block is 56.0 g. What is the mass density of the metal?*

## SOLUTION

Given the length, width, thickness, and mass of a rectangular metal block, we are asked to calculate the mass density of the metal. Since this problem involves mass density, mass, and volume, the equation for mass density is the basic equation.

Basic equation:    $D = \dfrac{m}{V}$

Since the volume is not given directly, however, we must use a working equation in which the given data for length, width, and thickness are shown.

Working equation: $D = \dfrac{m}{(l)(w)(h)}$

Now we are ready to substitute the given data into the working equation and to compute the answer.

$$D = \frac{56.0 \text{ g}}{(2.63 \text{ cm})(2.15 \text{ cm})(1.52 \text{ cm})}$$

$$D = 6.52 \text{ g/cm}^3$$

Determining the answer unit:

$$\frac{\text{g}}{(\text{cm})(\text{cm})(\text{cm})} = \frac{\text{g}}{\text{cm}^3}$$

Determining the magnitude:

$$\frac{56.0}{(2.63)(2.15)(1.52)} = \frac{56.0}{(5.654)(1.52)} = \frac{56.0}{8.594} = 6.52$$

$$\text{(Step 1)} \qquad \text{(Step 2)} \quad \text{(Step 3)}$$

Step 1: Multiplying the first two terms of the denominator and rounding to one more than the correct number of significant figures gives this denominator.

Step 2: Multiplying the terms in the denominator and again rounding to one more than the correct number of significant figures gives this denominator.

Step 3: Dividing the terms of the fraction and rounding to the correct number of significant figures gives this quotient.

# summary

The metric system of measurement is a decimal system. It has been adopted by almost all the countries of the world. The United States is in the process of converting to the metric system.

Physical quantities are aspects of the universe. They are measured in units. A unit based on a natural phenomenon is a conceptual unit. An arbitrary unit is called a standard unit. All units of measurement are derived from seven fundamental units that are used to measure length, mass, time, temperature, luminous intensity, electric charge, and molecular quantity. The names and symbols for physical quantities and units have been standardized in the International System of Units (abbreviated SI).

The SI standard unit of length is the meter. It is based on a specific wavelength of the light emitted by krypton-86 atoms. The standard unit of mass is the kilogram, which is based on the mass of a cylinder kept near Paris. The unit of force is the newton, which is a derived unit. The unit of time is the second, which is based on the vibrations of cesium-133 atoms.

All measurements in science are uncertain to some degree. The closeness of a measurement to an accepted value is called accuracy. It is expressed as absolute error or relative (percentage) error. Precision is the agreement among measurements that have been made in the same way. Precision is expressed as absolute deviation or relative deviation. It may also be shown by significant figures, which are all the digits of a measurement that are known with certainty plus the first digit that is uncertain. Specific rules govern operations with significant figures.

Scientific notation is a convenient way of writing very large and very small numbers. Such numbers have the form M × 10ⁿ, in which M is a number with one nonzero digit to the left of the decimal point and *n* is a positive or negative exponent. The order of magnitude of a number is the approximation of the number to the nearest power of ten.

Data is the term used for the numbers, units, and other information obtained in experiments. Tables, graphs, and equations are used to express the relationships among data. A straight-line graph illustrates a direct proportion. A hyperbola is indicative of an inverse proportion, in which the product of two quantities is a constant.

A scalar is a quantity that needs only a number with appropriate units to describe it. A quantity that re-quires magnitude and direction for its description is a vector quantity. It is usually represented by an arrow in which the length represents magnitude and the orientation of the arrow specifies direction. Vectors in the same or opposite direction can be combined by simple addition or subtraction. The resultant of vectors at other angles is found by the parallelogram or the end-to-end method.

The solving of a physics problem involves a number of logical steps. Among these are the use of a basic equation, which relates the known and unknown quantities of the problem, and a working equation, which expresses the unknown quantity in terms of the known ones. Another important step is dimensional analysis, in which the mathematical operations are performed with only the units.

# questions

## GROUP A

1. List three ways of expressing the precision of a measurement.

2. State the rule for the multiplication of significant figures.

3. (a) What is the shape of the graph of two quantities that are in direct proportion? (b) in inverse proportion?

4. (a) Should the curve pass through all the plotted points of a graph dealing with cause-and-effect relationships? (b) Explain.

5. What is the advantage of developing a working equation for a problem in physics before substituting the data given in the problem?

6. What is the value of estimating the order of magnitude of the answer in solving physics problems?

7. How can a graph be used to determine the precision of a series of measurements?

8. What is meant by dimensional analysis?

9. Describe two ways in which the resultant of three or more vectors can be found.

# problems

## GROUP A

1. How many significant figures are there in each of the following numbers? (a) 173.2; (b) 205; (c) 4000; (d) 0.025; (e) 700; (f) 0.09050.

2. Write each of the numbers in Problem 1 in scientific notation form.

3. Write each of the following numbers in scientific notation form:
   (a) 175,000,000
   (b) 602,300,000,000,000,000,000,000
   (c) 0.000047
   (d) 0.000,000,000,000,000,000,000,001,672,39

4. What is the order of magnitude of each of the numbers in Problem 3?

5. A substance has a mass density of 0.20 g/cm³. What is the volume in cm³ of a 100-g sample of the substance?

6. A sample of maple wood has a mass of 40 g. Read the volume of the sample from Figure 2-10.

7. The time required for a 100-km trip is 1.5 hours. Read the average speed from Figure 2-11.

8. Estimate the order of magnitude of the answer for each of the following calculations:
   (a) $(6.1 \times 10^8)(3.2 \times 10^{-2})$  (c) $(65)(32 \times 10^{-5})$
   (b) $\dfrac{5.92 \times 10^{-2}}{5.37 \times 10^8}$  (d) $\dfrac{(2.35)(0.45)(546)}{(379)(4.3 \times 10^4)}$

9. An airplane is heading westward at a velocity of 950 km/hr. The wind is blowing northward with a velocity of 55.0 km/hr. What is the resultant speed and direction of the airplane relative to the ground?

10. A vector with a magnitude of 5.0 units is directed northward. Another vector with a magnitude of 3.0 units is directed northeastward from the same

point. Draw these vectors to scale and measure the magnitude and direction of the resultant.

GROUP B

11. If the tension of a vibrating string is kept constant, the length of the string is related to the frequency of the tone it emits. Plot a graph of the following data for a typical vibrating string, using lengths as abscissas and frequencies as ordinates.

| Length (m) | Frequency $(s^{-1})$ | Length (m) | Frequency $(s^{-1})$ |
|---|---|---|---|
| 0.075 | 1024 | 0.60 | 128 |
| 0.15 | 512 | 0.80 | 96 |
| 0.20 | 384 | 1.20 | 64 |
| 0.30 | 256 | 2.40 | 32 |
| 0.40 | 192 | | |

(a) What is the shape of the graph? (b) What relationship exists between the length of the vibrating string and the frequency of the tone it emits? (c) From the graph interpolate the frequency the string would have if it were 0.75 m long. (d) How long must the string be to vibrate at the rate of 400/s?

12. In a laboratory experiment a student obtained the following values for the acceleration of gravity by timing a swinging pendulum: 9.796 m/s², 9.803 m/s², 9.825 m/s², and 9.801 m/s². For that location of the laboratory the accepted value is 9.801 m/s². (a) Give the absolute error of each reading. (b) Compute the relative error of each value. (c) What is the absolute deviation of each measurement? (d) Express the precision of the experiment in terms of relative deviation.

13. According to the laws of planetary motion, planetary orbits can be described by the following equation: $k = P^2/d^3$, where $k$ is a constant that is the same for all of the sun's planets, $P$ is the period of revolution for a specific planet, and $d$ is its average distance from the sun. The average distance between the sun and the earth is $1.496 \times 10^8$ km. Find the value of $k$ for the solar system.

14. Using the value of $k$ found in the previous problem, find the average distance between the sun and Jupiter if the period of revolution of that planet is equal to 11.86 earth years.

# 3 Nature and Cause of Motion

## 3.1 The nature of motion

If you see a car in front of your house and later see it further along the street, you are correct in saying that the car has moved. To reach this conclusion, you observed two positions for the car and you also noted the passage of time. You might not know how the car got from one position to the other. For all you know, it might have moved at a steady rate or it might have speeded up and then slowed down before it got to its second position. It might also have been moving when you first noticed it and might still have been moving at its second location. The car may have moved from one location to the other in a straight line, or it may not have. But none of these possibilities changes the truth of the statement that the car has moved.

Usually, when we see something move, we do not just make two observations. We observe the moving object continuously. However, even a case of continuous observation can be thought of as a series of observations in which the interval of time between two successive observations is small.

Figure 3-1 shows several important things about the nature of motion. First, it shows the changing positions of a moving ob-

**Figure 3-1** A study of motion. The disk was photographed every 0.1 s as it moved from left to right along the meter stick. Note that the displacement of the disk is equal in equal time periods.

ject. Such *a change of position in a particular direction is called a displacement*. A displacement has magnitude, direction, and a point of origin. Furthermore, displacements are vector quantities and can be added and subtracted like other vector quantities.

*Displacement is a change of position.*

Figure 3-1 also shows that relative motion can be detected by comparing the displacement of one object with respect to another. The reference object is usually considered to be stationary. Thus in the case of the moving car, the street and houses are the stationary references. So **motion** *may be defined as the displacement of an object in relation to objects that are considered to be at rest (stationary)*.

*Motion is relative displacement.*

This chapter deals with the simplest type of motion—the motion of an object along a straight line. More complicated types of motion will be discussed in Chapter 5.

## 3.2 Speed

*The time rate of motion is called* **speed**. This statement means that if you are walking at a speed of 3.0 m/s, in one second you travel 3.0 meters. In 2.0 seconds, you travel 6.0 meters, and in 3.0 seconds you travel 9.0 meters. A graph of this motion, and of several other motions with constant speeds, is shown in Figure 3-2. Notice that the lines that represent greater speeds are more steeply inclined. The *slope* of a line indicates how steep the line is. The slope is defined as the ratio of the change in the quantity plotted vertically divided by the corresponding change in the quantity plotted horizontally. For example, the distance marked in color on line **A** represents a change of 3.0 units on the vertical axis. The same distance on line **A** represents a change of 1.0 unit on the horizontal axis. The slope of the line is $\frac{3.0}{1.0} = 3.0$.

*Speed is the time rate of motion.*

This definition of the slope of a line on a graph may be used to represent a physical quantity such as speed. If the vertical axis represents path length and the horizontal axis represents time, then the ratio for the slope of the line represents speed. For each of the speeds graphed in Figure 3-2 the data for computing the slope of the line are given. A graph such as this and a single computation of the slope will determine the speed over the entire motion only if the speed is constant. *If the determination of speed over any randomly chosen interval gives the same value, the speed is constant*. The graph of constant speed is a straight line.

**Figure 3-2** Three graphs of motion with different constant speeds. A is for 3 m/s, B is for 1 m/s, and C is for ⅓ m/s. In each case, speed is represented by the slope of the line.

*Average speed is found by dividing the total path length by the elapsed time*. For example, if you run 112 m in 20.0 s, you might not run at constant speed. You might speed up and slow down. But as long as you move a total path length of 112 m in 20.0 s, your average speed is $\frac{112 \text{ m}}{20.0 \text{ s}} = 5.60$ m/s.

Suppose you ride a bicycle 120 m in $\overline{20}$ s. Your average

**Figure 3-3** A graph of motion with changing speed.

speed is $\dfrac{120 \text{ m}}{2\bar{0} \text{ s}} = 6.0$ m/s. A graph of your speed might look like the graph shown in Figure 3-3. You start at a speed of 0.0 m/s and increase your speed. Then from about 3 s to 15 s you travel at constant speed. Then at about 15 s you begin to tire and slow down until at $2\bar{0}$ s you stop. On this graph it can be seen that *instantaneous speed is the slope of the line that is tangent to the curve at a given point.* Without a speedometer it is difficult to determine your instantaneous speed. It can be defined, however, as the speed that you would have if your speed did not change from that point on.

Instantaneous speed is measured approximately by timing the motion over a short path length. In Figure 3-3 instantaneous speed is found approximately by dividing a small amount of time, measured on the graph, into the corresponding path length for that time. The region of the curve marked **A** represents your change in speed as you move faster. An interval of time of 2.3 s is indicated on the horizontal axis. The corresponding path length for this time interval, approximated to the nearest 0.1 m, is 9.0 m. The average slope of the colored line over the interval **A** is $\dfrac{9.0 \text{ m}}{2.3 \text{ s}} =$ 3.9 m/s. This method gives only an approximation of the instantaneous speed because we found the *average speed* for the time interval indicated. This value for the average speed is the same as the instantaneous speed (the slope of the tangent line) at some point in the indicated region, but we cannot precisely determine that point.

Since the graph of your motion is a straight line in the region **B**, it represents constant speed. The elapsed time in region **B** is 9.0 s − 7.0 s = 2.0 s. The corresponding path length is 56 m − 41 m = 15 m. The instantaneous speed in this case can be determined precisely because it is the same as the average speed. It is $\dfrac{15 \text{ m}}{2.0 \text{ s}} = 7.5$ m/s.

Region **C** on the graph is curved. The elapsed time is 18.0 s − 16.0 s = 2.0 s. The corresponding path length is 118.0 m − 109.0 m = 9.0 m. The average speed over the interval **C** (as an approximation of the instantaneous speed) is $\dfrac{9.0 \text{ m}}{2.0 \text{ s}} = 4.5$ m/s.

Both instantaneous speed and average speed are completely described in terms of magnitude alone. Hence speed is a scalar quantity.

## 3.3 Velocity

*Velocity is speed in a given direction.*

When both speed and direction are specified for the motion, the term *velocity* is used. In other words, **velocity** is speed in a particular direction. A person walking eastward does not have the same velocity as a person walking northward, even though

their speeds are the same. Two persons also have different velocities if they walk in the same direction at different speeds. As we
described in Section 2.6, velocities are vector quantities. Both
magnitude and direction are necessary to describe velocities,
and velocities behave like other quantities that can be represented by vectors.

For the simple cases of this chapter, in which the motion is
along a straight line, the word "velocity" and the symbol for
velocity will be used without specifically stating the direction.
The values given for velocity will indicate only the magnitude
and not the direction. In these cases the velocity may be either
a positive or a negative number to indicate in which direction
the object is moving. The speed is never a negative number; it
always represents the magnitude of the velocity. So the equations for velocity and speed appear the same.

Average velocity is defined as the total displacement divided
by the total elapsed time.

$$v_{av} = \frac{d_f - d_i}{t_f - t_i}$$

where $v_{av}$ is the average velocity, $d_i$ is the initial position at time
$t_i$, and $d_f$ is the final position at time $t_f$. This relationship may
also be written

$$v_{av} = \frac{\Delta d}{\Delta t}$$

where $\Delta d$ represents the *change* of position (displacement)
during the time interval $\Delta t$. The Greek letter $\Delta$ (delta) designates
a change in the quantity with which it is associated.

Graphic representations of the velocity of motion along a
straight line are shown in Figure 3-4 and Figure 3-5. These graphs
indicate that the direction of motion does not change in either
case because the magnitude of displacement is continuously increasing. (The direction of displacement is not shown in the
graph.) In Figure 3-4, $\Delta t$ for the entire range of the graph is $\bar{10}$ s
and $\Delta d$ is 5.0 m. Consequently, $v_{av} = \dfrac{5.0 \text{ m}}{\bar{10} \text{ s}}$ or 0.50 m/s. The
same value for $v_{av}$ is obtained by choosing any other two points on
the graph, such as **A** and **B**. In this case, $\Delta t$ is 2.0 s and $\Delta d$ is 1.0
m, and $v_{av}$ again equals 0.50 m/s. The velocity, represented by
the slope of the straight line, is constant. The motion of the object
is said to be *uniform*.

In Figure 3-5, the motion is *variable*. The average velocity for the
entire range of the graph is $\dfrac{5.0 \text{ m}}{\bar{10} \text{ s}}$ or 0.50 m/s, as before. However, the average velocity between points **C** and **D** is $\dfrac{2.0 \text{ m}}{2.0 \text{ s}}$ or
1.0 m/s. If a velocity at a specific time (such as point **C**) is sought,
$\Delta t$ is considered to be a very small interval, and consequently,

**Figure 3-4**  A graph of motion with uniform velocity.

*The Greek letter $\Delta$ in an equation
means "change of."*

**Figure 3-5**  A graph of motion with variable velocity.

$d$ will also be very small. The ratio of $\frac{d}{t}$ at the point **C** is called the *instantaneous velocity*. It can be shown that the instantaneous velocity at point **C** in Figure 3-5 is given by the slope of the line that is tangent to the curve at point **C.** The numerical value of this slope is found, as in the case of the uniform motion in Figure 3-4, by measuring $d$ and $t$ between two points on the tangent and calculating $d/t$. This gives a slope of 0.5 m/s.

### 3.4 Working velocity problems

Now let us expand on the parallelogram method for solving velocity vector problems that was illustrated in Section 2.6. In an example in that section, an airplane flies eastward with a velocity of 485 km/hr. The wind has a velocity of 42.0 km/hr southward. The resultant, found by the parallelogram method, is 487 km/hr in a direction 4.9° south of east. Now suppose the pilot of the airplane does not want to go 42.0 km south of the course for each hour of flight. What change must be made in the velocity of the airplane so that it stays on course despite the effects of the wind blowing from the north? The velocity we wish to obtain is 485 km/hr eastward. This situation is represented by $v_R$ in Figure 3-6. The desired velocity is the diagonal of the velocity parallelogram. We know one component of this velocity: that of the wind 42.0 km/hr southward represented by $v_S$. To complete the parallelogram, we first draw **SR**. Then from **O**, **OV** is drawn parallel and equal to **SR**. Connecting **V** with **R** completes the parallelogram. The vector $v_V$ represents the velocity the airplane must maintain, computed to be 487 km/hr 4.9° north of east. By heading the airplane in this direction and increasing the air speed to 487 km/hr, the pilot actually travels with a speed of 485 km/hr with respect to the ground in an easterly direction.

**Figure 3-6** The vector representing the velocity that the airplane must maintain is a side of the parallelogram of which the desired velocity is the diagonal.

**EXAMPLE**

*A person can row a boat at the rate of 8.0 km/hr in still water. The person heads the boat directly across a stream that flows at the rate of 6.0 km/hr. Find the resultant velocity (a) graphically and (b) trigonometrically.*

**SOLUTION**

(a) To solve this problem graphically, use a protractor and a ruler with a millimeter scale. Draw a velocity vector, **OB,** to represent the velocity of the boat in still water, $v_B$, using an appropriate scale such as $1\bar{0}$ mm = 1.0 km/hr. (See the accompanying figure, but bear in mind that the scale in the figure is smaller than the one suggested for your paper.) Draw the velocity vector, **OC**, to the same scale and at right angles to **OB** to represent the velocity of the stream, $v_c$.

Man rows 8.0 km/hr ($v_B$)

Current 6.0 <m/hr ($v_C$)

37°

Resultant velocity $1\bar{0}$ km/hr ($v_R$)

Complete the parallelogram **OBRC**, and draw in the diagonal **OR**. Place an arrowhead at **R**. The vector **OR** represents the resultant velocity, $v_R$. Using the same scale that you used in drawing **OB** and **OC**, read the magnitude of **OR** as precisely as possible. It should be about $1\bar{0}$ km/hr. Use the protractor to measure the direction of **OR**. It should be about 37° downstream from **OB**.

(b) The graphic solution of vector problems is limited by the precision with which the angles and lines are drawn and measured. This limitation is avoided by using the trigonometric method. In this method tables or a calculator are used to determine the lengths of vectors. The precision of the tables or calculator is usually greater than that of the estimated answers in a graphic solution. Nevertheless, the graphic solution serves as an important check against errors in the trigonometric solution.

The trigonometric solution is found by using the relationship

$$\tan \theta = \frac{\textbf{OC}}{\textbf{OB}} = \frac{v_C}{v_B} = \frac{6.0 \text{ km/hr}}{8.0 \text{ km/hr}} = 0.75$$

$$\theta = 37°$$

$$\sin \theta = \frac{\textbf{OC}}{\textbf{OR}} = \frac{v_C}{v_R}$$

$$v_R = \frac{v_C}{\sin \theta} = \frac{6.0 \text{ km/hr}}{0.602} = 1\bar{0} \text{ km/hr}$$

Hence, $v_R = 1\bar{0}$ km/hr at an angle of 37° downstream.

**EXAMPLE**

*Trigonometrically determine the resultant of the following two vectors, which are applied at the same point: 42 mm 35° north of east and 95 mm 26° east of south.*

**SOLUTION**

The accompanying diagram shows the angles that exist in this example. Carefully study the diagram to see how the value of each angle is obtained.

Since the vectors do not act at right angles, it is necessary to use the law of cosines and the law of sines in the solution. (Refer to the *Mathematics Refresher*.) Designate the 42 mm vector as **a**, the 95 mm vector as **b**, and the resultant as **c**. To determine the magnitude of **c**, use the law of cosines:

$$\mathbf{c} = \sqrt{\mathbf{a}^2 + \mathbf{b}^2 - 2\mathbf{ab} \cos \mathbf{C}}$$
$$\cos \mathbf{C} = \cos \angle \mathbf{OAC}$$
$$\angle \mathbf{OAC} = 180° - 35° - (90° - 26°)$$
$$\angle \mathbf{OAC} = 81°$$
$$\cos 81° = 0.156$$
$$\mathbf{c} = \sqrt{(42 \text{ mm})^2 + (95 \text{ mm})^2 - 2 \,(42 \text{ mm}) \,(95 \text{ mm}) \,(0.156)}$$
$$\mathbf{c} = 98 \text{ mm.}$$

To determine the direction of **c,** use the law of sines:

$$\mathbf{b}/\sin \mathbf{B} = \mathbf{c}/\sin \mathbf{C} \qquad\qquad \sin \mathbf{C} = \sin 81° = 0.988$$
$$\sin \mathbf{B} = \mathbf{b} \sin \mathbf{C}/\mathbf{c} = (95 \text{ mm}) (0.988)/98 \text{ mm} = 0.958$$
$$\mathbf{B} = 73° \qquad\qquad 73° - 35° = 38° \text{ south of east.}$$

# questions

**GROUP A**

1. Define motion.

2. (a) Define speed. (b) Distinguish between average and instantaneous speed. (c) What are the units of speed in the MKS system?

3. (a) What is velocity? (b) Distinguish between speed and velocity.

4. (a) Describe the motion of an object that has constant speed. (b) Describe the motion of an object that has uniform velocity.

**GROUP B**

5. Why is speed a scalar quantity but velocity a vector quantity?

6. How can the magnitude and direction of the resultant of two velocities that are directed at right angles to each other be determined?

7. (a) Does a change in the speed of an object always produce a change in its velocity? (b) Does a change in the velocity of an object always indicate a change in its speed? Explain.

# problems

*Note:* Problems 2 through 9 should be solved (a) graphically and (b) trigonometrically.

GROUP A

1. The highway distance from Indianapolis to Denver is 1712 km. If the driving time is 29.25 hr, what is the average speed for the trip?

2. A motorboat travels 25 km/hr in still water. What will be the magnitude and direction of the velocity of the boat if it is directed upstream on a river that flows at the rate of 4 km/hr?

3. An airplane has a velocity, with respect to the air, of 825 km/hr northward. What is the velocity of the airplane with respect to the ground if the wind is blowing with a velocity of 35 km/hr southward?

4. A person rows a boat at a speed of 5.0 km/hr in still water. The person heads directly across a river that flows at a speed of 5.0 km/hr. Determine the magnitude and direction of the boat's resultant velocity.

5. An airplane flies westward at 650 km/hr. If the wind has a velocity of 40.0 km/hr northward, determine the magnitude and direction of the resultant velocity.

6. An airplane is to maintain a velocity of 475 km/hr in a northeasterly direction. If the wind velocity is 50.0 km/hr southeast what should be the magnitude and direction of the velocity of the airplane to offset the effect of the wind?

GROUP B

7. Determine the magnitude and direction of the resultant velocity of 75.0 m/s, 25.0° east of north, and 100.0 m/s, 25.0° east of south.

8. A boat is to cross a river on a course directed 20.0° upstream to a dock 815 m distance in 10.0 min. If the river flows at a speed of 3.0 km/hr, at what angle upstream must the boat be headed and what must be its speed in km/hr relative to the moving water?

9. An airplane must fly at a ground speed of 125 km/hr in a direction of 10.0° east of south to be on course and on schedule. If the wind velocity is 25.0 km/hr 40.0° east of north, in what direction and at what speed relative to the air must the pilot fly?

# ACCELERATION

The gas pedal of a car is sometimes called the accelerator. When you drive a car along a level highway and increase the pressure on the accelerator, the speed of the car increases. The needle of the car's speedometer shows that for a certain amount of time the car's speed is increasing. For the time that its speed is increasing, we say it is *accelerating*. When you apply the brakes of the car you are driving, the speed of the car decreases. The speedometer indicates that the car's speed is decreasing, and we say that the car is *decelerating*.

**Acceleration** *is defined as the rate of change of velocity.* An automobile that goes from 0.0 km/hr to 60 km/hr in $1\overline{0}$ seconds has greater acceleration than a car that goes from 0.0 km/hr to $6\overline{0}$ km/hr in 15 seconds. The first car has an average acceleration of $\dfrac{6\overline{0} \text{ km/hr}}{1\overline{0} \text{ s}} = 6.0$ (km/hr)/s. The second car has an average acceleration of 4.0 (km/hr)/s.

Acceleration, like velocity, is a vector quantity. In the case of a car moving along a straight road, acceleration can be represented by a vector in the direction the car is moving. Deceleration occurs in the opposite direction. For the cases in which the motion is known to be along a straight line, the direction of the acceleration is specified by saying whether it is a positive or a negative

**3.5 The nature of acceleration**

*Acceleration is a change in velocity. It can be positive or negative.*

Figure 3-7 A graph of velocity versus time for uniformly accelerated motion.

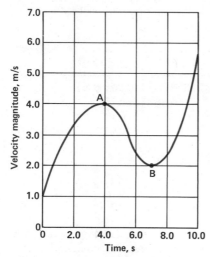

Figure 3-8 A graph of velocity versus time for motion with variable acceleration.

number. In Section 3.3 we saw that the equations for speed and velocity appear the same. For the same reasons, the equations for rate of change of speed and acceleration appear the same. These equations involve only the magnitude and not the direction of motion or displacement.

Average acceleration is found by the relationship

$$a_{av} = \frac{v_f - v_i}{t_f - t_i}$$

where $a_{av}$ is the average acceleration, $v_i$ is the initial velocity at time $t_i$, and $v_f$ is the final velocity at time $t_f$. This relationship may also be stated

$$a_{av} = \frac{\Delta v}{\Delta t}$$

where $\Delta v$ is the change in velocity during the time interval $\Delta t$.

Figures 3-7 and 3-8 are velocity-time graphs for accelerated motion. In Figure 3-7 the velocity curve is a straight line. Hence the acceleration is a constant. This is an illustration of *uniformly accelerated motion*. Also see Figure 3-9.

The motion illustrated in Figure 3-8 is an example of *variable acceleration*. As we mentioned in the case of finding instantaneous speed or instantaneous velocity, finding the average acceleration between two points on the curve only approximates the instantaneous acceleration. Instantaneous acceleration is equal to the slope of the line that is tangent to the curve at the given point.

Notice that the slope of the curve in Figure 3-8 is not always positive. That is, the velocity does not increase during all time intervals. For the interval between points **A** and **B**, for example, $\Delta t$ is 3.0 s and $\Delta v$ is $-2.0$ m/s. Consequently,

$$a_{av} = \frac{2.0 \text{ m/s}}{3.0 \text{ s}} = -0.67 \frac{\text{m/s}}{\text{s}}$$

This reduction in speed is deceleration.

Figure 3-9 Accelerated motion. The baseball was photographed at equal time periods as it rolled down a calibrated inclined plane. Note that the displacement of the ball increases by a constant amount. This is an example of uniform acceleration.

The dimensions of acceleration should be carefully examined. Acceleration is the rate of change of the rate of displacement, or $(\Delta d/\Delta t)/\Delta t$. If $\Delta d$ is in meters and $\Delta t$ is in seconds, acceleration is given in m/s/s, or m/s$^2$.

Galileo Galilei (1564–1642) was the first scientist to understand clearly the concept of acceleration. Galileo is pictured in Figure 3-10. He found that the acceleration of a ball rolling down an inclined plane and the acceleration of a falling object were both part of the same natural phenomenon and were described by the same mathematical rules.

Let us consider one of Galileo's experiments. One end of a board is raised so that it is just steep enough to allow a ball to roll from rest to the 0.5-m position in the first second. The apparatus is shown in Figure 3-11. As the ball rolls down the board, its position is determined at one-second intervals. The data obtained are shown in the first six columns of Table 3-1.

The data in the last four columns of Table 3-1 show that the velocity at the end of each second is 1.0 m/s greater than at the end of the previous second. Thus the acceleration is 1.0 (m/s)/s, or 1.0 m/s$^2$. The motion of a ball rolling down an inclined plane is an example of uniformly accelerated motion.

The initial velocity of the ball is zero. Its acceleration, or rate of gain in velocity, is 1.0 m/s$^2$. Therefore its velocity at the end of the *first second* is 1.0 m/s. (If the ball at that instant were no longer accelerated, it would continue to move with a constant velocity of 1.0 m/s.) At the end of the next second, its velocity is 2.0 m/s. (2.0 s × 1.0 m/s$^2$ = 2.0 m/s.) Similarly the ball's

## 3.6 Uniformly accelerated motion

**Figure 3-10** Galileo Galilei formulated the laws of accelerated motion and falling bodies.

*Galileo died during the year that Sir Isaac Newton, who further developed the laws of motion, was born.*

**Figure 3-11** The ball rolls down the plane with uniformly accelerated motion.

Table 3-1

| UNIFORMLY ACCELERATED MOTION | | | | | | | | | |
|---|---|---|---|---|---|---|---|---|---|
| Interval number | Time at start of interval | Time, $t$, at end of interval | Position at start of interval | Position at end of interval | Distance, $\Delta d$, traveled in interval | Average velocity, $v_{av}$, during interval | Instantaneous velocity, $v_i$, at start of interval | Instantaneous velocity, $v_f$, at end of interval | Average acceleration, $a_{av}$, during interval |
| | (s) | (s) | (m) | (m) | (m) | (m/s) | (m/s) | (m/s) | (m/s$^2$) |
| 1 | 0.0 | 1.0 | 0.0 | 0.5 | 0.5 | 0.5 | 0.0 | 1.0 | 1.0 |
| 2 | 1.0 | 2.0 | 0.5 | 2.0 | 1.5 | 1.5 | 1.0 | 2.0 | 1.0 |
| 3 | 2.0 | 3.0 | 2.0 | 4.5 | 2.5 | 2.5 | 2.0 | 3.0 | 1.0 |
| 4 | 3.0 | 4.0 | 4.5 | 8.0 | 3.5 | 3.5 | 3.0 | 4.0 | 1.0 |
| 5 | 4.0 | 5.0 | 8.0 | 12.5 | 4.5 | 4.5 | 4.0 | 5.0 | 1.0 |

*Galileo's experiment verified the property of inertia.*

*Galileo was among the first scientists to use experiments in testing hypotheses.*

velocity at the end of the fifth second is 5.0 m/s. These data show that *the final velocity of an object starting from rest and accelerating at a uniform rate equals the product of the acceleration and the elapsed time. If an object does not start from rest, its final velocity will equal the sum of its initial velocity and the increase in velocity produced by the acceleration.*

We may arrive at this same conclusion by mathematical reasoning. The equation defining acceleration is

$$a_{av} = \frac{v_f - v_i}{t_f - t_i}$$

For uniformly accelerated motion $a_{av}$ becomes $a$. Then assuming that $v_i$ is the velocity in the direction of the acceleration when $t_i = 0$ and $t_f$ is elapsed time $\Delta t$,

$$a = \frac{v_f - v_i}{\Delta t}$$

Multiplying both sides of the equation by $\Delta t$,

$$a \, \Delta t = v_f - v_i$$

Isolating the term $v_f$ yields

$$v_f = v_i + a \, \Delta t \qquad \text{(Equation 1)}$$

If the object starts from rest, $v_i = 0$

and

$$v_f = a \, \Delta t$$

In Section 3.3 we saw that

$$v_{av} = \frac{\Delta d}{\Delta t}$$

or

$$\Delta d = v_{av} \, \Delta t \qquad \text{(Equation 2)}$$

When an object is uniformly accelerated, the average velocity for any given interval of time can be found by taking one-half the sum of the initial and final velocities:

$$v_{av} = \frac{v_i + v_f}{2} \qquad \text{(Equation 3)}$$

By substituting the value of $v_f$ (obtained in Equation 1) in Equation 3,

$$v_{av} = \frac{v_i + (v_i + a \, \Delta t)}{2} \qquad \text{(Equation 4)}$$

Now, substituting the value of $v_{av}$ (obtained in Equation 4) in Equation 2 gives

$$\Delta d = v_i \Delta t + \tfrac{1}{2} a \, \Delta t^2 \qquad \text{(Equation 5)}$$

If the object starts from rest,

$$v_i t = 0$$

and

$$\Delta d = \tfrac{1}{2} a \, \Delta t^2$$

From this equation we see that if an object starts from rest and travels with uniformly accelerated motion, the displacement of the object during the first second is numerically equal to one-half the acceleration.

Now let us solve Equation 1 for $\Delta t$, and substitute this value of $\Delta t$ in Equation 5. From Equation 1,

$$\Delta t = \frac{v_f - v_i}{a}$$

*The Mathematics Refresher may come in handy here.*

Substituting in Equation 5,

$$\Delta d = v_i\left(\frac{v_f - v_i}{a}\right) + \tfrac{1}{2}a\left(\frac{v_f - v_i}{a}\right)^2$$

Multiplying by $2a$ and expanding terms,

$$2a\ \Delta d = 2v_iv_f - 2v_i{}^2 + v_f{}^2 - 2v_fv_i + v_i{}^2$$

Combining terms,

$$2a\ \Delta d = v_f{}^2 - v_i{}^2$$

Solving for $v_f$,

$$v_f = \sqrt{v_i{}^2 + 2a\ \Delta d} \qquad \text{(Equation 6)}$$

With uniform acceleration the final velocity equals the square root of the sum of the square of the initial velocity and twice the acceleration times the displacement.
If the object starts from rest,

$$v_i{}^2 = 0$$

and
$$v_f = \sqrt{2a\ \Delta d}$$

The equations just given apply whether the uniform acceleration is positive or negative, hence it is important to pay attention to the sign of the displacement. The equations may be used to calculate the distance an object will travel when its motion is uniformly decelerated and the time that elapses in bringing the object to a stop. The following examples show how the equations are used in problems dealing with both positively and negatively accelerated motion.

**EXAMPLE**

*A ball rolls down an inclined plane with a uniform acceleration of 1.00 m/s². At a certain instant its velocity is 0.50 m/s. (a) What is the velocity of the ball 10.0 s later? (b) How far has the ball traveled in that interval of 10.0 s? (c) How far did the ball travel during the eighth second?*

**SOLUTION**

(a) Assuming that time is measured from the moment that the velocity of the ball is observed to be 0.50 m/s,

$$v_f = v_i + a\Delta t = 0.50 \text{ m/s} + (1.00 \text{ m/s}^2)\,(10.0 \text{ s})$$
$$v_f = 10.5 \text{ m/s}$$

(b) $\Delta d = v_i \Delta t + \frac{1}{2} a \Delta t^2$
    $\Delta d = (0.50 \text{ m/s}) (10.0 \text{ s}) + \frac{1}{2} (1.00 \text{ m/s}^2)(10.0 \text{ s})^2$
    $\Delta d = 55.0 \text{ m}$

(c) The distance the ball travels during the eighth second equals the distance traveled in 8 s minus the distance traveled in 7 s.
    $\Delta d = v_i \Delta t_8 + \frac{1}{2} a \Delta t^2 - (v_i \Delta t_7 + \frac{1}{2} a \Delta t_7^2)$
    $\Delta d = v_i (\Delta t_8 - \Delta t_7) + \frac{1}{2} a (\Delta t_8^2 - \Delta t_7^2)$
    $\Delta d = (0.50 \text{ m/s}) (8.00 \text{ s} - 7.00 \text{ s}) + \frac{1}{2}(1.00 \text{ m/s}^2)(64.0 \text{ s}^2 - 49.0 \text{ s}^2)$
    $\Delta d = 8.00 \text{ m}$

**EXAMPLE**

*An automobile is traveling 65 km/hr. Its brakes decelerate it 6.0 m/s². (a) How long will it take to stop the car? (b) How far will the car travel after the brakes are applied?*

**SOLUTION**

(a)   $a = \dfrac{v_f - v_i}{\Delta t}$

   $\Delta t = \dfrac{v_f - v_i}{a} = \dfrac{(0 \text{ km/hr} - 65 \text{ km/hr}) (1000 \text{ m/km})}{(-6.0 \text{ m/s}^2) (3600 \text{ s/hr})}$

   $\Delta t = 3.0 \text{ s}$

(b)  $\Delta d = v_i \Delta t + \frac{1}{2} a \Delta t^2$

   $\Delta d = \dfrac{(65 \text{ km/hr}) (3.0 \text{ s}) (1000 \text{ m/km})}{3600 \text{ s/hr}} + \frac{1}{2}(-6.0 \text{ m/s}^2) (3.0 \text{ s})^2$

   $\Delta d = 27 \text{ m}$

(*Note:* Part B could also be solved by using the equation immediately preceding Equation 6.)

---

**3.7 Freely falling bodies**    In New York City if a body falls freely from rest, it reaches a velocity of 9.803 m/s in one second of time. Since $a = v_f/\Delta t$, the acceleration equals 9.803 m/s² at this location. We must consider the location because the value of the acceleration depends on the earth's gravity. As the earth's gravity may vary from place to place, the value of the acceleration may also vary. (The nature of gravity will be discussed more fully in Sections 3.11–3.13.) The rounded-off value of 9.80 m/s² is approximately valid for locations in the United States.

The equations for accelerated motion apply to freely falling bodies. Since the acceleration due to gravity, $g$, is the same for all objects at a given location, we may substitute $g$ for $a$ in these equations. Thus

$$v_f = v_i + g \Delta t$$
$$\Delta d = v_i \Delta t + \frac{1}{2} g \Delta t^2$$
$$v_f = \sqrt{v_i^2 + 2g \Delta d}$$

When freely falling bodies start from rest, $v_i = 0$, and the motion is described by the following equations:

$$v_f = g\,\Delta t$$
$$\Delta d = \tfrac{1}{2}g\,\Delta t^2$$
$$v_f = \sqrt{2g\,\Delta d}$$

In the case of freely falling bodies, $\Delta d$ is always a vertical distance. The vector quantities $v$ and $\Delta d$ in these equations are customarily assigned plus signs if they are directed downward and minus signs if they are directed upward. (The description of the motion is simplified by considering the downward direction of gravity as positive.) These equations apply only to objects that are falling freely in a vacuum because they do not take into consideration the resistance of air, as illustrated in Figure 3-12. These equations apply reasonably well to dense and compact objects, such as baseballs or lead shot falling through air (Figure 3-13). Of course, these equations do not apply to objects whose air resistance is great compared to their mass, such as leaves or feathers dropping through air.

An object thrown upward is uniformly decelerated by the force of gravity until it finally stops rising. Then as the object falls, it is uniformly accelerated by the force of gravity. If the effect of the atmosphere is neglected, then the time required for the object to fall is the same as the time required for it to rise. The following example shows how a problem of this type is solved.

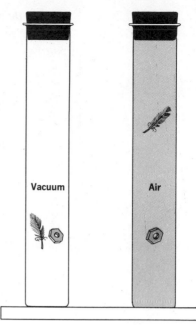

**Figure 3-12** Objects fall with the same acceleration in a vacuum (left) but with different accelerations through air (right).

*Since the force of gravity acts downward, vector quantities that have the same direction as the force of gravity are designated as positive.*

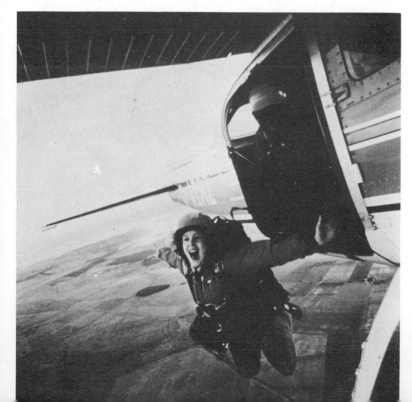

**Figure 3-13** A skydiver in free fall. Air resistance allows a skilled diver to control the orientation and direction of her body even before the parachute is opened.

EXAMPLE

*An object is projected upward with a velocity of 125 m/s. (a) To what height will it rise? (b) How long will it take to reach that height? (c) What will be the total time elapsed until it strikes the earth?*

SOLUTION

(a) $v_f = \sqrt{v_i^2 + 2g\,\Delta d}$

$\Delta d = \dfrac{v_f^2 - v_i^2}{2g}$

$\Delta d = \dfrac{0 - (-125\,\text{m/s})^2}{2 \times 9.80\,\text{m/s}^2}$ (The value for $v_i$ is negative because the velocity is upward.)

$\Delta d = -797\,\text{m}$ (The negative value obtained for $\Delta d$ indicates an upward displacement.)

(b) $v_f = v_i + g\,\Delta t$

$\Delta t = \dfrac{v_f - v_i}{g} = \dfrac{0 - (-125\ \text{m/s})}{9.80\,\text{m/s}^2} = 12.8\,\text{s}$

(c) Neglecting the effect of the atmosphere, the same amount of time is required for the object to fall as for the object to rise. Thus the total time elapsed will be $2 \times 12.8\,\text{s} = 25.6\,\text{s}$.

# questions

## GROUP A

1. (a) What is acceleration? (b) Why is the unit of time squared in the unit of acceleration?

2. How do the directions of an acceleration vector and its corresponding velocity vector compare for the uniformly accelerated linear motion of an object starting from rest?

3. Define the following: (a) uniformly accelerated motion; (b) variably accelerated motion; (c) uniformly decelerated motion; (d) variably decelerated motion.

4. What effect does the force of gravity have on a baseball thrown directly upward?

5. What is meant by instantaneous acceleration?

## GROUP B

6. What equation relates final velocity to initial velocity, acceleration, and elapsed time?

7. How would you calculate displacement when the initial velocity, final velocity, and elapsed time are known?

8. Give an example of an object moving at high speed with zero acceleration.

9. Give an example of an object starting with zero speed and high acceleration.

# problems

*Note:* Whenever necessary, use $g = 9.80\,\text{m/s}^2$. Disregard the effect of the atmosphere.

## GROUP A

1. If a ball is dropped and attains a velocity of 29.31 m/s in 3.00 s, what is the acceleration due to gravity?

2. An automobile can be accelerated from 95 km/hr to 142 km/hr in 8.1 s. What is the acceleration?

3. A large rock is dropped from a bridge into the river below. (a) If the time required for it to drop is 1.7 s, with what velocity, in m/s, does it hit the water? (b) What is the height, in meters, of the bridge above the water?

4. (a) How many seconds does it take for a metal ball to drop 145 m from rest? (b) What velocity does it attain?

5. An object with an initial velocity of 20.0 cm/s is accelerated at 8.0 cm/s² for 5.0 s. (a) What is the total displacement? (b) What is the displacement during the fifth second?

6. What velocity is attained by an object that is ac-

celerated at 0.30 m/s² for a distance of 54 m if its initial velocity is 0.50 m/s?

7. (a) If the brakes of an automobile can decelerate it at 7.00 m/s², what time is required to reduce the velocity of the automobile from 157.0 km/hr to 75.0 km/hr? (b) How many meters does the car travel during this deceleration?

GROUP B

8. A ball is thrown from the ground to the top of the school flagpole. If it returns to the ground after 4.0 s, what is the height of the flagpole in meters?

9. A stone is released from a balloon while the balloon is ascending at the rate of 5.0 m/s and when the balloon is 353 m above the ground. What time is required for the stone to reach the ground?

10. A baseball is thrown vertically downward from the top of a 155-m tower with an initial velocity of 25 m/s. (a) With what velocity does it reach the ground? (b) What time is required for it to reach the ground?

# NEWTON'S LAWS OF MOTION

Thus far in Chapter 3 we have largely discussed motion apart from other physical quantities. Now we shall study the relationship between forces and the motion of bodies. A *force is a physical quantity that can affect the motion of an object*. A push or a pull is a force. A force is a vector quantity. It requires magnitude, direction, and a point of application for its description. Forces behave like other quantities that can be represented by vectors. In the MKS system of measurement, forces are measured in *newtons* (n).

The relationships among force, mass, and motion were described clearly for the first time by Sir Isaac Newton (1642–1727) in three laws of motion that bear his name. While some aspects of Newton's laws of motion can be tested only under carefully controlled conditions, repeated experiments and observations have led scientists to believe that the laws are universally true. That is, the laws apply not only to objects on or near the earth, but to objects throughout the universe. See Figure 3-14.

Newton's first law of motion deals with the motion of a body on which no net force is acting. That is, either there is no force at all acting on the body or the *vector sum* of all forces acting on the body is zero. The word "net" refers to the second situation. Even though a body may have many forces acting on it, these forces may act against each other. They may balance each other in such a way that the body does not change its state of motion. If such a body is at rest, it will remain at rest. If it is in motion, it will continue in its motion *in a straight line with uniform speed. Newton's first law of motion* may therefore be summarized as follows: *If there is no net force acting on a body, it will continue in its state of rest or will continue moving along a straight line with uniform speed.*

At first glance, this law seems to contradict our everyday experiences. If a car is to be kept moving with a constant velocity, the car's engine must apply a constant force to it. If the engine stops applying this force, the car comes to a stop. Only then does the car seem to obey the part of Newton's law that states that

## 3.8 Inertia

**Figure 3-14** Sir Isaac Newton formulated the law of gravitation and three laws of motion that describe how forces act on matter.

*The law of inertia states that unless a net force acts on an object, the object keeps on doing the same thing so far as motion is concerned.*

**Figure 3-15** A diagram of Galileo's thought experiment. In the upper and middle drawings, the ball reaches almost the same height as that at which it started. In the lower drawing, the ball continues to move indefinitely at constant speed. In each drawing, the successive images show the positions of the ball after equal time intervals.

objects at rest will remain at rest unless acted upon by an unbalanced force.

Close study of a moving car shows, however, that it is the force of friction that brings the car to a stop and not the absence of the force provided by the engine. If it were possible to remove this friction, it would be reasonable to assume that the car would keep rolling without applying a constant force.

The study of the motion of a car in the absence of friction is an example of a *thought experiment* since the study cannot be performed under actual conditions. It was a thought experiment of this kind that led Galileo to an understanding of inertia even before Newton described it. Galileo noticed that if a ball rolls down one incline and up a second one, as shown in Figure 3-15, the ball will reach almost the same height on the second incline as the height from which it started on the first incline. Galileo concluded that the difference in height is caused by friction and that if friction could be eliminated the heights would be exactly alike. Then he reasoned that the ball would reach the same height no matter how shallow the slope of the second incline. Finally, if the second slope were eliminated altogether, the ball would keep rolling indefinitely with constant velocity. This is the same idea as the one expressed in Newton's first law of motion, which deals with the property of inertia. Inertia keeps a stationary object stationary, and it keeps a moving object moving. A demonstration of the first part of this statement is shown in Figure 3-16.

*Inertia can be verified more easily in space than on the earth's surface, where friction and gravity intervene.*

**Figure 3-16** A demonstration of inertia. As the table moves quickly to the right, the chicken dinner is momentarily suspended in midair.

The greater the inertia of an object, the greater is the force required to produce a given acceleration. A pencil lying on the floor has relatively little mass and therefore little inertia. You can produce acceleration easily by kicking it with your foot. A brick has much more mass and more inertia. You can easily tell its difference from the pencil if you try to kick it. Newton's first law specifies which aspects of motion have a *cause* and which aspects do not. Uniform motion in a straight line is the only motion possible for an object far removed from other objects. Nonuniform motion of an object is always *caused* by the presence of some other object.

---

Newton's first law of motion tells us how a body acts when there is no net applied force. Let us consider what happens when there *is* either a single applied force or two or more applied forces whose *vector sum* is not zero. In the following discussion, we shall use "applied force" or just "force" to mean the vector sum of all forces applied to the body.

**Newton's second law of motion** may be stated as follows: *The effect of an applied force is to cause the body to accelerate in the direction of the force. The acceleration is in direct proportion to the force and in inverse proportion to the mass of the body.*

If the body is at rest when the force is applied, it will begin to move in the direction of the force and will move faster and faster as long as the force continues.

If the body is moving in a straight line and a force is applied in the direction of its motion, it will increase in speed and continue to do so as long as the force continues. If the force is applied in the direction opposite to the motion, the acceleration will again be in the direction of the force, causing the body to slow down. If such a force continues long enough, the body will slow down to a stop and then begin to move with increasing speed in the opposite direction.

If the force applied to a moving object is not along the line of its motion, the acceleration will still be in the direction of the force. The effect in general will be to change both the direction and the speed of the motion. We shall postpone detailed consideration of this more complex case until Chapter 5. For the present we shall consider only the speed of an object initially at rest or one that is moving in a straight line that is changed only by a force acting along that line.

It should be emphasized again that a body to which no force is applied has zero acceleration. If such a body is in motion, its velocity does not change. If it is at rest, its velocity remains unchanged; its velocity stays at zero. And when there is no change in velocity, the acceleration is zero. When a force is applied to a body, the acceleration is not zero and the acceleration is in the direction of the applied force.

## 3.9 Law of acceleration

*Newton's second law of motion describes both the direction and the magnitude of acceleration.*

*Because of friction, stepping on the accelerator of a car does not necessarily accelerate the car.*

If different forces are applied to the same body, the magnitude of the acceleration is directly proportional to the amount of the force. That is, doubling the force causes the acceleration to double, and so on.

We can express such a direct proportion as an equation by saying that one of the quantities equals the other one times a constant, or

$$F = ka$$

in which $F$ is the applied force, $a$ is the resulting acceleration, and $k$ is the constant of proportionality. Since $F$ and $a$ are both vectors, this equation also says that the applied force and the resulting acceleration are in the same direction (which is a restatement of the first part of Newton's second law of motion).

What happens when forces are applied to *different* objects? This question brings us to the third part of Newton's second law. It turns out that the equation $F = ka$ is always true but that the value of $k$ is different for different objects. In fact, we find that if we properly define the units of force and mass, the value of $k$ for any object is identical with the mass, $m$, of that object. The equation may be written

$$F = ma$$

In the MKS system, the unit of mass is the kilogram and acceleration has the units of meters per second$^2$. (See Section 3.5.) The force required to accelerate 1 kilogram of mass at 1 meter per second$^2$ is 1 kg m/s$^2$. This force is called a *newton* (n) and is defined by the relationship

$$\mathbf{1\ n = 1\ kg\ m/s^2}$$

Since the acceleration acquired by a particular object is directly proportional to the amount of force applied, this law of acceleration can be expressed as the proportion

$$\frac{F}{F'} = \frac{a}{a'}$$

where $F$ and $F'$ are two different forces and $a$ and $a'$ are the corresponding accelerations.

In the case of a freely falling object, one of the forces is known. It equals the weight, $F_w$, of the object. The acceleration, $g$, is also known. It is the acceleration due to gravitation, 9.80 m/s$^2$. Making these substitutions, the proportion becomes

$$\frac{F}{F_w} = \frac{a}{g}$$

and

$$F = \frac{F_w a}{g}$$

Using this equation, we can calculate the force needed to give any desired acceleration to an object of known weight.

Since $F = ma$, we can substitute this value for $F$ in the above equation and get

$$ma = \frac{F_w a}{g}$$

Dividing both sides of the equation by $a$, we have

$$m = \frac{F_w}{g} \quad \text{and} \quad F_w = mg$$

See the following example.

*Notice the similarity between $F_w = mg$ and $F = ma$. Can you explain this similarity?*

**EXAMPLE**

*What force is required to accelerate a car weighing $2.00 \times 10^4$ n from 30.0 km/hr to 70.0 km/hr in 10.0 s?*

**SOLUTION**

*Basic equation:* $F = ma$

*but* $\quad m = \dfrac{F_w}{g}$

*and* $\quad a = \dfrac{\Delta v}{\Delta t} = \dfrac{v_f - v_i}{\Delta t}$

Substituting for $m$ and $a$ we get
*Working equation:*

$$F = \frac{F_w(v_f - v_i)}{g\,\Delta t}$$

$$F = \frac{2.00 \times 10^4 \text{ n } (70.0 \text{ km/hr} - 30.0 \text{ km/hr})(1000 \text{ m/km})}{(9.80 \text{ m/s}^2)(10.0 \text{ s})(3600 \text{ s/hr})}$$

$$F = 2.27 \times 10^3 \text{ n}$$

---

**3.10 Law of interaction**

*Newton's third law of motion* states the following: *When one body exerts a force on another, the second body exerts on the first a force of equal magnitude in the opposite direction.* To illustrate this law, consider some of the forces that are exerted when a book is resting on the top of a level table. The book exerts a downward force against the table. The table top exerts an upward force on the book. These forces are equal in magnitude and opposite in direction. When you walk forward on a level floor your feet exert a horizontal force against the floor. At the same time, the floor pushes against your feet with a force of equal magnitude, but in the opposite direction.

*For every action there is an equal and opposite reaction.*

In each of these situations we have two objects. In the first instance, the objects are the book and the table. In the second instance, they are the foot and the floor. Two forces are involved in each situation. In the first, they are the force of the book against the table and the force of the table against the book. In the second, they are the force of the foot against the floor and the force of the floor against the foot. In cases such as these, one force may be called the *action,* while the second force may be called the *reaction.* Thus unaccompanied forces do not exist in nature.

The law of reaction holds true for all objects at all times, whether they are stationary or moving. Let us consider another example. A boy rows a boat toward the shore of a lake and, when he is a meter or so from shore, he attempts to leap ashore. He exerts a force against the boat and the boat exerts an equal but opposite force against him. The force exerted by the boat against the boy accelerates him. The direction of his acceleration is opposite to the direction in which his force caused the boat to be accelerated. If we assume the resistance to the motion of the boat by the water to be negligible, the amount of acceleration of each object is inversely proportional to its mass. The boy might judge the force he must exert to reach shore on the basis of his experience in jumping the same distance from an object fixed to the earth. If so, when he jumps from the boat, he might not reach shore, but instead fall into the water.

Suppose we fasten one spring balance to a rigid support and hook another spring balance to it, as shown in Figure 3-17. If we pull on one balance, we find that both balance readings are the same. The pull of the first balance on the second equals the pull of the second on the first. The action is equal but opposite to the reaction.

You may argue that motion cannot occur if action and reaction are equal. If two people pull on a lightweight wagon with equal force in opposite directions, the wagon will not move. But this is not an example of action and reaction. There are two forces, it is true, and they have the same magnitude and opposite directions, *but they are both exerted on the same object.* Action and reaction apply when forces are exerted on different objects. For example, action and reaction are involved in the force that each one's feet exert against the ground and the equal but opposite force the ground exerts against the feet.

**Figure 3-17** An example of action-reaction. The readings on the two spring balances are equal because the force exerted by the person pulling on one balance is accompanied by an equal and opposite resisting force of the table.

# questions

GROUP A

1. If a steel ball is placed on the top of a level table, it will remain there. (a) What forces are acting on the ball in this situation? (b) Are there any unbalanced forces acting on the ball?

2. (a) If the steel ball of Question 1 is given a slight push, what happens to the ball? (b) What forces act on the ball after it has been pushed? (c) Are any of these unbalanced forces? (d) What is the effect of the various forces on the motion of the ball?

3. (a) State Newton's first law of motion. (b) Describe the motion of a body in equilibrium.

4. (a) If other conditions are constant, how does the acceleration of an object vary with the amount of force applied? (b) How does the direction of the acceleration compare with the direction of the applied force?

5. How does the acceleration produced on different objects by identical forces vary with the mass of the object?

6. (a) State Newton's second law of motion. (b) What equation expresses the relationship of force to mass and acceleration?

7. How can the amount of force required to produce a certain acceleration of an object of known weight be calculated?

8. Suppose a brick is suspended from a rigid support by a suitable length of cord. (a) What downward force acts on the brick? (b) If this force is the action force, what force is the reaction force?

9. (a) What upward force acts on the suspended brick in Question 8? (b) If this force is the action force, what is the corresponding reaction force?

GROUP B

10. (a) What is meant by a thought experiment? (b) Give an example.

11. Why does a falling object in a vacuum undergo constant acceleration?

12. (a) Does Newton's second law hold only when frictional forces are absent? (b) Explain.

13. A fishline will break when a force of more than 600 n is exerted on it. Two people pull on the line in opposite directions with a force of 400 n each. (a) Will the fish line break? (b) Explain.

14. Explain the thought experiment you could devise to determine the mass of an object if you had only the following objects: a frictionless horizontal plane, a 1-kilogram standard, a meter stick, a spring balance in which the scale is marked in units unknown to you, and a stopwatch.

15. A tractor is pulling a heavy load. (a) If, according to Newton's third law, the load is pulling back as hard as the tractor is pulling forward, then why does the tractor move? (b) Make a drawing of the situation and show the appropriate force vectors.

16. If a third spring balance is placed between the other two in Figure 3-17, what will be the reading on the center balance? Test your answer in the laboratory.

# problems

*Note:* Use $g = 9.80$ m/s². All forces are net forces.

GROUP A

1. What force is required to accelerate a 3.0-kg object (which is free to move) at 5.0 m/s²?

2. What is the mass of an object that is accelerated 3.00 m/s² by a force of 125 n?

3. What acceleration does an object, mass 15 kg, undergo when a force of 25 n acts on it?

4. What is the weight of a 24-kg block of stone at sea level?

GROUP B

5. What is the mass of a bag of cement that weighs 485 n at sea level?

6. What force is required to give a projectile weighing 475 n an acceleration of $3.00 \times 10^3$ m/s²?

7. A truck weighs $1.0 \times 10^5$ n. What force will give it an acceleration of 1.5 m/s²?

## 3.11 Newton's law of universal gravitation

*Newton developed his laws of motion and gravitation while he was home from college on an extended vacation during the Great Plague in 1665.*

In addition to formulating his three laws of motion, Newton described the force that makes falling bodies accelerate toward the earth. In doing so, he made use of the laws of planetary motion that were developed by Johannes Kepler almost a century before Newton's time. See Section 1.4. In Newton's own account of his study of falling bodies, he states that he wondered whether the force that makes an apple fall to the ground was related to the force that keeps the planets in their orbits. If so, a single law could be used to describe the attraction between objects in all parts of the universe.

From Kepler's laws, Newton deduced the fact that the *force of attraction between two objects is directly proportional to the product of the masses of the objects and inversely proportional to the square of the distance between their centers of mass.* (The center of mass of an object is that point at which all its mass can be considered to be concentrated. This concept is similar to that of "center of gravity," which will be discussed in Chapter 4.) Newton called this attractive force the *force of gravitation.* Hence the statement is known as Newton's **law of universal gravitation**. In equation form the law is

$$F = G \frac{m_1 m_2}{d^2}$$

where $F$ is the force of gravitation, $m_1$ and $m_2$ are the masses of the attracting objects, $d$ is the distance between their centers of mass, and $G$ is a proportionality constant called the *universal gravitational constant.*

Newton was only able to confirm his theory with astronomical observations. He was unable to confirm his theory in the laboratory or to measure $G$ with the instruments available to him at that time. The first determination of $G$ was made in 1797 by the English scientist Henry Cavendish (1731–1810). A schematic diagram of this experiment is shown in Figure 3-18. Two small lead balls are attached to the end of a lightweight rod that has a mirror attached to it. The rod is suspended by a thin quartz fiber. Two large lead balls are placed in fixed positions near the small balls. The gravitational force between the fixed and movable balls draws the movable balls toward the fixed ones. This motion causes the suspending fiber to twist. The fiber offers a slight resistance to twisting. The resistance increases as the twisting increases, and the angle of twist is proportional to the force of gravitation between the fixed and the movable balls. The angle of twist could be measured directly from the rod's movement, but the sensitivity of the instrument can be increased by shining a light into the mirror. The light is reflected onto a distant scale, and small movements of the mirror result in large movements of the reflected light across the

**Figure 3-18** A schematic diagram of the Cavendish experiment. The gravitation between the balls can be measured by observing, with the help of a light beam, the deflection of the rod carrying the small balls.

scale. Such an arrangement is called an optical lever. Since $G$ has a very small value, extreme care must be used to isolate the Cavendish apparatus from outside forces such as those produced by air currents and electric charges.

The value of $G$ has been found to be $6.67 \times 10^{-11}$ n m²/kg². But recent studies of bodies in the solar system, especially the moon, indicate that $G$ may not be constant. The force of gravitation between the earth and the moon moves large masses of water on the earth. (These movements of water are called tides.) Moving this mass on the earth causes the moon's rotation to slow down. However, the moon is slowing down at twice the rate that can be attributed to the tides. The extra decrease can be explained by a decrease in $G$ of about 1 part in 10 billion per year. See Figure 3-19. Similar evidence is seen in the orbits of binary stars (stars that revolve around each other). The rate of revolution of binary stars as well as the sizes of their orbits depend upon the value of $G$. The large number of binary stars having large orbits supports the idea that the value of $G$ is gradually decreasing.

**Figure 3-19** The earth as seen from lunar orbit by the Apollo 8 astronauts. Separated by 380,000 kilometers of space, the earth and moon are held by gravitation in a mutually revolving system.

## 3.12 The mass of the earth

Once $G$ has been measured, the equation for Newton's law of universal gravitation can be used to find the force of gravitation between any two objects of known mass with a known distance between their centers of mass. Or if the force of gravitation, the distance, and one of the masses are known, the equation can be used to find the value of the other mass. For example, the equation can be used to find the mass of the earth. In the equation, use $m_e$, the mass of the earth, for $m_1$. For $m_2$, use $m_p$, the mass of a particle on the earth's surface. In this case $d$ will be the radius of the earth. The force of gravitation, $F$, will be the weight of the particle, so we shall replace $F$ by $F_w$.

$$F_w = G \frac{m_e m_p}{d^2} \qquad \text{(Equation 1)}$$

Dividing both sides of the equation by $m_p$,

$$\frac{F_w}{m_p} = \frac{Gm_e}{d^2} \qquad \text{(Equation 2)}$$

But

$$F_w = m_p g \qquad \text{(Equation 3)}$$

Or

$$\frac{F_w}{m_p} = g \qquad \text{(Equation 4)}$$

Substituting Equation 4 in Equation 2,

$$g = \frac{Gm_e}{d^2} \qquad \text{(Equation 5)}$$

Since both $G$ and $m_e$ are constants, Equation 5 shows that the acceleration due to gravity in a given location depends only on the square of the distance from the center of the earth.

Equation 5 may be used to determine the mass of the earth. Solving this equation for $m_e$,

$$m_e = \frac{gd^2}{G}$$

*Compare this value with the one given in Section 2.4. Are they the same?*

Substituting 9.80 m/s² for $g$, $6.37 \times 10^6$ m for $d$, and $6.67 \times 10^{-11}$ n m²/kg² for $G$, $m_e = 5.96 \times 10^{24}$ kg, the mass of the earth.

## 3.13 Relation of gravity and weight

Table 3-2

| SURFACE GRAVITIES OF THE MOON AND PLANETS | |
|---|---|
| Body | Relative gravity (Earth = 1.00) |
| Jupiter | 2.54 |
| Neptune | 1.2 |
| Saturn | 1.07 |
| Uranus | 0.8 |
| Earth | 1.00 |
| Venus | 0.894 |
| Mercury | 0.378 |
| Mars | 0.379 |
| Pluto | uncertain |
| Moon | 0.165 |

*In space flight, forces are often described as multiples of the force of gravity on the earth's surface. Thus a force of $3g = 3 \times 9.8$ n = 29 n.*

*The term **gravity** is used to describe the force of gravitation on an object on or near the surface of a celestial body, such as the earth.* Thus we say that the moon has less gravity than the earth because the force of gravitation near the moon's surface is smaller than the force of gravitation near the earth's surface. A calculation of the gravity of a celestial body near the surface must take into consideration the size of the body since the force of gravitation varies inversely with the square of the distance to the center of mass of the body. The surface gravities of the moon and planets are compared in Table 3-2.

The value for the mass of the earth can be used to determine the theoretical value of the gravity at any given location on or above the earth's surface. Such factors as local variations in the composition of the earth's crust and the effect of the earth's rotation must be considered to obtain the actual value of the gravity at a particular location.

Equation 1, Section 3.12 shows that the weight of an object is the measure of the force of attraction between the object and the earth. When we say that a person weighs $9\overline{0}0$ n, we mean that the force exerted on that person by the earth is $9\overline{0}0$ n. The person also exerts a force of $9\overline{0}0$ n on the earth. Equation 3 tells us that the weight of an object equals the product of its mass and the acceleration due to gravity. The mass of an object is constant. But Equation 5 indicates that the acceleration due to gravity is inversely proportional to the square of the distance from the center of the body to the center of the earth. All parts of the earth's surface are not the same distance from its center. The variations range from 393 m below sea level at the shore of the Dead Sea to 8848 m above sea level at the top of Mount Everest. An object at the top of a mountain, where gravity is less, will weigh less there than it does at sea level. Also, since the earth is slightly flattened at the poles and since the earth's rotation counteracts the force of gravitation, an object weighs a little more at the North Pole than it does at the equator.

## 3.14 Gravitational fields

The value of $g$, the acceleration due to gravity, at a particular point is sometimes called the *gravitational field strength* at that point. The effect of rotation, if any, is usually included in determining $g$. *A region of space in which each point is associated with the value of g at that point is called a **gravitational field**.* Since $g$ is an acceleration, it is a vector. Hence a gravitational field is a region of space in which each point has associated with it a vector equal to the value of $g$ at that point and which is called the gravitational field strength.

If an object of mass $m$ is located at any point in a gravitational field, the force of gravitation on the object can be calculated by the equation in Section 3.9

$$F_W = mg$$

If the mass of the object is 1 kg, then $F_W$ is numerically equal to $g$. Another way to think of the gravitational field strength at a point is that it equals the force of gravitation that would be exerted on a mass of one kilogram if the mass were located at that point, or

$$g = \frac{F_W}{m}$$

The value of $g$ for the earth varies with the distance from the center of the earth and with certain other aspects of the earth's motion and composition. In Figure 3-20, vectors are used to represent the gravitational field strength at various altitudes. Table 3-3 lists the values of gravitational field strength for various locations on the earth's surface, as determined by careful measurements.

The concept of a field is more subtle and more complicated than the idea of direct forces acting between objects. Yet the field concept can explain more physical phenomena (such as electromag-

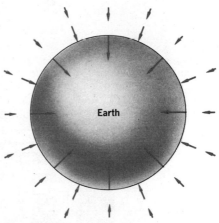

**Figure 3-20** Simplified diagram of the earth's gravitational field. The inner circle of vectors represents the magnitude and direction of the field at various places on the earth's surface. The outer vectors represent the field at different altitudes.

Table 3-3

| GRAVITATIONAL FIELD STRENGTH OF THE EARTH | | | |
|---|---|---|---|
| Location | Latitude | Altitude (m) | Field strength (n/kg) |
| North Pole | 90°N | 0 | 9.832 |
| Greenland | 70°N | 20 | 9.825 |
| Stockholm | 59°N | 45 | 9.818 |
| Brussels | 51°N | 102 | 9.811 |
| Banff | 51°N | 1376 | 9.808 |
| Chicago | 42°N | 182 | 9.803 |
| New York | 41°N | 38 | 9.803 |
| Denver | 40°N | 1638 | 9.796 |
| San Francisco | 38°N | 114 | 9.800 |
| Canal Zone | 9°N | 6 | 9.782 |
| Java | 6°S | 7 | 9.782 |
| New Zealand | 37°S | 3 | 9.800 |

netic waves) than the simpler concept of action at a distance. The field idea pictures objects as having associated regions such that a mass would be acted on by a force if it were placed in the region. Thus a ball falls to the earth because of the interaction between the gravitational field of the earth and the ball.

A gravitational field may be thought of as resulting from the fact that an object changes the properties of the space in its vicinity. It should not be supposed, however, that the field concept is an explanation of the cause of gravitation any more than the idea of acceleration is. Even though scientists are able to express certain aspects of gravitation in terms of acceleration and force fields, the real nature and origin of the force of gravitation are still unknown.

The concept of fields is not restricted to gravitation. The concept is useful when effects extend into the region surrounding their source. We will have occasion to use the idea of fields again in the discussion of magnetism, electricity, and nuclear structure.

**Figure 3-21** On the earth, this astronaut's gear would be too heavy for him to carry. On the moon, it weighs only about $\frac{1}{6}$ as much.

# summary

Displacement is a change of position of an object in a particular direction. Motion is the displacement of an object in relation to stationary objects. Speed is the time rate of motion. Velocity is speed in a particular direction. Speed is a scalar quantity, but velocity is a vector quantity. Graphs can be used to determine average and instantaneous speed and velocity. Velocity problems can be worked graphically, or they can be worked trigonometrically by use of the parallelogram method of vector addition.

Acceleration is the rate of change of velocity. The relationships among displacement, time, initial and final velocity, and acceleration can be expressed as equations. In the case of freely falling bodies, the acceleration caused by the earth's gravity is used.

A force is a physical quantity that can affect the motion of an object. Newton's laws of motion are (1) a body will continue in its state of rest or uniform motion in a straight line unless a net force acts on it; (2) the acceleration of a body is directly proportional to the net force exerted on it, inversely proportional to its mass, and in the same direction as the force; (3) when one body exerts a force on another body, the second body exerts an equal force on the first body but in the opposite direction.

The force of gravitation is the mutual force of attraction between bodies. Newton's law of universal gravitation states that the force of gravitation between two objects is directly proportional to the product of their masses and inversely proportional to the square of the distance between their centers of mass. The mass of the earth can be calculated by means of this law. The force of gravitation near the surface of a celestial body is called gravity. The values of gravity at various distances from a celestial body make up the gravitational field of the body.

# questions

GROUP A

1. (a) What force acts on an artificial satellite in orbit around the earth? (b) What force is the satellite exerting?

2. (a) On what factors does the magnitude of the force of gravitation depend? (b) How is the force of gravitation related to these factors?

3. Why must we exert five times as much force to lift a mass of 5 kg as we must to lift a mass of 1 kg?

4. Assuming your mass remains constant, how will your weight vary as you go from Colorado Springs, elevation 1800 m, to the top of Pikes Peak, elevation 4300 m?

5. Even though your mass remains constant, what happens to your weight as you drive from the entrance to Death Valley National Monument, eleva-

tion 1600 m, down to the lowest spot in Death Valley, 85 m below sea level?

6. Describe the method used by Cavendish to measure the universal gravitational constant.

GROUP B

7. (a) How does the weight of an object vary as it is transported from the earth to the moon? (b) How would its weight vary if it were transported to the center of the earth?

8. Why does the equation $g = Gm_e/d^2$ give a theoretical and not an actual value for the acceleration due to gravity at a given location?

9. (a) What is meant by a gravitational field? (b) How is gravitational field strength defined?

# problems

GROUP A

1. The acceleration due to gravity on the moon is 1.62 m/s². If a person weighs 795 n on the earth, what will the person's weight be on the moon?

2. The instrument-carrying payload of a rocket weighs 1058 n on the surface of the earth. What does it weigh $2.560 \times 10^4$ km above the earth?

3. The acceleration due to gravity at Hartford, Connecticut, is 9.80336 m/s². What is the force of gravitation in newtons on a mass of 0.250000 kg at this location?

GROUP B

4. What is the force of gravitation between two spherical $10\overline{0}$-kg masses whose centers are 2.00 m apart?

5. A 5.00 kg and a 10.0 kg sphere are 0.300 m apart. Find the force of gravitation between them.

6. Calculate the theoretical value for the acceleration due to gravity at a point $1.00 \times 10^7$ m from the center of the earth.

7. Show that the dimensions of $g$ in the equation $g = F_w/m$ are m/s².

# 4 Resolution and Composition of Forces

### 4.1 Describing forces

As we saw in Chapter 3, a force is a physical quantity that is required to change the motion of an object. Now we shall take a look at some other characteristics of forces, and see how these characteristics are used in solving force problems.

When you push a door shut with your hand, your hand exerts a force on the door. The door also exerts a force on your hand. When you sit in a chair, you push on the chair and the chair pushes on you. In both of these cases, there is physical contact between the objects that are exerting forces on each other. Another example of forces is illustrated in Figure 4-1.

Forces can also be exerted without such physical contact. While an object is falling toward the earth, the earth exerts a force on the object and the object exerts a force on the earth. Yet there is no physical contact between the earth and the falling object. These examples illustrate several important characteristics of forces:

*1. A net force will change the state of motion of an object.* The door moved because the force exerted by your hand was sufficient to overcome friction and other forces acting on the door. The falling object moved as it did because a force pulled it toward the earth. As we saw in Chapter 3, the application of a net force to an object always produces an acceleration.

*2. Forces can be exerted through long distances.* Gravitational forces and magnetic forces exhibit this characteristic.

*3. Forces always occur in pairs.* When one object pushes or pulls on another object, there is a force on *each* of the two objects. In the given examples, the two objects were your hand and the door, you and the chair, and the falling object and the earth.

**Figure 4-1** Large forces at work in an open-pit mine. This huge excavator, called a "walking dragline," handles with each bite about 168 cubic meters of earth and rock overlying a coal mine.

*4. In each pair of forces, the two forces act in exactly opposite directions.* You pushed on the door, and the door pushed back. You pushed down, and the chair pushed up. The earth pulled the falling object toward the earth's center, and the object pulled the earth toward the object's center.

*A force never exists by itself.*

*[handwritten: must be reactions to each other (3 & 4)]*

Now let us see how the magnitudes of forces are measured. (You will remember from Chapter 3 that forces are vector quantities and have both magnitudes and directions.) When an object is suspended from a spring, it is pulled toward the earth by the force of gravitation. The spring stretches until the restoring force of the spring is equal to the force of gravitation on the object. Another object having the same weight stretches the spring by the same amount. Both objects together stretch the spring twice as far, and an object with three times the weight stretches it three times as far, etc. This characteristic of coiled springs, that the amount of stretch is proportional to the force pulling on the spring, means that we may use the amount of stretch to measure the size of a force. A device that measures forces in this way is called a *spring balance.*

*Refer to Section 1.8 for a discussion of spring and platform balances.*

In physics, spring balances are often calibrated directly in newtons. Forces may also be measured with devices other than spring balances. But the results of such measurements can always be expressed in terms of a number of newtons.

---

In Section 2.6, vectors were introduced and used to solve velocity problems. Now vectors will be used to represent forces and to solve force problems. Vector quantities, such as forces, require a magnitude and a direction for their description. The magnitude of the force is represented by the length of the arrow. The line of action of the force, its direction, may be deduced from the physical situation. For example, suppose a barge is being towed through still water by a tugboat. The tugboat applies a force of 10,$\overline{0}$00 n to the barge through the towline. The length of the arrow representing the force is proportional to the magnitude of the force, 10,$\overline{0}$00 n. Figure 4-2 is a diagram of this example. The point of application of the force is the point at which the rope is attached to the barge. A long rope can transmit only a pull in a direction along its length. It cannot transmit a push or a sideways force. The rope is in the direction of the force. The arrow should represent this direction.

Force vectors are treated like velocity vectors. For example, suppose two tugboats are attached to the same barge. Tugboat **A** is pulling with a force of 10,$\overline{0}$00 n and tugboat **B** is pulling with a force of 7,500 n in the same direction. Figure 4-3 represents this situation with vectors. The resultant force vector is 17,500 n in the direction of the towline. Figure 4-4 shows a vector diagram representing two tugboats pulling in opposite directions on a barge.

## 4.2 Using vectors to represent forces

*[handwritten: e.g. $\vec{A} = A$]*

**Figure 4-2** A vector diagram of a force of 10,$\overline{0}$00 n applied by a tugboat to a barge through a towline. In such a diagram, the direction and point of application of the vector represent the line of action and point of application of the force. These may be reasoned from the direction and point of attachment of the towline.

10,$\overline{0}$00 n

**Figure 4-3** A vector diagram of two tug-boats applying forces to a barge at points $O_1$ and $O_2$. Tugboat **A** exerts a force of 10,000 n, and tugboat **B** exerts a force of 7,500 n. The resultant force vector is 17,500 n in the direction both tugs are pulling.

**Figure 4-4** A vector diagram of two tug-boats applying forces to a barge in op-posite directions. In many cases, even though the forces act on extended objects such as opposite ends of the barge as in our example, vectors may be considered as acting on the same point **O**. Tugboat **A** pulling west exerts a force of 10,000 n. Tugboat **B** pulling east exerts a force of 7,500 n. The resultant force vector is 2,500 n in the direction of tugboat **A**.

*The sum of two or more vectors is called the resultant.*

Even though the forces act on extended objects such as opposite ends of the barge, the vectors may be considered as acting at the same point, **O**. The resultant force vector is 2,500 n in the direction of tugboat **A**.

**EXAMPLE**

*Two tugboats are attached by separate towlines to the same point, **O**, on a barge. Tugboat **A** is pulling north with a force of 10,000 n. Tugboat **B** is pulling east with a force of 7,500 n. What is the magnitude and direction of the resultant force vector?*

**SOLUTION**

Figure 4-5 represents this situation. In the figure, the resultant force is represented by $F_R$. Since **AOB** is a right angle, the parallelogram is a rectangle and **OAR** is also a right angle. **AR** is equal in length to **OB**.

$$\tan \theta = \frac{\mathbf{AR}}{\mathbf{OA}} = \frac{F_B}{F_A} = \frac{7,500 \text{ n}}{10,000 \text{ n}} = 0.75$$

$$\theta = 37°$$

$$\cos \theta = \frac{\mathbf{OA}}{\mathbf{OR}} = \frac{F_A}{F_R}$$

$$F_R = \frac{F_A}{\cos \theta} = \frac{10,000 \text{ n}}{0.799} = 12,500 \text{ n}$$

Hence $F_R = 12,500$ n at an angle of 37° east of north.

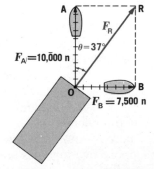

**Figure 4-5** A vector diagram of two tug-boats applying forces to a barge. Tugboat **A** exerts a force of 10,000 n north. Tug-boat **B** exerts a force of 7,500 n east. The resultant force vector is 12,500 n at an angle 37° east of north.

# RESOLUTION OF FORCES

Frequently a force acts on a body in a direction in which the body cannot move. For example, gravitational force pulls vertically downward on a wagon on an incline, but the wagon can move only along the incline. Finding the magnitude of the force that is pulling the wagon along the incline is an example of a problem of *resolution of forces*. Instead of a single force, two forces acting together can have the same effect as the original single force. One of the forces can be parallel to the surface of the incline and can pull the wagon along the incline. The other can be perpendicular to the surface of the incline. This force does not contribute to the force along the incline. These forces are at right angles to each other. The two forces that have the same effect as the single force are called the *components* of the original force. *This procedure of finding component forces is called resolution of forces*. Most of the examples we shall consider involve resolving a force into components that are at right angles to each other.

Before working problems with objects on an incline, study the following example, in which a force is resolved into two perpendicular components.

## 4.3 Components of force vectors

*A single force can be resolved into two or more components that have the same effect.*

**EXAMPLE**

*A force of 10.0 n acts on point **O** at an angle of 37.0° east of south, as shown in Figure 4-6. Find the magnitudes of the southward and eastward components of its force vectors graphically and trigonometrically.*

**SOLUTION**

$F_S = F_R \cos \theta$

$\cos \theta = \cos 37.0° = 0.799$

$F_S = (10.0 \text{ n})(0.799) = 7.99 \text{ n}$, the southward component

$\sin \theta = \dfrac{F_E}{F_R}$

$F_E = F_R \sin \theta$

$\sin \theta = \sin 37.0° = 0.602$

$F_E = (10.0 \text{ n})(0.602) = 6.02 \text{ n}$,

the eastward component

**Figure 4-6**  A diagram for the determination of the eastward and southward components of a 10.0-n force acting at an angle of 37° east of south.

## 4.4 Resolving the force vector of gravitational attraction

**Figure 4-7** Resolution of gravitational force. One component acts parallel to the plane while the other component acts normal (perpendicular) to the plane.

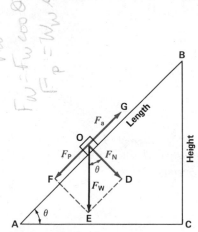

**Figure 4-8** When the angle of the incline increases, the component of the weight acting parallel to the plane increases, while the component that acts normal (perpendicular) to the plane decreases.

An object placed on an inclined plane is attracted by the earth. The force of attraction is the weight of the object. See Figure 4-7. The plane prevents the motion of the object in the direction of $F_W$, the direction in which the earth's attraction acts. The vector representing the force of attraction may, however, be resolved into two components. One component acts in a direction perpendicular to the surface of the plane. In physics, the term *normal* is often used to mean perpendicular. Hence we label the normal component $F_N$. The other component $F_P$, acts parallel to the plane. We choose these two components because they have physical significance. The vector $F_N$ represents the force exerted by the object perpendicular to the incline or the amount of the object's weight supported by the incline. The vector $F_P$ represents the component that tends to move the object down the incline. (The plane is assumed to be frictionless.)

Using $F_W$ as the diagonal, we can construct the parallelogram **ODEF** and find the relative values of the sides $F_P$ and $F_N$ by plotting to scale. We can also express these values trigonometrically. Since right triangles **ABC** and **OED** have mutually perpendicular, or parallel, sides, the triangles are similar and $\angle$ EOD = $\theta$. Hence sin $\theta$ can be expressed either as $\dfrac{BC}{AB}$ or $\dfrac{F_P}{F_W}$. This equation means that the force vector parallel to the plane, $F_P$, is smaller in magnitude than the weight vector, $F_W$, in the same ratio as the height of the plane, **BC**, is smaller than its length, **AB**.

By using cos $\theta$, it may be similarly shown that the magnitude of the force vector perpendicular to the plane, $F_N$, is related to the weight vector of the object in the same way that the base of the plane is related to its length.

If $\theta$ and $F_W$ are known,
$$F_P = F_W \sin \theta$$
and $F_N = F_W \cos \theta$

Making the plane steeper increases the component $F_P$ and decreases the component $F_N$. This steeper inclined plane is shown in Figure 4-8. The vector $F_a$, which is equal and opposite to $F_P$, represents the applied force needed to keep the object from sliding down the plane. The steeper the plane, the greater this force becomes. It should be noted that in both Figure 4-7 and Figure 4-8, the normal force that the plane exerts on the object in reaction to force $F_N$ is not shown. It does exist however.

# questions

GROUP A

1. (a) Define force. (b) Give examples of forces exerted by bodies in contact with each other. (c) What types of forces do not require such contact?

2. (a) What is the MKS unit of force? (b) From what fundamental units can it be derived?

3. What equation shows the relationship between force and mass?

4. What is the relationship between force and weight?

5. What properties of a force are represented by a force vector?

GROUP B

6. What type of motion is *not* the result of a net force?

7. (a) Describe two convenient components of the weight of an object lying on an inclined plane. (b) How are the magnitudes of these components related to the angle of the incline?

8. The transmitting tower of a TV station is held upright by guy wires that extend from the top of the tower to the ground. The wires make a 30.0° angle with the tower. Into what two convenient components can the force that the tower exerts on each guy wire be resolved?

9. An automobile is parked on a hill. (a) Into what two convenient components can the weight of the automobile be resolved? (b) Which component is counteracted by the brakes of the automobile?

# problems

Solve each of the following problems (a) graphically and (b) trigonometrically.

GROUP A

1. What single force is needed to support a stationary mass of 25.0 kg near the earth's surface?

2. A person pushes with 150.0 n of force along the handle of a lawn roller. The angle between the handle and the ground is 45.0°. Determine the magnitudes of the horizontal and vertical components of this force.

3. A truck weighing $1.00 \times 10^5$ n is parked on a hill that rises 3.00 m in each 100 m of road. What is the magnitude of the component of its weight that tends to make the truck roll down the hill?

4. A rectangular picture frame weighing 4.00 n is supported by a wire attached to its two top corners and passed over a nail in the wall. The top edge of the picture frame is horizontal. What force is exerted by

each half of the wire if the angle between them is (a) 60.0°; (b) 90.0°; (c) 120.0°?

GROUP B

5. A force of 25.0 n acts on point C at an angle of 35.0° west of north. What are the magnitudes of the northward and westward components of this force?

6. The rafters of a roof meet at an angle of 120.0°. What force is exerted along the rafters by an object weighing $6.00 \times 10^3$ n suspended from the peak?

7. A person pulls a sled along level ground. The rope with which the person pulls the sled makes an angle of 20.0° with the ground as the person pulls with a force of 78.0 n. What are the horizontal and vertical components of the force?

8. A crate having a mass of 114 kg rests on an inclined plane that makes an angle of 12.0° with the horizontal. (a) What force does the crate exert perpendicular to the plane? (b) What force tends to make the crate slide down the plane?

# COMPOSITION OF FORCES

skip

Just as it is possible to resolve a force into components, it is possible to combine several forces into a single force that produces the same effect. *When two or more forces have lines of action that pass through the same point, they are called **concurrent forces** and are said to act concurrently. A **resultant force** is a single force that produces the same effect as several forces acting concurrently.*

The resultant of two or more concurrent forces may be used as a substitute for those forces. The simplest example of such a resultant is that of two concurrent forces acting in the same direction. Suppose one girl pulls eastward with a force of 200 n and another girl joins her and pulls in the same direction with a force of 300 n. Refer to the vector diagram shown in Figure 4-9.

## 4.5 Resultant force of concurrent forces

*Concurrent forces act through the same point.*

*Several concurrent forces can be combined into a single resultant that has the same effect.*

**Figure 4-9** The resultant of two forces acting in the same direction has a magnitude equal to the sum of the forces and acts in the same direction.

**Figure 4-10** The resultant of two forces acting in opposite directions has a magnitude equal to the difference between the forces and acts in the direction of the greater force.

**Figure 4-11** A diagram for the graphic and trigonometric determination of the resultant force vector of two force vectors acting at right angles.

The resultant is the sum of the two forces, or $50\overline{0}$ n, acting eastward. One woman, taking the place of the two girls, could produce the same effect with a force of $50\overline{0}$ n.

Now suppose one girl pulls eastward with a force of $20\overline{0}$ n and another girl pulls westward on the same point with a force of $30\overline{0}$ n. This time the resultant force is $10\overline{0}$ n westward, as shown in Figure 4-10. *The resultant of two forces acting in the same or in opposite directions upon the same point has a magnitude equal to the algebraic sum of the forces and acts in the direction of the greater force.*

Suppose one force of 10.0 n, $F_E$, acts eastward upon an object at a point **O**. Another force of 15.0 n, $F_S$, acts southward upon the same point. Since these forces act concurrently upon point **O**, the vector diagram is constructed with the tails of both vectors at **O**. See Figure 4-11. $F_E$ tends to move the object eastward. $F_S$ tends to move the object southward. When the forces act simultaneously, the object tends to move along the diagonal of the parallelogram of which the two forces are sides. This is the vector $F_R$. *The resultant force vector of two forces acting at an angle upon a given point is equal to the diagonal of a parallelogram of which the two force vectors are sides.*

A graphic determination of the magnitude and direction of a resultant force can be made from a diagram constructed to scale. As in the problems of the resolution of forces in Section 4.4, the trigonometric solution makes use of the facts that the opposite sides of a parallelogram are equal and that the diagonal of a parallelogram divides it into two congruent triangles. If the two forces act at right angles, the magnitude and direction of the resultant $F_R$ can be determined as shown in the following example.

EXAMPLE

*Calculate the magnitude and direction of the resultant of the two forces acting on point **O** as shown in Figure 4-11.*

SOLUTION

Triangle **OSR** is a right triangle.

$$F_E = 10.0 \text{ n}$$
$$F_S = 15.0 \text{ n}$$
$$\tan \theta = \frac{F_E}{F_S} = \frac{10.0 \text{ n}}{15.0 \text{ n}} = 0.667$$
$$\theta = 33.7°$$
$$F_R = \frac{F_S}{\cos \theta} = \frac{15.0 \text{ n}}{0.833} = 18.0 \text{ n}$$

So $F_R = 18.0$ n 33.7° east of south

The angle between two forces acting on the same point is generally not a right angle. Figure 4-12 represents the vectors for the two forces 10.0 n east and 15.0 n 40.0° east of south acting on point **O**. The parallelogram is completed as shown. Observe that the diagonal vector representing the resultant *is drawn from the point on which the two original forces are acting since the resultant will also act on this point.* The magnitude of $F_R$ is found graphically to be 23 n. The direction is $\overline{30}°$ south of east.

The resultant is very different if the angle between the same two forces is 140.0°. The parallelogram is constructed to scale in the same manner. The force vectors are the sides and the angle between them 140.0°. This parallelogram is shown in Figure 4-13. The diagonal must be drawn from **O**, the point at which the two forces act. The graphic solution for $F_R$ yields $\overline{10}$ n 8° west of south.

The resultant of two forces acting at an acute or obtuse angle may be found trigonometrically by means of special formulas called the *law of sines* and the *law of cosines.* The use of these formulas is shown in the following example.

**Figure 4-12** A diagram for the graphic and trigonometric determination of the resultant of two force vectors acting at an acute angle.

**Figure 4-13** Diagram for the graphic and trigonometric determination of the resultant of two force vectors acting at an obtuse angle.

| | |
|---|---|
| **EXAMPLE** | *Trigonometrically determine the magnitude and direction of the resultant of the forces shown in Figure 4-12.* |
| **SOLUTION** | The magnitude and direction of $F_R$ can be found by the application of the law of cosines and the law of sines. |

$\angle$ **EOA** $= 50.0°$

$\angle$ **OER** $= 130.0°$

By the cosine law,

$F_R = \sqrt{F_E{}^2 + F_A{}^2 - 2\,F_E F_A \cos \angle \textbf{OER}}$

where $\cos \angle$ **OER** $= \cos 130.0° = -\cos(180.0° - 130.0°) = -\cos 50.0° = -0.643$

$F_R = \sqrt{(10.0 \text{ n})^2 + (15.0 \text{ n})^2 - 2(10.0 \text{ n})(15.0 \text{ n})(-0.643)} = 22.8 \text{ n}$

The magnitude of $F_R$ is 22.8 n.

By the sine law,

$\dfrac{\textbf{ER}}{\sin \angle \textbf{EOR}} = \dfrac{\textbf{OR}}{\sin \angle \textbf{OER}}$

$\sin \angle \textbf{EOR} = \dfrac{(\textbf{ER})(\sin \angle \textbf{OER})}{\textbf{OR}}$

$\sin \angle$ **OER** $= \sin 130.0° = \sin(180.0° - 130.0°) = \sin 50.0° = 0.766$

$\sin \angle \textbf{EOR} = \dfrac{(15.0 \text{ n})(0.766)}{22.8 \text{ n}} = 0.504$

$\angle$ **EOR** $= 30.3°$

The direction of $F_R$ is 30.3° south of east.

*4-6→4-9*
*no net force acting*

## 4.6 The equilibrant force

**Figure 4-14** The equilibrant of two forces acting at a point is applied at the same point. It equals the magnitude of their resultant but acts in the opposite direction.

*An equilibrant force is equal in magnitude to the resultant of two or more concurrent forces and acts in the opposite direction.*

**Equilibrium** *is the state of a body in which there is no change in its motion.* A body in equilibrium is either at rest or moving at constant speed in a straight line. In this section we shall discuss the conditions for equilibrium of bodies at rest. The same conditions hold for the equilibrium of bodies that are in motion. Examples of these conditions will be discussed in Chapter 5.

A body at rest must be in both translational and rotational equilibrium. *The first condition of equilibrium is that there are no unbalanced (net) forces acting on a body.* The second condition of equilibrium deals with rotation. It will be discussed in Section 4.13.

When there are no unbalanced forces acting on a body, the vector sum of all the forces acting on the body is zero. For example, if a person pulls on a rope with a force of $8\overline{0}$ n and another person pulls on the same rope in the opposite direction with a force of $8\overline{0}$ n, the vector sum of the two forces is zero and the system is in equilibrium. We can say also that each force is the *equilibrant* of the other.

To find the equilibrant of two forces, we first find their resultant. Then, since the equilibrant must balance the effect of this resultant, the equilibrant must have the same magnitude but act in the opposite direction. Figure 4-14 shows the equilibrant for the same force vectors that were used in the explanation of the resultant shown in Figure 4-11.

The equilibrant of three or more concurrent forces can be found in a similar way. The resultant of the concurrent forces is obtained by vector addition of their force vectors. Then the equilibrant is drawn from the origin of the resultant so that it is equal in magnitude to the resultant but extends in the opposite direction. *When two or more forces act concurrently at a point, the equilibrant force is that single force that if applied at the same point would produce equilibrium.*

*net force ≠ gross — tare = net*

## questions

### GROUP A

1. (a) What is a resultant force? (b) How is the resultant found when two forces act on the same point at the same time?

2. How can we determine mathematically the magnitude and direction of the resultant of two forces that act at right angles to each other on the same point?

3. (a) What is equilibrium? (b) What condition must be met for a body to be in equilibrium?

4. (a) What is an equilibrant force? (b) At what point must it be applied? (c) How does it compare with the resultant force?

### GROUP B

5. How can we determine mathematically the magnitude and direction of the resultant of two forces that act at any angle to each other on the same point?

6. What method can be used to find the magnitude of the resultant of three or more forces that act simultaneously on the same point?

7. How is the resultant affected when force vectors are added in different order?

# problems

## GROUP A

1. Two forces act simultaneously on point A. One force is 5.0 n south; the other is 15.0 n south. Determine the magnitude and direction of the resultant force vector.

2. Two forces act on point E. One is 20.0 n north; the other is 20.0 n 30.0° south of east. Determine the magnitude and direction of (a) the resultant, (b) the equilibrant.

3. A person weighs 612 n. If the person sits in the middle of a hammock that is 3.0 m long and sags 1.0 m below the points of support, what force would be exerted by each of the two hammock ropes?

## GROUP B

4. Trigonometrically determine the magnitude and direction of the resultant of the two force vectors shown in Figure 4-13.

5. Two forces of 10.0 n east and 30.0 n 30.0° south of west act on the same point. Determine the magnitude and direction of (a) the resultant, (b) the equilibrant.

6. Three forces act simultaneously on point J. One force is 10.0 n north; the second is 15.0 n west; the third is 15.0 n 30.0° east of north. Determine the magnitude and direction of the resultant.

7. A sign weighing 495 n is supported as shown in the diagram at the left. Determine the magnitudes and directions of the forces exerted by the chain and by the bracket. Assume that the horizontal rod cannot support vertical forces.

8. A block of stone having a mass of 2.00 × 10³ kg is to be raised by a crane. The angle between the load cable and the crane boom is 30.0°. The hinged boom is held in place by a tie cable that forms an angle of 20.0° with the boom. See the diagram at the right. Determine the magnitude of the thrust force (push) of the boom and of the tie force (pull) of the cable.

# FRICTION

## 4.7 The nature of friction

In Section 4.4 we discussed the resolution of the weight of an object resting on an incline. One of the components of the weight tends to pull the object down the incline. As the angle of the incline increases, this component also increases. The slightest angle of incline will produce the component that pulls the object down the incline *if* there is no restraining force on the object. However, in performing experiments of this type, we find that the object does not begin to slide until the component parallel to the incline reaches a certain value. This means that forces must exist between the object and the incline that prevent the object from sliding. These forces are called *forces of friction*, or simply *friction*. **Friction** *is a force that resists motion. It involves objects that are in contact with each other.*

The cause of friction is not simple. Some scientists believe that friction is caused mainly by the uneven surfaces of the touching objects. As the surfaces are rubbed together, they tend to interlock and thus offer resistance to being moved over each other. It has been shown that tiny particles are actually torn from one surface and become imbedded in the other.

*Friction resists the motion of objects that are in contact with each other.*

From this theory of friction one would expect that if the two surfaces are carefully polished, sliding friction between them would be lessened. Experiments have shown, however, that there is a limit to the amount by which friction may be reduced by polishing the surfaces. If they are made very smooth, the friction between them actually increases. This observation has led to the theory that some cases of sliding friction may be caused by the same forces that hold atoms and molecules together.

*Some of the causes of friction are difficult to explain.*

In many instances, friction is very desirable. We would be unable to walk if there were no friction between the soles of our shoes and the ground. There must be friction between the tires of an automobile and the road before the automobile can move. When we apply the brakes on the automobile, the friction between the brake linings and the brake drums or discs slows down the wheels. Friction between the tires and the road brings the car to a stop. In a less obvious way, friction holds screws and nails in place and it keeps dishes from sliding off a table if the table is not perfectly level. On the other hand, friction can also be a disadvantage, as it is when we try to move a heavy piece of furniture by sliding it across the floor.

*Without friction you couldn't write your homework.*

## 4.8 Principles of friction

Friction experiments are not difficult to perform but the results are not always easy to express as equations or laws. The following statements, therefore, should be understood as approximate descriptions only. Furthermore, they deal exclusively with solid objects. Frictional forces involving liquids and gases are beyond the scope of this book. Also, our discussion is restricted to starting and sliding friction. *Starting friction* is the maximum frictional force between stationary objects. *Sliding friction* is the frictional force between objects that are sliding with respect to one another. Static friction (which varies from 0 to the value of starting friction) and rolling friction are not considered in this introductory treatment.

**Figure 4-15** Forces on a block being pulled along a surface. $F_f$ is the force of sliding friction. The block does not move until $F_a$ exceeds the force of starting friction, which is usually greater than $F_f$.

*1. Friction acts parallel to the surfaces that are in contact and in the direction opposite to the motion of the object or to the net force tending to produce such motion.* Figure 4-15 illustrates this principle. The weight of the block, $F_W$, is balanced by the upward force of the table, $F_W'$. The force $F_a$ is sliding the block along the table top. In this case, $F_a$ is parallel to the table top. The sliding frictional force, $F_f$, also parallel to the table top, resists the motion and is exerted in a direction opposite to that of $F_a$.

*2. Friction depends on the nature of the materials in contact and the smoothness of their surfaces.* The friction between two

**Figure 4-16** The force of friction does not vary significantly with the area of contact if the two blocks have the same weight and all surfaces are equally smooth.

pieces of wood is different from the friction between wood and metal.

*3. Sliding friction is usually less than starting friction.* Starting friction prevents motion until the surfaces begin to slide. When the object begins to slide, less force is required to keep it sliding than was required to start it sliding.

*4. Friction is practically independent of the area of contact.* The force needed to slide a block along a table is almost the same whether the block lies on its side or on its end. Figure 4-16 illustrates this principle. The surfaces are in contact in more places when the area of contact is large, but the pressure is greater when the area is small.

*5. Starting or sliding friction is directly proportional to the force pressing the two surfaces together.* It does not require as much force to slide an empty chair across the floor as it does to slide the same chair when a person is sitting on it. The reason for this is that the extra force actually deforms the surfaces to some extent and thus increases the friction.

A simple way to measure starting and sliding friction is with a spring balance, as shown in Figure 4-16. By sliding blocks made of the same material and with equally smooth surfaces but of different sizes across the same surface, we can find the ratio between the force of sliding friction and the weight of the block. This ratio is called the ***coefficient of sliding friction***. It may be defined as *the ratio of the force of sliding friction to the normal (perpendicular) force pressing the surfaces together.* As an equation, it can be written as

*The coefficient of friction is always less than 1.*

*When an object rests on a horizontal surface, $F_N$ is the weight of the object, $F_W$.*

$$\mu = \frac{F_f}{F_N}$$

where $F_f$ is the force of sliding friction, $\mu$ (the Greek letter mu) is the coefficient of sliding friction, and $F_N$ is the normal (perpendicular) force between the surfaces. (Within certain limits, this equation is an approximate summary of friction measurements.) The coefficient of starting friction is determined in a similar fashion, except that $F_f$ is the force of starting friction. The approximate values for the coefficients of friction of various surfaces in contact with each other are given in Table 4-1.

Table 4-1

| COEFFICIENTS OF FRICTION | | |
|---|---|---|
| Surfaces | Starting friction | Sliding friction |
| steel on steel | 0.74 | 0.57 |
| glass on glass | 0.94 | 0.40 |
| wood on wood | 0.50 | 0.30 |
| rubber tire on dry road | | 0.70 |
| rubber tire on wet road | | 0.50 |
| Teflon on Teflon | 0.04 | 0.04 |

## 4.9 Changing friction

**Figure 4-17** Friction between skis and snow is appreciably reduced with the application of a wax layer on the wood or metal surface of the skis.

*The squeaking wheel gets the grease.*

In winter we sand icy sidewalks and streets in order to increase friction. Tire chains and snow tires are used for the same reason. In baseball, pitchers often use rosin to get more friction between their fingers and the ball. Many more examples could be given in which friction is purposely increased by changing the nature of the surfaces that are in contact.

The most common method of reducing sliding friction is by lubrication. The skier pictured in Figure 4-17 applied a layer of wax to the skis to reduce friction. A thin film of oil between rubbing surfaces reduces friction. The lesser friction between a liquid and a solid has replaced the greater friction between two solids. Alloys have also been developed that are in effect self-lubricating. For example, when steel slides over an alloy of lead and antimony, the coefficient of friction is less than when steel slides over steel. Bearings lined with such an alloy reduce friction. From Table 4-1 it is also obvious that if a bearing is coated with a plastic such as Teflon, there is very little friction. Such bearings are used in electric motors where the use of a liquid lubricant is undesirable.

Friction may also be greatly reduced through the use of ball bearings or roller bearings. Sliding friction is thereby changed to rolling friction, which has a much lower coefficient. Using steel cylinders to roll a heavy box along the floor is another example of changing sliding to rolling friction.

## 4.10 Solving friction problems

**Figure 4-18** A diagram for the determination of the coefficient of friction.

The force required to slide an object along a level surface can be computed easily from the weight of the object and the coefficient of sliding friction between the two surfaces. However, when the force applied to the object is not applied in the direction of the motion, it is necessary to resolve forces in the calculation. This resolution of forces is illustrated in the following example.

In the case of an object resting on an incline, the forces of starting and sliding friction will determine whether the object remains at rest, slides down the incline with constant speed, or accelerates as it descends. How the angle of the incline and coefficient of sliding friction are used in such a problem is illustrated in another example.

**EXAMPLE** | *A box weighing $45\overline{0}$ n is pulled along a level floor at constant speed by a rope that makes an angle of $30.0°$ with the floor, as shown in Figure 4-18. If the force on the rope is $26\overline{0}$ n, what is the coefficient of sliding friction?*

**SOLUTION**

*Basic equation:* $\mu = \dfrac{F_f}{F_N}$

Before we can use this equation, we must calculate the component of the applied force that acts parallel to the floor. Also, we must calculate the net normal force acting on the floor while the box is being pulled. This is done by finding the appropriate vector components.

The force $F_a$ has a horizontal component, $F_h$, which moves the object along the level floor. The force of friction, $F_f$, acts opposite to $F_h$. Since the speed is constant, $F_f = F_h$

$$F_f = F_h = F_a \cos 30.0°$$

The force between the surfaces, $F_N$, is due to the downward action of the weight that is decreased by the vertical upward component, $F_V$, of the force $F_a$.

$$F_N = F_W - F_V$$
$$F_V = F_a \sin 30.0°$$
$$F_N = F_W - F_a \sin 30.0°$$

Since $\mu = \dfrac{F_f}{F_N}$ while $F_f = F_a \cos 30.0°$ and $F_N = F_W - F_a \sin 30.0°$, substitution gives the

*Working equation:* $\mu = \dfrac{F_a \cos 30.0°}{F_W - F_a \sin 30.0°}$

$$\mu = \frac{(26\overline{0}\,\text{n})(0.866)}{45\overline{0}\,\text{n} - (26\overline{0}\,\text{n})(0.500)} = \frac{225\,\text{n}}{32\overline{0}\,\text{n}} = 0.703$$

**EXAMPLE**

*A wood block weighing $13\overline{0}$ n rests on an inclined plane, as shown in Figure 4-19. The coefficient of sliding friction between the block and the plane is 0.620. Find the angle of the inclined plane at which the block will slide down the plane at constant speed once it has started moving.*

**Figure 4-19** Diagram for the determination of the angle at which a block will slide down an incline.

**SOLUTION**

For the block to slide at constant speed, the net force in the direction of sliding must be zero. That is, the frictional force, $F_f$, must be just enough to equal and cancel the force $F_P$ that tends to pull the block downward along the incline.

*Basic equation:* $F_P = F_f$

But we know that the frictional force equals the coefficient of friction times the normal force, or $F_f = \mu F_N$. Substituting in the basic equation, we have

$$F_P = \mu F_N \qquad \text{or} \qquad \frac{F_P}{F_N} = \mu$$

From the diagram, we see that $\dfrac{F_P}{F_N} = \tan\theta$. Substituting in the previous equation, we now have $\tan\theta = \mu$. This is a useful result that holds for similar problems.

Since $\tan\theta = \mu$, then

*Working equation:* $\theta = \arctan\mu$. (This expression is read as $\theta$ is the angle whose tangent has a value of $\mu$.) Substituting the given value of $\mu$ in the equation,

$$\theta = \arctan 0.620$$

Looking up the angle whose tangent is 0.620 in Appendix B, Table 6, gives

$$\theta = 31.8°$$

In other words, the block will slide uniformly when the angle of the incline is 31.8°, no matter what the block weighs. (The weight of the block cancels out.) If the angle is less than 31.8°, the block will not slide at all. If the angle is greater than 31.8°, the block will accelerate as it slides down the plane. The angle at which the block slides depends only on the coefficient of friction.

# questions

## GROUP A

1. (a) What is friction? (b) What ideas have scientists presented to explain friction?
2. Give several examples of ways in which friction is helpful.
3. What methods are used to reduce friction?
4. How does sliding friction compare with starting friction?
5. (a) On what does the amount of sliding friction usually depend? (b) Of what is it independent?
6. What is meant by the coefficient of friction?

## GROUP B

7. What is the direction of the force of friction when two surfaces are moving over one another?
8. Name several devices that increase friction between the tires of a car and the pavement.
9. Why does a lubricant reduce friction in a bearing?
10. (a) Under what conditions is the weight of an object the same as the normal force pressing it to the surface over which it is moving? (b) How is the normal force component of the weight of an object determined under other conditions?

# problems

## GROUP A

*Note:* For each problem, draw a force diagram using a suitable scale, and then perform the necessary calculations.

1. A block weighs $2.00 \times 10^3$ n. If a horizontal force of $1.00 \times 10^2$ n is required to keep it in motion with constant speed on a horizontal surface, what is the coefficient of sliding friction?
2. In a coefficient of friction experiment, a horizontal force of 45 n was needed to keep an object weighing 125 n sliding at constant speed over a horizontal surface. Calculate the coefficient of sliding friction.
3. A crate weighing $1.25 \times 10^3$ n slides down an inclined plane at constant speed. The plane is 6.0 m long. Its height is 3.0 m. What is the coefficient of sliding friction between the crate and the inclined plane?

## GROUP B

4. The coefficient of sliding friction between a metal block and the inclined surface over which it will slide is 0.200. If the surface makes an angle of 20.0° with the horizontal and the block has a mass of 80.0 kg, what force is required to slide the block at constant speed up the plane?
5. A crate weighing $40\overline{0}$ n is pulled along a horizontal sidewalk at constant speed by a rope that makes an angle of 45.0° with the sidewalk. If a force of $15\overline{0}$ n is applied to the rope, what is the coefficient of sliding friction?
6. A box having a mass of 50.0 kg is dragged across a horizontal floor by means of a rope tied on the front of it. The coefficient of sliding friction between the box and the floor is 0.300. If the angle between the rope and the floor is 30.0°, what force must be

exerted on the rope to move the box at constant speed?

7. (a) If a crate slides down a 10.0° incline at constant speed, what is the coefficient of sliding friction between the crate and the incline? (b) What is the coefficient of sliding friction when a crate slides down a 20.0° incline at constant speed? (c) What is the coefficient of sliding friction for a crate moving at constant speed down an incline of x°?

8. A block weighing $13\overline{0}$ n is on an incline. It is held back by a weight of 45.0 n hanging from a cord

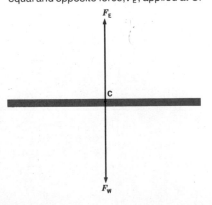

that passes over a frictionless pulley and is attached to the block as shown in the accompanying diagram. Find the angle at which the block will slide down the plane at constant speed. The coefficient of friction is 0.620.

# PARALLEL FORCES

Thus far in our study of forces, we have been treating all the forces acting on a body as if they were acting at a single point. In general, however, there may be many forces, each acting at a different point on the object. For example, Figure 4-20 represents a stone lying on the ground. Since every part of the stone has mass, every part is attracted to the center of the earth. Because of the large size of the earth, all the downward forces exerted on the stone are virtually parallel. The weight of the stone can be thought of as a force vector that is the vector sum, or resultant, of all these parallel force vectors. *Parallel forces act in the same or in opposite directions at different points on an object.* The resultant of parallel forces has a magnitude equal to the algebraic sum of all the forces. The resultant acts in the direction of this net force.

But where in the stone is this resultant force acting? Experiments show that if the proper point of application is chosen, the stone can be lifted without producing rotation. As shown in Figure 4-20, the equilibrant lifting force vector is then in line with the resultant (weight) vector of the stone. In other words, the stone acts as if all its weight were located at one point, which is called the *center of gravity*. *The center of gravity of any object is that point at which all of its weight can be considered to be concentrated.*

In Figure 4-21, the center of gravity of the bar is at **C**. In a bar of uniform construction, **C** is at the geometric center. But if the density or shape of the bar is not uniform, **C** is not at the geometric center.

Since the weight of the bar, $F_W$, can be considered to be acting at **C**, the bar can be suspended without changing its rotation by an equilibrant force, $F_E$, applied at **C**. Since $F_W$ and $F_E$ are equal but opposite vectors, they counterbalance each other. In this condition the bar is in both *translational and rotational equilibrium*. This expression means that the bar is not accelerating and that its rotation (if any) is uniform.

## 4.11 Center of gravity

**Figure 4-20** All the weight of the stone appears to be concentrated at the point called its center of gravity.

**Figure 4-21** The weight of the bar, $F_W$, is apparently concentrated at the center of gravity, C, and can be balanced by an equal and opposite force, $F_E$, applied at C.

Figure 4-22 Two parallel forces, $F_A$ and $F_w$, are applied at different points. A tendency to rotate results.

Suppose, however, that the upward force is not applied at **C** but at some other point, **A**, along the bar, as shown in Figure 4-22. In this condition a clockwise rotating effect is produced on the bar. This rotating effect is produced by *torque*.

## 4.12 The nature of torque

The two forces represented in Figure 4-22 by the vectors $F_A$ and $F_W$ are parallel. They do not act on the same point as did the concurrent forces we studied earlier in this chapter. To measure the rotating effect of such parallel forces in a given plane, it is first necessary to choose a stationary reference point for the measurements. We shall refer to this stationary reference point as the *pivot point*.

Sometimes, as in the case of a seesaw, there is a "natural" point about which the rotating effects can be measured. However, such a pivot point is "natural" only when the seesaw is in motion. When it is motionless there is no "natural" pivot point. Any point on the seesaw, or even beyond it, may be chosen.

Once a suitable pivot point is chosen, a perpendicular line is drawn on the vector diagram from it to each of the lines along which force vectors act on the object. Each such line is called a *torque arm*. In some cases, the force vectors must be extended in order to meet the perpendicular. ***Torque, T, is the product of a force and the length of its torque arm***. The unit of torque is the meter-newton.

To illustrate the concept of torque, consider the bar in Figure 4-22 with the application of an additional force, $F_B$, as shown in Figure 4-23. Choosing **A** as the pivot point, **CA** is the torque arm of $F_W$ and **BA** is the torque arm of the additional upward force, $F_B$. The clockwise torque around **A** is the product of $F_W$ and **CA**. The counterclockwise torque is the product of $F_B$ and **BA**. Since $F_A$ has a torque arm of zero, it produces no torque and does not enter into the calculations.

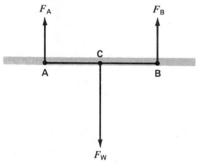

Figure 4-23 Rotational equilibrium results when the sum of the clockwise torques is equal to the sum of the counterclockwise torques. Any point may be chosen as the pivot point in making the computation provided the vector sum of the forces is zero.

To identify a torque as clockwise or counterclockwise, imagine that the bar is free to rotate around a stationary pivot point. Further imagine that the force producing the torque is the only force acting on the bar. The direction in which the bar would rotate is the direction of the torque.

## 4.13 The second condition of equilibrium

In Section 4.6 we discussed the conditions necessary for the translational equilibrium of an object. These conditions, however, do not prevent the *rotary motion* of an object that is subjected to torques. To prevent rotation in a given plane a second condition of equilibrium must be met. ***The second condition of***

Clockwise torques

$20$ n $\times$ 3.0 m = $60$ m n
$10$ n $\times$ 6.0 m = $60$ m n
$\phantom{10 n \times 6.0 m =}$ $120$ m n

Counterclockwise torque

$30$ n $\times$ 4.0 m = 120 m n

Clockwise torque

$10$ n $\times$ 2.0 m = $20$ m n

Counterclockwise torque

$20$ n $\times$ 1.0 m = $20$ m n

**Figure 4-24** The computation of torques can be simplified by setting one of the torque arms equal to zero. In the upper diagram, the left end of the bar is used as the pivot point. In the lower diagram, the point of application of the upward force is used, thereby shortening the computation.

*equilibrium* in a given plane is that the sum of all the clockwise torques equals the sum of all the counterclockwise torques about a pivot point.

Both conditions of equilibrium are illustrated in Figure 4-24. The sum of the force vectors is zero ($30$ n upward against $20$ n + $10$ n downward). The sum of the clockwise torques is equal to the sum of the counterclockwise torques. Two methods of computing the torques are shown. In the upper drawing of Figure 4-24, the left end of the bar is chosen as a pivot point. In the lower drawing, the point of application of the upward force is used as the pivot point. This simplifies the computation.

When a force is applied to a bar at an angle other than perpendicular, the distances along the bar measured from the points of application of the forces cannot be used to measure the torque arms. The torque arms must always be measured perpendicular to the directions of the forces. Figure 4-25 shows such a situation. A meter stick is under the influence of three parallel forces. To find the torque arms it is necessary to draw a horizontal line through the pivot point. Since the weights hang vertically, a horizontal line is perpendicular to the force vectors of the weights. The problem is simplified by locating the pivot point at the center of gravity. If the bar is not homogeneous, this center of gravity may not be located at the geometric center of the bar. (Experi-

**Figure 4-25** The torque arm is measured from the pivot point to the perpendicular intersection with the line indicating the direction of the applied force.

*The simplest way to solve a problem is the best way.*

Torque arm for $F_N$

$F_N$   $F_a$

$l$

$\theta$   $\theta$   $\theta$

$l \sin \theta$

Torque arm for $F_a$

**Figure 4-26** The resolution of forces is used to find the torque produced by a force acting on the bar at an angle other than perpendicular.

EXAMPLE     *A horizontal rod, **AB**, is 10.00 m long. It weighs $50\overline{0}$ n and its center of gravity, **C**, is 3.00 m from **A**. At **A** a force of $100\overline{0}$ n acts downward. At **B** a force of $75\overline{0}$ n acts downward. At **D**, 2.00 m from **B**, a force of $40\overline{0}$ n acts upward. At **E**, 1.00 m from **A**, a force of $75\overline{0}$ n acts upward. (a) What is the magnitude and direction of the force that must be used to produce equilibrium? (b) Where must it be applied?*

SOLUTION       Construct a diagram as shown in Figure 4-28.

**Figure 4-28**   A diagram for the determination of the conditions for equilibrium.

(a) Consider the known upward force vectors as being positive and the known downward force vectors as being negative. The algebraic sum of these force vectors will then be the resultant force vector. It is this resultant force vector that must be counterbalanced by a force vector in the opposite direction in order to establish translational equilibrium.

$$75\overline{0} \text{ n} + 40\overline{0} \text{ n} - 100\overline{0} \text{ n} - 50\overline{0} \text{ n} - 75\overline{0} \text{ n} = -110\overline{0} \text{ n}$$

Therefore $110\overline{0}$ n must be applied upward to establish translational equilibrium.

(b) Use **A** as the pivot point, and let $x$ be the distance from **A** to the point where the $110\overline{0}$-n force must be applied. To prevent rotary motion,

clockwise torque = counterclockwise torque
$$(50\overline{0} \text{ n})(3.00 \text{ m}) + (75\overline{0} \text{ n})(10.00 \text{ m}) = (75\overline{0} \text{ n})(1.00 \text{ m}) + (40\overline{0} \text{ n})(8.00 \text{ m}) + (110\overline{0} \text{ n})x$$
$$x = 4.59 \text{ m}$$

4.59 m is the distance from **A** to the point where the $110\overline{0}$-n upward force must be applied.

# summary

Forces are vector quantities. A net force will change the state of motion of an object. Forces can be exerted over long distances. Forces always occur in pairs in which the two forces act in opposite directions.

A single force may be resolved into two components, usually acting at right angles to each other. A resultant force is a single force that produces the same effect as several forces acting along lines that pass through the same point. Component and resultant forces are found by the parallelogram method. The equilibrant force is the single force that produces equilibrium when applied at a point at which two or more concurrent forces are acting.

Friction is a force that resists the motion of objects that are in contact with each other. It acts parallel to the surfaces that are in contact, depends on the nature and smoothness of the surfaces, is independent of the area of contact, and is directly proportional to the force pressing the surfaces together. Starting friction is usually greater than sliding friction. The coefficient of friction is the ratio of the force of friction to the perpendicular force pressing the surfaces together. The resolution of forces is used in solving friction problems.

Parallel forces act in the same or in opposite directions. The center of gravity of an object is that point at which all of the object's weight can be considered to be concentrated. A stationary object is in translational and rotational equilibrium. The torque produced by a force is the product of the force and the length of the torque arm on which it acts. To produce equilibrium in parallel forces, the sums of the forces in opposite directions must be equal and the sum of all the clockwise torques must equal the sum of all the counterclockwise torques about a pivot point. Two forces of equal magnitude that act in opposite directions but not along the same line is called a couple.

# questions

## GROUP A

1. Define center of gravity.
2. (a) What are parallel forces? (b) How is the resultant of two parallel forces that act in the same direction calculated? (c) How is the resultant of parallel forces that act in opposite directions calculated?
3. Explain how two children of unequal weight can be made to balance on a seesaw.
4. (a) A force acts at right angles to a pivoted bar. How is the torque produced by this force calculated? (b) What is the MKS unit of torque?
5. If a bar on which parallel forces act is to be in equilibrium, what conditions must be met?

## GROUP B

6. How can the choice of the pivot point simplify the calculations of the torques in a problem?
7. Distinguish between center of gravity and the pivot point.
8. Give an example of an object with a center of gravity that is not within the object.
9. A certain force does not act at right angles to a pivoted bar. How is the torque produced by this force calculated?
10. (a) What is a couple? (b) How is the torque of a couple calculated?

# problems

## GROUP A

*Note:* For each problem, draw a force diagram using a suitable scale and perform the necessary calculations. Unless otherwise noted, the center of gravity is at the geometric center of the object.

1. A steel beam of uniform cross section weighs $2.5 \times 10^5$ n. If it is 5.00 m long, what force is needed to lift one end of it?
2. A bar 4.0 m long weighs $40\overline{0}$ n. Its center of gravity is 1.5 m from one end. A weight of $30\overline{0}$ n is attached at the heavy end and a weight of $50\overline{0}$ n is attached at the light end. What are the magnitude, direction, and point of application of the force needed to achieve translational and rotational equilibrium of the bar?

3. A painter weighing 875 n stands on a plank 3.00 m long, which is supported at each end by a stepladder. The plank weighs 223 n. If the painter stands 1.00 m from one end of the plank, what force is exerted by each stepladder?
4. A bricklayer weighing $8.00 \times 10^2$ n stands 1.00 m from one end of a scaffold 3.00 m long. The scaffold weighs $75\overline{0}$ n. A pile of bricks weighing $3.20 \times 10^2$ n is 1.50 m from the other end of the scaffold.

What force must be exerted on each end of the scaffold in order to support it?

5. A bench is 2.40 m long and weighs $3.20 \times 10^2$ n. The legs are attached 0.30 m from each end and weigh 15.0 n each. If three persons weighing, in order, $5.00 \times 10^2$ n, $7.50 \times 10^2$ n, and $1.000 \times 10^3$ n, sit 0.40 m, 1.20 m, and 2.00 m respectively from one end of the bench, what downward force must each set of legs exert on the floor?

6. Give an example showing the correctness of the rule for finding the torque of a couple by placing the pivot point somewhere between the two force vectors.

7. The bridge **AB** in the accompanying figure is 36.5 m long. It weighs $2.56 \times 10^5$ n. A truck weighing $5.25 \times 10^4$ n is 10.2 m from one end of the bridge. Calculate the upward force that must be exerted by each pier to support this weight.

10.2 m — 26.3 m

A          B

2.56 × 10⁵ n

GROUP B

8. A bar 5.0 m long has its center of gravity 1.5 m from the heavy end. If it is placed on the edge of a block 1.5 m from the light end and a weight of 750 n is placed on the bar at the light end, it will be balanced. What is the weight of the bar?

9. A uniform bar 25.0 m long weighs $1.000 \times 10^4$ n. From end A a weight of $2.50 \times 10^3$ n is hung. At B, the other end of the bar, there is a weight of $3.50 \times 10^3$ n. An upward force of $3.00 \times 10^3$ n is ex-

erted 4.0 m from B, while an upward force of $4.00 \times 10^3$ n is exerted 8.0 m from A. Determine the magnitude, direction, and point of application of the force needed to establish translational and rotational equilibrium.

10. A door is 2.50 m high and 1.00 m wide. It weighs 204 n and its center of gravity is at its geometric center. The door is supported by hinges located 0.30 m from the top and bottom. If each hinge supports half the weight of the door, find the horizontal component of the force exerted by each hinge.

11. (a) Find the torques exerted on the rod in the accompanying drawing. (b) Find the magnitude and direction of the additional force that must be exerted at the right end, perpendicular to the rod, in order to prevent rotational equilibrium.

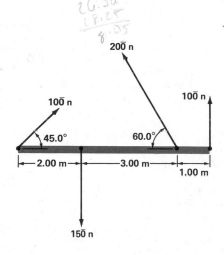

200 n

100 n

100 n

45.0°          60.0°

2.00 m          3.00 m

1.00 m

150 n

# 5 Curvilinear and Harmonic Motion

## 5.1 Motion in a curved path

*A light flashing at regular intervals is called a stroboscope, or strobe light.*

**Figure 5-1** Even though the ball at the right has a horizontal velocity, the force of gravity acts in the same way on both balls, causing them to move vertically with the same acceleration.

In Section 3.3 we described the motion of an object having uniform velocity. Such an object moves equal distances along a straight path in equal time intervals, as shown photographically in Figure 3-1. This photograph was taken using a light flashing at regular time intervals. Notice that the distances between adjacent images are equal.

In Section 3.5 we described the motion of an object having uniform acceleration. Such an object moves an increasing distance along a straight path in equal time intervals as shown by the ball at the left in the photograph, Figure 5-1. This photograph was also taken by flashing a light at regular time intervals. The ball on the left was accelerated downward from rest by the force of gravity. There is an increase in the vertical distance the ball travels in equal amounts of time.

Now let us examine what happens to the motion of an object that moves horizontally with uniform velocity but is also accelerated vertically. That is, there is a right angle between the direction of the uniform velocity and the direction of the acceleration. What will be the path of such an object? The ball at the right in Figure 5-1 illustrates such motion. It was released at the same time as the ball on the left, but had a uniform horizontal velocity. The horizontal distances between adjacent images of the right-hand ball are equal. This fact indicates that the ball is still traveling horizontally with uniform velocity. At the same time, the ball on the right covered the same vertical distance between each image as did the ball on the left, which had no horizontal velocity. Each position of the ball on the right

**90**

A ════════════════════════════════════  
Path of high velocity projectile which            } Projectile drops 4.90 m during first second  
travels this distance in one second

B ═════════════════════════════════════  
╳  
╳  
Path of low velocity projectile which             } Projectile drops 4.90 m during first second  
travels the same distance in four seconds

Projectile drops 14.70 m during second second

Projectile drops 24.50 m during third second

Projectile drops 34.30 m during fourth second

is the resultant of motion with uniform velocity in one direction and motion with uniform acceleration in the other. This combination produces motion along a curved path. *Motion along a curved path is called* **curvilinear motion**.

Suppose a rifle bullet is fired horizontally with a velocity of 1250 m/s. Neglecting air resistance, the bullet travels 1250 m by the end of the first second. Immediately after it leaves the muzzle of the gun, the force of gravity begins to accelerate the bullet toward the earth's center of gravity. This force is vertical. During the first second, a freely falling body drops 4.90 m. The bullet drops 4.90 m while traveling the first 1250 m horizontally. In two seconds the bullet travels 2500 m, but it also drops 19.6 m. Over short distances the path of a high-velocity projectile approximates a straight line, but over greater distances its path is noticeably curved. The path of a slow-moving projectile is curved, as is evident over shorter distances. See Figure 5-2.

If the line of sight to a target is horizontal, a rifle must be fired at a small upward angle in order to hit the target. This angle compensates for the downward acceleration due to the force of gravity on the bullet. Provided the same ammunition is used, the size of this angle depends upon the gun's distance from the target. The front sight of most rifles is fixed at the end of the barrel while the rear sight is movable. Since the line of sight is a straight line to the target, the angle the barrel makes with this line is increased by raising the rear sight. When the rifle is aimed, its muzzle is directed upward at the predetermined angle. When the gun is fired, this angle gives the bullet the upward velocity component necessary to compensate for the bullet's drop on its way to the distant target.

The path a projectile fired from a long-range field gun might take is shown in Figure 5-3. The muzzle velocity, $v_m$, is resolved into the horizontal component, $v_h$, and the vertical component, $v_v$. **AC** is the range. The path of the projectile, **ABC**, is the trajectory.

**Figure 5-2** The effect of the force of gravitation on high-velocity and low-velocity projectiles.

**Figure 5-3** When air resistance is not considered, the path of a projectile fired from a long-range field gun is a parabola.

## CHAPTER 5

## 5.2 Motion in a circular path

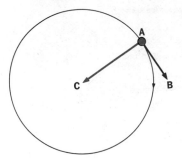

**Figure 5-4** Uniform circular motion. When the force along **AC** stops acting, the ball moves in a direction that is indicated by the tangent **AB**.

*In the absence of gravity, horizontal and vertical have no meaning.*

*Centripetal: toward a central point.*

**Figure 5-5** Diagrams for deriving the centripetal acceleration formula.

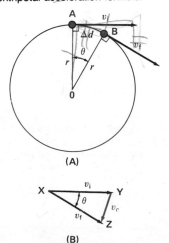

An important type of curvilinear motion is motion in a circular path. Figure 5-4 shows motion of this kind. Ball **A** is attached to the end of string **CA**. The string is fastened at **C**. If the speed of the ball in the circular path is constant, the ball is said to describe *uniform circular motion*. If the speed of the ball in the circular path varies, its motion is *variable circular motion*.

Imagine that you are at a location where there is no force of gravity. You attach a ball to a string as shown in Figure 5-4 and hold the string at **C**. Then you give the ball an initial velocity in the direction of **B**, tangent to the circumference of the circle. The ball whirls in a circular path around **C**. You can feel yourself pulling continuously on the string to keep the ball in the circular path.

Let us analyze what you would observe in this situation. We know that the radius of a circle, **AC** for example, is perpendicular to the tangent drawn through the end of the radius. If the string is in the direction of the radius and the velocity is always directed along a tangent, your pull on the string is always directed perpendicularly to the velocity. Your pull accelerates the ball into a circular path, but the ball does not speed up or slow down. Your pull changes only the direction of the velocity but not the magnitude of the velocity. If your pull were not perpendicular to the velocity, a component of the acceleration tangential to the ball's motion would exist and the speed of the ball would change.

In this example, the acceleration is directed toward the center of a circle. *Acceleration directed toward a central point is called* **centripetal acceleration**. (The word centripetal means ''directed toward a center.'')

This example can also be analyzed by means of velocity vectors. Even though the *speed* of the ball in its circular path is uniform, the *velocity* is constantly changing. In Figure 5-5(A), **A** and **B** represent two successive positions of an object moving with uniform circular motion about point **O**. The velocity vector $v_i$ indicates the velocity of the object when at point **A**, and the velocity vector $v_f$ indicates its velocity at point **B**. The velocity vectors, $v_i$ and $v_f$, are tangent to the circle at **A** and **B** respectively, and are thus perpendicular to the respective radii **OA** and **OB**.

In order to study the change of velocity between $v_i$ and $v_f$, a separate vector diagram, Figure 5-5(B), is drawn in which $v_i$ and $v_f$ originate at point **X**. If $v_f$ is considered the resultant and $v_i$ one of its components, then $v_c$ is the other component. This vector $v_c$ represents the change in velocity between $v_i$ and $v_f$. Because the vectors $v_i$ and $v_f$ are equal in magnitude and are perpendicular to their respective radii, $\angle\theta$ in Figure 5-5(A) equals $\angle\theta$ in Figure 5-5(B) and triangle **ABO** is similar to triangle **XYZ**. Then

$$\frac{v_c}{v_i} = \frac{\text{chord AB}}{r}$$

If angle $\theta$ is made smaller, arc $\Delta d$ becomes more nearly equal to chord **AB** and can be substituted for it.

$$\frac{v_c}{v_i} = \frac{\Delta d}{r}$$

But $v_i$ and $v_f$ are equal in magnitude and can be represented by $v$. If we let $\Delta t$ represent the time between $v_i$ and $v_f$ and use the equation $\Delta d = v\Delta t$, we can write

$$\frac{v_c}{v} = \frac{v\Delta t}{r}$$

Transposing terms

$$\frac{v_c}{\Delta t} = \frac{v^2}{r}$$

But $v_c/\Delta t$ is the centripetal acceleration directed along a radius of the circle and can be represented by $a$. Then

$$a = \frac{v^2}{r}$$

in which $a$ is the centripetal acceleration of the object, $v$ is its speed along the circular path, and $r$ is the radius of its circular path.

By Newton's second law of motion, $F = ma$. Thus the force producing centripetal acceleration can be written

$$F_c = \frac{mv^2}{r}$$

and is called the *centripetal force*. The centripetal force is the net force directed toward the center of the circle. The equation for centripetal force indicates that it is directly proportional to the mass of the object, directly proportional to the square of the object's speed along the circular path, and inversely proportional to the radius of the object's circular path.

Because matter has inertia, a centripetal force is required to produce the centripetal acceleration that changes the direction of a moving object. If the centripetal force applied on the ball by the string ceases to act (for example, the string breaks) the ball will move in a straight line tangent to the curved path at the point where the string breaks. This behavior is in accordance with Newton's first law of motion. When the string breaks, the centripetal force no longer acts on the ball; the ball has no unbalanced forces acting on it and thus moves in a straight line with constant speed.

*The equation $v = \dfrac{\Delta d}{\Delta t}$ is derived in Section 3.3. How is the form used here obtained?*

*Refer to Section 3.9.*

$$\frac{2\pi r}{360} = \frac{\Delta d}{\theta} \qquad \frac{2\pi r\theta}{360} = \Delta d$$

## 5.3 Motion in a vertical circle

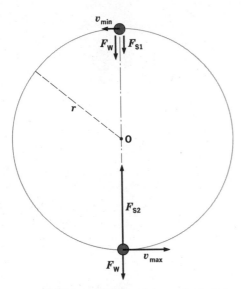

**Figure 5-6** Motion in a vertical circle. When the ball is at its highest point, the centripetal force on the ball equals the tension of the string plus the weight of the ball. At its lowest point, the weight of the ball must be subtracted from the tension to find the centripetal force.

Thus far, in describing the motion of an object in a circle, we have ignored the effect of the force of gravitation. This was done in order to simplify the analysis of the relationship between centripetal acceleration and the magnitude of the object's velocity. However, if the object moves in a vertical circle with gravity acting on it, the situation is not so simple.

Suppose a ball on the end of a string moves along a circular path. The plane of the circle is vertical. Figure 5-6 is a diagram of the ball's motion. Because of the force of gravity, the speed of the ball in the circular path is not uniform. The ball speeds up on the downward part of its path and slows down on the upward part. The speed of the ball is a minimum at the top of the circle and a maximum at the bottom. Consequently, the centripetal force is a minimum at the top of the circle and a maximum at the bottom. Let us see what forces comprise the centripetal force to make this so.

At the top of the circle the ball has velocity $v_{min}$. The centripetal force, $F_{c1}$, is the sum of the force the string exerts on the ball, $F_{s1}$, and the weight of the ball, $F_w$, since these both act toward the center of the circle.

$$F_{c1} = \frac{mv_{min}^2}{r} = F_{s1} + F_w \qquad \text{(Equation 1)}$$

At the bottom of the circle, the ball has velocity $v_{max}$. The centripetal force, $F_{c2}$, is the difference between the magnitude of the force the string exerts on the ball, $F_{s2}$, and the weight of the ball, $F_w$, since these forces now act in opposite directions. The force the string exerts is inward, and the weight of the ball acts outward.

$$F_{c2} = \frac{mv_{max}^2}{r} = F_{s2} - F_w \qquad \text{(Equation 2)}$$

Observe that since $v_{max}$ is greater than $v_{min}$, $F_{c2}$ is greater than $F_{c1}$. Further, since the weight of the ball is added in Equation 1, but subtracted in Equation 2, $F_{s2}$ is greater than $F_{s1}$ by a ratio greater than the ratio $F_{c2}/F_{c1}$.

When a ball on a string moves in a vertical circle, there is a certain velocity below which the ball will not describe a circular path—the string slackens as the ball approaches its highest point. To find this minimum value of the velocity, we shall use Equation 1. When the string begins to slacken, $F_{s1} = 0$ and

$$\frac{mv_{min}^2}{r} = F_w$$

But

$$F_w = mg$$

So

$$\frac{mv_{min}^2}{r} = mg$$

Solving for $v_{min}$

$$v_{min} = \sqrt{rg}$$

This value of $v_{min}$ is called the *critical velocity*. As the equation indicates, critical velocity depends only on the acceleration due to gravity and the radius of the vertical circle. The critical velocity does not depend on the mass of the object describing the motion. This is true because the force of gravity and the centripetal force are both proportional to the mass of the object. It can be shown that the same statements apply to projectiles.

*A satellite in circular orbit around a planet moves with critical velocity.*

Figure 5-7 shows a chamber attached to the end of a long boom. The boom is designed to rotate around a central point under the observation booth at the top of the picture. In operation, the chamber revolves at constant speed in a large circle around the central point.

Suppose you were an observer in the chamber conducting experiments while the chamber was revolving. You would still feel the pull of gravity. In addition, you would feel your body being pressed against the outside wall of the chamber. You would observe that a ball placed on the floor would move across the floor toward the outside wall of the chamber. If you dropped an object in the chamber, you would see it fall to the floor in a curved path.

## 5.4 Frames of reference

**Figure 5-7** This centrifuge is used to study the effects of angular acceleration on the human body. A volunteer is entering the test chamber of the centrifuge at the left.

From these observations it would seem that all Newton's laws of motion do not hold true in the revolving chamber. These observations can be explained, however, by attributing them to a force that tends to move all particles toward the outside wall of the chamber. This force moves the ball across the floor and accelerates the falling object so that its path is curvilinear. *A force that tends to move the particles of a rotating object away from the center of rotation is called* **centrifugal force**. Centrifugal force exists only for an observer in a rotating (or any accelerating) system who is considered to be stationary.

*Centrifugal: away from a central point.*

An observer in the booth above the revolving chamber in Figure 5-7 interprets the situation quite differently, however. To this observer, the chamber and its occupant tend to continue their motion in a straight line because of their inertia. A force in the boom, a centripetal force, causes the chamber to follow a circular path. And a force exerted by the chamber on its occupant causes the occupant also to follow a circular path. The observer in the booth can explain the behavior of objects in the chamber in terms of inertia and centripetal force. To the observer, centrifugal force is not involved.

To resolve this seeming contradiction, it is helpful to discuss this situation in terms of *frames of reference*. Each observer assumes that some surrounding objects are stationary because they do not move with respect to each other. To the observer in the revolving chamber, the walls and floor of the chamber are stationary and are used as the basis of measurements. Other objects, such as the ball on the floor, move with respect to these stationary objects. The walls and floor of the chamber are the basis for this observer's *frame of reference*.

*A* **frame of reference** *is a system for specifying precisely the location of objects*. It is used to describe the positions and relative motions of objects. A frame of reference in which Newton's first law holds true is called an *inertial frame*. An accelerating frame of reference is *noninertial* because Newton's first law does not hold true.

The observer in the booth in Figure 5-7 is stationary with respect to the earth. Strictly speaking, however, a frame of reference based upon the earth is not an inertial frame. The earth rotates and revolves around the sun and describes continuous acceleration in doing so. However, the earth is so close to being an inertial frame that we can consider a frame of reference based upon the booth as an inertial frame. (For practical purposes, we often neglect the accelerations of frames of reference that are stationary with respect to the earth.)

*Centripetal and centrifugal are never used to describe motion in the same frame of reference.*

The direction of motion of the revolving chamber is continually changing. With respect to the observer in the booth, the revolving chamber is accelerating. It is, therefore, a noninertial frame. Using such a frame, one can observe acceleration that cannot be attributed to such forces as friction or gravitation. The concept of centrifugal force is necessary. Centrifugal force is sometimes called fictitious because it is not involved when we decide to use an inertial frame to describe motion.

# questions

GROUP A

1. (a) What is curvilinear motion? (b) Describe how it can be produced.

2. (a) A projectile is fired horizontally. As the result of what motions can its path be described? (b) What effect does each of these motions have on the path of the projectile?

3. (a) What is uniform circular motion? (b) What force causes circular motion? (c) Why must a force be used to produce circular motion?

4. What factors determine the magnitude of a centripetal force?

5. (a) How does motion in a vertical circle differ from uniform circular motion? (b) What causes this difference?

6. (a) What is meant by critical velocity? (b) What happens to an object that does not have critical velocity?

7. (a) What is meant by a frame of reference? (b) List four frames of reference that could be used to describe the motion of an earth satellite.

GROUP B

8. (a) What adjustment is made on the rear sight of a rifle when the distance to the target is increased? (b) How would the use of a higher velocity bullet affect the adjustment?

9. Why does an astronaut experience large forces (a) during the launching of a space vehicle? (b) during the reentry of the vehicle?

10. (a) In what way is the motion of a satellite in a circular orbit similar to motion in a vertical circle? (b) How are the two motions different?

11. Evaluate the statements: (a) "An earth satellite is weightless." (b) "An earth satellite is continuously falling around the earth."

12. Describe the motion of a car rounding a turn in the road in terms of two different frames of reference.

# problems

GROUP A

1. What is the centripetal acceleration of an object moving along a horizontal circular path of 16.0-m radius with a speed of 40.0 m/s?

2. If the mass of the object in Problem 1 is 2.00 metric tons, what centripetal force is required to maintain it in a circular path?

3. A ball of mass $2.5 \times 10^{-2}$ kg is swung at the end of a string in a horizontal circular path at a speed of 5.0 m/s. If the length of the string is 2.0 m, what centripetal force does the string exert on the ball?

4. Calculate the centripetal force exerted on a 5.0-kg mass that is moving at a speed of 3.0 m/s in a horizontal circular motion if the radius of the circle is (a) 1.0 m; (b) 3.0 m.

5. Find the critical velocity of the mass in Problem 4 for both radii if the mass is moving (a) in a vertical circle at the earth's surface; (b) in a vertical circle $6.0 \times 10^2$ km above the earth's surface. The radius of the earth is $6.37 \times 10^6$ m.

GROUP B

6. An automobile weighs $6.0 \times 10^4$ n. If it is driven around a horizontal curve that has a radius of 250 m at the rate of 22 m/s, what is the centripetal force of the road on the automobile?

7. What is the orbiting speed of a satellite moving uniformly in a circular path $1.00 \times 10^3$ km above the earth?

8. A person has a mass of 75.0 kg. If the person is standing on the equator, by how much is the person's weight changed because of the earth's rotation?

9. A baseball player hits a fly ball to a height of 50.0 m. After the bat strikes the ball, how much time does a fielder have to get into position to make the catch?

10. A person throws a ball from the roof of a building. The ball has a velocity of 25 m/s horizontally when it leaves the person's hand, and the ball hits the ground 3.0 s later. (a) How far does the ball fall during each second? (b) How far does the ball move horizontally during each second?

## 5.5 Motion about an axis

*Rotary: turning about an internal axis.*

_Rotary motion_ is the motion of a body about an _internal_ axis. Rotary motion occurs in a turning bicycle wheel, the rotating crankshaft of an automobile engine, and a pulley wheel attached to the spinning shaft of an electric motor. Note the difference between circular motion and rotary motion. In circular motion the axis of the motion is outside the object. A spinning wheel is in rotary motion; an object on the rim of the wheel describes circular motion.

For rotary motion to be *uniform*, the object must spin about a fixed axis at a constant rate. The movement of the hands of an electric clock is an example of uniform rotary motion. If either the direction of the axis or the rate of spin varies, the rotary motion is *variable*. The movements of automobile wheels as a car is driven at different speeds and the movements of a spinning top as it slows down are examples of variable rotary motion.

## 5.6 Angular velocity

For uniform linear motion, velocity is defined as the time rate of displacement. Similarly, for uniform rotary motion, **angular velocity** is defined as *the time rate of angular displacement*. Angular displacement is the angle about the axis of rotation through which the object turns. The symbol for angular velocity is the Greek letter ω (omega). The equation for angular velocity, ω, is

$$\omega = \frac{\Delta \theta}{\Delta t}$$

where $\Delta \theta$ is an angular displacement and $\Delta t$ is the time interval in which the angular displacement occurs. The units of angular velocity are revolutions per second, degrees per second, or *radians per second*.

*An angle of one radian is the angle that, when placed with its vertex at the center of a circle, subtends on the circumference an arc equal in length to the radius of the circle.* Thus in Figure 5-8, if radius $r'$ is rotated from radius $r$ until arc $\Delta d$ = radius $r$, the angle $\theta$ is 1 radian. Since the circumference of a circle is $2\pi$ times the radius

**Figure 5-8** Since arc $\Delta d$ equals radius $r$, angle $\theta$ is 1 radian. There are $2\pi$ radians in one revolution.

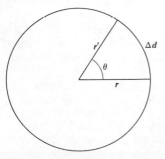

**1 revolution = 360° = 2π radians**

and

$$1 \text{ radian} = \frac{360°}{2\pi} = \frac{180°}{\pi}$$

$$1 \text{ radian} = 57.3°$$

Since an angle measured in radians equals the ratio of the length of the subtended arc to the length of the radius, the units cancel. An angle in radians is a pure number without dimensions.

The concept of angular velocity includes both the rate of rotation and the direction of the axis of rotation. Angular velocity is a vector quantity represented by a vector parallel to the axis of rotation. The length of the vector indicates the magnitude of the angular velocity. The direction of the vector is the direction in which the thumb of the right hand points when the fingers of the right hand encircle the vector in the direction in which the body is rotating. See Figure 5-9.

*right-hand rule*

**Figure 5-9** Angular velocity is represented by a vector parallel to the axis of rotation.

## 5.7 Angular acceleration

From the study of linear motion we have already recognized that a change of velocity defines acceleration. The same principle is true for rotary motion. Changing either the rate of rotation or the direction of the axis involves a change of angular velocity and thus defines angular acceleration. The uniform rate of change of linear velocity is known as linear acceleration (Section 3.5). Similarly, the uniform rate of change of angular velocity is known as angular acceleration. It is designated by the symbol $\alpha$ (alpha).

$$\alpha = \frac{\Delta\omega}{\Delta t}$$

The equations for uniformly accelerated linear motion can be transformed into the corresponding equations for uniformly accelerated rotary motion by substituting $\Delta\theta$ for $\Delta d$, $\omega$ for $v$, and $\alpha$ for $a$. These equations are shown in Table 5-1.

Table 5-1

| EQUATIONS FOR UNIFORMLY ACCELERATED MOTION | |
| --- | --- |
| Linear | Rotary |
| $v_f = v_i + a\Delta t$ | $\omega_f = \omega_i + \alpha\Delta t$ |
| $\Delta d = v_i\Delta t + \frac{1}{2}a\Delta t^2$ | $\Delta\theta = \omega_i\Delta t + \frac{1}{2}\alpha\Delta t^2$ |
| $v_f = \sqrt{v_i^2 + 2a\Delta d}$ | $\omega_f = \sqrt{\omega_i^2 + 2\alpha\Delta\theta}$ |

**EXAMPLE**

*Find the angular displacement in radians during the second 20.0-s interval of a wheel that accelerates from rest to 725 revolutions per minute in 1.50 min.*

**SOLUTION**

The angular displacement $\Delta\theta$ required for the second 20.0-s interval is equal to the difference between the angular displacement $\Delta\theta_2$ achieved during the first 40.0 s, $\Delta t_2$, and the angular displacement $\Delta\theta_1$ achieved during the first 20.0 s, $\Delta t_1$.

*Basic Equation:* $\Delta\theta = \Delta\theta_2 - \Delta\theta_1$

Since $\omega_i = 0$ for each time interval,

$$\Delta\theta_2 = \frac{1}{2}\alpha\Delta t_2^2 \quad \text{and} \quad \Delta\theta_1 = \frac{1}{2}\alpha\Delta t_1^2$$

$$\Delta\theta = \frac{1}{2}\alpha\Delta t_2^2 - \frac{1}{2}\alpha\Delta t_1^2$$

*Working Equation:* $\Delta\theta = \frac{1}{2}\alpha(\Delta t_2^2 - \Delta t_1^2)$

$$\Delta\theta = \frac{725/\text{min} \times 2\pi \text{ rad}}{2 \times 1.50 \text{ min}} \times \left(\frac{\text{min}}{60 \text{ s}}\right)^2 \times [(40.0 \text{ s})^2 - (20.0 \text{ s})^2]$$

$$\Delta\theta = 505 \text{ rad}$$

## 5.8 Rotational inertia

**Figure 5-10**  Apparatus for demonstrating rotational inertia.

A wheel mounted on an axle will not start to rotate unless a torque is applied to the wheel. A wheel that is spinning will continue to spin at constant angular velocity unless a torque acts on it. In both cases the wheel is in equilibrium. Thus if we replace "force" with "torque," Newton's first law of motion also applies to rotary motion.

If we wish to change the rate of rotation of an object about an axis—that is, change its angular velocity—we must apply a torque about the axis. The angular acceleration that this torque produces depends on the mass of the rotating object and upon the distribution of its mass with respect to the axis of rotation.

In Figure 5-10 two masses, $m_1$ and $m_2$, are mounted on a bar that is fastened to an axle. The masses can be placed on the bar at varying distances from the axle. If a cord is wrapped around the axle and attached to a weight that falls under the influence of gravity, a constant torque is applied to the axle. If different weights are attached to the cord, different torques are applied. If the masses mounted on the bar remain in a fixed position, the greater the torque, the greater will be the angular acceleration. If the masses are placed near the axis of rotation, the acceleration produced by a given torque is greater than if they are placed at the ends of the bar. Note that moving the masses farther apart does not change the amount of mass that is rotated. It does, however, change the distribution of mass; in this case we say that it increases the *rotational inertia*. The angular acceleration, $\alpha$, is directly proportional to the torque, $T$, but inversely proportional to the rotational inertia, $I$.

$$\alpha = \frac{T}{I}$$

Transposing

$$T = I\alpha$$

which for rotary motion is analogous to $F = ma$ for linear motion. The torque, $T$, is computed by

$$T = Fr$$

where $F$ is the force applied tangentially at distance $r$ from the axis of rotation. Like a force, a torque has magnitude and direction. As in the case of angular velocity, the direction of the torque vector is the direction in which the thumb of the right hand points when the fingers of the right hand encircle the vector in the direction in which the mass is rotating. Torques behave like other quantities that can be represented by vectors.

The rotational inertia in rotary motion takes into account both the shape and the mass of the rotating object. Equations for the rotational inertia of certain regularly shaped bodies are

Thin ring
$I = mr^2$

Disk
$I = \frac{1}{2} mr^2$

Cylinder
$I = \frac{1}{2} mr^2$

Thick ring
$I = \frac{1}{2} m(r_1{}^2 + r_2{}^2)$

Solid ball
$I = \frac{2}{5} mr^2$

Uniform thin rod
$I = \frac{1}{3} ml^2$

Uniform thin rod
$I = \frac{1}{12} ml^2$

Disk
$I = \frac{1}{4} mr^2$

**Figure 5-11** Equations for calculating the rotational inertia of certain regularly shaped bodies about the indicated axes of rotation.

given in Figure 5-11. Rotational inertia has the unit dimensions kg m². The following analysis illustrates this.

$$I = \frac{T}{\alpha} = \frac{\mathbf{m\ n}}{1/s^2} = \frac{\mathbf{kg\ m^2/s^2}}{1/s^2} = \mathbf{kg\ m^2}$$

Figure 5-12 shows a spinning bicycle wheel that seems to be defying gravity. The only means of support of the wheel is the cord that is holding up the left end of the axle. Yet if the wheel is spinning fast enough, its axle will remain almost horizontal in space. Instead of falling, the axle will slowly rotate counterclockwise (as seen from above) around the axis marked by the cord. This horizontal rotation of the axle is called *precession*.

To understand the behavior of a wheel that is spinning, particularly its precession, we will need to refer to Figures 5-12 and 5-13. In Figure 5-12, **OA** is the axle of a wheel spinning counterclockwise as seen from **A**. **OC** is the cord from which the wheel is suspended. The weight of the wheel produces a clockwise torque about **O** (as seen from the front). $\omega_S$ is the

## 5.9 Precession

**Figure 5-12** Precession. When the wheel rotates, the angular velocity combined with the torque produced by the weight of the wheel causes a precession.

**Figure 5-13** Vector analysis of precession. All vectors are in the same horizontal plane. When vector $\Delta\omega_\alpha$ is small, vectors $\alpha$, $\alpha\Delta t$, and $\Delta\omega_\alpha$ are all perpendicular to vectors $\omega_S$ and $\omega_S{}'$.

*A rotating wheel is sometimes called a gyroscope.*

vector representing the angular velocity of the spinning wheel.

In Figure 5-13, $\alpha$ describes the angular acceleration due to the torque produced by $F_w$. ($\alpha$ is horizontal and directed into the paper.) Because of this angular acceleration there will be a change in the angular velocity during the short time $\Delta t$ : $\Delta \omega_\alpha = \alpha \Delta t$. This added vectorially to $\omega_S$ results in a new angular velocity $\omega_S'$ of the same magnitude but different direction. (Remember that the change in angular velocity is small and it is therefore at right angles to both the initial and new angular velocities.) Because of the way the wheel is supported, if the new axis is now along $\omega_S'$, the axle of the wheel has to turn toward this new position. The analysis has to be repeated for successive time intervals and the result is the precessional motion of the wheel.

*A gyroscope does not precess in the absence of gravity or in a freely falling space ship.*

The earth is a good example of precession since it spins about an axis that is tilted with respect to its plane of revolution around the sun. The rotation of the earth produces an equatorial bulge. The gravitational pull of the sun on the part of the bulge closest to the sun is stronger than the pull on the part of the bulge on the other side of the earth. Because of the resulting torque, the earth's axis goes through a precessional motion and does not point continually at the same place in space. See Figure 5-14. It has been calculated that a period of about 26,000 years is required for the earth's axis to complete a single precessional cycle.

**Figure 5-14** At the present time, the northern end of the earth's axis points approximately toward the star Polaris. Hence it is called the North Star. As the earth's axis precesses, however, it points successively toward other regions of the sky. This precessional circle has a radius of $23\frac{1}{2}°$ and takes about 26,000 years to complete.

# questions

GROUP A

1. (a) What is rotary motion? (b) Give examples of uniform and variable rotary motion.
2. How is a 1-radian angle defined?
3. (a) What is angular velocity? (b) What is angular acceleration?
4. (a) Explain why angular velocity is a vector quantity. (b) How is a vector representing an angular velocity drawn?
5. How do equations for uniformly accelerated rotary motions compare with those for uniformly accelerated linear motions?

GROUP B

6. Explain how a revolving flywheel tends to maintain the fixed axle on which it is mounted at a constant angular velocity.
7. What is the result of the addition of two angular velocities about different axes?
8. In the case of precession, how do the directions of the angular acceleration vector and the angular velocity vector compare at the same instant of time?
9. For uniformly accelerated rotary motion how do the directions of an angular acceleration vector and its corresponding angular velocity vector compare?
10. (a) What causes precession? (b) How does precession affect the apparent location of the present-day North Star?

# problems

GROUP A

1. What is the angular velocity in radians per second of a flywheel that turns 4820 revolutions per minute?
2. If a wheel turns 625 rad/s, what is its angular velocity in revolutions per minute?
3. A net force of 10.0 n is applied tangentially to the rim of a wheel having a 0.25-m radius. If the rotational inertia of the wheel is 0.500 kg m², what is its angular acceleration?
4. Calculate the rotational inertia of a thin ring whose mass is 5.7 kg and whose radius is 0.15 m that rotates about an axis through the center perpendicular to the plane of the ring.
5. What is the rotational inertia of a solid ball 0.050 m in radius that weighs 80.0 n if it is rotated about a diameter?

GROUP B

6. Calculate the angular acceleration in radians per second² of a wheel that starts from rest and attains an angular velocity of 545 revolutions per minute in 1.00 minute.
7. (a) What is the angular displacement in radians of the wheel of Problem 6 during the first 0.500 min? (b) During the second 0.500 min?
8. (a) If a force of 25.0 n is applied tangentially to the rim of a uniform disk whose radius is 0.200 m and mass is 30.0 kg, what angular velocity will the disk attain in 0.200 min? (b) What is the angular displacement during this acceleration?
9. A disk-shaped wheel 1.00 m in radius weighs $2.00 \times 10^3$ n. A force of 50.0 n is applied tangentially to the rim. After how many seconds does it attain an angular velocity of 1200 rev/min?

# SIMPLE HARMONIC MOTION

*When a body continually moves back and forth over a definite path in equal intervals of time it is said to undergo **periodic motion**.* Figure 5-15 shows a mass attached to a spring that is supported from a horizontal beam. If we pull down on the mass and then let it go, it will vibrate up and down in periodic motion. Let us investigate quantitatively the periodic motion of this mass.

If we exert a force, $F$, acting downward on a mass, $m$, we displace it from its equilibrium position by a distance $d$. We also

### 5.10 Periodic motion

*Periodic: repeated in the same way in equal time intervals.*

*Handwritten annotations:*

max up

Fwe=ma

a=max V=0

Fs=Fw   a=0   F=ma V=ma E.P.

**Figure 5-15** Simple harmonic motion. The frequency of vibration of the mass depends on the stiffness of the spring and the magnitude of the mass.

a=max

max down   Fs=ma   V=0

find by experiment that if we exert force $2F$ we displace the mass a distance $2d$. The downward displacement from the equilibrium position is directly proportional to the downward force we exert.

In exerting this force downward we pull against the spring, and the spring also pulls against our hand with a force $-F$ (law of interaction). When we release the mass, the upward force of the spring exceeds the downward pull of gravity on the mass. An upward acceleration that is directly proportional to the excess force is produced (law of acceleration).

As the mass, $m$, returns to its equilibrium position, less and less force is exerted on it by the spring. Consequently the acceleration becomes less. The net force is zero when the mass is at its equilibrium position. The acceleration is also zero. The mass, $m$, has acquired its maximum velocity at this point. It moves past its equilibrium position because of its inertia. As this overshoot occurs, the upward pull of the spring becomes less than the downward force on the mass. There is a net downward force on the mass, and this downward force decelerates it. The mass stops. (During the upward movement of the mass, the spring's pull may change to a downward force due to compression.) The downward force then accelerates it again. As a consequence of the upward force exerted by the spring and the downward force due to gravity, the mass describes an up-and-down motion.

Assuming the ideal conditions of a frictionless spring, the mass moves above the equilibrium position the same distance it moves below the equilibrium position, and it completes each up-and-down cycle in the same amount of time. At each point in the up-and-down cycle, the force exerted on the mass, and therefore the resulting acceleration, are directly proportional to the displacement of the mass from the equilibrium position. Both the force and the acceleration are directed toward the equilibrium position. The type of periodic motion that has these particular characteristics is known as *simple harmonic motion*.

***Simple harmonic motion*** *is a type of linear motion of a particle in which the acceleration is proportional to the displacement of* *the particle from its equilibrium position and is always directed toward the equilibrium position.* The motion of a mass vibrating up and down on a spring, the motion of the prongs of a vibrating tuning fork, and the motion of a swinging pendulum bob are familiar examples of motion that is simple harmonic motion or very nearly so.

*Harmonic motion: acceleration directed toward an equilibrium position and proportional to the distance from that position.*

Simple harmonic motion can be analyzed in terms of circular motion. In Figure 5-16(A) a light is shining directly down on a rotating wheel. As the wheel turns, the handle on the wheel describes circular motion. The shadow of the wheel and handle falls perpendicularly on the horizontal surface below. The shadow of the handle will move back and forth along the shadow of the wheel. It can also be shown that the shadow of the handle slows down when it is going away from the center of the wheel's shadow and speeds up when it approaches the center point. This is the definition of simple harmonic motion given in the previous section.

The diagram in Figure 5-16(B) shows more clearly the relationship between the handle, **P**, and its projection, **P′**. **P** is moving with uniform speed in a circular path around point **O**. **P′** is the perpendicular projection of **P** along line **MN**. When **P** is at **a**, its projection is at **a′**; when it is at **b**, its projection is at **b′**, and so on. As **P** makes a complete revolution, **P′** describes a *complete vibration*. It can be shown that **P′** moves with an acceleration proportional to **O′P′**, and the acceleration is always directed toward **O′**. Thus the motion of **P′** along **MN** is simple harmonic motion. When **P′** is at **b′**, the *displacement* of **P′** is the distance **b′O′**—its distance from the midpoint of its vibration at that

## 5.11 The relationship between circular motion and simple harmonic motion

**Figure 5-16** Simple harmonic motion can be analyzed in terms of circular motion.

Light rays

Shadow of handle

(A)

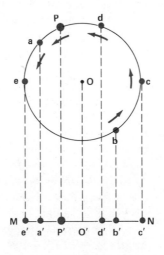

(B)

particular instant. The *amplitude* of the vibration is the maximum displacement **O'M** or **O'N**—it equals the radius of the reference circle. The *period* is the time of one complete vibration—the time required for the point to make one revolution on the reference circle. The *frequency* of a vibratory motion is the number of vibrations per second—the number of revolutions per second of a point on the reference circle. *The frequency is the reciprocal of the period.* The *equilibrium position* of an object that is describing simple harmonic motion is the midpoint of its path, **O'**.

## 5.12 The pendulum

*An object mounted so that it can swing back and forth about an axis is called a **pendulum**.* Figure 5-17 shows a simple pendulum in which a small dense mass, called the bob, is suspended by a cord. The mass of the cord is negligible when compared to the mass of the bob. If the displacement of the bob is small in comparison to the length of the pendulum, the motion of a pendulum very closely approximates simple harmonic motion.

As the pendulum bob moves from **A** to **B** and back again to **A**, it makes a complete vibration. The time required for a complete vibration is the period of the pendulum. The number of complete vibrations per second is the frequency. The displacement is the distance of the bob from the equilibrium position **C** at any instant. The amplitude is the maximum displacement.

Galileo was probably the first scientist to make quantitative studies of the motion of a pendulum. It is said that he observed the gentle swaying of a sanctuary lamp in the cathedral at Pisa. Using his pulse as a timer, he found that successive vibrations of the lamp were made in equal lengths of time, regardless of the amplitude of the vibrations. He later verified his observations experimentally and then suggested that a pendulum be used to time the pulse rates of medical patients.

In the simple pendulum shown in Figure 5-17, all the mass may be considered to be concentrated in the bob. For an ideal pendulum of this type, the following statements hold true.

*1. The period of a pendulum is independent of the mass or material of the pendulum.* This statement is strictly true only if the pendulum vibrates in a vacuum. Air resistance has more effect on a pendulum bob made of cotton than it does on a bob made of lead.

*2. If the arc is small, the period of a pendulum is independent of the amplitude.* The arc is considered small if it is a small fraction of one radian, that is, 10° or less.

*3. The period of a pendulum is directly proportional to the square root of its length.* If we have two pendulums 25 cm long and 100 cm long, the period of the longer one will be twice that

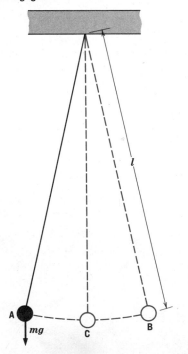

**Figure 5-17** The simple pendulum. The frequency of vibration depends only on the values of *l* and *g,* provided that the displacement is small compared to the length of the pendulum and air resistance is negligible.

of the shorter one. Since the square roots of 25 and 100 are 5 and 10 respectively, the periods are in the ratio of 5 to 10, or 1 to 2.

4. *The period of a pendulum is inversely proportional to the square root of the acceleration of free fall.* A pendulum vibrates slightly faster at the north pole than at the equator. If we use the letter *l* to denote the length of a pendulum and *g* to denote the acceleration due to gravity, the period, *T*, is

$$T = 2\pi \sqrt{\frac{l}{g}}$$

Any real object that can vibrate like a pendulum is called a *physical pendulum*, as distinguished from the ideal *simple pendulum*. For example, a baseball bat can be a physical pendulum as shown in Figure 5-18. When the bat is suspended from **O** and set in vibration, its period will be the same as that of a simple pendulum with a length equal to the distance **OC**. Consequently, **C** is called the *center of oscillation*. The interesting thing is that **O** and **C** are interchangeable; that is, if the bat is suspended from **C**, the center of oscillation will be at **O**.

An additional property of **C** is that it is the *center of percussion* of the bat. The batter's hands do not experience a "sting" if a ball strikes the bat at the center of percussion as the hands turn the bat about the center of oscillation. If the ball hits the bat at a point other than the center of percussion, the bat rotates about some point other than the center of oscillation. The part of the bat at the center of oscillation is quickly pushed against the hands, and this accounts for the "sting."

*The equation for the pendulum was developed by the Dutch physicist Christian Huygens (1629–1695).*

**Figure 5-18** A physical pendulum and simple pendulum with the same period of vibration. **O** is the point of suspension, **G** is the center of gravity, and **C** is the center of oscillation and percussion.

# summary

Uniform circular motion is motion at constant speed along a curved path of constant radius. An object moving in a curved path undergoes centripetal acceleration. Centripetal acceleration is produced by a force known as centripetal force which is directed toward a central point. When gravity is acting on an object, a minimum velocity is required to keep the object moving in a vertical circle.

A frame of reference is a system for specifying precisely the location of objects. Centrifugal forces are required to explain the curvilinear motions of objects in terms of a noninertial, or accelerating, frame of reference.

Rotary motion is the motion of a body about an internal axis. In such motion, the relationships among angular displacement, velocity, acceleration, and time are similar to the corresponding relationships for linear motion. The angular acceleration of a rotating body is directly proportional to the torque that produces motion and inversely proportional to the body's rotational inertia. The rotation of the axle of a rotating body that is under the influence of gravity is called precession.

Periodic motion occurs when a body continually moves back and forth over a definite path in equal intervals of time. Simple harmonic motion is a special type of periodic motion. Simple harmonic motion can be analyzed in terms of circular motion. A swinging pendulum describes simple harmonic motion. The period of a pendulum is directly proportional to the square root of its length and inversely proportional to the square root of the acceleration of gravity.

# questions

GROUP A

1. How is periodic motion related to simple harmonic motion?

2. Define the following terms as they apply to simple harmonic motion: (a) complete vibration; (b) displacement; (c) period; (d) frequency.

3. What factors determine the period of motion of a pendulum?

4. (a) What is a physical pendulum? (b) How is it related to a simple pendulum?

5. List two ways of finding the center of percussion of a baseball bat.

GROUP B

6. If a pendulum clock loses time, how should the pendulum be adjusted?

7. Describe a method of using the simple pendulum to find the value of $g$ for a given location.

8. Explain why less force is exerted on the mass in Figure 5-15 as the mass returns to its equilibrium position.

9. In what sense may the balance wheel of a wrist watch be compared with a simple pendulum?

# problems

GROUP A

1. A pendulum 0.25 m long has a period of 1.1 s. What is the period of a pendulum in the same location if it has a length of 0.10 m?

2. What is the period of a pendulum 1.5 m long at sea level?

GROUP B

3. What is the value of $g$ for a location where a pendulum 1.08 m long has a period of 2.05 s?

4. A seconds pendulum is one with a period of exactly two seconds. Find the length of a seconds pendulum at Denver, Colorado ($g = 9.79609$ m/s²).

# 6 Conservation of Energy and Momentum

## WORK, MACHINES, AND POWER

The word *work* has a very special meaning in physics. ***Work is done when a force is exerted on an object causing the object to move in the direction of a component of the applied force.*** If you remain stationary, no matter how long you hold a heavy load on your shoulder, in a scientific sense you are not doing any work on the load. You are merely exerting an upward force that counteracts the downward force of gravity on the load. You do work in a scientific sense when you raise the load to your shoulder, when you carry it up a flight of stairs, or when you pull it across the floor. In these cases, *you exert a force that has a component in the direction in which the object moves.*

Two factors must be considered in measuring work: the displacement of the object and the magnitude of the force in the direction of displacement. *The amount of work, W, equals the product of the force in the direction of displacement, F, and the displacement, $\Delta d$, of an object.*

$$W = F\Delta d$$

When the force is measured in newtons and the distance through which it acts is measured in meters, the work is expressed in *joules* (j). *A force of one newton acting through a distance of one meter does **one joule** of work.* This unit of work is named for the English physicist James Prescott Joule. Note that *a joule is a newton meter.*

For example, let us compute the work required to lift a 1.0-kg mass to a height of 5.0 m. From the relationship between mass and weight discussed in previous chapters, we know that a force of about 9.8 n must be exerted to lift a mass of 1.0 kg at sea level.

**6.1 Scientific definition of work**

*Work: the product of force and displacement.*

*Joule, following the experiments of Count Rumford described in Section 1.13, showed the relationship between heat and work.*

Thus, the amount of work involved is

$$W = F \Delta d$$

$$W = (9.8 \text{ n})(5.0 \text{ m})$$

$$W = 49 \text{ j}$$

If we merely slide the 1.0-kg mass along a horizontal surface having a coefficient of sliding friction, $\mu$, of 0.30 for a distance of 5.0 m, the work required is

$$W = F_f \Delta d$$

$$W = \mu F_N \Delta d$$

$$W = (0.30)(9.8 \text{ n})(5.0 \text{ m})$$

$$W = 15 \text{ j}$$

In both instances, the force is applied in the direction in which the object moves.

Suppose, however, that the force is applied to the object in a direction other than that in which it moves. In that case, only the component of the applied force that acts in the direction the object moves is used to compute the work done on the object. Thus in Figure 6-1, the relationship between the applied force, $F_a$, and the component in the direction of motion, $F$, is

$$F = F_a \cos \theta$$

This relationship is used in the following example.

*The relationship $F_f = \mu F_N$ is explained in Section 4.8.*

**Figure 6-1** Definition of work. The work done by the applied force, $F_a$, is equal to the product of $F$, the component of $F_a$ in the direction of the displacement, and $\Delta d$, the distance through which the mass moves.

## EXAMPLE

*A box with a mass of 115 kg is pushed up an inclined plane 10.0 m long. The push is applied parallel to the plane, which makes an angle of 15.0° with the horizontal. How much work is done if the coefficient of sliding friction between the box and plane is 0.30? (It is assumed that the box is moving with constant speed.)*

## SOLUTION

*Basic equation:*   $W = F \Delta d$

In this case, $F$ is the sum of the force of friction, $F_f$, and the component of the weight of the box parallel to the plane, $F_p$, so that $F = F_f + F_p$.

The weight of the box, $F_w = mg$.

The force of friction, $F_f = \mu F_N$

$F_N$ is the component of the weight of the box normal to the plane, or
$F_N = F_w \cos \theta = mg \cos \theta$. Thus $F_f = \mu mg \cos \theta$.

The component of the weight of the box parallel to the plane,
$F_p = F_w \sin \theta = mg \sin \theta$.

Substituting these values in the basic equation, we get the

*Working equation:*   $W = (\mu mg \cos \theta + mg \sin \theta)\Delta d$, or

$W = mg \Delta d (\mu \cos \theta + \sin \theta)$

$W = [(115 \text{ kg})(9.80 \text{ n/kg})(10.0 \text{ m})][(0.30)(0.966) + 0.259]$

$W = 6.20 \times 10^3 \text{ j}$

In the examples of work in Section 6.1, the forces involved did not vary. In many problems involving work, however, the forces may vary in direction, in magnitude, or in both during the time that they are acting on an object. For example, when a force is used to stretch a spring, the magnitude of the force increases as the spring gets longer.

An easy way to determine the amount of work done by a varying force is to use a graph. In Figure 6-2, the area under the curved line represents the work done by a force that varies in magnitude and direction. The horizontal axis is the distance, $\Delta d$, and the vertical axis is the force that acts in the direction of motion, $F$. The amount of work required to provide the displacement indicated by the curve up to point **A**, for example, is equal to the area bounded at the top by the curve, at the right by a vertical line from **A** to the horizontal axis, and at the left and bottom by the two coordinate axes.

To calculate the area of a geometric figure that is bounded by one or more curved lines requires special mathematical techniques. A good approximation is obtained, however, by the use of suitable rectangles. For example, the work indicated by the curve between points **B** and **C** is approximately equal to the area of the colored rectangle in the figure. Thus, if $\Delta d$ is in meters and $F$ is in newtons, the work is approximately equal to the product of 2.0 m and 6.5 n, or 13 j.

The total amount of work that may be represented by the area under the curve can be found by adding the areas of many rectangles formed in the same way as the one in the figure. If the rectangles are made very narrow, the answer will be more accurate. Calculus, a branch of mathematics, gives a method of finding the area under specific curves without using rectangles. An interesting way to measure the area under a curve is to cut it out of a piece of paper, weigh it, and compare it with the weight of a known area.

The problem of finding the total work done by a varying force is somewhat simpler in the case of the stretching spring, as long as the force is constantly applied in the direction of the stretching. The force required to stretch a spring depends on the stiffness of the spring, but the force is directly proportional to the amount of stretching. (The limits within which this relationship is true will be more fully discussed in Section 7.11.) Consequently, a graph of the work done in stretching a spring is shown in Figure 6-3. No approximations are required in computing the total work because the area of the triangle under the curve is exactly equal to one-half the product of its base and height.

## 6.2 Work done by varying forces

**Figure 6-2** Work done by a variable force. The area under the curve represents the total work.

*The mathematical term for finding the area under a curve is integration.*

**Figure 6-3** Work done by a constantly increasing force. The total work is represented by the colored triangle.

## 6.3 Work done in rotary motion

**Figure 6-4** Work done in rotary motion. A torque is required to increase the kinetic energy of the wheel.

To compute the work done in rotary motion, we make use of the principles of radian measure (Section 5.6). In Figure 6-4 the displacement of the rim of the wheel is designated by the arc $\Delta d$. If the angle $\Delta\theta$ is expressed in radians, then $\Delta d = r\Delta\theta$. Substituting this expression for $\Delta d$ in the work equation, we get

$$W = Fr\Delta\theta$$

Furthermore, in Section 4.12 we saw that a torque, $T$, is equal to the product of a force and the length of its torque arm. In Figure 6-4, the torque arm is the radius of the circle, so $T = Fr$. The work equation can now be written

$$W = T\Delta\theta$$

which means that the work done in rotary motion can be computed by finding the product of the torque producing the motion and the angular displacement in radians.

For example, if the radius of the wheel in Figure 6-4 is 2.0 m and a force of 12 n is applied tangentially to it, the work done in a single revolution is

$$W = T\Delta\theta$$

$$W = Fr\Delta\theta$$

$$W = 2\pi Fr$$

$$W = 2(3.14)(12\ \text{n})(2.0\ \text{m})$$

$$W = 150\ \text{j}$$

## 6.4 Machines

**Figure 6-5** The six simple machines. Each machine multiplies force at the expense of distance.

Six types of simple machines are shown in Figure 6-5. Each one can be used to multiply force. Other machines are either modifications of these simple machines or combinations of two or more of them. The six machines shown are actually variations of two basic types: the pulley and the wheel and axle are forms of the lever, and the wedge and screw are modified inclined planes.

Lever

Inclined plane

Wheel and axle

Wedge

Pulley

Screw

Although a machine can be used to multiply force, it cannot multiply work. Conservation laws hold true for machines; the work output of a machine cannot exceed the work input. In a frictionless machine, work output and work input would be exactly equal. In a machine that multiplies force, this equality means that the distance over which the input force moves is always greater than the distance over which the load moves. See Figure 6-6.

The ratio of the useful work output of a machine to total work input is called the *efficiency*.

$$\text{Efficiency} = \frac{W_{\text{output}}}{W_{\text{input}}}$$

The efficiency of all machines is less than 100% because the work output is always less than the work input. This is due to the force of friction.

Thus in using a machine to lift an object, the efficiency equation becomes

$$\text{Efficiency} = \frac{F_{\text{w}}\Delta h}{F_{\text{a}}\Delta d}$$

where $F_{\text{w}}$ is the weight of the object, $\Delta h$ is the height through which it is lifted, $F_{\text{a}}$ is the input force applied to the machine, and $\Delta d$ is the distance through which $F_{\text{a}}$ acts in the direction of the input motion.

The following example illustrates the use of the efficiency equation in solving problems dealing with simple machines.

*A gadget with gears and wheels is not necessarily a machine.*

*The ratio of the output force to the input force in a machine is called the mechanical advantage.*

**Figure 6-6** Principle of the simple machine. The efficiency of the machine is the ratio of the work output, $F_{\text{w}}\Delta h$, to the work input, $F_{\text{a}}\Delta d$.

---

**EXAMPLE**

*An inclined plane is 6.00 m long and 1.00 m high. The coefficient of friction is 0.050. (a) What force is required to pull a weight of $1.00 \times 10^4$n up the plane? (b) What is the efficiency of the plane?*

**SOLUTION**

(a) The required force is the sum of the useful input force and the force required to overcome the force of friction.

*Basic equation:*      $F = F_{\text{u}} + F_{\text{f}}$

$$W_{\text{input}} \text{ (useful)} = W_{\text{output}} \text{ (useful)}$$

$$F_{\text{u}}\Delta d = F_{\text{w}}\Delta h$$

$$F_{\text{u}} = \frac{F_{\text{w}}\Delta h}{\Delta d}$$

$$F_{\text{f}} = \mu F_{\text{N}}$$

*Working equation:*      $F = \dfrac{F_{\text{w}}\Delta h}{\Delta d} + \mu F_{\text{N}}$

$F_N$ is found by the method outlined in Section 4.4. $F_N = 9860$ n

$$F = \frac{(1.00 \times 10^4 \text{ n})(1.00 \text{ m})}{(6.00 \text{ m})} + (0.050)(9860 \text{ n})$$

$$F = 2160 \text{ n}$$

(b) *Working equation:*  Efficiency $= \dfrac{F_w \Delta h}{F_a \Delta d}$

Efficiency $= \dfrac{(1.00 \times 10^4 \text{ n})(1.00 \text{ m})}{(2160 \text{ n})(6.00 \text{ m})}$

Efficiency $= 0.772$, or $77.2\%$

## 6.5 The scientific meaning of power

*Power: work divided by time.*

Like the term *work*, the term *power* has a scientific meaning that differs somewhat from its everyday meaning. When we say a person has great power, we usually mean that the person has great strength or wields great authority. In physics, the term **power** means *the time rate of doing work*.

You do the same amount of work whether you climb a flight of stairs in one minute or in five minutes, but your power output is not the same. See Figure 6-7. Power depends upon three factors: the displacement of the object, the force in the direction of the displacement, and the time required.

Since power is the time rate of doing work,

$$P = \frac{W}{\Delta t}$$

where $P$ is power, $W$ is work, and $\Delta t$ is time. Or, because $W = F \Delta d$ and $v = \Delta d / \Delta t$,

$$P = \frac{F \Delta d}{\Delta t} = Fv$$

When work is measured in joules and time is measured in seconds, power is expressed in *watts* (w). *A **watt** is a joule per*

**Figure 6-7** A power comparison. In each case, the girl will do the same amount of work in climbing the stairs. However, on the right her output of power is greater and she accomplishes the climb in a shorter time. (Kinetic energy is disregarded by assuming that both girls start from rest and come to a stop at the top of the stairs.)

**Figure 6-8** James Watt, the Scottish inventor for whom the metric unit of power is named, in his workshop.

*second.* This unit is named in honor of James Watt who designed the first practical steam engine. Since the watt is an inconveniently small unit, power is more commonly measured in units of 1000 watts, or kilowatts (kw).

The terms watt and kilowatt are used frequently in connection with electricity but also apply to quantities of power other than electric power. The watt is the basic unit of power in the MKS system and can be used to express quantities of mechanical as well as electric power. You may be familiar with the unit called the "horsepower." It is equal to 746 watts.

*The wattage of a light bulb tells how much power the bulb uses, not how bright it is.*

## EXAMPLE

*A child's mass is 75.2 kg. If the child walks up a flight of stairs 12.6 m high in 28.0 s, what is the power output? Assume that the kinetic energy of the child is the same at the bottom and top of the stairs.*

## SOLUTION

*Basic equation:*
$$P = \frac{F \Delta d}{\Delta t}$$

In this case, $F$ is the weight of the child, $F_W$, which is found from the child's mass by the relationship
$$F_w = mg$$

The distance $\Delta d$ is the vertical height of the staircase.

*Working equation:*
$$P = \frac{mg \Delta d}{\Delta t}$$

$$P = \frac{(75.2 \text{ kg})(9.80 \text{ m/s}^2)(12.6 \text{ m})}{28.0 \text{ s}}$$

$$P = 332 \text{ w}$$

### 6.6 Power in rotary motion

By using radian measure, we can compute the power involved in rotary motion in the same way that we calculated the work done in rotary motion in Section 6.3. Substituting the expression for work in rotary motion, $T\Delta\theta$, the power equation becomes

$$P = \frac{T\Delta\theta}{\Delta t}$$

We saw in Section 5.6 that the time rate of angular displacement, $\Delta\theta/\Delta t$, is called the angular velocity, $\omega$. If $\Delta\theta$ is measured in radians, then $\omega$ is in radians per second.

For rotary motion, the expression for power can now be written

$$P = T\omega$$

which means that the power required to maintain rotary motion against an opposing torque is equal to the product of the torque maintaining the rotary motion and the constant angular velocity.

# questions

GROUP A
1. Give the scientific definition of "work."
2. (a) How is a graph used to find the work done by a varying force? (b) What method for finding the work done can easily be applied if the force varies constantly?
3. Is work done by the centripetal force that produces circular motion? Explain.
4. (a) List the six simple machines. (b) Into what two basic types can they be divided?
5. (a) Define efficiency for a machine. (b) How is it computed?
6. How does friction affect the efficiency of machines?
7. List the advantages and disadvantages of friction in the use of a screw.

8. (a) Give the scientific definition of "power." (b) What is the MKS unit of power?

GROUP B
9. How are the coordinates of a graph used to find the area under a given curve?
10. Suppose that you have two simple machines, each of which multiplies a force by a factor of three. By what factor will the force be multiplied if the two machines are used in series? Explain.
11. (a) What physical quantity is expressed in kilowatt-hours? (b) Use dimensional analysis to verify your answer.
12. Show how the formula for power in rotary motion is derived.

# problems

GROUP A
1. A person weighing 750 n climbs a flight of stairs that is 5.0 m high. What work does the person do?
2. What work is done when a person lifts a 2.5-kg package and places it on a shelf 2.2 m high?

3. How much work must be done to roll a metal safe, mass 116 kg, a distance of 15.0 m across a level floor? The coefficient of friction is 0.050.
4. A sled is pulled over level snow a distance of 0.500 km by a force of 124 n applied to a rope that makes

an angle of 35.0° with the snow. How much work is done?

5. A force of 18 n is required to stretch a spring 0.25 m from its equilibrium position. (a) Compute the amount of work done on the spring. (b) How much force is required to stretch the spring 0.50 m (assuming that the elastic limit of the spring is not exceeded)? (c) Compute the amount of work done.

6. A force of 545 n is exerted on the rope of a pulley system, and the rope is pulled in 10.0 m. This work causes an object weighing 2520 n to be raised 1.50 m. What is the efficiency of this machine?

7. Two people use a wheel and axle to raise a mass of 750 kg. The radius of the wheel is 0.50 m, and the radius of the axle is 0.040 m. If the efficiency of the machine is 62% and each person exerts an equal force, how much force must each apply?

8. The raised end of an inclined plane 4.0 m long is 0.90 m high. Neglecting friction, what force is required to push a steel box weighing 750 n up this plane?

9. A jackscrew has a lever arm 0.75 m long. The screw has 1.5 threads to the centimeter. If 320 n of force must be exerted in order to raise a load of $6.0 \times 10^3$ kg, calculate the efficiency.

10. What power is required to raise a mass of 47 kg to a height of 12 m in 15 s?

11. A loaded elevator has a mass of $2.50 \times 10^3$ kg. If it is raised in 10.0 s to a height of 50.0 m, how many kilowatts are required?

12. The mass of a large steel ball is 1500 kg. What power is used in raising it to a height of 33 m if the work is performed in 30.0 s?

GROUP B
13. A loaded trunk has a mass of 35 kg. The coefficient of friction between the trunk and the floor is 0.20. How much work is done in moving the trunk 8.0 m across a level floor and then lifting it into a truck 1.3 m above the floor?

14. A 75.0-kg crate is to be pushed up an inclined plane 3.00 m long that makes an angle of 20.0° with the horizontal. If the coefficient of friction between the crate and the inclined plane is 0.150, how much work must be done?

15. A tangential force of 7.5 n is applied to a wheel 0.25 m in radius to maintain it at a constant speed of 240 revolutions per minute. How much work is done per minute?

16. An unbalanced force of 5.0 n acts on a mass of 2.0 kg that is initially at rest. How much work is done (a) during the first two seconds; (b) during the tenth second?

17. A flywheel, mass 203 kg, is a uniform disk 1.00 m in radius. (a) What constant torque must be applied to bring the flywheel from rest to an angular velocity of 195 revolutions per minute in 60.0 s? (b) How much work is done during this time?

18. A loaded sled is pulled by means of a rope that makes an angle of 45.0° with the horizontal. If the mass of the sled is 60.0 kg and the coefficient of friction is 0.020, how much work is done in pulling the sled along a level road for a distance of 1.000 km?

19. A pump can deliver 20.0 liters of gasoline per minute. What power, in kilowatts, is expended by the pump in raising gasoline a distance of 6.00 m? One liter of gasoline has a mass of 0.700 kg. (The kinetic energy acquired by the gasoline may be disregarded.)

20. A motor is rated to deliver 10.0 kw. At what speed in m/min can this motor raise a mass of $2.75 \times 10^4$ kg?

21. What power will be required to move a locomotive weighing $1.00 \times 10^6$ n up a grade that rises 1.50 m for each $10\overline{0}$ m of track, so that it will move at a speed of 40.0 km/hr, if the frictional force opposing the motion is $2.00 \times 10^3$ n?

# ENERGY

In Chapter 1 we saw that there are two kinds of energy, potential and kinetic. In the following sections, we will deal quantitatively with these concepts and see how the various forms of energy are expressed in terms of work units.

The potential energy acquired by an object equals the work done against gravity or other forces to place it in position as shown in Figure 6-9. The equation for calculating work when the force acts in the same direction as the displacement is

$$W = F\Delta d$$

## 6.7 Gravitational potential energy

**Figure 6-9** Examples of potential energy. Can you give the reason for the difference in energy for each pair of situations?

Therefore

$$E_p = F\,\Delta d$$

In lifting an object, $F$ is its weight, which from Newton's second law of motion equals $mg$, and $\Delta d$ is the vertical distance $\Delta h$ through which it is lifted.

$$E_p = mg\,\Delta h$$

The gravitational potential energy defined by this equation is expressed in relation to an arbitrary reference level where $h = 0$. It makes no difference what level is chosen. Sea level, street level, ground level, or floor level are all useful reference levels.

When the mass of an object is given in kilograms, the height in meters, and the acceleration due to gravity in m/s², the gravitational potential energy is expressed in joules. Thus if a $\overline{50}$-kg mass of steel is raised 5.0 m, its gravitational potential energy is

$$E_p = mg\,\Delta h$$

$$E_p = \overline{50}\text{ kg} \times 9.8\text{ m/s}^2 \times 5.0\text{ m}$$

$$E_p = 2.5 \times 10^3 \text{ j}$$

## 6.8 Measurement of kinetic energy

At any particular instant, the velocity of a freely falling object that starts from rest, expressed in terms of the acceleration of gravity and the distance traveled, is given by the equation

$$v = \sqrt{2g\,\Delta d}$$

Solving for $\Delta d$, we obtain

$$\Delta d = \frac{v^2}{2g}$$

Since $\Delta d$ in this equation means the same quantity as $\Delta h$ in the equation $E_p = mg\,\Delta h$, let us substitute the expression we have just derived for $\Delta d$ in place of $\Delta h$. Since this object is moving with velocity $v$, it possesses kinetic energy. We then obtain

$$E_k = mg \times \frac{v^2}{2g}$$

$$E_k = \tfrac{1}{2}mv^2$$

Although this equation for kinetic energy was derived from the motion of a falling body, it can be shown that it applies to motion in any direction or from any cause.

As in the case of gravitational potential energy, kinetic energy is expressed in joules if the mass is given in kilograms and the velocity in meters per second. Thus if a baseball has a mass of 0.14 kg and is thrown with a velocity of 7.5 m/s, its kinetic energy is

$$E_k = \tfrac{1}{2}mv^2$$

$$E_k = \frac{0.14 \text{ kg } (7.5 \text{ m/s})^2}{2}$$

$$E_k = 3.9 \text{ j}$$

**Figure 6-10** Examples of kinetic energy. In each case, the energy is dependent upon the mass of the moving particle and its speed.

## 6.9 Kinetic energy in rotary motion

If a rotating object starts from rest, the angular velocity expressed in terms of angular acceleration and angular displacement is

$$\omega = \sqrt{2\alpha\Delta\theta}$$

For this same rotating object, the relationship among torque, rotational inertia, and angular acceleration is

$$T = I\alpha$$

Solving both of these expressions for angular acceleration,

$$\alpha = \frac{\omega^2}{2\Delta\theta} \text{ and } \alpha = \frac{T}{I}$$

Setting these two expressions equal

$$\frac{T}{I} = \frac{\omega^2}{2\Delta\theta}$$

Solving for $T\Delta\theta$,

$$T\Delta\theta = \frac{I\omega^2}{2}$$

When only the net force and torque are considered in these equations, all of the work done to produce rotation appears as kinetic energy. Since for rotary motion $W = T\Delta\theta$,

$$E_k = \tfrac{1}{2}I\omega^2$$

The wheel of a moving automobile has both linear motion and rotary motion. The wheel turns on its axle as the axle moves along parallel to the road. The kinetic energy of such an object is the sum of the kinetic energy due to linear motion and the kinetic energy due to rotary motion.

$$E_k = \tfrac{1}{2}mv^2 + \tfrac{1}{2}I\omega^2$$

**EXAMPLE**

*A metal ring, mass 2.50 kg, rolls along a horizontal surface with a velocity of 5.25 m/s. What is the total kinetic energy of the moving ring?*

**SOLUTION**

*Basic equation:* $E_k = \tfrac{1}{2}mv^2 + \tfrac{1}{2}I\omega^2$
The rotational inertia of a ring, $I = mr^2$ (See Figure 5-11)

By definition, $\omega = \dfrac{\Delta\theta}{\Delta t}$ and $\theta = \dfrac{\Delta d}{r}$ and $v = \dfrac{\Delta d}{\Delta t}$

Consequently, $\omega = \dfrac{\Delta d/r}{\Delta t} = \dfrac{\Delta d}{r\Delta t} = \dfrac{v}{r}$

Substituting, $\tfrac{1}{2}I\omega^2 = \tfrac{1}{2}mr^2\,(v/r)^2 = \tfrac{1}{2}mv^2$

*Working equation:* $E_k = \tfrac{1}{2}mv^2 + \tfrac{1}{2}mv^2 = mv^2$

$$E_k = (2.50 \text{ kg})(5.25 \text{ m/s})^2$$

$$E_k = 68.9 \text{ j}$$

When energy is supplied to an object and simultaneously gives it both linear and rotary motion, the energy division depends on the rotational inertia of the object. If a ring and a solid disk of equal mass and diameter roll down the same incline, the disk will accelerate more. Its rotational inertia is less than that of the ring, thus its rotational kinetic energy is less. Its linear kinetic energy is therefore greater than that of the ring; the disk acquires a higher linear velocity and reaches the bottom of the incline first. However, at the bottom of the incline the total kinetic energy of the ring will be the same as that of the disk since both ring and disk have the same gravitational potential energy at the top.

## 6.10 Elastic potential energy

When a spring is compressed, energy is stored in the spring. At any instant during the compression, the elastic potential energy in the spring is equal to the work done on the spring. The potential energy in a stretched or compressed elastic object is called *elastic potential energy*.

The work required to stretch or compress a spring does not depend on the weight of the spring. Consequently, gravity is not involved in the measurement of elastic potential energy. Instead, the work required to stretch or compress a spring is dependent upon a property of the spring known as the *force constant*. The force constant does not change for a specific spring so long as the spring is not permanently distorted.

The force required to stretch a spring is given by the equation

$$F = k\Delta d \qquad \text{(Equation 1)}$$

where $k$ is the force constant of the spring and $\Delta d$ is the distance over which $F$ is applied. We noted in Section 6.2 that the force is directly proportional to the length of the stretch (within definite limits). Consequently, the work done on the spring also varies directly with the amount of stretching. The total amount of work, therefore, is given by the equation

$$W = \tfrac{1}{2}F\Delta d \qquad \text{(Equation 2)}$$

where $F$ is the force exerted on the spring at the end of the stretch through distance $\Delta d$. Because the force varies from zero to $F$, the equation uses the average of these two values, or $\tfrac{1}{2}F$.

Substituting the expression for $F$ from Equation 1 in Equation 2, we get

$$W = \tfrac{1}{2}k(\Delta d)^2 \qquad \text{(Equation 3)}$$

This equation applies to the compression of a spring as well as the stretching of a spring. Since the potential energy of an object is equal to the work done on the object, Equation 3 can be rewritten as an elastic potential energy equation

$$E_\text{p} = \tfrac{1}{2}k(\Delta d)^2 \qquad \text{(Equation 4)}$$

This equation represents ideal conditions. In actual practice, a small fraction of the work of stretching or compression is converted into heat energy in the spring and thus does not show up as elastic potential energy.

*Compare this equation with the one for kinetic energy in Section 6.8. Why do you suppose they are similar?*

---

The vibration of a mass on a spring and the swinging of a pendulum are both examples of simple harmonic motion. Both can be used to illustrate an important principle of physics called the **law of conservation of mechanical energy**. This law states that *the sum of the potential and kinetic energy of an ideal energy system remains constant.*

Gravitational forces and elastic forces are *conservative forces* because they are responsible for the exchange between potential and kinetic energy in simple harmonic motion. There are forces, however, that produce deviations from the law of conservation of mechanical energy. The force of friction is one such example.

## 6.11 Conservation of mechanical energy

*This is a special case of the law of conservation of energy discussed in Section 1.12.*

**Figure 6-11** The work done by conservative forces is independent of the path. The potential energy of the man is, in each case, dependent only on his mass and the height above the reference level.

Forces of this type are called nonconservative, or *dissipative forces*.

The reason that friction is a dissipative force is that it produces a form of energy (heat) that is not mechanical. Energy is lost. When considered in light of the more comprehensive law of conservation of *total* energy, there is no "lost" energy, of course. The calculation of heat energy and its role in energy transformations will be discussed in Chapter 8.

Another way to distinguish between conservative and dissipative forces is to observe the relationship between the force and the path over which it acts. In the case of a conservative force, the work done and energy involved are completely independent of the length of the path, provided the paths have the same end point. For example, in the illustration of gravitational potential energy in Figure 6-11, the gravitational potential energy of both men is the same, provided they have equal masses, even though one of them traveled a greater distance than the other one. The mass of the men and their height above the reference level are the only factors necessary for the determination of gravitational potential energy.

The amount of heat energy lost through friction, a dissipative force, can be quite different for two objects descending from the same height, however. Where the path is longer, the amount of mechanical energy that is converted to heat energy will be greater. This is true even if the frictional forces were to remain constant. Thus the work done by a given dissipative force varies directly with the length of the object path.

# questions

GROUP A
1. Differentiate between (a) potential and kinetic energy; (b) gravitational potential energy and elastic potential energy.
2. Show how the formula for gravitational potential energy is derived from the work formula.
3. (a) Describe the kinetic energy of the wheel of a moving automobile. (b) Give the equations that can be used to calculate this energy.
4. (a) What determines the force required to stretch or compress a spring? (b) In what units is this factor expressed?

5. (a) Define mechanical energy. (b) How is it conserved in the motion of a pendulum?

GROUP B
6. (a) Show how the equation for kinetic energy is derived. (b) Use dimensional analysis to show that kinetic energy is expressed in work units.
7. Compare a swinging pendulum with the motion of a mass on the end of a horizontally compressed spring on a frictionless table.
8. (a) Distinguish between conservative and dissipative forces. (b) Why is the force of friction a dissipative force?

# problems

GROUP A
1. A mass of 2.00 kg is lifted from the floor to a table 0.80 m high. Using the floor as a reference, what potential energy does the mass have because of this change of position?

2. A large rock with a weight of 1470 n rests at the top of a cliff 40.0 m high. What potential energy does it have using the bottom of the cliff as a reference?
3. What is the kinetic energy of a baseball having a

mass 0.14 kg that is thrown with a speed of 18 m/s?

4. A meteorite weighing 1860 n strikes the earth with a velocity of 45.2 m/s. What is its kinetic energy?

5. A spring scale is calibrated from zero to $2\overline{0}$ n. The calibrations extend over a length of 0.10 m. (a) What is the elastic potential energy of the spring in the scale when a weight of 5.0 n hangs from it? (b) What is the elastic potential energy when the spring is fully stretched?

6. The force constant of a spring is 150 n/m. (a) How much force is required to stretch the spring 0.25 m? (b) How much work is done on the spring in that case?

## GROUP B

7. A stone having a mass 50.0 kg is dropped from a height of 197 m. What is the potential energy and the kinetic energy of the stone (a) at $t = 0$ s; (b) at $t = 1.00$ s; (c) at $t = 5.00$ s; (d) when the stone strikes the ground?

8. A car weighing $2.00 \times 10^5$ n is accelerated on a level road from 45.0 km/hr to 75.0 km/hr in 11.0 s. (a) What is its increase in kinetic energy?

(b) What force produces the acceleration? (c) What power is required?

9. What is the kinetic energy, in joules, of an electron that has a mass of $9.1 \times 10^{-31}$ kg and that moves at a speed of $1.0 \times 10^7$ m/s?

10. The rotor of an electric motor has a rotational inertia of 45 kg m². What is its kinetic energy if it turns at 1500 revolutions per minute?

11. A bowling ball has a mass of 8.00 kg. If it rolls down the alley, without slipping, at 7.00 m/s, calculate (a) the linear kinetic energy; (b) the rotational kinetic energy; (c) the total kinetic energy.

12. A solid ball, mass 10.0 kg, is at the top of an incline 2.00 m high and 10.00 m long. If it rolls down a frictionless incline, what is its linear speed as it reaches the bottom?

13. A 1.00-kg mass is placed at the free end of a compressed spring. The force constant of the spring is 115 n/m. The spring has been compressed 0.200 m from its neutral position. It is now released. Neglecting the mass of the spring and assuming that the mass is sliding on a frictionless surface, how fast will the mass move as it passes the neutral position of the spring?

# MOMENTUM

It is much harder to stop a train than it is to stop a car, even though both are moving with the same velocity. A bullet fired from a gun has more penetrating power than a bullet thrown by hand, even though both bullets have the same mass. The physical quantity that describes this aspect of the motion of an object is called *momentum*. **Momentum is the product of the mass of a moving body and its velocity**. The equation for momentum is

$$p = mv$$

where $p$ is the momentum, $m$ is the mass, and $v$ is the velocity of an object.

In the example of the car and train, the greater mass of the train gives it more momentum than the car. Consequently, a greater change of momentum is involved in stopping the train than in stopping the car. In the case of the bullets, the greater momentum of the fired bullet is due to its greater velocity; a large change of momentum takes place when the speeding bullet is stopped.

From Newton's second law of motion, we can derive an important relationship involving momentum. We know that over a short time interval $a_{av} = \Delta v / \Delta t$ (Section 3.5). If we substitute this value of acceleration for $a$ in $F = ma$, we get

$$F = \frac{m \Delta v}{\Delta t} \quad \text{or} \quad F \Delta t = m \Delta v$$

**6.12 The nature of momentum**

*The first of these equations states that force is the time rate of change of momentum.*

**Figure 6-12** During the moment of contact, much of the momentum of the bat is transferred to the baseball.

*Split-second timing was required for the photo in Figure 6-12. Compare it with the photo in Figure 2-4, which was taken by the same scientist.*

*The product of a force and the time interval during which it acts, $F \Delta t$, is called **impulse***. Hence from Newton's second law of motion we have established that impulse equals change in momentum. The equation $F = m \Delta v / \Delta t$ tells us that when a force is applied to a body, the body's rate of change of momentum is equal to the force. Since the equation is a vector equation, we also know that the body's rate of change of momentum is in the direction of the force.

A good example of the relationship between impulse and change in momentum is a bat hitting a baseball. See Figure 6-12. The impulse imparted to the ball depends on the force with which the ball is hit and the length of time during which the ball and bat are in contact. On leaving the bat, the ball has acquired a momentum equal to the product of its mass and its change of velocity. In a sense, the impulse produced the change of momentum; hence the two are equal.

## 6.13 The conservation of momentum

*This is also a special case of the law of conservation of energy.*

In Figure 6-13, a boy with a mass of $4\bar{0}$ kg and a man with a mass of $8\bar{0}$ kg are standing on a frictionless surface. When the man pushes on the boy from the back, the boy moves forward and the man moves backward.

The velocities with which the boy and the man move are specified by one of the most important principles of physics, the ***law of conservation of momentum***. This law states that *when no net external forces are acting on a system of objects, the total vector momentum of the system remains constant*.

Let us apply this law to the situation in Figure 6-13. Initially the man and the boy are at rest. The system, therefore, has zero momentum. When the man and the boy move apart, the law of conservation of momentum requires that the total vector momentum remain zero. Hence the momentum of the boy in one direction must equal that of the man in the other direction.

If the boy moves with a velocity of 0.50 m/s, the man will move with a velocity of 0.25 m/s since the mass of the man is

**Figure 6-13** A momentum experiment. On a frictionless surface, the momentum of the boy toward the left would equal the momentum of the man toward the right.

**Figure 6-14** The unbalanced force of the expanding gases inside the rocket engine pushes this model rocket upward.

twice as great as that of the boy. The momentum of the boy in one direction ($4\overline{0}$ kg × 0.50 m/s) must equal the momentum of the man in the opposite direction ($8\overline{0}$ kg × 0.25 m/s).

An important application of the law of conservation of momentum is the launching of a rocket. When a rocket fires, hot exhaust gases are expelled through the rocket nozzle. The gas particles have a momentum equal to the mass of the particles times their exhaust velocity. Momentum equal in magnitude is therefore imparted to the rocket in the opposite direction. See Figure 6-14. Newton's third law of motion (Section 3.10) is a special case of the law of conservation of momentum.

The law of conservation of momentum is very helpful in studying the motions of colliding objects. Collisions can take place in various ways, and we shall see how the momentum conservation principles apply in several such cases.

## 6.14 Inelastic and elastic collisions

**Figure 6-15** An inelastic collision. The carts have equal masses and approach each other with velocities of equal magnitude along the same straight line. The total momentum of the system is the same before and after the collision.

In Figure 6-15(A), two carts of equal mass approach each other with velocities of equal magnitude. A lump of putty is attached to the front of each cart so that the two carts will stick together after the impact. This situation is an example of *inelastic collision*. Since the carts are traveling along the same straight line, it is also an example of a *collision in one dimension*.

The momentum of cart **A** is $m_A v_A$. It is equal in magnitude to the momentum of cart **B**, $m_B v_B$. However, the direction of $v_A$ is opposite to the direction of $v_B$, so

$$v_A = -v_B$$

Consequently,

$$m_A v_A = -m_B v_B$$

and

$$m_A v_A + m_B v_B = 0$$

This means that the total vector momentum of the system of two moving carts is zero. (We assume that the system is *isolated*, that is, there are no net external forces acting on it. In actual collision studies, the external force of friction is usually minimized by the use of rolling carts or air tracks, such as the one shown in Figure 6-16.)

After the carts in Figure 6-15(B) collide, they both come to rest. The cart velocities, $v_A$ and $v_B$, are now both zero; the sum of the momenta of the two carts is zero, just as it was when the carts were in motion in opposite directions. Thus the total vector momentum of the system is unchanged by the collision.

If one of the carts has a greater mass than the other, although its velocity is still of equal magnitude but opposite sign, the outcome of the collision will be different. After impact, the combined carts will move in the direction of the cart with the larger

**Figure 6-16** An air track designed for collision experiments. Air jets minimize the friction between the track and the masses placed on it.

mass. The velocity of the combined carts will be such that the total momentum of the system remains unchanged.

For example, suppose

$$m_A = 2m_B$$

and

$$v_A = -v_B, \text{ as before.}$$

Then,

$$m_A v_A + m_B v_B \neq 0$$

Since $m_B = \dfrac{m_A}{2}$, by substitution,

$$m_A v_A - 1/2\, m_A v_A = 1/2\, m_A v_A$$

This means that the total momentum of the system, before and after the collision, is $1/2\ m_A v_A$; the combined carts will move with this momentum in the direction of the original velocity of cart **A**. The velocity after the collision can be found by dividing the total momentum by the total mass

$$\frac{1/2\, m_A v_A}{3/2\, m_A} = 1/3\, v_A$$

When carts of equal and opposite momenta collide inelastically, they come to rest. Before the collision they have kinetic energy; after the collision, they do not. When colliding objects rebound from each other without a loss of kinetic energy, a perfectly *elastic collision* has occurred. The only true perfectly elastic collisions occur between atomic and subatomic particles. The situation can be approximated, however, by the use of hard steel balls or springs on an air track. The momentum conservation law holds for elastic collisions as well as inelastic ones and for collisions that are partly elastic and partly inelastic.

The law also holds for *collisions in two dimensions*, that is, when the colliding objects meet at an angle other than head-on. Figure 6-17(A) shows the elastic, two-dimensional collision of two balls of equal mass. Ball **B** collides at an angle with ball **R**, which is initially at rest. Figure 6-17(B) is the vector diagram representing the momenta of the balls before and after collision.

*Review the parallelogram method of adding vectors explained in Section 2.6.*

(A)                                              (B)

**Figure 6-17** A vector diagram can be used to show that the total momentum of a system remains constant in a two-dimensional collision.

In Figure 6-17(B), $m_B v_B$ is the momentum of the black ball before the collision. Since the colored ball is stationary before the collision, its momentum is zero and is not represented by a vector. The total momentum of the system before collision is

$$m_B v_B + 0 = m_B v_B$$

After the collision, the measured velocities of the black and colored balls are $v_B'$ and $v_R'$ respectively, in the directions indicated. The total momentum now is the vector sum $m_B v_B' + m_R v_R'$. Since the momentum is conserved, the vector $m_B v_B$ must equal the vector sum of $m_B v_B'$ and $m_R v_R'$. The vector diagram therefore appears as a closed triangle.

The conservation of momentum also holds for collisions involving more than two bodies and in three-dimensional situations. The examples that follow show how collision problems can be solved by the principles just discussed.

**EXAMPLE**

*A ball having a mass of 0.25 kg and a velocity of 0.20 m/s eastward collides with another ball having a mass of 0.10 kg and a velocity of 0.10 m/s, also eastward and along the same straight line. After the collision the more massive ball has a velocity of 0.15 m/s eastward. What is the velocity of the less massive ball?*

**SOLUTION**

Let $\quad$ $m$ = the mass of the more massive ball
$m'$ = the mass of the less massive ball
$v_i$ and $v_f$ = the initial and final velocities of the more massive ball
$v_i'$ and $v_f'$ = the initial and final velocities of the less massive ball

The total vector momentum is the same after the collision as before the collision.

*Basic equation:* $\qquad m v_i + m' v_i' = m v_f + m' v_f'$

*Working equation:* $\qquad v_f' = \dfrac{m v_i + m' v_i' - m v_f}{m'}$

$$v_f' = \frac{(0.25 \text{ kg})(0.20 \text{ m/s}) + (0.10 \text{ kg})(0.10 \text{ m/s}) - (0.25 \text{ kg})(0.15 \text{ m/s})}{0.10 \text{ kg}}$$

$$v_f' = 0.22 \text{ m/s eastward}$$

**EXAMPLE**

*Two balls with equal masses collide in the way shown in Figure 6-17. Before the collision, the black ball moves with a speed of 0.80 m/s. After the collision, the balls are observed to move along paths that are perpendicular to each other. If the angle between $m_R v_R'$ and $m_B v_B$ in the vector diagram is $4\overline{0}°$, calculate the speed of each ball after the collision.*

**SOLUTION**

Since the balls have equal masses, we can ascribe any convenient mass to them for the purposes of the problem. If we choose 1.00 kg, then the numerical value of the momentum for each ball will equal the numerical value of the velocity. The vector diagram will then yield the velocities directly.

$$v_B = 0.80 \text{ m/s (the speed of the black ball before the collision)}$$
$$v_R' = v_B \times \cos 4\overline{0}° = (0.80 \text{ m/s}) (0.77)$$
$$\phantom{v_R'} = 0.62 \text{ m/s (the speed of the colored ball after the collision)}$$
$$v_B' = v_B \times \sin 4\overline{0}° = (0.80 \text{ m/s}) (0.64)$$
$$\phantom{v_B'} = 0.51 \text{ m/s (speed of the black ball after the collision)}$$

---

## 6.15 Angular momentum

For rotary motion, the relationship between impulse and the change of angular momentum is similar to that for linear motion. Using the symbols for rotary motion, the equation becomes

$$T\Delta t = I\omega_f - I\omega_i$$

where $T\Delta t$ is the *angular impulse* and $I\omega_f - I\omega_i$ is the change in *angular momentum*. The dimensions of both angular impulse and angular momentum are kg m²/s.

Just as the linear momentum of an object is unchanged unless a net external force acts on it, *the angular momentum of an object is unchanged unless a net external torque acts on it*. This is a statement of the *law of conservation of angular momentum*. A rotating flywheel, which helps maintain a constant angular velocity of the crankshaft of an automobile engine, is an illus-

**Figure 6-18** Angular momentum of a girl on ice skates. When she lowers her arms, her angular velocity increases. This experimental evidence supports the law of conservation of momentum.

tration. The rotational inertia of a flywheel is large. Consequently torques acting on it do not produce rapid changes in its angular momentum. As the torque produced by the combustion in each cylinder tends to accelerate the crankshaft, the rotational inertia of the flywheel resists this action. Similarly, as the torques produced in the cylinders where compression is occurring tend to decelerate the crankshaft, the rotational inertia of the flywheel resists this action also. Consequently the flywheel tends to maintain a uniform rate of crankshaft rotation.

If the distribution of mass of a rotating object is changed, its angular velocity changes so that the angular momentum remains constant. See Figure 16-18.

A skater spinning on the ice with arms folded turns with relatively constant angular velocity. If she extends her arms, her rotational inertia increases. Since angular momentum is conserved, her angular velocity must decrease.

# summary

Work is the product of a displacement and the component of the force in the direction of the displacement. The unit of work is the joule. Work done by varying forces can be found by calculating the area under the curve of a graph in which the horizontal axis denotes the displacement and the vertical axis denotes the force. Radian measure is used to compute work done in rotary motion.

Machines can be used to multiply force at the expense of distance. The efficiency of a machine is the ratio of the useful work output to the total work input and is expressed as a percentage. Power is the time rate of doing work. It is measured in watts. Radian measure is used to compute power in rotary motion.

Gravitational potential energy is equal to the work done against gravity to place an object in position. Thus energy is measured in units of work. The kinetic energy of a body moving in a straight line is directly proportional to the mass of the body and the square of its velocity. In rotary motion, the kinetic energy is directly proportional to the rotational inertia and the square of the angular velocity. Elastic potential energy is directly proportional to the force constant and the square of the amount of stretch. The law of conservation of mechanical energy states that the sum of the potential and kinetic energy of an ideal energy system remains constant.

Momentum is the product of the mass of a moving body and its velocity. The change of momentum of a moving body is equal to its impulse, which is the product of a force and the time interval during which the force acts. The momentum of a system of objects is conserved when no net external forces are acting on the system. This is the law of conservation of momentum. The reaction principle is an application of this law. The conservation of momentum also helps to describe the motion of objects colliding elastically or inelastically and in one, two, or three dimensions. Unless a net external torque acts on a rotating object, its angular momentum is also conserved.

# questions

GROUP A

1. (a) What is impulse? (b) What is momentum? (c) How are impulse and change of momentum related?

2. Why do both a slowly docking ferryboat and a speeding rifle bullet have a large amount of momentum?

3. Are impulse and momentum scalar or vector quantities?

4. What is the law of conservation of momentum?

5. How does an aerial display of fireworks illustrate conservation of momentum?

6. Distinguish between elastic and inelastic collisions.

7. What is meant by an isolated system? Consider torques as well as forces in your answer.
8. Give examples of one-dimensional and two-dimensional collisions.

GROUP B

9. Explain why it is impossible for a moving ocean liner or a speeding airplane to make an abrupt turn.

10. What happens to the momentum of a car when it stops?
11. How can you explain the precession of a spinning gyroscope in terms of angular momentum and the torque produced by gravity?
12. (a) What external forces other than friction are acting on the moving carts in Figure 6-15? (b) Why can they be ignored in the experiment?

# problems

GROUP A

1. A 50̄0-kg mass is at rest and is free to move. At a certain time, 25.0 s after a force acts on it, the mass has a velocity in the direction of the force of 15̄0 m/s. What is the magnitude of the force?
2. A bullet, mass 60.0 g, is fired from a gun that is suspended by wires and is free to move. The mass of the gun is 5.00 kg. The speed of the bullet is 615 m/s. What is the speed of recoil of the gun?
3. A 1.50-kg ball whose velocity is 8.00 m/s southward collides with a 2.00-kg ball traveling along the same path with a velocity of 3.00 m/s southward. If the velocity of the 2.00-kg ball is 4.50 m/s southward after impact, what is the velocity of the 1.50-kg ball?
4. A proton (mass = $1.67 \times 10^{-27}$ kg) moves with a velocity of $6.00 \times 10^6$ m/s. Upon colliding with a stationary particle of unknown mass, the proton rebounds on its own path with a velocity of $4.00 \times 10^6$ m/s. The collision sends the unknown particle forward with a velocity of $2.50 \times 10^6$ m/s. What is the mass of the unknown particle?
5. An object with a mass of 15.0 kg and a velocity of 2.00 m/s collides with a stationary object having the same mass. After the collision the first object moves along a line that makes an angle of 4̄0° to the right of its original path. The second object moves at an angle of 10̄0° to the left of the path of the first object after the collision. (a) Graphically determine the momentum of each object after the collision. (b) Calculate the speed of each object after the collision.

GROUP B

6. A freight car with a mass of $3.0 \times 10^5$ kg travels at a velocity of 2.5 m/s. It collides with a stationary car having a mass of $1.5 \times 10^5$ kg on a horizontal track. The cars connect and roll together after impact. What is the velocity of the connected cars?
7. Benjamin Franklin once said that light could not consist of particles because if a particle would travel at such tremendous speeds ($3 \times 10^8$ m/s), it would have the impact of a 10-kg cannon ball fired from a cannon with a velocity of 100 m/s. According to this comparison, what is the mass of Franklin's particle of light?
8. A person is skiing down a hill. The person's mass, including skis, is 65 kg. When the person reaches the bottom of the hill the speed is 15 m/s. The person hits a snowdrift and stops in 0.30 s with uniform deceleration. (a) How far does the person penetrate the snowdrift? (b) With what average force does the person hit the drift?
9. Show that angular momentum has the unit dimensions kg m²/s.
10. Two balls collide head-on with equal velocity. One ball has three times the mass of the other. After the elastic collision, the more massive ball stops and the less massive one moves back along its original path with twice its original velocity. Show that momentum is conserved in the collision.
11. In the multiple-exposure photograph accompanying this problem, a large ball approaches from the top and a smaller one from the bottom. The mass of the large ball is 15̄0 g. The photo shows the balls at equal time intervals. By means of an appropriate vector diagram, find the mass of the smaller ball.

# careers

**P**hysics is more than a course of study. It is a foundation of information upon which careers are built. The people pictured here are applying the concepts and principles of physics daily in their work. From their endeavors have come useful products and important solutions to interesting problems. These diverse applications are supplying the research and technology vital to the future progress of our society.

*Top right: Combining computer and audio technology, the effects of radio, TV, and radar signals are measured.*

*Bottom right: Solar energy applications show great potential as a future energy source. This technician examines the installation and operation of a solar energy cell.*

*Right: Analysis of nozzle and turbine blade designs will help achieve maximum efficiency in exploiting the energy in the liquid and vapor phases of geothermal brine deposits.*

*Right: A surveyor uses many of the principles of physics in determining the optimal sites and conditions for construction.*

*Right: The combined efforts of these scientists led to the discovery of the J/psi particle.*

*Below: This civil engineer is involved in the design phase of the construction of a U.S. submarine.*

*Above: A scientist at the U.S. Department of Energy's Argonne National Laboratory discusses the newly developed lithium/sulfur battery with a student who may become one of tomorrow's scientists.*

*Left: At the Johnson Space Center, TX, this NASA astronaut-candidate, seated in a T-38 jet trainer aircraft, prepares for a familiarization flight under the guidance of a veteran astronaut.*

*Bottom, left to right:*

*The Telstar II satellite is checked out by NASA scientists. This active repeater satellite is used for trans-Atlantic radio, TV, and telephone transmission.*

*The principles of electronics have made possible the vast array of computer applications. Here a computer programmer works at a cathode-ray tube.*

*The development of a clean, inexhaustible source of electrical energy involves laser fusion research. The assembly of neodymium glass disks will amplify a .001-j pulse of laser light 250,000 times before it reaches the fusion target. Such research must be done in a dust-free environment.*

*Members of the collaboration team of experimenters that discovered the Upsilon particle pose in the apparatus used for their research at the Fermi National Accelerator Laboratory, IL.*

# 7 Phases of Matter

## MOLECULES AND ATOMS

### 7.1 The structure of matter

When a sample of matter such as a lump of sugar is crushed into smaller particles, each of these particles is still a particle of sugar. Only the size of the particle of sugar is changed. If the subdividing process is continued by grinding the material into a fine powder, the results are the same. Even when the sugar is dissolved in water and the particles are too small to be seen with a microscope, the identifying properties of the substance are retained. Evaporation of the water returns the solid sugar's identifying properties, such as color, crystalline shape, and density. Observations such as these, together with the quantitative evidence supporting the laws of definite and multiple proportions, which you may have already studied in chemistry, lead to these conclusions about the nature of matter:

1. *Matter is composed of particles.*
2. *The ultimate particles of matter are extremely small.*

As early as 400 B.C., Greek philosophers formulated ideas about the ultimate composition of matter. Democritus (460–370 B.C.) believed that matter was indestructible and that the subdividing process mentioned above would reach a limit beyond which no further separation was possible. He called these ultimate particles *atoms*, after the Greek word *atomos* meaning indivisible. This idea was largely the result of rational thinking. Democritus had no direct evidence with which to back up his concept of atoms.

The Greek philosopher Aristotle (384–322 B.C.) suggested that all matter can be reduced eventually to four basic *elements*: air, earth, fire, and water. The reasoning that was used to sup-

*We still refer to wind and rain as the "elements of nature," especially during a storm.*

port this idea was often quite complex, but it was a beginning in the attempt to list the ultimate particles of the universe.

It was a long time before the idea of atoms and ultimate particles was actively studied again. Near the beginning of the 19th century, the English scientist John Dalton (1766–1844) conducted a series of experiments with gases that added greatly to our knowledge of the nature of atoms. Dalton's *atomic theory* explained the mechanisms of known reactions between substances and made it possible to extend the list of known elements.

The atomic theory has been modified and expanded many times since Dalton's day. Almost two hundred years of investigation has added much information to our knowledge of the makeup and properties of atoms, the way in which they interact, and the nature of the compounds they form. Modern theory includes data concerning the mass and size of atoms as well as the energy relationships among atoms. Experiments have also revealed the fact that atoms are not ultimate particles of matter after all. A whole array of subatomic particles is presently being studied by scientists. (These are described in Chapters 23–25.)

## 7.2 Molecules

A *molecule* is the smallest particle of a substance that is capable of stable, independent existence. Thus in the example in the previous section, the smallest particle of sugar that retains the identifying properties of the substance is a molecule of sugar. Not all substances, however, are composed of molecules. Some substances are composed of electrically charged particles known as ions.

A molecule of sugar is so small that it has never been seen, even with the help of the most powerful microscope. To get an idea of the extremely small size of molecules, imagine a drop of water magnified until it is as large as the earth. With this tremendous increase in size, a single molecule of water would be about one meter in diameter. A simple molecule, like that of water, is about $3 \times 10^{-10}$ m, or 3 angstroms (Å) in diameter.

Molecules of more complex substances may have sizes of more than 200 Å. The electron microscope, which is capable of magnifications of several million times, can be used to photograph some of these "giant" molecules.

*$1 \text{ Å} = 10^{-10}$ m. The angstrom is named after the Swedish physicist Anders Ångstrom (1841–1874). The angstrom is not an SI unit, but it continues to be used because of its convenient size for atomic dimensions.*

## 7.3 Atoms

If a molecule of sugar is analyzed, it is found to consist of particles of three simpler kinds of matter: carbon, hydrogen, and oxygen. These simpler forms of matter are called *elements*. An *atom is the smallest particle of an element that can exist either alone or in combination with other atoms of the same or*

**Figure 7-1** Single uranium atoms. These atoms have been magnified more than five million times by a scanning transmission electron microscope developed at the University of Chicago by A. Crewe, M. Isaacson, M. Utlaut, and M. Ohtsuki. The small bright spots are single uranium atoms. The larger white spots are clusters of uranium atoms. The background is a thin carbon filament, about six atoms thick, that supports the uranium atoms.

*different elements*. A molecule of sugar, therefore, is made up of atoms of carbon, hydrogen, and oxygen.

Since atoms make up molecules, atoms are usually smaller than molecules. The smallest atom, an atom of hydrogen, has a diameter of about 0.6 Å. The largest atoms are a little more than 5 Å in size. The hydrogen atom is also the lightest atom. It has a mass of $1.67343 \times 10^{-27}$ kg. The most common uranium atom, which is one of the heaviest atoms, has a mass of $3.95268 \times 10^{-25}$ kg. There is about a tenfold range in the sizes of atoms and about a 250-fold range in their masses.

Even with the use of scientific notation, it is difficult to express conveniently the masses of individual atoms. Consequently, scientists express the *atomic mass* of an atom in **atomic mass units** *(u)*. One $u$ is equal to $1.6605655 \times 10^{-27}$ kg. This is $\frac{1}{12}$ the mass of a carbon-12 atom; carbon-12 is the most abundant form of carbon atoms. In other words, scientists use carbon-12 as the standard of mass for atoms.

In atomic mass units, the atomic mass of the most abundant form of hydrogen is 1.007825 while that of the most abundant form of uranium is 238.0508. You will notice that atomic masses are known very accurately. *The integer nearest to the atomic mass is called the **mass number** of an atom*. The mass number is represented by the symbol $A$. Thus for the common hydrogen atom, $A = 1$; for the common uranium atom, $A = 238$.

In 1970 the American scientist Albert Crewe (b. 1927) took the first photos of atoms. In 1976 Dr. Crewe obtained black and white motion pictures of atoms. Two years later, Crewe used an electron microscope to take color movies of atoms. The concept of atoms is very useful in the study of chemical reactions. When substances interact chemically, atoms are regrouped, but the number of the various kinds of atoms does not change during the reaction.

## 7.4 Kinetic theory of matter

So far in our study of physics, we have been concerned almost entirely with the behavior of solid particles of matter. A solid is one of the three *phases* (or states) of matter—the solid phase, the liquid phase, and the gas phase. In the description of matter *phase* indicates the way in which particles group together to form a substance. The structure of a substance can vary from compactly arranged particles to highly dispersed ones.

In a *solid*, the particles are close together in a fixed pattern. In a *liquid*, the particles are not usually as close together as in a solid and are not held in any fixed pattern. In a *gas*, the average separation of the particles is relatively large, and as in a liquid, the particles are not held in any fixed pattern. (Frequently the term *vapor* is used to describe a gas that under ordinary conditions of temperature and pressure is in the liquid phase.)

To explain the motions of molecules and the energy molecules possess, particularly in the gaseous phase, scientists have developed the **kinetic theory of matter**. Two basic concepts of this theory are:

*1. The molecules of a substance are in constant motion.* The amount of motion depends upon the average kinetic energy of the molecules; this energy depends upon the temperature.

*2. Collisions between molecules are perfectly elastic* (except when chemical changes or molecular excitations occur).

*The kinetic theory was developed independently of the atomic theory.*

## 7.5 Forces acting between molecules

The forces required to pull a solid apart are generally much greater than the forces required to separate a similar amount of liquid. The fact that liquids separate into drops indicates that the forces of attraction between the molecules of liquids are not as great as the attractive forces of solids. Most liquids occupy a larger volume than the same mass of solid. The size of a molecule of a substance in one phase does not differ appreciably from its size in another phase. Thus molecules of liquids must be farther apart than molecules of solids. In a gas, molecules separate from each other spontaneously; this accounts for the fact that a gas occupies a volume of the order of $10^3$ times that of an equal mass of liquid. This spontaneous separation of gas molecules indicates that the kinetic energy of the molecules is great enough to keep them separated. We may conclude that forces between molecules decrease as the distance between them increases.

Solids and liquids are not easily compressed. Apparently, when molecules in solids and liquids are pushed closer together than their normal spacing, they repel each other. As the molecules are pushed closer together, the repulsive forces become greater.

Intermolecular forces are predominantly electric. If we compare the strength of intermolecular forces with the gravitational forces between molecules at the typical distances found in solids and liquids, we find that the intermolecular forces are of the order of $10^{29}$ times as strong. Thus gravitational forces between molecules are negligible in comparison with intermolecular forces. Intermolecular forces are small compared to the weight of objects we can see and handle; however, the masses these intermolecular forces act on—the masses of molecules—are small, too. These forces can impart instantaneous accelerations $10^{14}$ times the acceleration of gravity. Such accelerations last only a very short time since one molecule, so accelerated, moves very quickly out of the range of another.

Figure 7-2 shows how the force of interaction between molecules varies with the distance between their centers. If we imagine

*The forces that hold molecules together in crystals are known as van der Waals forces, after the Dutch scientist Johannes Diderik van der Waals (1837–1923).*

**Figure 7-2** The force between molecules varies with the distance between molecular centers.

one molecule to be fixed at the intersection of the axes, the other molecule will be repelled until the distance of separation is such that their outer charges do not overlap. This condition occurs at $r_0$ where no net force acts between the molecules. The distance to $r_0$ is often called the equilibrium distance. This distance (about $2.5 \times 10^{-10}$ meter) is, therefore, the distance between the centers of two "touching" molecules and is the diameter of a single molecule. As the separation between the molecules increases, the force of attraction between opposite charges first increases and then approaches zero. Different molecules have different sizes and charge configurations, but they always show the qualitative behavior indicated by Figure 7-2.

In the solid phase, molecules vibrate about the equilibrium position $r_0$. They do not have enough energy to overcome the attractive force. The equilibrium positions are fixed. In a liquid the molecules have greater vibrational energy about centers that are free to move, although the average distance between the centers of the molecules remains nearly the same. The average distance of separation between gas molecules is considerably greater than the range of intermolecular forces, and the molecules move in straight lines between collisions.

# SOLIDS

## 7.6 The nature of solids

Solids have definite shapes and definite volumes. Scientists usually describe solids as either *crystalline* or *amorphous*. Crystalline solids have a regular arrangement of particles; amorphous solids have a random particle arrangement.

In addition to the forces that bind particles of a solid together, the motion of particles of a solid is an important consideration. Particles of a solid are held in relatively fixed positions by the binding forces. However, they do have a vibratory motion about their fixed positions. The amplitude of their vibration and their resulting vibratory energy are related to the temperature of the solid. At low temperatures the kinetic energy is small, at higher temperatures it is larger.

*Diffusion is the penetration of one type of particle into a mass consisting of a second type of particle.* If a lead plate and a gold plate are in close contact for several months, particles of gold may be detected in the lead, and vice versa. This demonstrates that even solids may diffuse. Diffusion is slow in solids because of the limited motion of the particles and their close-packed, orderly arrangement.

## 7.7 Cohesion and adhesion

The general term for *the force of attraction between molecules of the same kind is cohesion*. Cohesion, the force that holds the close-packed molecules of a solid together, is a short-range force. If a solid is broken, layers of gas molecules from the air cling to the broken surfaces. These gas molecules prevent the rejoining of the solid surfaces. The molecules of the broken surfaces are not close enough to have sufficient attraction to hold. However, if the surfaces of two like solids are polished and then slid together, cohesion causes the solids to stick together.

Molecules of different kinds sometimes attract each other strongly. Water wets clean glass and other materials. Glue sticks to wood. *The force of attraction between molecules of different kinds is called* **adhesion**. The forces of cohesion and adhesion have definite values for specific molecules.

*Why is the tape used to hold a bandage in place called adhesive tape?*

## 7.8 Tensile strength

Several properties of solids depend on cohesion; one of these is tensile strength. Suppose two wires of the same diameter, one copper and one steel, are put in a machine that pulls the wires until they break. When tested in this manner, steel wire proves stronger than copper wire of the same diameter. Therefore we say that steel has a higher *tensile strength* than copper. *The* **tensile strength** *of a material is the force per unit cross-sectional area applied perpendicularly to the cross section that is required to break a rod or wire of that material.* See Figure 7-3 and Appendix B, Table 7. Tensile strength is a measure of cohesion between adjacent molecules over the entire cross-sectional area.

**Figure 7-3** Tensile test of steel exhibiting high ductility. Note localized reduction of area in center of specimen.

## 7.9 Ductility and malleability

If a metal rod can be drawn through a die to produce a wire, the metal is said to be *ductile* (*duk*-til) or to possess *ductility*. As the metal is pulled through the die, pressure decreases its diameter and increases its length and the rod becomes a wire. See Figure 7-4(A). In one industrial application of ductility,

Casing

Die of tungsten carbide

Direction of pull

Slab of metal

Rolls

Direction of rolling

**(A)**

**(B)**

**Figure 7-4** During the process of drawing (A) and rolling (B), the atoms of a metal are forced to move over each other from one position in the crystal pattern to another.

more than 1000 meters of wire are extruded per minute from a device in which the necessary pressure is exerted by a fluid and the extruded wire never touches the solid die.

Metals that can be hammered or rolled into sheets are said to be *malleable* (*mal*-ee-uh-bul) or to have *malleability*. During the hammering or rolling, the shape of the metal is greatly changed. See Figure 7-4(B).

In the process of hammering, rolling, or drawing, layers of atoms of a metal are forced to slide over one another, thus changing their positions in the crystal pattern. Since the cohesive forces are strong and the atoms do not become widely separated from each other during their rearrangement, the metal holds together while its shape is being changed. Silver, gold, platinum, copper, aluminum, and iron are all highly malleable and ductile.

## 7.10 Elasticity

*Elastic potential energy was discussed in Sections 1.11 and 6.10.*

When opposing forces are applied to an object, the object becomes deformed. The deformation can be a change in its dimensions or its shape. *The ability of an object to return to its original size or shape when the external forces are removed* is described as its **elasticity**. In the deformed configuration the intermolecular forces are not in equilibrium, while in the original configuration they are. There exists a limit beyond which the deformation produced by the applied forces does not disappear when the forces are removed. The object is then said to be permanently deformed. Ductility and malleability are properties of substances that can undergo such permanent deformations without fracturing. *When a substance is on the verge of becoming permanently deformed*, we say it has reached its **elastic limit**.

At the elastic limit, molecular forces are overcome to such an extent that particles slide past each other. Particles shift places in the crystal, and the shape of the material is altered. Such a drastic change cannot be reversed by molecular forces. Every solid has a certain range through which it can be deformed and yet return to its original condition before its elastic limit is reached.

In order to make quantitative measurements of the elastic properties of a substance we shall introduce two new terms: *stress* and *strain*.

*Stress is the ratio of the internal force, F, that occurs when a substance is deformed in any way to the area, A, over which the force acts.*

$$stress = \frac{F}{A}$$

Stress represents the tendency of a substance to recover its normal configuration. The deforming force changes the distance between molecules by either pulling them farther apart or pushing them closer together. When the deforming force is removed, molecular forces restore the molecules to their normal spacing.

The *relative amount of deformation produced in a body under stress is called* **strain**. There are various kinds of deformation, or strain, but its measure is always an absolute ratio—a number without units. When a rod is placed under tension or stretched, it elongates. *The ratio of the increase in length to the unstretched length is called the* **elongation strain** *and can be expressed as* $\Delta l/l$. Linear compression strain is the reverse of elongation. These processes are illustrated in Figure 7-5. Both of these processes are accompanied by small changes in the cross-sectional area. We will not consider these changes further because their effect is small in situations where elastic limits are not exceeded.

In an *elongation strain*, the particles have been moved in a direction perpendicular to the area over which the forces act. In a *shear strain*, the particles move in a direction parallel to the area over which the forces act. An imaginary cube of unstrained material will take the shape of a rhombic prism when shear forces are applied to it. *The measure of shear is the ratio of the amount the top of the imaginary cube is moved to the side to the dimension of one side of the cube*. This ratio, shear, is expressed as the tangent of the angle through which the oblique edges of the imaginary cube have been rotated from their original direction, as shown in Figure 7-6.

*Volume strain* is the ratio of the decrease in volume to the volume before the stress was applied.

Flexure (bending) and torsion (twisting) are combinations of elongation and compression strains. A straight beam bent into a plane curve undergoes compression on the concave side and elongation on the convex side. The layer of material down the center of the beam undergoes neither compression nor elongation.

**Figure 7-5** Strain may be a change in the length of a rod resulting from applied forces. (A) Elongation strain equals $\Delta l/l$. (B) Linear compression strain also equals $\Delta l/l$.

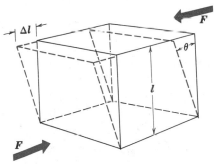

**Figure 7-6** This is an imaginary cube of a substance within a larger body of material to which shear forces are applied. Shear strain = $\tan \theta = \Delta l/l$.

Beams and girders of buildings and bridges are often subjected to varying forces or stresses. It is important for engineers to know what deformation, or strain, these forces will produce. In order to do this, they must have a way of measuring the elasticity of materials.

If a coiled spring is stretched by a weight, as shown in Figure 7-7(A), it will probably return exactly to its original form after the stretching force is removed. If it does, it is said to be *perfectly elastic*. If the spring is stretched too far, it remains permanently deformed; its elastic limit has been exceeded.

Suppose we fasten one end of a steel wire to a beam, as in Figure 7-7(B). Now suppose we add weights to the hanger attached to the lower end. As we add the weights one by one, the

## 7.11 Hooke's law and Young's modulus

**Figure 7-7** In the figures above, the pointers stood at zero before the weights were applied. (A) If the pointer returns to the zero mark after the weight is removed, the spring is perfectly elastic. (B) If weights stretch a wire beyond its elastic limit, the pointer will not return to zero when the weights are removed.

*Young's modulus is named after the English physicist Thomas Young, who also did experiments with light. Values of Young's modulus for various substances are given in Appendix B, Table 8.*

wire stretches gradually. We find that the wire elongates by an amount that is exactly proportional to the weight pulling on it, and that it returns to its original length when the weight is removed. If we continue to apply more weights, eventually we reach the elastic limit. Then when we remove the weights, the wire remains deformed; it does not return to its original length.

By making such measurements, the English philosopher and scientist Robert Hooke (1635–1703) found that the amount of elongation in elastic solids is directly proportional to the deforming force provided the elastic limit is not exceeded. The elongation also depends on the length and cross-sectional area of the wire or rod. It is possible to combine all these facts into one simple law given by Hooke. ***Hooke's law*** states that *within certain limits strain is directly proportional to stress*.

The value of the ratio stress/strain is different for different solids. However, the ratio is constant for a given substance, even when the substance is fashioned into different shapes. This ratio gives us a means of comparing the elasticity of various solids. The numerical value of Hooke's law is called *Young's modulus*, $Y$, and is defined by the equation

$$Y = \frac{\text{stress}}{\text{strain}}$$

From the definitions of stress and strain we get

$$Y = \frac{F/A}{\Delta l/l}$$

and

$$Y = \frac{Fl}{\Delta lA}$$

As an example, the steel "A" string of a piano is 43.0 cm long. It has a cross-sectional area of $6.50 \times 10^{-7}$ m². How much will it elongate when a force of $7\overline{1}0$ n is applied to it by the piano tuner to bring it up to pitch?

$$\Delta l = \frac{Fl}{YA} = \frac{(7.10 \times 10^2 \text{ n})(4.30 \times 10^{-1} \text{ m})}{(20.0 \times 10^{10} \text{ n/m}^2)(6.50 \times 10^{-7} \text{ m}^2)} = 2.38 \times 10^{-3} \text{ m}$$

# questions

GROUP A

1. List two basic concepts of the kinetic theory.
2. (a) What is meant by the phase of matter? (b) Describe the three phases of matter.
3. What types of collision do molecules undergo? (See Section 6.14.)
4. Under what circumstances are the forces between molecules in a solid (a) attractive, (b) repulsive?
5. (a) What are the two classes of solids? (b) What is the particle arrangement in each?
6. (a) Describe the motion of the particles of a solid.

(b) What experimental evidence supports this description?

7. What name is given to the force of attraction between (a) like molecules, (b) unlike molecules?

8. (a) What is tensile strength? (b) In what units is the value for tensile strength usually expressed?

9. Define elasticity.

10. Distinguish between stress and strain.

11. What is meant by the elastic limit?

12. State Hooke's law.

13. (a) What is Young's modulus? (b) State the equation and identify each term.

GROUP B

14. For a given mass of matter that can exist as a solid, a liquid, and a gas, what does the volume indicate about the spacing between molecules in these three phases?

15. (a) What is the magnitude of an atomic mass unit? (b) How is this value established?

16. What direct evidence do we have that matter is composed of molecules?

17. Distinguish between a molecule and an atom.

18. What happens to the crystal pattern of an elastic material when its elastic limit is exceeded?

# problems

GROUP A

1. A coiled spring is stretched 0.050 m by a mass weighing 0.500 n that is hung from one end. How far will it be stretched by a mass weighing 1.000 n?

2. The hook of a spring balance is pulled down 5.00 cm by a mass weighing 40.0 n. (a) If a mass weighing 125.0 n is substituted for the previous mass, how far is the hook pulled down? (b) How far apart are the 5.00-n graduations?

3. Two identical wires are 125.0 cm and 375.0 cm long. The first wire is broken by a force of 489.0 n. What force is needed to break the other?

4. A copper wire 100.0 cm long and 0.200 cm in diameter is suspended from a solid support. A 10.00-kg mass is hung from the lower end of the wire. (a) Determine the stress in the wire. (b) Determine the strain in the wire.

5. The cross-sectional area of an aluminum wire is $2.50 \times 10^{-3}$ cm². What force will break it?

6. A brass wire 2.57 m long and 2.00 mm in diameter is suspended from a fixed support. A mass of 8.25 kg is hung from the lower end. Determine the increase in the length of the brass wire.

7. A brass wire 215 cm long and $5.00 \times 10^{-2}$ cm² in cross-sectional area supports a mass weighing 1.25 n. How far is the wire stretched?

GROUP B

8. An aluminum wire 2.00 m long and 0.400 mm in diameter is attached to a firm support. Masses weighing 1.00 n each are added to it one at a time. The measured changes in the length of the wire as determined by a microscope and scale are 0.0224 cm, 0.0464 cm, 0.0681 cm, 0.0897 cm, and 0.1128 cm. Plot a graph with the stresses as ordinates and the strains as abscissas. From the information given above and the graph, determine Young's modulus. How is the graph used to determine Young's modulus?

9. A rod 6.00 mm in diameter is composed of a material having a Young's modulus of $9.00 \times 10^{10}$ n/m². What force will stretch it by 0.02% of its length?

# LIQUIDS

In 1827 the English botanist Robert Brown (1773–1858) placed some pollen grains in water. He dropped a bit of this suspension on a small glass slide. When he examined the suspension through a microscope, he found that the pollen grains moved in a very random way. The path of one particle resembled that shown in Figure 7-8. This *Brownian movement* is caused by the ceaseless bombardment of the suspended particles by molecules

**7.12 The nature of liquids**

**Figure 7-8** The haphazard movement of the white particle is the result of its bombardment by the molecules of the liquid in which it is suspended. The black arrows indicate the directions of the liquid molecules after the collisions. (The relative distances between collisions have been exaggerated for clarity.)

*Brownian movement is also exhibited by solid particles, such as smoke, suspended in the atmosphere.*

**Figure 7-9** Diffusion in liquids. Ions of water diffuse downward into the heavier copper(II) sulfate solution, and vice versa.

of the suspending liquid. It indicates that molecules of a liquid are in continuous, rapid, and random motion.

Liquids diffuse. This effect can be demonstrated by the following experiment. Enough concentrated copper(II) sulfate solution is poured into a tall cylinder to form a layer of colored liquid several centimeters deep. A flat cork is floated on the surface of the solution. Water is carefully poured through a funnel tube onto the top of the cork, as shown in Figure 7-9. The water flows around the edge of the cork and spreads out over the surface of the colored liquid, producing two distinct layers. The water "floats" on the copper(II) sulfate solution because the water has a lower density than the copper(II) sulfate solution. After the cylinder stands for a few days, the interface between the layers is less distinct. Some of the colored solution diffuses into the water above, and some of the water molecules diffuse into the copper(II) sulfate solution below. Even though weeks may pass before the diffusion is complete, we can see that diffusion does occur in liquids despite the force of gravity. Because of the slightly more open molecular arrangement and greater molecular mobility of liquids, their rate of diffusion is considerably faster than that of solids.

## 7.13 Cohesion and adhesion in liquids

If you push a spoon into a jar of honey and then pull it out, you discover that a certain amount of force is needed to pull apart the molecules that make up the honey. If you lick the honey from the spoon, you realize that force is required to pull the molecules of the honey away from the molecules of the spoon. This observation demonstrates cohesion within a liquid and adhesion between a liquid and a solid. The relative strength of these forces determines what occurs at the surface of a liquid and a solid.

If a clean glass rod is dipped into water and then removed, some of the water clings to the glass rod. We say that the water wets the glass. The adhesion of water molecules to glass must therefore be greater than the cohesion between water molecules.

If the glass rod is dipped into mercury and then removed, the mercury does not cling to the glass. The cohesion between mercury molecules is greater than their adhesion to glass. Cohesive forces vary in different liquids. They are usually smaller in liquids than in solids.

## 7.14 Surface tension

**Figure 7-10** Surface tension keeps a razor blade afloat even though its mass density is much greater than that of water.

Have you ever seen a sewing needle or a razor blade floating on the surface of water? Even though they are about seven times as dense as water, if they are placed carefully on the surface, they remain there. A close look at the water surface shows that the needle or razor blade is supported in a hollow in the water surface, as seen in Figure 7-10. *The water acts as though it has a thin, flexible surface film.* The weight of the needle or razor blade is counterbalanced by the upward force that is exerted by the surface film. This property of liquids is due to *surface tension*.

All liquids show surface tension. Mercury has a very high surface tension. In many liquids the surface film is not as strong as that of water or mercury. Part of the cleaning action of detergents is due to their ability to lower the surface tension of water. This makes it possible for the water and detergent to penetrate more readily between the fibers of the substances being cleaned and the dirt particles.

Since particles in a liquid attract similar liquid particles that are nearby, they tend to arrange themselves so that they are as close together as possible. Hence the surface will tend to have a minimum area. The effect of this attraction is to make the liquid behave as if it were contained in a stretched elastic skin. The *tension* in this "skin" is the *surface tension*. When a force acts on a liquid surface film and distorts that film, the cohesion of the liquid molecules exerts an equal and opposite force that tends to restore the horizontal surface. Thus the weight of a supported needle produces a depression in the water surface film that increases the area of the film. Because of its tendency to restore the surface of the liquid to its original horizontal condition, the

*Surface tension also helps ducks float on water.*

Center film broken.
Thread pulled to
form circle.

(A)

(B)

**Figure 7-11 (left)** (A) A soapy-water film is formed across the ring. (B) When the center of the film is broken, the outer portion of the film contracts and pulls the loop of thread into a circle.

**Figure 7-12 (right)** Small drops of mercury assume a spherical shape because of surface tension. Large drops are flattened because the downward force of gravitation is greater than the upward force produced by surface tension.

*Handle mercury with care. Mercury is poisonous. It can be absorbed through the skin or by breathing its vapor.*

cohesion of the water molecules exerts a counterbalancing upward force on the needle.

*Surface tension produces contraction forces in liquid films.* A liquid film has two free surfaces on which molecules are subject to an unbalanced force toward the inside of the film. Thus both free surfaces tend to assume a minimum area. The contraction of the film can be demonstrated by the device shown in Figure 7-11. If a wire ring containing a loop of thread, Figure 7-11(A), is dipped into a soap solution, a film is formed across the ring. If the film inside the loop of thread is broken with a hot wire, the unbroken film outside the loop contracts and pulls the thread equally on all sides to form a circle, as shown in Figure 7-11(B).

*Surface tension causes a free liquid to assume a spherical shape.* A free liquid is one that is not acted upon by any external force. This is an ideal condition, but it can be approximated by small drops of mercury on a table top, as shown in Figure 7-12. A sphere has the smallest surface area for a given volume. The unbalanced force acting on liquid surface molecules tends to pull them toward the center of the liquid, reducing the surface area and causing the liquid to assume a spherical shape. Since the cohesive force between mercury molecules is great and mercury has a very high surface tension, small drops of mercury are almost spherical. Larger drops of mercury, on which the effect of the force of gravity is greater, are noticeably flattened.

### 7.15 The shape of liquid surfaces

If you examine the surface of water in a glass container, you will find that it is not exactly level. It is very *slightly concave* when viewed from above. The edge of the surface where water comes in contact with the glass is lifted a little above the general level, as shown in Figure 7-13(A). *The crescent-shaped surface of a liquid column is called the meniscus* (meh-*niss*-kus). The water at the edge is lifted above the normal level because adhesion between water and glass is greater than cohesion between water molecules.

If the container is filled with mercury instead of water, the edges of the liquid are depressed and the surface is *slightly convex*. See Figure 7-13(B). In this case, cohesion between mercury molecules is greater than adhesion between mercury and glass.

**Figure 7-13** (A) Liquids that wet the surfaces of their containers have surfaces with concave edges. (B) Liquids that do not wet the surfaces of their containers have surfaces with convex edges.

*Meniscus comes from a Greek word meaning crescent moon.*

## 7.16 Capillarity

When the lower ends of several tubes are immersed in water, the water will rise to the same height in each tube only if the tubes have large enough diameters so that the centers of the menisci are relatively flat. *Water does not rise to the same height in tubes of varying small diameters*. The height to which it rises increases as the diameter of the tube decreases. See Figure 7-14(A). When mercury is used, the depression of the surface is greater as the diameter of the tube is reduced. See Figure 7-14(B). *This elevation or depression of liquids in small diameter or capillary tubes is called* **capillarity**.

Water rises                                    Mercury is depressed

(A)                                            (B)

**Figure 7-14** (A) Capillary action of water. (B) Capillary action of mercury. The elevation or depression is inversely proportional to the diameter of the tube. (The tube diameters and magnitudes of capillarity are exaggerated for clarity.)

Capillarity depends on both adhesion and surface tension. Adhesion between water and glass causes water to creep up the glass walls and produce a concave surface; surface tension tends to flatten this surface by contraction. The combined action of these two forces raises the water above its surrounding level. The water level rises until the upward force is counterbalanced by the weight of the elevated liquid.

Several conclusions about capillarity have been verified by experiment. *(1) Liquids rise in capillary tubes they wet and are depressed in tubes they do not wet. (2) Elevation or depression is inversely proportional to the diameter of the tube. (3) The elevation or depression decreases as the temperature increases. (4) The elevation or depression depends on the surface tension of the liquid.*

---

### 7.17 Melting

*The change of phase from a solid to a liquid is called* **melting**. Melting involves the breaking of bonds between the particles of a solid. The temperature at which this change occurs is called the **melting point**. Pure *crystalline* solids have definite melting points, and different solids have different melting points.

When a substance changes from a liquid to a solid, it is said to *freeze*. The temperature at which freezing occurs is known as the **freezing point**. For pure crystalline substances, the melting point and the freezing point are the same temperature at any given pressure.

*Noncrystalline solids*, like paraffin, have no definite melting point. When they are heated, they soften gradually. The temperature at which noncrystalline solids first soften and the temperature at which they flow freely are often greatly different.

*Butter and glass do not have definite melting points.*

In order for a solid to melt, energy must be supplied to it. This energy increases the energy of the particles of the solid and gives them the freedom of motion characteristic of the particles of a liquid. As the temperature of a solid increases, the vibrations of its particles increase in amplitude; thus more and more potential energy is stored in the average stretching of the bonds between the particles. Finally a point is reached at which the bonds between the particles cannot absorb any more energy without breaking. Thus crystalline solids have a definite melting point. When the liquid formed by melting a crystalline solid cools to a certain temperature, the energy of the liquid particles is reduced to such an extent that the forces between the particles draw them into fixed positions in a crystal. Thus a liquid that forms a crystalline solid freezes at a definite temperature.

All the energy supplied to a substance during melting appears as work done by the particles in changing from a solid crystal structure to a liquid structure. The kinetic energy of the particles does not change. Since average kinetic energy depends on temperature, melting is a constant temperature process.

Usually, the particles of noncrystalline solids are held together by forces of attraction and by the physical entanglement of long-chain molecules. The bonding combination is not of such definite strength that the bonds are broken when the particles acquire a fixed amount of energy. The energy required to overcome these bonds varies with the extent of the bonding and entanglement of each molecule. As they are heated, non-crystalline substances soften at a lower temperature first. At some higher temperature, they flow freely. Similarly, as they are cooled, the molecules become bonded at various kinetic energies and the liquid does not solidify at a definite temperature.

The degree of separation of particles of a substance is different in the solid and liquid phases because of the difference in the potential energy of the particles. If melted paraffin is poured into a vessel and allowed to harden, the center becomes indented, or depressed, as shown in Figure 7-15(A). The paraffin cools and contracts as it solidifies. Both kinetic energy and potential energy are lost in the process. The loss of kinetic energy is indicated by the decrease in temperature. Loss of potential energy permits the particles to move closer together and take up less space. Almost all substances behave in this manner; the particles of most substances are closer in the solid phase than in the liquid phase.

Water is the most important exception to the rule that a substance contracts when it changes from a liquid to a solid. See Figure 7-15(B). When an ice cube tray is placed in the freezing compartment of a refrigerator, the level of the water in the sections of the tray is uniform. When the ice cubes are formed, however, each one has a slightly raised spot in the center. The volume occupied by ice is about 1.1 times that occupied by the water from which it was formed. The force of expansion when water freezes is enormous. Antifreeze is used in water-cooled cars that are driven in areas where the atmospheric temperature drops below the freezing point of water. As its name suggests,

(A)

(B)

**Figure 7-15** (A) Most substances, like paraffin, contract when they solidify. (B) Water is one of the few substances that expands on solidification.

a mixture of antifreeze and water freezes at a lower temperature and does not expand significantly in freezing if the mixture is sufficiently concentrated.

Bismuth and antimony are two metals that expand rather than contract when they solidify. Substances such as ice, bismuth, and antimony have open crystal structures in which the particles are more widely separated than they are in the liquid phase. That is why the solid occupies a larger volume than the liquid.

## 7.18 Effect of pressure on the freezing point

Freezing above wire

Melting beneath wire

Weights

**Figure 7-16** Melting under pressure and freezing again after the pressure is released is called regelation.

*For best results, the experiment in Figure 7-16 should be conducted in slightly subfreezing temperatures.*

**Figure 7-17** Mobile regelation. A thin film of water forms as the skates press on the ice. As the skates pass, the water film freezes again.

In substances that contract when they solidify, like the paraffin in Figure 7-15(A), the molecules of the solid are closer together than the molecules of the liquid. If additional pressure is exerted, such a liquid can be made to solidify at a higher temperature than its normal freezing point under atmospheric pressure. An increase in pressure raises the freezing (melting) point of most substances.

Some of the rock in the interior of the earth is hot enough to melt at normal pressure, but most of it remains solid because of the tremendous pressure. If the pressure is released, as when a volcano erupts, more of the rock melts and forms lava.

An increase in pressure has the opposite effect on the freezing point of a substance like water that expands as it freezes. In such a substance the molecules are farther apart in the solid than they are in the liquid. Since an increase in pressure makes formation of the solid more difficult, the freezing point is lowered if the pressure is raised.

We can illustrate this effect by suspending two weights over the surface of a cake of ice by means of a strong wire. See Figure 7-16. The pressure of the wire on the ice lowers the melting point of the ice immediately below the wire. If the surrounding temperature is above the new melting point, this part of the ice melts, and the molecules of water are forced upward around the wire. When they reach a spot above the wire, the pressure returns to normal, the melting point rises, and the water freezes again. When the wire is embedded in the ice, the extra heat needed to melt the ice below the wire is supplied by the freezing of the water above the wire. In this way, the wire may cut its way through the cake of ice, and yet leave the ice in one piece. This process of melting under pressure and freezing again after the pressure is released is called *regelation* (ree-jeh-*lay*-shun).

When the pressure of ice-skate blades on ice is sufficient to melt the ice at its existing temperature, the blades slide along with very little friction on a thin layer of water. However, if the ice is so cold that the pressure of the skate blades cannot melt the ice, the blades are retarded by the higher friction of steel on ice and skating is difficult.

The freezing point of a liquid is lowered when another substance is dissolved in it. The extent of the lowering depends on the nature of the liquid, the nature of the dissolved substance, and the relative amounts of each. The greater the amount of the substance dissolved in a fixed amount of liquid, the lower the freezing point of the liquid. We apply this principle when we use rock salt to prevent the formation of ice on roads and sidewalks and to melt the ice that has formed. The dissolved substance interferes with crystal formation as the liquid cools. Before crystals form, the kinetic energy of the liquid particles must be reduced to a level below that at which they normally go into a crystal pattern.

## 7.19 Effect of dissolved materials on the freezing point

# GASES

Gas molecules are mostly independent particles traveling at high speed. Evidence for this concept comes from observing three properties of gases:

*1. Expansion.* A gas has neither a definite shape nor a definite volume; rather it expands and completely fills any container. This observation indicates that gas molecules are independent particles.

*2. Pressure.* An inflated balloon may burst from the force that the air inside it exerts on its inside surface. This force is a result of the continual bombardment of the inside surface by billions of moving molecules. If we increase the number of molecules within the balloon by blowing more air into it, the number of collisions against the inside surface increases, the pressure on the inside surface thus increases, and the balloon expands.

*3. Diffusion.* Hydrochloric acid is a water solution of the high-density gas hydrogen chloride; ammonia water is a water solution of the low-density gas ammonia. When these gases react chemically, they form a cloud of fine, white particles of solid ammonium chloride. Suppose we put a few drops of hydrochloric acid in a warm bottle and an equal amount of ammonia water in a second warm bottle. We then cover the mouth of each bottle with a glass plate and invert the bottle containing ammonia over the one containing hydrogen chloride, as shown in Figure 7-18(A). After the bottles have stood this way for a minute or two, we remove the glass plates so that the bottles are now mouth-to-mouth. The formation of white smoke indicates that the less dense ammonia descends and mixes with the more dense hydrogen chloride. The hydrogen chloride also rises and mixes with the ammonia in the upper bottle. The movement of each of these gases is opposite to that which would

## 7.20 The nature of gases

**Figure 7-18**   (A) When the glass plates are removed, the gases mix by diffusion. (B) The difference in diffusion rates causes pressure differences that result in bubbles in the liquid. (C) The liquid in the lower vessel rises as a result of a pressure difference caused by differing diffusion rates.

be caused by the density of the gases. The movement must be due to molecular motion. Thus diffusion of gases is evidence of the rapid movement of gas molecules.

Gases diffuse through porous solids. In the apparatus shown in Figure 7-18(B), an inverted, unglazed earthenware cup is closed with a rubber stopper through which passes a glass tube that dips into a colored liquid. When a low-density gas, such as hydrogen, is led into a beaker placed over the cup, air immediately begins to bubble through the colored liquid. Evidently the lighter molecules of hydrogen move in through the porous walls of the cup faster than the heavier molecules in the air move out. Thus there is an accumulation of hydrogen molecules inside the cup. This accumulation increases the pressure inside the cup, thus pushing the liquid down the tube and forcing some of the air and hydrogen mixture in the tube to escape. In a similar way, the porous cup is now surrounded with a dense gas, such as carbon dioxide. See Figure 7-18(C). Since carbon dioxide is denser than air, the apparatus must be modified; the vessel surrounding the porous cup must be closed at the bottom and open at the top. When this vessel is filled with carbon dioxide, molecules from the air flow out through the porous cup faster than carbon dioxide molecules enter. This difference reduces the pressure inside the cup, and the colored liquid rises in the tube. Thus we see that there is an inverse relation between the rate of diffusion of a gas and its density.

Diffusion of gases through porous solids is an important process. Such diffusion occurs through the membranes of plants, animals, and humans, allowing oxygen to reach living cells and carbon dioxide to escape. Uranium isotopes are separated by means of the different rates of diffusion of $^{235}_{92}UF_6$ and $^{238}_{92}UF_6$, two gaseous hexafluorides of uranium, through a suitable porous barrier.

*Nuclear power on a large scale was first released by the splitting of U-235 atoms that were concentrated by diffusion.*

## 7.21 Vaporization

If some ether is placed in a shallow dish, within a short time the quantity of liquid decreases and the odor of ether becomes quite strong near the dish. Apparently molecules of ether liquid become molecules of ether vapor and mix with molecules of the gases in the surrounding air. In a similar manner, but at a much slower rate, moth balls left out in the air become smaller and smaller and eventually disappear while their characteristic odor is noticed in the air nearby. In this case, molecules of the solid moth balls turn into vapor and diffuse into the surrounding air. These are two examples of **vaporization**, *the production of a vapor or gas from matter in another phase.* See Figure 7-19.

As in the case of melting (Section 7.17), vaporization is a constant-temperature process. All the energy supplied during vaporization goes to increase the potential energy of the particles. The average kinetic energy of the particles is unchanged.

The particles of all liquids and solids have an average kinetic energy that depends on the temperature of the liquid or solid. However, because of random collisions and vibratory motion, some particles have energies higher than average and others have energies lower than average. When the particle on the surface of a liquid or solid acquires enough energy to overcome the forces that hold it as part of the substance, the particle escapes and becomes a particle in the vapor phase. When vaporization occurs from liquids it is known as *evaporation*; when vaporization occurs from solids, it is known as **sublimation**. Sublimation is a direct change from solid to vapor without passing through the liquid phase.

The energy of the particles that evaporate from a liquid is obtained either from the surrounding atmosphere or from the remaining liquid. In either case, evaporation has a cooling effect on the environment. When perspiration evaporates from the skin, the process cools the skin. When rubbing alcohol is applied to the skin, the cooling effect is even greater because alcohol evaporates more rapidly than water.

Since the rate of evaporation or sublimation depends on the energy of the particles undergoing the change and in turn their energy depends upon their temperature, evaporation and sublimation occur more rapidly at higher temperatures and more slowly at lower temperatures.

**Figure 7-19** Vaporization. Water molecules (black circles) escape into the air at the surface of the liquid. Some of them collide with molecules of gases in the air (colored circles) and rebound.

The tendency of liquids to evaporate and of solids to sublime is determined by a property called *equilibrium vapor pressure*. A bell jar covering a container of water is shown in Figure 7-20. There are as many molecules of the gases of the air within the bell jar as there are in an equal volume of air outside it. The pressure (force per unit area) exerted by the gas molecules on the inside walls of the bell jar is the same as the pressure that such molecules exert on the outside walls.

When a molecule at the surface of the water within the bell jar acquires sufficient kinetic energy, it escapes and becomes a water vapor molecule. As the water evaporates, water vapor molecules mix with the gas molecules in the bell jar. These water vapor molecules collide with gas molecules, with the walls of the bell jar, with the outside surface of the container of water, and with the surface on which the bell jar rests. They can also touch the water surface, be held by it, and become molecules of liquid again. The conversion of molecules of vapor to molecules of liquid is called **condensation**. Eventually the rate of evaporation equals the rate of condensation, and a condition of equilibrium prevails. At equilibrium, evaporation and con-

## 7.22 Equilibrium vapor pressure

**Figure 7-20** When the number of water molecules evaporating from the liquid equals the number of water vapor molecules returning to the liquid, the pressure exerted by the water vapor molecules against the walls of the bell jar is the equilibrium vapor pressure.

densation do not cease; they occur at the same rate. The number of water vapor molecules in the air in the bell jar remains constant. At equilibrium, the space above the water in the vessel is said to be *saturated* with water vapor.

The collision of water vapor molecules against the walls of the bell jar increases the pressure on the bell jar so that it exceeds the pressure exerted by the gases of the air. *Added pressure exerted by vapor molecules in equilibrium with liquid* is called **equilibrium vapor pressure**.

Since the kinetic energy of the particles of the liquid depends on both the temperature and mass of the particles, the equilibrium vapor pressure of a liquid depends on the composition as well as the temperature of the liquid. As the kinetic energy of the particles increases, so does the vapor pressure.

The ratio of the water vapor pressure in the atmosphere to the equilibrium vapor pressure at that temperature is called the *relative humidity*. Relative humidity is usually expressed as a percentage. For example, suppose that the air temperature on a given day is $3\overline{0}°C$ and that the water vapor pressure is 15.5 mm of mercury. The equilibrium vapor pressure at $3\overline{0}°C$ (as given in Appendix B, Table 12) is 31.8 mm of mercury. The relative humidity is

$$\frac{15.5 \text{ mm}}{31.8 \text{ mm}} \times 100\% = 48.7\%$$

*In summer, the humidity is often more oppressive than the temperature. Why?*

Relative humidity depends on both the temperature and the amount of water vapor in the atmosphere. The temperature at which a given amount of water vapor will exert equilibrium vapor pressure is called the *dew point*. In the above example, the dew point is 18°C because at that temperature the equilibrium vapor pressure of water is 15.5 mm of mercury.

**7.23 Boiling**      When water is heated sufficiently its vapor pressure will eventually equal the combined pressure of the atmosphere and the liquid pressure of the water. Vaporization then occurs at such a rapid rate throughout the water that the water becomes agitated. *This rapid vaporization that disturbs the liquid and that occurs when the vapor pressure of the liquid equals the pressure on its surface is called boiling.* If the pressure on the liquid surface is one atmosphere (760 mm of mercury), the temperature at which boiling occurs is called the *normal boiling point*. If the pressure on the liquid surface is greater than one atmosphere, boiling occurs at a higher temperature than the normal boiling point; if the pressure on the liquid surface is less than one atmosphere, boiling occurs at a lower temperature than the normal boiling point. Greater pressure is largely the result of the greater number of collisions of the particles against the surface of the liquid. Consequently, the kinetic energy of the liquid, and thus its temperature, must be raised to make boiling possible. The opposite is true when the pressure on a liquid is decreased.

Water or any other liquid that is boiling rapidly does not get hotter when it is boiling than when it is simmering. While a liquid is boiling away, the boiling temperature remains constant until all the liquid has been vaporized.

Solids or gases dissolved in a liquid change the liquid's boiling temperature. For example, salt water boils at a higher temperature than pure water. In general, solids dissolved in liquids raise the boiling temperature and gases dissolved in liquids lower the boiling temperature.

**Figure 7-21** Castle Geyser in Yellowstone National Park.

# summary

The smallest particle of any substance that is capable of stable, independent existence is a molecule. Molecules are composed of atoms. Atoms are the smallest particles of elements that can exist either alone or in combination with other atoms of the same or different elements. The masses of individual atoms are usually expressed in atomic mass units, rather than kilograms. The atomic mass unit is based on the mass of the carbon-12 atom.

The kinetic theory of matter states that molecules of matter are in constant motion and undergo perfectly elastic collisions. The phase of matter (solid, liquid, or gas) is determined by the forces acting between molecules and the energy the molecules possess.

Properties of solids such as diffusion, cohesion, adhesion, tensile strength, ductility, malleability, and elasticity depend on molecular forces and/or molecular motion. Hooke's law states that, within limits, strain (the deformation of a solid) is directly proportional to

stress. The ratio of stress to strain is called the Young's modulus of the substance.

Molecular forces, molecular motion, and the weight of molecules are factors on which liquid properties such as diffusion, cohesion, adhesion, surface tension, and capillarity depend. Melting is the change of phase from a solid to a liquid. Crystalline solids have characteristic melting points; noncrystalline solids do not have definite melting points. Most substances expand upon melting. Water is an important exception. Pressure and dissolved materials change the melting point and freezing point of substances.

Gases expand, exert pressure, and diffuse. Vaporization is the change of phase from a solid or liquid to a gas or vapor. The added pressure exerted by vapor molecules in equilibrium with liquid molecules is called equilibrium vapor pressure. Boiling is rapid vaporization that occurs when the vapor pressure of a liquid is equal to the pressure on its surface.

# questions

GROUP A

1. What characteristic of liquid molecules did Brown's experiment reveal?

2. Describe a demonstration that shows that molecules of liquids diffuse.

3. In terms of adhesion and cohesion, explain why alcohol clings to a glass rod and mercury does not.

4. What is the effect of adding a detergent to the water on which a needle is supported?

5. Why is a soap bubble floating through the air spherical in shape?

6. What determines whether a meniscus is concave or convex when viewed from above?

7. Water rises to a certain height in a capillary tube of given diameter. What is the effect on the amount of rise if (a) the tube is lengthened, (b) the diameter of the tube is decreased, (c) the temperature of the water is raised?

8. (a) Which change of phase is called melting? (b) What name is given to the temperature at which melting occurs? (c) What is freezing? (d) What name is given to the temperature at which freezing occurs?

9. (a) Which has a greater density, water or ice? (b) Explain in terms of molecular configuration.

10. What is the meaning of the term "regelation"?

11. In terms of the kinetic theory, explain why gases (a) expand when heated, (b) exert pressure, (c) diffuse through porous substances.

GROUP B

12. Describe the characteristics of the particles of a substance that is liquid at room temperature.

13. Describe the forces that are acting when a razor blade is supported on water.

14. Why is lead shot made by allowing melted lead to fall through cool air?

15. In terms of adhesion and cohesion, explain why mercury is depressed in capillary tubes.

16. Describe the forces that cause water to rise in a capillary tube.

17. Why do crystalline solids have a definite melting point and noncrystalline solids do not?

18. What is the effect of increased pressure on the freezing point of (a) substances that contract as they freeze, (b) substances that expand as they freeze?

19. Why do sharp ice skates melt the ice better than dull ones?

20. What would happen if the gas introduced into the large beaker of the apparatus shown in Figure 7-18(B) were (a) helium, (b) argon?

# Thermal Effects

## HEAT AND TEMPERATURE UNITS

We know from experience that heat and temperature are related. They are not the same, however. A burning match has a much higher temperature than a steam radiator, but the match does not give out enough heat to warm a room. Suppose we have a large cup filled with boiling water, as shown in Figure 8-1. If we pour some of the water into a smaller cup, the temperature of the water in that cup will be about the same as that in the large cup. However, the water in the large cup could melt more ice than the water in the small cup because the water in the large cup gives out more heat. (Ice absorbs heat as it melts.) It is possible for a material to be at a high temperature and give out little heat; to be at a high temperature and give out a large quantity of heat; to be at a low temperature and give out little heat; or to be at a low temperature and give out a large quantity of heat.

When a material is hot, it has more *thermal energy* than when it is cold. We do not know the exact relationship between thermal energy and the structure of matter, but we define *the **thermal energy** of a material as the total potential and kinetic energy associated with the random motion and arrangements of its particles*.

What we call temperature is simply the "hotness" or "coldness" of a material. The quantity of thermal energy possessed by a body affects its temperature. The same quantity of thermal energy possessed by different bodies, however, does not give each the same temperature. The ratio between temperature and thermal energy is different for different materials.

### 8.1 Thermal energy, heat, and temperature

**Figure 8-1**   The water in the two cups is at the same temperature, but the water in the large cup can give off more heat.

We saw in Chapter 7 that the temperature of a substance will rise if the average kinetic energy of its particles is increased. If the average kinetic energy is decreased, the temperature goes down. On the other hand, when the potential energy of the particles is increased or decreased without a change in the average kinetic energy, a change of phase takes place without a change in temperature.

*Refer to Sections 7.17 and 7.21.*
*Heat is thermal energy in motion.*

*Thermal energy that is absorbed, given up, or transferred from one material to another is* **heat**. The temperature of a body is a measure of its ability to give up heat to or absorb heat from another body. Thus, the temperature of a body determines whether or not heat will be transferred to or from any nearby body.

The classical experiments of Count Rumford and James Prescott Joule (Section 1.13) show that mechanical energy and heat are equivalent and that *heat must be a form of energy*.

Since thermal energy has also been defined as a form of energy, you may wonder why two different terms—thermal energy and heat—are used. The distinction is not essential, but the following example will serve to illustrate the usage of these terms. The temperature of the air in a bicycle tire will rise when the tire is being pumped up. It will also rise when the tire is out in the sun. In both cases the thermal energy and the temperature of the air are increased. In the first case the work done in pumping was converted to thermal energy. In the second case the rise in temperature was due to energy transferred from the sun to the tire. The term *heat* is used when the transfer of thermal energy from one body to another body at a different temperature is involved.

Although temperature is actually defined in terms of measurements made by idealized thermometers, the known relationships among temperature, the structure of matter, and energy are consistent with the following definition of temperature: *Temperature is a physical quantity that is proportional to the average kinetic energy of translation of particles in matter.*

## 8.2 Measuring temperature

To measure temperature it is necessary to introduce a fourth fundamental unit. The unit of temperature difference, the degree, cannot be derived from length, mass, and time; a measurable physical property that changes with temperature is used.

There are many physical properties that change with temperature. The linear dimension of a solid, the volume of a liquid, the pressure of a gas held at constant volume, the volume of a gas held at constant pressure, the resistance of an electric conductor, and the color of a solid heated to a high temperature are examples. Some of these properties of matter could be used in developing a temperature scale and constructing a thermometer.

To establish a temperature scale it is necessary to identify a process that occurs without a change in temperature. The temperature at which such a process takes place can then be used as a fixed point on a temperature scale. A change of phase of a substance, such as melting or boiling, can be used. The temperature at which the solid phase of a substance is in thermal equilibrium with its liquid phase is a fixed value at a given pressure. This is the melting point. Similarly, at the boiling point the liquid is in thermal equilibrium with its vapor, and this point has a fixed value at a given pressure. The boiling temperature of the substance is always higher than the melting temperature.

There is only one pressure at which the solid, liquid, and vapor phases of a substance can be in contact and in thermal equilibrium. This equilibrium occurs at only one temperature, which is known as the *triple-point temperature*. For example, there is only one pressure and temperature condition at which ice, liquid water, and water vapor can exist in a vessel in thermal equilibrium. The ice, liquid water, and vapor are all at the same temperature and can continue to exist indefinitely in the constant volume of the sealed vessel. A device for determining the triple point of water is shown in Figure 8-2.

The temperature of the triple point of water is of particular significance because in 1954 the Tenth Conference on Weights and Measures adopted this temperature as the single fixed point for defining temperature. This conference assigned the numerical value of 273.16°K, Kelvin, to this temperature.

Before 1954, two fixed points were used to define the standard temperature interval. They were the *steam point* (the boiling point of water at standard atmospheric pressure) and the *ice point* (the melting point of ice when in equilibrium with water saturated with air at standard atmospheric pressure). The Celsius scale (formerly called the centigrade scale), devised by the Swedish astronomer Anders Celsius (1701–1744), assigned the value 0°C to the ice point and 100°C to the steam point, as shown in Figure 8-3. Thus the interval between the two fixed points was 100C°. Note that specific temperatures on the Celsius scale are expressed in the unit °C. Temperature differences or intervals on the Celsius scale are expressed in the unit C°. Kelvin scale temperatures have the unit °K; Kelvin scale temperature differences are expressed in K°.

In the temperature scale adopted in 1954, the magnitude of the Kelvin degree (K°) is the same as that of the Celsius degree (C°). These are arbitrarily established units for the measurement of temperature difference. 0°K is called the *absolute zero of temperature*. Absolute zero should not be thought of as a condition of matter with zero energy and no molecular motion. Molecular action does not cease at absolute zero. The molecules of a substance at absolute zero have a minimum amount of kinetic

**Figure 8-2** The National Bureau of Standards triple-point cell. Pure water with air removed is sealed permanently in the cell, which is then immersed in a water-ice bath. The system is at the triple point when ice, water, and vapor are all present within the cell. A central well is provided for the immersion of the thermometer to be calibrated.

*The triple point of water is the reference standard for temperature scales. The Kelvin scale was invented by Sir William Thomson (1824–1907), who is better known by his title, Lord Kelvin.*

*0°K (−273°C) is the coldest possible temperature because at that temperature molecular energy is at a minimum.*

100 — Boiling point
         of water
90
80
70
60
50
40
30
20 — Room temperature
10
0 — Freezing point
       of water
−10
−20

**Figure 8-3** The Celsius thermometer shown is one type used in laboratory work.

energy, known as the zero-point energy. Molecular energy is a minimum, but not zero, at absolute zero.

Now let us consider the results obtained when a temperature is measured using any of the thermometers in common use. To assign numbers on the temperature scale, it is assumed that a measurable physical property of a substance that changes with temperature, $X$, is proportional to the Kelvin temperature, $T$; thus $X \propto T$. If $X_t$ is the measurement of the physical property at the standard fixed temperature, $T_t$, which is the triple point of water, and $X$ is the measure of the same property of the same substance at the unknown temperature, $T$, then we can write the proportion

$$\frac{X}{X_t} = \frac{T}{T_t}$$

Since $T_t$ is 273.16°K, we can rewrite the proportion as

$$T = 273.16°\text{K}\frac{X}{X_t} \qquad \text{Equation 1}$$

Because $X$ and $X_t$ are measurable quantities, we can use this expression to compute the value of the temperature, $T$.

When a temperature is measured by different thermometers using different thermometric properties, the results may vary considerably. The most consistent results are obtained by using thermometers that measure the pressure, $p$, of a definite volume of gas. When a constant-volume gas thermometer is used, Equation 1 becomes

$$T = 273.16°\text{K}\frac{p}{p_t}$$

where $p$ is the pressure of the gas at the temperature, $T$, being measured, and $p_t$ is the pressure of the gas at the temperature of the triple point of water.

Even with constant-volume gas thermometers there is some variation in the measured value of the temperature of a substance. These variations result from the nature of the gas used and its pressure at the triple-point temperature of water. Because of intermolecular attraction, different gases have slightly different rates of expansion with increased temperature and reduced pressure. By decreasing the quantity of gas used in the thermometer, we reduce the pressure at the temperature of the triple point, $p_t$, further separate the gas molecules, and partially eliminate the differences observed with different gases. As the internal gas pressures of different constant-volume gas thermometers are reduced, the measured values of the temperature of a substance approach the same value.

A set of readings of the temperature of a substance taken by a constant-volume gas thermometer may be extrapolated to give the reading of $T$ when $p_t$ is theoretically equal to zero. In order to do this, the gas pressure $p_t$ is reduced toward zero by withdrawing the gas from the thermometer between readings. This procedure gives the temperature of the ice point on the Kelvin scale as 273.15°K. (Note that the difference in temperature between the ice point and the triple point of water is 0.01 K°.) When determined by this same method, the temperature of the steam point of water is 373.15°K. The temperature difference between the ice point and the steam point of water is 100.00 K°. This is numerically equal to the difference in temperature as measured on the Celsius scale. Thus 1 K° = 1 C°.

The degrees between the ice and steam points are numbered from zero degrees Celsius, 0°C, to one hundred degrees Celsius, 100°C. From one degree to the next is a temperature interval of one Celsius degree, 1 C°. Temperatures below 0°C and above 100°C are measured by extending the scale in 1 C° intervals. Temperatures below 0°C are represented by negative values.

The relationship between the Celsius and Kelvin temperature scales is given by

$$°K = °C + 273.15°$$

Since we normally use three significant figures in our work, we can use 0°C = 273°K and write the conversion equation as

$$°K = °C + 273°$$

The most commonly used thermometers contain either mercury or alcohol. In both cases, the liquid volume increases rather uniformly with temperature over the useful range of the instruments.

*Gabriel Fahrenheit (1686–1736) is credited with the first use of mercury in thermometers. He invented the temperature scale that bears his name.*

## 8.3 Heat units

The expansion of mercury in a thermometer provides a convenient and accurate method of measuring temperature. The measurement of heat is not so simple; there is no instrument that directly measures the amount of thermal energy a body gives out or absorbs. Therefore, *quantities of heat must be measured by the effects they produce.* For example, the amount of heat given out when a fuel burns can be measured by measuring the temperature change in a known quantity of water that the burning produces. If one sample of coal warms 1.0 kg of water 1.0 C°, and another sample warms 1.0 kg of water 2.0 C°, then the second sample gives out twice as much heat.

In the past, water was the standard substance for defining heat units. In the MKS system of units, the *kilocalorie* (kcal) was defined as the quantity of heat needed to raise the temper-

*The Calorie used in dietary tables is equal to one thousand of the calories used by physicists.*

ature of one kilogram of water one Celsius degree. The *calorie* (cal) was defined as the quantity of heat needed to raise the temperature of one gram of water one Celsius degree. Observe that a unit mass of water was used for defining each heat unit. Also note that the kilocalorie is one thousand times larger than the calorie. The kilocalorie is the "Calorie" used by biologists and dietitians to measure the fuel value of foods.

The foregoing definition of the calorie is still used in many laboratory measurements. However, as thermal measurements increased in precision, these older definitions became inadequate. Physicists are now sure that heat is a form of energy. Consequently there is no need to define an arbitrary heat unit that must then be related to the joule experimentally. Instead, heat units can be defined independently of mechanical energy. Another reason the older definitions have been found inadequate is that the quantity of heat required to raise the temperature of 1 gram of water through 1 Celsius degree varies slightly for different water temperatures.

Today, by international agreement, *the calorie is defined as a specific number of joules*.

$$\text{1 calorie} = \text{4.18605 joules}$$

Since the kilocalorie equals $10^3$ calories, it follows that

$$\text{1 kilocalorie} = \text{4.18605} \times 10^3 \text{ joules}$$

Defined in this way, the size of the calorie is very nearly the same as the original calorie. When taken to three significant figures, 4.19 joules, this slight difference disappears. Thus the relationships stated in the original definition, while no longer valid for defining purposes, are still useful in the measurement of thermal properties.

The MKS units the kilocalorie and the kilogram are consistent with the units of measurement we have stressed throughout this book. They are often inconveniently large for laboratory and discussion purposes, however. We shall use calorie and gram units in our consideration of the thermal properties of matter because of their more practical size.

# questions

GROUP A

1. Distinguish between thermal energy and heat.
2. How do heat and temperature differ?
3. Why were the temperature of the melting point of ice and the temperature of the boiling point of water called "fixed points" in defining a temperature scale?

4. What single fixed point is now used for the definition of temperature scales?
5. Compare the magnitude of a Celsius degree with that of a Kelvin degree.
6. (a) What is the Celsius temperature at absolute zero? (b) What would be the thermal energy of a material at absolute zero?

7. Compare the amount of thermal energy possessed by each of the following: (a) a soldering iron and a needle, both at 150°C, (b) a 4-section radiator and a 10-section radiator, (c) a kettle of boiling water and cup of boiling water, (d) 20.0 kg of ice at −10.0°C and 10.0 kg of ice at −10.0°C, (e) a liter of liquid air and a milliliter of liquid air, both at −189°C.

8. How are quantities of heat measured?

9. What is a kilocalorie?

GROUP B

10. How does the thermal energy of a material determine its temperature?

11. Describe a triple-point scale.

12. How can the boiling points of substances be determined from the triple point of water?

13. If you examine several similar laboratory thermometers, you may find that the distance between 0°C and 100°C is not exactly the same on all of them. Why is there such a difference when they are all the same make and model?

# problems

## GROUP A

1. The temperature in a classroom is 24.0°C. What is the Kelvin reading?

2. Liquid nitrogen boils at 77.0°K. What is the reading on the Celsius scale?

3. The boiling point of liquid oxygen is −183°C. What is this temperature in °K?

4. What is the boiling point of helium on the Celsius scale if its boiling point is 4.1°K?

5. How many calories will be needed to change the temperature of 500 g of water from 20°C to 100°C?

6. The stem of a thermometer is marked off in 150 equal scale divisions. When the bulb of this thermometer is placed in melting ice, the mercury stands at 30.0. When the bulb is suspended in the steam from water boiling at standard pressure, the mercury stands at 80.0. To what Celsius temperature does a reading of 125 on this thermometer correspond?

# THERMAL EXPANSION

*With few exceptions, solids expand when heated and contract when cooled.* They not only increase or decrease in length but also in width and thickness.

The atoms and molecules of a crystalline solid are constantly vibrating. They are held in place by electric forces. When a solid is heated, the increase in thermal energy increases the average distance between the atoms and molecules of the solid, and the solid expands.

The expansion of solids can be measured experimentally. A metal rod is heated in an apparatus that has a precise measuring device. If the temperature of an aluminum rod 1.0 m long is raised 1.0C°, the increase in length is $2.3 \times 10^{-5}$ m. An iron rod of the same length expands only $1.1 \times 10^{-5}$ m when its temperature is raised 1.0C°. For the same increase in temperature, different materials of the same length expand different amounts. *The change in length per unit length of a solid when its temperature is changed one degree is called its coefficient of linear expansion.* See Figure 8-4. While the coefficient of linear expansion of most solids varies with temperature, the change is slight and we shall neglect it in our discussion.

## 8.4 Thermal expansion of solids

*Why should ovenware be made of a substance with a low coefficient of linear expansion?*

**Figure 8-4** The change per unit length of a solid when its temperature is changed one degree is the coefficient of linear expansion. The total increase in the length of a solid when it is heated equals the product of its length, its change in temperature, and its coefficient of linear expansion. The change in length illustrated here is greatly exaggerated. The actual change in length that would occur is too small to be visible in this drawing.

As mentioned, 1.0 m of aluminum expands $2.3 \times 10^{-5}$ m when its temperature is raised $1.0 \text{C}°$. The coefficient of linear expansion of aluminum is therefore $2.3 \times 10^{-5}/\text{C}°$. Likewise the coefficient of linear expansion of iron is $1.1 \times 10^{-5}/\text{C}°$. Since the coefficient of linear expansion is defined as *the change in length per unit length,* its value does not depend upon any particular length unit. Appendix B, Table 14, gives the value of the coefficient of linear expansion of several solids.

So far, we have been discussing 1.0-m lengths of aluminum and iron and a rise in temperature of $1.0 \text{C}°$. If the temperature of 10.0 m of aluminum rod is raised $1.0 \text{C}°$, the expansion is $\overline{10}$ times as much as the expansion of the 1.0-m length: $\overline{10} \times 2.3 \times 10^{-5}$ m $= 2.3 \times 10^{-4}$ m. If the temperature of this 10.0 m of aluminum is raised $10.0 \text{C}°$, the increase is $\overline{10}$ times as great as for $1.0 \text{C}°$: $\overline{10} \times 2.3 \times 10^{-4}$ m $= 2.3 \times 10^{-3}$ m. We can conclude from these observations that *the change in length of a solid equals the product of its original length, its change in temperature, and its coefficient of linear expansion.*

This can be given by the equation

$$\Delta l = \alpha l \Delta T$$

where $\Delta l$ is the change in length, $\alpha$ is the coefficient of linear expansion, $l$ is the original length, and $\Delta T$ is the difference between the final temperature, $T_f$, and the initial temperature, $T_i$.

In most practical situations, we are interested in the amount of linear expansion of solids. We must bear in mind, however, that when solids are heated they increase in all dimensions. The **coefficient of area expansion**, or *the change in area per unit area per degree change in temperature,* is defined to be *twice* the coefficient of linear expansion. The **coefficient of cubic expansion**, or *the change in volume per unit volume per degree change in temperature,* is defined to be *three times* the coefficient of linear expansion.

Expansion of solids is considered in the design and construction of any structure that will undergo temperature changes. When a concrete road is laid, provision is made for expansion by pouring the concrete in sections that are separated by small spaces. Steel rails for railroads can be laid with small spaces between the ends of the rails for the same reason. Bridges are also built so that the parts can expand and contract without distorting the entire structure, as shown in Figure 8-5.

Suitable allowance must be made not only for changes in size due to expansion and contraction, but also for the different rates of expansion and contraction of different materials. For a tight seal, the wires that lead into the filament of an incandescent lamp must have the same coefficient of expansion as the glass of which the lamp is made. The principle of the expansion of solids is also applied in metallic thermometers, thermostats, and the compensated balance wheels of watches.

**Figure 8-5** Expansion and contraction of the roadway is compensated for by this special joint.

If the gasoline tank of an automobile is filled on a cool morning and the car is then parked in the sun, some of the gasoline may overflow the tank. Heat causes the gasoline to expand. Here again the increased thermal energy of the molecules and their resultant increase in amplitude of vibration cause them to move away from each other slightly. The principle of expansion of liquids has many useful applications. Thermometers contain either mercury or colored alcohol because these liquids expand and contract quite uniformly as the temperature changes.

Since liquids do not have a definite shape, but take the shape of their container, we are concerned only with their volume expansion. An apparatus like that shown in Figure 8-6 can be used to measure the volume expansion of a liquid.

Liquids expand more than solids; consequently they have higher coefficients of volume expansion. If this were not so, the liquid in a thermometer would not rise. The coefficients of volume expansion for some common liquids are given in Appendix B, Table 15.

The change in volume of a liquid can be given by the formula

$$\Delta V = \beta V \Delta T$$

where $\Delta V$ is the change in the volume, $\beta$ is the coefficient of volume expansion, $V$ is the original volume, and $\Delta T$ is the difference between the final and initial temperatures.

## 8.5 Thermal expansion of liquids

**Figure 8-6** A tube for measuring the volume expansion of liquids. The scale takes into account the expansion of the container.

Narrow tube makes it possible to read even a slight expansion

## 8.6 Abnormal expansion of water

**Figure 8-7**  The density of water is greatest at 4°C.

**Figure 8-8**  A graph showing the variation in the volume of one gram of water as it is cooled from 10$\bar{0}$°C (on the right) to 0°C, frozen to ice, and further cooled from 0°C to −2$\bar{0}$°C.

*How does the expansion of water between 4°C and 0°C help to keep fish alive in the winter?*

Suppose an expansion bulb, like that shown in Figure 8-6, is filled with pure water at 0°C. As the bulb and water are warmed, the water gradually *contracts* until a temperature of 4°C is reached. As the temperature of the water is raised above 4°C, the water *expands*. Because the volume of water decreases as the temperature is raised from 0°C to 4°C, the mass density of the water increases. (The mass of the water is constant.) Above 4°C, the volume of water increases as the temperature is raised, and the mass density decreases. Therefore, *water has its maximum mass density,* 1.0000 g/cm³, *at 4°C*. The variation of the density of water with the temperature is shown in Figure 8-7. The temperature range of the graph was chosen to include the temperature at which the density of water is a maximum.

This unusual variation of the density of water with the temperature can be explained as follows. When ice melts to water at 0°C, the water still contains groups of molecules bonded in the open crystal structure of ice. These flow over one another and give the water fluidity. As the temperature of water is raised from 0°C to 4°C, these open crystal fragments begin to collapse and the molecules move closer together. The molecular speeds of the molecules also increase during the 0°C to 4°C interval, but the effect of the collapsing crystal structure predominates and the density increases. Above 4°C the effect of increasing molecular speed exceeds the effect of collapsing crystal structure and the volume increases, as shown in Figure 8-8.

If water did not expand slightly as it is cooled below 4°C and expand much more as it freezes, the ice that forms on the surface of a lake would sink to the bottom. During the cold winter months, ice would continue to form until the lake was frozen solid. In the summer months only a few feet of ice at the top of the lake would melt. However, because of the unusual properties of ice and water, no ice forms at the surface of a pond until all the water in it is cooled to 4°C. At 4°C water is more dense than at any other temperature. As the surface water cools below 4°C, it expands slightly and floats on the 4°C water. Upon freezing at 0°C, further expansion takes place and the ice floats on the 0°C water.

The graph in Figure 8-8 shows from right to left the gradual contraction of a given mass of water as it is cooled. The sharp expansion on freezing and the slight contraction as ice is cooled below 0°C is evident. The slight expansion that occurs during cooling from 4°C to 0°C is too small to show in this graph.

## 8.7 Variation of gas volume with temperature

Gases expand when heated because the increase in the thermal energy of the gas molecules results in an increase in the kinetic energy of the molecules.

Different solids and liquids have different coefficients of expansion, but *all gases have approximately the same coefficient of expansion*. Also, *the coefficient of expansion of gases is nearly constant at all temperatures*, except for those near the liquefying temperature of the gas.

In 1787, the French scientist Jacques Charles (1746–1823) performed experiments that showed that if the pressure is kept constant, all gases expand the same amount when heated one Celsius degree.

In order to determine the rate at which gases expand, apparatus such as that shown in Figure 8-9 is used. A mass of air is trapped by a globule of mercury in a capillary tube that is sealed at one end. The length of the air column is measured when the tube is immersed in a mixture of ice and water. Then the length of the air column is measured when the tube is surrounded by steam. Comparing these two readings, we find that the air column increases by $\frac{100}{273}$ of its original length when heated from 0°C to 100°C. For each degree of temperature change the expansion is $\frac{1}{273}$ of the volume at 0°C. When gases other than air are used, similar results are obtained. The same fractional contraction occurs when gases are cooled below 0°C.

The coefficient of volume expansion for gases is $\frac{1}{273}$ of the volume at 0°C or $3.663 \times 10^{-3}/C°$. This is about 20 times the volume expansion of mercury and almost 60 times that of aluminum. All gases have approximately the same coefficient of expansion because they all consist of widely separated, exceedingly small molecules that are, in effect, independent particles. Gas molecules are separated by distances much greater than their molecular diameters. Consequently, the forces acting between them, and their volume in relation to the total gas volume, are negligible. For these reasons all gases have similar physical properties except at temperatures and pressures near those at which they liquefy.

If a gas is confined so that it cannot expand when it is heated, it exerts a greater pressure. An increase in the pressure of the air in an automobile tire accompanies an increase in temperature. The temperature increase may result from exposure to the sun or from the flexing of the tire as it is driven over the highway. When a gas is heated, the speed of the molecules becomes greater. The molecules bombard the inner walls of the tire more vigorously and produce a higher pressure.

Table 8-1 gives the volume occupied by a certain mass of gas at various Celsius and Kelvin temperatures. From the table we see that the volume of a gas varies directly with the Kelvin temperature. **Charles' law** states the following: *The volume of a dry gas is directly proportional to its Kelvin temperature, provided the pressure is held constant.*

$$\frac{V}{T} = k$$

Thermometer reading 0°C

Length of air column
273 mm

Ice water

(A)

Thermometer reading 100°C

Length of air column
373 mm

Boiling water

Electric hot plate

(B)

**Figure 8-9** For each degree rise in temperature, a gas expands 1/273rd of its volume at 0°C.

Table 8-1

| THE VOLUME-TEMPERATURE RELATIONSHIP OF A GAS | | |
|---|---|---|
| Volume (cm³) | Temperature | |
| | (°C) | (°K) |
| 373 | $10\overline{0}$ | 373 |
| 323 | $5\overline{0}$ | 323 |
| 273 | $\overline{0}$ | 273 |
| 223 | $-5\overline{0}$ | 223 |
| 173 | $-10\overline{0}$ | 173 |

Unless a gas is under very high pressure or at very low temperature,

$$\frac{V}{T_K} = \frac{V'}{T_K'}$$

and

$$V' = \frac{VT_K'}{T_K}$$

where $V$ is the original volume, $T_K$ is the original Kelvin temperature, $V'$ is the new volume, and $T_K'$ is the new Kelvin temperature.

Plotting the gas volumes given in the table as a function of the Kelvin temperatures produces the curve shown in Figure 8-10. This linear relationship between the volume of a gas and its Kelvin temperature shows that these two quantities are directly proportional. Since 0°C, (273°K) is frequently used as a reference point in calculations that involve temperature, this value is called *standard temperature*.

**Figure 8-10**  At constant pressure, the volume of a dry gas varies directly with the Kelvin temperature.

## 8.8 Variations of gas volume with pressure

The English scientist Robert Boyle (1627–1691) was the first person to investigate what he called the "spring [elasticity] of the air." Other scientists at that time knew about compressed air, but none of them had performed experiments to learn how the volume of a gas is affected by the pressure exerted on it.

In his experiments, Boyle used a large J-shaped glass tube similar to that shown in Figure 8-11. He set up the apparatus in the stairwell of his laboratory at Oxford. The straight portion of the shorter arm was about one-third meter in length, while the longer arm had a length of about twenty-five meters. Enough mercury was poured into the tube to fill the bent portion. By tipping the tube to allow air to escape from the small arm, the mercury levels were then adjusted so that the mercury would stand at the same height in both arms. In this way Boyle trapped a column of air in the short arm of the tube. Next he measured the height of this air column. By assuming that the bore of the tube was uniform, Boyle used the height of the air column as a measure of the volume of air. The air must have been under atmospheric pressure because the mercury levels were the same in both arms of the tube. See Figure 8-11(A). By reading the height of the mercury in a Torricellian apparatus (an early-style mercurial barometer), Boyle found the pressure exerted by the atmosphere on the volume of air.

In successive steps Boyle added more mercury to the long arm of the tube, as shown in Figure 8-11(B). By measuring the

**Figure 8-11**  J-tube apparatus used to demonstrate Boyle's law. This is similar to the apparatus actually used by Boyle.

(A)

(B)

height of the column of air in the short arm, he could determine each new volume. He found the corresponding pressure on this volume of air by measuring the height of the mercury column **ab**, and adding that height to the height of the mercury in the Torricellian apparatus.

Boyle cooled the trapped, compressed air with a wet cloth, warmed it with a candle flame, and noted small changes in volume as a result. These changes were so slight, however, that while it was obvious to Boyle that the temperature of the air during the experiment should be kept constant, he recognized that small changes in temperature would not seriously affect the experimental results. Boyle's data, though not exceedingly accurate, convinced him and other scientists of his time that "the pressures and expansions . . . [are] in reciprocal proportion." Increasing the pressure on a column of confined air reduces its volume correspondingly. To reduce the volume to one-half, it is necessary to double the pressure; to reduce the volume to one-third, it is necessary to triple the pressure. Today we state **Boyle's law** as follows: *The volume of a dry gas varies inversely with the pressure exerted on it, provided the temperature remains constant.*

Boyle's data are plotted in the graph shown in Figure 8-12. The total pressures are the abscissas, and the heights of the air columns (volumes) are the ordinates. You will recall from Chapter 2 that a graph of this shape, a hyperbola, suggests an inverse proportion.

When two quantities are in inverse proportion, their product is a constant. At any given temperature, *the product of pressure and volume is always a constant.*

$$pV = k$$

With the exception of the conditions of very high pressure, very low temperature, or both, it is true in all cases that

$$pV = p'V'$$

and

$$V' = V\frac{p}{p'}$$

Here $p$ is the original pressure and $V$ is the original volume; $p'$ represents the new pressure and $V'$ the new volume.

The pressure of a column of mercury exactly 760 mm high is called *standard pressure*. It is approximately equal to the average pressure of the atmosphere at sea level. Standard temperature, 0°C, and standard pressure are frequently designated as STP.

There is no change in the mass of a gas when its volume is changed by a difference in the exerted pressure. Since an increase in pressure produces a decrease in the volume of a gas,

**Figure 8-12** Graph of Boyle's original pressure-volume data. This is the graph of two quantities that are inversely proportional.

*STP = exactly 760 mm pressure and 0°C.*

it must also increase the density of the gas. *The density of a gas varies directly with the pressure exerted on it.*

$$\frac{D}{D'} = \frac{p}{p'}$$

A cubic meter of air has a mass of 1.29 kg at a pressure of one atmosphere. A container having a volume of one cubic meter can hold four times 1.29 kg, or 5.16 kg, of air under a pressure of four atmospheres because the air is four times as dense.

---

**8.9 The general gas law**   It frequently happens that both temperature and pressure conditions affecting a gas change. To find the new volume that a gas will occupy in such a case, we must consider the effects of both Boyle's and Charles' laws. This calculation can be made in separate steps by first correcting the original volume to the new pressure conditions and then correcting this volume for the temperature change. Usually, however, these two steps are carried out simultaneously.

We can derive an equation that combines Boyle's and Charles' laws. At constant Kelvin temperature, $T_{K1}$, a certain mass of gas occupying volume $V_1$ is subject to a change in pressure from $p_1$ to $p_2$. The new volume, $V_2$, from Boyle's law, is

$$V_2 = \frac{p_1 V_1}{p_2} \qquad \text{(Equation 1)}$$

Now if $V_2$ is subject to an increase in temperature from $T_{K1}$ to $T_{K2}$ at constant pressure, $p_2$, the new volume, $V_3$, from Charles' law is

$$V_3 = \frac{V_2 T_{K2}}{T_{K1}} \qquad \text{(Equation 2)}$$

Substituting the value of $V_2$ in Equation 1 into Equation 2, $V_3$ becomes

$$V_3 = \frac{p_1 V_1 T_{K2}}{p_2 T_{K1}}$$

and rearranging the terms, this expression becomes

$$\frac{p_1 V_1}{T_{K1}} = \frac{p_2 V_3}{T_{K2}}$$

But $V_3$ is the volume at pressure $p_2$ and temperature $T_{K2}$, and therefore we can write

$$\frac{pV}{T_K} = \frac{p'V'}{T_K'}$$

where $p$, $V$, and $T_K$ are original pressure, volume, and Kelvin temperature; and $p'$, $V'$, and $T_K'$ are the new pressure, volume, and Kelvin temperature of a given mass of gas. This last equation is one form of the general gas law.

---

The quantity $pV/T_K$ can be evaluated for any mass of gas provided we know its pressure, volume, and Kelvin temperature. The value, however, has no significance for other than the specific sample.

It is possible to select a sample of gas such that the number of molecules will be independent of the gas selected. In 1811 the Italian physicist Amedeo Avogadro (1776–1856) recognized that at the same temperature and pressure, mass densities of different gases are proportional to their molecular weights. The molecular weight of a gas is the sum of the atomic weights of all the atoms comprising a molecule of that particular gas. He also postulated that the number of molecules in one gram-molecular weight (mole) of any substance was the same as that in a mole of any other substance. The number of molecules in one gram-molecular weight of a substance is called the *Avogadro number*. *A **mole** is the amount of a substance containing the Avogadro number of particles of that substance.*

The value of $pV/T_K$ is designated by the symbol $R$ and is the same for one mole of any gas. The value of $R$ is independent of the chemical nature of the gas, except at very high pressure, and is known as the *universal gas constant*. If $n$ moles are present in the sample we write

$$pV = nRT_K$$

This equation is called the *ideal gas equation*. It is the relationship that defines the behavior of an ideal gas. An ideal gas is imagined to consist of infinitely small molecules that exert no forces on each other. The ideal gas equation describes the behavior of real gases with reasonable accuracy except at low temperatures, extreme pressures, or both.

The numerical value of the universal gas constant $R$ can be determined from the relationship $pV = nRT_K$. If the pressure is exactly one atmosphere, exactly one mole of an ideal gas will have a volume of 22.414 liters at the standard temperature of 273.15°K

$$R = \frac{pV}{nT_K} = \frac{(1 \text{ atm})(22.414 \text{ L})}{(1 \text{ mole})(273.15° \text{ K})}$$

$$R = 8.2057 \times 10^{-2} \text{ L atm/mole °K}$$

Note that in the above expression the pressure is exactly one atmosphere, and the value of $n$ is exactly one mole by definition.

From the ideal gas equation we may calculate the pressure, volume, mass, molecular weight, or Kelvin temperature of a gas provided four of these five quantities are known. To do this we must recognize that $n = m/M$ where $m$ is the mass and $M$ is the gram-molecular weight.

## 8.10 The universal gas constant

*The Avogadro number is $6.02 \times 10^{23}$.*

EXAMPLE

*11.0 g of carbon dioxide ($CO_2$) occupy a volume of 10.0 L at a temperature of 350.0°K. Find the pressure exerted by the $CO_2$.*

SOLUTION

The gram-molecular weight of $CO_2$ is $(12.0 + 16.0 + 16.0)$ g = 44.0 g; therefore, $n = 11.0$ g/44.0 g = 0.250 mole. $V = 10.0$ L and $T_K = 350.0°$K. Solving the ideal gas equation for $p$,

$$p = \frac{nRT_K}{V}$$

$$p = \frac{(0.250 \text{ mole})(8.21 \times 10^{-2} \text{ L atm/mole }°K)(350.0°K)}{10.0 \text{ L}}$$

$$p = 0.717 \text{ atm}$$

# questions

GROUP A
1. What is meant by the coefficient of linear expansion?
2. What provision is made to allow for the expansion of (a) concrete highways, (b) bridges, (c) piston rings?
3. A hole 1.00 cm in diameter is drilled through a piece of steel at 20.0°C. What happens to the diameter of the hole as the steel is heated to 100.0°C?
4. A platinum wire can be easily sealed into a glass tube, but a copper wire does not form a tight seal with glass. Explain.
5. How does the coefficient of volume expansion of mercury compare with the coefficient of volume expansion of glass?
6. Why are mercury and alcohol used in making thermometers?
7. Why does the pressure of a confined gas increase as its temperature is raised?
8. What is the meaning of STP?
9. (a) What is a mole? (b) How is the mole related to Avogadro's number?

10. How does the density of a gas vary with the pressure exerted on it?

GROUP B
11. Does the coefficient of linear expansion depend on the unit of length used? Explain.
12. Why do solids expand when their temperature is raised?
13. (a) Why does water contract as its temperature is raised from 0°C to 4°C? (b) Why does it expand when heated above 4°C?
14. Why does the measurement of the expansion of a liquid contained in a bulb or tube fail to give a true value for the expansion of the liquid?
15. A brass disk fits a hole in a steel plate snugly at 20.0°C. In order to make the disk drop out of the plate, should the disk and plate combination be heated or cooled?
16. Why are the coefficients of volume expansion very nearly the same for all gases?
17. Why do real gases within the usual experimental ranges of temperature and pressure conform to the behavior of an ideal gas?

# problems

GROUP A
1. A piece of copper pipe is 5.00 m long at 20.0°C. If it is heated to 70.0°C, what is the increase in its length?
2. A rod of silver is 100.0 cm long at 0.0°C. What is its increase in length when heated to 100.0°C?
3. A steel pipeline is $150\overline{0}$ m long at 30.0°C. What is its length when the temperature is 10.0°C?

4. The diameter of a hole drilled through a piece of brass is 1.500 cm when the temperature is $2\overline{0}$°C. What is its diameter when the brass is heated to $15\overline{0}$°C?
5. What is the increase in volume of 15.0 liters of ethyl alcohol when it is heated from 15.0°C to 25.0°C?
6. A quantity of carbon tetrachloride occupies a vol-

ume of 500.00 mL at 20.0°C. What is its volume at 45.0°C?

7. A sample of oxygen occupies a volume of 5.00 liters at 27°C. If the pressure is unchanged, what volume does it occupy at 77°C?

8. A gas occupies a volume of 250.0 cm³ at 37°C. What is its volume at 67°C if the pressure is not changed?

9. A gas occupies 2.00 liters at 73.5 mm pressure. What is the volume at standard pressure if the temperature is unchanged?

10. A gas occupies 625 mL at 745 mm pressure. What is the volume at 815 mm pressure? The temperature remains constant.

11. A volume of 465 cm³ of a gas is at a pressure of 725 mm of mercury. What volume will the gas occupy if the pressure is increased to 825 mm?

12. A certain gas has a density of 1.55 g/liter at a pressure of $76\overline{0}$ mm. What is the density if the pressure is decreased to 725 mm?

**GROUP B**

13. The spaces between 12.0-m steel rails are 0.0075 m at −18.0°C. If the rails close up at 32.0°C, what is their coefficient of linear expansion?

14. Mercury has a mass density of 13.6 g/cm³ at 20.0°C. Find its mass density at 100.0°C.

15. What must be the length of a steel rod if its length increases by 0.00102 m as a result of a 20.0-C° change in temperature?

16. A steel steam pipe is 100.0 m long. How much room must be provided for expansion if its temperature change varies from $-1\overline{0}$°C to 105°C?

17. A steel tape is correctly calibrated in metric units

at 0.00°C. It is used at a temperature of 25.00°C to measure the distance between two lines on a cement floor. The reading obtained is 25.000 m. (a) What is the actual distance between the lines? (b) What would the reading of the tape have been if its temperature had been 0.00°C?

18. A copper ring has an inside diameter of 3.980 cm at 20.0°C. To what temperature must it be heated to fit exactly on a shaft 4.000 cm in diameter?

19. A Pyrex glass vessel has a volume of 1.0000 liter at 20.0°C. What volume will it have at 50.0°C?

20. The pressure exerted on a volume of gas at 0°C is $60\overline{0}$ mm of mercury. The temperature of the gas is increased to $3\overline{0}$°C, while the volume is held constant. What will the new pressure be?

21. A constant-pressure air thermometer contains a mass of air whose volume is $60\overline{0}$ cm³ at 0°C. What will be its volume at $8\overline{0}$°C?

22. A calibrated Pyrex glass flask is filled to the 1000.0 cm³ level with water. Both flask and water are at a temperature of 20.0°C. The system is heated to 80.0°C. Determine what the volume reading will be at this new temperature. (Bear in mind that both the water and the flask will expand.)

23. A certain mass of gas has a volume of 1.25 liters at a pressure of 76.0 cm of mercury and a temperature of 27.0°C. The gas expands to a volume of 1.55 liters at which time its pressure is 80.0 cm of mercury. What is the final temperature?

24. What volume will 5.00 moles of oxygen occupy at 77.0°C and 80.0 cm pressure? The gram-molecular weight of oxygen is 32.0 g.

25. How many moles of argon occupy a volume of 1.75 L at 25.0°C and 75.0 cm pressure? The gram-molecular weight of argon is 39.9 g.

# MEASURING HEAT

Blocks of five different metals—aluminum, iron, copper, zinc, and lead—are shown in Figure 8-13. They all have the same mass and the same cross-sectional area, but the pieces have different heights because these metals have different densities. First the blocks are put in a pan of boiling water to heat them all to the same temperature. Then they are transferred to a block of paraffin. The diagram shows the relative depths to which they melt the paraffin. The aluminum block melts the most paraffin, iron follows as a poor second, copper and zinc are tied for third, and lead melts the least paraffin. This demonstration shows that different materials absorb or give out different amounts of heat, even though the materials have the same

**8.11 Heat capacity**

**Figure 8-13** Because metals have different heat capacities, these blocks, all of equal mass and heated to the same temperature, melt the paraffin to different depths.

mass and undergo the same temperature change. Similarly, different amounts of heat are absorbed by blocks of the same material if their mass is different and their temperature change the same, if their mass is the same and their temperature change is different, or if they have different masses and undergo different temperature changes. Such objects are then said to differ in *heat capacity*. Those with a high heat capacity warm more slowly because they must absorb a greater quantity of heat; they also cool more slowly because they must give out more heat. *The **heat capacity** of a body is the quantity of heat needed to raise its temperature 1°.*

*Different substances have different heat capacities.*

$$\text{heat capacity} = \frac{Q}{\Delta T}$$

where $Q$ is the quantity of heat needed to produce a change in the temperature of the body, $\Delta T$. The units we shall use for heat capacity are cal/C°.

## 8.12 Specific heat

The heat capacity of an object does not indicate much about the thermal properties of the material of which it is made. For example, the heat capacity of 1.0 kg of copper differs from that of 1.0 kg of aluminum, but the heat capacity of 1.0 kg of aluminum also differs from that of 2.0 kg of aluminum. In order to obtain a quantity that is characteristic of copper, aluminum, or any material, the heat capacities of equal masses of the materials must be compared. This comparison yields a more useful quantity known as *specific heat*.

The specific heat of a body is characteristic of the material of which the body is composed. ***Specific heat** is the heat capacity of a material per unit mass*. It is numerically equal to the quantity of heat that must be supplied to a unit mass of a material to raise its temperature one degree. If $Q$ represents the quantity of heat needed to produce a temperature change, $\Delta T$, in a quantity of material of mass $m$, the specific heat, $c$, is given by

$$c = \frac{Q/\Delta T}{m}$$

which when simplified yields

$$c = \frac{Q}{m\Delta T}$$

Since 1 calorie of heat raises the temperature of 1 g of water 1 C°, the specific heat of water is 1 cal/g C°. In MKS units the specific heat of water is 1 kcal/kg C°. Appendix B, Table 13, shows that the specific heat of most substances is less than that of water.

Let us solve the specific heat equation for $Q$.

$$Q = mc\Delta T$$

Thus the quantity of heat needed to produce a certain temperature change in a body equals the product of the mass of the material, its specific heat, and its temperature change. If $m$ is in g, $c$ in cal/g C°, and $\Delta T$ in C°, $Q$ will be expressed in calories.

*$\Delta T$ is always positive. Its value is found by subtracting the lower temperature from the higher temperature, regardless of which one is the initial or final temperature.*

---

If water is too hot for washing, you may cool it quickly by adding cold water. As the two mix, the temperature of the hot water is lowered while the temperature of the added cold water is raised. The final temperature of the mixture lies between the original temperatures of the hot and cold water. Each time two substances of unequal temperature are mixed, the warmer one loses heat and the cooler one gains heat until both finally reach the same temperature. *A process that absorbs energy as it progresses is* **endothermic**. *An* **exothermic** *process liberates heat as it progresses.*

No thermal energy is lost when substances of unequal temperatures are mixed. *In any heat-transfer system, the heat lost by hot substances equals the heat gained by cold substances.* This is known as the *law of heat exchange*. The total number of heat units liberated by warmer substances equals the total number of heat units absorbed by cooler substances. This can be expressed as

$$Q_{lost} = Q_{gained}$$

This equality is the basis of a simple technique known as the *method of mixtures* for measuring a quantity of heat in transit from one substance to another. The method of mixtures and the law of heat exchange can be used to determine the specific heat of a solid, as shown in Figure 8-14. The hot solid of unknown

## 8.13 Law of heat exchange

**Figure 8-14** Apparatus for measuring the specific heat of a metal by the method of mixtures.

specific heat, but of known mass and temperature, is "mixed" with water of known mass and temperature in a *calorimeter* (usually nested metal cups separated by an insulating air space) of known mass and temperature. The final temperature of the mixture is measured. All the data for the law of heat exchange equation are known except the specific heat of the solid; it can be calculated as in the example that follows.

*Heat lost = heat gained.*

In practical situations, some heat is usually transferred to the surroundings. This decrease in the amount of thermal energy that can be measured affects the accuracy of most heat experiments in the high school laboratory.

## EXAMPLE

*A laboratory experiment to determine the specific heat of a sample of brass yielded the following data:*

| | |
|---|---|
| *Mass of calorimeter* | *160.0 g* |
| *Specific heat of calorimeter* | *0.0930 cal/g C°* |
| *Mass of water* | *225.0 g* |
| *Specific heat of water* | *1.00 cal/g C°* |
| *Mass of brass* | *184.7 g* |
| *Initial temperature of water and calorimeter* | *18.0°C* |
| *Initial temperature of brass* | *99.5°C* |
| *Final temperature of water, calorimeter, and brass* | *23.5°C* |

## SOLUTION

To calculate the specific heat of the brass from these data, first identify the substances losing and gaining heat. The brass cylinder lost heat while the water and the calorimeter gained heat. It is assumed that the inner cup of the calorimeter, which has a mass of 160.0 g and is in direct contact with the water, will always be at the temperature of the water. Since this cup is thermally insulated from the outer cup by a fiber ring and an air space, we can disregard at this level of accuracy any heat transfer to or from the inner cup system.

Now apply the basic idea that heat lost by the brass in cooling, $Q_b$, will equal heat gained by the water, $Q_w$, and the calorimeter, $Q_c$, in warming.

*Basic Equation:* $Q_b = Q_w + Q_c$

Since $Q = mc\Delta T$ in each case, we can substitute for $Q_b$, $Q_w$, and $Q_c$.

$$m_b c_b \Delta T_b = m_w c_w \Delta T_w + m_c c_c \Delta T_c$$

Solving for $c_b$

*Working Equation:* $c_b = \dfrac{m_w c_w \Delta T_w + m_c c_c \Delta T_c}{m_b \Delta T_b}$

Substituting the given data and solving

$$c_b = \frac{[225.0 \text{ g} \times 1.00 \text{ cal/g C}° \times (23.5 - 18.0) \text{C}°] + [160.0 \text{ g} \times 0.093 \text{ cal/g C}° \times (23.5 - 18.0) \text{C}°]}{184.7 \text{ g} \times (99.5 - 23.5) \text{C}°}$$

$$c_b = \frac{1240 \text{ cal} + 82 \text{ cal}}{14,\overline{0}00 \text{ g C}°} = \frac{1320 \text{ cal}}{14,\overline{0}00 \text{ g C}°}$$

$$c_b = 0.0943 \text{ cal/g C}°$$

**EXAMPLE**    *In a laboratory experiment, 100.0 g of iron at 80.0°C was added to 53.5 g of water at 20.0°C. What is the final temperature of the mixture?*

**SOLUTION**    From Appendix B, Table 13, we learn that the specific heat of iron is 0.108 cal/g C°, and the specific heat of water is 1.00 cal/g C° Using $T_f$ as the final temperature of the mixture, the heat lost by the iron is

$$Q_i = m_i c_i \Delta T_i = m_i c_i (T_i - T_f)$$

and the heat gained by the water is

$$Q_w = m_w c_w \Delta T_w = m_w c_w (T_f - T_w)$$

These expressions are equal. Therefore

$$m_i c_i (T_i - T_f) = m_w c_w (T_f - T_w)$$

Solving for $T_f$

$$T_f = \frac{m_i c_i T_i + m_w c_w T_w}{m_i c_i + m_w c_w}$$

$$T_f = \frac{100.0 \text{ g} \times 0.108 \text{ cal/g C}° \times 80.0°C + 53.5 \text{ g} \times 1.00 \text{ cal/g C}° \times 20.0°C}{100.0 \text{ g} \times 0.108 \text{ cal/g C}° + 53.5 \text{ g} \times 1.00 \text{ cal/g C}°}$$

$$T_f = 30.0°C$$

# questions

GROUP A
1. What is the heat capacity of a body?
2. (a) Give a word definition for specific heat. (b) What is the formula that defines specific heat?
3. How do the specific heats of most common substances compare with the specific heat of water?
4. How is the amount of thermal energy required to produce a given temperature change in a substance calculated?
5. What is the law of heat exchange?
6. What data are required for the determination of specific heat by the method of mixtures?
7. On what basic law are experiments with calorimeters based?

# problems

## GROUP A

1. How much heat is given out when 85 g of lead cools from 200°C to 1$\bar{0}$°C?

2. If 10.0 g of water at 0.0°C is mixed with 20.0 g of water at 30.0°C, what is the final temperature of the mixture?

3. What is the final temperature of a mixture of 135 g of water at 21.0°C in a 45.0-g brass calorimeter and 20$\bar{0}$ g of silver at 100.0°C?

4. An aluminum calorimeter has a mass of 60.0 g. Its temperature is 25.0°C. What is the final temperature attained when 75.0 g of water at 95.0°C is poured into it?

5. A piece of tin weighing 225 g and having a temperature of 100.0°C is dropped into 10$\bar{0}$ g of water at a temperature of 10.0°C. If the final temperature of the mixture is 20.0°C, what is the specific heat of the sample of tin?

## GROUP B

6. A block of metal has a mass of 100$\bar{0}$ g. It is heated to 300.0°C and then put in 100.0 g of water at 0.0°C in a calorimeter. The calorimeter's mass is 50.0 g and its specific heat is 0.200 cal/g C°. If the final temperature is 70.0°C, calculate the specific heat of the metal.

7. A block of brass, mass 500.0 g, temperature 100.0°C, is put in 300.0 g of water, temperature 20.0°C, in an aluminum calorimeter, mass 75.0 g. If the final temperature is 30.0°C, what is the specific heat of the brass?

8. A cylinder of copper has a mass of 95.3 g and a specific heat of 0.092 cal/g C°. It is heated to 90.5°C and then put in 75.2 g of turpentine, temperature 20.5°C. The temperature of the mixture after stirring is 35.5°C. What is the specific heat of the turpentine?

9. A metal cylinder, mass 450.0 g, temperature 100.0°C, is dropped into a 150.0-g iron calorimeter, specific heat 0.100 cal/g C°, that contains 300.0 g of water at 21.5°C. If the resulting temperature of the mixture is 30.5°C, what is the specific heat of the metal cylinder?

# CHANGE OF PHASE

## 8.14 Phase equilibrium

The phase and density of any pure substance are determined by its temperature and pressure. When temperature and pressure are completely controlled, it is possible to cause a pure substance to pass from any one phase to either of the other two phases. The substance can undergo the phase change directly by a simple transition or by passing through the third phase with two transitions.

Figure 8-15 represents the temperature-pressure equilibrium curves for a *pure, waterlike* substance. At the pressure and temperature of the triple point, **T**, the three phases of the substance, solid, liquid, and vapor, can exist in equilibrium. This substance exists as a solid for temperature-pressure values lying in the area between the curves **TC** and **TB**. It is a liquid when these values lie in the area between **TB** and **TA**. In the area below the **ATC** curve it is a vapor. If the temperature-pressure values fall anywhere on the curve **TA**, the substance can exist with its vapor and liquid phases in equilibrium. Similarly, if these values fall on the curve **TB**, the solid and liquid phases can exist in equilibrium. For values on the curve **TC** the solid and vapor phases can exist in equilibrium. When there are two or more phases of a substance in equilibrium at any given temperature and pressure, there will always be interfaces separating the phases.

**Figure 8-15** Temperature-pressure curve for a substance like water. **T** is the triple point. At this point all three phases of the substance are in equilibrium.

Figure 8-15 with the solid-liquid curve **TB**, the liquid-vapor curve **TA**, and the solid-vapor curve **TC** plotted on a single graph is typical of pure crystalline materials. However, each substance has a different set of curves. This is because the temperatures at which changes of phase occur (at a given pressure) are different for each substance.

---

Figure 8-16 is also a temperature-pressure curve. It is for water, which has a triple point at a temperature of 0.01°C and a pressure of 4.58 mm of mercury. A point on any curve represents a condition of equilibrium between two phases at a definite temperature and pressure. At the triple point **T**, ice, water, and water vapor can coexist in a sealed vessel. If the system varies in either temperature or pressure from the triple-point value, at least one of the three phases disappears. For example, if the temperature is raised and the pressure reduced from their triple-point values, the ice and water will change to vapor.

For most pure substances the triple-point diagram differs slightly from that of water because the temperature of the melting point usually increases with an increase in pressure. Thus for most crystalline substances the solid-liquid curve **TB** would have a positive rather than a negative slope.

## 8.15 Triple point of water

**Figure 8-16**    Temperature-pressure curves for pure water, also known as the triple-point diagram for water. The temperature and pressure scales have been condensed in order to fit the critical point into the diagram.

---

Figure 8-16 is the temperature-pressure curve for water. At the temperature and pressure indicated by point **a** on line **af**, water exists as ice, a solid. Let us assume that we keep the pressure constant as we apply heat at a uniform rate. The ice will be warmed from its initial temperature to the temperature at point **b** where the **af** line intersects the **TB** (fusion) curve. At this temperature the ice will begin to melt. Melting is an endothermic process. The application of more heat will melt more ice, but the temperature will not rise until all the ice is melted.

Following this change in phase, the temperature of the liquid water will rise. The horizontal line **abcdef** shows the temperature values as heat is applied first to the ice, then to the water, and finally to the vapor while the pressure on the system is held constant. This information can be shown more strikingly in another way. Assume that we start with a block of ice at $-20$°C and add heat at a constant rate while holding the pressure constant at a value indicated by the line **af**. A plot of temperature readings against time during which heat is being applied at a uniform rate gives us the graph of Figure 8-17. The line **ab** in each figure represents the warming of the ice without change of state; **bc** represents the heat required to change the solid to a

## 8.16 Heat of fusion

*In melting, a substance absorbs heat without a rise in temperature.*

**Figure 8-17** Temperature vs. time of heating for a constant input of heat of $10\overline{0}$ cal per minute, starting with $10\overline{0}$ g of ice at $-2\overline{0}°C$.

liquid without a change of temperature (note that **b** and **c** of Figure 8-16 are the same point); **cd** represents the warming of the water. The addition of heat to a solid at its melting point produces a change of phase instead of a rise in temperature. All the heat energy is used to increase the potential energy of the particles. The average kinetic energy is unchanged. Thus the addition of heat to ice at a pressure of one atmosphere and a temperature of 0°C causes the ice to change into water at 0°C.

*The heat of fusion of ice is $8\overline{0}$ calories per gram at 0°C.*

*The amount of heat needed to melt a unit mass of a substance at its melting point is called its **heat of fusion**, $L_f$. $L_f$ for ice is* approximately 80 cal/g at 0°C, meaning that this quantity of heat must be added to each gram of ice at 0°C to convert it to water at 0°C. Heats of fusion of various substances are given in Appendix B, Table 13.

The method of mixtures can be used to determine the heat of fusion of a solid. Suppose we wish to determine experimentally the heat of fusion of ice. Since hot water melts ice, we find the mass of ice at a known temperature that can be melted by a known mass of water at a known temperature. The example following illustrates these calculations.

**EXAMPLE**

*A calorimeter has a mass of 100.0 g and a specific heat of 0.900 cal/g C°. It contains 400.0 g of water at 40.0°C. When 91.0 g of ice at 0.0°C is added and completely melted, the temperature of the water is 18.2°C. What is the heat of fusion of ice?*

**SOLUTION**

*Basic Equation:* $Q_1 = Q_g$

Heat lost by water + heat lost by calorimeter = heat gained by melting ice + heat gained by ice water.

$$(mc\,\Delta T)_w + (mc\,\Delta T)_c = (mL_f)_i + (mc\,\Delta T)_{iw}$$

*Working Equation:*  $L_f = \dfrac{(mc\Delta T)_w + (mc\Delta T)_c - (mc\Delta T)_{iw}}{m_i}$

$(mc\Delta T)_w = [400.0 \text{ g} \times 1.00 \text{ cal/g C}° \times (40.0 - 18.2) \text{ C}°] = 8720 \text{ cal}$
$(mc\Delta T)_c = [100.0 \text{ g} \times 0.0900 \text{ cal/g C}° \times (40.0 - 18.2) \text{ C}°] = 196 \text{ cal}$
$(mc\Delta T)_{iw} = [91.0 \text{ g} \times 1.00 \text{ cal/g C}° \times (18.2 - 0.0) \text{ C}°] = 1660 \text{ cal}$
$\qquad m_i = 91.0 \text{ g}$

Then  $L_f = \dfrac{8720 \text{ cal} + 196 \text{ cal} - 1660 \text{ cal}}{91.0 \text{ g}} = \dfrac{7260 \text{ cal}}{91.0 \text{ g}}$

$\qquad L_f = 79.8 \text{ cal/g}$

---

The heat added to ice to make it melt increases the thermal energy of its molecules and changes it into water. This same amount of heat is evolved when water freezes because this process is a reversible energy change. Freezing is an exothermic process. Each gram of water at 0°C that forms ice at 0°C liberates approximately 80 calories of heat. When the molecules of water return to their fixed positions in ice, they give up in the form of heat the energy that enabled them to slide over one another. The reversible energy change between 1 g of ice and 1 g of water at 0°C is shown in Figure 8-18. To change the ice to water, it is necessary to add $8\bar{0}$ cal; to change the water to ice, it is necessary to take away $8\bar{0}$ cal. A more precise value for the heat of fusion of ice is 79.71 cal/g.

If pure water is very carefully cooled without being disturbed, it can reach temperatures as low as $-20°$C without freezing. Water that is cooled below the normal freezing point is said to be *supercooled*. If a piece of ice or a speck of dust is added to such water, freezing takes place rapidly and the temperature rises to 0°C, the normal freezing point. The formation of ice takes place readily at 0°C if there is some dust or other foreign matter on which the first crystals of ice can form. Supercooling occurs when no such foreign matter is present. Supercooling is of particular interest in meteorology because the process of supercooling takes place in the formation of some clouds and when "freezing rain" turns to ice as it hits trees, telephone wires, and other surfaces.

## 8.17 The freezing process

*In freezing, a substance gives off heat without a drop in temperature.*

**Figure 8-18** It takes 80 calories to change 1.0 g of ice at 0°C to water. Water at 0°C sets free this much heat in freezing to ice.

---

When the temperature of water is raised, its molecules acquire more kinetic energy and the water evaporates more rapidly. More water vapor molecules become mixed with gas molecules before the rate of condensation once again equals the rate of evaporation. When the water temperature is raised, the water vapor molecules exert a greater pressure and the equilibrium

## 8.18 Vapor pressure

*Equilibrium vapor pressure is defined in Section 7.22. Boiling point is defined in Section 7.23.*

**Figure 8-19** The equilibrium vapor pressure of water increases rapidly as the temperature is raised.

vapor pressure is greater. This point will lie somewhat higher and farther to the right on the **TA** curve in Figure 8-16. Of course, if the temperature is lowered, the equilibrium vapor pressure decreases; the point still lies on the **TA** curve but nearer the triple point **T**.

The equilibrium vapor pressure of a liquid is a characteristic of the liquid that depends on the temperature only. Appendix B, Table 12 gives the equilibrium vapor pressure of water at various temperatures. The vapor pressure curve for water is shown in Figure 8-19. This curve shows the relationship between the pressure and temperature of water and its saturated vapor. Any point on the curve or on **TA** (Figure 8-16) represents a definite temperature and pressure at which water is in equilibrium with its saturated vapor. Figure 8-19 is simply a portion of the curve **TA** of Figure 8-16 drawn to specific temperature and pressure scales. Other liquids show vapor pressure curves that are similar.

Solids, like liquids, exert a vapor pressure. The equilibrium vapor pressure of ice at 0°C is about 4.5 mm of mercury. The vapor pressure of solids is much less than that of liquids because solids sublime more slowly, if at all, at normal temperatures. Evaporation of both solids and liquids can occur at temperatures and pressures other than the equilibrium values that fall on the curves **TC** and **TA** of Figure 8-16. A solid at any temperature and pressure to the left of the curve **TA** can be evaporating to some degree depending upon the nature of the substance. Under these conditions the vapor pressure of the substance will be less than the pressure at saturation, however.

At 100.0°C the vapor pressure of water is 760 mm of mercury. 100.0°C is the *normal boiling point* of water. If the air pressure is reduced to 525.8 mm of mercury, water boils at 90.0°C because at this temperature the vapor pressure of water is 525.8 mm of mercury. In order to make water boil at 50.0°C, the pressure must be reduced to 92.5 mm of mercury. If the pressure is increased to 787.5 mm of mercury, water will not boil until its temperature reaches 101°C.

Strong-walled pressure cookers, in which water is boiled at pressures up to about 2 atmospheres and at temperatures up to about 120°C, are useful for rapid cooking of foods. Special pans in which water is boiled at room temperature or slightly above are used in the production of sugar crystals.

If a mixture of ethyl alcohol and water is boiled, the boiling temperature is not the same as the boiling point of either liquid by itself. Alcohol boils at 78°C and water at 100°C; the boiling temperature of the mixture is between 78° and 100°C, depending on the proportions of alcohol and water in the mixture. The boiling temperature of a mixture of two or more liquids each having different boiling points is different from that of any of the liquids used.

A liquid can be separated from a nonvaporizing dissolved solid by *distillation*. Distillation involves evaporation followed by condensation of the vapor in a separate vessel. Liquids that have different boiling points can be separated by *fractional distillation*. As the mixture boils, more of the component with the lower boiling point vaporizes and the boiling point of the resulting mixture rises. Samples collected at different temperatures are then redistilled.

*Mixtures of liquids having different boiling points can be separated by fractional distillation.*

---

If a liter of water at 0°C is heated to 100°C, each gram of water will absorb $10\overline{0}$ cal. If heat is supplied at a constant rate, it takes more than five times as long to boil the water away as it did to heat it from 0°C to $10\overline{0}$°C. (See Figure 8-17.) Each gram of water absorbs more than 500 calories of heat as it is changed into steam. The temperature of the water remains constant during boiling, and the steam produced has the same temperature as the boiling water. *The heat required per unit mass to vaporize a liquid at its boiling point is called its* **heat of vaporization**, $L_v$.

The heat required for vaporization gives the particles of liquid sufficient thermal energy to overcome the energy binding them to the liquid, and so enables them to separate from one another and move among the molecules of the gases above the liquid. As noted in Section 7.21, all the energy is used to increase the potential energy of the particles. Their average kinetic energy is not changed. Since the energy required for vaporization varies with temperature, the heat of vaporization varies with temperature. The heat of vaporization for water is about 540 cal/g at 100°C. For calculation purposes the more precise value of 539 cal/g should be used. Water boiling under reduced pressure at a lower temperature has a heat of vaporization that is somewhat higher; at boiling temperatures above the normal boiling point, the heat of vaporization is lower.

The method of mixtures is used to determine the heat of vaporization of water. As shown in Figure 8-20, a known mass of steam is passed into a known mass of cold water at a known temperature, and the increase in temperature is measured. To ensure that only steam enters the water in the calorimeter, a trap is used to catch any condensed water from the steam generator. The calculations for this method are given in the following example.

## 8.19 Heat of vaporization

*Boiling is an endothermic process.*

*The heat of vaporization of water is 540 calories per gram at $10\overline{0}$°C.*

**Figure 8-20** Laboratory apparatus that may be used for finding the heat of vaporization of water by the method of mixtures.

EXAMPLE

Given the following data:
| | |
|---|---|
| Mass of calorimeter | 120.0 g |
| Specific heat of calorimeter | 0.100 cal/g C° |
| Mass of water | 402.0 g |
| Mass of steam | 23.5 g |
| Initial temperature of cold water | 6.0°C |
| Temperature of steam | 100.0°C |
| Final temperature of water | 40.0°C |

Calculate the heat of vaporization of water

SOLUTION

Basic Equation: $Q_1 = Q_g$
Heat lost by steam in condensing + heat lost by resulting water = heat gained by calorimeter + heat gained by water.

$$(mL_v)_s + (mc\Delta T)_{sw} = (mc\Delta T)_c + (mc\Delta T)_w$$

Working Equation:  $L_v = \dfrac{(mc\Delta T)_c + (mc\Delta T)_w - (mc\Delta T)_{sw}}{m_s}$

$(mc\Delta T)_c = [120.0 \text{ g} \times 0.100 \text{ cal/g C}° \times (40.0 - 6.0)\text{C}°] = 408 \text{ cal}$
$(mc\Delta T)_w = [402.0 \text{ g} \times 1.00 \text{ cal/g C}° \times (40.0 - 6.0)\text{C}°] = 13,700 \text{ cal}$
$(mc\Delta T)_{sw} = [23.5 \text{ g} \times 1.00 \text{ cal/g C}° \times (100.0 - 40.0)\text{C}°] = 1410 \text{ cal}$
$\qquad m_s = 23.5 \text{ g}$

Then

$$L_v = \frac{408 \text{ cal} + 13,700 \text{ cal} - 1410 \text{ cal}}{23.5 \text{ g}} = \frac{12,700 \text{ cal}}{23.5 \text{ g}}$$

$L_v = 54\overline{0} \text{ cal/g}$

## 8.20 The condensing process

*Condensation is an exothermic process.*

**Figure 8-21**  It takes 539 calories to change 1.0 g of water at 10$\overline{0}$°C into steam. Steam at 10$\overline{0}$°C sets free this much heat in condensing to water.

Heat is absorbed during vaporization. This increase in the thermal energy of the molecules of a liquid enables them to break away from the liquid and become molecules of vapor. When the vapor condenses to a liquid, this thermal energy is evolved as heat. This reversible energy change, shown in graphic form in Figure 8-21, is useful in a steam heating system. The heat of vaporization changes water to steam in the boiler. The steam passes into radiators where it gives up its heat of vaporization and condenses to a liquid.

Even though steam and boiling water are at the same temperature, steam can produce a more severe burn. One reason is that steam at 100°C has acquired about 540 more calories of heat per gram than water at 100°C. When steam condenses, this heat of vaporization is given out. As it cools, this water that is formed gives out the same amount of heat that water at 100°C does during cooling.

Let us return to Figures 8-16 and 8-17 and continue the discussion concerning fusion. As heat is applied to the mass of water formed from the melted ice, the temperature of the water rises to that of point **d**, its boiling point. The line **de** of Figure 8-17 represents the heat required to change the liquid to a vapor (steam) without producing a change in temperature. Note that points **d** and **e** on Figures 8-16 and 8-17 represent the same values. After all the water is converted to steam, the addition of heat energy causes the temperature of the steam to rise as indicated by **ef** in both figures.

In order to keep the pressure constant while heat is applied to change ice from −20°C to steam at 120°C, the volume of the container must be greatly increased. In our previous discussions we noted that ice expands slightly as its temperature is raised to 0°C, it contracts as it is melted to water at 0°C, the water formed contracts to its minimum volume at 4°C, and above 4°C the water expands as its temperature is raised to 100°C. At constant pressure, as the water at 100°C is changed to steam at 100°C by the addition of heat the expansion is about 1700 times. As the vapor (steam) is heated further, it continues to expand at a rate that would be somewhat like, but not the same as, a Charles' law expansion. The vapor is too near its condensation temperature to obey Charles' law closely.

## 8.21 A further look at the triple-point diagram

The vaporization curve **TA** in Figure 8-16 is not unlimited in extent. The lower limit is the temperature and pressure of the triple point. The upper limit is the *critical point*. The temperature and pressure of the critical point are called the *critical temperature* and the *critical pressure*. A substance cannot exist as a liquid at a temperature above its critical temperature; no matter how great the pressure, it cannot be condensed to the liquid state. At the critical point the densities of the liquid and the vapor are equal and the heat of vaporization is zero. At temperatures above the critical temperature a substance is usually called a gas, while at temperatures below the critical temperature it is called a vapor. The critical temperature of water is 374°C, and the critical pressure is 218 atmospheres. This means that the temperature of liquid water cannot be raised to 374°C unless it is under a pressure of 218 atmospheres, and that at any higher temperature water can exist only in its gaseous phase, no matter how high the pressure.

Gaseous substances, such as oxygen and nitrogen, have very low critical temperatures. The critical temperature of oxygen is −119°C and of nitrogen is −174°C. These gases must first be cooled to their low critical temperatures before they can be liquefied. Helium has the lowest critical temperature, −268°C.

## 8.22 The critical point

*The lower limit of the vaporization curve of a substance is the triple point. The upper limit is the critical point.*

## 8.23 Summary of effects of heat on water

We have described several effects of addition or loss of heat on water. In Figure 8-22 these are summarized in a somewhat different manner than has been shown previously. The graph shows the relationship among temperature, thermal energy, and phase as ice at $-2\overline{0}°C$ is heated to steam at $12\overline{0}°C$. Since the specific heat of ice is 0.53 cal/gC°, 1.0 g of ice absorbs 11 cal in being warmed to 0°C. As this ice melts there is *no temperature change* while $8\overline{0}$ cal of heat is being absorbed. There is a phase change only. As heating continues, the next $10\overline{0}$ cal increases the temperature to $10\overline{0}°C$. As the water boils, 539 cal of heat converts the water into steam at 100°C; during this change of phase there is *no temperature change*. If the steam is under one atmosphere pressure, its specific heat is 0.48 cal/gC°, and 9.6 cal is needed to heat it to 120°C. Thus 740 cal is required to change 1.0 g of ice at $-2\overline{0}°C$ into 1.0 g of steam at $12\overline{0}°C$. Conversely, 740 cal is evolved if 1.0 g of steam at $12\overline{0}°C$ is changed into 1.0 g of ice at $-2\overline{0}°C$.

**Figure 8-22** Graph showing the heat absorbed as 1.0 g of ice at $-2\overline{0}°C$ is converted into steam at $12\overline{0}°C$.

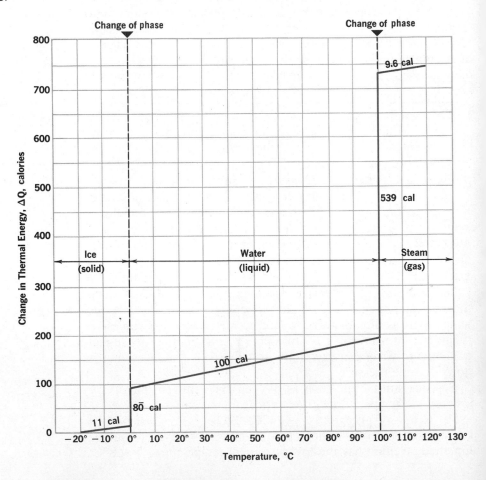

By the process of evaporation, perspiration or an alcohol rub helps to cool the human body. This cooling occurs because much of the heat of vaporization comes from the skin. If you sit in a breeze, where evaporation can occur even more rapidly, you cool off faster.

The cooling effect of evaporation is the basis of mechanical refrigeration. In a refrigerator, a gas that is easily liquefied by pressure at room temperature is compressed and then cooled by air circulated by a fan. When the gas loses enough heat, it condenses to a liquid. The liquid is then allowed to move into coils inside the storage area of the refrigerator where it evaporates and expands. During evaporation and expansion, the liquid absorbs heat from the interior of the refrigerator. The gas is then drawn back to the compressor where it is compressed again, and the cycle is repeated.

A refrigerator absorbs heat from the inside of the unit and transfers it to the air of the room. This movement of heat energy from a region of low temperature to one of higher temperature requires mechanical work. In most refrigerators the work is supplied by an electric motor that runs the compressor.

Refrigerators cool things; in effect, however, refrigerators also heat their surroundings. The same device is a heater as well as a cooler. When the device is used as a heater it is called a *heat pump*. A heat pump absorbs heat from a cool environment, usually the outside air, and gives it off to a region of higher temperature, such as the inside of a house. The same apparatus can, in fact, be used as an air conditioner in the summer and as a heat pump in the winter. Figure 8-23 shows such a unit.

Heat pumps can result in greatly reduced home energy costs when used alone or in conjunction with conventional heating systems. This is because the electric motor in a heat pump is a more efficient user of energy than are electric heaters or furnaces that use fossil fuels.

## 8.24 Cooling effects of evaporation

*The most commonly used refrigerants are the Freons, ammonia, and sulfur dioxide.*

**Figure 8-23** A heat pump is an air conditioner working in reverse. Refrigerant in the coils (A) absorbs heat from the air outside the house. The compressor (B) pressurizes the refrigerant and sends it to the indoor coils (C). There the heat flows to the air that is circulated through the house by a fan (D). The refrigerant then flows back outside and the process is repeated.

# summary

The thermal energy of a material is the potential and kinetic energy of its particles. Heat is the thermal energy that is absorbed, given up, or transferred from one material to another. Thus heat is a form of energy. Temperature is the physical quantity that is proportional to the average kinetic energy of the particles of a substance.

Temperature is measured in degrees. The Celsius and Kelvin temperature scales are based on the triple point of water, which is the temperature at which the solid, liquid, and vapor phases of water can coexist. Absolute zero (0° K) is the temperature at which the kinetic energy of the molecules of a substance is at a minimum. Heat is measured in calories. A calorie is equivalent to 4.19 joules of energy.

The change in unit length of a solid when its temperature is changed one degree is its coefficient of linear expansion. The expansion of most liquids is proportional to their increase in temperature. The expansion of water is abnormal. Water reaches its maximum density at 4°C. Gases expand uniformly except at very high pressures and very low temperatures. According to Charles' law, the volume of a dry gas is directly proportional to its Kelvin temperature, provided the pressure is constant. Boyle's law states that if the temperature is constant, the volume of a dry gas is inversely proportional to the pressure. The ideal gas equation relates the pressure, volume, Kelvin temperature, number of moles, and universal gas constant of an ideal gas. Since the behavior of a real gas is similar to that of an ideal gas except at extreme pressures and low temperatures, the gas laws can be used with reasonable exactness with real gases.

The heat capacity of a body is the quantity of heat needed to raise its temperature one degree. Its specific heat is the ratio of its heat capacity to its mass. The heat given off by hot materials equals the heat received by cold materials.

The heat of fusion is the amount of heat needed to bring about fusion in a unit mass of a substance at its melting point. The pressure exerted by vapor molecules in equilibrium with the liquid is the equilibrium vapor pressure. The heat required to vaporize a unit mass of liquid at its boiling point is the heat of vaporization. The temperature to which any gas must be cooled before it can be liquefied by pressure is called its critical temperature; the pressure needed to liquefy a gas at this temperature is called its critical pressure.

Heat pumps make use of the cooling effect of evaporation to transfer heat from an environment at a lower temperature to an environment at a higher temperature.

# questions

GROUP A

1. Draw the temperature-pressure equilibrium curves for a waterlike substance.
2. (a) What is heat of fusion? (b) What is the value for the heat of fusion of ice?
3. What is supercooling?
4. For what purposes are (a) pressure cookers, (b) vacuum pans used?
5. Explain the processes of (a) distillation, (b) fractional distillation.
6. (a) What is heat of vaporization? (b) What is the magnitude of heat of vaporization of water?
7. Why does steam at 100°C produce a more severe burn to the skin than the same mass of water at 100°C?
8. Why does an easily vaporized liquid, such as acetone or ether, feel cool to the skin?
9. The air above the ice of a pond is −10°C. What is the probable temperature of (a) the upper surface of the ice; (b) the lower surface; (c) the water just beneath the surface; (d) the water at the bottom of the pond?

GROUP B

10. How do the curves drawn in Question 1 differ from those that would be drawn for a substance that contracts as it changes from a liquid to a solid?
11. Assume you have a sample of pure water at the triple point. What happens if you (a) increase the pressure while the temperature is held constant? (b) increase the temperature while the pressure is held constant? (c) reduce the temperature while the pressure is held constant? (d) reduce the pressure while the temperature is held constant?
12. Refer to Figure 8-15. What is the location of the set of points that indicate the temperature-pressure values for situations where the solid and vapor of this waterlike substance are in equilibrium?
13. Isolate one point of the set referred to in Question 12. Assume that the pressure is held constant while the temperature of the substance is increased. What happens?
14. (a) Why does the boiling temperature of a liquid depend on the pressure exerted on its surface? (b) How does the boiling temperature of a liquid vary with the pressure exerted on its surface?

15. How is fractional distillation used in separating the different materials found in petroleum?

16. What data are required in order to determine the heat of vaporization of water by the method of mixtures?

17. Why does the heat of vaporization vary with the boiling temperature?

18. What are the limits of the vaporization curve **TA** in Figure 8-16?

19. What is the physical meaning of the critical point?

# problems

## GROUP A

1. How many calories will be absorbed by 1.50 kg of ice at 0.0°C as it melts?

2. To what temperature must a 2270-g iron ball be heated so that it can completely melt 1150 g of ice at 0.0°C?

3. A 50$\overline{0}$-g aluminum block is heated to 35$\overline{0}$°C. How many grams of ice at 0.0°C will the aluminum block melt on cooling?

4. A copper calorimeter has a mass of 220.0 g. It contains 450.0 g of water at 21.0°C. How many grams of ice at 0.00°C must be added to reduce the temperature of the mixture to 5.00°C?

5. To what temperature must a 500.0-g brass weight be heated to convert 60.0 g of ice at −20.0°C to water at 20.0°C?

6. How many calories are given off by 50.0 g of steam at 10$\overline{0}$°C when it condenses?

7. How many calories are used to vaporize 20.0 kg of water at 10$\overline{0}$°C?

8. Calculate the number of calories evolved when 4.00 kg of steam at 10$\overline{0}$°C is condensed, cooled, and changed to ice at 0°C.

9. How many grams of mercury can be vaporized at its boiling point, 356.58°C, by the addition of $1.00 \times 10^3$ calories?

10. What is the final temperature attained by the addition of 11.4 g of steam at 100.0°C to 681.0 g of water at 25.0°C in an aluminum calorimeter having a mass of 182.0 g?

11. A calorimeter contains 400.0 g of water at 20.0°C. How many grams of steam at 100.0°C are needed to raise the temperature of the water and calorimeter to 80.0°C? The calorimeter has a mass of 100.0 g; its specific heat is 0.100 cal/gC°.

## GROUP B

12. What is the final temperature of a mixture of 50.0 g of ice at 0.00°C and 50.0 g of water at 80.0°C?

13. What is the final temperature if 300.0 g of ice at 0.00°C, 500.0 g of ice water at 0.00°C, and 120$\overline{0}$ g of water at 100.0°C are mixed?

14. A calorimeter, specific heat 0.100 cal/gC°, mass 200.0 g, contains 300.0 g of water at 40.0°C. If 50.0 g of ice at 0.0°C is dropped into the water and stirred, the temperature of the mixture when all the ice has melted is 23.8°C. Calculate the heat of fusion of ice.

15. A block of silver, mass 500.0 g, temperature 100.0°C, is put in a calorimeter with 300.0 g of water, temperature 30.0°C. The mass of the calorimeter is 50.0 g, and its specific heat is 0.100 cal/gC°. A 50.0-g mass of ice at −10.0°C is also put in the calorimeter. Calculate the final temperature.

16. What is the final temperature attained when 90$\overline{0}$ g of ice at 0.0°C is dropped into 340$\overline{0}$ g of water at 93.3°C in a calorimeter having a mass of 135$\overline{0}$ g with specific heat 0.090 cal/gC°?

17. In an experiment to determine the heat of vaporization of water, 15.0 g of steam at 100.0°C is added to 150.0 g of water at 20.0°C in a calorimeter. The mass of the calorimeter is 75.0 g; its specific heat is 0.100 cal/gC°. The equilibrium temperature of the mixture is 73.9°C. What is the heat of vaporization of water?

18. A mixture of ice and water, mass 200.0 g, is in a 100.0-g calorimeter, specific heat 0.200 cal/gC°. When 40.0 g of steam is added to the mixture, the temperature is raised to 60.0°C. How many grams of ice were originally in the calorimeter?

19. An aluminum cylinder, mass 50.0 g, is placed in a 100.0-g brass calorimeter with 250.0 g of water at 20.0°C. What equilibrium temperature is reached after the addition of 25.0 g of steam at 120.0°C?

20. A copper ball with a mass of 4.54 kg is removed from a furnace and dropped into 1.36 kg of water, temperature 22.0°C. After the water stops boiling, the combined mass of the ball and water is 5.45 kg. What is the furnace temperature?

# Heat and Work

## 9.1 Relationship between heat and work

*Refer to Section 1.13.*

**Figure 9-1** The English physicist James Prescott Joule who is credited with the first determination of the mechanical equivalent of heat.

The temperature of two wooden blocks can be raised by briskly rubbing them together. The temperature of a nail can be raised by pounding it with a hammer. This is evidence that work and heat are related.

It was not until 1800 that Count Rumford discovered that work done against friction produces heat. From 1842 to 1870 James Prescott Joule carefully conducted a series of work and heat experiments. The aim of these experiments was to determine the amount of mechanical work that must be done on a body to produce the same temperature change as that produced by the addition of a given quantity of heat to the body. These experiments were called *mechanical equivalent of heat* experiments. Joule found that the heat produced by a definite quantity of mechanical energy was always the same. These discoveries showed that heat was another form of energy and could therefore be related to work.

*The study of the quantitative relationships between heat and other forms of energy is called* **thermodynamics**. In this chapter we shall be concerned with the relationship of heat energy to mechanical energy. In discussing energy transformations, we shall also use the term *internal energy*. **Internal energy** *is the total potential and kinetic energy of the particles of a substance*. These particles include molecules, ions, atoms, and subatomic particles. Heat is one form of internal energy.

Joule used an apparatus similar to that shown in Figure 9-2 to determine the relationship between mechanical energy and heat energy. The system on which work was done was a mass of water in an insulated vessel designed to reduce the transfer of heat from the vessel to a minimum. A set of movable paddles was attached to a shaft that was turned by a falling mass also attached to the shaft by a cord. The paddles turned past stationary vanes, churned the water, and increased its temperature from $T_i$ to some final value $T_f$. The work done on the water equals the loss of potential energy of mass $m$ as it descends through a distance $d$, less the kinetic energy it possesses as it reaches the bottom of its path. The loss in potential energy is $mgd$. The final kinetic energy of the mass is $\frac{1}{2}mv^2$. (In these experiments, $v$ was small.) Hence, the amount of work, $W$, done on the system by the falling mass is

$$W = mgd - \tfrac{1}{2}mv^2$$

The amount of heat that would be needed to produce the observed temperature change in the water is

$$Q = m_w c_w (T_f - T_i)$$

$W$, the work done on the system, is expressed in units of mechanical energy. $Q$ is the equivalent energy expressed in heat units. The results of many careful experiments have shown that

$$\text{1 calorie} = \text{4.19 joules}$$

This equality is shown in Figure 9-3 and is known as the *mechanical equivalent of heat.*

If we wish to set up an equation involving $W$ and $Q$, we must introduce a conversion factor. $J$, the symbol for the *mechanical equivalent of heat,* is used. Thus

$$W = JQ \quad \text{where} \quad J = \text{4.19 joules/calorie}$$

Dimensionally, $W = $ (joules/calorie)(calories), and $W$ is expressed in joules.

Just as in the case of the hot brass chips in Count Rumford's cannon-boring experiments, it is possible to produce internal energy indefinitely in the Joule apparatus provided we continue to supply mechanical energy to it. Thus we must conclude that heat is a form of energy and not a substance.

A different kind of energy transformation takes place in the gasoline engine. As shown in Figure 9-4(A), as the piston moves down, air and gasoline vapor are brought into the cylinder through a valve. As the piston moves up again, Figure 9-4(B), the valve closes and the air-vapor mixture is compressed to a fraction of its original volume. This compression causes the temperature of the mixture to rise. A spark then starts a chemical reaction between the gasoline vapor and the oxygen in the air, as shown in Figure 9-4(C). Heat produced by the chemical reaction increases the pressure of the gas in the cylinder. The heated gas does work by pushing the piston. Changing some of the internal

**Figure 9-2** A simplified diagram of Joule's apparatus for observing the conversion of mechanical energy into internal energy.

**Figure 9-3** The mechanical equivalent of heat in the metric system.

*In the diesel engine, the heat of compression alone is enough to ignite the air-vapor mixture. No spark is required.*

**Figure 9-4** The four strokes of a conventional gasoline engine: intake (A), compression (B), power (C), and exhaust (D).

energy into mechanical energy causes the temperature of the gases to decrease, but not to a temperature as low as the temperature of the outside air. The heat that was added from the chemical reaction was partly converted to work and partly used to increase the internal energy of the gases that escape through the exhaust, as shown in Figure 9-4(D).

## 9.2 First law of thermodynamics

*The first law of thermodynamics is a more general form of the law of conservation of energy.*

We can now broaden the statement of the conservation of energy in Section 1.12 to include internal energy as well as mechanical energy. This follows from the work of Count Rumford, Joule, and others, and is known as the ***first law of thermodynamics****: The quantity of energy supplied to any isolated system in the form of heat is equal to the work done by the system plus the change in internal energy of the system.* Thus the energy input to an isolated system equals the energy gained by the system plus the energy output in the form of work. We may also state the first law of thermodynamics as follows: *When heat is converted to another form of energy or when other forms of energy are converted to heat, there is no loss of energy.*

As an application of the first law of thermodynamics, let us assume that an amount of heat, $Q$, is added to a substance whose total internal energy is $E_i$. Generally we would find that the addition of this heat energy increases the internal energy of the substance to $E_f$ and also causes the substance to do a quantity of work, $W$, on its surroundings. This can be stated algebraically as

$$Q = (E_f - E_i) + W$$

$Q$ is positive when heat is added to the substance, and $W$ is positive when the body does work on surrounding objects. All quantities must be expressed in the same units. If $E_f$ and $E_i$ are expressed in calories, the expression becomes

$$Q = (E_f - E_i) + \frac{W}{J}$$

When $E_f$ and $E_i$ are expressed in joules the equation becomes

$$JQ = (E_f - E_i) + W$$

In situations where no work is done by or on the substance, the change in internal energy equals the quantity of heat added to or removed from the substance. Adding heat to water that undergoes no change of phase will cause each gram of water to increase in temperature by one Celsius degree for each calorie of heat added. Here, we neglect the very small amount of work involved in changing the volume of the water. We know that the internal energy of the water is changed because we observe that the temperature of the water is changed.

*A process in which no heat is added to or removed from a substance* is called an **adiabatic process**. In such a case, $Q = 0 = (E_f - E_i) + W$. Thus $W = E_f - E_i$. An example is the Joule experiment for determining the mechanical equivalent of heat. When the vessel containing the water permits no heat to enter or leave during the churning process, the work done on the water equals the change in its internal energy.

*Adiabatic: no heat is added or removed.*

In another example let us assume that we have a quantity of air trapped in an *insulated* cylinder with a tight-fitting but freely moving piston. When the air is compressed by pushing the piston into the cylinder, the change in the internal energy of the air must equal the work done on it. This relationship is shown by the change in volume, pressure, and temperature of the air. This situation is similar to that in a diesel engine cylinder where the compression of the air occurs so rapidly that practically no heat escapes. Under these conditions the temperature of the air becomes high enough to ignite the gas-air mixture produced when the fuel is injected.

## 9.3 Conversion of heat into work

The conversion of work to heat is reversible—heat can be changed to work. One calorie of heat can be converted to 4.19 joules of work. There are several methods by which this conversion can be accomplished. Two examples are:

*1. By means of steam.* Heat from burning wood, coal, or oil is used to generate steam. Since this is usually done by burning the fuel outside the engine, most steam engines and steam turbines are *external combustion engines*. When water is changed to steam under normal atmospheric pressure it expands about 1700 times. In a boiler, however, the steam is confined and exerts pressure in all directions. Steam under pressure can do work by moving the piston of a steam engine or the blades of a steam turbine. In either case, a portion of the heat of the burning fuel is transformed into work through the use of steam. A modern steam turbine is shown in Figure 9-5. Nuclear power plants use heat from a nuclear reactor to produce steam.

*2. By means of burning gases.* When heat is obtained through the combustion of gases, we can eliminate the need for a boiler. The pressure built up by burning compressed gases converts heat to work by exerting a force that moves a piston or turns the blades of a turbine. Since the burning of the fuel occurs within the cylinder or turbine chambers, such engines are *internal combustion engines*. An automobile engine is an internal combustion engine.

**Figure 9-5** (Top) Principle of the turbine. The force of steam moves the wheel, which turns the generator, creating electricity. (Bottom) This fossil-fuel steam turbine-generator is capable of producing more than 250,000 kilowatts of electric power, enough to supply the power demands of a city of over a quarter-million people.

In nearly all situations involving gases, the gases are confined by barriers on which they exert a force and which, in turn, exert an equal and opposite force on the gases. A gas may be under pressure in a storage tank or in a cylinder above a movable piston of an internal combustion engine. A quantity of air (an air mass) in the atmosphere is under pressure exerted by the air around it. In any of these cases, expansion of the gas requires it to do work against an external force; thus work is done on the external medium. On the other hand, the quantity of gas may be compressed by the action of an outside force; work may be done on the gas.

To calculate the work done by a gas in expanding, let us imagine the gas enclosed in a cylinder with a tight-fitting piston, as illustrated in Figure 9-6. The piston rod is connected to a device on which it may exert a force. The force, $F$, acting on the piston due to the pressure, $p$, exerted by the gas on area $A$ of the piston head is

$$F = pA$$

Suppose the piston is moved a distance $d$ by the expanding gas in the cylinder. Suppose further that heat is applied to the gas while the pressure remains constant during the expansion. The work done by the expanding gas in moving the piston will be

$$W = Fd = pAd$$

where the quantity $Ad$ is the change in volume of the expanding gas. Thus the work done by the gas expanding at constant pressure is

$$W = p(V_f - V_i)$$

where $V_f$ and $V_i$ are the final and initial volumes, respectively, of the confined gas. We may conveniently show the work done by the gas expanding at constant pressure by using a graph, as shown in Figure 9-7. On this graph volumes are plotted as abscissas and pressures as ordinates. The expansion at constant pressure is represented by a colored horizontal line extending from $V_i$ to $V_f$. The work, $W$, done by the gas in expanding is given by the area between this line and the $X$ axis and between $V_i$ and $V_f$ (the colored portion shown in Figure 9-7). This graph is for the *expansion* of a gas at constant pressure. If the gas is *compressed* at constant pressure, the work done is represented in the same manner. It is considered negative, however, because the volume is decreasing as a result of work being done on the gas.

If during the expansion the pressure of the gas changes, the calculation becomes somewhat more complicated. Let us consider a situation where sufficient heat is supplied to keep the

## 9.4 Work done by a gas

**Figure 9-6**  Expansion of a burning gas at constant pressure.

**Figure 9-7**  Graphic representation of work done by a gas expanding at constant pressure.

**Figure 9-8** Graphic representation of work done during the expansion of a gas kept at constant temperature.

*Isothermal: constant temperature.*

temperature constant during an expansion. For a dry gas, the relationship between pressure and volume is given by Boyle's law

$$pV = \text{constant}$$

This relationship can be shown graphically, as in Figure 9-8. The area under the $pV$ curve between $V_f$ and $V_i$ represents the work involved. This work can be computed by dividing the total volume change into a number of very small volume changes. Each of these volume changes must be so small that the pressure remains practically constant for the change. The work associated with each minute change in volume is determined by multiplying the change in volume by the pressure at the volume at which the change takes place. The sum of all these quantities of work equals the total work involved. *A process that takes place at constant temperature is known as an* **isothermal process**.

The common methods of converting heat to work make use of the expansion of hot compressed gases. To understand this better we must further describe the isothermal and adiabatic processes.

As stated earlier, isothermal expansion and compression of ideal gases occur in accordance with Boyle's law. If the volume of an ideal gas increases at constant temperature, its pressure decreases. Similarly, if the volume of an ideal gas decreases at constant temperature, its pressure increases. Since the internal energy of an ideal gas is determined by its temperature, there can be no change in the internal energy of an ideal gas during isothermal processes. However, work is done by a gas during expansion. Since the volume occupied by the gas becomes greater, work is done on the gas molecules against external pressure. (In a real gas, some work is also done on the gas molecules, increasing their potential energy by moving them farther apart.) The heat equivalent of the work done isothermally *by* an ideal gas during expansion *must be absorbed from its surroundings*. In a similar manner, work must be done *on* an ideal gas during isothermal compression and the equivalent amount of heat *must be transferred to its surroundings*.

A sealed plastic bag containing air will increase in volume as the atmospheric pressure drops during an approaching storm, even if the room temperature remains constant. The air in the plastic bag pushes out against the atmosphere and does work, yet there are no temperature changes.

During an adiabatic expansion of an ideal gas, work is done just as it is during an isothermal expansion. Now, however, the equivalent amount of heat is not withdrawn from the surroundings but is obtained at the expense of the thermal energy of the gas. Thus during adiabatic expansion the temperature as well as the pressure of the ideal gas is lowered. Similarly, when work is done on a gas as it is adiabatically compressed, the heat equivalent of the work is not lost to the surroundings but is used to increase the internal energy of the gas. Hence, during adiabatic compression both the pressure and the temperature of the gas increase.

Practical examples of adiabatic changes are not common because there is no perfect heat insulator. They do occur in fast processes when there is not enough time for much heat to be lost. Adiabatic expansion occurs in any large atmospheric up-current. An imaginary cubic meter of air in the center of such an up-current is surrounded by a huge volume of air undergoing the same temperature change. Thus there is no transfer of heat to or from this central cubic meter. Its changes in pressure and volume are strictly adiabatic, though they may be slow.

## 9.5 Specific heats of gases

*Refer to Section 8.12 for a definition of specific heat.*

While the specific heat of a solid or liquid is a fixed value to several significant figures for the substance at a given temperature, this is not true for gases. When heat is added to a mass of gas, its pressure, volume, or both may change and its temperature may rise. Let us select the conditions for addition of heat to a unit mass of gas and describe special but significant cases.

First the volume of a unit mass of gas is held constant as heat is added. The quantity of heat required to change the temperature of this unit mass of gas by $1 C°$ is called its *specific heat at constant volume, $c_v$*.

Second the pressure of the same unit mass of gas is held constant as heat is applied to raise its temperature $1 C°$. The quantity of heat required in this case is called its *specific heat at constant pressure, $c_p$*.

The numerical value of $c_v$ differs from that of $c_p$ even though the same mass of the same gas is taken through the same temperature interval. This difference can be easily explained. The internal energy of the unit mass of gas must be changed by the same amount in each instance. Where the pressure is held constant, added energy must be provided to do the work required to produce the volume increase. That is, work must be done on the movable part of the gas container or the surrounding atmosphere. This added work equals the pressure times the change in volume. As a result $c_p$ is greater than $c_v$. In addition to increasing the internal energy, as evidenced by the increased temperature of the gas, some of the added heat energy is transformed into mechanical energy as a result of the expansion.

The same situation exists for liquids and solids. However, the amount of expansion is so small that the two specific heats are numerically the same to the number of significant figures with which we work, even in most research situations.

Table 9-1

| SPECIFIC HEATS OF GASES | | |
| --- | --- | --- |
| Gas | $c_p$ $\left(\dfrac{\text{cal}}{\text{g C°}}\right)$ | $c_v$ $\left(\dfrac{\text{cal}}{\text{g C°}}\right)$ |
| air | 0.242 | 0.173 |
| ammonia | 0.523 | 0.399 |
| carbon dioxide | 0.200 | 0.154 |
| hydrogen | 3.40 | 2.40 |
| nitrogen | 0.248 | 0.176 |
| oxygen | 0.218 | 0.156 |

The values of $c_p$ and $c_v$ for some common gases at room temperature and atmospheric pressure are given in Table 9-1.

## 9.6 Efficiency of ideal heat engines

The processes occurring in the operation of an engine that converts heat energy into mechanical work are complex. However, we can simplify things by replacing the actual heat-engine cycle with an ideal cycle that can produce the same transformations of heat and work. We need not be concerned here with the fact that there are many different types of heat engines utilizing a variety of working substances such as steam, a mixture of fuel and air, or a mixture of fuel and oxygen.

In an engine, the working substance is taken through a series of operations known as a *cycle*. The result is that some of the heat supplied to the substance from a high temperature source is converted into work that is delivered to an external object. For example, high temperature steam drives a turbine that in turn does work on an electric generator. Experimental and theoretical evidence indicate that not all the heat supplied to the engine can be converted into work. The heat that is not converted into work is delivered by the engine to some external reservoir at lower temperature. Such a reservoir is called a *heat sink*. It is a system that absorbs the exhausted heat, preferably without a significant increase in its own temperature.

*A heat sink is the opposite of a heat source.*

In an ideal heat engine, the working substance is a gas that is returned at the end of the cycle to its original pressure, volume, and temperature conditions. There is no permanent loss or gain of internal energy; the internal energy of the working substance remains unchanged.

The operation of an ideal heat engine is schematically shown in Figure 9-9. A quantity of heat, $Q_1$, is delivered to the engine during the beginning of a cycle. This heat comes from a high temperature heat source. The engine performs an amount of work, $W$, on some outside object and exhausts an amount of heat, $Q_2$, to a low temperature heat sink. Low temperature in this case means any temperature below that of the heat source, and ideally much lower. Applying the first law of thermodynamics to this cycle,

$$W = J(Q_1 - Q_2)$$

The thermal efficiency, $e$, of the heat engine is defined as

$$e = \frac{\text{work done during one cycle}}{\text{heat added during one cycle}}$$

or

$$e = \frac{W}{JQ_1}$$

**Figure 9-9** Schematic diagram of the operation of a heat engine.

High temperature heat source

$Q_1$

$W$

$Q_2$

Low temperature heat sink

Since

$$W = J(Q_1 - Q_2)$$

then

$$e = \frac{J(Q_1 - Q_2)}{JQ_1} = 1 - \frac{Q_2}{Q_1}$$

From this equation we see that the thermal efficiency of an operating heat engine must always be less than 100%.

*The efficiency of a heat engine is always less than 100%.*

It can be shown that the ratio $Q_2/Q_1$ is always equal to the ratio of the absolute temperatures $T_2/T_1$, provided that the engine is considered frictionless. Therefore we can write

$$e = \frac{T_1 - T_2}{T_1} = 1 - \frac{T_2}{T_1}$$

By examining the above equation we can see that the efficiency of a heat engine may be increased by making the temperature of the heat source as high as possible and the temperature of the heat sink as low as possible.

From experience we know that gasoline and steam engines expel some heat during the exhaust part of the cycle. The efficiency of any real heat engine will be less than the efficiency of an ideal heat engine because of heat loss from engine parts and friction.

It is interesting to note that the efficiency of steam engines has increased from 0.17% for the first steam engines of the seventeenth century to 40% for the 1,000,000-kilowatt turbines used in modern power plants.

**Figure 9-10** A wood engraving of the Corliss engine, an early form of steam engine, as exhibited at the Philadelphia Centennial Exhibition of 1876.

## 9.7 Second law of thermodynamics

*The second law of thermodynamics is another way of saying that heat flows from objects with higher temperatures to objects with lower temperatures.*

We have already seen that not all the heat supplied to a heat engine can be converted into mechanical work. This fact is true for all types of heat engines and is the basis for a far-reaching generalization known as the ***second law of thermodynamics:*** *It is not possible to construct an engine whose sole effect is the extraction of heat from a heat source at a single temperature and the conversion of this heat completely into mechanical work.* Thus if a heat engine takes a quantity of heat from a heat source at a high temperature, it must transfer some of this heat to a heat sink at a lower temperature.

One interpretation of the second law of thermodynamics is that it is impossible to attain the absolute zero of temperature. There is simply no place to which heat can be transferred in order to cool a substance to exactly 0°K. Values only a few thousandths of a degree above absolute zero have been attained. The experimental difficulties increase enormously as still lower temperatures are sought. The unattainability of absolute zero is sometimes called the third law of thermodynamics.

Some have considered extracting heat from the internal energy of the ocean and using this to operate the engines of a ship. If the water surrounding the ship is considered a heat source at a single temperature, the second law of thermodynamics indicates that it would be impossible to operate the engines of the ship from the internal energy of the sea water.

It also follows from the second law of thermodynamics that transfer of internal energy from a low temperature heat source to a high temperature heat sink requires work. This type of internal energy transfer takes place in refrigerators, air conditioners, and heat pumps.

In order to express the second law of thermodynamics in quantitative form, we must be able to measure the amount of mechanical work a system can do. For example, consider placing a hot and a cold body in thermal contact. After a time they will reach thermal equilibrium; the two bodies will come to the same temperature. There is no loss of energy in the process, but the system as a whole loses its capacity for doing work. (The temperature of the environment is disregarded in this discussion.) A heat engine connected between the two bodies before the bodies were placed in contact could have done useful work. After contact of the two bodies, when a temperature difference no longer exists between them, work cannot be done by an engine connected between the two.

*The amount of energy that cannot be converted into mechanical work is related to **entropy**.* Entropy is a measurable property as important in the study of thermodynamics as is energy. As with potential energy or internal energy, it is the *difference* in entropy that is significant rather than the actual value of entropy.

If an amount of heat, $\Delta Q$, is added to a system that is at a Kelvin temperature, $T$, the change in entropy, $\Delta S$, is

$$\Delta S = \frac{\Delta Q}{T}$$

If heat is removed from the system, the quantity $\Delta Q$ is negative and the change in entropy is also negative. Note that this equation defines the change in entropy and not entropy itself. Common units for denoting the change in entropy are calories per degree or joules per degree.

Let us again refer to the heat transfer taking place between the two bodies of different temperature that were brought into thermal contact. Assume that these bodies are insulated from their surroundings and the initial temperature, $T_1$, of the first body is greater than the initial temperature, $T_2$, of the second body. The moment they touch, a small quantity of heat, $\Delta Q$, will be transferred from body 1 to body 2. The entropy change is $+\dfrac{\Delta Q}{T_2}$ for body 2 and $-\dfrac{\Delta Q}{T_1}$ for body 1. The net change in entropy for the system is $\dfrac{\Delta Q}{T_2} - \dfrac{\Delta Q}{T_1}$. Since $T_1 > T_2$, the change in entropy is positive; the entropy of the system increased. This is an example of an irreversible process in which a loss of capacity for work results in an increase in entropy for the system. It can be shown that for any transformation occurring in an isolated system, the entropy of the final state can never be less than that of the initial state. Only in cases where the transformation is reversible will the system undergo no change in entropy.

The *second law of thermodynamics* can now be restated as **the law of entropy**: *A natural process always takes place in such a direction as to cause an increase in the entropy of the universe. In the case of an isolated system it is the entropy of the system that tends to increase.*

All natural processes are irreversible and therefore involve increases in entropy. Thus the second law of thermodynamics is equivalent to the statement that the entropy of the universe is increasing, and the first law of thermodynamics is equivalent to the statement that the total energy of the universe is constant.

Heat can be considered disordered energy. An example of ordered energy is a flying rifle bullet that has kinetic energy. When the bullet is stopped suddenly by impact, the energy of its motion is transformed to random motion of atoms. This disordered energy is evidenced by the heating of both the bullet and the area of impact.

Work involves orderly motion. But when work is done against friction and is dissipated into internal energy, the disorderly motion of molecules is increased. There is an accompanying increase in disorder.

*The law of entropy states that the available energy of the universe is diminishing.*

There are many examples in nature where energy processes are observed to go toward a state of greater disorder. The melting of an isolated crystalline solid is an example. When heat is added, the system goes from a well-ordered array of molecules in a crystal to a less well-ordered array of molecules in a liquid without a change in the temperature of the sample. Entropy may thus be thought of as a measure of the order-disorder in the system.

Most natural processes proceed toward a state of greater entropy as well as toward increased disorder. It is not surprising to note that physicists have found a connection between the thermodynamic concept of entropy and the statistical concept of disorder.

Two quantities can be used to describe heat. One quantity describes the energy and is measured in calories or joules. The other quantity describes the amount of disorder and is expressed as entropy, which is a mathematical concept.

# summary

The study of the quantitative relationships between heat and other forms of energy is called thermodynamics. One calorie of heat is equal to 4.19 joules of mechanical energy. The first law of thermodynamics states that the quantity of heat supplied to a system is equal to the work done by the system plus its change in internal energy. The second law of thermodynamics states that it is impossible to make an engine that will extract heat from a heat source at a single temperature and convert this heat completely into mechanical work.

The expansion of a gas may be an adiabatic or an isothermal process. Adiabatic processes are those in which no heat is added to or removed from a substance. Isothermal processes take place at constant temperatures. The efficiency of an ideal heat engine increases as the difference between the temperatures of the heat source and heat sink increases.

The amount of energy that cannot be converted into mechanical work is related to entropy. The change in entropy of a system is equal to the amount of heat added to the system divided by its Kelvin temperature. The entropy of a system always tends to increase.

# questions

GROUP A

1. What is thermodynamics?
2. State (a) the first law of thermodynamics, (b) the second law of thermodynamics.
3. What is the meaning of the term *mechanical equivalent of heat*?
4. What is the metric value for the mechanical equivalent of heat?
5. What is (a) an isothermal process, (b) an adiabatic process?
6. What is the purpose of (a) a heat source, (b) a heat sink?
7. On what does the efficiency of an ideal engine depend?

8. How can we cause heat to flow from a body at a lower temperature to one at a higher temperature?

GROUP B

9. How does the first law of thermodynamics differ from the mechanical conservation of energy principle?
10. Describe Joule's method for determining the mechanical equivalent of heat.
11. What physical law governs the isothermal expansion and compression of an ideal gas?
12. What physical laws govern the adiabatic expansion and compression of an ideal gas?
13. (a) What is the source of the heat equivalent of the work done by an ideal gas during isothermal

expansion? (b) What happens to the heat equivalent of the work done on an ideal gas during isothermal compression?

14. (a) What is the source of the heat equivalent of the work done by an ideal gas during adiabatic expansion? (b) What happens to the heat equivalent of the work done on an ideal gas during adiabatic compression?

15. When an ideal gas expands isothermally, it does work on its surroundings. (a) Does the energy of the gas change during this process? (b) What is the source of the energy by which the gas can do this work?

16. (a) Does a gas do work on its surroundings when it expands adiabatically? (b) What is the source of energy by which the gas can do this work?

# problems

## GROUP A

1. How many joules can ideally be obtained from $1.00 \times 10^4$ cal?

2. Gasoline, mass density 0.700 g/cm³, liberates $1.15 \times 10^4$ cal/g when it is burned. How many joules of work can be obtained by burning 1.00 liter of gasoline?

3. The water going over Niagara Falls drops 50.6 m. How much warmer is the water at the bottom of the falls than it is at the top? Disregard any possible effects of evaporation of water during the fall.

## GROUP B

4. The natural gas burned in a gas turbine has a heating value of $1.00 \times 10^5$ cal/g. If 2.00 g of gas are burned in the turbine each second and the efficiency of the turbine is 25.0%, what is the output in kilowatts?

5. How much heat will be produced if a 1.25-kg mass moving at 26.6 m/s strikes a wall and all the energy is converted to heat?

6. The powder used in firing a 5.00-g bullet from a rifle produces 750 calories of heat when burned. In the process of firing the rifle, 30.0% of the energy is converted into the kinetic energy of the bullet. Determine the muzzle speed of the bullet.

7. A lead block falls from a height of 125 m and strikes a cement block. Assume that half the energy of the lead block is converted into internal energy in the lead. Determine the rise in temperature of the lead block.

8. What must be the speed in meters per second of a snowball at 0°C if the snowball is completely melted by its impact against a wall? Assume that all the energy is absorbed by the snowball.

9. The following data were obtained by the use of an apparatus similar to that shown in Figure 9-2: descending mass, 2.50 kg; distance moved, 1.50 m; number of descents, 25; temperature rise of water and calorimeter, 0.31 C°; mass of water, 0.700 kg; mass of copper calorimeter, 0.150 kg. Calculate the mechanical equivalent of heat. (Assume that the mass has no kinetic energy when it stops descending.)

10. What is the theoretically highest efficiency of a steam engine that has a steam input temperature of 200.0°C and a steam exhaust temperature of 100.0°C?

11. Referring to Problem 10, assume the temperature of the heat sink to remain at 100.0°C. What input temperature would be required to increase the efficiency of this engine to 30.0%?

# 10
# Waves

### 10.1 Energy transfer

We know that some mechanism must be provided to transport energy from one point to another. The place where energy is available is often different from the place where it is needed. One way of transporting energy is by the movement of materials or objects from one place to another. Winds and projectiles in flight are well-known examples. When a baseball strikes a window, the glass is shattered by energy transferred from the ball during impact. Thermal convection is a familiar process for transferring heat energy from one point to another by the gross movement of quantities of heated gas or liquid between the points.

A more interesting but more complicated way of transporting energy involves *waves*. We shall recognize several natural phenomena that are examples of waves. We study these phenomena all together because of a very important simplifying fact: The ideas and language used to describe waves are the same, regardless of the kind of wave involved. The basic concept in our use of the term *wave* is that the wave involves some quantity or disturbance that *changes in magnitude with respect to time at a given location* and *changes in magnitude from place to place at a given time*. We shall recognize that some wave disturbances occur only in material media and others are not restricted in this way. In general, *a wave is a periodic disturbance that propagates itself through a medium or space*. Figure 10-1 shows ocean waves and their periodic character. The common characteristic of all types of waves is that energy is transferred by the wave without the transport of matter.

A stone dropped into a quiet pond produces a familiar wave pattern on the surface of the water. A sound is heard because a

**Figure 10-1** The periodic nature of water waves is evident in the surface waves of the ocean.

wave travels from the source through the intervening atmosphere. The energy released by a great explosion can shatter windows far from its source because a wave of compression moves out from the source in all directions. The ''shock wave'' of a sonic boom can have similar destructive effects. *These waves are disturbances that move through a material medium.*

We are able to explain some properties of light by means of waves. Physicists have demonstrated that light waves, radio waves, infrared and ultraviolet waves, X rays, and gamma rays are fundamentally similar. They are *electromagnetic waves.* Although they can travel through matter, their transmission from one place to another does not require a material medium, that is, a medium composed of matter.

The nature of electromagnetic waves will be discussed in detail in later chapters. For the present, we shall be concerned with waves that travel in a material medium. We call these waves *mechanical waves.* Such wave motion is related to harmonic motion. However, when we described harmonic motion in Section 5.10, we were concerned with a single particle vibrating about its equilibrium position. Now we must consider many particles vibrating about their respective equilibrium positions as the wave travels through the medium. It is important to understand the behavior of waves because the language and ideas of wave motion are needed to correctly describe the motions of very small particles of matter.

As particles at some distance away from a source of vibrational energy are made to vibrate, their vibration shows that they possess energy. The energy has been transmitted to particles far from the source. This behavior reveals a very important characteristic of waves: Waves provide a mechanism by which energy is transmitted from one place to another *without the physical transfer of matter between these places.*

*Periodic motion: the motion of a particle is repeated in each of a succession of equal time intervals.*

*Simple harmonic motion: linear motion in which the acceleration of a particle is proportional to its displacement and is directed toward its equilibrium position.*

---

*A **mechanical wave** is a disturbance in the equilibrium positions of matter, the magnitude of which is dependent on location and on time.* To produce mechanical waves, we need a *source of energy* that produces a disturbance and an *elastic medium* to transmit the disturbance. An elastic medium behaves as if it were an array of particles connected by springs with each particle having an equilibrium position. A simple model of such a medium is shown in Figure 10-2.

If particle **1** is displaced from its equilibrium position by being pulled away from particle **2,** it is immediately subjected to a force from particle **2** that attempts to restore particle **1** to its original

## 10.2 Mechanical waves

*Elastic forces obeying Hooke's law have the character that gives rise to simple harmonic motion.*

**Figure 10-2** An elastic medium behaves as if it were an array of particles connected by springs, with each particle occupying an equilibrium position.

position. At the same time, particle **1** exerts an equal but opposite force on particle **2** that attempts to displace it from its equilibrium position. Similar events occur but in opposite directions if particle **1** is displaced from its equilibrium position by being pushed toward particle **2**.

Suppose particle **1** is displaced by an energy source. Then particle **1** exerts a force that displaces particle **2**. Particle **2,** in turn being displaced from its equilibrium position, exerts a force on particle **3,** which is in turn displaced. In this way, the displacement travels along from particle to particle. Because the particles have inertia, the displacements do not all occur at the same time but successively as the disturbance affects particles farther and farther from the source. The energy initially imparted to particle **1** by the energy source is transmitted from particle to particle in the medium.

## 10.3 Transverse waves

**Figure 10-3**   A transverse pulse traveling along an elastic medium.

*The disturbance actually moves in both directions, but for simplicity the one to the left is not shown.*

Now let us use a long spiral spring stretched between two rigid supports as an elastic medium as shown in Figure 10-3 (A). A portion of the spring is displaced at point **2** to form a *crest,* or upward displacement. See Figure 10-3 (B). To force the spring into this shape, we have to pull up on point **2** while points **1** and **3** are held in place. When we suddenly release the spring at points **2** and **3,** point **2** accelerates downward and point **3** accelerates upward. The crest moves toward the right as in Figure 10-3 (C). Similarly, as the spring in the region of point **3** moves downward, the spring in the region of point **4** is displaced upward. In this manner the crest travels along the spring as shown in Figure 10-3 (D) and (E). A *trough,* or downward displacement, formed at **2** travels along the spring in a similar fashion.

A single nonrepeated disturbance such as a single crest is called a single-wave pulse, or, simply, a *pulse*. The displacements of the particles of the medium (the coiled spring) caused by the pulse are *perpendicular* to the direction in which the pulse travels. Such a pulse is said to be *transverse*.

If a regular succession of pulses is applied to the coiled spring, a series of crests and troughs travels through the medium. This wave disturbance is called a *continuous wave,* or a *wave train*. Again, the displacements of the particles of the medium are perpendicular to the direction in which the wave train travels. The wave motion is transverse. **Transverse waves** *are those in which the displacements of particles of the medium are perpendicular to the direction of propagation of the wave.*

## 10.4 Longitudinal waves

Now, let us use a similar spiral spring, but instead of pulling the spring out of line, we pinch several coils closer together at one end as in Figure 10-4 (A). Such a distortion is called a *compression*. When these compressed coils are released, they attempt

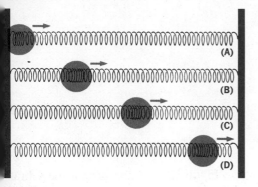

**Figure 10-4** A compression pulse traveling along an elastic medium.

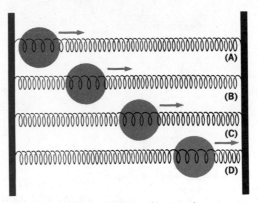

**Figure 10-5** A rarefaction pulse traveling along an elastic medium.

to spread out to their equilibrium positions. In doing so, they compress the coils immediately to the right. In this way the compression moves toward the right. See Figure 10-4 (B), (C), and (D).

If the coils at the left end of the spring are stretched apart instead of compressed a *rarefaction* is formed. When released, the rarefaction travels along the spring just as the compression did. This effect is shown in Figure 10-5.

These pulses propagate along the spring by displacing the particles of the spring in directions *parallel* to the direction the pulses are traveling. They are examples of *longitudinal pulses.* Similarly, a continuous wave disturbance of this type gives rise to *longitudinal wave motion.* Energy is transferred from particle to particle along the medium without motion of the medium as a whole. **Longitudinal waves** are those in which the displacements of particles of the medium are parallel to the direction of propagation of the wave.

*Transverse   displacements   are across the path of propagation.*

*Longitudinal   displacements   are along the path of propagation.*

## 10.5 Periodic waves

We have examined the effect of a single, nonrecurring wave disturbance on one end of a long, rigidly mounted spring. Now let us consider what happens if similar disturbances are repeated periodically.

Suppose we attach the left end of a long spring to a weight suspended by a second spring as in Figure 10-6. Assume that the weight can move up and down without friction between its vertical guides. If the weight is pulled down slightly and then released, it will vibrate within the guides with simple harmonic motion. Such a motion is *periodic.* That is, the weight repeats its motion once every certain time interval *T*, called the *period* of vibration. Since the vibrating weight is attached to the end of the long spring, it acts as a source of periodic disturbances. A *transverse wave train* is generated, which moves to the right along the spring. The

*All simple harmonic motions are periodic; not all periodic motions are simple harmonic. For example, doing push-ups at a constant repetition rate is a periodic phenomenon, but it is not simple harmonic motion.*

**Figure 10-6** The oscillating weight generates a periodic transverse wave. The waves in color and the black waves represent a time different of one-half period ($T/2$).

transverse wave is shown in Figure 10-6 at the instant the vibrating weight is at the upper limit of its excursion and again at the instant it is at the lower limit of its excursion.

This periodic transverse wave carries energy away from the vibrating weight. Unless energy is supplied to it, the weight loses amplitude and comes to rest. In order for a source to generate a continuous wave of uniform amplitude, energy must be supplied to the source at the same rate as the source transmits energy to the medium. Then the successive wave disturbances will be identical. When the periodic wave is a simple harmonic wave, it gives each particle of the medium a simple harmonic motion.

A periodic longitudinal wave can be generated by the apparatus shown in Figure 10-7 (A). The long spring is attached to a metal ball fastened to one end of a hacksaw blade. The other end of the blade is rigidly clamped. If the metal ball is displaced slightly to one side and released, it vibrates with simple harmonic motion.

**Figure 10-7** (A) An apparatus for generating longitudinal waves. (B) A periodic longitudinal wave in a section of the spring.

(A)

(B)

This motion produces a series of periodic compressions and rarefactions in the spring, and thus a periodic longitudinal wave. This is illustrated in Figure 10-7 (B). In order for the successive wave disturbances to be identical, energy must be provided to the source at the same rate it is transmitted by the wave.

---

All waves have several common characteristics in addition to that of transferring energy without the transport of matter. As a periodic wave travels through a medium, the particles of the medium vibrate about their equilibrium positions in identical fashion. Generally, however, the particles are in corresponding positions of their vibratory motion at different times. The position and motion of a particle indicate the *phase* of the wave. Particles that have the same displacement and are moving in the same direction are said to be *in phase*. Particles **a** and **b** in both waves in Figure 10-8 are in phase. Those with opposite displacements and moving in opposite directions, such as particles **b** and **c** in both waves, are in *opposite phase*, or 180° out of phase.

The *frequency, f,* of a periodic wave is the number of crests (or troughs) passing a given point in unit time. It is the same as the frequency of the simple harmonic motion of the source and is conventionally expressed in terms of the vibrating frequency

## 10.6 Characteristics of waves

Figure 10-8 Characteristics of transverse and longitudinal waves. The black open circles show the equilibrium positions of the particles of the medium. The white dots show their displaced positions. The black arrows indicate the displacements of the particles from their equilibrium positions. The white arrows are the velocity vectors for the particles above them.

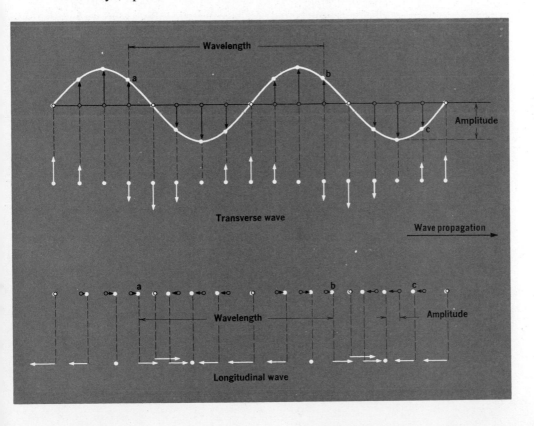

of the source. Thus the frequency of a motion is the number of vibrations, oscillations, or cycles per unit of time. The MKS unit of frequency is the *hertz* (hz). One hz is equivalent to the expression "one cycle per second." Note that "cycle" is an event, not a unit of measure. Therefore it is not a part of the dimensional structure of the hertz. The dimension of the hertz is simply $s^{-1}$. For example, a wave generated at 60 cycles per second has a frequency of 60 hz, which is expressed dimensionally as 60/s.

$$f = \textbf{60 cycles per second} = \textbf{60 hz} = \textbf{60/s}$$

The *period, T,* of a wave is the time between the passage of two successive crests past a given point. It is the same as the period of the simple harmonic motion of the source. Period is therefore the reciprocal of frequency.

*If $f = 100/s$, $T = 0.01$ s.*

$$f = \frac{1}{T} \qquad \text{and} \qquad T = \frac{1}{f}$$

The *wavelength,* represented by the Greek letter $\lambda$ (lambda), is the distance between any particle in a wave and the nearest particle that is in phase with it. The distance between particles **a** and **b** in either of the waves shown in Figure 10-8 is one wavelength. It is the distance advanced by the wave motion in one period, $T$.

An advancing wave has a finite *speed, v,* for a given transmitting medium. Wave speed may be quite slow, as that of water waves. It may be moderately fast, as that of sound waves that travel with speeds of the order of $10^2$–$10^3$ m/s. It may be the speed of light or radio waves in a vacuum, $3 \times 10^8$ m/s. The speed of a wave depends primarily on the nature of the wave disturbance and on the medium through which it passes. In certain media, wave speed may also depend on wavelength.

When the speed of a wave depends on its wavelength (or frequency), the transmitting medium is said to be *dispersive.* A glass prism disperses (separates) a beam of white light into a color spectrum as the light of different wavelengths emerges along diverging paths. Glass is a dispersive medium for light waves. We can observe rainbows because water droplets in the atmosphere disperse sunlight in the same way. In fact, all electromagnetic waves propagating through matter, but not through a vacuum, show dispersion.

Water is highly dispersive for surface waves, and the wave speed can change significantly with wavelength. Ripples produced by a very gentle wind or vibrations of high frequency have very short wavelengths. The wave speed is governed by the surface tension of the liquid, which is a measure of the tendency of the surface to resist stretching. In this case, the *shorter* the wavelength, the higher is the wave speed.

A strong steady wind may produce surface waves of very long wavelength. Here, the wave speed is governed by gravity, which provides a restoring force. Such waves are called *gravity waves*. In this case, the *longer* the wavelength, the higher is the wave speed.

Since a wave travels the distance λ in the time $T$ for a complete vibration of the source, its speed $v$ is given by the expression

$$v = \frac{\lambda}{T}$$

and because

$$f = \frac{1}{T}$$

then

$$v = f\lambda$$

*The wave equation $v = f\lambda$ is true for all wave systems.*

This important equation is true for all periodic waves, whether transverse or longitudinal, no matter what the medium is.

The maximum displacement of the vibrating particles of the medium from their equilibrium positions is called the *amplitude* of the wave. It is related to the energy flow in the system.

## 10.7 Amplitude and energy

In all forms of traveling waves, energy is transmitted from one point to another. By expending energy, a vibrating source can cause a harmonic disturbance in a medium. The energy expended per unit of time depends on the amplitude, the frequency, and the mass of the particles of the medium at the source. Simple harmonic motion (vibrational motion) of a particle of the medium is characterized by an amount of energy, part kinetic and part potential, that the particle has at any instant. The disturbance is transferred through the medium because of the influence that a particle has on other particles adjacent to it. Thus the wave carries energy away from the source.

Assuming no losses in the system, the energy transported by the advancing wave during a given time is the same as the energy expended by the source during that time. The energy transported, or the energy expended, per unit of time is the *power* transmitted by the wave.

If the wave amplitude is doubled, the vibrational energy is increased fourfold. Doubling the vibrating frequency has the same effect. *The rate of transfer of energy, or the power transmitted by a wave system, is proportional to the square of the wave amplitude and also to the square of the wave frequency*.

Surface waves on water that emanate from a point source undergo a decrease in amplitude as they move away from their source. Each advancing wave crest is an expanding circle. The energy contained in each crest is a fixed amount, and the crest is expanding. The energy per unit length of crest must decrease. Thus the amplitude of the wave must diminish. This effect is

**Figure 10-9** The surfer makes use of the energy transported in an ocean wave.

greater for sound waves as the advancing crests are expanding spheres.

We know from experience that the amplitude of a vibrating pendulum or spring gradually decreases with time and the vibrations eventually stop. Frictional and resistance effects that oppose the motion slowly remove energy from the vibrating system. Similarly, in a wave system energy is dissipated and the wave amplitude gradually diminishes. *The reduction in amplitude of a wave due to the dissipation of wave energy as it travels away from the source is called* **damping.** Damping effects may be quite small over relatively short distances.

# questions

GROUP A

1. In what ways may energy be transferred?
2. Distinguish between mechanical waves and electromagnetic waves.
3. What are three requirements for the production of mechanical waves?
4. (a) What is a disturbance? (b) What constitutes the disturbance when a wave moves across the surface of a pond? (c) What constitutes the disturbance when a longitudinal wave travels through the air?
5. How does an elastic material behave as a wave medium?
6. (a) Distinguish between transverse and longitudinal waves. (b) Give an example of each.
7. Define (a) pulse; (b) crest; (c) trough; (d) compression; (e) rarefaction.

8. For wave motion, define (a) speed; (b) phase; (c) frequency; (d) period; (e) wavelength; (f) amplitude.
9. What does a wave source supply to the medium through which the wave passes?
10. A pebble is dropped into a quiet pond of water. Neglecting damping losses, how does the amplitude of the resulting wave disturbance vary with the distance from the source?
11. Neglecting damping losses, would you expect the amplitude of an advancing surface wave on a pond to diminish with distance from its point source at the same rate as an advancing sound wave diminishes with distance from its point source in air? Justify your conclusion qualitatively.

# problems

GROUP A

1. What is the speed of a periodic wave disturbance, frequency 2.5 hz and wavelength 0.60 m?
2. Calculate the wavelength of water waves that have frequency 0.50 hz and speed 4.0 m/s.
3. The speed of transverse waves in a string is 15 m/s. If a source produces a disturbance, frequency 5.0 hz, what is the wavelength of the wave produced?
4. A periodic transverse wave, frequency 10.0 hz, travels along a string. The distance between a crest and either adjacent trough is 1.50 m. What is (a) the wave length, (b) the speed of the wave?

5. A periodic longitudinal wave, frequency $2\overline{0}$ hz, travels along a coil spring. If the distance between successive compressions is 0.40 m, calculate the speed of the wave.
6. What is the wavelength of a periodic longitudinal wave in a coil spring, frequency 8.0 hz, and speed $2\overline{0}$ m/s?
7. A wave generator produces 16 pulses in 4.0 seconds. (a) What is its period? (b) What is its frequency?
8. One pulse is generated every 0.10 s in a tank of water, and the wavelength of the surface wave measures 3.3 cm. What is the propagation speed?

# WAVE INTERACTIONS

In any study of wave behavior, the various properties common to all kinds of waves should be recognized. These common properties are: *rectilinear* (straight line) *propagation, reflection, refraction, diffraction,* and *interference.* Being familiar with the properties of waves helps to determine whether an observed phenomenon involves a wave or not.

Surface waves on water are particularly useful in studying wave properties. A surface wave is easily generated, its speed is quite slow, and the transparency of the water to light allows the wave pattern to be projected on a screen. A continuous wave can be established on the water surface by allowing a probe to dip into the surface periodically. An apparatus for observing wave motion on the surface of water is shown in Figure 10-10. It is called a ripple tank.

The diagram in Figure 10-11 shows how images of surface wave crests can be projected on a screen. The ripple tank has a glass bottom that allows light to be projected down through the water and the glass onto a screen below the tank. The crests appear on the screen as bright regions, and troughs appear as dark regions.

## 10.8 Properties of waves

**Figure 10-10 (left)** The ripple tank provides a means of observing the properties of waves in the laboratory.

**Figure 10-11 (right)** A functional diagram of a ripple tank.

We can generate a train of straight waves in a ripple tank by placing a long straight edge, like that of a ruler, along the surface of the water and causing it to vibrate up and down. A photograph of the image of such a continuous wave is shown in Figure 10-12. The wave crests are the parallel white lines. The wave troughs are the dark spaces separating the crests. The surfaces whose particles are all in the same phase of motion are called *wave fronts.* The paths of the two points **a** and **b** show that *the direction of propagation of the advancing straight wave is perpendicular to the wave front.*

## 10.9 Rectilinear propagation

*The convex surface of a wave crest serves as a converging lens to focus light.*

*The concave surface of a wave trough serves to diverge light.*

**Figure 10-12 (left)** Periodic straight wave moving across a ripple tank. The wavelength is the distance between adjacent troughs.

**Figure 10-13 (right)** Periodic circular wave generated by a point source in a ripple tank. The wave moves outward from the point of generation in everwidening circles.

*Light regions of a ripple-tank image relate to wave crests, and dark regions of a ripple-tank image relate to wave troughs.*

By changing from a straight to a pointed probe such as the tip of a pencil, we can generate a train of circular waves. See Figure 10-13. Here the advancing wave crests are expanding circles; the wave fronts are moving out in all directions from the center of disturbance. The letters **a** and **b** locate two points on an expanding crest. Their paths show that *the directions of propagation of these two segments of the advancing circular wave lie along radial lines away from the center of disturbance*. The same is true of all other points on any circular wave crest. The radial lines are perpendicular to the segments of the wave front through which they pass.

From these experiments with the ripple tank we observe that *continuous waves traveling in a uniform medium propagate in straight lines perpendicular to the advancing wave fronts*. The uniform spacing between the wave crests suggests that the wave speed in the medium is constant. Considering the speed and direction of propagation of traveling waves, we can state that *the wave velocity at every point along the advancing wave front is perpendicular to the wave front*.

## 10.10 Reflection

*The illusion of reversal occurs because of the left-right symmetry of the body.*

Familiar examples of reflection are the sound echoes that return from a distant canyon wall, the reflection of light from a mirror, and the reflection of waves from the edge of a pool. Our image as seen in a mirror appears to be reversed, right for left. The crest of a water wave is reflected from the pool side as a crest traveling in a different direction. The echo of a sound retains the character of the original sound.

About the only inference we can draw from these casual observations is that *a wave is turned back, or **reflected**, when it encounters a barrier that is the boundary of the medium in which the wave is traveling*. A close examination of the boundary conditions can reveal much more about the nature of reflection.

Suppose we generate a single straight pulse in a ripple tank that has a straight barrier placed across the tray parallel to the advancing wave front. When the pulse reaches the barrier, it is re-

---

flected back in the direction from which it came. No disturbance appears in the water behind the barrier. The paths of the incident pulse (approaching the barrier) and the reflected pulse lie perpendicular to the surface of the barrier.

The angle formed by the path of incidence and the perpendicular (normal) to the reflecting surface at the point of incidence is called the *angle of incidence, i*. The angle formed by the path of reflection and the normal is the *angle of reflection, r*. In this instance both the incident and reflected angles are 0°, and *i* is equal to *r*.

Certainly *i* and *r* equal 0° only when the incident wave approaches the barrier along a line perpendicular to it. We may then ask whether the equality between *i* and *r* is coincidental in this situation, or whether it is characteristic of reflection in general. To investigate the relationship of *i* and *r* further, we need to change the position of the barrier so that it is no longer parallel to the wave fronts and then send more pulses against it. Figure 10-14 shows the reflection of a single pulse from a diagonal barrier.

Reasonably good measurements can be made of the angles that the incident and reflected pulses make with the barrier by placing suitable markers on the screen parallel to the projected images of the pulse. We shall call these angles *i'* and *r'* respectively. Measurements of *i'* and *r'* for several positions consistently indicate that these angles are equal. From Figure 10-15 it is evident that angles

**Figure 10-14** A single straight pulse being reflected from a diagonal barrier. The reflected part of the pulse is moving to the right.

$$r + y = 90°$$
$$y + r' = 90°$$
$$r = r'$$

$$i + x = 90°$$
$$x + i' = 90°$$
$$i = i'$$

Incident pulse approaching barrier

**Figure 10-15** The geometry of reflection. A straight pulse is reflected from a straight barrier in a ripple tank. The angle of incidence, *i*, equals the angle of reflection, *r*.

**Figure 10-16** Reflection of a periodic straight wave train from a diagonal barrier. The left portion of each wave crest has already been reflected toward the right.

**Figure 10-17** A circular wave generated at the center of the photograph is reflected from a straight barrier.

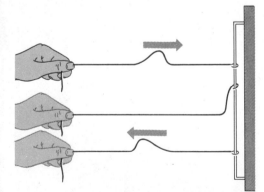

**Figure 10-18** Reflection of a pulse at the "free" end of a taut string. The string is shown terminated in a frictionless ring that allows the end segment unrestrained displacement in the plane of the pulse.

$i + x = 90°$ because the incident path **bb′** is perpendicular to the incident segment **b′c** of the pulse. Also, angles $x + i' = 90°$ because they form the angle between the barrier and its normal. Thus $i$ and $i'$ are equal angles. Similar reasoning shows that $r$ and $r'$ are also equal angles. From measurement, $i'$ and $r'$ are equal. Thus the angle of incidence, $i$, and the angle of reflection, $r$, are equal.

$$i = r$$

We can state this relationship as a ***law of reflection***. *When a wave disturbance is reflected at the boundary of a transmitting medium, the angle of incidence, i, is equal to the angle of reflection, r.* A photograph of a periodic straight wave train reflected from a diagonally placed barrier is shown in Figure 10-16.

The reflection of a circular wave from a straight barrier is shown in Figure 10-17. Each segment of the expanding wave front reflected from the barrier surface rebounds according to the principle just stated. Observe that the reflected portions of the wave crests are arcs of circles. The apparent center of these reflected wave crests is as far behind the reflecting surface as the real center of disturbance is in front of it.

Reflection may be partial or complete depending on the nature of the reflecting boundary. If there is no boundary mechanism for extracting energy from the wave, all the energy incident with the wave is reflected back with it.

When a surface wave in the ripple tank encounters the straight barrier, which is a rigid vertical bulkhead, the vertical transverse component of the wave is unrestrained. The wave crest is reflected *as a crest,* and the trough is reflected *as a trough.* The surface wave is reflected without a change in phase. *A boundary that allows unrestrained displacement of the particles of a medium reflects waves with no change in phase.* The bulkhead acts as a *free-end* or *open-end* termination to the wave medium.

Suppose we send a transverse pulse traveling along a stretched string of which the far end is free. Having such a string presents no problem in a "thought" experiment. In practice, the free-ended termination might be approximated as shown in Figure 10-18. To the extent that the termination is frictionless, the end of the string is free to move in the plane of the pulse.

After arriving at the free end of the string, the pulse is reflected as shown in Figure 10-18. Observe that it has not been inverted. Displacement of the particles of the string is in the same direction as that for the incident pulse. During the time interval that the pulse is arriving at the free end of the string and the reflected pulse is leaving it, the combined effect of the two pulses causes the free end to experience twice the displacement as from either pulse alone. *Reflection at the free-end termination of a medium occurs without a change in phase.*

Now suppose we clamp the far end of the string in a fixed position and send a transverse pulse toward this termination. See Figure 10-19. When the pulse arrives at the fixed end, it applies an upward force to the clamp. An equal but opposite reaction force is applied to the string generating a reflected pulse that is inverted with respect to the incident pulse. *Reflection at the fixed termination of a medium occurs with a phase shift of 180°.* In general, we may conclude that *a boundary that restrains the displacement of the particles of a medium reflects waves inverted in phase.*

Some examples of reflecting terminations for different kinds of wave disturbances are given in Table 10-1. The first three systems listed summarize the phase relations discussed in this section.

Generally, something less than total reflection occurs at the termination of a transmitting medium. The "free" end of a vibrating string, as well as the fixed end, must be supported in some manner, and some of the wave energy is transferred to the medium providing this support.

The speed of the wave disturbance depends on the properties of the transmitting medium. Thus waves in the string and in the terminating medium travel at different speeds. If this difference in speed is very great, the portion of wave energy reflected at the boundary will be very large. If the two wave speeds are very similar, little reflection will occur at the boundary. An intermediate effect is seen in Figure 10-21 (page 221), where partial reflection is evident at the boundary of the deep and shallow water. Light is partially transmitted and partially reflected when it passes from air into glass because of the difference in the transmission speeds in the two media.

**Figure 10-19** Reflection of a pulse at the clamped end of a taut string. The string is terminated in a fixed position and displacement of the end segment is restrained.

Table 10-1

| | | Termination | |
|---|---|---|---|
| **Type of wave** | **Example** | For in-phase reflection | For out-of-phase reflection |
| transverse (mechanical) | stretched string | free-ended | fixed ended |
| longitudinal (sound) | air motion in organ pipe | open pipe | closed pipe |
| liquid surface (vertical component) | water | solid bulkhead | (no simple analog) |
| optical (electromagnetic) | light | (no simple analog) | mirror |
| electric | transmission line | short circuit | open circuit |

REFLECTION BEHAVIOR

If we were to apply the same wave-producing force to a light string and to a heavy rope, two entirely different *displacement velocities* would result. The string would experience a very large displacement velocity compared to that of the rope. We could say that the ratio of the *wave producing force* to the *displacement velocity* is quite small for the string and quite large for the rope.

## 10.11 Impedance

In the study of waves, this *ratio of the applied wave-producing force to the resulting displacement velocity is called the **impedance** of the medium.*

$$\text{Impedance} = \frac{\text{wave-producing force}}{\text{resulting velocity of the medium}}$$

By this definition, the string is said to have a relatively low impedance and the rope a relatively high impedance. The impedance of a wave medium denotes the ease or difficulty with which a wave disturbance of given amplitude can be launched in it.

The concept of impedance is quite general and can be applied to wave media of all kinds. For a stretched string, the wave-producing force is the transverse oscillatory force applied to the end of the string. The displacement velocity is the oscillating transverse velocity imparted to the particles of the first portion of the string. In an organ pipe, the ratio of the alternating compressional force applied to the molecules of the air to the longitudinal oscillating velocity acquired by these molecules defines the acoustic impedance of the air column.

In cases of *total* in-phase reflection discussed in Section 10.10, the impedance of the terminating medium may be considered to be zero. For *total* out-of-phase reflection, the impedance of the terminating medium is infinite. In systems having infinite or zero impedance terminations, reflection is complete and no wave energy is transferred to the terminating medium.

If the terminating impedance exactly matches that of the transmitting medium, the wave energy is completely transferred to the terminating medium and there is no reflection. What about systems that fall in between the extreme impedance mismatch, zero or infinite impedance terminations, and the perfect impedance match? In these cases some energy is transferred to the terminating medium and some is reflected back through the medium of the incident wave.

In practical energy transfer systems, an abrupt impedance discontinuity between two wave propagation media causes unwanted wave reflection that wastes energy. Numerous devices and techniques are used to smooth over an impedance mismatch and reduce or prevent reflections. They are called *impedance transformers*.

A cheerleader's megaphone is a simple approximation of an acoustic impedance transformer. It effectively matches the impedance of the air column of the throat and mouth to the free air. The coating on an optical lens acts as an impedance transformer. It reduces reflection at the air-glass boundary and causes a greater portion of the total incident light energy to be transmitted through the lens. There are many applications of impedance transformers in electric and electronic systems. In general, whenever a device intended to receive wave energy efficiently cannot be designed to have the same impedance as the transmitting medium, it must be coupled to the medium by means of an impedance transformer.

*"Impedance" is a more common term in alternating-current electricity and electronics.*

*An impedance transformer is an energy-transfer device.*

The properties of the medium through which a certain wave disturbance moves determine the propagation speed of that disturbance. It is not surprising therefore to find that traveling waves passing from one medium into another experience a change in speed *at the interface (boundary)* of the two media.

From the wave equation, $v = f\lambda$, we see that the wavelength, $\lambda$, for a wave disturbance of a given frequency, $f$, is a function of its speed, $v$, in the medium through which it is propagating. If the speed decreases when the wave enters a second medium, the wavelength is shortened proportionately. If the speed increases, the wavelength is lengthened proportionately.

A useful aspect of water waves is the relation of the speed of surface waves to the depth of the water. Such wave disturbances travel faster in deep water than in shallow water. For a given wave frequency, the wavelength in deep water is longer than it is in shallow water. Therefore water of two different depths acts just like two different transmitting media for wave propagation.

This difference is easily observed in the ripple tank by arranging the tray so that it has two different depths of water. Then surface waves are generated that travel across the boundary of the two regions. In Figure 10-20 the deep water representing the medium of higher propagating speed is in the lower portion of the photograph. The wave moves toward the shallow water in the upper portion. The boundary between the deep and shallow water is parallel to the advancing wave front. Thus each incident wave crest approaches the shallow region along the normal to the boundary.

Observe that the change in wavelength is abrupt. It occurs simultaneously over the entire wave front at the boundary of the deep and shallow water. All segments of the advancing wave front change speed at the same time, and the wave continues to propagate in its original direction.

Suppose we adjust the deep and shallow regions of the tray so that the boundary is no longer parallel to the advancing straight wave but cuts diagonally across its path. This arrangement is shown in Figure 10-21. Each advancing wave crest now approaches the boundary obliquely. Adjacent segments of the wave front pass from deep to shallow water successively rather than simultaneously. At the boundary, the direction of the wave front changes; the advancing wave has undergone *refraction*. *Refraction is the bending of the path of a wave disturbance as it passes obliquely from one medium into another of different propagation speed.*

The refraction of surface waves on water is shown by diagram in Figure 10-22. As the wave passes into the shallow water where its speed is less and its wavelength is shorter, it is refracted *toward* the normal drawn to the deep-shallow boundary. The angle of refraction, *r,* is smaller than the angle of incidence, *i*. (The angle

## 10.12 Refraction

**Figure 10-20** The passage of a surface wave from deep to shallow water. The shallow water is at the top of the picture.

**Figure 10-21** Refraction of a surface wave at the boundary of deep and shallow water in a ripple tank.

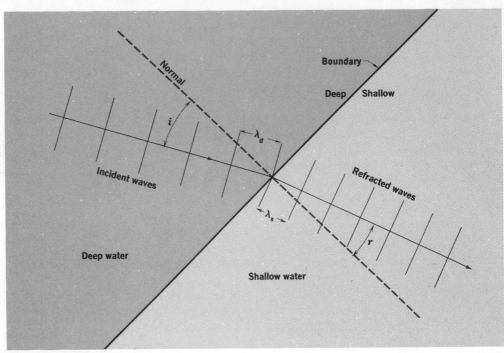

**Figure 10-22** The geometry of refraction. Water of two depths in the ripple tank represents two media of different speeds.

*r* is the angle between the path of the refracted wave and the normal.)

Had we generated the wave in the shallow region and directed it obliquely toward the boundary, it would have been refracted *away from* the normal on entering the deep water. Angle *r* would have been larger than *i*. The change in direction and the change in speed occur simultaneously. How are these two changes related? We shall investigate this question quantitatively later when we study optical refraction. The measurements we need there can be made with reasonable precision.

## 10.13 Diffraction

Sounds can be heard even though they may originate around the corner of a building. However, the source of the sound disturbance cannot be seen around the corner. Rectilinear propagation appears to hold in this situation for light but not for sound. The building is an obstruction that prevents the straight-line transmission of light from the source of the sound disturbance to the observer.

Perhaps, where sound waves are concerned, the corner of the building creates a discontinuity in the transmitting medium that causes the waves to *spread*. Even if we find support for this idea, the question of the different behavior of light remains to be answered.

We will again use the ripple tank to observe wave behavior, this time with obstructions inserted into the transmitting medium. This may be done by placing two straight barriers across the tray on a line parallel to the straight-wave generator. An *aperture*, or opening, is left between them approximately equal to the wavelength of the wave to be used. When a periodic straight wave is sent out, the wave pattern beyond the barrier opening appears as shown in Figure 10-23. As a segment of each wave crest passes through the aperture, it clearly spreads into the region beyond the barriers. *This spreading of a wave disturbance beyond the edge of a barrier is called* **diffraction.**

Sound waves spread around the edges of doorways in the same way that water waves spread around the edges of obstructions. Audible sounds have wavelengths in air ranging from a few centimeters to several meters. The doorway of a room or building has dimensions within this range. This suggests, but does not prove, that a discontinuity such as an aperture in the path of an advancing wave will diffract the wave if its dimensions are comparable to the wavelength of the oncoming wave.

We produced the diffraction pattern in the ripple tank with a barrier aperture approximately the same width as the wavelength of the surface wave used. Suppose we shorten the wavelength by increasing stepwise the frequency of the wave generator. We would observe a series of patterns with waves of decreasing wavelengths.

The spreading of the wave at the edges of the aperture diminishes as the wavelength of the wave sent against them is shortened. When the wavelength is a small fraction of the width of the opening between the barriers, the wave segments passing through show little tendency to spread into the shadow regions beyond the barriers. These observations suggest that if the wavelength is very much smaller than the width of the aperture, there will be no diffraction. The part of the straight wave that passes through the opening will continue in straight-line propagation.

How are these observations related to the fact that light is not diffracted at the edges of a doorway as is sound? The speed of light in air is high, being of the order of $3 \times 10^8$ m/s. We have not yet dealt with light frequencies, but if they were extremely high, light wavelengths ($v/f$) would be very short. Then it would not be surprising to find that light is diffracted only by apertures having very small dimensions.

Indeed, the wavelength of visible light ranges from approximately $7.5 \times 10^{-7}$ m down to about $4 \times 10^{-7}$ m. This range of wavelengths suggests that the diffraction of light occurs in the realm of extremely small dimensions. Diffraction phenomena associated with light waves will be presented in Chapter 15.

**Figure 10-23** The diffraction of a periodic straight wave as it passes through a small aperture. Observe the decrease in the diffraction effect as the wavelength sent against the barrier is shortened.

*An open doorway diffracts sound, but it does not diffract light.*

## 10.14 The superposition principle

We have described the passage of a single pulse and a continuous wave through a medium. It is possible for two or more wave disturbances to move through a medium at the same time. Sound waves from all the musical instruments of an orchestra move simultaneously through the air to our ears. Electromagnetic waves from many different radio and television stations travel simultaneously through regions of space to our receiving antennas. Nevertheless, we can listen to the sound of a particular musical instrument or select a particular radio or television station. These facts suggest that each wave system proceeds independently along its pathway as if the other wave systems were not present.

Let us consider the effects of two periodic transverse waves traveling along a taut string in the same direction. The displacements they produce *at a particular instant* are shown in Figure 10-24. These two waves have different amplitudes and frequencies. The displacements $y_1$ produced by one wave are represented by the black solid curve. The displacements $y_2$ produced by the other wave are represented by the black dashed curve. The resultant displacements $Y$ all along the string at this instant are represented by the colored curve. These resultant displacements are determined by algebraically adding the displacements $y_1$ and $y_2$ for every point along the string.

In effect, the displacement of any particle of the medium by one wave at any instant is superimposed on the displacement of that particle by the other wave at that instant. The action of each wave on a particle is independent of the action of the other, and the particle displacement is the resultant of both wave actions. This phenomenon is known as *superposition*. The two waves are said to *superpose*.

*The superposition principle: When two or more waves travel simultaneously through the same medium, (1) each wave proceeds independently as though no other waves were present and (2) the resultant displacement of any particle at a given time is the vector sum of the displacements that the individual waves acting alone would give it.*

**Figure 10-24** An instantaneous view of the superposition of two periodic transverse waves of different amplitude and frequency. The component waves $y_1$ and $y_2$ are shown in black; the resultant wave $Y$ is in color.

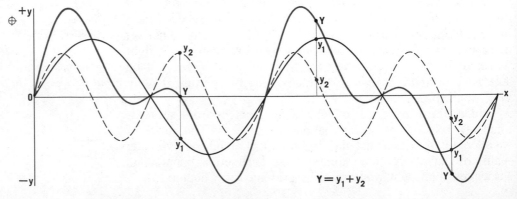

Providing the displacements are small, this principle holds for light and all other electromagnetic waves as well as for sound waves and waves on a string or on a liquid surface. For example, this principle does not hold for "shock waves" produced by violent explosions.

The component waves $y_1$ and $y_2$ in Figure 10-24 are simple sine waves. Either wave alone would cause each particle of the string to undergo simple harmonic motion about its equilibrium point as the wave traveled along the string. The resultant wave is periodic. However, it has a complex, or complicated, wave form. The superposition principle makes it possible to analyze a complex wave in terms of a combination of simple waves.

Actual wave disturbances generally have complex wave forms. For example, the sound waves produced by musical instruments may be very complicated compared to simple sine wave variations. Wave forms of musical tones from a French horn and a trumpet are shown in Figure 11-15 in Chapter 11. Each of these complex waves can be represented by a certain combination of simple waves that by superposition yield the complex wave form.

---

## 10.15 Interference

The general term *interference* is used to describe the *effects* produced by two or more waves that superpose while passing through a given region. Special consideration is given to *waves of the same frequency*, particularly in the case of sound and light. Interference phenomena are exclusively associated with waves. In fact, the existence of interference in experiments with light first established the wave character of light.

Let us consider two waves of the same frequency traversing the same medium simultaneously. *Each particle* of the medium is affected by *both* waves. Suppose the displacement of a particular particle caused by one wave at any instant is in the same direction as that caused by the other wave. Then the total displacement of *that particle at that instant* is the *sum* of the separate displacements (superposition principle). The resultant displacement is *greater* than either wave would have caused separately. This effect is called *constructive interference*.

On the other hand, if the displacement effects of the two waves on the particle are in opposite directions, they tend to cancel one another. The resultant displacement of *that particle at that instant* is the *difference* of the two separate displacements and is in the direction of the larger (superposition principle). The resultant displacement is *less* than one of the waves would have caused separately. This effect is called *destructive interference*.

If two such opposite displacement effects are equal in magnitude, the resultant displacement is zero. The destructive interference is complete. The particle is not displaced at all but is in its equilibrium position *at that instant*.

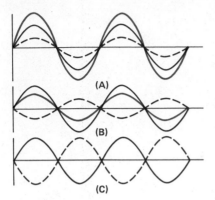

**Figure 10-25** Interference of two periodic waves of the same frequency and traveling in the same direction. The component waves are in black, and the resultant wave is in color. (A) Constructive interference. (B) Destructive interference. (C) Complete destructive interference.

Notice that we have been considering the effect of two waves on the position of just *one particle* of the medium at *one particular instant*. We shall continue to fix our attention on one instant in time as we consider the displacements of many *different* particles of the medium in which the two waves are propagating. We find that the interference effects on different particles are different. There is constructive interference at some locations and destructive interference at others.

In Figure 10-25 (A) two periodic waves with the same frequency and in phase are traveling in the same direction. They interfere constructively. The resultant periodic wave, shown in color, has the same frequency as the component waves but has an amplitude equal to the sum of the component amplitudes.

In Figure 10-25 (B) the two periodic waves have the same frequency but are opposite in phase, that is 180° out of phase. The displacements of the two waves are opposite in sign, and they interfere destructively. In Figure 10-25 (C) the amplitudes of the two waves are equal and the destructive interference is complete.

The arrangement of interference effects (called an *interference pattern*) depends on the relative characteristics of the interfering waves. Figure 10-26 is a photograph of an interference pattern produced in a ripple tank by two identical circular waves emanating from two points. The two waves are in phase at their sources. That is, the two probes that generate the waves by their vibrations are moving up and down together.

A diagram of this interference pattern is shown in Figure 10-27. Points **A** and **B** are the sources of two periodic circular waves of the same frequency and amplitude. The sources are acting in phase. Solid circular lines represent wave crests and dashed circular lines represent wave troughs.

**Figure 10-26** A photograph of the interference pattern of water waves from two point sources. Locate the nodal and antinodal lines.

**Figure 10-27** A diagram of the interference pattern of two periodic circular waves of the same frequency emanating in phase from points A and B.

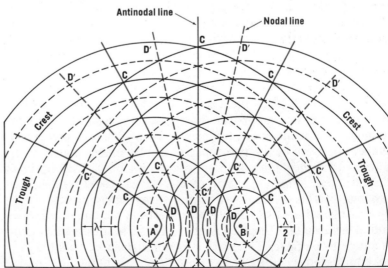

At each point similar to those marked **C** the crest of a wave from one source is superposed with the crest of a wave from the other source. At points similar to **C'** the troughs are superposed. A half period later the crests are at **C'** and the troughs are at **C.** Constructive interference occurs along the lines **CC'** giving the resultant wave an amplitude twice the amplitudes of the individual waves.

At each point similar to those marked **D** the crest of a wave from one source is superposed with the trough of a wave from the other source. Destructive interference occurs along the lines **DD'**, displacements being reduced to zero.

Points of zero displacement in the interference pattern are called *nodes*. The lines **DD'** along which they occur are *nodal lines*. Similarly, points of maximum displacement are called *antinodes* (or loops) and the lines **CC'** along which they occur are *antinodal lines*. Observe these nodal and antinodal regions in the photograph of the interference pattern shown in Figure 10-26.

At any nodal point where the destructive interference is complete, there is no motion of the medium and no energy. This does not mean that the energy of the two interfering waves has been destroyed or otherwise lost. Instead, it appears at points of constructive interference, such as points **C** in Figure 10-27. Recall from Section 10.7 that where the amplitude of the resultant wave crest is double that of a single interfering wave, the energy is four times greater. The total energy of the two wave systems remains unchanged, but the *energy distribution* resulting from the interference is different.

## 10.16 Standing waves

We found in Section 10.10 that a transverse pulse traveling on a taut string is inverted when reflected at the clamped end. This inversion upon reflection at a clamped end occurs also with a train of transverse waves. If no energy is lost in reflection at the fixed end, a continuous wave will be reflected back upon itself giving two wave trains of the same wavelength, frequency, and amplitude but traveling in opposite directions.

Portions of two such wave trains are shown at a certain instant in time in Figure 10-28 (A) and (B). If their displacements are added at this instant, as in (C), the resultant displacement is zero. When the wave patterns have moved $\frac{1}{4}$ wavelength, each in its own direction of travel, superposition gives the resultant shown in (D). Another $\frac{1}{4}$ wavelength of movement gives the resultant in (E), and an additional movement of $\frac{1}{4}$ wavelength gives the resultant displacement in (F). Such a wave pattern is a *standing wave*. The particles in a standing wave vibrate in simple harmonic motion with the same frequency as each of the component waves. The amplitude of their motion is not the same for all points along the string. It varies from a minimum of zero amplitude at scale

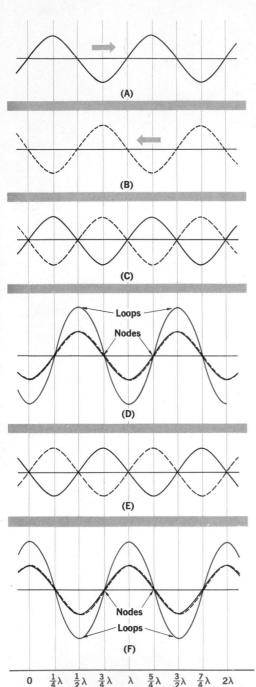

positions $\frac{1}{4}\lambda$, $\frac{3}{4}\lambda$, $\frac{5}{4}\lambda$, $\frac{7}{4}\lambda$, etc., to a maximum of twice the amplitude of one component wave at $0\lambda$, $\frac{1}{2}\lambda$, $1\lambda$, $\frac{3}{2}\lambda$, etc.

In the displacement shown in Figure 10-28 (F) the motions of all the particles between $0\lambda$ and $\frac{1}{4}\lambda$ are exactly in phase with one another and with the motion of particles between $\frac{3}{4}\lambda$ and $\frac{5}{4}\lambda$. They are 180° out of phase with the motion of particles between $\frac{1}{4}\lambda$ and $\frac{3}{4}\lambda$ and with the motion of particles between $\frac{5}{4}\lambda$ and $\frac{7}{4}\lambda$. When particles in a length of string equal to one-half wavelength are going up, the particles in the immediately adjacent parts of the string are going down.

Certain parts of a string vibrating with a standing wave pattern never move from their equilibrium positions. These parts are the *nodes*. Halfway between the nodes, where the amplitude of vibration is maximum, are the *loops*. The wavelength of the component periodic transverse waves that produce the standing wave is *twice* the distance between the adjacent nodes or the loops in a standing wave.

*A standing wave is produced by the interference of two periodic waves of the same amplitude and wavelength traveling in opposite directions.* No standing wave can be produced if the two waves have different wavelengths.

When a stretched string is clamped at both ends, a standing wave pattern can be formed only for certain definite wavelengths. In such a vibrating string both ends must be nodes. Four possible standing wave patterns in a stretched string are shown in Figure 10-29. Loops are indicated by the letter **L** and nodes by the letter **N**. The wavelength, $\lambda$, for each standing wave is expressed in terms of the length of the string, $l$. Figure 10-29 (A) is a time-exposure view showing the envelopes of the standing waves. Part (B) is a strobe-flash view showing positions of the strings at different instants of time.

In a standing wave, particles of the string at the nodes are continuously at rest. Energy is not transported along the string, but remains "standing" in the string. The energy of each particle remains constant as that particle executes its simple harmonic motion. When the string is straight, or undistorted, particles have their maximum velocities and the energy is all kinetic. The energy is all potential when the string has its maximum displacement and all particles are momentarily at rest.

Standing waves are established in water, in air, or in other elastic bodies just as they are in taut strings. Standing waves can also be produced with electromagnetic waves. A standing wave pattern can occur in a circular ripple tank in which a periodic circular wave is generated at the center of the tank. Nodal rings appear where the surface of the water is at rest. The surface oscillates up and down between the nodal rings. Many vibrating objects vibrate normally in a way that establishes standing waves in the object. The strings or the air columns of musical instruments establish various modes of standing waves.

**Figure 10-28** Standing wave (shown in color) produced by the interference of two periodic waves of the same frequency and amplitude traveling in opposite directions.

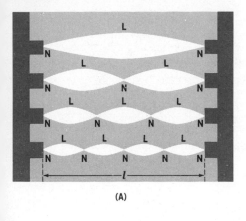

$\lambda = 2l$

$\lambda = l$

$\lambda = \frac{2}{3}l$

$\lambda = \frac{1}{2}l$

(A)

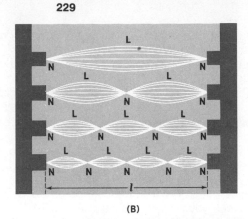

(B)

**Figure 10-29** Standing wave patterns in a stretched string. (A) A time-exposure view. (B) A strobe-flash view. Wavelength $\lambda$ is expressed in terms of the length, $l$, of the string. Labels L and N identify loops and nodes.

# summary

Energy can be transferred by the movement of materials or objects, by the motion of particles, by the flow of gases or liquids, and by waves. Energy is transferred by waves without the transport of matter. Waves that require a material medium for their transmission are called mechanical waves. Electromagnetic waves can travel through matter but a material medium is not required for their transmission. A pulse is a single nonrecurring wave disturbance. A continuous wave results from a wave disturbance that recurs periodically.

Mechanical waves in which the particles of the transmitting medium are displaced perpendicular to the direction in which the wave travels are called transverse waves. Those in which the particles of the medium are displaced parallel to the wave direction are longitudinal waves.

Waves have common characteristics such as phase, frequency, period, wavelength, speed, and amplitude. The velocity of a wave is the product of the frequency and its wavelength in the medium. Transmission media in which the speed of a wave is dependent on its frequency are said to be dispersive.

Common properties of waves are rectilinear propagation, reflection, refraction, diffraction, and interference. Superposition occurs when two or more wave disturbances move through a medium at the same time. Standing waves are produced by the interference of two periodic waves of the same amplitude and wavelength and traveling in opposite directions.

# questions

GROUP B

1. How does a pulse on a taut string differ from the incident pulse after being reflected at a fixed termination?

2. List the common properties of waves and give an illustration of each.

3. Make a drawing showing two transverse waves of the same wavelength but of different amplitudes that are in phase. Graphically find the wave pattern that results if these two waves are superposed.

4. Repeat Question 3 with waves of the same amplitude but with one having twice the wavelength of the other. At $t = 0$, the displacement of both waves is zero. At $t = T/4$ later for each, the displacement is maximum positive.

5. Repeat Question 4, but take the displacement as zero for the wave of longer wavelength and as positive maximum for the wave of shorter wavelength at $t = 0$ while the reverse applies at $t = T/4$.

6. In your drawings of Questions 4 and 5 mark the points of maximum displacement and zero displacement. Do they occur at the same points at $t = 0$ as at $t = T/4$? Would you consider the resulting pattern as a standing wave or a progressing wave?

7. What are the requirements for production of a standing wave pattern?

8. What are *loops* and *nodes* in a standing wave pattern?

9. When two waves interfere, what influence does each exert on the progress of the other? Explain.

10. When two waves interfere, is there a loss of energy in the system? Explain.

11. Distinguish between the effects of a fixed and a free termination at the interface of a medium.

12. Two rooms are separated by a special sound-proof partition except for a connecting doorway. How can you explain the fact that a sound produced anywhere in one room can be heard anywhere in the other?

13. A new phenomenon has been observed in which there is a transfer of energy. What type of experiments would you propose to determine whether it is a particle or wave phenomenon?

14. What is an impedance transformer?

15. A wave disturbance travels through a uniform medium to its termination where a small part of the wave energy is transferred to the terminating medium and the remainder is reflected. How would you describe the impedance of the terminating medium relative to the impedance of the transmitting medium?

16. Suggest two possible ways of modifying the wave-transfer system described in Question 15 to eliminate the reflection of wave energy.

# problems

GROUP B

1. Electromagnetic waves travel through space at a speed of $3.0 \times 10^8$ m/s. The visible region of the spectrum has wavelengths ranging from about $4.0 \times 10^{-7}$ m in the violet region to about $7.6 \times 10^{-7}$ m in the red region. What is the frequency range of visible light?

2. A string stretched between two clamps is 2.0 m long. When plucked at the center, a standing wave is produced that has nodes at the clamped ends and a single loop at the center. By means of a stroboscope, the string is observed to complete 7.0 vibrations per second. (a) What is the wavelength of the component traveling waves? (b) What is the speed of the transverse waves in the string?

3. Periodic longitudinal waves are generated in a coil spring from a vibrating source at one end of the spring as shown in Figure 10-7. The frequency of the vibrating source is 15.0 hz. The distance between successive compressions is 41.0 cm. What is the speed of each compression moving along the spring?

4. An observer determined that 2.5 m separated a trough and an adjacent crest of surface waves on a lake and counted 33 crests passing in 30 s. What was the speed of these surface waves?

5. Two physics students were fishing from a boat anchored in a lake 24 m from shore. One student observed that the boat rocked through 11 complete oscillations in 19 s and that one wave crest passed the boat with each oscillation. The other student noted that each crest required 6.5 s to reach the shore. (a) What was the period of the surface wave? (b) What was the wavelength?

# 11 Sound Waves

## THE NATURE OF SOUND

The energy-transfer mechanism of compression waves is a major interest of physicists. In a medium having elastic and inertial properties, compression waves propagate as longitudinal disturbances. The disturbances consist of *compressions* and *rarefactions* that give rise to elastic forces in the propagating (transmitting) medium. Through these elastic forces the energy of the wave is transferred to the particles of the medium that are next in line. The energy exchange is continuous as particles receive wave energy and pass it along.

The frequency range over which such longitudinal waves occur is very large. It is called the *sonic spectrum*. There is no clearly defined lower limit of frequency of the sonic spectrum. However, the frequency of an earthquake wave may be a fraction of a cycle per minute and its wavelength may be measured in kilometers.

The upper limit of the sonic spectrum is well defined. For a constant-velocity condition, periodic waves of increasing frequency have proportionally decreasing wavelength. A wave is not transported by a medium in which the wavelength is small compared to the inter-particle spacing of the medium. For a gas the mean free path of the molecules is the limiting dimension. Thus at ordinary temperatures and pressures the upper range of sonic frequencies is of the order of $10^9$ hertz in a gaseous medium. In liquids and solids the upper frequency limit is higher because of the smaller inter-particle spacing.

Within the sonic spectrum lies the region of *sound, a range of compression-wave frequencies to which the human ear is sen-*

### 11.1 The sonic spectrum

**Figure 11-1** Photograph of a sound, circa 1930. Dr. A. L. Foley devised a technique for photographing the sound from a loud electric spark. Light from a second spark discharge cast a shadow on photographic film of the shock wave traveling outward in the air as a spherical shell. This photograph shows the wave being reflected from a plane surface.

231

*sitive.* This audible range of frequencies, called the *audio range* or the *audio spectrum,* extends from approximately 20 to 20,000 hertz. Compression waves at frequencies above the audio range are referred to as *ultrasonic;* those below the audio range are referred to as *infrasonic.*

## 11.2 The production of sound

**Figure 11-2** Sounds are produced by vibrating matter.

*Recall that sounds are produced by vibrating matter.*

*A sound wave may be thought of as a displacement wave or as a pressure wave. The displacement wave is 90° out of phase with the pressure wave.*

A sound is produced by the initiation of a succession of compressive and rarefactive disturbances in a medium capable of transmitting these vibrational disturbances. Particles of the medium acquire energy from the vibrating source and enter the vibrational mode themselves. The wave energy is passed along to adjacent particles as the periodic waves travel through the medium.

Such vibrating elements as reeds (clarinet, saxophone), strings (guitar, vocal cords), membranes (drum, loudspeaker), and air columns (pipe organ, flute) initiate sound waves. Sound waves are transmitted outward from their source by the surrounding air. When they enter the ear, they produce the sensation of sound.

Suppose we clamp one end of a thin strip of steel in a vise to serve as a vibrating reed. When struck sharply, the free end vibrates to and fro, as shown in Figure 11-2. If the reed vibrates rapidly enough, it produces a humming sound.

When the reed vibrates, its motion approximates simple harmonic motion. See Figure 11-3 (A). A graph of its displacement with time produces the sine wave shown in Figure 11-3 (B). As the vibrating reed moves from **a** to **b** it compresses the gas molecules of the air immediately to the right. The reed transfers energy to the molecules in the direction in which the compression occurs. At the same time the air molecules to the left expand into the space behind the moving reed and become rarefied. Thus the movement of the reed from **a** to **b** produces a compression and rarefaction simultaneously with a net transfer of energy to the right, the direction of the compression.

As the reed moves in the reverse direction from **b** to **a** it compresses the gas molecules to the left, while those to the right become rarefied. The combined effect of this simultaneous compression and rarefaction transfers energy to the left, again the direction of the compression.

If we consider just the series of compressions and rarefactions produced to the right, it is apparent that the maximum compression occurs as the reed moves through its equilibrium position **o** traveling from **a** to **b**. See Figure 11-3 (C). The maximum rarefaction occurs as the reed moves through its equilibrium position **o** traveling from **b** to **a**. This is shown in (D) as a plot of the variation of pressure with time.

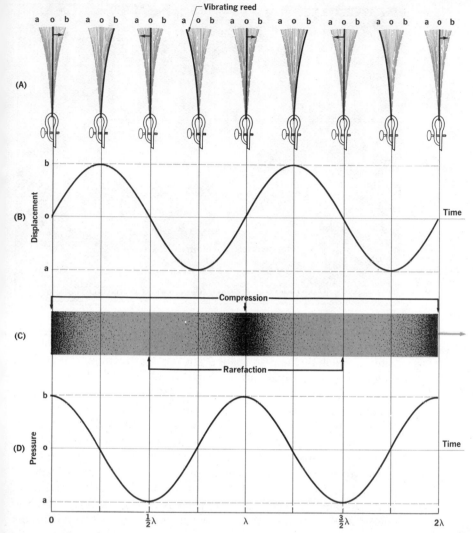

Simultaneously, of course, a corresponding series of rarefactions and compressions is produced to the left. The vibration of the reed thus generates longitudinal trains of waves. In these longitudinal waves, vibrating gas molecules move back and forth along the path of the traveling waves, receiving energy from adjacent molecules nearer the source and passing it on to adjacent molecules farther from the source. *Sound waves are longitudinal waves.*

Variations in the work done in setting the reed in vibration alter the amplitude of the vibration but not the frequency. The greater the energy of the moving reed, the greater is the amplitude of its vibrations and the amplitude of the resulting longitudinal waves.

**Figure 11-3** Variations of the vibrating reed in (A) produce the displacement variations with time in (B). The regions of compression and rarefaction of the longitudinal sound wave produced to the right of the reed are shown in (C). The pressure, or density, variations of the sound wave with time are plotted in (D). Observe that the displacement and pressure curves are 90° out of phase.

**Figure 11-4** In this specially designed room, 99.9% of reflected sound is eliminated. The acoustical conditions here are similar to those in the atmosphere 1.6 km above the earth's surface.

## 11.3 Sound transmission

To produce sound waves, we must have a source that initiates a mechanical disturbance and an elastic medium through which the disturbance can be *transmitted*. Most sounds come to us through the air, and it is the air that acts as the transmitting medium. At low altitudes, we usually have little difficulty hearing sounds. At higher altitudes where the density of the air is lower, less energy may be transferred from the source to the air. Dense air is a more efficient transmitter of sound than rarefied air.

The following experiment provides evidence that a material is required for the transmission of sound. As shown in Figure 11-5, an electric bell under a bell jar is connected to a source of energy so that it rings. While it is ringing, air is removed from the bell jar. As the remaining air becomes less and less dense, the sound becomes fainter and fainter. When air is allowed to re-enter, the sound becomes louder. These effects show that it is increasingly difficult to get sound energy transferred to the air as the density of the air decreases. This demonstration suggests that if all the air could be removed from the bell jar, no sound would be heard. *Sound does not travel through a vacuum; it is transmitted only through a material medium.*

The sound of two rocks being struck together under water can be heard quite plainly by a swimmer submerged in the water. If the swimmer is near the source of the disturbance, the effect can be painful. Liquids are efficient transmitters of sound.

Sometimes a loose faucet washer vibrates when water is drawn from a water pipe. The sound of this vibration is carried to all parts of the house by water pipes and wood framework. A train

**Figure 11-5** As air is pumped from the bell jar, the sound of the bell becomes fainter. Such a demonstration is evidence that a material medium is needed for the transmission of sound.

To vacuum pump

can be heard from a great distance by the sound transmitted through the rails. Many solids are efficient sound transmitters. In long rods or pipes, the sound propagation may be restricted to one dimension instead of spreading in space.

During a thunderstorm, a distant lightning flash can be seen several seconds before the accompanying thunder is heard. The timer at the finish line during a track meet may see the smoke from the starter's gun before he hears the report. Over short distances, light travels practically instantaneously. Therefore, the time that elapses between a lightning flash being seen and the thunder being heard or between a gun being fired and the report being heard must be the time required for the sound to travel from its source to the observer. The speed of sound in air is 331.5 m/s at 0°C. This speed increases with temperature about (0.6 m/s)/C°.

The speed of sound in water is about four times the speed in air. In water at 25°C sound travels about 1500 m/s. In some solids, the speed of sound is even greater. In a steel rod, for example, sound travels approximately 5000 m/s—about 15 times the speed in air. In general the speed of sound varies with the temperature of the transmitting medium. For gases the change in speed is rather large. For liquids and solids, however, this change in speed is small and is usually neglected. Representative values for the speed of sound waves in various media are given in Table 11-1. A more extensive list will be found in Appendix B, Table 17.

## 11.4 The speed of sound

Table 11-1

| SPEED OF SOUND (25°C) | |
|---|---|
| Medium | Speed (m/s) |
| air | 346 |
| hydrogen | 1339 |
| alcohol | 1207 |
| water | 1497 |
| glass | 4540 |
| aluminum | 5000 |
| iron (steel) | 5200 |

A nearby clap of thunder is loud; a whisper is soft. A cricket has a shrill, high chirp; a bulldog has a deep growl. A violin string bowed by a virtuoso produces a note of fine quality and is far more pleasing to hear than that produced by the novice. Each of these sounds has characteristics clearly associated with it. Sounds differ from each other in several fundamental ways. We shall consider three physical properties of sound waves: *intensity, frequency,* and *harmonic content.* The effects of these properties on the ear are called, respectively, *loudness, pitch,* and *quality.*

## 11.5 The properties of sound

*The **intensity** of a sound is the time rate at which the sound energy flows through a unit area normal to the direction of propagation.* Intensity thus has the dimension of power/area.

$$I = \frac{P}{A}$$

Where $P$ is sound power in watts and $A$ is area in square centimeters, the sound intensity $I$ is expressed in watts per square

## 11.6 Intensity and loudness

*Recall that* $P = \dfrac{E}{t}$.

*Review Section 10.7.*

*We interpret the intensity of a sound in terms of its loudness.*

*The ear is a nonlinear device.*

centimeter. The intensity of a sound wave of given frequency is dependent on its amplitude; it is proportional to the square of the amplitude.

Sound waves that emanate from a vibrator approximating a point source and that travel in a uniform medium spread out in a spherical pattern. Thus the area of the expanding wave front is directly proportional to the square of its distance from the source. Since the total power of the wave is constant the intensity of the wave diminishes as it moves away from the source. The sound produced by a whistle is only one-fourth as intense at a distance of one kilometer as it is at a distance of half a kilometer from the source. The intensity of sound in a uniform medium is inversely proportional to the square of its distance from the point source.

*The **loudness** of a sound depends on an auditory sensation in the consciousness of a human listener.* In general, sound waves of higher intensity are louder, but the ear is not equally sensitive to sounds of all frequencies. Consequently a high or a low frequency sound may not seem as loud as one of mid-range frequency having the same intensity.

An increase in the intensity of a sound of fixed frequency causes it to seem louder to the listener. Suppose we generate a 1000-hz tone of such low intensity that it is barely audible. The intensity can be increased approximately $10^{12}$ times before the tone becomes so loud that it is painful to the listener. The degree of loudness of a sound is not directly measurable with instruments since it depends on the ear and subjective judgment of the listener.

## 11.7 Intensity level measurements

Intensity is measured with acoustical apparatus and does not depend on the hearing of an observer. At 1000 hz the intensity of the average faintest audible sound, called the *threshold of hearing,* is $10^{-16}$ watt/cm$^2$. In measuring the *intensity level* of a sound, its intensity is compared with the intensity of this threshold of hearing. Because of the great range of intensities over which the ear is sensitive, a *logarithmic* rather than an arithmetic intensity scale is used. The intensity level of a sound is given by the equation

$$\beta = 10 \log \frac{I}{I_0}$$

where $\beta$ (the Greek letter beta) is the intensity level in *decibels* (db) of a sound of intensity $I$. $I_0$ is the intensity of the threshold of hearing. $I$ and $I_0$ are measured in the same units, usually watt/cm$^2$. Therefore the decibel is a dimensionless quantity. The following example illustrates the use of this equation. Intensity levels of several familiar sounds are listed in Table 11-2.

Table 11-2

| INTENSITY LEVELS OF SOUNDS (at 1000 hz) | |
|---|---|
| Type of sound | Intensity (db) |
| threshold of hearing | 0 |
| whisper | 10–20 |
| very soft music | 30 |
| average residence | 40–50 |
| conversation | 60–70 |
| heavy street traffic | 70–80 |
| thunder | 110 |
| threshold of pain | 120 |
| jet engine | 170 |

EXAMPLE

*Sound energy is radiated uniformly in all directions from a small source at a rate of 1.2 watts. (a) What is the intensity of the sound at a point 25 m from the source? (b) What is the intensity level at this reception point?*

SOLUTION

Assuming no absorption of sound energy by the transmitting medium, the 1.2 watts of sound power is associated with a spherical area having a radius of 25 m.

(a) $I = \dfrac{P}{A} = \dfrac{1.2 \text{ w}}{4\pi(2500 \text{ cm})^2} = 1.5 \times 10^{-8} \text{ w/cm}^2$

(b) $\beta = 10 \log \dfrac{I}{I_0} = 10 \log \dfrac{1.5 \times 10^{-8} \text{ w/cm}^2}{10^{-16} \text{ w/cm}^2} = 10 \log (1.5 \times 10^8) = 82 \text{ db}$ *8.2 bels*

The decibel is the practical unit for sound intensity levels. The word decibel means one-tenth of a *bel*, a unit named in honor of Alexander Graham Bell (1847–1922).

*Originally the bel was defined as the unit for intensity level differences, but it was too large to be practical.*

$$\textbf{Intensity level in bels} = \log \dfrac{I}{I_0}$$

In the human sensory response, a change in the sound power level of 1 db is just barely perceptible. This change of 1 db represents a change in sound intensity of 26%. Table 11-3 shows several power ratios and their decibel equivalents.

We stated in Section 11.1 that the audio spectrum extends from approximately 20 to 20,000 hz. The lower frequency is called the *lower limit of audibility* and the higher frequency the *upper limit of audibility*. However, there is considerable variation in the ability of individuals to hear sounds of high or low frequencies.

The graph in Figure 11-6 shows the characteristics of audible sound waves. Since the graph is a composite of results obtained

Table 11-3

| RELATIVE INTENSITIES | | |
|---|---|---|
| $I/I_0$ | bel | db |
| 10 | 1 | 10 |
| 4 | | 6 |
| 2 | | 3 |
| 1 | 0 | 0 |
| 0.5 | | -3 |
| 0.25 | | -6 |
| 0.1 | -1 | -10 |

**Figure 11-6** The range of audibility of the human ear.

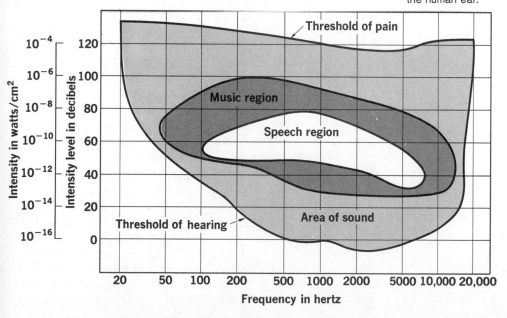

by testing many persons, it refers to the performance of the "average" ear.

The lower curve, the *threshold of hearing,* shows the minimum intensity level at which sound waves of various frequencies can be heard. Observe that the lowest intensity that will produce audible sound is for frequencies between 2000 and 4000 hz. The ear is most sensitive in this frequency range. At the lower and upper limits of audibility the intensities of sound waves must be greater to be heard.

The upper curve, the *threshold of pain,* indicates the upper intensity level for audible sounds. Sounds of greater intensity produce pain rather than hearing.

The graph shows the general frequency limits for the audio range to be between 20 and 20,000 hz. The intensity limits in the region of maximum sensitivity are between 0 and 120 decibels, corresponding to intensities of from $10^{-16}$ watt/cm$^2$ to $10^{-4}$ watt/cm$^2$.

## 11.8 Frequency and pitch

**Air**

11-5 The pitch of a sound depends on the frequency of the sound waves received by the ear.

*We interpret the frequency of a sound in terms of its pitch.*

*Noise: sounds with nonperiodic wave forms.*

A perforated disk, as shown in Figure 11-7, can be used to show that the frequency of a sound determines its *pitch.* The disk has five concentric rings of holes. The holes of the innermost ring are irregularly spaced. The holes in the other four rings are regularly spaced, and, respectively, there are 24, 30, 36, and 48 holes in them.

A stream of air directed against a ring of holes is interrupted by the metal between the holes as the disk rotates rapidly at constant speed. The interruptions give rise to a series of air blasts that produce a sound characteristic of the frequency of the blasts. A sound of constant pitch is heard if the holes are evenly spaced. The pitch rises as the disk rotation is accelerated; it falls as the disk rotation is decelerated. If the stream of air is directed at the 24-, 30-, 36-, and 48-hole rings successively as the disk rotates at a constant rate, tones of successively higher pitch are produced. ***Pitch** is the identification of a certain sound with a definite tone and depends on the frequency that the ear receives.*

We usually distinguish between a musical tone and a noise by the fact that the former is a pleasing sound, and the latter is a disagreeable one. When the stream of air is directed at the innermost ring of holes, an unpleasant noise is heard. The noise is characterized by a random mixture of frequencies and is not easily identified in terms of pitch.

The pitch of a tone produced by directing the air against one of the regularly spaced rings of holes is appropriately described in terms of the frequency of the sound produced. If the disk is rotating at the rate of 20 revolutions per second, the frequency of the tone produced by the ring with 24 holes is 480 hertz. The ring with 30 holes produces a tone having a frequency of 600 hertz;

the 36-hole ring, a frequency of 720 hertz; and the 48-hole ring, 960 hertz.

The two tones produced by the outermost and innermost of these four regularly spaced rings are an *octave* apart, their frequencies being in the ratio of 2:1. The four tones have frequencies in the ratios 4:5:6:8. When these tones are produced simultaneously, they comprise a musical sound known as a *major chord*.

*Music: sounds with approximately periodic wave forms unless their intensity is too high.*

## 11.9 The Doppler effect

In our discussion of frequency and pitch in Section 11.8, both the source of the emission and the listener were assumed to be stationary. In that case the pitch of the sound heard is characteristic of the frequency of the emission. If the source emits 1000 vibrations per second, the listener hears a 1000-hz tone.

When there is relative motion between the source of sound and the listener, the pitch of the sound heard is not the same as that when both listener and source are stationary. Two situations are common: The source may be moving and the listener is stationary, and the listener may be moving and the source is at rest.

The first situation prevails when the listener stands at a railroad crossing while a train passes. The pitch of the warning horn of the locomotive drops abruptly as it passes the observer's position. The second situation prevails when the listener rides in the train as it passes through a highway intersection. In this instance the pitch of the warning bell at the crossing drops abruptly as the observer passes through the intersection.

In both situations the steady pitch of the sound heard by the observer is *higher* than the actual frequency of the source would indicate as the distance between the listener and the source *decreases* at a constant rate. Also, the steady pitch of the sound heard is *lower* than the actual frequency of the source would indicate as the distance between the listener and the source *increases* at a constant rate. *The change in pitch produced by the relative motion of the source and the observer is known as the Doppler effect.* Of course, the frequency of the sound emitted by the source remains unchanged as does the velocity of the sound in the transmitting medium. Figure 11-8 illustrates this principle.

Let us suppose that a source of sound is stationed at **S** in Figure 11-9 and that one listener is at $L_F$ and another is at $L_B$. If the source emits a sound of frequency $f_S$ and the velocity of sound in the medium is $v$, the wavelength $\lambda$ is

$$\lambda = \frac{v}{f_S} \qquad \text{(Equation 1)}$$

The time $t$ in this diagram is unit time of 1 second. Thus the distance $SL_F = SL_B = vt$, that is, the distance the sound travels

*The Doppler effect is named for the Austrian physicist Christian Johann Doppler (1803–1853).*

**Figure 11-8** Doppler effect. The pitch of the horn on the speeding diesel locomotive sounds normal to the listeners $L_X$ and $L_Y$ off to the sides, higher to the listener $L_F$ in front, and lower to the listener $L_B$ in back.

**Figure 11-9** Sound waves emitted in unit time by the source **S** during its movement from **S** to **S₁** with speed $v_S$ are contained within the distance $\mathbf{S_1L_F}$ in the direction of listener $\mathbf{L_F}$ in front of the source and within the distance $\mathbf{S_1L_B}$ in the direction of the listener $\mathbf{L_B}$ behind the source.

in 1 second. Then there are $f_S$ waves in both distances $\mathbf{SL_F}$ and $\mathbf{SL_B}$, each of wavelength $\lambda$.

Now suppose that the source is moving toward $\mathbf{L_F}$ and away from $\mathbf{L_B}$ with speed $v_S$ and in 1 second travels from $\mathbf{S}$ to $\mathbf{S_1}$, a distance $v_S t$. During this time, $f_S$ vibrations are emitted by the source. The first vibration is emitted at $\mathbf{S}$. At the end of the 1-second interval this vibration is at $\mathbf{L_F}$ in front of the source, and also at $\mathbf{L_B}$ behind the source. Remember that the advancing wave fronts are spherical. The last vibration just emitted at the end of the 1-second interval is at $\mathbf{S_1}$. Therefore, the same number of vibrations, $f_S$, are in the front region $\mathbf{S_1L_F}$ and the back region $\mathbf{S_1L_B}$ in the 1-second interval. These two distances are respectively

$$\mathbf{S_1L_F} = (v - v_S)t \qquad \text{(Equation 2a)}$$

and
$$\mathbf{S_1L_B} = (v + v_S)t \qquad \text{(Equation 2b)}$$

*The wavelength $\lambda'$ of the sound reaching the stationary listener in front of the moving source is shorter than $\lambda$ of Equation 1* and is given by

$$\lambda' = \frac{v - v_S}{f_S} \qquad \text{(Equation 3)}$$

The velocity of the sound in the medium, $v$, is independent of the motion of the source. Thus the frequency of the sound reaching the stationary observer in front of the moving source, $f_{LF}$, is

$$f_{LF} = \frac{v}{\lambda'} \qquad \text{(Equation 4)}$$

Substituting the expression for $\lambda'$ given in Equation 3 in Equation 4 yields

$$f_{LF} = \frac{v}{\dfrac{v - v_S}{f_S}}$$

or
$$f_{LF} = f_S \frac{v}{v - v_S} \qquad \text{(Equation 5)}$$

Equation 5 shows us that *the frequency of the sound reaching the stationary listener in front of the moving source is higher than the frequency of the source.* Therefore, the sound that is heard has a higher pitch than that emitted by the source.

We shall now turn to the other listener, $L_B$, in Figure 11-9 and show how the pitch of the sound heard is related to the frequency of the source. *The wavelength $\lambda'$ of the sound reaching the stationary listener behind the moving source is longer than $\lambda$ of Equation 1* and can be expressed as

$$\lambda' = \frac{v + v_S}{f_S} \qquad \text{(Equation 6)}$$

As in Equation 4 the frequency of the sound reaching the observer behind the moving source, $f_{LB}$, is

$$f_{LB} = \frac{v}{\lambda'} \qquad \text{(Equation 7)}$$

Substituting the expression for $\lambda'$ given in Equation 6 in Equation 7, we get

$$f_{LB} = f_S \frac{v}{v + v_S} \qquad \text{(Equation 8)}$$

Equation 8 indicates that *the frequency of the sound reaching the stationary listener behind the moving source is lower than the frequency of the source.* Thus the sound that is heard has a lower pitch than that emitted by the source.

If the listener is moving toward a stationary source, the pitch of the sound heard will be higher than $f_S$, but it will not be exactly that indicated by Equation 5. If the listener has a closing velocity $v_{LC}$, $v_{LC}/\lambda$ waves per second are received in addition to the $f_S$ emitted by the source. From Equation 1,

$$f_S = \frac{v}{\lambda}$$

so,

$$f_{LC} = \frac{v}{\lambda} + \frac{v_{LC}}{\lambda}$$

or

$$f_{LC} = \frac{v + v_{LC}}{\lambda} \qquad \text{(Equation 9)}$$

Substituting the expression for $\lambda$ given in Equation 1 in Equation 9, we have

$$f_{LC} = f_S \frac{v + v_{LC}}{v} \qquad \text{(Equation 10)}$$

*Equation 10 shows the frequency of the sound reaching the listener moving toward the stationary source.* Thus a sound is heard that has a higher pitch than that emitted by the source but not the same pitch as given in Equation 5.

The listener moving away from the stationary source with an

opening velocity $v_{LO}$ will receive $v_{LO}/\lambda$ waves per second fewer than $f_S$ emitted by the source.

$$f_{LO} = \frac{v - v_{LO}}{\lambda} \qquad \text{(Equation 11)}$$

Substituting for $\lambda$ as before,

$$f_{LO} = f_S \frac{v - v_{LO}}{v} \qquad \text{(Equation 12)}$$

*From Equation 12 we can determine the frequency of the sound reaching a listener moving away from the stationary source.* Observe that the pitch is lower than that emitted by this source, but is not the same pitch as given in Equation 8.

We have considered the special cases in which the velocities of the source and the observer lie along the line common to both. If the medium has a velocity along this line joining the source and the listener, it must be considered also.

The Doppler effect is most easily observed in connection with sound waves. Astronomers have observed slight changes in the wavelength of light received from distant stars, and interpret this as being a Doppler effect caused by the relative motions of the stars toward or away from the earth. Light from many distant stars is shifted to longer wavelengths, or toward the red region of the light spectrum. This effect, called the *red shift,* suggests that the universe is expanding. Doppler radar techniques can be used to detect moving objects, and some satellite tracking systems also use the Doppler principle.

**Figure 11-10** Doppler effect due to motion of the source. The Doppler effect observed in a ripple tank in which the source of the disturbance is moving from left to right.

# questions

GROUP A
1. How are sounds produced?
2. Why is sound not transmitted through a vacuum?
3. (a) What is the speed of sound in air at 0°C in the MKS system of measurement? (b) What is the rate of increase of speed with rise in temperature?
4. Distinguish between intensity and loudness.
5. Distinguish between frequency and pitch.
6. The engineer of a diesel locomotive sounds the horn as the train approaches you. How does the pitch you hear compare with the pitch the engineer hears?
7. How do the vibrations of the source of a musical tone differ from the vibrations of the source of a noise?
8. (a) What is the range of audio frequencies? (b) What name is applied to sound vibrations below the audio range? (c) What name is applied to sound vibrations above the audio range?
9. (a) What is the threshold of hearing? (b) What is

the threshold of pain? (c) From Figure 11-6, what is the threshold of hearing at 1000 hz? (d) What is the threshold of pain at 1000 hz?

GROUP B
10. Describe how a vibrating reed sets up longitudinal waves in the air surrounding it and thereby transfers its energy to the surrounding air.
11. (a) How does variation in the work done in setting a reed in vibration affect the sound produced? (b) How does variation in the length of the vibrating portion of the reed affect the sound?
12. Explain why the audibility of a sound disturbance in an enclosed gaseous medium diminishes as the density of the gas is lowered.
13. Why is the intensity level of sound measured on a logarithmic scale?
14. What condition determines the upper limit of the sonic spectrum in a given transmitting medium?
15. Explain the meaning of the statement, "the sound level in the room is 40 db."

# problems

**GROUP A**

1. What time is required for sound to travel 5.00 km if the temperature of the air is 10.0°C?

2. What is the wavelength, in meters, of the sound produced by a tuning fork that has a frequency of $32\overline{0}$ hz? The temperature of the air is 15°C.

3. The echo of a ship's fog horn, reflected from an iceberg, is heard 5.0 s after the horn is sounded. The temperature is −10.0°C. How many meters away is the iceberg?

4. A rifle is fired in a valley with parallel vertical walls. The echo from one wall is heard in 2.0 s; the echo from the other wall 2.0 s later. The temperature is 20°C. What is the width of the valley?

5. What is the intensity level in decibels of a sound that has an intensity of $10^{-11}$ watt/cm²?

**GROUP B**

6. A stone is dropped into a mine shaft $25\overline{0}$ m deep. The temperature is 5.0°C. How many seconds

pass before the stone is heard to strike the bottom? (Neglect the effect of air resistance on the stone.)

7. A stone is thrown out horizontally over a cliff and is heard to strike the ground after 8.00 s. The temperature is 25°C. What is the height of the cliff in meters? (See note in Problem 6.)

8. A locomotive approaches a crossing at 95.0 km/hr. Its horn has a frequency of 288 hz and the temperature is 15°C. What is the frequency of the sound heard by the guard at the crossing?

9. What is the drop in frequency of the sound a listener hears as a train with its horn sounding passes at 145 km/hr? The frequency of the horn is $32\overline{0}$ hz; the temperature is 25.0°C.

10. What is the intensity in w/cm² of a sound that has an intensity level of $3\overline{0}$ db?

11. The intensity of a sound is determined to be $10^{-14}$ w/cm². What is its intensity level?

# CHARACTERISTICS OF SOUND WAVES

Suppose a piano wire is stretched about a meter in length between two clamps and drawn tight enough to vibrate when plucked. If plucked in the middle, the wire vibrates *as a whole*, as shown in Figure 11-11(A). *A taut wire or string that vibrates as a single unit produces its lowest frequency, called its* **fundamental**.

**11.10 Fundamental tones**

(A) Fundamental mode

(B) Second harmonic

(C) Third harmonic

(D) Fourth harmonic

**Figure 11-11** A strobe-flash view of some vibration modes of a single string.

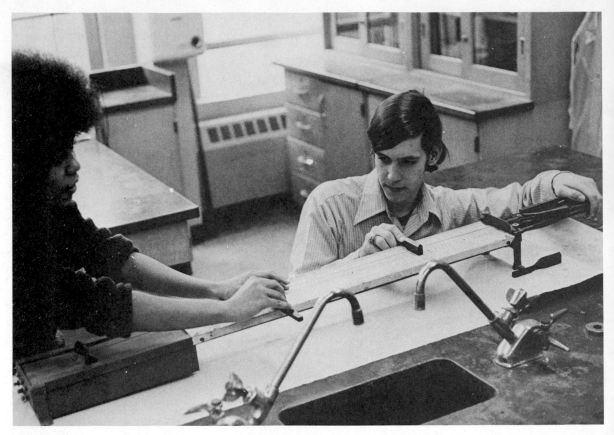

**Figure 11-12** The sonometer can be used to study the vibrational characteristics of strings and wires.

The properties of vibrating strings and the sounds they produce can be studied using an instrument called a *sonometer,* which is shown in Figure 11-12. The sonometer may have two or more wires or strings stretched over a sounding board, which reinforces the sound produced by the wires. Because wires may vary in diameter, tension, length, and composition, a sonometer is useful for studying the effects of these variables on the vibrational characteristics of the wires.

By plucking a string, energy is transferred to the string and causes it to vibrate in transverse wave motion. Just as a vibrating reed transfers energy to molecules of air gases and causes them to exhibit longitudinal wave motion, so a vibrating string transfers energy to these gas molecules and causes them to vibrate and transmit a longitudinal wave. The frequency of the longitudinal vibration of the molecules, which is the frequency of the sound wave, is the same as the frequency of the transverse vibration of the string. Since the production of sound by a vibrating string dissipates energy, energy must be continuously supplied to the string by plucking or bowing to maintain the sound.

A string may vibrate as an entire unit and may also vibrate in two, three, four, or more segments depending on the standing wave pattern that is established on the string. See Figure 11-11(B–D). When a string is plucked or bowed, not only the fundamental mode but other higher modes of vibration may be present.

Suppose a string vibrates in two segments with a node in the middle as in Figure 11-11(B). Its vibrating frequency is twice that of the string vibrating as a single segment. Doubling the frequency of a sound wave raises the pitch one *octave*. When the string vibrates in four segments, its vibrating frequency (and that of the sound waves produced) is four times its fundamental frequency. The pitch of the sound produced is then two octaves above the fundamental. *The fundamental and the vibrational modes having frequencies that are whole number multiples of the fundamental are called* **harmonics.**

By this definition the fundamental is the *first harmonic* because it is *one* times the fundamental. The vibrational mode having a frequency twice that of the fundamental is the *second harmonic*. The vibrational mode of frequency *three* times that of the fundamental is the *third harmonic*, and so on. Oscillograms of a fundamental mode and several harmonics are shown in Figure 11-13.

## 11.11 Harmonics

**Figure 11-13** Oscillograms of (A) a fundamental, (B) the second harmonic, (C) the third harmonic, and (D) the fourth harmonic.

## 11.12 The quality of sound

**Figure 11-14** A strobe-flash view of a single string vibrating in its fundamental and second harmonic modes simultaneously.

*We interpret the harmonic content of a sound in terms of its quality.*

**Figure 11-15** Oscillograms of (A) a fundamental and second harmonic, (B) a fundamental and fourth harmonic, (C) the sound of a French horn, and (D) the sound of a trumpet.

It is not difficult to pick out the sounds produced by different instruments in an orchestra, even though they may be producing the same tone with equal intensity. The difference is a property of sound called *quality,* or *timbre*.

If the string of a sonometer is touched very lightly in the middle while being bowed near one end, it will vibrate in two segments and as a whole at the same time, as Figure 11-14 illustrates. The fundamental is audible, but added to it is the sound of the second harmonic. The combination is richer and fuller; the quality of the sound is improved by the addition of the second harmonic to the fundamental. See Figure 11-15(A). *The **quality** of a sound depends on the number of harmonics produced and their relative intensities*. When stringed instruments are played, they are bowed, plucked, or struck near one end to enhance the production of harmonics that blend with the fundamental and give a richer sound. See Figure 11-15(B).

The quality of the tones produced by orchestral instruments varies greatly. For example, the tone produced by a French horn consists almost entirely of the fundamental and the second harmonic. This harmonic content can be recognized by comparing Figures 11-15(A) and 11-15(C). The tonal quality of the trumpet is due to the intensity of its high-frequency harmonics. See Figure 11-15(D).

The frequency of a vibrating string is determined by its *length, diameter, tension,* and *density*. The strings of a piano produce tones with a wide range of frequencies. If we examine them we find that the strings that produce low-frequency tones are long, thick, and loose, while the strings that produce high-frequency tones are short, thin, and taut. One string produces a tone loud enough for the low notes, but three strings are needed to produce high notes of comparable loudness.

The conditions affecting the frequency of vibrating strings are summarized in four *laws of strings*.

*1. Law of lengths.* A musician may raise the pitch produced by a stringed instrument by shortening the vibrating length of the string. A violinist shortens the length of the A string about 2.5 cm to produce the note B. *The frequency of a string is inversely proportional to its length if all other factors are constant.*

$$\frac{f}{f'} = \frac{l'}{l}$$

Here $f$ and $f'$ are the frequencies corresponding to the lengths $l$ and $l'$.

*2. Law of diameters.* In a piano and other stringed instruments like the cello and the guitar, the strings that produce higher frequencies have smaller diameters. A string with a diameter of 0.1 cm has twice the frequency of a similar string 0.2 cm in diameter. *The frequency of a string is inversely proportional to its diameter if all other factors are constant.*

$$\frac{f}{f'} = \frac{d'}{d}$$

Here $f$ and $f'$ are the frequencies corresponding to the diameters $d$ and $d'$.

*3. Law of tensions.* When stringed instruments are tuned, the strings are tightened to increase their frequency or loosened to decrease it. *The frequency of a string is directly proportional to the square root of the tension on the string if all other factors are constant.*

$$\frac{f}{f'} = \frac{\sqrt{F}}{\sqrt{F'}}$$

Here $f$ and $f'$ are the frequencies corresponding to the tensions $F$ and $F'$. See the following example.

*4. Law of densities.* The more dense a string is, the lower its frequency. Usually three of the strings on a violin are of plain gut; the fourth is wound with fine wire to increase its density

## 11.13 The laws of strings

**Figure 11-16** How are the laws of strings used by the guitarist?

so that it can produce the low-frequency tones. *The frequency of a string is inversely proportional to the square root of its density if other factors are constant.*

$$\frac{f}{f'} = \frac{\sqrt{D'}}{\sqrt{D}}$$

Here $f$ and $f'$ are the frequencies corresponding to the densities $D$ and $D'$.

| | |
|---|---|
| **EXAMPLE** | *A string stretched with a force of 50.0 n produces the note C, 261.6 hz. What force must be applied to this string to make it produce the note C', one octave higher in frequency?* |
| **SOLUTION** | The frequency of C is 261.6 hz; that of C' is 523.2 hz. |

Basic equation:     $\dfrac{f}{f'} = \dfrac{\sqrt{F}}{\sqrt{F'}}$

Working equation:     $F' = \dfrac{f'^{2}F}{f^{2}} = \dfrac{(523.2 \text{ hz})^2 \times 50.0 \text{ n}}{(261.6 \text{ hz})^2} = 20\overline{0} \text{ n}$

---

**11.14 Forced vibrations**    When a tuning fork is struck with a rubber hammer, it vibrates at its fundamental frequency together with some low-order harmonics. The fundamental has a natural frequency that depends upon the fork length, thickness, and composition. When a key on a piano is struck, the piano string vibrates at its fundamental frequency and at harmonics of this frequency. The only external forces that affect these natural rates of vibration are friction and gravitation.

Suppose we strike a tuning fork and then press its stem against a table top. The tone becomes louder when the fork is in contact with the table because the fork *forces* the table top to vibrate with the same frequency. Since the table top has a much larger vibrating area than the tuning fork, these *forced vibrations* produce a more intense sound.

A vibrating violin string stretched tightly between two clamps does not produce a very intense sound. When the string is stretched across the bridge of a violin, however, the wood of the violin is forced to vibrate in response to the vibrations of the string; the intensity of the sound is increased by these forced vibrations. The sounding board of a piano acts in the same way to intensify the sounds produced by the vibrations of its strings.

Matched tuning forks

Resonant air column

Sound waves from nearby fork

## 11.15 Resonance

The two tuning forks in Figure 11-17 have the same frequency. They are mounted on sounding boxes that increase the intensity of the sound through forced vibrations. One end of each sounding box is open. Suppose we place these forks a short distance apart, with the open ends of the boxes toward each other. Now let us strike one fork and, after it has vibrated several seconds, touch its prongs to stop them. We find that the other fork is vibrating weakly. The compressions and rarefactions produced in the air by the first tuning fork act on the second fork in a regular fashion, causing it to vibrate. Such action is called *resonance,* or *sympathetic vibration.* A person who sings near a piano may cause the piano strings that produce similar frequencies to vibrate. Resonance occurs when the natural vibration rates of two objects are the same or when the vibration rate of one of them is equal to one of the harmonics of the other. If we changed the frequency of one of the tuning forks by adding mass to one of its prongs, we would alter the conditions of the experiment and no resonance would be evident. Both forks should have the same natural frequency to produce this resonant effect.

Figure 11-18 illustrates a method of producing resonance between a tuning fork and a column of air. The vibrating fork is held above the hollow cylinder immersed in water. The length of the air column is gradually increased by raising the cylinder. At the position shown in Figure 11-18(A) there is a marked increase in the loudness of the sound. Here the column of air in the tube vibrates vigorously at the frequency of the tuning fork and the two are in resonance.

This behavior is similar to the production of a standing wave on a stretched string. During resonance, a compression of the reflected wave unites with a compression of the direct wave and a rarefaction of the reflected wave unites with a rarefaction of the direct wave. The constructive superposition of the two waves in phase amplifies the sound.

The resonant air column is simply a standing longitudinal wave system. The water surface in Figure 11-18(A) closes the

**Figure 11-17** Resonance between two matched tuning forks.

**Figure 11-18** Resonance between a tuning fork and a vibrating air column. (A) and (B) give greater sound reinforcement than would any in-between positions.

(A)      (B)

lower end of the tube and prevents longitudinal displacement of the molecules of the air immediately adjacent to it. This termination effectively clamps the air column at the closed end and gives rise to a displacement node. Because the upper end of the tube is open it provides a free-ended termination for the air column and gives rise to a displacement antinode or loop. These are, respectively, shown in Figure 11-18(A) as **N** and **L.**

Because the air particles at the closed end of the tube are unable to undergo longitudinal displacement, they experience maximum changes in pressure. This position of a displacement node is also a pressure antinode, or a point of maximum pressure change. (Refer to Figure 11-3 for the phase relationship between displacement and pressure waves.) Compressions are reflected as compressions and rarefactions are reflected as rarefactions. This behavior amounts to a change in phase upon reflection from a rigid termination in the sense that the displacement vector of the air particles is inverted. See Figure 11-19(A).

The open end of the tube is a displacement loop and, consequently, a pressure node. Here the pressure remains at the constant value of the outside atmosphere and air rushes into and out of the tube as the column vibrates. It is this large movement of air at the open end of the tube that transfers energy to the atmosphere and provides the reinforcement of the sound produced by the tuning fork.

The fundamental frequency of the resonant column corresponds approximately to a displacement node at the closed end and an adjacent displacement loop at the open end, as shown in Figure 11-18(A). Since the distance separating a node and an adjacent loop of a standing wave is one-fourth wavelength, *the length of the closed tube is approximately one-fourth the wavelength of its fundamental resonant frequency*.

$$\lambda \simeq 4l$$

By applying a small empirical correction proportional to the diameter of the tube (because the motion of molecules of the air at the open end of the tube is not strictly in one dimension), we can state the relationship more precisely as follows:

$$\lambda = 4(l + 0.4d)$$

in which $\lambda$ is the wavelength of the fundamental resonant frequency, $l$ is the length of the closed tube, and $d$ is its diameter.

If the cylinder of Figure 11-18(A) is lifted higher out of the water, resonance will occur again when the length is three-

**Figure 11-19** A compression traveling from left to right is reflected at the right end as a compression in (A) and as a rarefaction in (B). The particle displacement vector is inverted by reflection in the closed tube, but it remains unchanged in the open tube because displacement of air layers in this tube is in the same direction for a rarefaction traveling to the left as for a condensation traveling to the right.

**Figure 11-20** The pipe organ uses many open and closed tubes or "pipes." How does the harmonic content of the resonant air columns differ in the open and closed pipes?

quarters of a wavelength. This length of air column also corresponds to a displacement node at the closed end and a loop at the open end and allows a standing wave to develop. See Figure 11-18(B). For a tube that is long enough, successively weaker resonance points could be found at $5/4\lambda$, $7/4\lambda$, etc. Thus *a closed tube is resonant at odd quarter-wavelength intervals.*

The quarter-wave resonant column for the fundamental frequency of the tuning fork of Figure 11-18(A) is three-quarters of a wavelength long for the third harmonic of this frequency. It is $5/4\lambda$ for the fifth harmonic and is $7/4\lambda$ for the seventh harmonic. Therefore *the resonant frequencies of a closed tube are harmonics, but only odd harmonics of the fundamental mode are present.* This relationship is illustrated in Figure 11-21.

Many musical instruments employ vibrating air columns open at one end and closed at the other *(closed tube)* or open at both ends *(open tube)*. From the above discussion we have shown that the normal modes of oscillation of air columns are characterized by

*1. a displacement node (or pressure loop) at a closed end,* and
*2. a displacement loop (or pressure node) at an open end.*

Compressions traveling in an open tube are reflected at the open ends as rarefactions and rarefactions are reflected as compressions. In such reflections, the longitudinal displacement vector of the air particles is *not* inverted and in this sense there is

**Figure 11-21** The normal modes of oscillation of a closed tube. The fundamental frequency is half that of an open tube of the same length, and only odd harmonics are produced.

Figure 11-22 The normal modes of oscillation of an open tube. The fundamental frequency is twice that of a closed tube of the same length, and all harmonics are produced.

no change in phase at the open termination of the air column. This condition is illustrated in Figure 11-19(B).

The fundamental frequency of a resonant air column in an open tube corresponds approximately to displacement loops at opposite ends and a displacement node in the middle as shown in Figure 11-22(A). Since adjacent loops of a standing wave are one-half wavelength apart, *the length of an open tube is approximately one-half the wavelength of its fundamental resonant frequency.*

$$\lambda \simeq 2l$$

Again, by applying a small empirical correction proportional to the diameter of the tube, we can state the relationship more precisely as follows:

$$\lambda = 2(l + 0.8d)$$

in which $\lambda$ is the wavelength of the fundamental resonant frequency, $l$ is the length of the open tube, and $d$ is its diameter.

An open tube, which is a half-wave resonant column at its fundamental frequency, is a full wavelength long at the second harmonic of this frequency. It is $3/2\,\lambda$ at the third harmonic. In each case displacement loops occur at both open ends and the column resonates in these modes. Therefore *the resonant frequencies of an open tube are harmonics, and all harmonics of the fundamental mode are present.* See Figure 11-22.

The quality of a musical tone is generally enhanced by its harmonic content. The open tube resonator has both odd and even harmonics of the fundamental mode present, whereas the closed tube resonator has only odd harmonics. Thus the quality of the sounds from open tubes and closed tubes is not the same.

## 11.16 Beats

We have already discussed interference of transverse waves in strings and of water waves in the ripple tank in Chapter 10. We have been concerned with standing waves in resonant air columns in the preceding section. There is abundant experimental evidence that two or more wave disturbances can travel through the same medium independently of one another. The superposition principle shows us that the displacement of a particle of a medium at any time is the vector sum of the displacements it would experience from the individual waves acting alone.

A standing wave is formed by two wave trains of the same frequency and amplitude traveling through a medium in opposite directions. We are generally concerned with the conditions or behavior of the space in which the standing wave exists. This generalization is true for resonant air columns used in musical instruments. The standing wave is characterized by an amplitude *that varies with distance, or position in space.*

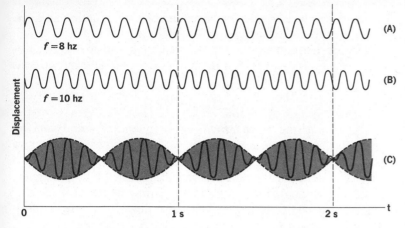

**Figure 11-23** Beats. Waves (A) and (B) of slightly different frequencies combine to give a wave (C) that varies in amplitude with time.

Two wave trains of slightly different frequencies traveling in the same direction through a medium will interfere in a different way. At any fixed point in the medium through which the waves pass, their superposition gives a wave characterized by an amplitude *that varies with time*.

In Figure 11-23 the resultant displacement of two wave trains of slightly different frequencies is plotted as a function of time. In curve (A) the frequency is 8 hz, and in (B) it is 10 hz. Curve (C) shows the combined effect of these two waves at a fixed point in their pathway. This resultant wave varies periodically in amplitude with time. Such amplitude pulsations are called *beats*.

Observe that waves (A) and (B) come into phase two times each second and out of phase the same number of times each second. The *beat frequency* can be described as *two beats per second*. *The number of beats per second equals the difference between the frequencies of the component waves*.

When the interfering frequencies are audible sounds, the amplitude variations, or beats, are recognized as variations in loudness. The average human ear can distinguish beats up to a frequency of approximately ten per second.

The beat phenomenon is frequently used to tune vibrating systems with great precision. Two vibrating strings can be tuned to the same frequency by adjusting the tension of one until the beats disappear. This procedure is called "zero beating." The piano tuner adjusts frequencies precisely by systematically beating harmonics of notes against each other.

To illustrate, let us assume that two vibrating strings have fundamental frequencies of 165 hz and 325 hz respectively. A person (who possesses a "trained" ear) may distinguish 5 beats per second as a consequence of the 325-hz tone beating against the second harmonic of the 165-hz tone.

A precision tuning fork vibrates only in its fundamental mode and produces a tone that is free of harmonics. Suppose a tuning fork of frequency 260 hz is sounded together with one of 264 hz.

A listener will hear 4 beats each second of sound having an average frequency of 262 hz.

If the lower frequency is represented by $f_l$ and the higher frequency by $f_h$, the average frequency $f_{av}$ can be expressed as follows:

$$f_{av} = 1/2(f_l + f_h)$$

The sound is a sine wave of average frequency $f_{av}$ and varying amplitude that reaches a maximum $(f_h - f_l)$ times each second (the beat frequency). When the frequency separation of the two tones is too large for the beats to be distinguished by the listener, a difference *tone* of frequency $(f_h - f_l)$ may be heard if the difference frequency falls within the audio range.

# summary

Sound is a longitudinal disturbance consisting of a succession of compressions and rarefactions to which the ear is sensitive. The term also applies to similar disturbances above and below the normal range of hearing. A medium having elastic and inertial properties is required for its propagation. The intensity of a sound is the rate at which the wave energy flows through a unit area. The sensory response to sound intensity is loudness, the sensory response to frequency is pitch, and the sensory response to harmonic content is tonal quality.

The sensory response to sounds is nonlinear. Minimum intensity levels for hearing various sound frequencies define the threshold of hearing. Upper intensities that produce pain rather than increased loudness define a threshold of pain. The change in pitch heard when there is relative motion between an observer and a constant-frequency source is called the Doppler effect.

When set in motion, sound generators such as taut strings and air columns vibrate at their fundamental and various harmonic frequencies. The greater the harmonic content of a sound produced by a musical instrument, the higher is its quality and the more pleasing is the auditory response. The frequency of a vibrating string is determined by its length, diameter, tension, and density. The laws of strings enunciate the relationships between frequency and these physical factors.

The intensity of a sound generated by a vibrating source can be increased by a sounding board forced to vibrate at the sound frequency. When forced vibrations are at the natural frequency of the reinforcing body (resonance), maximum reinforcement occurs.

Resonant air columns in the form of open and closed tubes are standing longitudinal wave systems. The resonant length of a closed tube is approximately one-fourth the wavelength of its fundamental frequency, and it resonates at odd harmonics of the fundamental mode. The resonant length of an open tube is approximately one-half the wavelength of its fundamental frequency, and it resonates at all harmonics of the fundamental mode.

Two wave trains of slightly different frequencies traveling in the same direction in a medium interfere in a way characterized by an amplitude that varies with time at any fixed point in the medium. The amplitude pulsations are called beats. The number of beats per second is the difference between the frequencies of the interfering waves.

# questions

GROUP A

1. (a) Why does a tuning fork sound louder when its stem is pressed against a table top? (b) Why doesn't its sound last as long?
2. What conditions are necessary to produce resonance?
3. To produce the best resonance, how must the length of a closed tube compare with the wavelength of the sound?
4. To produce the best resonance, how must the length of an open tube compare with the wavelength of the sound?

5. How do the frequencies of notes an octave apart compare?

6. (a) What is a fundamental? (b) How does a string vibrate to produce the fundamental?

7. Which law of strings is used (a) in tuning a guitar; (b) in playing the instrument?

8. In sound waves, what is (a) constructive interference; (b) destructive interference? (c) What are beats?

GROUP B

9. Why is it easy to distinguish between the sound produced by a piano and a trombone even if both play the same note?

10. How do the strings on a piano illustrate the laws of strings?

11. Suggest a function of the bridge between the strings and the sounding board of a musical instrument such as a cello.

12. Suppose a piano tuner has tuned the notes middle C and G to frequencies of 262 hz and 392 hz respectively. The note G is then beat against low C, which is one octave below middle C. What should be heard to indicate that low C has been adjusted to its proper frequency?

13. Given two tuning forks that vibrate at the same frequency, suggest a way to hear beats between them.

# problems

GROUP A

1. What is the frequency of a tuning fork that resonates with an open tube 25.0 cm long and 2.0 cm in diameter when the temperature is 20°C?

2. A tuning fork, frequency 384 hz, produces resonance with a closed tube 20.0 cm long and 4.0 cm in diameter. What is the speed of sound?

3. A tuning fork has a frequency of 440 hz. If another fork of slightly lower pitch is sounded at the same time, the beats produced are 5/s. What is the frequency of the second tuning fork?

4. How many beats will be heard each second when a string, frequency 288 hz, is plucked simultaneously with another string, frequency 296 hz?

5. If the string on a violin is 25.4 cm long and produces a fundamental tone of frequency $44\overline{0}$ hz, by how much must it be shortened to produce a tone of frequency 523.3 hz?

6. Compare the frequency of one string 25 cm long and 0.50 mm in diameter with that of another 100 cm long and 0.25 mm in diameter, assuming all other factors are constant.

7. Two tuning forks of $32\overline{0}$ hz and 324 hz are sounded simultaneously. What sound will the listener hear?

GROUP B

8. When a string 0.500 m long is stretched with a force of $2.50 \times 10^2$ n, its frequency is $44\overline{0}$ hz. If the string is shortened to 0.400 m and the stretching force is increased to $5.00 \times 10^2$ n, what is the new frequency?

9. Sound intensity at the hearing threshold is approximately $10^{-14}$ w/cm² for a sound frequency of 200 hz. The pain threshold is reached for sound at this frequency when the intensity is increased by 110 db. Calculate the intensity of this sound at the pain threshold.

10. Middle C on the piano keyboard is tuned to 261.6 hz when the temperature is 20.0°C. Calculate (a) the frequency, and (b) the wavelength in air of the highest note on the keyboard that is exactly 4 octaves above middle C.

11. An organ pipe open at both ends is 1.23 m long and has a diameter of 10 cm. (a) What is its fundamental frequency when the air temperature is 15°C? (b) What are the frequencies of the two lowest harmonics produced along with the fundamental tone?

12. An organ pipe closed at one end is 0.76 m long and has a diameter of 5.0 cm. The air temperature is 12°C. (a) Determine its fundamental frequency. (b) What are the frequencies of the two lowest harmonics produced along with this fundamental tone?

# technology

the engineer's most powerful scientific tool is physics. Through the knowledge and application of the principles of physics, technological achievements in civil and automotive engineering are continually being made. The cars in which we ride; the roads, tunnels, and bridges we traverse; and the dams that control our water supply and provide hydroelectric power are examples. Bridges must be designed to withstand tension and compression. The type of bridge—beam, arch, suspension, cantilever—is determined by span and weight requirements. Every bridge has a theoretical span limit. Dams can be of two types—embankment or concrete. The design depends on the dam's location, and consideration must be given to drainage, water pressure, rock structure and fissures, and the construction of an interim dam. Tunnels through hard rock are usually built by drilling and blasting. In underwater tunnels pressurization of the work area is necessary so that the internal air pressure exceeds the water pressure. Prefabricated steel or concrete sections of tunnel are increasingly being used. They are floated into position and sunk into a trench dredged in the lake or river bed.

*Top: The Poughkeepsie Railroad Bridge, completed in 1889, is a steel, cantilever, truss bridge crossing the Hudson River, NY.*

*Center: The Chesapeake Bay Bridge-Tunnel, VA, is a 28.4-km crossing that includes 2 bridges, 2 tunnels, and 4 specially constructed islands. This engineering feat took 3½ years to complete.*

*Bottom: The Normandy Dam, part of the TVA, under construction.*

*Above: Aided by a computer, an automotive engineer reviews and alters specifications for the purpose of improving car design.*

*Top right: Artist's concept of an electric test car to be built as part of the U.S. Department of Energy's electric vehicle technology program. The car features a flywheel for better acceleration.*

*Right: This artist's concept of a truck of the future utilizes aerodynamic principles to achieve clean, smooth shapes that will greatly reduce cost-per-mile operation.*

*Below: Aerial view of the intricate Interstate 26/U.S. Route 176 interchange, SC.*

**PHOTO ESSAY**

# The Nature of Light

## WAVES AND PARTICLES

### 12.1 Properties of light

The general properties of waves were described in Chapter 10. They may be summarized as follows:

*1. Propagation* within a uniform medium is along straight lines.

*2. Reflection* occurs at the surface, or boundary, of a medium.

*3. Refraction,* or bending, may occur where a change of speed is experienced.

*4. Interference* is found where two waves are superposed.

*5. Diffraction,* or bending around corners, takes place when waves pass the edges of obstructions.

These properties are easily recognized in the behavior of sound and water waves. Such disturbances occur in matter, the particles of the medium being set in motion about their equilibrium positions by the passing waves.

Matter is not required for the propagation of light. While light does pass readily through certain kinds of matter, its transmission is unhindered in interstellar space or through an evacuated vessel.

The regular reflection of light from smooth surfaces was known in the time of Plato, almost twenty-four hundred years ago. (Reflection is the subject of Chapter 13.)

The refraction of light at the interface (boundary) of two transparent media of different optical densities was observed by the Greeks as early as the second century A.D. The Arabian mathematician Alhazen (965–1038) studied the refraction of light and disputed the ancient theory that visual rays emanated from the eye. He demonstrated the refractive behavior of light as it passed from one medium into another of greater optical density. See Figure 12-1. He believed that the angles of incidence and refraction were

**Figure 12-1** The Arabian mathematician Alhazen studied the refraction of light nearly a thousand years ago.

related, but was unable to determine how they were related. This relationship, now known as *Snell's law*, was established six hundred years later. (Refraction and Snell's law are discussed in Chapter 14.)

The shapes of shadows and the practical use of sight lines for placing objects in a straight line give evidence of the straight-line, or rectilinear, propagation of light. Greek philosophers were familiar with this property of light. Sir Isaac Newton conducted experiments on the separation of light into colors by means of a prism and was aware of the colors produced by thin films.

Rectilinear propagation, reflection, and refraction are the principal light phenomena that were familiar to observers in the seventeenth century. It must have been evident to Newton and his contemporaries that since the transmission of energy from one place to another was involved, only two general theories could explain these properties of light.

*Sir Isaac Newton lived from 1642 to 1727.*

In general, energy can be propagated either by particles of matter or by wave disturbances traveling from one place to another. A window pane may be shattered by a moving object, such as a baseball thrown from a distance, or by the concussion ("shock wave") from a distant explosion.

Arguments favoring both a particle (corpuscular) theory and a wave theory were plausible when applied to the properties of light observed in the seventeenth century. The principal advocate of the corpuscular theory was Newton, whose arguments were supported by the French mathematical physicist and astronomer Laplace (1749–1827). The wave theory was upheld principally by Christian Huygens (*hi*-ganz) (1629–1695), a Dutch mathematician, physicist, and astronomer. He was supported by Robert Hooke of England. Because of the plausibility of both theories a scientific debate concerning the nature of light developed between the followers of Newton and the followers of Huygens and continued unresolved for more than a century. What are some of the arguments that support each of these classical theories of light?

*The light phenomena known in Newton's time are rectilinear propagation, reflection, and refraction.*

## 12.2 The corpuscular theory

Sir Isaac Newton believed that light consists of streams of tiny particles, which he called "corpuscles," emanating from a luminous source. Let us examine the arguments used by those who believed the particle theory best explained the various light phenomena known to them.

*1. Rectilinear propagation.* A ball thrown into space follows a curved path because of the influence of gravity. Yet if the ball is thrown with greater and greater speed, we know that its path curves less and less. We can easily imagine minute particles traveling at such enormous speed that their paths form essentially straight lines.

Newton experienced no difficulty in explaining the rectilinear

**(A)**

**(B)**

**Figure 12-2** The rebound of a steel ball from a resilient surface resembles the reflection of light from a mirror surface. This example was used as an early argument to "prove" that light rays were streams of tiny particles.

propagation of light by means of his particle model. In fact, this property of light provided the supporters of the corpuscular theory with one of their strongest arguments against a wave theory. How, they asked, could waves travel in straight lines? A sound can easily be heard around the corner of an obstruction, but a light certainly cannot be seen from behind an obstruction. The former is unquestionably a wave phenomenon. How can the latter also be one?

The simple and direct explanation of rectilinear propagation provided by the particle model of light, together with the great prestige of Sir Isaac Newton, were largely responsible for the preference shown for the corpuscular theory during the seventeenth and eighteenth centuries.

*2. Reflection.* Where light is incident on a smooth surface, such as a mirror, we know that it is regularly reflected. How do particles behave under similar circumstances? Steel ball bearings thrown against a smooth steel plate rebound in much the same way light is reflected. Perfectly elastic particles rebounding from a resilient surface, then, could provide a suitable model for the reflection of light. See Figure 12-2.

*3. Refraction.* Newton was able to demonstrate the nature of refraction by means of his particle model. We can duplicate this experimentally by arranging two level surfaces, one higher than the other, with their adjacent edges joined by an incline, as shown in Figure 12-3. A ball may be rolled across the upper surface, down the incline, and across the lower surface. Of course, it will experience an acceleration due to the force of gravity while rolling down the incline and will move across the lower surface at a higher speed than it had initially.

Suppose the ball is set rolling on the higher surface toward the incline at a given angle with the normal to the edge. At the incline, the accelerating force exerts a pull on the ball causing it to roll across the lower surface at a smaller angle with the normal to its edge. Now if we think of the upper surface as representing air, the lower surface as an optically more dense medium like water, and

**Figure 12-3** A ball bearing rolling from a higher to a lower surface illustrates one aspect of the refraction of light. In what way does this rolling-ball model of refraction fail?

the incline as the interface of the two transmitting media, the rolling ball behaves as particles of light being redirected, or refracted, as they pass from air into water.

By varying the grade of the incline while maintaining both constant rolling speed and constant angle with the normal on the upper surface, the refractive characteristics of different transmitting media can be illustrated by the rolling-ball model.

Newton believed that water attracted the approaching particles of light in much the same way gravity attracts the rolling ball on the incline. The rolling-ball experiments imply, as they did to Newton, that light particles accelerate as they pass from air into a medium of greater optical density like water or glass. The corpuscular theory required that the speed of light in water be higher than the speed of light in air. Newton recognized that if it should ever be determined that the speed of light in water is lower than the speed of light in air, his corpuscular theory would have to be abandoned. This uncertainty about the speed of light in water remained unresolved for one hundred twenty-three years after Newton's death. In 1850 the French physicist Jean Foucault (foo-*koh*) (1819–1868) demonstrated experimentally that the speed of light in water is indeed lower than the speed of light in air. This condition was predicted by the wave theory.

*Physicist Foucault is recognized primarily for his pendulum experiment, which demonstrates that the earth rotates on its axis in space. The Foucault pendulum experiment is now repeated daily in science museums throughout the world.*

## 12.3 The wave theory

Christian Huygens is generally considered to be the founder of the wave theory of light. Although somewhat different in its modern form, Huygens' basic concept is still very useful to us in predicting and interpreting the behavior of light. Let us recall a familiar characteristic of water waves as an introduction to this important principle.

If a stone is dropped into a pool of quiet water, it creates a disturbance in the water and a series of concentric waves travels out from the disturbance point. The stone quickly comes to rest on the bottom of the pool, so its action on the water is of short duration. However, wave disturbances persist for a considerable time thereafter and cannot reasonably be attributed to any activity on the part of the stone. It must be that the disturbances existing at all points along the wave fronts at one instant of time generate those in existence at the next instant.

Huygens recognized this logical deduction as a basic aspect of wave behavior and devised a geometric method of finding new wave fronts. His concept, published in 1690 and now recognized as **Huygens' principle,** may be stated as follows: *Each point on a wave front may be regarded as a new source of disturbance.*

According to this principle, a wave front originating at a source **S** in Figure 12-4(A) arrives at the position **AB.** Each point in this wave front may be considered as a secondary source sending out wavelets. Thus from points **1, 2, 3,** etc., a series of wavelets

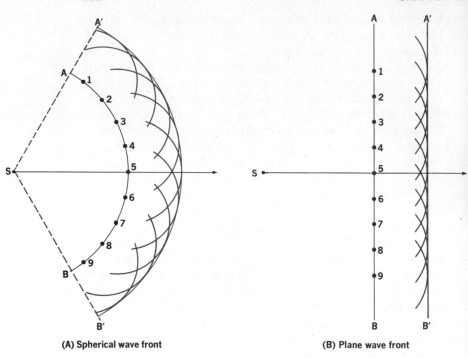

(A) Spherical wave front                    (B) Plane wave front

**Figure 12-4** By Huygens' principle, every point on an advancing wave front is regarded as a source of disturbance.

develops simultaneously. After a time, $t$, these wavelets have a radius equal to $vt$, where $v$ is the velocity of the wave.

The principle further states that the surface **A′B′**, tangent to all the wavelets, constitutes the new wave front. It is apparent from Figure 12-4 that spherical wave fronts are propagated from spherical waves and plane wave fronts from plane waves.

The wave theory treats light as a train of waves having wave fronts perpendicular to the paths of the light rays. In contrast to the particle model discussed earlier, the light energy is considered to be distributed uniformly over the advancing wave front. Huygens thought of a ray merely as a line of direction of waves propagated from a light source.

The supporters of the wave theory were able to satisfactorily explain reflection and refraction of light. The explanation of refraction required that the speed of light in optically dense media such as water and glass be *lower* than the speed of light in air. They had trouble, however, explaining rectilinear propagation. This was the primary reason Newton rejected the wave theory.

Before the nineteenth century, interference of light was unknown and the speed of light in such media as water and glass had not been measured. Diffraction fringes or shadows had been observed as early as the seventeenth century. In the absence of knowledge of interference, however, neither Newton nor Huygens attached much significance to this diffraction phenomenon.

In 1801 the interference of light was discovered. This was followed in 1816 by the explanation of diffraction based on interference principles. (Interference and diffraction are discussed in Chapter 15.)

These two phenomena imply a wave character and cannot be satisfactorily explained by the behavior of particles. Thus despite the great prestige of Sir Isaac Newton, the corpuscular theory was largely abandoned in favor of the wave theory. The final blow to the corpuscular theory came when Foucault found that the speed of light in water was lower than the speed of light in air. Through the remainder of the nineteenth century the wave concept supplied the basic laws from which came remarkable advances in optical theory and technology.

*The corpuscular theory was largely abandoned in favor of the wave theory following the discovery of interference and diffraction of light. Note that the speed of light in water had not yet been measured.*

## 12.4 The electromagnetic theory

Hot objects transfer heat energy by radiation. If the temperature is high enough, these objects radiate light as well as heat. If a light source is blocked off from an observer, its heating effect is cut off as well. For this reason, a cloud that obscures the sun's light cuts off some of the sun's heat at the same time.

The English physicist Michael Faraday (1791–1867) became concerned with the transfer of another kind of energy while investigating the attraction and repulsion of electrically charged bodies. In 1831 these experiments led him to the principle of the electric generator.

Faraday's practical mind required a model to interpret and explain physical phenomena. It was difficult for him to visualize electrically charged objects attracting or repelling each other at some distance with nothing taking place in the intervening space. Thus he conceived a space under stress and visualized *tubes of force* between charged bodies.

Faraday was not an astute mathematician and so did not put his model for this "transmission of electric force" into abstract mathematical form.

The Scottish mathematical physicist James Clerk Maxwell (1831–1879) set out to determine the properties of a medium that would transmit the energies of heat, light, and electricity. By the year 1865 he had developed a series of mathematical equations from which he predicted that all three are propagated in free space at the speed of light as *electromagnetic disturbances*. This unification, the *electromagnetic theory,* brought into common focus the various phenomena of radiation. Maxwell determined that the energy of an electromagnetic wave is equally divided between an electric field and a magnetic field, each perpendicular to the other, and both perpendicular to the direction of propagation of the wave. In Section 10.1 we defined a wave as a periodic disturbance that propagates itself through a medium or space. In this sense, *an electromagnetic wave is a periodic disturbance involving electric*

**Figure 12-5** Before he was fifteen years old, James Clerk Maxwell (1831–1879), the Scottish theoretical physicist, wrote papers that were recognized for their scientific value. His laws of electromagnetic waves (Maxwell's equations) have the same role in electromagnetism that Newton's laws of gravitation and motion have in mechanics.

**Figure 12-6** Electromagnetic wave. The electric and magnetic fields are each at right angles to the direction of propagation. This is a graph of the two fields at a given instant.

**Figure 12-7** Heinrich Hertz, the German experimental physicist whose research provided the experimental confirmation of the electromagnetic waves predicted by Maxwell.

*and magnetic forces*. A model of an electromagnetic wave at a given instant is shown in Figure 12-6.

By 1885 experimental confirmation of the electromagnetic theory was achieved by the German physicist Heinrich Rudolph Hertz (1857–1894). Hertz showed that light transmissions and electrically generated waves are of the same nature. Of course, many of their properties are quite different because of the very great differences in frequency.

Maxwell's theory of electromagnetic waves seemed to provide the final architecture for optical theory; all known optical effects could now be fully explained. Many physicists felt at this time that all the significant laws of physics had been discovered and that there was little left to do other than develop new and more sophisticated techniques for measuring everything more accurately. In this connection Hertz stated, ''The wave theory of light is, from the point of view of human beings, a certainty.'' Ironically, it was Hertz who was soon to discover a most important phenomenon having to do with the absorption of light energy, one that would create a dilemma involving the wave theory and at the same time set the stage for the *new physics* that was to emerge in the early years of the twentieth century.

## 12.5 The electromagnetic spectrum

Electromagnetic energy can be detected and measured by physical means only when it is intercepted by matter and changed into another form of energy such as thermal, electric, kinetic, potential, or chemical energy. Today, the electromagnetic spectrum is known to consist of a tremendous range of radiation frequencies extending from about 10 hz to more than $10^{25}$ hz. Since all electromagnetic radiations travel in free space with a speed of $3 \times 10^8$ meters per second, the range of wavelengths is from about $3 \times 10^7$ meters in the low-frequency region to less than $3 \times 10^{-17}$ meters in the high-frequency region. See Figure 12-8. In angstroms (Å), the units commonly used to express the wave-

HARD GAMMA RAYS (cosmic rays) are extremely high energy protons moving through space. When they collide with nuclei in the earth's atmosphere, a descending shower of high-energy particles occurs.

GAMMA RAYS are photons of great penetrating power emitted by radioactive elements and as a byproduct of a nuclear reaction.

X RAYS are high-energy radiations created by a stream of high-speed electrons bombarding a metal plate in a vacuum. Wavelengths are comparable to the size of atoms.

ULTRAVIOLET RADIATION from the sun is largely absorbed in the atmosphere. It has germicidal, photochemical, photoelectric, and fluorescent effects. Sun lamps and arc lights are sources also.

OPTICAL SPECTRUM includes the visible light region, and the near infrared and near ultraviolet which are invisible but can be recorded on photographic film.

INFRARED RADIATION is freely transmitted through haze and is widely used for heating and drying.

RADIO WAVES cover a broad band of the spectrum from a few millimeters to approximately 10 kilometers wavelengths and accomodate numerous modes of communication.

POWER FREQUENCIES are produced by electric generators and, since wavelengths range from about $10^2$ to $10^4$ kilometers, the energy is transferred by transmission lines.

**Figure 12-8**  The electromagnetic spectrum.

**Figure 12-9** X-ray photograph of a sea horse. Locate the X-ray region of the electromagnetic spectrum in Figure 12-8.

lengths of electromagnetic radiations, the range is from $3 \times 10^{17}$ Å to $3 \times 10^{-7}$ Å. One angstrom equals $10^{-10}$ m.

Eight major regions of the electromagnetic spectrum are commonly recognized. These regions are based on the general character of the radiations and are identified in Figure 12-8. All kinds of electronic transmissions are accommodated in the *radio-wave* region. Commercial electricity falls within the *power* region. Observe the very small region occupied by the *visible spectrum*.

The optical spectrum includes those radiations, commonly referred to as light, that can be detected visually. They range from approximately 7600 Å to 4000 Å. Accordingly, **light** *may be defined as radiant energy that a human observer can see*. The optical spectrum also extends into the near infrared and into the near ultraviolet. Although our eyes cannot see these radiations, they can be detected by means of photographic film.

## 12.6 The photoelectric effect

As mentioned in Section 12.4, Hertz conducted experiments that led to confirmation of the electromagnetic theory. While studying the radiation characteristics of oscillatory discharges, he observed that a spark discharge occurred more readily between two charged spheres when they were illuminated by another spark discharge. At about the same time other investigators found that negatively charged zinc plates lost their charge when illuminated by the ultraviolet radiations from an arc lamp. Positively charged plates, on the other hand, were not discharged when similarly illuminated.

Observations of the peculiar effects of ultraviolet radiation on metal surfaces led to the discovery of the photoelectric effect, a phenomenon that defied explanation based on the electromagnetic wave theory of light.

Figure 12-10 shows two freshly polished zinc plates **A** and **B** that are sealed in an evacuated tube having a quartz window and are connected externally to a battery and galvanometer (a sensitive current-indicating meter). The quartz window transmits ultraviolet radiation, which does not pass through glass. The galvanometer indicates a small current in the circuit when ultraviolet light falls on the negative plate **A.** If a sensitive electrometer circuit is substituted for the battery, it may be shown that the plate exposed to the ultraviolet light acquires a positive charge.

The results of these experiments imply that the action of the light on the zinc plate causes it to lose electrons. The German physicist Philipp Lenard (1862–1947) published the results of the first quantitative studies of the photoelectric phenomenon in 1902. By measuring the charge-to-mass ratio of the negative electricity derived from an aluminum plate illuminated by ultraviolet light, he was able to prove that electrons were ejected from the metal surface. Such electrons are called *photoelectrons*. Subsequent

**Figure 12-10** Apparatus for demonstrating the photoelectric effect.

investigations have shown that all substances exhibit photo-emission of electrons. *The emission of electrons by a substance when illuminated by electromagnetic radiation is known as the* **photoelectric effect.**

---

Plate **B** of Figure 12-10, having a positive potential $V$ with respect to the emitter plate **A,** acts as a collector of photoelectrons ejected from the emitter. If the positive potential is increased enough, all photoelectrons are collected by plate **B** and the photoelectric current $I$ reaches a certain limiting or *saturation* magnitude.

Curve **a** of Figure 12-11 is a graph of photoelectric current as a function of collector plate potential for a given source of light. Curve **b** shows the result of doubling the intensity of the light. Observe that the magnitude of the saturation current is doubled. This means, of course, that the rate of emission of photoelectrons is doubled. Here we have evidence of the *first law of photo-electric emission: The rate of emission of photoelectrons is directly proportional to the intensity of the incident light.*

For an electron to escape through the surface of a metal, work must be done against the forces that bind it within the surface. This work is known as the *work function*. Photoelectrons must acquire from the incident light radiation the energy needed to overcome this surface barrier. If electrons acquire less energy than the work function of the metal, they cannot be ejected. On the other hand, if they acquire more energy than is required to pass through the surface, the excess appears as kinetic energy and consequently as velocity of the photoelectrons.

We may assume that light penetrates a few atom layers into the metal and that the photoelectric effect will occur at varying depths beneath the surface. Photoelectrons ejected from atom layers below the surface will lose energy through collisions in reaching the surface and must then give up energy equal to the work function of the metal in escaping through the surface. Photoelectrons ejected from the surface layer of atoms lose only the energy necessary to overcome the surface attractions. Thus in any photoelectric phenomenon we should expect photoelectrons to be emitted at various velocities ranging up to a maximum value possessed by electrons having their origin in the surface layer of atoms.

We can test the logic of these deductions by experimenting further with the photoelectric cell of Figure 12-10. A positive potential of a few volts on the collector plate **B** produces a saturation current as shown in Figure 12-11. If the collector plate potential is lowered towards zero, the photoelectric current decreases slightly, but at zero potential may still be close to the saturation magnitude.

## 12.7 Laws of photoelectric emission

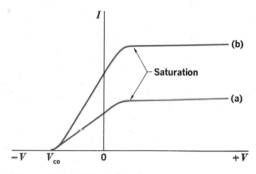

**Figure 12-11** Photoelectric current as a function of collector plate potential. Curve (b) shows the effect of doubling the intensity of the same incident light.

As the collector plate potential is made slightly negative with respect to the emitter, the photoelectric current decreases also. By increasing this negative potential a value is reached where the photoelectric current drops to zero. This is called the *stopping,* or *cut-off,* potential $V_{co}$ and is shown in Figure 12-11.

A negative potential on the collector plate repels the photoelectrons, tending to turn them back to the emitter plate. Only those electrons having enough kinetic energy and velocity to overcome this repulsion reach the collector. As the cut-off potential is approached, only those photoelectrons with the highest velocity reach the collector. These are the electrons with the maximum kinetic energy that are emitted from the surface layer of the metal. At the cut-off potential even these electrons are repelled and turned back to the emitter.

Thus the negative collector potentials, which repel rather than attract photoelectrons, reveal something about the kinetic energy distribution of the ejected electrons. As this potential is made more negative a nearly linear decrease in photoelectron current shows us that the photoelectrons do have a variety of velocities. The cut-off potential measures the kinetic energy of the *fastest* photoelectrons.

From curves **a** and **b** shown in Figure 12-11 observe that the photoelectric currents produced by different intensities of incident light from a certain source reach zero at the same collector potential. Thus the cut-off potential for a given photoelectric system and *the velocity of the electrons expelled* are independent of the intensity of the light source. From these observations we may formulate a **second law of photoelectric emission:** *The kinetic energy of photoelectrons is independent of the intensity of the incident light.*

The American physicist Robert A. Millikan (1868–1953) performed many experiments with various emitters and light sources. By illuminating emitters made of sodium metal with light radiations of different frequencies, Millikan found that the cut-off potential had different values for the various frequencies of incident light. By plotting the cut-off potentials $V_{co}$ as a function of light frequencies $f$ the straight line shown in Figure 12-12 is obtained. Millikan demonstrated that *the cut-off potential depends only on the frequency of the incident light.*

Recalling that the cut-off potential measures the kinetic energy of the fastest photoelectrons ejected in a particular photoelectric system, we must conclude that the *maximum kinetic energy of photoelectrons increases with the frequency of the light illuminating the emitter.*

Other physicists, notably A. L. Hughes at the Cavendish Laboratory in England and K. T. Compton at Princeton University, obtained similar results in numerous experiments. All these experiments further showed that *for each kind of surface*

---

*The cut-off potential "cuts off" the photoelectric current at the collector plate.*

*The cut-off potential measures the maximum kinetic energy of photoelectrons.*

*The second law of photoelectric emission will make trouble for the wave theory.*

**Figure 12-12** A plot of cut-off potentials for sodium as measured by Millikan at various frequencies of illumination. The cut-off frequency of sodium is 4.4 × 10¹⁴ hz.

*there is a characteristic threshold or cut-off frequency $f_{co}$ be-low which the photoelectric emission of electrons ceases* no mat-ter how intense the illumination.

Only a few elements, in particular the alkali metals, exhibit photoelectric emission with ordinary visible light. The cut-off frequency of cesium is in the infrared region of the electromag-netic spectrum. Millikan determined the $f_{co}$ of sodium to be $4.4 \times 10^{14}$ hz, which is red light with a wavelength of about 6800 Å. The cut-off frequency of potassium is in the visible green region. Those of copper and platinum are in the ultraviolet and deep ultraviolet.

For photoelectric emission from any surface, the incident light radiation must contain frequencies higher than the cutoff fre-quency characteristic of that surface. The maximum kinetic energy of photoelectrons emitted from any surface can be in-creased only by raising the frequency of the light illuminating the surface. These facts provide us with a ***third law of photo-electric emission:*** *Within the region of effective frequencies, the maximum kinetic energy of photoelectrons varies directly with the difference between the frequency of the incident light and the cut-off frequency.*

*The number of materials available as photoelectric emitters with visible light is limited.*

## 12.8 Failures of the wave theory

The experiments of Hertz, together with those which followed, confirmed that Maxwell's electromagnetic theory correctly de-scribes the transmission of light and other kinds of radiation. This wave theory requires the radiated energy to be distributed uniformly and continuously over a wave front. The higher the intensity of the radiating source, the greater should be the energy distributed over the wave front.

The first law of photoelectric emission does not imply any deviation from the electromagnetic theory since the magnitude of the photoelectric current is proportional to the incident light intensity. The surprising thing is that the velocity of the photo-electrons is not raised with an increase in the intensity of the illumination on the surface of an emitter, contrary to what the wave theory suggests. Measurements of emission cut-off poten-tials over very large ranges of intensities show that the maximum kinetic energy of photoelectrons is independent of the light intensity.

According to the wave theory, light of any frequency should cause photoelectric emission provided it is intense enough. Ex-periments show, however, that all substances have characteristic cut-off frequencies below which emission does not occur, no matter how intense the illumination. On the other hand, a very feeble light containing frequencies above the threshold value causes the ejection of photoelectrons.

Again, from the wave theory we could argue that given enough time an electron in an area illuminated by a very feeble light would "soak up" enough energy to escape from the surface. No such time lag between the illumination of a surface and the ejection of a photoelectron has ever been measured. If emission of photoelectrons occurs at all, it begins simultaneously with the illumination of a photosensitive surface.

*The wave theory does not provide an explanation for the photoelectric effect.*

The wave theory, which serves so well in the explanation of radiation transmission phenomena, is incapable of describing the processes of radiation absorption observed in the photoelectric effect. In this instance a particle model of light appears to be useful. Had Newton perhaps been on the right track after all? The classic particles of Newton's theory could explain the relation between photoelectron emission rate and intensity of illumination but not that between photoelectron velocities and frequency of illumination.

The discovery of the photoelectric effect, coming as it did from the experiments that established the correctness of the electromagnetic wave theory, presented a paradox to twentieth-century physicists. Was there no theory to explain these widely divergent phenomena?

## 12.9 The quantum theory

Aside from the disturbing implications that the photoelectric effect introduced into twentieth-century physics, physicists were much concerned about discrepancies between their experimental studies of absorption and emission of radiant energy and the requirements derived from the electromagnetic radiation theory.

The first great step toward the resolution of these discrepancies was taken by the German theoretical physicist Max Planck (1858–1947). See Figure 12-13. In 1900 Planck was investigating the spectral distribution of electromagnetic radiation from a hot body. Classic electromagnetic theory predicted that the emission intensity would increase continuously as the radiation frequency increased. The spectral distribution of radiated energy measured experimentally was very different from that predicted by theory at the higher frequencies. It approached zero rather than infinity as the frequency increased without limit. Clearly something was wrong in this prediction that the radiated energy would keep on increasing with frequency without limit.

Planck found that he could bring radiation theory and experiment into agreement by assuming the energy emitted by the radiating sources to be an integral multiple of a fundamental quantity $hf$, where $h$ is a universal constant now known as *Planck's constant,* and $f$ is the frequency of these radiating sources. To explain why this bold assumption worked, he postulated that light is radiated and absorbed in indivisible packets, or quanta. We now call these packets, or quanta, *photons.*

**Figure 12-13** Max Planck, the German physicist, developed the initial assumptions on which the quantum theory is based. He did this while studying radiation phenomena.

The amount of energy comprising a photon is determined by the frequency of the radiation. It is directly proportional to this frequency since

$$E = hf$$

When $f$ is given in hertz and $h$ in joule seconds ($h = 6.63 \times 10^{-34}$ j s), the energy, $E$, of a photon is expressed in joules.

Planck published his quantum hypothesis in 1901 and, although not immediately accepted, it was destined to profoundly influence the *new physics* emerging with the twentieth century. Certainly there is nothing in the classical physics of Newton to suggest that certain values of energy should be allowed and others should not.

Albert Einstein recognized the value of Planck's quantum hypothesis in connection with the photoelectric effect. He reasoned that since emission and absorption of light radiation occur discontinuously, certainly the transmission field should be discontinuous. Proceeding with this hypothesis, in 1905 Einstein published a very simple and straightforward explanation of the photoelectric effect. A few years later, the very accurate experimental work of Millikan, Hughes, and Compton established the correctness of Einstein's explanation. The bold extension of Planck's quantum ideas by Einstein firmly established *the quantum theory,* which assumes that the transfer of energy between light radiations and matter occurs in discrete units called quanta, the magnitude of which depends on the frequency of the radiation.

---

### 12.10 Einstein's photoelectric equation

According to Einstein, light radiation illuminating an emitter surface consists of a stream of photons. When a photon is absorbed by the emitter, its quantum of energy $hf$ is transferred to a single electron within the surface. If the acquired energy is sufficient to overcome the surface barrier and the electron is moving in the right direction, the electron will escape from the surface. In penetrating the surface, the electron must give up a certain energy $w$, the work function of the substance. If the energy $hf$ imparted by the photon is greater than $w$, the electron will have kinetic energy as indicated by its velocity after leaving the surface.

The maximum kinetic energy possessed by photoelectrons ejected from an emitter illuminated by light of frequency $f$ was given by Einstein as

$$\tfrac{1}{2}mv^2_{max} = hf - w$$

where $m$ and $v$ are the mass and velocity, respectively, of the photoelectrons, $h$ is Planck's constant, $f$ is the frequency of the impinging light radiation (the product $hf$ is the energy of the photon), and $w$ is the work function of the emitting material.

Now, recalling the failures of the wave theory to explain photoelectric emission, we find no such difficulties in the application of Einstein's photon hypothesis. A lower light intensity means fewer photons impinging on the emitter surface in a given period of time and fewer photoelectrons ejected. However, as long as the frequency of the incident light remains unchanged, each photon transfers the same energy $hf$ to the electron when a collision occurs.

Einstein's photoelectric equation shows clearly why light of too low a frequency will not cause photoelectric emission from a given material no matter how intense the illumination. Photon energy is a linear function of the frequency of the light since it equals the product $hf$. Now if $\frac{1}{2}mv^2_{max} = 0$, it follows that

*Recall that $f_{co}$ for an emitting surface is the illumination frequency below which the photoemission of electrons ceases.*

$$hf_{co} = w$$

Here the photon can impart to the electron just enough energy for it to penetrate the surface barrier. No energy is left over to appear as electron velocity. The frequency in this situation is the cut-off frequency $f_{co}$. Illumination of any lower frequency on this emitter will consist of photons with energy $hf < w$, and photoelectric emission cannot occur no matter how many photons there are.

If photons have enough energy to eject electrons, no "soaking up" time is required before a feeble light can start the photoelectric emission process. This is true because the ejection energy for each photoelectron is delivered in a single concentrated bundle.

The quantum theory, which provides a particle model of light, meets every objection raised when the electromagnetic wave theory is employed to interpret photoelectric emission phenomena. Yet many experiments have proved the correctness of the wave theory. When we consider the full range of radiation phenomena, light must have a dual character. In some circumstances it behaves like waves, and in other circumstances it behaves like particles. *The modern view of the nature of light recognizes this dual character: Radiant energy is transported in photons that are guided along their path by a wave field.*

*Light exhibits a dual character: that of waves and of particles.*

## 12.11 The quantized atom

Striking evidence favoring the quantum theory was given by Niels Bohr (1885–1962), who in 1913 devised a model of the atom based on quantum ideas. Ernest Rutherford (1871–1937), the English physicist, had conducted experiments (described in Section 23.7) that in 1911 led him to postulate the nuclear atom with its planetary arrangement of electrons. This model of Rutherford's immediately encountered difficulties when subjected to the classical laws of physics, that is, the known laws of mechanics and electromagnetism as formulated by Newton and Maxwell.

The electromagnetic theory predicts that charged particles undergoing acceleration must radiate energy. Indeed, this ac-

counts for the radiation of energy from a radio transmitting antenna. A planetary electron moving about the nucleus of an atom
experiences acceleration and accordingly should radiate energy.
As energy is drained from the electron it should spiral in toward
the nucleus causing the atom to collapse. Of course atoms do not
collapse, and so this classical model cannot be correct.

Bohr assumed that an electron in an atom can move about the
nucleus in certain discrete orbits without radiating energy. Such
orbits represent ''allowable'' energy levels in the Planck concept. The level closest to the nucleus corresponds to the orbit of
lowest energy. This postulate could account for the stability of
an atom. However, atoms do radiate energy. Bohr assumed
further that an electron may ''jump'' from one discrete orbit to
another of lower energy. In the process a photon is emitted. Its
energy represents the difference between the energies of the
levels involved in the transition. The frequency of the emission
is proportional to this energy difference, the proportionality
factor being Planck's constant $h$. Thus the frequency of the
photon emission depends on the magnitude of this energy change
$\Delta E$ and can be expressed as $\Delta E/h$.

The return of excited atoms to their stable state results in the
emission of *bright line spectra*. (See Color Plate VII, Chapter
14.) Excited hydrogen atoms produce the simplest such atomic
spectra. Hydrogen lines appear in several series in and beyond
the visible region of the radiation spectrum. These include the
*Balmer series* in the visible region, the *Lyman series* in the ultraviolet region, and the *Paschen series* in the near infrared region.
See Figures 12-15 and 12-16.

Numerous attempts had been made to account for the discrete frequencies of the bright lines observed in these spectra.
It was Bohr who first associated spectral lines with pairs of energy levels, thus marking the initial step in the development of
the *quantum mechanics* of atomic structure.

Bohr's atom model provided no information about the mechanics of photon emission when an electron passes from a
higher to a lower energy level; but his concept of energy levels
provided a great stimulus for theoretical studies in this field. In
about 1924 the French physicist Louis de Broglie (b. 1892) suggested that the dual particle-and-wave nature of light provided
evidence of the wave nature of particles as well. Accepting
Einstein's idea of the equivalence between mass and energy,
he postulated that *in every mechanical system, waves are associated with matter particles*. The application of this concept
of matter waves to the study of the structure of matter is known
as *wave mechanics*. Just as the ordinary laws of mechanics are
essential to any explanation of the behavior of objects of large
dimensions, *wave mechanics* is necessary in dealing with objects that have atomic and subatomic dimensions.

**Figure 12-14** Niels Bohr, the Danish
physicist, received the Nobel Prize in
1922 for his work in atomic physics.

*Excited atom: one that has acquired
more energy than a normal, or
stable, atom of the same species.*

**Figure 12-15** An electronic energy-level
diagram for hydrogen showing some of
the transitions that are possible in this
atom.

**Figure 12-16** Representative lines in the hydrogen spectrum. The small letter below each line indicates which of the energy-level transitions in Figure 12-15 produces it.

A photon has energy that is the product of Planck's constant and its radiation frequency.

$$E = hf$$

In Einstein's equation $E = mc^2$ for mass-energy equivalency, $m$ is the mass of the particle while in motion. When at rest its mass $m_0$, known as the rest mass, is smaller than $m$.

If we consider the energy of the photon to be equivalent to that of a moving particle, then

$$hf = mc^2$$

and we could solve for $m$. However, this would imply also a certain rest mass for the photon. But a photon is never at rest; it always moves with the speed $c$. Photons do have momentum and can transfer it to any surface on which they impinge. Calculating this momentum $mc$ we get

$$mc = \frac{hf}{c}$$

Since

$$c = f\lambda$$

by substitution,

$$mc = \frac{h}{\lambda}$$

or

$$\lambda = \frac{h}{mc}$$

The wavelength of the photon may be expressed in terms of its momentum $mc$. Similarly, the wavelength of any matter particle having a velocity $v$ may be expressed in terms of its momentum $mv$.

$$\lambda = \frac{h}{mv}$$

There is abundant evidence today of the wave nature of subatomic particles. Accelerated electrons have been found to behave like X rays. The electron microscope is an application of electron waves. The development of the quantum theory and the system of wave mechanics have provided physicists with their most powerful means of studying the structure and properties of matter. Matter waves will be discussed more extensively in Chapter 25.

## 12.12 Coherent light; the laser

Common light sources like fluorescent and incandescent lamps radiate light in all directions over a wide range of frequencies with random phase relationships. Even groups of waves of the same frequency have random phase relationships. These disordered light waves are said to be *incoherent*.

*Incoherent waves differ in frequency or phase, or both.*

In Section 10.15 we described a stationary interference pattern (Figure 10-27). To produce such a pattern, it is necessary to employ two wave trains with identical wavelengths, or frequencies, and a constant phase relationship. Such wave trains have *coherence;* they are said to be *coherent* waves.

It is not difficult to obtain coherence from two sources in the case of sound waves. But to produce a stationary interference pattern with light waves in the high school laboratory, one will undoubtedly resort to a subtle arrangement using a single source of incoherent light.

*Coherent waves have the same frequencies and a constant phase relationship.*

Coherent light is produced by a remarkable instrument called a *laser*. It is a light amplifier that functions because of stimulated emissions of radiation. The term "laser" is an acronym derived from Light Amplification by Stimulated Emission of Radiation. The laser output is a single-frequency (monochromatic) radiation of in-phase parallel waves.

The first successful laser produced a coherent red beam from a ruby crystal. Today there are many different types of lasers using gases, liquids, crystals, semiconductors, glass, and plastics. These lasers produce coherent beams in different spectral colors. Laser research is continuing on a broad front. Industry, engineering, medicine, communications, photography, and the military are areas in which lasers are being used. Scientists are constantly finding new applications.

The basic ruby laser system consists of a pencil-shaped ruby crystal and an external flash lamp. The ends of the ruby crystal are optically flat, silvered reflecting surfaces. One end may be only half silvered to allow some light to emerge. The flash lamp surrounds the ruby crystal as illustrated in Figure 12-17. When this lamp flashes, photons enter the ruby crystal and initiate the laser action.

The effect of the flash lamp is to "pump" energy into the crystal. Some atoms of the crystal become excited by absorbing

**Figure 12-17** An operating laser beam (left). Diagram of a ruby laser (right).

photons and are elevated to a higher energy state. They may then emit some of the energy and make a transition to an intermediate state. From this intermediate state an atom may return to its stable state either by spontaneous or stimulated emission of a photon of light energy equal to its energy level difference.

Suppose one atom emits a photon spontaneously. The photon is reflected at the end of the ruby crystal. As it travels back through the crystal, the photon stimulates another atom in the intermediate state to emit a photon. This process continues, and the intensity of the photon beam in the crystal is *amplified*.

With the reflective ends of the crystal the proper distance apart, a standing wave of single-frequency red light is set up in the ruby rod. This particular standing light wave is analogous to the standing sound wave in an organ pipe. As the photon beam is amplified, photons pass through the partially reflective end of the rod in the form of intense pulses of coherent red light. Gaseous lasers produce a continuous but less intense beam of coherent light. The laser provides practical evidence of the quantized energy levels of atoms as proposed by Bohr in 1913. See Section 12.11.

## 12.13 Production of X rays

In the photoelectric effect, photons of frequency $f$ cause the ejection of electrons from atoms of a substance with a maximum velocity given by the equation

$$\tfrac{1}{2}mv^2{}_{\text{max}} = hf - w$$

It is not surprising that the converse of this phenomenon can be produced also. High-speed electrons projected against the surface of a target with velocity $v$ cause the emission of photons of radiation having a maximum frequency given by the photoelectric equation

$$\tfrac{1}{2}mv^2 = hf_{\text{max}} - w$$

The work function $w$ of target material is negligible compared to the photon energy at X-ray frequencies and is usually omitted from the above equation.

This phenomenon is sometimes referred to as the *inverse photoelectric effect*. A well-known example is the production of accelerated electrons. Each electron that strikes the target loses its energy, and this energy reappears as photons of radiation. Neglecting the work-function energy, as previously indicated, no more than the full kinetic energy of the electron can appear in the X-ray photons as the energy $hf$. Since $h$ is constant, the maximum frequency $f_{max}$ of the X-ray radiation is determined by the velocity $v$ of the electron.

The penetrating properties of X rays and their many practical uses stemming from these properties are well known. X rays lie deep in the high frequency end of the electromagnetic spectrum beyond the ultraviolet region. The energy $hf$ of X-ray photons is very high, being of the order of $10^4$ times the energy of photons in the visible region. As a consequence of this high photon energy and the very short wavelengths, X rays are used extensively in numerous areas of research. Table 12-1 gives photon energies for important regions of the spectrum.

Table 12-1

| PHOTON ENERGIES | | |
|---|---|---|
| Radiation | Typical value of $f$ (hz) | $hf$ (j) |
| gamma rays | $3.0 \times 10^{19}$ | $2.0 \times 10^{-14}$ |
| X rays | $3.0 \times 10^{18}$ | $2.0 \times 10^{-15}$ |
| visible light | $6.0 \times 10^{14}$ | $4.0 \times 10^{-19}$ |
| heat waves | $3.0 \times 10^{13}$ | $2.0 \times 10^{-26}$ |
| radio waves | $3.0 \times 10^{15}$ | $2.0 \times 10^{-28}$ |

## 12.14 The pressure of light

The electromagnetic theory of Maxwell predicted that incident light should exert a pressure applied in the direction of the radiation. According to Maxwell, the pressure on a totally reflecting surface should be twice that on a totally absorbing surface illuminated by the same radiation.

In 1901 Nichols and Hull in the United States and Lebedev in Russia succeeded experimentally in measuring the pressure of light. Their results were in such close agreement with theory as to provide proof of the existence of light pressure.

What does the particle model tell us about the pressure of light? Our common experiences with pressure are those involving collisions of particles in motion. Since particle collisions are momentum problems, conservation of momentum applies.

A perfectly elastic ball rebounding from an object transfers twice the momentum that a perfectly inelastic ball having the same mass and velocity would transfer. In Section 12.11 we expressed the momentum of a photon in terms of its frequency as

$$mc = \frac{hf}{c}$$

When a beam of photons is incident on a totally absorbing surface, the pressure exerted depends on the rate of change of photon momentum per unit area of illuminated surface.

*Pressure, p, is force per unit area. Force, F, is time rate of change of momentum.*

$$p = \frac{F}{A} = \frac{\Delta(hf/c)}{\Delta t \times A} = \frac{\Delta hf}{c \, \Delta t A}$$

In the MKS system, $p$ has the dimensions

$$p = \frac{j\ s/s}{m/s \times s \times m^2} = \frac{j}{m^3} = \frac{n}{m^2}$$

If the photon energy $hf$ is totally reflected from the surface of a body, the momentum change is $2hf/c$ and the pressure of light is twice that for the totally absorbing surface illuminated by the same beam.

The pressure of light is exceedingly small in comparison to pressures we commonly experience. The pressure of sunlight on the earth is approximately $4 \times 10^{-11}$ standard atmosphere. The tails of comets always point away from the sun, apparently due to the pressure of sunlight and solar particles on the extremely diffuse matter in comet tails.

# questions

GROUP A

1. What is the modern view of the nature of light?

2. Arrange the following in order of increasing wavelength: visible light, infrared radiations, ultraviolet radiations, X rays, radio waves, gamma rays.

3. Compare visible light and sound as to: (a) origin, (b) transmitting media, (c) wavelength, (d) type of wave, (e) speed.

4. How does an atom of a substance radiate energy according to the quantum theory?

5. The flatiron is a source of radiations that cannot be detected by the eye. (a) Would you expect an ordinary photoelectric cell to detect these radiations? Explain. (b) Suggest a way to prove that such radiations are emitted.

GROUP B

6. A beam of light passes through a small aperture and illuminates the blackened bulb of a thermometer. A piece of ordinary glass is placed over the aperture and the thermometer reading drops two degrees. The glass is replaced by a quartz window and the thermometer reading returns approximately to the original value. What do the results suggest concerning the nature of the light source? Explain.

7. (a) State the three laws of photoelectric emission. (b) To what extent is a wave model of light successful in explaining these laws?

8. Given a monochromatic (single frequency) light source to illuminate a photocell, how can you explain the fact that photoelectrons are ejected at various velocities ranging up to a maximum value?

9. How does the pair of curves shown in Figure 12-11 show that the velocity of photoelectrons is independent of the intensity of the light illuminating the photocell?

10. What special significance can you attach to the photoelectric situation in which the photon energy $hf$ transferred to an electron is just equal to the work function $w$ of the emitter?

11. How would you defend the assertion that the production of X rays illustrates the inverse photoelectric effect?

12. (a) Distinguish between coherent and incoherent light waves. (b) Describe the light emitted by a laser.

# ILLUMINATION

Nearly all the natural light we receive comes from the sun. Distant stars account for an extremely small amount of natural light. Of course, moonlight is sunlight reflected from the surface of the moon.

We produce light from artificial sources in several ways. Materials may be heated until they glow, or become incandescent, as in an electric lamp. Molecules of a gas at reduced pressure may be bombarded with electrons to produce light, as in a neon tube. Most of the visible light from fluorescent tubes results from the action of ultraviolet radiations on phosphors that coat the inside surface of the glass tubes. The firefly produces light by means of complex chemical reactions.

Most artificial sources of light are hot bodies that radiate energy in the infrared region of the spectrum as well as visible light. The energy of the *thermal radiation* emitted by hot bodies depends upon the temperature of the body and the nature of its surface.

At a temperature of 300°C the most intense radiation emitted by a hot body has a wavelength of about $5 \times 10^{-4}$ cm, well down in the infrared region of the electromagnetic spectrum. As the temperature is raised to 800°C, enough radiation is emitted in the visible region to cause the body to appear "red hot" although the bulk of the energy radiated is still in the infrared region. If the temperature of the body is raised to 3000°C, the most intense emission remains in the near infrared region; however, there is enough blue visible radiation to cause the body to appear "white hot."

This last temperature is near that of the filament of an incandescent lamp. Hence such lamps have low efficiencies as producers of visible radiation. Generally the efficiency improves as the filament temperature is raised.

The white-hot filament of an incandescent lamp is said to be *luminous*. It is visible primarily because of the light it emits. *An object that gives off light because of the energy of its accelerated particles is said to be **luminous**.* The sun and the other stars are luminous objects.

Just as radiant heat may be reflected, light may be reflected from the surfaces of objects. Mirrors reflect a beam of light in a definite direction. Other surfaces scatter the light that is incident on them in all directions. *An object that is seen because of the light scattered from it is said to be **illuminated**.* The moon is illuminated, for it reflects radiant energy from the sun. Some of the light energy arriving at the surface of a substance is reflected, some of it is transmitted, and some of it is absorbed by the substance.

## 12.15 Luminous and illuminated objects

*Visible spectrum: $7.6 \times 10^{-5}$ cm to $4.0 \times 10^{-5}$ cm.*

**Figure 12-18** The formation of beams and pencils of light.

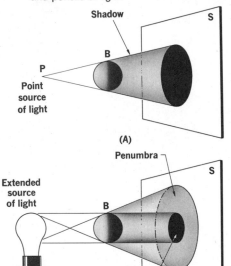

**Figure 12-19** An obstruction in the path of light from a point source (A) casts a shadow of uniform density. If the light is from an extended source (B), the shadow is of varying density.

**Figure 12-20** A diagram of a total solar eclipse showing the umbral and penumbral regions of the moon's shadow. CC′ is the region of totality on the earth; CH and C′H′ are the regions from which a partial eclipse is seen. (Sizes and distances are not to scale.)

Any dark-colored object absorbs light, but a black object absorbs nearly all the light it receives. When the rays of the sun strike a body of water vertically, most of them are either absorbed or transmitted. Most of the rays are reflected, however, when they strike the water at an oblique angle. For this reason the image of the sun can be seen in the water without discomfort when the sun is directly overhead, but not when the sun is near the horizon.

Air, glass, and water transmit light readily and are said to be *transparent*. Other substances transmit light but scatter or diffuse it so that objects seen through them cannot be identified. Such substances are *translucent*. Typical examples are frosted electric lamps and parchment lampshades. *Opaque* substances do not transmit light at all.

From a luminous point source, light waves travel outward in all directions. If the medium through which they pass is of the same nature throughout, the light progresses along the normal to the wave front. A single line of light from a luminous point is called a *ray;* a group of closely spaced rays forms a *beam* of light. Small beams are referred to as *pencils*. See Figure 12-18. Light coming from the sun is in rays so nearly parallel that it may be considered as a parallel beam. When several rays of light come from a point, they are called a *diverging* pencil, while rays proceeding toward a point form a *converging* pencil. When the sun's rays pass through a magnifying glass, they converge at a point called a *focus*.

Because an opaque object absorbs light it casts a shadow in the space behind it. When the source of light is a point, as in Figure 12-19(A), an opaque ball, **B,** cuts off all the rays that strike it and produces a shadow of uniform darkness on the screen, **S.** If the light comes from an extended source, the shadow varies in intensity, as shown in Figure 12-19(B). The part from which all the rays of light are excluded is called the *umbra;* the lighter part of the shadow is the *penumbra*. Within the region of the penumbra the luminous source is not entirely hidden from an observer. The umbral and penumbral regions of the moon's shadow cast during a solar eclipse are shown in Figure 12-20.

The speed of light is one of the most important constants used in physics, and the determination of the speed of light represents one of the most precise measurements ever achieved. Before 1675 light propagation was generally considered to be instantaneous, although Galileo had suggested that a finite time was required for it to travel through space. In 1675 the Danish astronomer Olaus Roemer (1644–1710) determined the first value for the speed of light to be 140,000 miles per second. This is approximately equivalent to 225,000 kilometers per second. He had been puzzled by a variation in his calculations of the time of eclipse of one of Jupiter's satellites as seen from different positions of the earth's orbit about the sun. Roemer concluded that the variation was due to differences in the distance that the light traveled to reach the earth.

Very precise modern measurements of the speed of light are made using laboratory methods. The most notable experiments were performed by Albert A. Michelson (1852–1931), a professor of physics at the University of Chicago, who measured the speed of light in air and in a vacuum with extraordinary precision.

*1. The speed of light in air.* Michelson measured the speed of light over the accurately determined distance between Mt. Wilson and Mt. San Antonio, California. His method is illustrated in principle by Figure 12-21. The light source, octagonal mirror, and telescope were located on Mt. Wilson and the concave mirror and plane mirror were located on Mt. San Antonio, 35.4 km (approximately 22 mi) away. The octagonal mirror, **M**, could be rotated rapidly under controlled conditions and was timed very accurately.

With mirror **M** stationary, a pencil of light from the slit opening was reflected by **M₁** to the distant mirror **M′**, from which it was returned to **M₃**. The image of the slit in the mirror at the **M₃** position could be observed accurately through the telescope. The

## 12.16 The speed of light

*Foucault first used a rotating mirror in 1850 to compare the speed of light in water and in air.*

S •

**Figure 12-21** Michelson's octagonal-mirror method for measuring the speed of light.

octagonal mirror was then set in motion and the speed of rotation brought up to the value that moved $M_2$ into the position formerly occupied by $M_3$ during the time required for the light to travel from $M_1$ to Mt. San Antonio and return. The slit image was again seen in the telescope precisely as it was when the octagon was stationary. The light traveled twice the optical path of 35.4 km in one-eighth of the time of one revolution of the octagonal mirror. Thus

$$c = \frac{2MM'}{t}$$

where $MM'$ is the optical path, $t$ is the time of one-eighth revolution of the octagon, and $c$ is the speed of light in air.

Michelson's investigation of the speed of light in air required several years to complete and extremely high precision was attained in making the necessary observations. The optical path was measured by the U. S. Coast and Geodetic Survey and found to be 35,385.5 meters, accurate to about one part in seven million. The rate of the revolving mirror was measured by stroboscopic comparison with an electric signal of standard frequency. The average of a large number of determinations yielded a speed of light in air of 299,729 km/s.

2. *The speed of light in a vacuum.* Michelson conducted similar experiments using an evacuated tube one mile long to eliminate the problems of haze and variations in air density. In these investigations he determined the speed of light to be 299,796 km/s, which he believed to be accurate to within 1 km/s.

**Figure 12-22** A laser beam is directed down a 30-meter vacuum tube in an experiment to measure the speed of light. The apparatus is installed in an abandoned gold mine and is so sensitive that it records "tides" in the earth's crust caused by the sun and moon.

Modern laboratory methods of measuring the speed of light require very complex apparatus and are considered to be more accurate than the methods used by Michelson. In some experiments, electromagnetic waves much longer than light waves have been used and good agreement has been found between their speed and that of visible light. These findings provide experimental confirmation of Maxwell's electromagnetic theory, which requires that all electromagnetic waves throughout the electromagnetic spectrum have the same speed $c$ in free space. Thus we must consider the speed of light within the larger framework of the speed of electromagnetic radiations in general.

As Michelson's figures show, the speed of light is slightly higher in a vacuum than in air. The speed in free space generally accepted as most accurate is

$$c = 2.99792458 \times 10^8 \text{ m/s}$$

with an uncertainty of 1.2 m/s. New laser experiments may soon provide the physicist with the techniques for measuring the speed of light with even greater accuracy, as shown in Figure 12-22.

---

## 12.17 Light measurements

*The quantitative study of light is called* **photometry**. Three quantities are generally measured in practical photometry: the *luminous intensity* of the source; the *luminous flux,* or light flow, from a source; and the *illumination* on a surface.

*1. Luminous intensity.* In order to derive a set of photometric units it is necessary to introduce an additional fundamental unit into our measurement system. The unit for luminous intensity, $I$, is the arbitrary choice. It is the *candle,* cd. The candle is known internationally as *candela.*

*The original standard candle was one made of spermaceti (wax from sperm oil) that burned 120 grains per hour.*

Originally the light from a certain type of candle was used as a standard, but this has been replaced by a more readily reproducible source of luminous intensity. *The* **candle** *is one-sixtieth of the luminous intensity of a square centimeter of a black-body radiator maintained at the temperature of freezing platinum* (2046°K). In practice it is convenient to use incandescent lamps that have been rated by comparison with the standard.

Incandescent lamps used for interior lighting generally have an intensity ranging from a few candles to several hundred candles. The common 40-watt lamp has an intensity of about 35 candles; a 100-watt lamp gives about 130 candles. Note that a 40-watt fluorescent lamp has an intensity of about 200 candles. The intensity of any lamp depends on the direction from which it is measured; the average candle power in all directions in space (spherical candle power) is often given.

*2. Luminous flux.* Not all of the energy radiated from a luminous source is capable of producing a visual sensation. Most of the radiation is in the infrared region, and a small amount is in

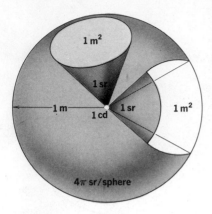

**Figure 12-23** A 1-candle point source radiates luminous flux at the rate of $4\pi$ lumens.

the ultraviolet region. The rate of flow of visible radiation is called *luminous flux,* the symbol for which is the Greek letter $\Phi$ (phi). ***Luminous flux*** *is that part of the total energy radiated per unit of time from a luminous source that is capable of producing the sensation of sight.* The unit of luminous flux is the *lumen,* lm.

Suppose a standard light source of 1 candle is placed at the center of a hollow sphere having a radius of 1 meter, as illustrated in Figure 12-23. The luminous source is presumed to radiate light equally in all directions and to have such small dimensions that it may be termed a "point source." The area of the surface of a sphere of radius $r$ is equal to $4\pi r^2$. Since the radius of the unit sphere is 1 meter, its surface area is $4\pi \times (1 \text{ m})^2$. One lumen of flux is radiated by the 1-candle source to each square meter of inside surface of the sphere. *The **lumen** is the luminous flux on a unit surface all points of which are at unit distance from a point source of one candle.* The lumen is not a measure of a total quantity of luminous energy but a *rate* at which luminous energy is being emitted, transmitted, or received.

The unit surface area of the unit sphere is intercepted by a solid angle, $\omega$, of 1 *steradian,* sr. The unit surface area of a sphere of radius $r$ is intercepted by a solid angle of $1/r^2$ steradians. *The ratio of the intercepted surface area of a sphere to the square of the radius is the measure of the solid angle in steradians.*

$$\omega = \frac{A}{r^2} \text{ (in sr)}$$

Observe that the steradian is dimensionless.

The luminous flux of the standard light source of 1 candle is 1 lumen per steradian.

Since the unit sphere has $4\pi$ unit areas of surface, there are $4\pi$ steradians per sphere. The total luminous flux emitted by a point source is therefore $4\pi$ lumens per candle of luminous intensity.

$$\Phi = \frac{4\pi \text{ lm}}{\text{cd}} \times I \text{ cd}$$
$$\Phi = 4\pi I \qquad \text{(in lumens)}$$

Thus a luminous source having an intensity of 1 candle emits light at the rate of $4\pi$ lm, or 12.57 lumens. In fact, light sources are usually rated in terms of the total flux emitted, with 12.57 lumens being radiated by 1 candle. A 40-watt incandescent lamp is rated at about 450 lumens and a 40-watt fluorescent lamp at about 2600 lumens.

*3. Illumination.* In Figure 12-23 it is evident that as the intensity of the source is increased, the luminous flux transmitted to each unit area of surface and the flux on each unit area are similarly increased. The *illumination* on the surface is said to be increased. ***Illumination*** *is the density of the luminous flux on a* *surface*. When the surface is uniformly illuminated, the illumination $E$ is the quotient of the flux on the surface divided by the area of the surface and is expressed as the luminous flux per unit area.

$$E = \frac{\Phi}{A}$$

Where $\Phi$ is the luminous flux in lumens and $A$ is the area in square meters, the illumination $E$ is in *lumens per square meter*.

Suppose the radius of the unit sphere shown in Figure 12-23 is increased to 2 meters. The surface area is $4\pi(2m)^2$, or approximately 50 m², and is *four* times the area of the unit sphere. Similarly, a radius of 3 meters gives an area of $4\pi(3m)^2$, which is *nine* times the area of the unit sphere. It is apparent that as the radial distance from the luminous source is increased, the area illuminated is increased in proportion to the *square* of the distance.

If a point source of constant intensity is located at the center of the sphere, *the illumination decreases as the square of the distance from the source*. See Figure 12-24. If the intensity of the source is doubled, of course the luminous flux transmitted to the surface is doubled and the illumination is doubled. Thus the illumination $E$ on a surface perpendicular to the luminous flux falling on it is dependent on the intensity $I$ of the source and its distance $r$ from the source.

The distance $r$ from the point source is the radius of a spherical surface of area $4\pi r^2$ illuminated by the source $I$ at its center. Thus the proper dimensions of $E$ become apparent from the following:

$$E = \frac{\Phi}{A} = \frac{4\pi I}{4\pi r^2}$$
$$E = \frac{I}{r^2}$$

If $r$ is expressed in meters and $I$ in candles, then

$$E = \frac{4\pi \text{ lm/cd} \times I \text{ cd}}{4\pi r^2 \text{m}^2}$$
$$E = \frac{I}{r^2} \text{ (in lm/m}^2\text{)}$$

The *inverse square law* is used to calculate the illumination from an individual point source on planes perpendicular to the beam. In practice, if the dimensions of the source are negligible compared with its distance from the illuminated surface, it is considered a point source. For long fluorescent tubes, the illumination varies inversely as the distance, over distances somewhat smaller than the length of the tube.

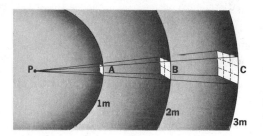

**Figure 12-24** The illumination on a surface varies inversely as the square of the distance from the luminous point source.

**Figure 12-25** The illumination on a surface varies directly with the cosine of the angle between the luminous flux and the normal to the surface.

When a surface is not perpendicular to the beam of light illuminating it, the luminous flux spreads over a greater area and the level of illumination is reduced. In Figure 12-25 the perpendicular surface **ABC** illuminated by the beam is square, having an area equal to **AB** × **BC.** As the surface is tilted away from the source, the illuminated area becomes rectangular, the width remaining the same and the length increasing to **BD.** In the right triangle **ABD**

$$BD = \frac{AB}{\cos \theta}$$

where $\theta$ equals the tilt angle of the surface from its perpendicular position with respect to the beam. (It is evident that $\theta$ also represents the angle that the light beam makes with the perpendicular to the illuminated surface.)

As $\theta$ reaches 60°, cos $\theta$ equals 0.5 and the length **BD** becomes twice the width **AB.** Thus the area is doubled and, since the same flux is spread over twice the area, the illumination is reduced to half the original level. In the general case,

$$E = \frac{I \cos \theta}{r^2}$$

*The illumination on a surface varies inversely with the square of the distance from the luminous source and directly with the cosine of the angle between the luminous flux and the normal to the surface.* A surface that is perpendicular to the luminous flux is simply a special case of the general expression for illumination in which the angle $\theta$ becomes zero and cos $\theta = 1$. See the following example.

**EXAMPLE**

(a) *What illumination is provided on the surface of a table located 4.00 m directly below a 1610-lumen incandescent lamp?*

(b) *What is the illumination on the surface of the table at a spot 3.00 m to one side of its original position?*

**SOLUTION**

(a) $E = \dfrac{I}{r^2}$      information given in lm

$\Phi = 4\pi I$, $I = \dfrac{\Phi}{4\pi}$      express $I$ in terms of $\Phi$

$E = \dfrac{\Phi}{4\pi r^2} = \dfrac{1610 \text{ lm}}{4\pi \times (4.00 \text{ m})^2}$      substitute $\Phi/4\pi$ for $I$

$E = 8.00 \text{ lm/m}^2$

(b) $E = \dfrac{I \cos\theta}{r^2}$

$I = \dfrac{\Phi}{4\pi}$

$E = \dfrac{\Phi \cos\theta}{4\pi r^2}$

$E = \dfrac{1610 \text{ lm} \times 0.800}{4\pi \times (5.00 \text{ m})^2}$      $\cos\theta = 4.00 \text{ m}/5.00 \text{ m } (3 - 4 - 5 \text{ rt } \triangle)$

$E = 4.08 \text{ lm/m}^2$

---

The candle power of a light source can be measured by comparing its intensity with that of a standard light source having the same color quality. This is done by using an instrument called a *photometer*. See Figure 12-26. Photometric measurements are made in a darkened room.

## 12.18 The intensity of a source

**Figure 12-26** A photoelectric photometer.

*1. Bunsen photometer.* The Bunsen photometer is sometimes called the grease-spot photometer. If a disk of white paper with a grease spot in the center is held toward a light, the grease spot will appear lighter than the rest of the paper because it transmits more light. On the other hand, because it is a poorer reflector of light than the paper, the grease spot will appear darker than the paper when held away from a light. In that case it is seen by reflected light. A laboratory model of the Bunsen photometer consists of such a paper screen supported on a meter stick between a standard lamp and a lamp of unknown candle power. The paper screen is moved back and forth along the meter stick until it is equally illuminated on both sides. At this point the grease spot seems to disappear. When the screen is correctly positioned, illuminations $E_1$ and $E_2$ of the two sides of the screen are equal.

$$\text{Since} \qquad E_1 = E_2 \qquad \text{then} \qquad \frac{I_1}{r_1{}^2} = \frac{I_2}{r_2{}^2}$$

$I_1$ and $I_2$ are the intensities of the two sources producing illuminations $E_1$ and $E_2$, and $r_1$ and $r_2$ are their respective distances from the screen. Each distance $r$ is a radial distance from a source.

*2. Joly photometer.* The Joly photometer generally gives more satisfactory results than the grease-spot photometer. It consists of two blocks of paraffin separated by a thin sheet of metal. The light from either side is transmitted by the paraffin, but is stopped by the metal. By looking at the edges of the blocks of paraffin it is easy to adjust the photometer so that both sides are equally illuminated. Then distances from the sheet of metal to the lamps are measured and calculations made as with the Bunsen photometer.

*3. Photoelectric photometer.* The Bunsen or Joly photometer head can be replaced by a photoelectric cell connected to a meter suitable for measuring the photoelectric current of the cell. The photoelectric cell is then placed a given distance from a standard lamp of known luminous intensity, and the photocurrent is measured. An unknown lamp is then substituted for the standard lamp, and the position of the photocell is adjusted to give the same photocurrent as for the standard lamp. The luminous intensity of the unknown lamp can then be calculated as with the Bunsen photometer.

*4. Spherical photometer.* The light source being tested is placed in the center of a large sphere that is painted white on the inside. The luminous flux is received by a photocell located inside the sphere but shielded from direct light from the source. The light on this cell is equal to that received by any other similar portion of the sphere interior, due to cross-reflections, and is therefore proportional to the total light emitted by the test source. A meter outside the sphere is connected to the cell and is calibrated to read the mean spherical candle power or lumens directly. This accurate photometer is used commercially.

# summary

A particle model and a wave model were developed in the seventeenth century to explain the properties of light known at that time. The particle model failed after additional properties of light were discovered. The wave model prevailed, and with the experimental confirmation of the electromagnetic theory the wave model of light was thought to be complete. The discovery of the photoelectric effect, the failure of the electromagnetic theory, and the success of the quantum theory in explaining photoemission established the dual character of light.

An object is luminous if it is visible because of the light it emits. An object is illuminated if it is visible because of the light it reflects. An object may reflect, absorb, or transmit the light it receives. Opaque objects cast shadows when illuminated. Shadows may consist of umbras and penumbras.

Photometry is the quantitative study of light. Three quantities measured in practical photometry are luminous intensity, luminous flux, and illumination. The intensity of a light source can be measured by means of a photometer.

# questions

## GROUP A

1. Distinguish between luminous and illuminated objects.
2. Define and illustrate the following terms: (a) transparent, (b) translucent, (c) opaque.
3. What are the physical quantities generally measured in practical photometry?
4. Define luminous flux.
5. (a) Which of the quantities from Question 3 is measured in fundamental units? (b) Which are measured in derived units?
6. What is our chief method of providing artificial light?

## GROUP B

7. By using Figure 12-21, explain how Michelson determined the speed of light in air.
8. Devise an experiment that would enable you to verify the inverse-square law with a light meter. Describe it.
9. Suggest a procedure by which a light meter with an arbitrary scale could be used in the absence of a photometer to determine the intensity of an unknown light source.
10. A member of a television studio audience in New York sits 30 m from the performer. A viewer observes the performance at home in Chicago, 1200 km away. Who hears the performer first?

# problems

## GROUP A

*Note:* Assume filament lamps to be point sources.

1. The distance from the earth to the sun is approximately $1.5 \times 10^8$ km. What time, in minutes, is required for light from the sun to reach the earth?
2. What is the illumination on the page of a book 1.20 m directly below a source whose intensity is 125 cd?
3. It is recommended that the illumination be 540 lm/m² for newspaper reading. How far from the paper should a 265-cd source be placed to provide this illumination? (Assume the paper to be perpendicular to the luminous flux reaching it.)
4. What is the maximum illumination 1.50 m from a lamp whose intensity is 150 cd?
5. The amount of illumination thrown on a screen by two sources of light is the same when the distances from the lamps to the screen are 3.0 m and 2.0 m respectively. If the intensity of the first lamp is $2\overline{0}$ cd, what is the intensity of the second lamp?
6. A lamp, intensity 16.0 cd, is placed at the 0.0-cm mark on a meter stick. A lamp of unknown intensity is placed at the 100.0-cm mark. If a Bunsen photometer is equally illuminated at the 60.0-cm mark, what is the intensity of the unknown lamp?
7. A photometer is in balance on a meter stick when a 40.0-cd lamp and a second lamp are 100.0 cm apart, and the grease spot is 30.0 cm from the second lamp. Find the intensity of this lamp.
8. The illumination on a screen located 3 m from a source of light is 4 times as much as that on a second screen that is illuminated by the same source. The intensity of the source is 25 cd. How far is the second screen from the source?

GROUP B

9. The intensity of a lamp is 60.0 cd. At what distance does it provide an illumination of 10.0 lm/m² on a table located directly beneath it?

10. How far away is the nearest star if it takes 4.3 years for the light from the star to reach the earth?

11. An incandescent lamp of 30.0 candles is placed at the 0-cm mark on a meter stick and a lamp of 20.0 candles is placed at the opposite end. Where must the screen of a photometer be placed so that both sides are equally illuminated?

12. A 100-watt lamp placed at one end of a meter stick and a 10-candle source placed at the other end equally illuminate a photometer that is 75 cm from the 100-watt lamp. How many candles per watt does the lamp supply?

13. How many revolutions per second did Michelson's octagonal mirror make if light traveled 70.8 km while the mirror made one-eighth of a revolution?

14. What is the range of frequencies of visible light?

15. A surface is 75 cm from a luminous source of 150 cd. At what angle can it be tilted and still have an illumination of 0.025 lm/cm²?

# 13 Reflection

A light beam passing through any material medium will become progressively weaker due to two effects. Part of the light beam's energy will be *absorbed* by molecules of the medium and part will be *scattered* in all directions by the molecules. A light beam striking the boundary between two media can be partly *transmitted* and partly returned to the first medium. See Figure 13-1. Light returned to the first medium is said to be *reflected* at the boundary. Reflection is described as a wave property in Section 10.10.

Part of the reflected light proceeds in a common direction but part can be reflected in all possible directions as scattered light.

## 13.1 Reflectance

**Figure 13-1** A diagram showing the effects on light rays of a material medium and an interface, or boundary, between two media. Note that the two bottom light rays are absorbed.

(A) Negligible scattering

(B) Complete scattering

**Figure 13-2** Reflecting surfaces vary in the extent to which reflected rays are scattered.

These effects are shown in Figure 13-2. The fact that a portion returns in a common direction provides us with a method for controlling the reflection of a light beam.

The amount of light reflected at the surface of an object, whether by scattering or by unidirectional reflection, depends on the kind of material underlying the surface, the smoothness of the surface, and the angle at which the light strikes it. *The ratio of the light reflected from a surface to the light falling on the surface is called* **reflectance**. This ratio is commonly expressed as a percentage. Materials differ widely in their reflectance. The material of highest reflectance is magnesium carbonate, a white chalky substance that reflects about 98% of incident light with practically complete scattering. The reflectance of a smooth surface of silver is about 95% with negligible scattering. Some black surfaces have reflectances of 5% or less.

## 13.2 Regular and diffused reflection

**Figure 13-3** Regular reflection of light from a specular surface.

**Figure 13-4** Irregular reflection promotes the diffusion of light.

The reflection of sunlight by a mirror produces a blinding glare. The rays of the sun reaching the earth are practically parallel and thus have the same angle of incidence. They remain practically parallel after being reflected from a plane mirror. Such reflection, in which scattering of the reflected rays is negligible, is called *regular* reflection. Polished, or *specular,* surfaces cause regular reflection and the image of the luminous source is sharply defined. The regular reflection of a narrow beam of light is in one direction with no appreciable loss of definition or intensity. The nature of regular reflection is shown in Figure 13-3.

Regular reflection from highly polished surfaces provides for relatively accurate control of light rays. Searchlights, beacons, and automobile spotlights use concentrated light sources of high intensity and highly-polished regular reflectors to redirect light rays in the desired direction.

In Figure 13-4 we observe what happens to a beam of light incident on an irregular surface. The laws of reflection hold true for each particular ray of light, but the normals to the surface are not parallel and the light is reflected in many directions. Such scattering, or *diffusion,* of light is extremely important.

If the sun's rays were not diffused by rough and irregular surfaces and by dust particles in the air, the corners of a room and the spaces under shade trees would be in almost total darkness and the glare would be dazzling in sunlit areas. Astronauts have found that it is possible for them to see in the shadows on the lunar surface where there is no air, but they cannot see as easily as we can on the surface of the earth.

The reflection of light is similar to the reflection of sound or to the rebound of an elastic ball. The line **MN** in Figure 13-5(A) represents a reflecting surface; **AD** is a ray of light incident upon the reflector at **D**; **DB** is the path of the reflected ray. The line **CD** perpendicular to the reflecting surface at the point of incidence is called a *normal*. In Figure 13-5(B) the normal is perpendicular to the tangent to the curved reflecting surface at the point of incidence. Recall from Section 10.10 that the *angle of incidence (i)* is the angle between the incident ray and the normal at the point of incidence [angle **ADC** in Figure 13-5(A)]. In Chapter 10 we examined the nature of reflection by sending water waves against a barrier in the ripple tank. At that time we recognized *the **first law of reflection**: The angle of incidence, i, is equal to the angle of reflection, r*. The *angle of reflection, r,* is the angle between the reflected ray and the normal at the point of incidence [angle **BDC** in Figure 13-5(A)].

The relationships between an incident ray of light and the reflected ray and between the angles they form with the normal are easily determined in the laboratory. Critical observation of the specular reflection of light reveals a ***second law of reflection:*** *The incident ray, the reflected ray, and the normal to the reflecting surface lie in the same plane.* As mentioned in Section 10.10 these laws are true for all forms of wave propagation.

Any highly polished surface that forms images by the regular reflection of light can act as a mirror. A *plane mirror* of plate glass is silvered on one surface to reflect light efficiently. Its reflectance may be nearly 100%. The plane parallel surfaces of the plate glass allow an essentially distortion-free image to be observed.

A *spherical mirror* is a small section of the surface of a sphere. One side of the section is polished or coated with a reflective material. If the *inside* (concave) surface is made reflective, it is a *concave mirror,* as shown in Figure 13-6(A). If the *outside*

## 13.3 Mirrors as reflectors

**Figure 13-5** Reflections from plane and curved surfaces.

*The reflective coating is commonly placed on the back surface of a plane mirror to protect the coating from damage.*

**Figure 13-6** Spherical mirrors are circular sections of spheres.

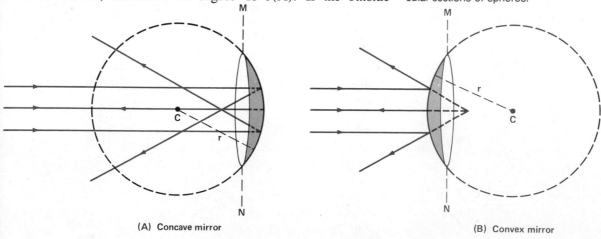

(A) Concave mirror

(B) Convex mirror

(convex) surface is made reflective, it is a *convex mirror,* as in Figure 13-6(B).

The laws of reflection hold for spherical mirrors just as they do for plane mirrors. However, the size and position of the images formed by spherical mirrors are quite different from the size and position of images formed by plane mirrors.

## 13.4 Images by reflection

Light rays reflected from a concave mirror may meet in front of the mirror and form an image of the object from which the light comes. Such an image can be projected on a screen placed at the image location. *An image formed by converging rays of light actually passing through the image point is called a **real image**.* Real images are inverted relative to the object and can be larger or smaller than the object.

Your image observed in a plane mirror seems to be behind the mirror, although the rays forming it actually are reflected forward from the mirror surface. *This image is called a **virtual image**. Rays of light that appear to have diverged from the image point do not actually pass through that point.* Virtual images cannot be projected on a screen. They are erect with respect to the object and can be enlarged or reduced in size.

In Figure 13-7 light traveling from a point source in spherical wave fronts is reflected from a plane mirror. At the instant that points **A** and **C** on the wave front reach the mirror, point **B** has been reflected back towards the source at **S**, having traveled the distance **VB**. The reflected wave front **ABC** has an apparent source **S'** at an apparent distance **VS'** behind the mirror. Note that **VS'** is equal to the distance **VS** of the source in front of the mirror. The reflected wave front approaches an observer, the eye, as though its source were **S'**, **S'** being the virtual image of the source **S**.

**Figure 13-7** A wave-front diagram of reflection of light from a point source by a plane mirror.

## 13.5 Images formed by plane mirrors

**Figure 13-8** The image formed by a plane mirror appears to be reversed right and left. Observe that the image of the right hand has the symmetry of a left hand.

The image formed by a plane mirror is neither enlarged nor reduced but is always virtual, erect, and appears to be as far behind the mirror as the object is in front of it. The image differs from the object in that right and left appear to have been interchanged. In Figure 13-8 the image of the right hand has the appearance of a left hand. If an object is spinning clockwise about its axis, its image appears to be spinning counterclockwise about its image axis.

Let us examine the ray diagram in Figure 13-9 for a simple graphical method of locating the image formed by a plane mirror. The triangle **ABC**, drawn on paper, is used as the object in front of a mirror, **MN**. A pin is placed at each vertex of the triangle. Rays **AO₁** and **AO₂** from pin **A** strike the mirror so as to be reflected to the two eyes, **E₁** and **E₂**, of the observer. When the sight lines $E_1O_1$ and $E_2O_2$ are produced (extended) behind the mirror, they intersect at $A'$, which is the location of the image of pin $A$. A comparison of triangles $AO_2O_1$ and $A'O_2O_1$ makes it apparent that $A'$ is as far behind the mirror as $A$ is in front of it.

The images of $B$ and $C$ are located in similar fashion at $B'$ and $C'$. In each instance *the image appears to be as far behind the mirror as the object is in front of it*. When the image points $A'B'C'$ are joined, it becomes evident that *the image is the same size as the object*.

This method of constructing images is based on the laws of reflection. The light ray $AO_1$ is reflected at point $O_1$ and is sighted at $E_1$. By drawing a normal to the mirror at $O_1$, the angle $AO_1E_1$ is bisected and the angle of reflection $E_1O_1R$ is equal to the angle of incidence $AO_1R$. The incident ray $AO_1$, the reflected ray $O_1E_1$, and the normal $O_1R$ all lie in the same plane.

Sound waves bound and rebound between parallel cliffs or walls and produce multiple echoes. In a similar fashion, light reflects back and forth between parallel mirrors or mirrors set at an acute angle and forms multiple images. The image formed in one mirror appears to act as the object forming the image in the next mirror. Because some light energy is absorbed and some is scattered at each mirror, the succeeding images become fainter. A thick plate-glass mirror produces multiple reflection, as shown in Figure 13-10, due to some light being reflected each time a boundary is encountered.

Multiple reflections can be avoided by aluminizing or silvering the front surface of a glass mirror. Mirrors for astronomical telescopes and other precision instruments are usually coated with aluminum in this manner. Such reflecting surfaces are exposed and can be easily damaged.

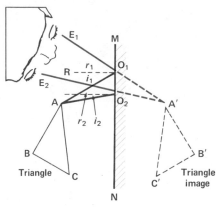

**Figure 13-9** A ray diagram used to construct an image formed by a plane mirror.

**Figure 13-10** Multiple reflections result from the use of a back-silvered mirror.

## 13.6 Curved-mirror terminology

In order to discuss image formation by spherical mirrors, we must first identify several terms associated with this process. We shall refer in this discussion to the diagrams of spherical mirrors shown in Figures 13-11 and 13-12.

The arc $MVN$ is the portion of the spherical surface separated from the sphere by a cutting plane represented by the line $MN$.

*1.* The *center of curvature,* $C$, is the center of the original sphere. The radius of the sphere is also the *radius* $CV$ of the spherical mirror.

*2.* The *vertex,* $V$, is the center of the mirror.

*3.* The *principal axis* of the mirror is the line $PV$ drawn through the center of curvature and the vertex.

*4.* A *secondary axis* is any other line drawn through the center of curvature to the mirror: $SS'$ for example.

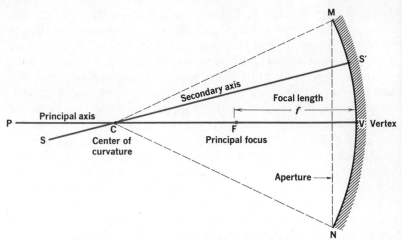

**Figure 13-11** A plane diagram for defining terms used with curved mirrors.

5. A *normal* to the surface of a spherical mirror is a radius drawn from the point of incidence of a light ray. Therefore the normal is perpendicular to the mirror surface at the incidence point. (Normals are illustrated in Figure 13-12.)

6. The *principal focus,* **F**, is the point on the principal axis where light rays close to and parallel to the principal axis converge, or from which they appear to diverge.

7. The *focal length, f,* is the distance from the vertex of the mirror to its principal focus.

8. The *aperture* determines the amount of light intercepted by the mirror. The length **MN** is called the *linear aperture* of the mirror, and the angle **MCN** is called the *angular aperture*. For a spherical mirror to be capable of forming sharp images, its aperture must be small compared with its focal length.

*The aperture size relative to focal length in mirror diagrams is exaggerated for the sake of clarity.*

## 13.7 Rays focused by spherical mirrors

In Figure 13-12(A) the rays **AD** and **BE**, parallel to the principal axis, are shown incident on a concave spherical mirror at points **D** and **E** respectively. The normals **CD** and **CE** are drawn to the points of incidence. By the second law of reflection, the reflected rays converge on the principal axis at **F**, the principal focus.

**Figure 13-12** Locating the principal focus of spherical mirrors.

(A) Concave mirror          (B) Convex mirror

Because the incident rays converge upon being reflected, concave mirrors are also known as *converging* mirrors. The distance **FV** is the *focal length* of the mirror. For spherical mirrors of small aperture, the focal length is one-half the radius of curvature.

Parallel rays incident on the surface of a convex spherical mirror are shown in Figure 13-12(B). The normals **CD** and **CE** produced beyond the mirror surface show the reflected rays to be divergent along the lines **FD** and **FE** produced, **F** being the principal focus of the mirror. Rays parallel to the principal axis appear to diverge from the principal focus of a convex mirror. Because incident rays diverge on being reflected, convex mirrors are known as *diverging* mirrors.

Diverging rays from a point **S** incident on a concave mirror, Figure 13-13, converge to a focus at some point **S′** beyond the principal focus of the mirror. If **S** is located on the principal axis, the image **S′** is also on the principal axis. Suppose the source of diverging rays is now moved to position **S′**. The image formed by the mirror will be at **S**.

Converging rays are also focused by concave mirrors. As shown by Figure 13-14, the point of focus is between the vertex and the principal focus. In every instance the direction of a reflected ray is determined by the laws of reflection.

We observed in Figure 13-12(A) that incident parallel rays that are also parallel to the principal axis of the concave mirror are reflected and converge at the principal focus. The image is ideally a point of light at the principal focus. If the parallel rays are not parallel to the principal axis but are incident at a small angle with the principal axis, they do not converge at the principal focus. Instead they are focused at a point in a *plane* that contains the principal focus and is perpendicular to the principal axis. This plane is called the *focal plane* of the mirror. Figure 13-15 illustrates the reflection of a bundle of parallel light rays incident on a

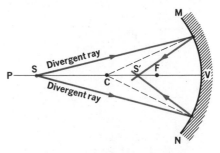

**Figure 13-13** The reflection of diverging rays by a concave mirror.

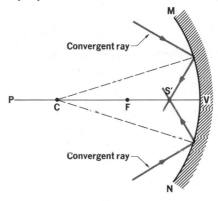

**Figure 13-14** The reflection of converging rays by a concave mirror.

**Figure 13-15** In (A) parallel rays are shown incident on a concave mirror parallel with its principal axis. The reflected rays converge at the principal focus. In (B) the parallel rays are incident at a small angle α with the principal axis. Here the reflected rays are focused at a point in the focal plane F′ F″ of the mirror.

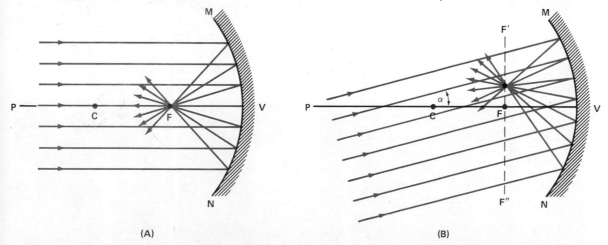

(A)                    (B)

concave mirror. In Figure 13-15(A) the rays are parallel to the principal axis of the mirror, and in Figure 13-15(B) the rays are at a small angle $\alpha$ (the Greek letter alpha) with the principal axis.

If the aperture of a spherical mirror is large, the parallel rays of light striking the mirror near its edge are not reflected through the principal focus but are focused at points nearer the mirror, as shown in Figure 13-16(A). Only those parallel rays that are incident on the mirror near its vertex are reflected to the principal focus. This characteristic of spherical mirrors of large aperture is known as *spherical aberration* and results in the formation of fuzzy images.

**Figure 13-16**  Spherical aberration is a characteristic of spherical mirrors with large apertures. This defect is avoided by the use of parabolic mirrors.

(A)  **Spherical aberration**

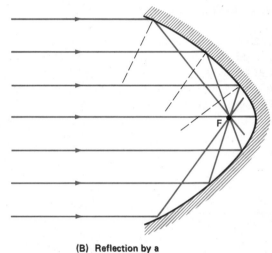

(B)  **Reflection by a parabolic mirror**

In order to reduce spherical aberration, the aperture of the spherical mirror must be small. For angular apertures no larger than about 10°, the distortion of the image is negligible. Spherical aberration can be avoided for parallel rays if the mirror surface is made parabolic instead of spherical. See Figure 13-16(B). The parabolic mirror shown in Figure 13-17 reflects light rays originating at the focus as parallel rays. Parabolic reflectors are used in automobile headlights, microwave communication relays, radar, and radiotelescopes. Parabolic mirrors are also used in large reflecting telescopes to collect and focus light rays from distant objects.

*A parabola is formed by a plane parallel to one side of a cone.*

**Figure 13-17**  Reflections from a parabolic mirror.

SOURCE AT FOCUS

AHEAD OF FOCUS

BEHIND FOCUS

In Figure 13-18 the image of point **S** formed by a concave mirror is to be located. First the principal axis **PV** is drawn through **C**. Because light is given off in all directions from point **S**, *any two lines* can be drawn from **S** to represent rays of light incident on the mirror. The point of intersection of the *reflected* rays locates the image of **S** at **S'**.

The construction is greatly simplified if incident rays are selected for which the directions of the reflected rays are known from the geometry of the system. Three such special rays are shown in Figure 13-18. Ray **SA**, *parallel to the principal axis*, is reflected through the principal focus. Ray **SB** *passes through the principal focus* and is reflected parallel to the principal axis. Ray **SC** *lies along the secondary axis*. It is reflected back along its path of incidence because the angle of incidence is zero. *Note that the convergence of any two of these three reflected rays at a common point S' forms the image of S.*

If the object were located at **S'** the image would be formed at **S**. The object and image are thus interchangeable, or *conjugate*. The positions of the object and its image, **S** and **S'**, are called conjugate points.

## 13.8 Constructing the image of a point

**Figure 13-18**  Locating an image formed by a concave mirror.

*Conjugate points: any two points so situated that light from one is concentrated at the other.*

We can construct the image formed by a concave mirror by locating the images of enough different points on the object. If the object is an arrow, the entire image can be located by finding the positions of the images of the head and tail of the arrow. Concave mirror images may be grouped into six cases.

*Case 1. Object at an infinite distance.* Rays emanating from an object at an infinite distance from a mirror are parallel at the mirror. If the rays are parallel to the principal axis, they are reflected through the principal focus. See Figure 13-19(A). We therefore conclude that *the image formed by a concave mirror of an object an infinite distance away is a point at the principal focus.* The rays of the sun reaching the earth are practically parallel and provide a simple method for finding the approximate focal length of a concave mirror.

*Case 2. Object at a finite distance beyond the center of curvature.* In Figure 13-19(B) the image of the object arrow can be located using the method illustrated in Section 13.8. Two known rays, **1** and **2**, emanating from the head of the arrow, intersect after reflection to locate the image of the arrowhead. The image of the tail lies on the principal axis as shown earlier in Figure 13-13. *The image in this case is real, inverted, reduced in size, and located between the center of curvature and the principal focus.* The nearer the object approaches the center of curvature, the larger the image becomes and the nearer the image approaches **C**.

## 13.9 Images formed by concave mirrors

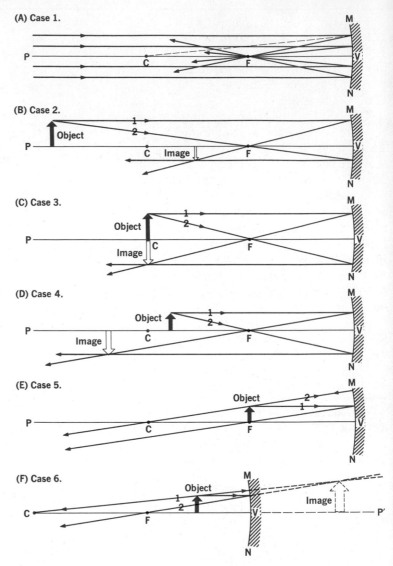

**Figure 13-19** Ray diagrams of image formation by concave mirrors.

*Case 3. Object at the center of curvature.* When the object arrow is at the center of curvature, as shown in Figure 13-19(C), the image of the arrowhead is found inverted at **C**. *When the object is at the center of curvature, the image is real, inverted, the same size as the object, and located at the center of curvature.*

*Case 4. Object between the center of curvature and principal focus.* This case is the converse of Case 2 and is shown in Figure 13-19(D). *The image is real, inverted, enlarged, and located beyond the center of curvature.* The nearer the object approaches the principal focus of the mirror, the larger the image becomes and the farther it is beyond **C**.

*Case 5. Object at principal focus.* This case is the converse of Case 1; all rays originating from the same point on the object are reflected from the mirror as parallel rays. See Figure 13-19(E). *When the object is at the principal focus, no image is formed.* If the object is a point source, all reflected rays are parallel to the principal axis.

*Case 6. Object between principal focus and mirror.* The reflected rays from any point on the object are divergent; they can never meet to form a real image. They appear to meet behind the mirror, however, to form a virtual image as shown in Figure 13-19(F). In this case, *the image is virtual, erect, enlarged, and located behind the mirror.*

---

A convex mirror forms an erect image of reduced size. The diagram shown in Figure 13-20 can be used to show how such an image is formed. The arrow **AB** represents the object. The secondary axes and the normals at the points of incidence of the parallel rays are *radii produced.* The parallel rays are reflected from the surface of the mirror as divergent rays. When produced behind the mirror, the reflected parallel rays *appear to meet* at the principal focus. The image is formed where parallel and secondary-axis rays *emanating from the same object point* appear to intersect behind the mirror. In a convex mirror, *all images are virtual, erect, smaller than the object, and located behind the mirror between the vertex and the principal focus.* The size of the image increases as the object is moved closer to the mirror, but it can never become as large as the object itself.

## 13.10 Images formed by convex mirrors

**Figure 13-20** The only image formed by a convex mirror is virtual, erect, reduced, and located behind the mirror.

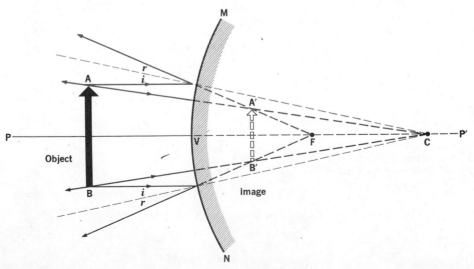

## 13.11 The reflecting telescope

The largest optical telescopes are reflecting telescopes. Large concave parabolic mirrors are used to collect and focus light rays. See Figure 13-21. Reflecting telescopes can be made much larger than refracting (lens) telescopes. It is difficult to obtain a large piece of glass of sufficiently high optical quality for a lens, grind and polish two surfaces with precision, and support it appropriately.

When objects being viewed with a reflecting telescope are at a finite distance beyond the center of curvature of the mirror, Case 2 (Section 13.9) applies. The image is real, inverted, and located near the principal focus of the mirror. This real image can be reflected out of the path of the rays of light incident on the mirror so that it can be viewed or photographed from a position outside the telescope. The inversion of the image is not objectionable when reflecting telescopes are used for viewing astronomical objects.

**Figure 13-21** The 200-inch mirror of the observatory on Mt. Palomar, California. Visible in the huge reflector are various images, all silhouetted against a day-time sky.

## 13.12 Object-image relationships

A simple relationship exists among the distance of an object $d_o$ from a curved mirror, the distance of its image $d_i$ from the mirror, and the focal length $f$ of the mirror. This relationship, known as the *mirror equation,* can be derived by considering the diagram shown in Figure 13-22 in which a real image of the object **AB** is formed by a concave mirror. (In this derivation we will consider as insignificant the very slight error introduced by the curvature **MV**.)

**Figure 13-22** A diagram for the derivation of the mirror equation for curved mirrors.

In similar triangles **A′ B′ F** and **MVF**

$$\frac{\mathbf{A'\,B'}}{\mathbf{MV}} = \frac{\mathbf{B'\,F}}{\mathbf{VF}}$$                    (Equation 1)

Taking $MV = AB$, $VF = f$, and $B'F = d_i - f$, we have

$$\frac{A'B'}{AB} = \frac{d_i - f}{f} = \frac{d_i}{f} - 1 \qquad \text{(Equation 2)}$$

In similar triangles $ABV$ and $A'B'V$,

$$\frac{A'B'}{AB} = \frac{B'V}{BV} \qquad \text{(Equation 3)}$$

Taking $BV = d_o$ and $B'V = d_i$,

$$\frac{A'B'}{AB} = \frac{d_i}{d_o} \qquad \text{(Equation 4)}$$

Substituting in Equation 2

$$\frac{d_i}{d_o} = \frac{d_i}{f} - 1$$

Dividing by $d_i$,

$$\frac{1}{d_o} = \frac{1}{f} - \frac{1}{d_i} \qquad \text{(Equation 5)}$$

Or,

$$\frac{1}{f} = \frac{1}{d_o} + \frac{1}{d_i} \qquad \text{(Equation 6)}$$

where $d_o$ is the distance of the object from the mirror, $d_i$ the image distance, and $f$ the focal length of the mirror.

Equation 6, the mirror equation, is applicable to all concave and convex mirrors. When an object is located less than one focal length in front of a concave mirror, the image is virtual. It appears to be located behind the mirror, and the image distance $d_i$ is a *negative* quantity. In the case of convex mirrors, the radius of curvature is negative and the image is virtual. Therefore, both the focal length $f$ and the image distance $d_i$ are *negative* quantities. For concave mirrors, the radius of curvature and the focal length are *positive*. The image distance can be either positive or negative —being *positive* for real images and *negative* for virtual images. The significance of these negative quantities is illustrated in the following example.

**EXAMPLE**

*An object located $2\overline{0}$ cm in front of a convex mirror forms an image $1\overline{0}$ cm behind the mirror. What is the focal length of the mirror?*

**SOLUTION**

$$\frac{1}{d_o} + \frac{1}{d_i} = \frac{1}{f}$$

Solving for $f$:

$$f = \frac{d_o d_i}{d_o + d_i} = \frac{2\overline{0} \text{ cm} \times (-1\overline{0} \text{ cm})}{2\overline{0} \text{ cm} + (-1\overline{0} \text{ cm})} = -2\overline{0} \text{ cm}$$

The relative heights of an object and its image formed by a curved mirror depend on their respective distances from the center of curvature of the mirror. This can be seen from similar triangles **ABC** and **A′B′C** of Figure 13-22.

We can demonstrate that for mirrors of small aperture the relative heights of the object and image also depend on their respective distances from the vertex of the mirror. If the height of object **AB** in Figure 13-22 is represented by $h_o$ and the height of the image **A′B′** is represented by $h_i$, Equation 4 of Section 13.12 becomes

$$\frac{h_i}{h_o} = \frac{d_i}{d_o}$$

A negative numerical value for $h_i$ merely signifies that the image is virtual. The ratio $h_i/h_o$ gives the magnification $M$ of the image. For example, suppose a magnification is determined to be

$$M = \frac{h_i}{h_o} = \frac{-12 \text{ cm}}{6.0 \text{ cm}} = -2.0$$

The virtual image is 2 times the height of the object. The magnification is commonly expressed as 2X.

The sign conventions for spherical mirror computations using the mirror equation are summarized as follows:

1. The numerical value of the focal length $f$ of a concave mirror is positive.

2. The numerical value of the focal length $f$ of a convex mirror is negative.

3. The numerical value of the real object distance $d_o$ is positive.

4. The numerical value of the real image distance $d_i$ is positive.

5. The numerical value of the virtual image distance $d_i$ is negative.

# summary

The amount of incident light reflected from the surface of an object depends on the composition of the object, the character of its surface, and the angle at which the light rays strike the surface. The ratio of the reflected light to the incident light is known as reflectance. The angle of reflection and the angle of incidence are equal, and both angles lie in the same plane.

Images may be either real or virtual. Real images are inverted with respect to the object and can be projected onto a screen. Virtual images are erect and cannot be projected onto a screen. Images formed by plane mirrors are virtual, erect, and the same size as the object. Images formed by plane mirrors appear to be the same distance behind the mirror as the object is in front of the mirror.

Concave mirrors cause reflected rays of light to converge. These mirrors can form real images. The size and position of an image are related to the size of the object and its position relative to the mirror. A virtual image is formed by a concave mirror if the object is less than a focal length away from the mirror. Convex mirrors cause reflected rays of light to diverge. They form virtual images of objects irrespective of the object distance from the mirror.

Spherical mirrors of large aperture form indistinct images. The spherical-mirror defect responsible for fuzzy images is known as spherical aberration. Parabolic mirrors do not show this aberration defect. When mirrors of large aperture are required, parabolic surfaces rather than spherical surfaces are used to reflect incident light.

# questions

GROUP A

1. What three factors determine the amount of light an object will reflect?
2. What are the two laws of reflection?
3. When you look in a plane mirror, do you see yourself as others see you? Explain.
4. Illustrate the following by diagram as they are related to curved mirrors: center of curvature, vertex, principal axis.
5. What type of mirror produces real images?
6. In what ways can spherical aberration in mirrors be reduced?

GROUP B

7. Suppose we write the word "light" on a mirror with white paint. When the mirror is placed in a beam of sunlight, the reflection of the sunlight on a smooth wall consists of a bright area in which the letters of the word "light" appear dark. Explain.

8. What kind of trick mirror produces (a) a short, fattened image; (b) a tall, thin image?
9. What kinds of mirrors could be used and where should the object be placed to produce (a) an enlarged real image, (b) a reduced real image, (c) a real image the same size as the object, (d) an enlarged virtual image, (e) a reduced virtual image?
10. (a) Construct a ray diagram to show the formation of an image by a concave mirror when the object is at a finite distance beyond the center of curvature. (b) Describe fully the image that is formed.
11. (a) Construct a ray diagram to show the formation of an image by a concave mirror when the object is between the principal focus and the center of curvature. (b) Describe the image formed.
12. (a) Construct a ray diagram to show the formation of an image by a convex mirror. (b) Describe fully the image that is formed.

# problems

GROUP A

1. A concave mirror has a focal length of 10.0 cm. What is its radius of curvature?
2. If the radius of curvature of a curved mirror is 8 cm, what is its focal length?
3. While you are looking at the image of your feet in a plane vertical mirror, you see a scratch in the glass. Assuming your height to be 1.76 m, what is the approximate height of the scratch from the floor?
4. The light from a distant star is collected by a concave mirror. If the radius of curvature of the mirror is 150 cm, how far from the mirror is the image?
5. An object is placed 25.0 cm from a concave mirror whose focal length is 5.00 cm. Where is the image located?
6. An object 25.4 cm high is located 91.5 cm from a concave mirror, focal length 15.0 cm. (a) Where is the image located? (b) How high is it?
7. An object placed 50.0 cm from a spherical concave mirror gives a real image 33.3 cm from the mirror. (a) What is the radius of curvature of the mirror? (b) If the image is 30.5 cm high, what is the height of the object?
8. An object and its image in a concave mirror are the same height when the object is 36.4 cm from the mirror. What is the focal length of the mirror?

GROUP B

9. An object is placed 5.0 cm from a concave mirror whose focal length is 15 cm. (a) Where is the image located? (b) If the object is 2.0 cm high, what is the height of the image?

10. An object 5.00 cm tall stands at the 0.0-cm mark on a meter stick. (a) If a convex mirror having a focal length of 25.0 cm is placed at the 50.0-cm mark, where is the image? (b) How tall is it?
11. The image of the moon is formed by a concave mirror whose radius of curvature is 4.00 meters at a time when the distance to the moon is 380,000 km. What is the diameter of the image in centimeters if the diameter of the moon is 3480 km?
12. The image of an incandescent lamp filament is to be formed on a screen 5.00 m from a concave mirror. The lamp filament is 5.00 mm long and the image is to be 50.0 cm long. (a) What should be the radius of curvature of the mirror? (b) How far in front of the vertex should the filament be?
13. A shaving mirror has a radius of curvature of 30.0 cm. When the face is 10.0 cm from the vertex of the mirror, what is its magnification?
14. A physics student 1.80 m tall stands in front of a mirror admiring the reflected image. Assume the student's eyes are 10 cm below the top of the head. (a) What is the smallest vertical mirror that will enable the entire image to be seen? (b) Is the length of the mirror dependent upon the distance between the student and the mirror? (c) Construct a ray diagram that supports your answers.
15. The mirror for Problem 14 is hung at an angle of 30.0° from the vertical toward the student. What is the minimum length mirror that will allow the student to see the full image if the line of vision cannot be depressed below the horizontal? Assume that the eyes are at the top of the head.

# 14 Refraction

## 14.1 The nature of optical refraction

In Section 10.12 we discussed refraction as a property of waves. Now we shall examine the refractive behavior of light and relate this behavior to its wave-like nature.

When aiming a rifle at a target, one relies on the common observation that light travels in straight lines. It does so, however, only if the transmitting medium is of the same *optical density* throughout. **Optical density** *is a property of a transparent material that is an inverse measure of the speed of light through the material.*

Consider a beam of light transmitted through air and directed onto the surface of a body of water. Some of the light is reflected at the interface (boundary) between the air and water; the remainder enters the water and is transmitted through it. Because water has a higher optical density than air, the speed of light is reduced as the light enters the water. This change in the speed

**Figure 14-1** A beam of light from a laser is reflected by two plane mirrors and is then refracted as it enters and leaves a semicircular piece of clear plastic.

of light at the air-water interface is shown diagrammatically in Figure 14-2.

A ray of light that strikes the surface of the water at an *oblique* angle (less than 90° to the surface) changes direction abruptly as it enters the water because of the change in speed. The reason for this change in direction with a change in speed can be illustrated if we redraw the wave-front diagram of Figure 14-2(A) to make the angle of the incident ray oblique, as in Figure 14-2(B). When interpreting this diagram, you should remember that a light ray indicates the direction the light travels and is perpendicular to the wave front. We have already defined refraction as a bending of a wave disturbance. (See Section 10.12.) This bending of a light ray is called *optical refraction*. **Optical refraction** *is the bending of light rays as they pass obliquely from one medium into another of different optical density.*

(A)

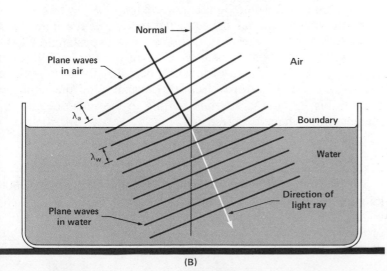

(B)

**Figure 14-2** Wave-front diagrams illustrating (A) the difference in the speed of light in air and in water and (B) the refraction of light at the air-water boundary.

Because of refraction, a fish observed from the bank appears nearer to the surface of the water than it actually is. A stick or teaspoon in a tumbler of water appears to be bent or broken at the surface of the water. A coin in the bottom of an empty teacup that is out of the line of vision of an observer may become visible when the cup is filled with water.

## 14.2 Refraction and the speed of light

Line **MN** of Figure 14-3 represents the surface of a body of water. The line **AO** represents a ray of light through the air striking the water at **O**. Some of the light is reflected along **OE**. Instead of continuing in a straight line along **OF**, the light ray entering the water is bent as it passes from air into water, taking the path **OB**.

The incident ray **AO** makes the angle **AOC** with the normal. Angle **AOC** is the *angle of incidence, i*. Recall that the angle of incidence is defined as the angle between the incident ray and the normal at the point of incidence. The refracted ray **OB** makes the angle **DOB** with the normal produced. *The angle between the refracted ray and the normal at the point of refraction is called the **angle of refraction**, r.*

In the examples given so far, the light rays have passed from one medium into another of *higher* optical density, with a resulting reduction in speed. When a ray enters the denser medium normal to the interface, no refraction occurs. When a ray enters the denser medium at an oblique angle, refraction does occur and the ray is bent *toward* the normal.

What is the nature of the refraction if the light passes obliquely from one medium into another of *lower* optical density? Suppose the light source were at **B** in Figure 14-3. Light ray **BO** then meets the surface at point **O**, and angle **BOD** is the angle of incidence. Of course some light is reflected at this interface. However, on entering the air the refracted portion of the light takes the path **OA**. The angle of refraction in this case is angle **COA**. It shows that the light is bent away from the normal. When a light ray enters a medium of lower optical density at an oblique angle, the ray is bent *away* from the normal. Had the light ray entered this less dense medium normal to the interface, no refraction would have occurred.

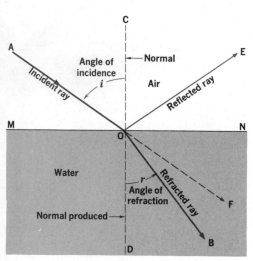

**Figure 14-3** A ray diagram of refraction showing the angle of incidence and the angle of refraction.

## 14.3 The index of refraction

The speed of light in a vacuum is approximately 300,000 kilometers per second. The speed of light in water is approximately 225,000 kilometers per second or just about three-fourths of that in a vacuum. The speed of light in ordinary glass is approximately 200,000 kilometers per second or about two-thirds of that in a vacuum. *The ratio of the speed of light in a vacuum to its speed in a substance is called the **index of refraction** for that substance.* For example:

$$\text{Index of refraction (glass)} = \frac{\text{speed of light in vacuum}}{\text{speed of light in glass}}$$

Using the approximate values just given, the index of refraction for glass would be about 1.5 and for water about 1.3. The index of refraction for a few common substances is given in Appendix B, Table 18. The speed of light in air is only slightly different from the speed of light in a vacuum. Therefore, with negligible error, we can use the speed of light in a vacuum for cases where light travels from air into another medium.

The fundamental principle of refraction was discovered by the Dutch mathematician and astronomer Willebrord Snell (1591–1626). See Figure 14-4. He did not publish his discovery, but his work was taught at the University of Leyden where he was a professor of mathematics and physics. The French mathematician and philosopher René Descartes (1596–1650) published Snell's work in 1637.

Snell's discoveries about refraction were not stated in terms of the speed of light. The speed of light in empty space was not determined until 1676, and the speed in water was not measured until 1850. From his observations, however, Snell defined the index of refraction as the ratio of the sine of the angle of incidence to the sine of the angle of refraction. This relationship is known as Snell's law. If *n* represents the index of refraction, *i* the angle of incidence, and *r* the angle of refraction,

$$n = \frac{\sin i}{\sin r}$$

The sines of angles from 0° to 90° are given in Appendix B, Table 6.

The relationship between Snell's law and the ratio of the speeds of light in air and a refracting medium can be recognized from Figure 14-5. Rays of light travel through the first medium (air) with a speed $v_1$ and enter the refracting medium in which their speed is $v_2$.

A wave front **MP** approaches the refracting interface **MN** in the first medium at an incident angle $i$. The wave front at **P** travels to **N** in the time $t$ with a speed $v_1$. Simultaneously the wave front at **M** travels in the second medium to **Q** in the same time $t$ but with a speed $v_2$. The new wave front is **NQ**, which travels forward in the second medium at a refractive angle $r$. The distances **PN** and **MQ** are respectively $v_1 t$ and $v_2 t$, so that

$$\frac{\textbf{PN}}{\textbf{MQ}} = \frac{v_1 t}{v_2 t} = \frac{v_1}{v_2}$$

**Figure 14-4** Willebrord Snell became a professor of mathematics and physics at the University of Leyden at the age of 21. He discovered the law of refraction now known as Snell's Law.

**Figure 14-5** A wave-front diagram of refraction.

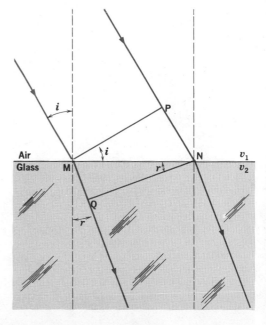

In triangle **MNP**

$$\sin i = \frac{PN}{MN}$$

In triangle **MNQ**

$$\sin r = \frac{MQ}{MN}$$

The ratio

$$\frac{\sin i}{\sin r} = \frac{PN/MN}{MQ/MN} = \frac{PN}{MQ} = \frac{v_1}{v_2}$$

From Snell's law

$$n = \frac{\sin i}{\sin r}$$

Therefore

$$n = \frac{v_1}{v_2}$$

These relationships are illustrated in the following example.

**EXAMPLE**

*A ray of light travels from air into water at an angle with the surface of 60.0°. The index of refraction of the water is 1.33. Find (a) the angle of refraction and (b) the speed of light in the water.*

**SOLUTION**

(a) From Snell's law,

$$n = \frac{\sin i}{\sin r} \text{ and } \sin r = \frac{\sin i}{n}$$

($i = 90.0° - 60.0° = 30.0°$ and $n = 1.33$)

$$\sin r = \frac{\sin 30.0°}{1.33} = \frac{0.500}{1.33} = 0.376$$

$$r = 22.0°$$

(b) From the definition of the index of refraction,

$$n = \frac{v_1}{v_2} \text{ and } v_2 = \frac{v_1}{n}$$

($v_1 = 3.00 \times 10^8$ m/s and $n = 1.33$)

$$v_2 = \frac{3.00 \times 10^8 \text{ m/s}}{1.33} = 2.26 \times 10^8 \text{ m/s}$$

The index of refraction of a homogeneous substance is a constant quantity that is a definite physical property of the substance. Consequently, the identity of such a substance can be determined by measuring its index of refraction with an instrument known as a *refractometer*. For example, butterfat and margarine have different indexes of refraction. One of the first tests made in a food-testing laboratory to determine whether butter has been mixed with margarine is the measurement of the index of refraction. The exceedingly high index of refraction of a diamond furnishes one of the most conclusive tests for its identification.

Because light travels very slightly faster in outer space than it does through air, light from the sun or the stars is refracted when it enters the earth's atmosphere obliquely. Since the atmosphere is denser near the earth's surface, a ray of light from the sun or a star striking the atmosphere obliquely follows a path suggested by the curve shown in Figure 14-7. There is no abrupt refraction such as that which occurs at the interface between two media of different optical densities.

Atmospheric refraction prevents the sun and stars from being seen in their true positions except when they are directly overhead. In Figure 14-7, the sun appears at **S′** instead of **S**, its true position. Since the index of refraction from outer space to air is only 1.00029, the diagram is greatly exaggerated to show the bending. Refraction of sunlight by the earth's atmosphere causes the sun to appear about one diameter (½°) higher than it really is. About 2 minutes are required for the earth to move through ½° of arc. Consequently, we gain about 4 minutes of additional daylight each day because of atmospheric refraction at sunrise and sunset.

**Figure 14-6** Parallel beams of light incident upon a rectangular glass plate. The beams are mainly refracted at both surfaces. Some reflection occurs at each surface, however.

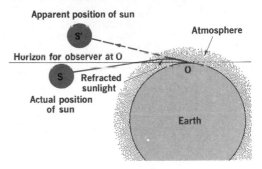

**Figure 14-7** The sun is visible before actual sunrise and after actual sunset because of atmospheric refraction.

---

If the index of refraction of a transparent substance is known, it is possible to trace the path that a ray of light will take in passing through the substance. In Figure 14-8 rectangle **ABCD** represents a piece of plate glass with parallel surfaces. The line **EO** represents a ray of light incident upon the glass at point **O**. From point **O** as a center, two arcs are drawn. The radii of these arcs are in the ratio 3/2 based on the index of refraction of the glass being 1.5 and that of the air being 1. The normal **OF** is drawn. Then a line is drawn parallel to **OF** through the point **H** where the incident ray intersects the *smaller* arc. This line intersects the *larger* arc at point **G**. The line **OP**, determined by points **G** and **O**, marks the path of the refracted ray through the glass.

If the ray were not refracted as it leaves the glass, it would proceed along the line **PK**. To indicate the refraction at point **P**, this point is used as a center and arcs are drawn having the same

## 14.4 The laws of refraction

Ray is refracted as it enters and as it leaves the glass plate

**Figure 14-8** A method of tracing a light ray through a glass plate.

*Test the validity of this construction using Figure 14-5 and Snell's law.*

ratio, 3/2, as before. The normal **PL** and a line **MN** parallel to the normal are drawn. The parallel line is drawn this time through point **N** where the larger arc is intersected by the extension of refracted ray **OP**. This line intersects the smaller arc at point **M**. Points **P** and **M** determine the path of the refracted ray as it enters the air.

In Figure 14-9 line **AD** represents a light ray incident upon a triangular glass prism at point **D**. Passing obliquely from air into glass, the ray is refracted toward the normal along line **DB**. Observe that at point **D** angle $i$ in air is larger than angle $r$ in glass. As light ray **DB** passes obliquely from glass into air at point **B**, it is refracted away from the normal along line **BC**. At point **B** angle $i$ in glass is smaller than angle $r$ in air.

**Figure 14-9** The path of a light ray through a prism. As the light ray AD passes from the optically less dense to the optically more dense medium at D, its path is refracted toward the normal. As the beam passes out of the glass at B, its path is refracted away from the normal.

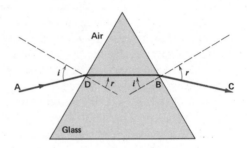

Refraction of light can be summarized in *three laws of refraction*:

*1. The incident ray, the refracted ray, and the normal to the surface at the point of incidence are all in the same plane.*

*2. The index of refraction for any homogeneous medium is a constant that is independent of the angle of incidence.*

*3. When a ray of light passes obliquely from a medium of lower optical density to one of higher optical density, it is bent toward the normal to the surface. Conversely, a ray of light passing obliquely from an optically denser medium to an optically rarer medium is bent away from the normal to the surface.*

## 14.5 Total reflection

Suppose an incident ray of light, **AO**, passes from water into air and is refracted along the line **OB**, as shown in Figure 14-10. As the angle of incidence, $i$, is increased, the angle of refraction, $r$, also increases. When this angle approaches the limiting value, $r_l = 90°$, the refracted ray emerges from the water along a path that gets closer to the water surface. As the angle of incidence continues to increase, the angle of refraction finally equals 90° and the refracted ray takes the path **ON** along the water surface. *The limiting angle of incidence in the optically denser medium that results in an angle of refraction of 90° is known as the **critical angle**, $i_c$.* The critical angle for water is reached when the inci-

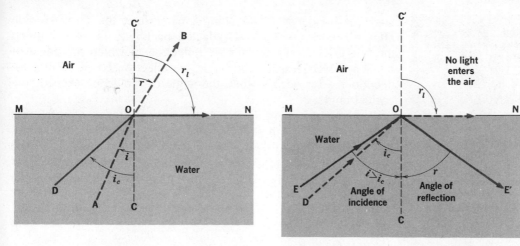

**Figure 14-10 (left)**   The critical angle $i_c$ is the limiting angle of incidence in the optically denser medium that results in an angle of refraction of 90°.

**Figure 14-11 (right)**   Total reflection at the water-air interface occurs when the angle of incidence exceeds the critical angle.

dent ray **DO** makes an angle of 48.5° with the normal; the critical angle for crown glass is 42°, while that for diamond is only 24°.

In Section 14.3 we defined the index of refraction of a material as the ratio of the speed of light in a vacuum (air) to the speed of light in the material or as the ratio $\sin i / \sin r$. In Figure 14-10 the light passes from the optically denser water to the air. Thus in the form of Snell's law, the roles of the angles of incidence and refraction are reversed. Here the angle of refraction, $r$, is related to the speed of light in air. The angle of incidence, $i$, is associated with the speed of light in water. The index of refraction of the water in this instance is

$$n = \frac{\sin r \ \textbf{(air)}}{\sin i \ \textbf{(water)}}$$

At the critical angle, $i_c$, $r$ is the limiting value $r_l$, which equals 90°. Thus

$$n = \frac{\sin r_l}{\sin i_c} = \frac{\sin 90°}{\sin i_c} = \frac{1}{\sin i_c}$$

Therefore, in general

$$\sin i_c = \frac{1}{n}$$

where $n$ is the index of refraction of the optically denser medium relative to air and $i_c$ is the critical angle of this medium.

If the angle of incidence of a ray of light passing from water into air is increased beyond the critical angle, no part of the incident ray enters the air. The incident ray is *totally reflected* from the water interface. In Figure 14-11 **EO** represents a ray of light whose angle of incidence exceeds the critical angle, the

*Some reflection (but not total reflection) occurs for angles of incidence equal to or less than $i_c$.*

**Figure 14-12** The meter stick appears to be bent at the surface of the water because of refraction. Can you account for the second image of the end of the meter stick at the lower left?

angle of incidence **EOC** being greater than the critical angle **DOC**. The ray of light is reflected back into the water along the line **OE′**, a case of simple reflection in which the angle of incidence **EOC** equals the angle of reflection **E′OC**. Total reflection always occurs when the angle of incidence exceeds the critical angle.

A diamond is a brilliant gem because its index of refraction is exceedingly high and its critical angle is therefore correspondingly small. Very little of the light that enters the upper surface of a cut diamond passes through the diamond; most of the light is reflected internally (total reflection), finally emerging from the top of the diamond.

# questions

**GROUP A**
1. Define (a) refraction, (b) angle of refraction, and (c) index of refraction.
2. What property of a transparent substance causes the refraction of light rays that strike it at an oblique angle?
3. What are the three laws of refraction?
4. What is meant by the terms (a) critical angle and (b) total reflection?
5. What practical use is made of the index of refraction of a substance?

**GROUP B**
6. You are looking diagonally down at a fish in a pond. To the fish, assuming that it can see you, does your head appear higher or lower than it actually is?
7. Explain why we see the sun before it actually rises above the horizon in the morning, and why we see it after it has dropped below the horizon in the evening.
8. Which is the better reflector of light, a right-angle prism or a plane, silvered mirror? Explain.
9. Why are totally reflecting prisms usually designed so that light enters and leaves the prism at an angle 90° with respect to the surface?
10. Why is a diamond more brilliant than a glass imitation cut the same way?

# problems

**GROUP A**
1. The speed of light in chloroform is $1.99 \times 10^8$ m/s. What is its refractive index?
2. What is the speed of light in kilometers per second in a diamond that has a refractive index of 2.42?
3. A penny at the bottom of a glass cylinder is 30.0 cm below the eye. If water is poured into the cylinder to a depth of 16.0 cm, how much closer does the coin appear?

**GROUP B**
4. A ray of light passes from a medium of refractive index 1.33 into a medium of refractive index 1.50. The angle of incidence is 45.0°. (a) By the construction method, determine the angle of refraction. (b) Compute the angle of refraction.
5. The angles of incidence and refraction of a ray of light passing from air into water are 60.0° and 41.0°. Find the index of refraction of the water.
6. Find the critical angle for a carbon tetrachloride-to-air surface.

# LENS OPTICS

A lens is any transparent object having two nonparallel curved surfaces or one plane surface and one curved surface. The curved surfaces can be spherical, parabolic, or cylindrical; spherical surfaces are the most common. Lenses are usually made of glass but can be made of other transparent materials. There are two general classes of lenses based upon their effects on incident light.

*1. Converging lenses.* Cross sections of converging lenses are shown in Figure 14-13(A). All are thicker in the middle than at the edge. The concavo-convex lens is known as a meniscus lens.

Recall that light travels more slowly in glass and other lens materials than it does in air. Light passing through the thick, middle region of a converging lens is retarded more than light passing through the thin, edge region. Consequently, a wave front of light transmitted through a converging lens is bent as shown in Figure 14-14(A). The plane wave in this diagram is incident on the surface of the converging lens parallel to the lens plane. The wave is refracted and converges at the point **F** beyond the lens.

## 14.6 Types of lenses

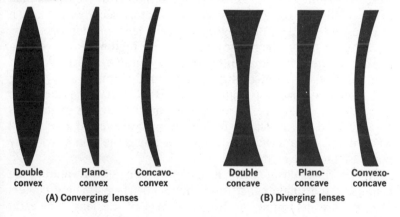

| Double convex | Plano-convex | Concavo-convex | | Double concave | Plano-concave | Convexo-concave |

**(A) Converging lenses**  **(B) Diverging lenses**

**Figure 14-13** Common lens configurations.

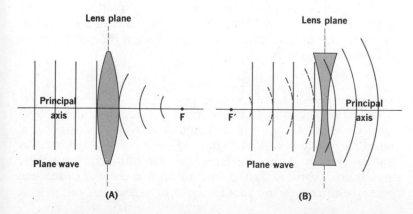

**(A)**  **(B)**

**Figure 14-14** Refraction of a plane wave (A) by a converging lens and (B) by a diverging lens. The incident wave is perpendicular to the lens axis.

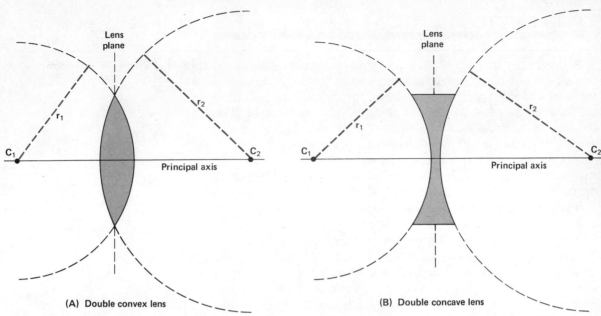

(A) Double convex lens        (B) Double concave lens

**Figure 14-15** The geometry of lens surfaces that have different radii of curvature. Observe that the surfaces of the double convex lens are sections of intersecting spheres.

2. *Diverging lenses.* Lenses that are thicker at the edges than in the middle are diverging lenses. Their cross sections are shown in Figure 14-13(B). The convexo-concave lens is a meniscus lens.

Light passing through the thin, middle region of a diverging lens is retarded less than light passing through the thick, edge region. A wave front of light transmitted through a diverging lens is bent as shown in Figure 14-14(B). Observe that the plane wave in this diagram is also incident on the surface of the lens parallel to the lens plane. In this case, however, the refracted wave diverges in a way that makes it appear to come from the point $\mathbf{F'}$ in front of the lens.

A spherical lens usually has two centers of curvature—the centers of the spheres that form the lens surfaces. These centers of curvature determine the principal axis of the lens. The radii of curvature of the two surfaces of double convex and double concave lenses are not necessarily equal, although for convenience they are so drawn in the ray diagrams in this chapter. The geometry of lens surfaces having different radii of curvature is shown in Figure 14-15.

## 14.7 Ray diagrams

The nature and location of the image formed by a lens is more easily determined by a ray diagram than by a wave-front diagram. The plane waves of Figure 14-14 can be represented by light rays drawn perpendicular to the wave fronts. Since these wave fronts approaching the lens are shown parallel to the lens plane, their ray lines are parallel to the *principal axis* of the lens.

(A)

(B)

**Figure 14-16** The ray diagram in (A) shows how rays parallel to the principal axis of a converging lens are brought to a real focus. In (B) a photograph of pencils of light shows a similar convergence.

Observe that the principal axis passes through the center of the lens and is perpendicular to the lens plane.

In Figure 14-16(A) these parallel rays (which are also parallel to the principal axis) are shown incident on a converging lens. They are refracted as they pass through the lens, and they converge at a point on the principal axis that locates the *principal focus* **F** of the lens. At point **B** the incident ray is bent toward the normal drawn to the front surface of the lens. At point **D** the incident ray is bent away from the normal drawn to the back surface of the lens. Because the rays of light actually pass through the principal focus **F**, it is called the *real focus*. *Real* images are formed on the same side of the lens as the real focus. Had these rays approached the lens from the right parallel to the principal axis, they would have converged at a point on the principal axis that located the principal focus **F′**.

*Real images can be projected on a screen.*

**Figure 14-17** (A) A ray diagram showing the refraction of light rays incident on a diverging lens parallel to its principal axis. (B) A photograph of a similar divergence of light pencils.

Rays parallel to the principal axis are shown incident on a diverging lens in Figure 14-17(A). The rays of light are refracted as they pass through the lens and diverge as if they had originated at the principal focus **F'** located in front of the lens. Because the rays do not actually pass through this principal focus, it is called a *virtual focus*. *Virtual* images are formed on the same side of the lens as the virtual focus.

In general, lenses refract rays that are parallel to the principal axis and the refracted rays either converge at the real focus behind the (converging) lens or diverge as if they originated at the virtual focus in front of the (diverging) lens. However, these foci are not midway between the lens and the center of curvature as they are in spherical mirrors. *The positions of the foci on the principal axis depend on the index of refraction of the lens.* A common double convex lens of crown glass has principal foci and centers of curvature that practically coincide and a focal length that is approximately equal to its radius of curvature. The

(A)　　　　　　　　(B)

**Figure 14-18** In (A) parallel rays are shown incident on a converging lens parallel to its principal axis. The refracted rays converge at its principal focus. In (B) the rays are incident at a small angle $\alpha$ with the principal axis. Here the refracted rays are focused at a point in the focal plane F'F" of the lens.

*focal length, f,* of a lens is the distance between the optical center of the lens and the principal focus. The focal length of any lens depends on its index of refraction and the curvature of its surfaces. The higher its index of refraction, the shorter is its focal length. The longer its radius of curvature, the longer is its focal length.

A "bundle" of parallel light rays incident on a converging lens parallel to its principal axis is refracted and converges at the principal (real) focus behind the lens. The image is ideally a point of light at the real focus. This refraction is shown in Figure 14-18(A).

Bundles of parallel rays are not always incident on a lens parallel to its principal axis. If such rays are incident on a converging lens at a small angle with the principal axis, they converge at a point in the plane that contains the principal focus of the lens and is perpendicular to the principal axis. This plane is called the *focal plane* of the lens. A bundle of parallel rays incident on a converging lens at a small angle $\alpha$ (alpha) with its principal axis is shown in Figure 14-18(B).

*The focal length of a lens is the same for light traveling in either direction even if the two lens surfaces have different radii of curvature.*

*Bundle of rays: the essentially parallel rays in a beam or a pencil of light.*

*The focal plane of a concave mirror is described in Section 13.7.*

---

The image of a point on an object is formed by intersecting refracted rays emanating from the object point. In Section 13.8 we recognized that the task of locating graphically an image formed by reflection is simplified if we select incident rays that have known paths after reflection. These rays, called *principal rays,* are shown with their *reflected* paths in Figure 13-18. Their paths after refraction are also known. They are shown with their *refracted* paths in Figure 14-19.

The image **S'** of point **S** (the object in Figure 14-19) is formed by the converging lens when the refracted rays from point **S** intersect behind the lens. Ray **1**, *parallel* to the principal axis, is refracted through the real focus, **F**. See Figure 14-16. Ray **2**, along the *secondary axis,* passes through the optical center of the lens, **O**, without being appreciably refracted. Ray **3** passes

## 14.8 Images by refraction

*Review Figure 13-18.*

**Figure 14-19** The principal rays used in ray diagrams. Any two of these three rays from the same point on an object locate the image of that point.

through the principal focus, **F′**, and is refracted parallel to the principal axis. The three refracted rays intersect at the image point **S′**. Observe that any two of the principal rays *emanating from the same object point* are sufficient to locate the image of that point.

Lenses and mirrors differ in several ways.

1. Secondary axes pass through the optical center of a lens and not through either of its centers of curvature.

2. The principal focus is usually near the center of curvature, depending on the refractive index of the glass from which the lens is made. Thus the focal length of a double convex lens is generally about equal to its radius of curvature.

3. Since the image produced by a lens is formed by rays of light that actually pass through the lens, a *real* image is formed on the side of the lens opposite the object. *Virtual* images formed by lenses appear to be on the same side of the lens as the object.

4. Convex (converging) lenses form images in almost the same manner as concave mirrors, while concave (diverging) lenses are like convex mirrors in the manner in which they form images.

Spherical lenses, like spherical mirrors, have aberration defects. See Figure 14-20. When such lenses are used with large

**Figure 14-20** (A) Rays parallel to the principal axis but near the edge of a converging lens are not refracted through the principal focus. (B) An aperture can be used to block these rays from the lens.

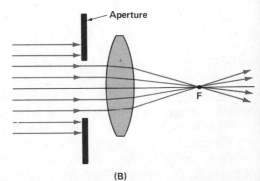

(A)                                                                                            (B)

apertures, images are generally sharp and well defined at the center but blurred near the edges because of *spherical aberration*.

Similarly, rays of light from horizontal and vertical lines in a plane in the object are not focused in the same plane on the edges of the image. This defect of lenses is known as *lens astigmatism*. By using a combination of lenses of suitable refractive indexes and focal lengths, lens makers produce *anastigmatic* lenses. Such lenses give good definition over the entire image even when used with large apertures.

A lens of short focal length that can be used with a large aperture has a large light-gathering capability. It is said to be a "fast" lens. The light-gathering power of a camera lens is given in terms of its $f$/-*number*. This number is determined by the focal length of the lens and its effective diameter. The effective diameter is the diameter of the camera aperture (diaphragm) that determines the useful lens area. The light-gathering power, or "speed," of a lens is expressed as the ratio of its focal length to its effective diameter. If the speed of a lens is given as $f/4$, it means that its focal length is 4 times its effective diameter.

Since the useful area of a lens is proportional to the square of its effective diameter, the light-gathering power of a lens increases four times when its effective diameter is doubled. An $f/4$ lens is 4 times as fast as an $f/8$ lens, and is 16 times as fast as an $f/16$ lens. It follows that the required time of exposure increases as the square of the $f$/-number.

*The area of a circle:*

$$A = \pi r^2 = \frac{\pi d^2}{4}. \textit{ Thus, } A \propto d^2.$$

## 14.9 Images formed by converging lenses

We shall consider six different cases of image formation. These cases are illustrated in Figure 14-21.

*Case 1. Object at infinite distance.* The use of a small magnifying glass to focus the sun's rays upon a point approximates this first case. While the sun is not at an infinite distance, it is so far away that its rays reaching the earth are nearly parallel. When an object is at an infinite distance and its rays are parallel to the principal axis of the lens, *the image formed is a point at the real focus.* See Figure 14-21(A). This principle can be used to find the focal length of a lens by focusing the sun's rays on a white screen. The distance from the screen to the optical center of the lens is the focal length of the lens.

*Case 2. Object at a finite distance beyond twice the focal length.* Case 2 is illustrated in (B). Rays parallel to the principal axis, along the secondary axis, and emanating from a point on the object are used to locate the corresponding image point. *The image is real, inverted, reduced, and located between F and 2F on the opposite side of the lens.* The lenses of the eye and the camera, and the objective lens of the refracting telescope are all applications of this case.

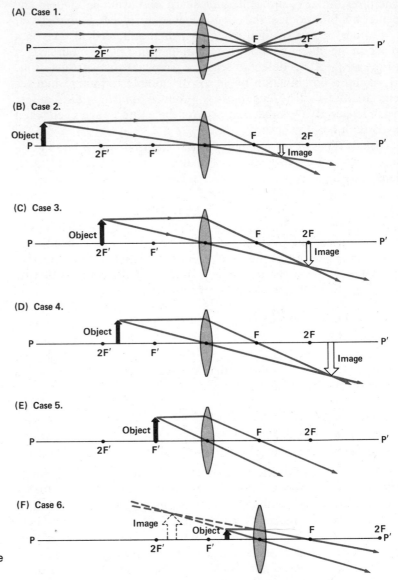

**Figure 14-21** Ray diagrams of image formation by converging lenses.

*Case 3. Object at a distance equal to twice the focal length.* The construction of the image is shown in (C). *The image is real, inverted, the same size as the object, and located at 2F on the opposite side of the lens.* An inverting lens of a field telescope, which inverts an image without changing its size, is an application of Case 3.

*Case 4. Object at a distance between one and two focal lengths away.* This is the converse of Case 2 and is shown in (D). *The image is real, inverted, enlarged, and located beyond 2F on the opposite side of the lens.* The compound microscope, slide projector, and motion picture projector are all applications of a lens used in this manner.

Case 5. *Object at the principal focus.* This case is the converse of Case 1. *No image is formed,* since the rays of light are parallel as they leave the lens (E). The lenses used in lighthouses and searchlights are applications of Case 5.

Case 6. *Object at a distance less than one focal length away.* The construction in (F) shows that the rays are divergent after passing through the lens and cannot form a real image on the opposite side of the lens. These rays appear to converge behind the object to produce *an image that is virtual, erect, enlarged, and located on the same side of the lens as the object.* The simple magnifier and the eyepiece lenses of microscopes, binoculars, and telescopes form images as shown in Case 6.

---

The only kind of image of a real object that can be formed by a diverging lens is one that is *virtual, erect, and reduced in size.* Diverging lenses are used to neutralize the effect of a converging lens, or to reduce its converging effect to some extent. The image formation is shown in Figure 14-22.

## 14.10 Images formed by diverging lenses

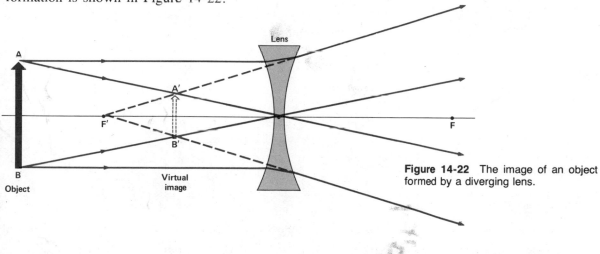

**Figure 14-22** The image of an object formed by a diverging lens.

---

For thin lenses, the ratio of object size to image size equals the ratio of the object distance to image distance. This rule is the same as the rule for curved mirrors. Thus

## 14.11 Object-image relationships

$$\frac{h_i}{h_o} = \frac{d_i}{d_o}$$

where $h_o$ and $h_i$ represent the heights of the object and the image respectively, and $d_o$ and $d_i$ represent the respective distances of the object and image from the optical center of the lens.

The equation used to determine the distances of the object

*Observe that the lens equations are the same as the mirror equations of Section 13.12.*

and image in relation to focal length for curved mirrors applies also to lenses. It can be restated here as

$$\frac{1}{f} = \frac{1}{d_o} + \frac{1}{d_i}$$

where $d_o$ represents the distance of the object from the lens, $d_i$ the distance of the image from the lens, and $f$ the focal length.

The numerical value of the focal length $f$ is *positive* for a converging lens and *negative* for a diverging lens. For real objects and images, the object and image distances $d_o$ and $d_i$ have *positive* values. For virtual objects and images, $d_o$ and $d_i$ have *negative* values.

*The lens equation is valid providing these sign conventions are followed:*

$d_o$ is $\left[\begin{array}{l} \textit{positive for real objects} \\ \textit{negative for virtual objects} \end{array}\right.$

$d_i$ is $\left[\begin{array}{l} \textit{positive for real images} \\ \textit{negative for virtual images} \end{array}\right.$

$f$ is $\left[\begin{array}{l} \textit{positive for converging lenses} \\ \textit{negative for diverging lenses} \end{array}\right.$

## 14.12 The simple magnifier

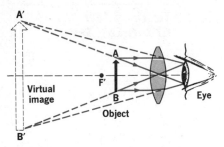

**Figure 14-23** The simple magnifier.

A converging lens of short focal length can be used as a simple magnifier. The lens is placed slightly nearer the object than one focal length and the eye is positioned close to the lens on the opposite side. This is a practical example of Case 6; the image is virtual, erect, and enlarged as shown in Figure 14-23. A reading glass, a simple microscope, and an eyepiece lens of a compound microscope or telescope are applications of simple magnifiers.

Magnification $M$ is simply the ratio of the image height to the object height.

$$M = \frac{h_i}{h_o}$$

But,

$$\frac{h_i}{h_o} = \frac{d_i}{d_o}$$

So,

$$M = \frac{d_i}{d_o}$$

Suppose an object is viewed by the unaided eye. As it is moved closer and closer to the eye, the image formed on the retina becomes larger and larger. Eventually, a *nearest* point is reached for the object at which the eye can still form a clear image. This minimum distance for distinct vision is approximately 25 cm from the eye. Although this nearest point varies among individuals, 25 cm is taken as the standard distance for most distinct vision; it is called the *near point*. As a person grows older the muscles of the eye, which thicken the lens and thus increase its convergence (shorten its focal length), gradually weaken. Consequently the near point moves out with aging.

When a converging lens is placed in front of the eye as a simple magnifier, the object can be brought much closer and the eye focuses on the virtual image. The lens is used to best advantage when the object is just inside the principal focus ($d_o \simeq f$). The image is then formed approximately at the near point. Magnification, shown above to be equal to the ratio $d_i/d_o$, can now be expressed for a simple magnifier as the ratio of the distance for most distinct vision to the focal length of the lens. When $f$ is given in centimeters, the magnification becomes approximately

$$M = \frac{25 \text{ cm}}{f}$$

Magnifiers are sometimes labeled to show their magnifying power. Thus a magnifier with a focal length of 5 cm would be marked 5X. One with a focal length of 2.5 cm would be marked 10X, etc. Observe that the shorter the focal length of a converging lens, the higher is its magnification.

---

The compound microscope, thought to be invented in Holland by Zacharias Janssen about 1590, uses a lens, the *objective*, to form an enlarged image as in Case 4. This image is then magnified, as in Case 6, by a second lens, called the *eyepiece*.

In Figure 14-24 a converging lens is used as the objective, with the object **AB** just beyond its focal length. At **A′B′**, a distance greater than twice the focal length of the objective lens, an enlarged, real, and inverted image is formed. The eyepiece lens acts as a simple magnifier to enlarge this image.

The magnifying power of the objective is approximately equal to the length of the tube, $l$, divided by the focal length, $f_o$, of the objective, or $l/f_o$. The magnifying power of the eyepiece, acting as a simple magnifier, is approximately 25 cm/$f_e$. The total magnification is the product of the two lens magnifications. (The equation is again an approximation.)

$$M = \frac{25 \text{ cm} \times l}{f_e \times f_o}$$

## 14.13 The microscope

**Figure 14-24** Image formation by a compound microscope.

---

A refracting astronomical telescope has two lens systems. The *objective lens* is of large diameter so that it will admit a large amount of light. The objects to be viewed in telescopes are always more distant than twice the focal length of the objective lens. As a consequence the image formed is smaller than the

## 14.14 Refracting telescopes

**Figure 14-25** Image formation in a terrestrial telescope.

object. The *eyepiece lens* magnifies the real image produced by the objective lens. The magnifying power is approximately equal to the focal length of the objective, $f_o$, divided by the focal length of the eyepiece, $f_e$, or $f_o/f_e$.

The lenses of a *terrestrial,* or field, telescope form images just as their counterparts do in the refracting astronomical telescope. Since it would be confusing to see objects inverted in a field telescope, another lens system is used to reinvert the real image formed by the objective. This additional inverting lens system makes the final image erect, as shown in Figure 14-25. The inverting lens system does not magnify the image because the lens system is placed exactly its own focal length from the image formed by the objective.

The *prism binocular* is actually a double field telescope that uses two sets of totally reflecting prisms instead of a third lens system to reinvert the real images formed by the objective lenses. This method of forming final images that are upright and correctly oriented also has the effect of folding the optical path, thus making binoculars more compact and easier to use than telescopes.

The prism binocular customarily has descriptive markings stamped on its case, such as $7 \times 35$, $8 \times 50$, etc. The first number gives its magnification, and the second number gives the diameters (in mm) of its objective lenses.

**Figure 14-26** A pair of totally reflecting prisms reinvert the image in binoculars.

# questions

GROUP A

1. (a) What causes spherical aberration in lenses? (b) How can it be remedied?
2. Of which case of converging lenses is the simple magnifier an application?
3. Explain the lens system and image formation of a compound microscope in terms of the lens cases used.
4. Explain the lens system and image formation of

a refracting astronomical telescope in terms of the lens cases used.
5. How does a terrestrial telescope compare with a refracting astronomical telescope?

GROUP B

6. What kinds of lenses could be used and where should the object be placed to produce (a) an enlarged real image, (b) a reduced real image,

(c) a real image the same size as the object, (d) an enlarged virtual image, (e) a small virtual image?

7. When the distance between a projector and the screen is increased, what adjustment must be made in the distance between the film and the objective lens to bring the image back into focus?

8. Is the focal length of a crown-glass diverging lens changed when the lens is immersed in water? Justify your answer.

9. A double convex lens in air acts as a converging lens. (a) Can it act as a diverging lens in another medium? (b) Construct a ray diagram to illustrate your response to (a).

10. Suppose you were going to use a clear plastic bag inflated with air as an underwater converging lens. (a) What shape should the inflated bag have? (b) Illustrate your response to (a) with an appropriate ray diagram.

# problems

## GROUP A

1. A converging lens has a focal length of 20.0 cm. If it is placed 50.0 cm from an object, at what distance from the lens will the image be?

2. If an object is $1\overline{0}$ cm from a converging lens of 5 cm focal length, how far from the lens will the image be formed?

3. The focal length of the lens in a box camera is 10.0 cm. The fixed distance between the lens and the film is 11.0 cm. If an object is to be clearly focused on the film, how far must it be from the lens?

4. An object 3.0 cm tall is placed $2\overline{0}$ cm from a converging lens. A real image is formed $1\overline{0}$ cm from the lens. What is (a) the focal length of the lens, (b) the size of the image?

5. An object $3\overline{0}$ cm from a converging lens forms a real image $6\overline{0}$ cm from the lens. (a) Find the focal length of the lens. (b) What is the size of the image if the object is 5 cm high?

6. The focal length of a camera lens is 5.00 cm. How far must the lens be from the film to produce a clear image of an object 3.00 m away?

7. What is the focal length of the lens in your eye when you read a book 35.0 cm from your eye? Distance from lens to retina is 19.0 mm.

8. What is the focal length of the lens in your eye when you are looking at a person standing 15.0 m away? The distance from the lens to the retina is 19.0 mm.

9. What is the magnifying power of a simple magnifier whose focal length is $1\overline{0}$ cm?

## GROUP B

10. An object 3 cm tall is placed 16 cm from a converging lens with a focal length of 24 cm. (a) Find the location of the image. (b) What is its size?

11. When an object 5.0 cm tall is placed 12 cm from a converging lens, an image is produced on the same side of the lens as the object but 61 cm away from the lens. What is (a) the focal length of the lens, (b) the size of the image?

12. An optical bench pointer 1.0 cm tall is placed at the 55.0-cm mark on the meter stick. When a diverging lens is placed at the 0.0-cm mark, an image is formed at the 5.0-cm mark. What is (a) the focal length of the lens, (b) the size of the image?

13. The objective lens of a compound microscope has a focal length of 0.500 cm. The eyepiece has a focal length of 2.00 cm. If the lenses are 15.0 cm apart, what is the magnifying power of the microscope?

14. The dimensions of the picture on a slide are 6.4 cm by 7.6 cm. This slide is to be projected to form an image 1.5 m by 1.8 m at a distance of 9.0 m from the objective lens of the projector. (a) What is the distance from the slide to the objective lens? (b) What focal length objective lens must be used?

15. The tube of a microscope is $16\overline{0}$ mm long. If the focal length of the eyepiece is 30.0 mm and the focal length of the objective is 5.00 mm, find the magnifying power.

16. What is the distance between the objective lens and the eyepiece lens of a terrestrial telescope when an object 1.5 kilometers away is being observed? The focal length of the objective lens is 15 cm and the focal length of the eyepiece lens is 5 cm. Each lens of the two-lens inverting system has a focal length of 3 cm, and these two lenses are 6 cm apart.

### 14.15 Dispersion by a prism

Suppose a narrow beam of sunlight is directed onto a glass prism in a darkened room. If the light that leaves the prism falls on a white screen, a band of colors is observed, one shade blending gradually into another. *This band of colors produced when sunlight is dispersed by a prism is called a **solar spectrum**.* The dispersion of sunlight was described by Newton, who observed that the spectrum was "violet at one end, red at the other, and showed a continuous gradation of colors in between."

We can recognize six distinct colors in the visible spectrum. These are *red, orange, yellow, green, blue,* and *violet.* Each color gradually blends into the adjacent colors giving a *continuous* spectrum over the range of visible light. A continuous spectrum is shown in **Plate VII** of the color insert between pages 332 and 333. *Light consisting of several colors is called **polychromatic** light; light consisting of only one color is called **monochromatic** light.*

The dispersion of light by a prism is shown in **Plate I** of the color insert. It is evident that the refraction of red light by the prism is not as great as that of violet light; the refractions of other colors lie between these two. Thus the index of refraction of glass is not the same for light of different colors. If we wish to be very precise in measuring the index of refraction of a substance, monochromatic light must be used and the monochrome color must be stated. Some variations in the index of refraction of glass are given in Table 14-1.

Table 14-1

| VARIATION OF THE INDEX OF REFRACTION | | |
|---|---|---|
| Color | Crown glass | Flint glass |
| red | 1.515 | 1.622 |
| yellow | 1.517 | 1.627 |
| blue | 1.523 | 1.639 |
| violet | 1.533 | 1.663 |

### 14.16 The color of light

A hot solid radiates an appreciable amount of energy that increases as the temperature is raised. At relatively low temperatures, the energy is radiated only in the infrared region. As the temperature of the solid is raised, some of the energy is radiated at higher frequencies. These frequencies range into the red portion of the visible spectrum as the body becomes "red hot." At still higher temperatures the solid may be "white hot" as the major portion of the radiated energy shifts toward the higher frequencies.

Suppose we have a clear-glass tungsten-filament lamp connected in an electric circuit so that the current in the filament, and thus the temperature of the filament, can be controlled. A small electric current in the filament does not change the filament's appearance. As we gradually increase the current, however, the filament begins to glow with a dark red color. To produce this color electrons in the atoms of tungsten must have been excited to sufficiently high energy levels so that upon de-excitation they emit energy with wavelengths of about 7600 Å.

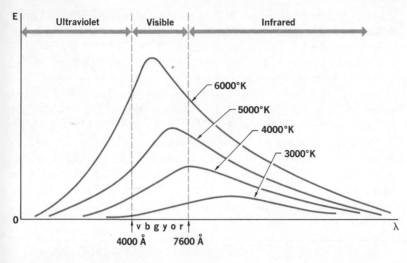

**Figure 14-27** Distribution of radiant energy from an ideal radiator.

Even before the lamp filament glows visibly, experiments show that it radiates infrared rays that can be detected as heat. As the current is increased further, the lamp filament gives off orange light in addition to red; then the filament adds yellow, and finally at higher temperatures it adds enough other colors to produce white light.

A photographer's tungsten-filament flood lamp operates at a very high temperature. If the white light of such a lamp is passed through a prism, a band of colors similar to the solar spectrum is obtained. Figure 14-27 shows the distribution of radiant energy from an "ideal" radiator for several different temperatures.

Considering the wavelengths of various colors shown in **Plate I**, it is evident that our eyes are sensitive to a range of frequencies equivalent to about one octave. The wavelength of the light at the upper limit of visibility (7600 Å) is about twice the wavelength of the light at the lower limit of visibility (4000 Å). We use the word *color* to describe a psychological sensation through the visual sense related to the physical stimulus of light. The color perceived for monochromatic light depends on the wavelength of the light. For example, when light of about 6500 Å enters the eye, the color perceived is red.

## 14.17 The color of objects

Color is a property of the light that reaches our eyes. Objects may absorb certain wavelengths from the light falling upon them and reflect other wavelengths. For example, a cloth that appears blue in sunlight appears black when held in the red portion of a solar spectrum in a darkened room. A red cloth held in the blue portion of the solar spectrum also appears black. *The color of an opaque object depends upon the frequencies of light it reflects.* If all colors are reflected, we say it is *white*. It is *black* if it absorbs

*Actually, in order to be reflected the red light must interact with the object. The interaction consists of a resonant absorption by electrons of the object's atoms. The energy is immediately re-emitted or "reflected."*

all the light that falls upon it. It is called *red* if it absorbs all other colors and reflects only red light. The energy associated with the colors absorbed is taken up as heat.

A piece of blue cloth appears black in the red portion of the spectrum because there is no blue light there for it to reflect and it absorbs all other colors. For the same reason, a red cloth appears black in the blue portion of the spectrum. *The color of an opaque object depends on the color of the light incident upon it.*

Ordinary window glass, which transmits all colors, is said to be colorless. Red glass absorbs all colors but red, which it transmits. The stars of the United States flag would appear red on a black field if viewed through red glass. *The color of a transparent object depends upon the color of the light that it transmits.*

## 14.18 Complementary colors

*The term "color" refers to the color of light.*

*Combining colored lights is an additive process.*

*Become familiar with the six elementary colors and their complements, illustrated in **Plate II**.*

Since polychromatic light can be dispersed into its elementary colors, it is reasonable to suppose that we can combine elementary colors to form polychromatic light. There are three ways in which this can be done.

1. A prism placed in the path of the solar spectrum formed by another prism will recombine the different colors to produce white light. Other colors can be compounded in the same manner.

2. A disk that has the spectral colors painted on it can be rotated rapidly to produce the effect of combining the colors. The light from one color forms an image that persists on the retina of the eye until each of the other colors in turn has been reflected to the eye. If pure spectral colors are used in the proper proportion, they will blend to produce the same color sensation as white light.

3. Wavelengths from the middle region of the visible spectrum combined with wavelengths from the two end regions produce white light. This method is described in Section 14.19.

Two prisms are used as described above, but with the red light from the first prism blocked off from the second prism. The remaining spectral colors are recombined by the second prism to produce a blue-green color called *cyan*. Red light and cyan should therefore combine to produce white light, and a rotating color wheel shows this to be true. *Any two colors that combine to form white light are said to be **complementary**.*

In similar fashion it can be shown that blue and yellow are complementary colors. White fabrics acquire a yellowish color after continued laundering. A blue dye added to laundry detergents neutralizes the yellow color and the fabrics appear white. Iron compounds in the sand used for making glass impart a green color to the glass. Manganese gives glass a *magenta,* or purplish-red, color. However, if both these elements are present in the right proportion, the resulting glass will be colorless. Green and magenta are complementary colors. The complements of the six elementary spectral colors are shown in **Plate II**.

The six regions of color in the solar spectrum are easily observed by the dispersion of sunlight. Further dispersion within a color region fails to reveal any other colors of light. We generally identify the range of wavelengths comprising a color region by the color of light associated with that region. These are the six *elementary* colors of the visible spectrum; they combine to produce white light. However, the complement of an elementary color is not monochromatic but is a mixture of all of the elementary colors remaining after the one elementary color has been removed.

Experiments with beams of different colored lights have shown that most colors and hues can be described in terms of three different colors. Light from one end of the visible spectrum combined with light from the middle region in various proportions will yield all of the color hues in the half of the spectrum that lies in between them. Light from the opposite end, when combined with light from the middle region, will also yield all hues in the half of the spectrum that lies in between them. Colored light from the two end regions and the middle region can be combined to match most of the hues when mixed in the proper proportions. The three colors that can be used most successfully in color matching experiments of this sort are *red, green,* and *blue.* Consequently these have been called the **primary colors**.

Suppose we project the three primary colors onto a white screen as shown in **Plate III(A)**. The three beams can be adjusted to overlap, producing additive mixtures of these primary colors. Observe that green and blue lights combine to produce cyan, the complement of red; green and red lights combine to produce yellow, the complement of blue; and red and blue lights combine to produce magenta, the complement of green. Thus two primary colors combine to produce the complement of the third primary color. Where the three primary colors overlap, white light is produced.

### 14.19 The primary colors

*Combining primary colors is an additive process.*

When the complements blue light and yellow light are mixed, white light results by an additive process. If we mix a blue pigment with a yellow pigment, a green mixture results. This process is subtractive since each pigment subtracts or absorbs certain colors. For example, the yellow pigment subtracts blue and violet lights and reflects red, yellow, and green. The blue pigment subtracts red and yellow lights and reflects green, blue, and violet. Green light is the only color reflected by both pigments; thus the mixture of pigments appears green under white light.

The subtractive process can be demonstrated by the use of various color filters that absorb certain wavelengths and transmit others from a single white-light source.

When pigments are mixed, each one subtracts certain colors from white light, and the resulting color depends on the light

### 14.20 Mixing pigments

*Combining primary pigments is a subtractive process.*

*Compare the additive combinations of primary colors in **Plate III(A)** with the subtractive combinations of primary pigments in **Plate IV(A)**.*

waves that are not absorbed. *The **primary pigments** are the complements of the three primary colors*. They are cyan (the complement of red), magenta (the complement of green), and yellow (the complement of blue). When the three primary pigments are mixed in the proper proportions, all the colors are subtracted from white light and the mixture is black. See **Plate IV**.

---

### 14.21 Chromatic aberration

Because a lens configuration has some similarity to that of a prism, some dispersion occurs when light passes through a lens. Violet light is refracted more than the other colors and is brought to a focus by a converging lens at a point nearer the lens than the other colors. Because red is refracted the least, the focus for the red rays is farthest from the lens. See Figure 14-28(A). Thus images formed by ordinary spherical lenses are always fringed with spectral colors. *The non-focusing of light of different colors is called **chromatic aberration***. Sir Isaac Newton developed the reflecting telescope to avoid the objectionable effects of chromatic aberration that occur when observations are made through a refracting telescope.

The English optician John Dollond (1706–1761) discovered that the fringe of colors could be eliminated by means of a combination of lenses. A double convex lens of crown glass used with a suitable plano-concave lens of flint glass corrects for chromatic aberration without preventing refraction and image formation. A lens combination of this type is shown in Figure 14-28(B). It is called an *achromatic* (without color) lens.

**Figure 14-28** (A) Chromatic aberration is caused by unequal refraction of the different colors. (B) A two-lens combination of crown and flint glass corrects chromatic aberration.

(A) Chromatic aberration

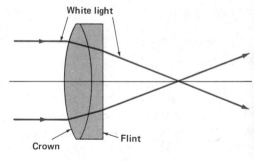

(B) Achromatic lens

## summary

The laws of refraction describe the behavior of light rays that pass obliquely from one medium into another of different optical density. The index of refraction of any transparent material is defined in terms of the speed of light in a vacuum and the speed of light in the material. The index of refraction is also expressed

in terms of Snell's law. Total reflection is explained on the basis of the critical angle of a material and the limiting value of the angle of refraction.

Converging lenses have convex surfaces and form images in a manner similar to that of concave mirrors. Diverging lenses have concave surfaces and form

**A.** The prism spreads a narrow beam of white light out into the visible spectrum, the shorter wavelengths being bent more than the longer wavelengths.

**B.** A red filter between the prism and the screen allows only light of the longer wavelengths to pass.

**C.** A green filter allows only light from the middle region of the spectrum to pass.

**D.** A blue filter passes only light of the shorter wavelengths.

(Adapted from COLOR AS SEEN AND PHOTOGRAPHED, Eastman Kodak)

Plate I

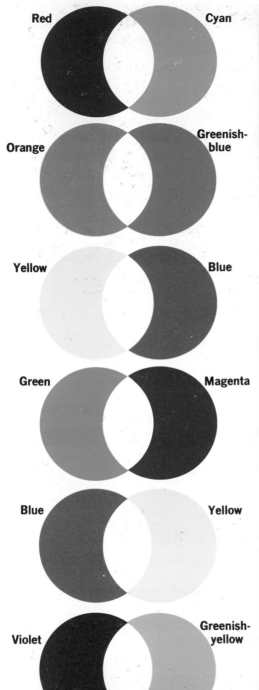

Red  Cyan

Orange  Greenish-blue

Yellow  Blue

Green  Magenta

Blue  Yellow

Violet  Greenish-yellow

**A.  Complementary colors.**

**B.  A cyan filter absorbs its complement, red light, and transmits blue and green light.**

**C.  A magenta filter absorbs its complement, green light, and transmits red and blue light.**

**D.  A yellow filter absorbs its complement, blue light, and transmits red and green light.**

**(Adapted from COLOR AS SEEN AND PHOTOGRAPHED, Eastman Kodak)**

Plate II

A. Primary colors. The additive mixture of red, green, and blue lights produces white light. Combined in pairs, two primaries give the complement of the third: cyan, magenta, and yellow. (Adapted from COLOR AS SEEN AND PHOTO-GRAPHED, Eastman Kodak)

B. Interference produced by reflecting white light from a soap film. The picture on the right shows the fringes produced by red light.

Plate III

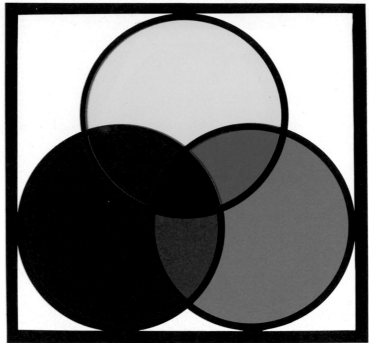

**A. Primary pigments.** The subtractive combination of cyan, magenta, and yellow filters transmits no light. Combined in pairs, two primary pigments give the complement of the third by subtraction: red, green, and blue.

**B. Subtractive process.** The range of colors produced by mixing the three primary pigments is shown on the left. The quantities are decreased toward the center allowing the white background to show through. At the right, magenta, yellow, and cyan water colors are mixed in varying amounts to give black shading through gray to white. (Adapted from COLOR AS SEEN AND PHOTOGRAPHED, Eastman Kodak)

Plate IV

Unpackaged

Sunlight

Molecule of atmospheric gas

Transmitted yellow-red
light partially polarized

Scattered blue
light, plane
polarized

B.  The appearance of the blue sky is due to the scattering of the shorter
wavelengths of the sunlight passing overhead in the atmosphere.

**A.** A continuous spectrum is produced by incandescent solids, liquids, and gases under high pressure. The very dense incandescent gases in the main body of the sun and stars produce continuous spectra.

**B.** A bright-line spectrum is produced by incandescent gases of low density. Each chemical substance yields a characteristic pattern of lines that differ from all others.

**C.** A dark-line spectrum is produced by a nonluminous (cooler) gas in front of an incandescent source of a continuous spectrum. The cooler gas absorbs light energy from the parts of the spectrum where it would emit bright lines if heated to incandescence. (Adapted from THE UNIVERSE, Time, Inc.)

Plate VI

# EMISSION SPECTRA

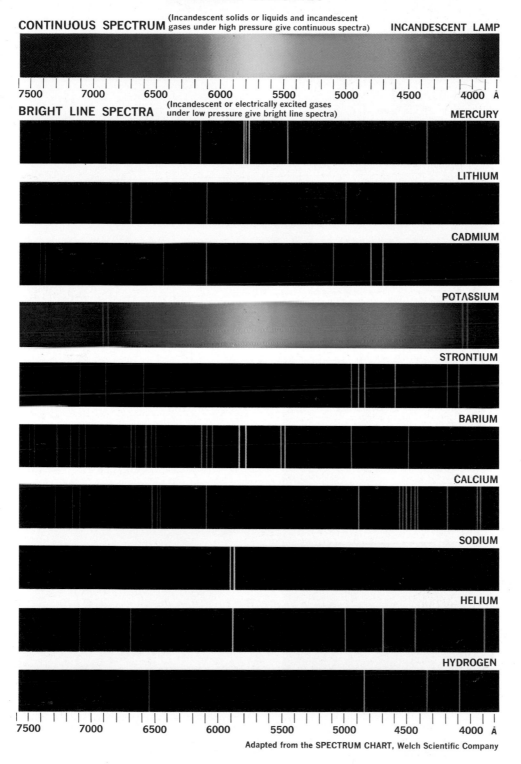

**CONTINUOUS SPECTRUM** (Incandescent solids or liquids and incandescent gases under high pressure give continuous spectra) **INCANDESCENT LAMP**

7500   7000   6500   6000   5500   5000   4500   4000 Å

**BRIGHT LINE SPECTRA** (Incandescent or electrically excited gases under low pressure give bright line spectra) **MERCURY**

LITHIUM

CADMIUM

POTASSIUM

STRONTIUM

BARIUM

CALCIUM

SODIUM

HELIUM

HYDROGEN

7500   7000   6500   6000   5500   5000   4500   4000 Å

Adapted from the SPECTRUM CHART, Welch Scientific Company

**Plate VII**

A. Interference pattern produced by light of a single spectral color passing through two narrow slits.

B. Passing white light through a single slit produces this diffraction pattern.

Red light passed through the same slit produces this pattern.

C. Mercury light through a diffraction grating. First and second order spectra appear to the right of the central image.

Plate VIII

images in a manner similar to that of convex mirrors. The general lens equations correspond to those for curved mirrors. These equations relate object and image sizes with their respective distances from the lens and object and image distances with the focal length of the lens.

A converging lens forms either real or virtual images of real objects depending on the position of the object relative to the principal focus of the lens. A diverging lens forms only virtual images of real objects. Lens functions in common types of refractive instruments such as microscopes and telescopes can be analyzed by considering each lens separately.

Sunlight is composed of polychromatic light that undergoes dispersion when refracted by a prism. Six elementary colors are recognized in dispersed white light. The visual perception of color is related to the wavelength of visible light.

The removal of an elementary color from white light leaves a polychromatic color that is the complement of the color removed. Addition of complementary colors produces white light. White light is produced by adding the primary colors. Any two of the three primary colors add to produce the complement of the third. The primary pigments are complements of the primary colors. Their combination is a subtractive process.

# questions

## GROUP A

1. Why does a prism disperse sunlight into a band of colors?

2. What property of light determines its color?

3. What name is given to electromagnetic radiations having wavelengths slightly (a) longer and (b) shorter than visible light?

4. If a black object absorbs all light rays incident upon it, how can it be seen?

5. What is the appearance of a red dress in a closed room illuminated only by green light? Explain.

6. (a) What are the primary colors? (b) Define a complementary color. (c) Name the complement of each primary color.

## GROUP B

7. Why can't white paint be made from orange paint by adding a pigment of another color?

8. How could you demonstrate that a piece of white-hot iron gives off red light?

9. The focal length of a converging lens is determined experimentally using red light. (a) How will this focal length compare with that for green light? (b) Construct a ray diagram to support your conclusion in (a).

10. Suppose a diverging lens is substituted for the converging lens in Question 9. (a) How will the focal length of the lens for red light compare with that for green light? (b) Construct an appropriate diagram to support your conclusion.

# 15

# Diffraction and Polarization

## INTERFERENCE AND DIFFRACTION

### 15.1 Double-slit interference

The superposition of two identical wave trains traveling in the same or opposite direction illustrates the phenomenon of *interference*. Sound waves of the same amplitude and wavelength projected in the same direction by two loudspeakers provide an interference pattern in which alternate regions of reinforcement and cancellation can be found. Two identical waves traveling in opposite directions on a stretched string interfere to produce a standing wave pattern.

The interference of two water waves of identical wavelength is easily observed in the laboratory using the ripple tank. More precise studies of such wave behavior are made by photographing light reflections from the surface of a mercury ripple tank. Interference and superposition topics can be reviewed by referring to Sections 10.14 through 10.16.

The superposition principle holds for these wave disturbances in material media and for light waves and other electromagnetic waves in free space. Thus light shows **interference**: *the mutual effect of two beams of light that results in a loss of intensity in certain regions (destructive interference) and a reinforcement of intensity in other regions (constructive interference).*

The English physician and physicist Thomas Young (1773–1829) first demonstrated interference of light in 1801 and showed how this phenomenon supports the wave theory of Huygens. Two narrow slits, as shown in Figure 15-1, about 1 mm apart in a piece of black paper are used to observe a narrow source of light, **S**, placed 2 or 3 meters away. A series of narrow bands alternately dark and light is seen in the center of a fairly wide

**Figure 15-1** A method of observing double-slit interference.

334

band of light. See Figure 15-2. If a red filter is placed between the source and the slits so that a single spectral color is the light source, a series of red and black bands is seen. A double-slit interference pattern from a monochromatic light is shown in **Plate VIII(A)**.

A wave-front diagram of double-slit interference with a monochromatic light source is shown in Figure 15-3. Slits $S_1$ and $S_2$ are equidistant from the source $S$. As light from $S$ reaches $S_1$ and $S_2$, each slit serves as a new light source producing new wave fronts in phase with each other. These waves travel out from $S_1$ and $S_2$ producing bright bands of light due to reinforcement where constructive interference occurs and dark bands due to cancellation where destructive interference occurs.

**Figure 15-2** A double-slit interference pattern.

*Compare the diagram in Figure 15-3 with the photograph in Figure 10-26.*

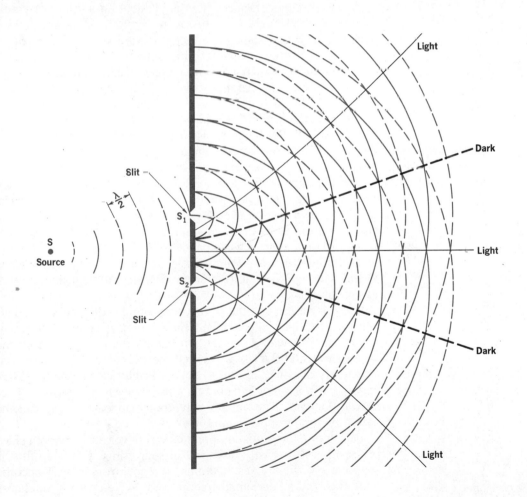

**Figure 15-3** A wave-front diagram of double-slit interference.

## 15.2 Interference in thin films

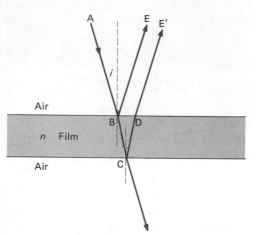

**Figure 15-4** Partial reflection and refraction of light in a thin film results in interference.

*The two reflected waves, BE and DE', are coherent because they both originate from the same point A on the monochromatic source.*

*The wavelength referred to is the wavelength of the monochromatic light in the thin film. Since the index of refraction of the film is higher than that of air, the wavelength of the light is shorter in the film than in the air.*

*Camera lenses are often coated with transparent thin films to reduce stray reflected light and increase image contrast.*

Sir Isaac Newton knew about the color fringes produced by thin films. He devised experiments to determine the film thickness that corresponds to a specific color. Interference of light was unknown in his time however. His corpuscular explanation of the partial reflection and partial refraction of light at the interface of two different transmitting media is inadequate in view of modern theories of light.

When viewed by reflected white light, thin transparent soap films, oil slicks, and wedge-shaped films of air show varying patterns of colors. When illuminated by monochromatic light, alternate bright and dark regions are observed, and the positions of the bands shift as the color of the monochromatic light is changed. Thomas Young explained this thin-film phenomenon in terms of the interference of light waves.

A ray of monochromatic light is incident on a thin transparent film at a small angle *i* as shown in Figure 15-4. Some light is reflected at **B** and some is refracted toward **C**. The index of refraction, *n,* of the transparent film is higher than that of air. The refracted light is then partially reflected at **C**, emerging from the film along **DE'** parallel to **BE**. If the wave fronts traveling along **BE** and **DE'** reach the eye, interference is observed. This is because the paths **ABE** and **ACE'** differ in length and the partial path **BCD** of **ACE'** is in a medium of different optical density. The nature of the interference depends on the phase relation between the waves arriving at the eye.

For the monochromatic light that is used, assume that the incidence angle *i* is very small and the film at **B** has an optical thickness of a quarter wavelength. Thus the optical path *in the thin film* from **B** to **C** is one-quarter wavelength. From **C** to **D** is another one-quarter wavelength. Light emerging from the film at **D** is therefore one-half wavelength behind that reflected at **B** and will be expected to interfere destructively causing the film to appear dark.

Now if we assume the film has an optical thickness of a half wavelength, light reflected from the lower surface of the film will emerge at **D** a whole wavelength behind that reflected from the upper surface at **B**. The waves will be expected to interfere constructively causing the film to appear bright at this point. *Observation of reflected light from thin films shows that a reverse effect actually occurs.* The quarter-wave point appears *bright* and the half-wave point appears *dark*.

This anomalous situation prevails whenever air is on both sides of the film. It is easily observed in soap films. If a soap film is supported vertically, as it drains its upper region will become quite thin and a very small fraction of a wavelength in thickness just before it breaks. If observed by reflected monochromatic light at this moment, this upper region appears dark. See **Plate III(B)**.

Applying the same line of argument to this film of almost negligible thickness, we would expect the light reflected from the front surface and that reflected from the back surface to reach the eye so nearly in phase that this upper region of the film would appear bright by reflected light. Here is a clear-cut discrepancy between observation and theory. How can it be reconciled?

Thomas Young resolved the discrepancy by suggesting that *one of the interfering waves undergoes a phase inversion during reflection*. This phase inversion gives a phase difference associated with a reflecting interface difference of a half wavelength between the two reflected waves. This phase difference is in addition to the phase difference that results from the unequal lengths of their optical paths. The phase inversion occurs during one reflection and not the other because the two reflections are opposite in kind. One reflection takes place at an interface where the medium beyond has a higher index of refraction. This corresponds to **B** in Figure 15-4. *The reflected wave is inverted in phase*. The other reflection occurs at an interface where the medium beyond has a lower index of refraction. This corresponds to **C** in Figure 15-4. *The reflected wave experiences no change in phase*.

Because of the phase-inverting effect of one of the two reflecting interfaces, the rules for constructive and destructive interference for thin films *bounded on both sides with a medium of lower index of refraction* are just the opposite from those we might expect. *Maximum constructive interference occurs with such thin films if the optical path difference is an odd number of half wavelengths*. This happens where the film thickness is an *odd* number of quarter wavelengths. *Maximum destructive interference occurs if the optical path difference is a whole number of wavelengths*. Here the film thickness is an *even* number of quarter wavelengths.

The vertically supported soap films of **Plate III(B)** gradually increase in thickness toward the bottom as they drain. A vertical cross section of such a film would have a wedge-like appearance. As the thickness increases the odd $\lambda/4$ requirement for the reinforcement of different colors and the even $\lambda/4$ requirement for their cancellation are met at successive intervals down the film. The soap film shown on the left of **Plate III(B)** therefore reflects white light as a succession of colors at intervals down the film.

An air film between two optically flat glass plates produces a regular pattern of interference fringes. Irregular surfaces produce irregular patterns of interference fringes. Using interference patterns, inspection techniques have been developed that make extremely high precision measurements possible. Test plates can be polished optically flat with a tolerance of approximately $5 \times 10^{-7}$ cm. Interference techniques are used to establish standards of measurement in many mechanical

*See Section 10.10 for a review of incident and reflected waves at a reflecting interface.*

**Figure 15-5** Interference patterns. (left) Straight interference fringes obtained from an optical flat. (right) An interference pattern obtained from a spherical mirror being tested in an interferometer. The white spots are reflections from the interferometer light source.

processes. The *interferometer* is an instrument that uses interference in the measurement of distance in terms of known wavelengths of light or in the measurement of wavelengths in terms of a standard of length.

## 15.3 Diffraction of light

*Review diffraction as observed in the ripple tank in Section 10.13.*

**Figure 15-6** A master diffraction grating being ruled by a diamond-pointed scribe.

According to the wave theory, light waves should bend around corners although our common experience with light shows that it travels in straight lines. Under some conditions light waves do bend out of their straight paths. When light waves encounter an obstruction with dimensions comparable to their wavelengths, the light spreads out and produces spectral colors due to interference. *The spreading of light into a region behind an obstruction is called **diffraction**.* A slit opening, a fine wire, a sharp-edged object, or a pinhole can serve as a suitable obstruction in the path of a beam of light from a point source. It is possible to see diffraction fringes if one peers between two fingers at a distant light source. With the fingers held close to the eye and brought together to form a slit opening, dark fringes will be seen just before the light is shut out.

Diffraction effects, such as indistinct edges of shadows and shadow fringes, are known to have been observed as early as the seventeenth century. However, before the discovery of interference in 1801, neither the wave theory nor the corpuscular theory could offer a suitable explanation for these diffraction effects. In 1816 the French physicist A. J. Fresnel (fray-*nel*) (1788–1827) demonstrated that the various diffraction phenomena are fully explained by the interference of light waves.

Very useful diffraction patterns can be produced by illuminating an optical surface, either plane or spherical concave, that has many thousands of straight, equally-spaced parallel grooves ruled on it. These ruled surfaces are known as *diffraction gratings*. Light is diffracted when it is transmitted through or reflected from the narrow spaces between the ruled lines.

Standard gratings can have as many as 12,000 ruled lines per centimeter of grating surface. X rays are investigated with ordinary diffraction gratings set with their surface at a low angle to the rays. The gratings thus have the equivalent of many lines per centimeter. Gratings are generally superior to optical prisms for displaying the length or spread of spectra. However, grating spectra tend to be less intense than those formed by prisms.

---

A transmission grating placed in the path of plane waves disturbs the wave front because the ruled lines are opaque to light and the narrow spacings between the lines are transparent. These spaces provide a large number of fine, closely-spaced transmission slits. New wavelets generated at these slits interfere in such a way that several new wave fronts are established. One wave front travels in the original direction and the other wave fronts travel at various angles from this direction depending on their wavelength.

Suppose a single narrow slit is illuminated by white light and viewed through a transmission grating. A white image of the illuminated slit is seen directly in line with the slit opening. In addition, pairs of continuous spectra are observed, each pair equally spaced on opposite sides of the principal image.

If we illuminate the slit with monochromatic light, successive pairs of slit images of decreasing intensity will appear on opposite sides of the principal image. The two images forming the first pair are known as *first order* images, those forming the second pair as *second order* images, etc.

Referring to Figure 15-7, **A** and **B** are parallel spaces between the ruled lines on a diffraction grating. They act as adjacent transmission slits, being uniformly separated by the distance $d$, called the *grating constant*. Monochromatic light from a distant illuminated slit traveling normal to the grating surface produces secondary wavelets simultaneously at **A** and **B**. A new wave front of these wavelets proceeds along **MN** and produces the principal image of the distant slit at **N**.

A given wavelet from **B** and the first preceding wavelet from **A** produce a wave front **CB** that travels along **MO** and gives a *first order* image of the slit at **O**. Similarly, a given wavelet from **B** and the second preceding wavelet from **A** give a wave front **DB** that yields a *second order* image at **P**, etc. Of course, corresponding images appear at **O′**, **P′**, etc., on the other side of **N**.

In the right triangle **ABC**, side **AC** equals the wavelength $\lambda$ of the incident light and angle $\theta_1$ is the angle of the first order

## 15.4 Wavelength by diffraction

*Recall Huygens' principle explained in Section 12.3: Each point on a wave front may be regarded as a new source of disturbance.*

**Figure 15-7** The optical geometry of a transmission grating.

diffracted wave front from the grating plane, the *diffraction angle*. It is evident that

$$\lambda = d \, \sin \, \theta_1$$

Side **AD** of triangle **ABD** is equal to $2\lambda$ and $\theta_2$ is the second order diffraction angle. Thus for second order images,

$$\lambda = \frac{d \, \sin \, \theta_2}{2}$$

In the general case, for *n* orders, the grating equation becomes

$$\lambda = \frac{d \, \sin \, \theta_n}{n}$$

The diffraction angle $\theta$ can be determined experimentally. Knowing the order of image *n* observed, the diffraction angle $\theta$, and the grating constant *d*, the wavelength of the light can be calculated from this equation. Of course, if the grating constant of a particular diffraction grating is not known, it can be calculated from an experimental determination of $\theta_n$ in which a monochromatic light of known wavelength is used. In the example, the grating equation is used to determine the wavelength of a monochromatic light from experimental data.

*Reliable measurements of the wavelengths of light from various sources can be made in the laboratory using this diffraction method.*

**EXAMPLE**

*An optical grating with $6.00 \times 10^3$ lines/cm gives a second order image at a diffraction angle of $44.8°$. Calculate the wavelength of the light used.*

**SOLUTION**

$$\lambda = \frac{d \sin \theta_n}{n}$$

where

$$n = 2 \quad \text{and} \quad d = \frac{1}{6.00 \times 10^3/\text{cm}} = 1.67 \times 10^{-4} \text{ cm}$$

$$\lambda = \frac{1.67 \times 10^{-4} \text{ cm} \times \sin 44.8°}{2}$$

$$\lambda = \frac{1.67 \times 10^{-4} \text{ cm} \times 0.705}{2} \times \frac{\text{Å}}{10^{-8} \text{ cm}}$$

$$\lambda = 5890 \text{ Å}$$

According to Huygens' principle, every point on an advancing wave front can be regarded as a new source of disturbance from which secondary waves spread out as spherical wavelets. If a barrier with a narrow slit opening is placed in the path of advancing plane waves, the disturbance will be transmitted by the slit to the region beyond the barrier. See Figure 15-8(A). When the width of the slit opening is reduced to only a few wavelengths of the light, a broad region **MN** is illuminated by the slit. Experiments show that the central portion of this region is always brighter than the remote portions that reveal diffraction fringes of diminishing intensity. Examples of single-slit diffraction patterns are shown in **Plate VIII(B)**.

In Figure 15-8(B) the point $b_0$ lies on the perpendicular bisector of the slit and is equidistant from points **B** and **C**. Because the distance from the slit to the screen is very large compared to the width of the slit, point $b_0$ is essentially equidistant from all points along the line **BAC**. Thus the wavelets originating simultaneously from all points along **BA** and from all points along **AC** will reach $b_0$ in phase and the screen in this region will be bright.

At points $d_1$, above and below $b_0$, where the distance from **B** and **C** is different by a whole wavelength, the distance from **A**

## 15.5 Single-slit diffraction

(A)                (B)

**Figure 15-8**  Single-slit diffraction. Slit size is exaggerated relative to the lines and screen.

and **C** is different by a half wavelength. For every point along **CA** there is a corresponding point along **BA** that is a half wavelength different in distance from $d_1$. Therefore wavelets arriving at $d_1$ from one half of the slit will be annulled by the wavelets arriving from the other half of the slit. The region of $d_1$ will be dark.

Beyond points $d_1$ there are points $b_1$ where the distance from **B** and **C** is different by 1.5 wavelengths. Now we can think of the slit opening as being divided into three equal parts. Wavelets from one part arrive at $b_1$ a half wavelength behind wavelets from the second part. Thus wavelets from these parts of the slit opening interfere destructively, while wavelets arriving from the third part produce brightness at $b_1$. However, the illumination at $b_1$ will be lower than that at $b_0$ since only one-third of the slit opening contributes to the brightness of these regions.

By the same reasoning the regions of $d_2$, where the difference in distance from **B** and **C** is 2 wavelengths, will be dark. Similarly, the regions of $b_2$ will be bright. Thus a series of alternate bright and dark regions appears on either side of $b_0$. The intensity of these regions decreases as the distance from $b_0$ increases.

# questions

## GROUP A

1. How do the colors of a soap bubble originate?
2. Why are the various colors of white light separated by a diffraction grating?
3. Will the angular separation between red and blue rays be greater in the first-order or second-order spectrum of white light produced by a diffraction grating?
4. You are given two diffraction gratings, one with 400 lines per centimeter and the other with 4000 lines per centimeter. Which grating yields more orders of images of an illuminated slit?
5. What advantage is realized by increasing the number of ruled lines per centimeter of grating surface?

## GROUP B

6. Explain why the following appear red: (a) glow-ing charcoal, (b) a ripe cherry, (c) a neon sign, (d) the sunrise, (e) objects viewed through red sunglasses.
7. How can you explain that in observations of thin films by reflected light the interference effects are the reverse of those we would normally expect?
8. You are given two optical gratings, one with fewer lines per centimeter than the other, and a single monochromatic light source. For which grating will the angular separation of orders be greater? Justify your conclusion.
9. What part of Young's double-slit experiment depended on diffraction and what part depended on interference?
10. Monochromatic light of known wavelength was transmitted by a grating and the diffraction angle of a first order image was determined. Derive the equation for the grating constant of the transmission grating.

# problems

## GROUP B

1. A transmission grating with $58\overline{0}0$ lines/cm is illuminated by monochromatic light with a wavelength of 4920 Å. What is the diffraction angle for the first order image?

2. In Problem 1, the perpendicular distance from the grating to the image screen was 34.5 cm. How far from the principal image was the first order image found?
3. Monochromatic light illuminates a grating having

5900 lines/cm. The diffraction angle for a second order image is 38.0°. (a) Determine the wavelength of the light in angstroms. (b) What is its color?

4. White light falls on a grating that has 3500 lines/cm. The perpendicular distance from the grating to the image screen is 50.0 cm. (a) Find the distance of the near edge of a first order image from the prin-cipal image on the screen. (b) Find the distance of the far edge of the same image.

5. In the experiment of Problem 4, a marker was placed in the first order image on the screen 9.25 cm from the principal image. (a) Determine the wavelength (in angstroms) at the marker position. (b) What color corresponds to this wavelength?

# POLARIZATION

The general wave properties of rectilinear propagation in a homogeneous medium—reflection, refraction, interference, and diffraction—are clearly recognized in the behavior of light as well as in sound and water disturbances.

In Chapter 12 we considered a particle model of light that at one time was as successful as the wave model in explaining recti-linear propagation, reflection, and refraction. Only interference and diffraction failed to accommodate the particle model. They required a wave model for explanation. Thus interference and diffraction give the best evidence that light has wave-like characteristics.

Before the introduction of the electromagnetic theory, light was generally assumed to be a longitudinal wave disturbance. Electromagnetic theory predicts that light is a transverse wave. Sound waves are longitudinal disturbances and water waves have both transverse and longitudinal characteristics. From inter-ference or diffraction experiments, we can infer nothing con-cerning the transverse nature of light waves since both sound and water waves show these properties. What experimental basis do we have that supports the theoretical prediction that light waves are transverse?

Fresnel observed that a beam of light falling on a calcite crystal was separated into two beams that were incapable of producing interference fringes. Thomas Young suggested that this could be explained by assuming that the light consisted of transverse waves that were separated into component waves having oscillating planes at right angles to each other. He called this *a plane-polarization effect*.

Many experiments with calcite and other similar materials have demonstrated the correctness of Young's polarization hypothesis. **Plane-polarized light** *is light in which the oscil-lations are confined to a single plane that is perpendicular to the line of propagation*. Transverse waves but not longi-tudinal waves can be polarized. This is because the oscilla-tions of transverse waves are independent and randomly

## 15.6 Polarization of transverse waves

*electric vector must ∥ major*

*must be ⊥*

**Figure 15-9** The vectors representing random oscillation planes of unpolarized light. (A) may be arbitrarily resolved into vertical and horizontal component vectors as in (B) for an end-on view, and as in (C) for a side view.

*Polaroid sunglasses are perhaps the most familiar optical polarizing device.*

oriented. Longitudinal waves vibrate along only one line of direction, and that direction is parallel to its propagation.

Light radiated by ordinary sources is unpolarized since the primary radiators, the atoms and molecules of the light source, oscillate independently. Beams of unpolarized light are made up of independent wave trains with oscillation planes oriented in a random manner about the line of propagation. Diagrammatically, we can represent unpolarized light being propagated in space by a system of *light vectors* as shown in Figure 15-9. It is customary to resolve these vectors into vertical and horizontal components, which is a convenient but entirely arbitrary orientation.

Ordinary light can become plane-polarized through interactions with matter. The scattering effect of small particles (see Section 15.11) is accompanied by a polarization effect. Polarization can also result from reflection of light from various surfaces, from refraction of light through some crystals, and from selective absorption of light in some crystals.

A simple mechanical model can be used to illustrate the polarization concept. Suppose we set up transverse waves in a rope passed through a slot as shown in Figure 15-10. We can readily see that vibrations are transmitted beyond the slot only when the vibrating plane of the rope and the plane of the slot are aligned. We shall call this frame of slots the *polarizer*. A second slot, parallel to the first, will transmit the waves. See Figure 15-10(A). If the second slot is perpendicular to the first slot, it obstructs them, as Figure 15-10(B) shows. We shall call this second frame of slots the *analyzer*.

If the rope is replaced by a long coiled spring, longitudinal waves set up in the spring will pass through both slots regardless of their orientation. *Polarization is a property of transverse waves*.

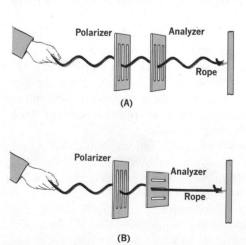

**Figure 15-10** A mechanical analogy of polarization.

It has long been known that certain crystalline substances transmit light in one plane of polarization and absorb light in other polarization planes. Tourmaline is such a material. Unpolarized light incident on a tourmaline crystal emerges as green, plane-polarized light of low intensity. This property of crystals in which one polarized component of incident light is absorbed and the other is transmitted is called *dichroism*. See Figure 15-11.

Dichroic crystals of quinine iodosulfate transmit plane-polarized light very efficiently but the crystals are too small for practical use. In 1935 Edwin H. Land developed a method of imbedding these crystals in cellulose film so that the dichroic properties of the crystals were retained. This highly efficient polarizing film is known commercially as Polaroid. Improved Polaroid sheets have now been developed in which polarizing molecules, rather than crystals, are imbedded in appropriate films.

## 15.7 Selective absorption

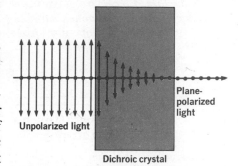

**Figure 15-11** Polarization by selective absorption.

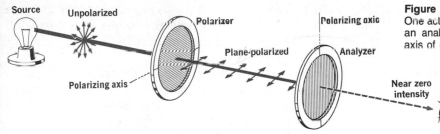

**Figure 15-12** Polaroid disks in use. One acts as a polarizer and the other as an analyzer. Notice that the polarizing axis of each disk is marked on the rim.

Sunlight reflected from the surface of calm water or from a level highway can be quite objectionable to the observer. Sunglasses made of polarizing films reduce the intensity of these reflections. By rotating the lenses slightly from side to side the reflections are seen to pass through a minimum, indicating that these rays are partially polarized.

Ordinary light incident obliquely on the surface of a glass plate is partly reflected and partly refracted. Both the transmitted and the reflected beams are partly polarized. This can be verified by observing the light through a polarizing disk used as an analyzer. By rotating the disk in a plane perpendicular to the light axis, one can determine the direction of the dominant light vectors in each beam.

The component of the incident light lying in the plane parallel to the surface of the glass is largely reflected. The component lying in the plane perpendicular to the surface is largely refracted. A particular angle of incidence at which polarization of the reflected light is complete, known as the *polarization angle,* can be found experimentally. Polarization by reflection is illustrated in Figure 15-13.

## 15.8 Polarization by reflection

**Figure 15-13** At the polarizing angle, the reflected light is completely polarized but of low intensity.

*Polarization by reflection does not occur for metals and other good conductors. Polarizing glasses can reduce glare from painted surfaces of automobiles, but not from chrome-plated bumpers.*

At the polarizing angle the reflected beam is of low intensity and the reflectance is about 15%. The refracted beam, which is not completely polarized, is bright. The intensity of the plane-polarized reflected beam can be increased by combining reflections as a result of stacking several plates. The combined refracted beam becomes less intense but more completely plane-polarized.

## 15.9 Polarization by refraction

If a thick glass plate is placed on a printed page, the print viewed through the glass may appear displaced due to refraction. A natural crystal of calcite placed on the page shows *two* refracted images of the print, as shown in Figure 15-14. Calcite and many other crystalline materials exhibit this property of *double refraction*.

Upon entering a doubly refracting crystal such as calcite, a beam of unpolarized light can divide into two beams at the crystal surface. This separation is shown diagrammatically in Figure 15-15. Analysis of these separate beams with polarizing disks reveals that they are plane-polarized with their planes of polarization perpendicular to each other.

Experimentally, one of the polarized beams can be shown to follow Snell's law; the other beam does not. Using monochromatic sodium light of 5893 Å and measuring the angles of incidence and refraction, one beam yields a constant index of refraction of 1.66. However, the other beam shows an index of refraction that varies from 1.49 to 1.66 depending on the angle of incidence. This difference suggests that the light energy is propagated through the crystal at different speeds that are determined by the orientation of the light planes with the crystal lattice.

**Figure 15-14** Double refraction in calcite.

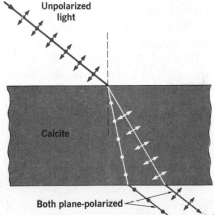

**Figure 15-15** Double refraction. Light in one polarization plane conforms to Snell's law; light in the other plane does not.

Calcite crystals are sometimes polished, cut through, and cemented back together in such a way that one of the polarized beams is totally reflected at the cemented face. Such a crystal, known as a *Nicol prism,* can be used to produce a beam of completely polarized light.

## 15.10 Interference patterns

The two plane-polarized beams of light that emerge from a doubly refracting crystal cannot be made to interfere with each other even though they are transmitted through the crystal at different speeds. This is because their planes of polarization are perpendicular to each other. It follows that *if two light waves interfere, their oscillations (or components of these oscillations) must lie in the same plane.*

If *polarized light* is incident on a doubly refracting crystal at the proper angle, the emerging beams *are* found to interfere as they pass through an analyzer disk. The analyzer passes only the components of these perpendicularly polarized rays that lie in its transmission plane. Those waves from the two beams having a phase difference of an odd number of half wavelengths interfere destructively, the corresponding color is removed, and its complement is observed.

Materials, such as glass and lucite, that become doubly refracting when subjected to mechanical stress are said to be *photoelastic*. When a photoelastic material is placed between polarizing and analyzing disks, the strain patterns (and thus the stress distributions) are revealed by interference fringes as shown in Figure 15-16.

**Figure 15-16** Strain patterns in a cylindrical disk subjected to diametrical compression.

## 15.11 Scattering

A beam of light traveling in dust-free air cannot be seen even in a darkened room. If, however, there is dust or smoke in the path of the beam, it becomes visible by reflection of light from the surface of the particles.

Suppose a beam of white light travels in a medium containing suspended particles that have diameters smaller than the mean wavelength of visible light. When observed at right angles to its path, the beam has a distinctly bluish cast. When observed in its path, the remaining transmitted beam has a red-orange cast. With certain concentrations of suspended particles, the bluish light sent off radially becomes quite intense and the transmitted light acquires a more intense red-orange color. An excess of shorter wavelengths is emitted at right angles to the path of the beam and an excess of longer wavelengths is transmitted along the path of the beam. This phenomenon, known as *scattering,* occurs when a beam of light encounters suspended particles with dimensions that are small compared to the wavelengths of the light.

If we look at blue skylight through a polarizing disk, we observe

*Horseshoe crabs and bees are said to navigate by the sun; they have analyzer capabilities with respect to polarized light.*

**Figure 15-17** Scattering of light by particles in the air brightens the daytime sky on earth (left). An observer on the lunar surface, however, sees a dark daytime sky (right) because the moon has almost no atmospheric particles.

*Atmospheric scattering accounts for our colorful sunsets and our blue sky.*

that it is plane polarized. By selecting a point in the blue sky near the horizon with the sun overhead, we find the scattered light to be horizontally polarized.

In the late afternoon near the time of sunset, sunlight must travel a maximum distance through the atmosphere to reach an observer. The setting sun has a yellow to red hue. The sunlight reflected to an observer from clouds near the sight line of the observer has the yellow or red hue characteristic of the sunset. Much of the energy in the blue region of the sunlight has been removed by the scattering effect of the atmospheric gas molecules. Under these conditions the transmitted light is largely yellow-red. This accounts for the blue appearance of the sky and the reddish appearance of the setting sun. See **Plate V(B)**.

If the earth had no envelope of atmospheric gases, the sky would appear black to an observer on the surface of the earth since there would be no scattering of sunlight passing overhead. Astronauts have observed the blackness of outer space while in flight beyond the earth's atmosphere.

Scattering is responsible for certain other natural color phenomena known as *structural colors* (in contrast to the pigment colors that we have already considered). The colors of many minerals are structural. The blue color of a bluejay's feathers results from scattering of light by tiny bubbles of air dispersed through the feather structure. The blue color in the eyes of a human being is also a structural color since there is no blue pigment in the irises of blue eyes.

## 15.12 Optical rotation

A number of substances, such as quartz, sugar, tartaric acid, and turpentine, are said to be *optically active* because they rotate the plane of polarized light. A water solution of cane sugar (sucrose) rotates the plane of polarization to the right. For a given path length through the solution, the angle of rotation is proportional to the concentration of the solution.

In analytical procedures chemists find numerous applications of this property of optically active substances. Instruments for measuring the angle of rotation under standard conditions are known as *polarimeters;* those used specifically for sugar solutions are called *saccharimeters*.

**Figure 15-18** A modern polarimeter in use.

# summary

Interference of light can be compared with interference in other wave disturbances. It is interpreted in terms of the superposition principle. Thomas Young first demonstrated interference of light and related double-slit interference and thin-film interference to Huygens' wave theory.

The analysis of thin-film interference requires an understanding of the nature of wave reflections at interfaces where the medium beyond has the higher or the lower index of refraction.

The various diffraction phenomena are explained by the interference of light waves. Diffraction gratings produce diffraction patterns by the reflection or transmission of incident light. The wavelength of light can be determined experimentally from measurements of grating spectra.

Polarization of light depends on the transverse nature of light waves. Polarization is a property of transverse waves. Light may be plane polarized by the selective absorption of certain crystals, by reflection from certain smooth surfaces, and by doubly refracting crystals. Photoelastic substances become doubly refracting when subjected to mechanical stress.

The scattering of sunlight accounts for the blue appearance of skylight and the reddish appearance of sunset and sunrise. Substances that rotate the plane of polarized light are said to be optically active.

# questions

## GROUP A

1. What phenomenon provides evidence of the transverse wave character of light?
2. How do Polaroid sunglasses reduce the glare of bright sunlight?
3. Distinguish between a structural color and a pigment color.
4. Define the polarizing angle.
5. How could you determine whether a beam of light is plane polarized or unpolarized?
6. Suggest a way to identify the polarizing axis of a sheet of Polaroid film.

## GROUP B

7. Explain why a Polaroid disk used as an analyzer blocks the beam of light transmitted by the polarizer disk when it is properly oriented?
8. The two beams of light that emerge from a doubly refracting crystal travel through the crystal at different speeds. Can they be made to produce an interference pattern? Explain.
9. A physics student observes that the setting sun near the horizon is red while the sky overhead is blue. Explain.
10. For a given optically active substance, upon what does the magnitude of the rotation angle for the plane of polarized light passing through the substance depend?
11. If scattering of sunlight is more pronounced in the shorter wavelength regions, violet light must be scattered more than blue. Why does the sky appear to be light blue rather than violet?
12. A tube filled with a sucrose solution is placed between two crossed polarizing disks. (a) Explain why some light is transmitted through the analyzer. (b) In what direction must the analyzer be rotated to reduce the light intensity to a minimum? (c) The tube is now filled with a more dilute solution of the same substance. How must the analyzer be adjusted to reestablish the light minimum?

# telescopes

telescopes are certainly the most important tools of the astronomer. The first telescope, a refractor, was made in Holland in 1608. Isaac Newton made the first reflecting telescope in 1668. In 1931 the American engineer Karl Jansky first detected radio waves coming from sources beyond the earth. This led to the construction of large radio telescopes and the beginning of radio astronomy. To avoid distortion and absorption of electromagnetic waves by the earth's atmosphere, large telescopes are now mounted on orbiting space vehicles.

*Bottom left: The world's largest solar telescope is housed in this building near Tucson, AZ. The telescope mirror is 203 cm in diameter.*

*Above: The Trifed Nebula, which contains millions of relatively young stars. The dark regions are masses of nonluminous gas and dust.*

*Left: The 48-inch Schmidt camera on Mt. Palomar, CA, is used primarily to map the sky for larger instruments. A correcting lens near the top minimizes spherical aberration.*

*Right, top to bottom:*

*A storm in the sun's atmosphere is seen here rising 260,000 km above the solar surface.*

*A portion of a large spherical radio telescope in France.*

*The Ring Nebula is a shell of gas that was formed when the star at the center exploded.*

*This 100-inch telescope on Mt. Wilson provided the first evidence of galaxies beyond the Milky Way.*

351

*Right: The globular cluster M-13 in the constellation Hercules, more than 3 x $10^{17}$km away, contains more than 100,000 stars.*

*Bottom left: Five 18-m dishes, used simultaneously, comprise the high resolution radio interferometer at Stanford Radioscience Laboratory.*

*Bottom right: The 36-inch refracting telescope at Lick Observatory is one of the largest of its kind in the world.*

*Above: The spiral galaxy in Ursa Major is sp far away that its light takes $10^7$ years to reach the earth. The other stars in the photo are members of the Milky Way.*

*Right: This 8-inch reflecting telescope is ideal for amateur astronomers because it is compact and portable.*

# 16
# Electrostatics

## 16.1 Charges at rest

*The ancient Greeks knew that when amber is rubbed, it attracts lightweight objects.*

We can observe about us a number of physical effects that are sometimes produced by rubbing pieces of dry matter. Sometimes an annoying shock is felt when the door handle of an automobile is touched after one slides over the plastic-covered seat. We may feel a shock after we walk on a woolen carpet and then touch a doorknob or other metal object. The slight crackling sound heard when dry hair is brushed and the tendency of thin sheets of paper to resist separation are other common observations of these physical effects.

When an object shows effects of the type we have described, we say that it has an *electric charge*. *The process that produces electric charges on an object is called* **electrification**. Electrification is most apparent when the air is dry. An object that is electrically charged can attract small bits of cork, paper, or other lightweight particles. Because the electric charge is confined to the object and is not moving, it is called an *electrostatic charge*. Thus **static electricity** *is stationary electricity in the form of an electric charge at rest*. Static electricity is commonly produced by friction between two surfaces in close contact.

## 16.2 Two kinds of charge

*A pith ball coated with aluminum or graphite is not appreciably more massive, but it can acquire a higher electric charge.*

We can detect the presence of an electrostatic charge by means of an instrument called an *electroscope*. The simplest kind of electroscope is a small ball of wood pith or Styrofoam suspended by a silk thread. This electroscope is more sensitive if the pith ball is coated with aluminum or graphite. Such an instrument is shown in Figure 16-1.

Suppose a hard rubber or Bakelite rod is charged by stroking it with flannel or fur. If the end of the charged rod is then held near a simple electroscope, the pith ball is attracted to the rod.

If the pith ball is allowed to come in contact with the charged rod, it immediately rebounds and is then repelled by the rod. We can reasonably assume that some of the *charge* has been transferred to the pith ball so that both the rod and the ball are now similarly charged.

Now suppose a glass rod is charged by stroking it with silk. If the glass rod is held near the charged electroscope, the pith ball is attracted rather than repelled as it was with the charged rubber rod. These effects of attraction and repulsion can be explained if we assume that there are two kinds of electric charge.

The electric charge produced on the rubber rod when the rod is stroked with flannel or fur is called a *negative* charge. The rod is said to be charged negatively. The electric charge produced on the glass rod when the rod is stroked with silk is called a *positive* charge. The rod is said to be charged positively.

From a study of atomic structure it is known that all matter contains both positive and negative charges. For simplification, however, the diagrams that follow show only the excess charge. If an object has an excess negative charge, the *net* charge will be indicated by negative (−) signs. If it has an excess positive charge, the *net* charge will be indicated by positive (+) signs. A neutral object will have no sign because it has the same amount of each kind of charge and therefore *a net charge of zero*.

Two pith balls that are negatively charged by contact with a charged rubber rod repel each other. Similarly, two pith balls that are positively charged by contact with a charged glass rod also repel each other. However, if a negatively charged pith ball is brought near a positively charged pith ball, they attract each other. See Figure 16-2. These observations are summarized in a ***basic law of electrostatics***: *Objects that are similarly charged repel each other; objects that are oppositely charged attract each other.*

**Figure 16-1** The pith-ball electroscope may be used to detect an electrostatic charge.

**Figure 16-2** Like charges repel each other and unlike charges attract each other.

## 16.3 Electricity and matter

*Objects that are electrically neutral have equal numbers of protons and electrons.*

*Objects that are electrically neutral have zero net charge.*

*A net negative charge results from electrons being deposited on an isolated neutral body.*

*A net positive charge results from electrons being removed from an isolated neutral body.*

As an understanding of the nature of static electricity requires a knowledge of the basic concepts regarding the structure of matter, we will briefly discuss these concepts now. (These concepts will be discussed more fully in Chapter 23.) All matter is composed of atoms, of which there are many different kinds. Each atom consists of a positively charged nucleus surrounded by negatively charged electrons.

Protons and neutrons are tightly packed into the very dense nucleus. Because each proton possesses a single unit of positive electric charge and neutrons, as their name suggests, are neutral particles, the nucleus is positively charged. This charge is determined by the number of protons the nucleus contains.

All electrons surrounding the nucleus are alike. They all carry the same amount of negative electric charge—one unit of negative charge per electron. Because an atom is electrically neutral, we know that the nucleus has a positive charge equal in size to the total negative electronic charge. Thus the number of electrons of a neutral atom equals the number of protons.

The rest mass of an electron is $9.1095 \times 10^{-31}$ kg. The mass of a proton is $1.6726 \times 10^{-27}$ kg and that of a neutron is $1.6750 \times 10^{-27}$ kg. Both the proton and the neutron have masses that are nearly 2000 times greater than the mass of an electron. The mass of an atom is almost entirely concentrated in the nucleus.

Protons and neutrons are bound together within the nucleus by strong forces acting through very short distances. By comparison, the repulsions between protons that are due to their similarity of charge are weak forces.

The electrons are retained in the atom structure by the electric attraction exerted by the positive nuclear charge. In general the outermost electrons of higher energies are held less firmly in the atom structure than inner electrons of lower energies. The outer electrons of the atoms of metallic elements in particular are loosely held and are easily influenced by outside forces.

When two appropriate materials are brought into close contact, some of the loosely held electrons can be transferred from one material to the other. If a hard rubber rod is stroked with fur, some electrons can be transferred from the fur to the rod. The rubber rod becomes negatively charged because it has a *net excess of electrons,* and the fur becomes positively charged because it has a *net deficiency of electrons*.

Similarly, when a glass rod is stroked with silk, some electrons are transferred from the glass to the silk. The glass is positively charged because it has a *net deficiency of electrons,* and the silk is negatively charged because it has a *net excess of electrons*. All these charged states result from *the transfer of electrons*.

Electric charge is a scalar quantity. The net charge on an object is the sum of its positive charges minus the sum of its negative charges.

Two common types of electroscopes that are more sensitive than the simple pith-ball device are shown in Figure 16-3.

The *vane electroscope* consists of a light aluminum rod mounted by means of a central bearing on a metal support that is insulated from its metal stand. When charged, the vane is deflected at an angle by electrostatic repulsion. The angle of deflection depends on the magnitude of the charge.

The *leaf electroscope* consists of very fragile strips of gold leaf suspended from a metal stem that is capped with a metal knob. The leaves are enclosed in a metal case with glass windows for their protection, and the metal stem is insulated from the case. When electrified, the leaves diverge because of the force of repulsion due to their similar charge. Good sensitivity is realized because of the very low mass of the gold leaf.

A *proof plane* is frequently used with an electroscope to test or transfer charges. The proof plane is a small metal disk with an insulating handle. One can easily be made by cementing a small coin to a glass rod. When the proof plane is used to transfer a charge, the metal disk is brought in contact with the charged object and then with an electroscope.

When used to test a charge, the charged disk of the proof plane is brought in contact with an electroscope previously electrified with a known charge. If the charge on the electroscope increases, the test charge is of the same sign as that on the electroscope. If the charge on the electroscope decreases, the test charge is of the opposite sign as that on the electroscope.

## 16.4 The electroscope

Metal knob
Insulator
Metal stem
Metal vane support
Aluminum vane
Metal ring support

Gold foil
Metal case (glass window)

Aluminum vane

Gold leaf

**Figure 16-3** Two types of sensitive electroscopes.

## 16.5 Conductors and insulators

Let us suspend an aluminum-coated pith ball by a silk thread and then join the ball to the knob of a leaf electroscope by means of a copper wire as shown in Figure 16-4. If we now place a charge on the ball, the leaves of the electroscope diverge. Apparently the charge on the ball is transferred to the electroscope by the copper wire.

Suppose we substitute a silk thread for the copper wire. Now

**Figure 16-4** A charge is conducted to the electroscope by the copper wire.

(A)

(B)

**Figure 16-5** Free electrons of a conductor surge in the direction that reduces the net charge.

when we charge the ball the leaves of the electroscope do not diverge. The charge has not been conducted to the electroscope by the silk.

*A **conductor** is a material through which an electric charge is readily transferred.* Most metals are good conductors. At normal temperatures, silver is the best solid conductor; copper and aluminum follow in that order.

*An **insulator** is a material through which an electric charge is not readily transferred.* Good insulators are such poor conductors that for practical purposes they are considered to be nonconductors. Glass, mica, paraffin, hard rubber, sulfur, silk, shellac, dry air, and many plastics are good insulators.

Liquid solutions and confined gases conduct electricity in a different way than solids. At this time we are primarily interested in the conductivity of solids. We can use our knowledge of the structure of matter to describe why some materials are conductors and why some are insulators.

A few grams of matter contain a very large number of atoms and, except for hydrogen, an even larger number of electrons. For example, 27 g of aluminum consists of $6.02 \times 10^{23}$ aluminum atoms containing $7.83 \times 10^{24}$ electrons. On an atomic scale, there is one electron in approximately 2.2 atomic mass units of matter. (One atomic mass unit $= 1.66 \times 10^{-24}$ g of matter.)

Metals have close-packed crystal structures in which the crystal lattice consists of positively charged particles permeated by a cloud of *free electrons*. This cloud of free electrons is commonly referred to as the *electron gas*. The binding force in such structures is the attraction between the positively charged metal ions and the electron gas. The loosely held outermost electrons of the metal atoms have been "donated" to the electron gas and belong to the crystal as a whole. These electrons are free to migrate throughout the crystal lattice. Their migration gives rise to the high electric conductivity commonly associated with metals.

A good conductor contains a large number of free electrons whose motions are relatively unimpeded within the material. Since like charges repel, the free electrons spread throughout the material in order to relieve any local concentration of charge. If such a material is brought into contact with a charged body, the free electrons surge in a common direction. If the charged object is deficient in electrons (positively charged), this surge is in the direction of the object. If the charged object has an excess of electrons (negatively charged), the surge is away from the object. See Figure 16-5. In either case a transfer of electric charge continues until the repulsive forces between the free electrons are in equilibrium throughout the entire system.

An insulator is characterized by a lack of free electrons because even the outermost electrons are rather firmly held within the atom structure. Thus the transfer of charge through an insulator is usually negligible. If an excess of electrons is transferred to one particular region of such a material, the extra electrons remain in that region for some time before they gradually leak away.

*Recall that insulators are actually extremely poor conductors.*

Suppose we charge a rubber rod negatively by stroking it with fur. If the rod is brought near the knob of an electroscope, the leaves diverge. If the rod is removed, the leaves collapse; no charge remains on the electroscope. The charge that makes the leaves diverge is called an *induced* charge. The electroscope is said to be charged temporarily by *induction*.

We can reason that the negative charge on the rod when brought near the metal knob of the electroscope repels free electrons in the knob and metal stem and forces them down to the leaves. See Figure 16-6(A). The force of repulsion of the extra electrons on the leaves causes them to diverge. The knob is then deficient in electrons and is consequently positively charged. As soon as the force of repulsion exerted by the charged rod is withdrawn, the excess free electrons on the leaves scatter throughout the stem and knob, restoring the normal uncharged state throughout the electroscope.

Similarly, a glass rod that has been stroked with silk temporarily induces a positive charge on the leaves of an electroscope by attracting electrons up through the stem to the knob. See Figure 16-6(B).

Electrostatic experiments are best performed in dry air. In moist air an invisible film of water condenses on the surfaces of objects, including those of charged insulators. Dissolved impurities in the film make these surfaces conductive, and an isolated charge cannot be maintained for any length of time.

Any conducting object when properly isolated in space can be temporarily charged by induction. The region of the object nearest the charged body will acquire a charge of the *opposite* sign; the region farthest from the charged body will acquire a

## 16.6 Transferring electrostatic charges

(A)                             (B)

**Figure 16-6** An electroscope may be charged temporarily by induction due to a redistribution of the free electrons of the metallic conductor.

**Figure 16-7** A charged rod brought near an isolated conductor induces electricity of the same sign in the far end of the conductor.

charge of the same sign. See Figure 16-7. This statement is consistent with the basic law of electrostatics stated in Section 16.2.

A charge can be transferred by *conduction*. If we touch the knob of an electroscope with a negatively charged rubber rod, the leaves diverge. When the rod is removed, the leaves remain apart, indicating that the electroscope retains the charge. How can we determine the nature of this residual charge on the electroscope?

We can reason that some of the excess electrons on the rod have been repelled onto the knob of the electroscope. This would be true only for the region of the rod immediately in contact with the electroscope since rubber is a very poor conductor and excess electrons do not migrate freely through it. Any free electrons thus transferred to the electroscope, together with other free electrons of the electroscope itself, would be repelled to the leaves by the excess electrons remaining on the parts of the rod not in contact with the electroscope.

When the rod is removed, and with it the force of repulsion, the electroscope is left with a residual negative charge of a somewhat lower density. This deduction can be verified by bringing a positively charged glass rod near the electroscope to induce a positive charge on the leaves. The leaves collapse and diverge again when the glass rod is removed. See Figure 16-8. *Any conducting object, properly isolated in space and charged by conduction, acquires a residual charge of the same sign as that of the body touching it.*

An electroscope with a known residual charge can be used to identify the nature of the charge on another object. This second object merely needs to be brought near the knob of this charged electroscope.

**Figure 16-8** The residual charge on an electroscope, when charged by conduction, is of the same sign as the charge on the object that touches it.

## 16.7 Residual charge by induction

When a charged rubber rod is held near the knob of an electroscope, there is no transfer of electrons between the rod and the electroscope. If a path is provided for electrons to be repelled from the electroscope while the repelling force is present, free electrons escape. Then if the escape path is removed before

| Uncharged electroscope | Leaves charged negatively by induction | Electrons repelled to earth | Electroscope deficient in electrons | Positively charged electroscope |

removing the repelling force, the electroscope is left with a deficiency of electrons, giving it a residual positive charge. We can verify this conclusion by bringing a positively charged glass rod near the knob of the charged electroscope. The leaves of the electroscope diverge even more. When the charged rod is withdrawn, the leaves fall back to their original divergence and remain apart. The steps in placing a residual charge on an electroscope by induction are shown in Figure 16-9.

Similarly, we can induce a residual negative charge on an electroscope using a positively charged glass rod. *When an isolated conductor is given a residual charge by induction, the charge is opposite in sign to that of the object inducing it.*

**Figure 16-9**  Steps in placing a residual charge on an electroscope by induction.

## 16.8 The force between charges

From the basic law of electrostatics stated in Section 16.2, we recognize that like charges repel and unlike charges attract. If a charge is uniformly dispersed over the surface of an isolated sphere, its influence on another charged object some distance away is the same as if the charge were concentrated at the center of the sphere. Thus the charge on such an object is considered to be located at a particular point and is called a *point charge*.

The quantity of charge on a body, designated by the letter $Q$, is determined by the number of electrons in excess of (or less than) the number of protons. In the MKS system of units, the quantity of charge is expressed in *coulombs* (c) named for the French physicist Charles Augustin de Coulomb (1736–1806).

$$\textbf{1 coulomb} = \textbf{6.25} \times \textbf{10}^{18} \textbf{ electrons}$$

Thus the charge on one electron, expressed in coulombs, is the reciprocal of this number and the sign of $Q$ is $-$.

$$\textbf{e}^- = \textbf{1.60} \times \textbf{10}^{-19} \textbf{ c}$$

Similarly, the charge on the proton is $1.60 \times 10^{-19}$ coulomb and the sign of $Q$ is $+$.

(A) Unlike charges

(B) Like charges

**Figure 16-10**  When $Q_1$ and $Q_2$ are of opposite sign, $F$ is negative and is interpreted as a force of attraction. When $Q_1$ and $Q_2$ are of the same sign, $F$ is positive and is interpreted as a force of repulsion.

*Note that Coulomb's law of electrostatics has the same form as Newton's law of universal gravitation, Section 3.11.*

The coulomb is a very large unit of charge for the study of electrostatics. Frequently it is convenient to work with a fraction of this unit called the microcoulomb ($\mu$c).

$$1 \; \mu c = 10^{-6} \; c$$

Coulomb's many experiments with charged bodies led him to conclude that the forces of electrostatic attraction and repulsion obey a law similar to Newton's law of universal gravitation. We now recognize his conclusions as **Coulomb's law of electrostatics:** *The force between two point charges is directly proportional to the product of their magnitudes and inversely proportional to the square of the distance between them.* Charged bodies approximate point charges if they are small compared to the distances separating them. See Figure 16-10.

Coulomb's law can be expressed as:

$$F \propto \frac{Q_1 Q_2}{d^2}$$

If we use a proportionality constant that takes into account the properties of the medium separating the charged bodies and that has the proper dimensions, Coulomb's law becomes

$$F = k \frac{Q_1 Q_2}{d^2}$$

In the MKS system, $k$ has the numerical value $8.987 \times 10^9$ for vacuum and $8.93 \times 10^9$ for air. The dimensions of $k$ are n m²/c². The point charges $Q_1$ and $Q_2$ are in coulombs and are of proper sign to indicate the nature of each charge. As $d$ is distance in meters, $F$ is expressed in newtons of force.

In Figure 16-10(A) the charges $Q_1$ and $Q_2$ have opposite signs and the force $F$ acts on each charge to move it toward the other. In Figure 16-10(B), charges $Q_1$ and $Q_2$ have the same sign and the force $F$ acts on each charge to move it away from the other. The force between the two charges is a vector quantity that acts on each charge.

Suppose the objects in Figure 16-10(B) are charged to 0.01 coulomb each and placed 10 meters apart. Since the charges are of like sign, the force between them is one of repulsion. Using $k$ for air (to one significant figure it is $9 \times 10^9$ n m²/c²), the Coulomb's law expression for this force becomes

$$F = 9 \times 10^9 \; \frac{n \; m^2}{c^2} \times \frac{(10^{-2} \; c)(10^{-2} \; c)}{(10 \; m)^2}$$

$$F = 9 \times 10^9 \; \frac{n \; m^2}{c^2} \times \frac{10^{-4} \; c^2}{10^2 \; m^2}$$

$$F = 9 \times 10^3 \; n \; \textbf{of repulsive force}$$

**EXAMPLE**

*Find the force between charges of + 100.0 μc and − 50.0 μc located 50.0 cm apart in air.*

**SOLUTION**

Two unlike charges are separated by a given distance in air. We are asked to determine the force acting on them through this distance. Coulomb's law applies.

$$F = k \ \frac{Q_1 Q_2}{d^2}$$ where $k$ is the constant for air.

Since $k$ has the dimensions n m²/c², the quantities of charge must be converted to coulombs and the distance to meters. Force will then be calculated in newtons.

$$F = 8.93 \times 10^9 \ \frac{\text{n m}^2}{\text{c}^2} \times \frac{(100.0 \ \mu c \times c/10^6 \ \mu c)(-50.0 \ \mu c \times c/10^6 \ \mu c)}{(50.0 \ \text{cm} \times \text{m}/10^2 \ \text{cm})^2}$$

$$F = 8.93 \times 10^9 \ \frac{\text{n m}^2}{\text{c}^2} \times \frac{(1.000 \times 10^{-4} \ \text{c})(-5.00 \times 10^{-5} \ \text{c})}{(5.00 \times 10^{-1} \ \text{m})^2}$$

$$F = 8.93 \times 10^9 \ \frac{\text{n m}^2}{\text{c}^2} \times \frac{-5.00 \times 10^{-9} \ \text{c}^2}{2.50 \times 10^{-1} \ \text{m}^2}$$

$$F = -1.78 \times 10^2 \ \text{n}$$ (the negative sign indicating *attraction* between the two charges)

## 16.9 Electric fields

The concept of a field of force will be helpful as we consider the region surrounding an electrically charged body. A second charge brought into this region experiences a force according to Coulomb's law. Such a region is an *electric field. An electric field is said to exist in a region of space if an electric charge placed in that region is subject to an electric force.*

Let us consider a positively charged sphere +**Q** of Figure 16-11(A) isolated in space. A small positive charge +**q**, which we shall call a *test charge,* is brought near the surface of the sphere. Since the test charge is in the electric field of the charged sphere and the charges are similar, it experiences a repulsive force directed radially away from +**Q**. Were the charge on the sphere negative, as in Figure 16-11(B), the force acting on the test charge would be directed radially toward −**Q**.

**Figure 16-11** The electric field surrounding a charged sphere isolated in space.

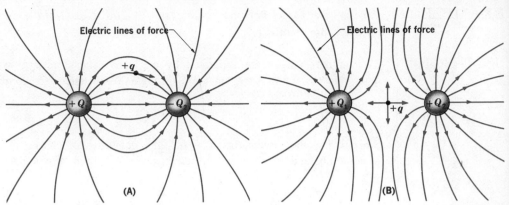

**Figure 16-12** Lines of force show the nature of the electric field near two equal charges of opposite sign (A), and near two equal charges of the same sign (B).

*An **electric line of force** is a line so drawn that a tangent to it at any point indicates the orientation of the electric field at that point.* We can imagine a line of force as the path of a test charge moving slowly in a very viscous medium in response to the force of the field. By convention, electric lines of force *originate* at the surface of a positively charged body and *terminate* at the surface of a negatively charged body, each line of force showing the direction in which a positive test charge would be accelerated in that part of the field. A line of force is *normal* to the surface of the charged body where it joins that surface.

The *intensity,* or strength, of an electrostatic field, as well as its direction, can be represented graphically by lines of force. *The electric field intensity is proportional to the number of lines of force per unit area normal to the field.* Where the intensity is high, the lines of force will be close together. Where the intensity is low, the lines of force will be more widely separated in the graphical representation of the field.

In Figure 16-12(A), electric lines of force are used to show the electric field near two equally but oppositely charged objects. At any point in this field the resultant force acting on a test charge +q can be represented by a vector drawn tangent to the line of force at that point.

The electric field near two objects of equal charge of the same sign is shown by the lines of force in Figure 16-12(B). The resultant force acting on a test charge +q placed at the midpoint between these two similar charges would be zero.

*The **electric field intensity**, $\mathscr{E}$, at any point in an electric field is the force per unit positive charge at that point.* In the MKS system the electric field intensity has the dimensions *newton per coulomb.* Thus

$$\mathscr{E} = \frac{F}{q} = \frac{kQ}{d^2}$$

where $\mathscr{E}$ is the electric field intensity and $F$ is the force in newtons acting on the test charge $q$ in coulombs.

The following example illustrates the use of this equation.

| | |
|---|---|
| EXAMPLE | *A charge of 2 μc placed in an electric field experiences a force of 0.08 n. What is the magnitude of the electric field intensity?* |

| | |
|---|---|
| SOLUTION | The charge of 2 $\mu$c expressed in coulombs becomes 2 $\mu$c $\times$ c/$10^6$ $\mu$c or $2 \times 10^{-6}$ c. The force of 0.08 n is most conveniently expressed as $8 \times 10^{-2}$ n. |

$$\mathscr{E} = \frac{F}{q} = \frac{8 \times 10^{-2} \text{ n}}{2 \times 10^{-6} \text{ c}}$$

$\mathscr{E} = 4 \times 10^4$ n/c, the electric field intensity.

# questions

## GROUP A

1. List five examples (other than those given in this chapter) in which electrification occurs.

2. A hard rubber rod is rubbed with fur. What kind of charge is acquired (a) by the rubber rod, (b) by the fur?

3. A glass rod is rubbed with silk. What kind of charge is acquired (a) by the glass rod, (b) by the silk?

4. A pith ball suspended on a silk thread is attracted to a charged rubber rod. Does this indicate that the pith ball is oppositely charged? Explain.

5. State the law of electrostatics that reveals the nature of the attraction and repulsion of charged objects.

6. Why do the leaves of an uncharged electroscope diverge when a charged object is brought near?

7. Why is it necessary to ground an electroscope temporarily while inducing a residual charge on it with a negatively charged object?

8. What determines the property of a metal as a conductor of electricity?

9. Explain why sulfur is a very poor conductor.

10. What is the unit of electric charge in the MKS system?

11. State Coulomb's law of electrostatics.

12. Define an electric field.

## GROUP B

13. How can you explain (a) the presence of a charge on a rubber rod after it has been rubbed with fur, (b) the charge remaining on the fur?

14. Which do you think offers the more conclusive proof of the presence of a charge on a pith-ball electroscope: an observed force of repulsion on it or one of attraction? Explain.

15. Given a charged sphere, describe a simple experiment that would enable you to determine conclusively the nature of the charge on the sphere.

16. A negatively charged rod is brought near the knob of a charged electroscope. The leaves first collapse and then as the rod is brought nearer they again diverge. (a) What is the residual charge on the electroscope? (b) Explain the action of the leaves.

17. (a) In order for a coulomb force to be expressed in newtons, what must be the dimensions of the MKS proportionality constant in the Coulomb's law equation, $F = k \ Q_1 Q_2/d^2$? (b) Verify your answer.

18. A very small sphere is given a positive charge and is then brought near a large negatively charged plate. Draw a diagram of the system showing the appearance of the electric lines of force.

19. An electron of mass $m$ and charge $e^-$ is projected into a uniform electric field with an initial velocity $v_i$ at right angles to the field. Describe its motion in the electric field.

# problems

## GROUP B

1. A small sphere is given a charge of $+2\bar{0}$ $\mu$c and a second sphere of equal diameter located $1\bar{0}$ cm away is given a charge of $-5.0$ $\mu$c. What is the force of attraction between the charges?

2. The two spheres of Problem 1 are allowed to touch and are again spaced $1\bar{0}$ cm apart. What force exists between them?

3. Two small spheres each having a mass of 0.050 g are suspended by silk threads from the same

point. When given equal charges, they separate, the threads making an angle of $1\overline{0}°$ with each other. What is the force of repulsion acting on each sphere? (Suggestion: Construct a vector diagram and solve for the horizontal component of the force on one thread.)

4. Two small spheres each having a mass of 0.10 g are suspended from the same point on silk threads $2\overline{0}$ cm long. When given equal charges, they repel each other, coming to rest 24 cm apart. Find the charge on each sphere. (Suggestion: Construct a vector diagram and find the force of repulsion by similar triangles.)

5. A charge of 0.52 $\mu$c is placed in an electric field where the field intensity is $4.5 \times 10^5$ n/c. What is the magnitude of the force acting on the charge?

# POTENTIAL DIFFERENCE

## 16.10 Electric potential

read

*The idea of a field of force was introduced by Faraday.*

Let us consider the work done by gravity on a wagon coasting down a hill. The wagon is within the gravitational field of the earth and experiences a gravitational force causing it to travel downhill. Work is done by the gravitational field, so the energy expended comes from within the gravitational system. The wagon has less potential energy at the bottom of the hill than it had at the top; in order to return the wagon to the top, work must be done on it. However, in this instance, the energy must be supplied from an outside source to pull against the gravitational force. The energy expended is stored in the system, imparting to the wagon more potential energy at the top of the hill than it had at the bottom.

Similarly, a charge in an electric field experiences an electric force according to Coulomb's law. If the charge moves in response to this force, work is done by the electric field. Energy is removed from the system. If the charge is moved against the coulomb force of the electric field, work is done on it using energy from some outside source, this energy being stored in the system.

If work is done as a charge moves from one point to another in an electric field or if work is required to move a charge from one point to another, these two points are said to *differ in electric potential. The magnitude of the work is a measure of this difference of potential.* The concept of potential difference is very important in the understanding of electric phenomena. *The **potential difference**, V, between two points in an electric field is the work done per unit charge as a charge is moved between these points.*

**Figure 16-13** A strand of copper wire is completely vaporized as a potential difference of 5,000,000 volts (5Mv) is placed across it.

$$\text{potential difference } (V) = \frac{\text{work } (W)}{\text{charge } (q)}$$

The unit of potential difference in the MKS system is the *volt (v).* One **volt** *is the potential difference between two points in an electric field such that 1 joule of work is done in moving a charge of 1 coulomb between these points.*

$$1 \text{ volt} = \frac{1 \text{ joule}}{1 \text{ coulomb}}$$

Small differences of potential are commonly expressed in *millivolts* (mv) or *microvolts* ($\mu$v). Large differences of potential are measured in *kilovolts* (kv) and *megavolts* (Mv).

$$1\ \mu v = 10^{-6}\ v$$
$$1\ mv = 10^{-3}\ v$$
$$1\ kv = 10^{3}\ v$$
$$1\ Mv = 10^{6}\ v$$

Suppose the potential difference between two points in an electric field is 6.0 v. The work required to move a charge of $3.00 \times 10^2\ \mu c$ between these points can be determined as follows.

$$V = \frac{W}{q}$$

$$W = Vq = 6.0\ v \times 3.00 \times 10^2\ \mu c \times c/10^6\ \mu c$$
$$W = 6.0\ v \times 3.00 \times 10^{-4}\ c$$
$$W = 1.8 \times 10^{-3}\ j$$

Since a joule of work is a force of 1 newton applied through a distance of 1 meter, it follows that

$$v = \frac{j}{c} = \frac{n\ m}{c}$$

and

$$\frac{v}{m} = \frac{n}{c}$$

In Section 16.9 it was shown that $\mathscr{E}$, the electric field intensity, is expressed in newtons per coulomb. Thus,

$$\mathscr{E} = \frac{n}{c} = \frac{v}{m}$$

The electric field intensity is commonly expressed in terms of *volts per meter* and can be referred to as the *potential gradient*. *The **potential gradient** of an electric field is the change in potential per unit of distance.*

We can consider the earth to be an inexhaustible *source* of electrons, or limitless *sink* into which electrons can be "poured" without changing its potential. For practical purposes, the potential of the earth is arbitrarily taken as *zero*. Any conducting object connected to the earth must be at the same potential as the earth; that is, the potential difference between them is zero. Such an object is said to be *grounded*.

The potential at any point in an electric field is the potential difference between the point and earth taken as zero. This potential can be either positive or negative depending on the nature of the charge producing the electric field.

## 16.11 Distribution of charges

**Figure 16-14** The type of conical silk bag used by Faraday to demonstrate that electric charges reside on the outside.

*Electric force is a conservative force: if it acts alone on a charge, the total energy is conserved.*

Michael Faraday performed several experiments to demonstrate the distribution of charge on an isolated object. He charged a conical silk bag like that shown in Figure 16-14 and found that the charge was on the outside of the bag. By pulling on the silk thread, he turned the bag inside out and found that the charge was again on the outside. The inside of the bag showed no electric charge in either position.

Faraday connected the outer surface of an insulated metal pail to an electroscope by means of a conducting wire, as shown in Figure 16-15(A). He then lowered a positively charged metal ball supported by a silk thread into the pail. The leaves of the electroscope diverged (B), indicating a charge by induction. The positive charge on the ball attracted free electrons in the pail to the inner surface, leaving the outside of the pail and the electroscope positively charged. When the ball was allowed to come in contact with the inside of the pail (C) and was then removed, the leaves remained apart without change. It was found that the ball no longer had a charge after its removal. The fact that the electroscope remained unchanged after the ball was removed (D) indicated *(1)* that there was no redistribution of positive charge on the outside surface of the pail and *(2)* that the outside of the pail (and the electroscope) had acquired a net charge equal to the charge originally placed on the ball.

From these and other experiments with isolated conductors we can conclude that:

*1. All the static charge on a conductor lies on its surface.* Electrostatic charges are at rest. If the charge were beneath the

**Figure 16-15** Faraday's ice-pail experiment.

surface so that an electric field existed within a conductor, free electrons would be acted upon by the coulomb force of this field. Work would be done, the electrons would move because of a difference of potential, and energy would be given up by the field. Since movement is not consistent with a static charge, the charge must be on the surface and the electric field must exist only externally to the surface of a conductor. See Figure 16-16.

*2. There can be no potential difference between two points on the surface of a charged conductor.* A difference of potential is a measure of the work done in moving a charge from one point to another. As no electric field exists within the conductor, no work is done in moving a charge between two points on the same conductor. No difference of potential can exist between such points.

*3. The surface of a conductor is an equipotential surface.* All points on a conductor are at the same potential and no work is done by the electric field in moving a charge residing on a conductor. If points of equal potential in an electric field near a charged object are joined, an *equipotential line* or *surface* within the field is indicated. No work is done when a test charge is moved in an electric field along an equipotential surface.

*4. Electric lines of force are normal to equipotential surfaces.* A line of force shows the direction of the force acting on a test charge in an electric field. It can be shown that there is no force acting normal to this direction. Thus no work is done when a test charge is moved in an electric field normal to the lines of force. See Figure 16-17.

*5. Lines of force originate or terminate normal to the conductive surface of a charged object.* Since the surface of a conductor is an equipotential surface, lines of force must start out perpendicularly from the surface. For the same reason, a line of force cannot originate and terminate on the same conductor.

**Pith balls inside are not affected**

**To electrostatic generator**

**Figure 16-16** When the metal cylinder is charged by the electrostatic generator, the pith balls outside diverge, while those inside are not affected. What does this tell us about the location of the charge?

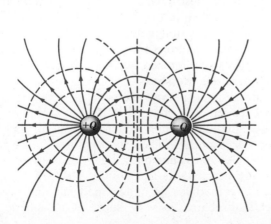

**Figure 16-17** Lines of force (solid lines) and equipotential lines (dashed lines) define the electric field near two equal but opposite charges.

## 16.12 Effect of the shape of conductors

A charged spherical conductor perfectly isolated in space has a uniform charge density, or charge per unit area, over the outer surface. Lines of force extend radially from the surface in all directions and the equipotential surfaces of the electric field are spherical and concentric. Such symmetry is not found in all cases of charged conductors.

A charge acquired by a nonconductor such as glass is confined to its original region until it gradually leaks away. The charge placed on an isolated metal sphere quickly spreads uniformly over the entire surface. If the conductor is not spherical, the charge distributes itself according to the surface curvature, concentrating mainly around points. The pear-shaped conductor illustrated in Figure 16-18 shows the charge more concentrated on the curved regions and less concentrated on the straight regions. If the small end is made more pointed, the charge density will increase at that end.

## 16.13 Discharging effect of points

Figure 16-18 The charge density is greatest at the point of greatest curvature.

——— Lines of force
– – – Equipotential lines

In Figure 16-18 the lines of force and equipotential lines are shown more concentrated at the small end of the charged conductor. This geometry indicates that the intensity of the electric field, or potential gradient, in this region is greater than elsewhere around the conductor. If this surface is reshaped to a sharply pointed end, the field intensity can become great enough to cause the gas molecules in the air surrounding the pointed end to *ionize*. Ionized air consists of gas molecules from which an outer electron has been removed, thus allowing both the positively charged *ion* and the freed electron to respond to the electric force. When the air is ionized, the point of the conductor is rapidly discharged.

There are always a few positive ions and free electrons present in the air. The intense electric field near a sharp point of a charged conductor will set these charged particles in motion such that the electrons are driven in one direction and the positive ions in the opposite direction. Violent collisions with other gas molecules will knock out some electrons and produce more charged particles. In this way air can be ionized quickly when it is subjected to a sufficiently large electric stress.

In dry air at atmospheric pressure, a potential gradient of 30 kv/cm between two charged surfaces is required to ionize the intervening column of air. When such an air gap is ionized, a *spark discharge* occurs. There is a rush of free electrons and ionized molecules across the ionized gap, discharging the surfaces and producing heat, light, and sound. Usually the quantity of static electricity involved is quite small and the time duration of the spark discharge is very short. Atmospheric lightning, however, is a spark discharge in which the quantity of charge is great.

The intensity of an electric field near a charged object can be sufficient to produce ionization at sharp projections or sharp corners of the object. A slow leakage of charge can occur at these locations producing a *brush* or *corona discharge*. A faint violet glow is sometimes emitted by the ionized gases of the air. A glow discharge known as St. Elmo's fire can sometimes be observed at night at the tips of ship masts and at the trailing edges of wing and tail surfaces of aircraft. The escape of charges from sharply pointed conductors is of great importance in the operation of electrostatic generators and in the design of lightning arresters.

Lightning is a gigantic electric discharge in which electric charges rush to meet their opposites. The interchange can occur between clouds or between a cloud and the earth. See Figure 16-19. According to the Lightning Protection Institute, one hundred bolts of lightning strike the earth every second, each bolt initiated by a potential difference of millions of volts.

There are no known ways of preventing lightning. However, there are effective means of protection from its destructiveness. Lightning rods, invented by Benjamin Franklin, are often used to protect buildings made of nonconducting materials from lightning damage. Sharply pointed rods are strategically located above the highest projections of the building, and by their discharging effect, they normally prevent the accumulation of a dangerous electrostatic charge. Lightning rods are thoroughly grounded. If lightning strikes, the rods provide a good conducting path into the ground. Being well grounded, the steel frames of large buildings offer excellent protection from lightning damage.

Television receiving antennas, even though equipped with lightning arresters, do not protect a building from lightning. Without lightning arresters they are a distinct hazard since they are not grounded.

*A lightning bolt transfers an average of about 1 coulomb of charge between a cloud and the earth.*

**Figure 16-19** Streaks of lightning brighten the nighttime sky. Each flash requires a potential difference of millions of volts.

### 16.14 Capacitors

Any isolated conductor is able to retain an electrostatic charge to some extent. If we place a positive charge on such a conductor by removing electrons, the potential is raised to some positive value with respect to ground. Conversely, a negative charge placed on the conductor results in a negative potential with respect to ground. By increasing the charge, we increase the potential of the conductor since the potential of an isolated conductor is a measure of the work done in placing a charge on the conductor. It is evident that we can continue to increase the charge until the potential with respect to ground or other conducting surface becomes so high that corona or spark discharges occur. However, if the conductor were in an evacuated space, it could have been raised to a much higher potential by continuing the addition of charge.

Suppose a charged conductor is connected to an electroscope, as shown in Figure 16-20(A). The leaves of the electroscope will diverge indicating the potential of the charged conductor. The electroscope is now a part of the conducting surface and there can be no difference of potential between different regions of a single charged conducting surface.

Now suppose a grounded conductor is brought near the charged conductor, as shown in Figure 16-20(B). A positive charge is induced on this second conductor as free electrons are repelled to ground by the negative field of the first conductor. The leaves of the electroscope partially collapse. The closer we move the grounded plate to the charged conductor, the more pronounced is this effect. Because of the attractive force of the induced charge on the grounded plate, less work is required to place the same negative charge on the first conductor. Its potential is consequently reduced accordingly. A greater charge can now be placed on this conductor to raise the potential back to the initial value.

**Figure 16-20** The principle of operation of a capacitor.

(A)                                                              (B)

*A combination of conducting plates separated by an insulator that is used to store an electric charge is known as a **capacitor**.* The area of the plates, their distance of separation, and the character of the insulating material separating them determine the charge that can be placed on a capacitor. The larger the charge, the greater is the potential difference between the plates of a capacitor. The ratio of charge $Q$ to the potential difference $V$ is a *constant* for a given capacitor and is known as its *capacitance, C*. ***Capacitance** is the ratio of the charge on either plate of a capacitor to the potential difference between the plates.* Thus

$$C = \frac{Q}{V}$$

where $C$ is the capacitance of a capacitor, $Q$ is the quantity of charge on either plate, and $V$ is the potential difference between the conducting plates.

In the MKS system, the unit of capacitance is the *farad* (f) named in honor of Michael Faraday. *The capacitance is 1 **farad** when a charge of 1 coulomb on a capacitor results in a potential difference of 1 volt between the plates.* The farad is an extremely large unit of capacitance. Practical capacitors have capacitances of the order of *microfarads* ($\mu$f) or *picofarads* (pf).

$$1\ \mu f = 10^{-6}\ f$$
$$1\ pf = 10^{-12}\ f$$

**Figure 16-21** A two-section, air-dielectric, variable capacitor. The capacitance of each section is varied by rotating the shaft to which the rotor (movable) plates are attached, thereby altering the area of rotor plates that engage the stator (fixed) plates.

## 16.15 Dielectric materials

Faraday investigated the effects of different insulating materials between the plates of capacitors. He constructed two capacitors with equal plate areas and equal plate spacing. Using air at normal pressure in the space between the plates of one and an insulating material between the plates of the other, he charged both to the same potential difference.

These capacitors are shown as $C_1$ and $C_2$ respectively in Figure 16-22. Faraday measured the quantity of charge on each capacitor and found that $C_2$ had a greater charge than $C_1$ by a factor $K$.

$$Q_2 = KQ_1$$

Air

$C_1$

Battery  +

$K$

$C_2$

**Figure 16-22** Capacitors $C_1$ and $C_2$ have identical dimensions and are charged to the same potential difference by the battery. $C_2$ accumulates the larger quantity of charge.

Except for the material separating the plates, the two capacitors are identical and have the same potential difference across their plates. The factor $K$ by which the charge on $C_2$ exceeds the charge on $C_1$ must be due to a property of the insulating material of $C_2$. The ratio $Q_2/V$ is larger than $Q_1/V$ by this factor $K$.

$$\frac{Q_2}{V} = K\frac{Q_1}{V}$$

Thus the capacitance of $C_2$ is larger than the capacitance of $C_1$ by the factor $K$.

$$C_2 = KC_1$$

Many materials such as mica, paraffin, oil, waxed paper, glass, plastics, and ceramics can be used instead of air in the space between the plates of a capacitor. For each material, the resulting capacitance $Q/V$ will have a different value.

Materials used to separate the plates of capacitors are known as *dielectrics*. *The ratio of the capacitance with a particular material separating the plates of a capacitor to the capacitance with a vacuum between the plates is called the **dielectric constant**, K, of the material.* Dry air at atmospheric pressure has a dielectric constant of 1.0006. In practice this is taken as *unity* (the same as vacuum) for dielectric constant determinations. Dielectric constants are dimensionless numbers ranging from 1 to 10 for materials commonly used in capacitors. The dielectric constant, $K$, of the dielectric material used in Figure 16-22 is

$$K = \frac{C_2}{C_1}$$

Typical dielectric constants for some common dielectric materials are given in Table 16-1.

Instead of charging the identical capacitors of Figure 16-22 to the same potential difference, suppose we place the same charge $Q$ on them. The experiment now shows that the potential difference across $C_2$ is smaller than that across $C_1$ by the factor $1/K$.

$$V_2 = \frac{V_1}{K}$$

This leads us to our previous conclusion about the influence of the dielectric material separating the plates of a capacitor. Since $C = Q/V$ and $Q_1$ and $Q_2$ are equal,

$$\frac{Q_2}{V_2} = \frac{Q_1}{V_1/K} \quad \text{and} \quad C_2 = KC_1$$

Table 16-1

| DIELECTRIC CONSTANTS | | |
| --- | --- | --- |
| Dielectric material | Dielectric constant $K$ | Proportionality constant $k$ (n m²/c²) |
| air | 1.0 | $8.9 \times 10^9$ |
| paper (oiled) | 2.0 | $4.5 \times 10^9$ |
| paraffin | 2.2 | $4.1 \times 10^9$ |
| polyethylene | 2.3 | $3.9 \times 10^9$ |
| polystyrene | 2.5 | $3.6 \times 10^9$ |
| hard rubber | 2.8 | $3.2 \times 10^9$ |
| mica | 6.0 | $1.5 \times 10^9$ |
| glass | 8.0 | $1.1 \times 10^9$ |

The molecules of some dielectrics have a permanent separation of their positive and negative centers of charge. This property is described as a permanent *electric dipole moment*. These molecules are called *polar* molecules, or simply *dipoles*. When placed in an electric field, polar molecules tend to become aligned with the external field to a degree characteristic of the molecules.

Other dielectrics are composed of molecules that are essentially *nonpolar* and that show no permanent electric dipole moments. When placed in an electric field, these molecules can acquire a temporary polar character by *induction*. While in the electric field, they have induced electric dipole moments.

The space between the plates of a charged capacitor is permeated by a uniform electric field. If a dielectric slab is inserted into such an electric field denoted by the potential gradient $\mathscr{E}_0$, the slab as a whole becomes polarized by induction. The surface near the positive plate of the capacitor acquires a negative charge and the surface near the negative plate acquires a positive charge. See Figure 16-23. These surface charges result from the dipole moments of the dielectric molecules and not from the transfer of electrons as in the case of metallic conductors.

The electric field established in the dielectric slab by the surface charge *opposes* the external field $\mathscr{E}_0$ of the capacitor. This opposing field is shown in Figure 16-20(B) as $\mathscr{E}_d$. Its effect is to weaken the original field within the dielectric. The net electric field $\mathscr{E}$ is the vector sum of the two fields $\mathscr{E}_0$ and $\mathscr{E}_d$ and is always a weaker field in the direction of $\mathscr{E}_0$.

$$\mathscr{E} = \mathscr{E}_0 + \mathscr{E}_d$$

The net effect of a dielectric between the plates of a charged capacitor is to lower the potential gradient of the electric field. If a parallel-plate capacitor with an air dielectric is charged and then isolated, a potential difference of $Q/C$ volts remains across the plates. The introduction of a dielectric slab between the

## 16.16 The effect of dielectrics

**Figure 16-23** A dielectric slab placed in an electric field tends to weaken the field within the dielectric. What should be the effect on the potential differences across the plates?

plates causes a decrease in this potential difference and reveals its weakening effect on the electric field of the capacitor.

If the charged spheres of Figure 16-10 are immersed in some dielectric medium, the medium would also become polarized by induction. Clustered around each of the charged spheres would be opposite charges from the medium. The result would be an effective reduction in the values of $Q_1$ and $Q_2$. A rigorous analysis shows that the force between the two spheres is reduced in value by the factor $K$, which is the dielectric constant of the medium. Thus in the equation for Coulomb's law

$$F = k \ \frac{Q_1 Q_2}{d^2}$$

*In Table 16-1 observe that the value of k for air divided by K for another dielectric material yields k for that material.*

the value of $k$ is $8.987 \times 10^9$ n m²/c² for vacuum but is reduced by the factor $K$ for material media. Its value for various materials is given in the last column of Table 16-1.

Capacitors find wide application in all kinds of electronic circuits, ignition systems, and telephone and telegraph equipment. Large capacitances are achieved by using large plate areas, insulators with high dielectric constants, and small separation of the plates. Physical size limits the plate area while cost limits the choice of dielectric. *Dielectric strength* of the insulator limits the reduction in spacing between the plates.

Dielectric strength should not be confused with the dielectric constant of a material. The dielectric strength defines the quality of the material as an insulator; that is, the potential gradient it will withstand without being punctured by a spark discharge. Some typical values are given in Table 16-2.

Table 16-2

| DIELECTRIC STRENGTHS | |
|---|---|
| Dielectric material | Dielectric strength (kv/cm to puncture) |
| air | 30 |
| oil | 75 |
| paraffin | 350 |
| paper (oiled) | 400 |
| mica | 500 |
| glass | 1000 |

## 16.17 Combinations of capacitors

Suppose we connect three capacitors in *parallel*, that is, with one plate of each capacitor connected to one conductor while the other plate is connected to a second conductor. See Figure 16-24(A).

The plates connected to the + conductor are parts of one conducting surface. Those connected to the − conductor form the other conducting surface. If the three capacitors are charged, it is apparent that they must have the same difference of potential, $V$, across them. The quantity of charge on each must be respectively

$$Q_1 = C_1 V, \ Q_2 = C_2 V, \ \text{and} \ Q_3 = C_3 V$$

The total charge, $Q_T$, must be the sum of the separate charges on the three capacitors,

$$Q_T = Q_1 + Q_2 + Q_3$$

then

$$Q_T = C_1 V + C_2 V + C_3 V$$

(A)

(B)

**Figure 16-24** Capacitors connected in parallel (A) and in series (B).

Since the total charge is equal to the product of the total capacitance, $C_T$, and the potential difference, $V$, it is evident that

$$Q_T = C_T V$$

Substituting,

$$C_T V = C_1 V + C_2 V + C_3 V$$

and

$$C_T = C_1 + C_2 + C_3$$

*For capacitors connected in parallel, the total capacitance is the sum of all the separate capacitances.*

Now suppose we connect the three capacitors in *series* as shown in Figure 16-24(B). A positive charge placed on $C_1$ from the + source induces a negative charge on the second plate as the electrons are attracted away from the plate $C_2$, which is connected to $C_1$. A positive charge of the same magnitude is left on the + plate of $C_2$. Similarly the plates of $C_3$ acquire the same magnitude of charge. Thus

$$Q = Q_1 = Q_2 = Q_3$$

The negative plate of $C_1$ must be at the same potential with respect to ground as the positive plate of $C_2$ since they are connected and are parts of the same conducting surface. Similarly the negative plate of $C_2$ must be at the same potential as the positive plate of $C_3$. The total difference of potential, $V_T$, across the three series capacitors must be equal to the sum of the separate potential differences across each capacitor: $V_1$, $V_2$, and $V_3$.

$$V_T = V_1 + V_2 + V_3$$

Since the charge received from the source is $Q$, then by definition

$$V_T = \frac{Q}{C_T}$$

and

$$V_1 = \frac{Q}{C_1}, \ V_2 = \frac{Q}{C_2}, \ V_3 = \frac{Q}{C_3}$$

Substituting,

$$\frac{Q}{C_T} = \frac{Q}{C_1} + \frac{Q}{C_2} + \frac{Q}{C_3}$$

or

$$\frac{1}{C_T} = \frac{1}{C_1} + \frac{1}{C_2} + \frac{1}{C_3}$$

*For capacitors connected in series, the reciprocal of the total capacitance is equal to the sum of the reciprocals of all the separate capacitances.* See the following example.

**EXAMPLE**

*Three capacitors have capacitances of 0.200 μf, 0.300 μf, and 0.500 μf. (a) If they are connected in parallel and charged to a potential difference of $10\overline{0}$ v, what is the charge on each capacitor? (b) What is the total charge acquired? (c) If these three capacitors are discharged, then connected in series, and a charge of +30.0 μc is transferred to the ungrounded terminal, what potential difference appears across each? (d) What total potential difference exists across the three capacitors?*

**SOLUTION**

(a) The diagram shown in Figure 16-24(A) applies to this part of the problem. In parallel,

$$V = V_1 = V_2 = V_3 = 10\overline{0} \text{ v}$$

Then

$$Q_1 = C_1 V = 0.200 \text{ μf} \times 10\overline{0} \text{ v} = 20.0 \text{ μc}$$
$$Q_2 = C_2 V = 0.300 \text{ μf} \times 10\overline{0} \text{ v} = 30.0 \text{ μc}$$
$$Q_3 = C_3 V = 0.500 \text{ μf} \times 10\overline{0} \text{ v} = 50.0 \text{ μc}$$

(b) In parallel,

$$Q_T = Q_1 + Q_2 + Q_3 = (20.0 + 30.0 + 50.0) \text{ μc}$$
$$Q_T = 100.0 \text{ μc}$$

(c) The diagram shown in Figure 16-24(B) applies to this part of the problem. In series,

$$Q = Q_1 = Q_2 = Q_3 = 30.0 \text{ μc}$$

Thus each capacitor is charged to 30.0 μc, the ungrounded terminal being positive. Then,

$$V_1 = \frac{Q}{C_1} = \frac{30.0 \text{ μc}}{0.200 \text{ μf}} = 15\overline{0} \text{ v}$$
$$V_2 = \frac{Q}{C_2} = \frac{30.0 \text{ μc}}{0.300 \text{ μf}} = 10\overline{0} \text{ v}$$
$$V_3 = \frac{Q}{C_3} = \frac{30.0 \text{ μc}}{0.500 \text{ μf}} = 60.0 \text{ v}$$

(d) In series,

$$V_T = V_1 + V_2 + V_3 = 15\overline{0} \text{ v} + 10\overline{0} \text{ v} + 60.0 \text{ v}$$
$$V_T = 31\overline{0} \text{ v (positive with respect to ground)}$$

# summary

Electric charges are of two kinds, negative and positive. Like charges repel and unlike charges attract. Electrification is the process that produces electric charges on an object. The process involves the transfer of free electrons. An electroscope may be used to indicate the presence of an electric charge and to provide a rough measurement of its magnitude.

Substances are classified as conductors or insulators based on their ability to conduct an electric charge. Most metals are good conductors. Most nonmetals are good insulators because they are poor conductors of electric charges. The conduction of electric charge by solids is related to the availability of free electrons in their structures. Isolated bodies with conducting surfaces can be charged by either induction or conduction.

The force of attraction or repulsion between point charges is enunciated in terms of Coulomb's law. Charged bodies approximate point charges if they are small in comparison with the distance separating them. The region about a charged body in which the coulomb force exists is an electric field. The path along which a positive test charge is driven by an electric field is called a line of force. Lines of force are used to represent both the direction and intensity of the field.

The difference in potential between two points in an electric field is defined in terms of work expended in moving a charge between two points and quantity of charge moved between these points.

Many experiments with isolated conductors have shown that (1) the residual charge on a conductor resides on its surface; (2) there can be no difference of potential between two points on the surface of a charged conductor; (3) the surface of a conductor is an equipotential surface; (4) electric lines of force are normal to equipotential surfaces; and (5) lines of force originate and terminate normal to the conductive surface of a charged object.

Charge density on the conductive surface of a charged body varies with the surface curvature. The intensity of the electric field near sharp points may be great enough to ionize the surrounding air, thus discharging the body.

An arrangement of conducting surfaces separated by insulators and used to store electric charge is called a capacitor. The capacity for storing electric charge is its capacitance. The dielectric constant of an insulating material is determined by comparing the material's effect on capacitance with the effect of air. Capacitors may be connected in series or in parallel. The total capacitance of the capacitor network is dependent upon the kind of connection used.

# questions

## GROUP A

1. In what region of an insulated ellipsoidal conductor is the greatest charge density concentrated?
2. What determines whether a difference of potential exists between two points?
3. Define (a) potential difference, (b) the MKS unit of potential difference.
4. A conducting object connected to the earth is at zero potential. Explain.
5. Is work required to move a charge along the surface of a charged conductor isolated in space? Explain.
6. How does a spark discharge occur between two charged surfaces?
7. (a) Define capacitance. (b) What is the MKS unit of capacitance?
8. What is the effect of connecting capacitors (a) in parallel, (b) in series?

## GROUP B

9. (a) Express the dimensions of the volt in fundamental MKS units. (b) Demonstrate that the electric field intensity can have the dimensions of volt per meter.
10. (a) Why is it not possible to maintain a charge on an electroscope indefinitely? (b) What shape should the knob have for a minimum rate of loss of charge?
11. Why are the tips of lightning rods shaped into sharp points?
12. Why are the occupants of a modern steel-frame building not harmed when the building is struck by lightning?
13. Would you expect to be very successful in conducting experiments with static electricity on a humid day? Explain.
14. The electrostatic force between two charges immersed in oil is found to be one-half of the electrostatic force when the same two charges are in air. Explain.
15. A solid metal sphere and a hollow metal sphere have the same dimensions, both perfectly insulated. Which will hold the larger maximum charge in air without breaking down?

# problems

1. A force of 0.032 n is required to move a charge of 42 $\mu$c in an electric field between two points 25 cm apart. What potential difference exists between the two points?

2. An electron is accelerated in a machine in which it is subjected to a potential difference of 5.0 megavolts. What energy has the electron acquired?

3. (a) What is the potential gradient between two parallel plates 0.50 cm apart when charged to a potential difference of 1.2 kv? (b) Convert your result to an expression of electric field intensity in terms of n/c.

4. A capacitor consisting of two parallel plates separated by a layer of air 0.3 cm thick and having a capacitance of 15.0 pf is connected across a 150-volt source. (a) What is the charge on the capacitor? The air dielectric is replaced by a sheet of mica 0.3 cm thick. (b) What is the capacitance with the mica dielectric? (c) What additional charge does the capacitor take up?

5. Three paper capacitors having capacitances of 0.15 $\mu$f, 0.22 $\mu$f, and 0.47 $\mu$f are connected in parallel and charged to a potential difference of 240 volts. (a) Determine the charge on each capacitor. (b) What is the total capacitance of the combination? (c) What is the total charge acquired?

# Direct-Current Circuits

## SOURCES OF DIRECT CURRENT

The quantity of charge on a capacitor is indicated by the potential difference between the plates.

$$Q = CV$$

If the capacitance, $C$, for a given capacitor is a constant, then the charge $Q$ is proportional to the potential difference, $V$, across it.

$$Q \propto V \quad (C \text{ constant})$$

A potential difference across a charged capacitor, and therefore a charge on the capacitor, can be indicated by an electroscope connected across the capacitor plates. See Figure 17-1. Suppose the two plates of the capacitor are now connected by a heavy copper wire as in Figure 17-2(A). The leaves of the electroscope immediately collapse, indicating that the capacitor has been discharged rapidly. Free electrons flow from the negative plate of the capacitor and from the electroscope, through the copper wire to the positive plate. This action quickly establishes the normal distribution of electrons characteristic of an uncharged capacitor.

Considering the charged capacitor of Figure 17-1 again, suppose the plates are connected by means of a long, fine wire made of nichrome, which has few free electrons compared to copper. The leaves of the electroscope collapse more gradually than before. See Figure 17-2(B). This delay means that a longer time is required to discharge the capacitor completely. When any conductor connects the plates of the capacitor, elec-

**17.1 Electric charges in motion**

**Figure 17-1** The charge on a capacitor can be indicated by an electroscope.

**Copper wire**

**(A)**

**Nichrome wire**

**(B)**

**Figure 17-2** The rate of discharge of a capacitor depends on the conducting path provided.

trons move from the negative plate through the conductor to the positive plate. This transfer decreases the charge on each plate and the difference of potential between the plates.

The charge, $Q$, on either plate of a capacitor is proportional to the potential difference, $V$, between the plates. The *rate* at which the charge decreases, in c/s, is proportional to the rate at which the potential difference decreases, in v/s. Now, the rate of decrease of charge on the capacitor must represent the rate of flow of the charge, in c/s, through the conductor. Thus the rate at which the leaves of the electroscope collapse indicates the rate of flow of the charge through the conductor. During the time the capacitor is discharging, a *current* is said to exist in the conducting wire. *An **electric current**, I, in a conductor is the rate of flow of charge through a cross section of the conductor.*

$$\text{current } (I) = \frac{\text{charge } (Q)}{\text{time } (t)}$$

The unit of current in the MKS system is the *ampere* (a), named for the French physicist André Marie Ampère (1775–1836). *One ampere is a current of 1 coulomb per second.*

$$1 \text{ a} = \frac{1 \text{ c}}{\text{s}}$$

Recall that 1 coulomb is the charge of $6.25 \times 10^{18}$ electrons or a like number of protons. Small currents can be expressed in *milliamperes* (ma) or *microamperes* ($\mu$a).

$$1 \text{ ma} = 10^{-3} \text{ a}$$
$$1 \text{ }\mu\text{a} = 10^{-6} \text{ a}$$

A moving charge is basic for an electric current. The character of a conducting substance determines the nature of the charge set in motion in an electric field. In solids the charge carriers are electrons; in gases or electrolytic solutions the charge carriers can be positive ions, negative ions, or both. *An **electrolyte** is a substance whose solution conducts an electric current.*

A negative charge moving in one direction in an electric circuit is equivalent to a positive charge moving in the opposite direction insofar as external effects are concerned. Negative charges departing from a negatively charged surface and arriving at a positively charged surface leave the former surface less negative and the latter surface less positive. Positive charges departing from the positively charged surface and arriving at the negatively charged surface would have a similar effect, leaving the positively charged surface less positive and the negatively charged surface less negative.

If both positive and negative charges are set in motion in a conducting medium, the current in the medium is the sum of the currents due to the motion of the positive charges in one direction and the negative charges in the opposite direction.

The directional sense of electron flow through an electric field in a metallic conductor is from negative to positive. The directional sense of a positive ion flow in an ionized gas is from positive to negative. In our study of electric circuits we will be concerned generally with current in metallic conductors and will deal mainly with electron flow in which the directional sense is from negative to positive. In any case, confusion about current direction can be avoided by indicating the directional sense of the charge carriers that are in motion.

The above reference to an electric field in a conductor does not contradict the assertions of Section 16.11, which require the electric field in a conductor to equal zero. In this earlier discussion we were concerned with static electric charges on an isolated conductor. The charges reside on the surface of such a conductor and there is no net charge motion on this equipotential surface. We are presently dealing with moving charges and with conductors across the ends of which potential differences are deliberately maintained. Thus this earlier restriction does not apply.

Free electrons in empty space are accelerated by an electric field. The effect of an electric field on the free electrons of a metallic conductor is quite different. An acceleration of extended duration of these electrons is not realized because of their frequent collisions with the fixed particles of the conductor, the metallic ions. With each collision the electron loses whatever velocity it had acquired in the direction of the accelerating force, transfers energy to the fixed particle, and makes a fresh start.

The kinetic energy transferred in these collisions increases the vibrational energy of the conductor particles and heat is given up to the surroundings. The free electrons move in the direction of the accelerating force with an average velocity called the *drift velocity*. This drift velocity has a constant average value for a given conductor carrying a certain magnitude of current. It is much smaller than the speed with which changes in the electric field propagate through the conductor, which is approximately $3 \times 10^8$ m/s.

It has been estimated that the free electrons of a copper conductor of 1 mm$^2$ cross section have an average drift velocity of about 1 mm/s when a current of 20 a is in the conductor. The situation is somewhat analogous to that of a ball rolling down a flight of stairs. With the proper conditions, the successive collisions of the ball with the steps effectively cancel the acceleration it acquires between steps and it rolls down with a constant average speed.

As we have seen, collision between the free electrons and the fixed particles of a conductor is an energy-dissipating process that opposes the flow of charge through the conductor. *This*

*The electric current in metallic conductors is an electron flow from negative to positive.*

*opposition to the electric current is called* **resistance**, *R*. The practical MKS unit of resistance is the *ohm,* represented by the Greek letter Ω (omega). The laws of electric resistance will be discussed in Section 17.11.

## 17.2 Continuous current

The current from a discharging capacitor persists for a very short interval of time; it is known as a *transient* current. The effects of such a current are also transient, but those effects are very important in certain types of electronic circuits. In the general applications of electricity, more continuous currents are required.

The effects of current electricity are quite different from those of static electricity. The electric current is one of our most convenient means of transferring energy. A *closed-loop* conducting path is needed if energy is to be utilized outside the source; this conducting loop is known as an *electric circuit*. The device or circuit component utilizing the electric energy is called the *load*. The basic components of an electric circuit are illustrated in simple form in Figure 17-3. Some conventional symbols used in schematic diagrams of electric circuits are shown in Figure 17-4.

A capacitor would be useful as a source of continuous current over a prolonged period of time only if some means were available for keeping it continuously charged. We would need to supply electrons to the negative plate of the capacitor as rapidly as they were removed by the current in the conducting loop. Similarly, we would need to remove electrons from the positive plate of the capacitor as rapidly as they were deposited by the current. This is to say we must maintain the potential difference across the source during the time a continuous current is in the circuit.

Maintaining a potential difference across a source of current in an operating circuit is an energy-consuming process; work is done on the electrons in opposition to the force of an electric field. In the process the potential energy of electrons is raised,

**Figure 17-3** An electric circuit is a conducting loop in which a current can transfer electric energy from a suitable source to a useful load.

(A) BLOCK DIAGRAM                    (B) PICTORIAL DIAGRAM                    (C) CIRCUIT DIAGRAM

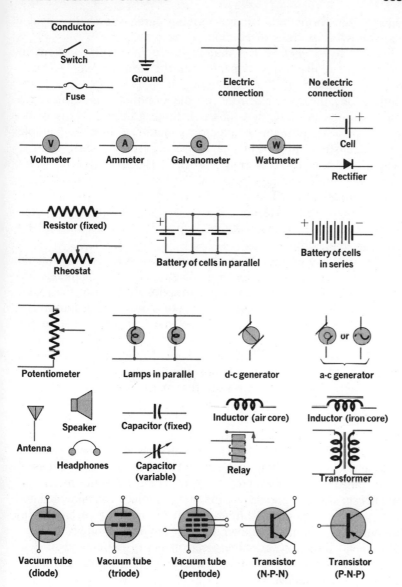

**Conductor**

**Switch**

**Fuse**

**Ground**

**Electric connection**

**No electric connection**

**Voltmeter** (V)  **Ammeter** (A)  **Galvanometer** (G)  **Wattmeter** (W)

**Cell**

**Rectifier**

**Resistor (fixed)**

**Rheostat**

**Battery of cells in parallel**

**Battery of cells in series**

**Potentiometer**

**Lamps in parallel**

**d-c generator**

**a-c generator** (or)

**Antenna**

**Speaker**

**Headphones**

**Capacitor (fixed)**

**Capacitor (variable)**

**Inductor (air core)**

**Inductor (iron core)**

**Relay**

**Transformer**

**Vacuum tube (diode)**

**Vacuum tube (triode)**

**Vacuum tube (pentode)**

**Transistor (N-P-N)**

**Transistor (P-N-P)**

**Figure 17-4** Conventional symbols used in schematic diagrams of electric circuits.

and this energy is available to do useful work in the external circuit. What is needed is some kind of "electron pump." Several practical energy sources are available to maintain a difference of potential across an operating electric circuit.

## 17.3 Sources of continuous current

The transformation of available energy into electricity is accomplished by one of two basic methods: *dynamic conversion* or *direct conversion*. Dynamic converters are rotating machines, and it is these machines that supply most of our requirements for electric energy today. Direct conversion methods produce energy transformations without moving parts. We shall consider the following sources of continuous current:

*1. Electromagnetic.* The major source of electric current in practical circuits today depends on the principle of *electromagnetic induction.* If a conducting loop is rotated in a magnetic field, the free electrons of the conductor are forced to move around the loop and thus constitute a current. This is the basic operating principle of electric generators. It is an example of the transformation of mechanical energy into electric energy, which is a dynamic conversion process. Electromagnetic induction and the electric generator will be studied in Chapter 20.

*2. Photoelectric.* The photoelectric effect was first observed by Heinrich Hertz. He noticed that a spark discharge occurred more readily when charged metal spheres were illuminated by another spark discharge.

Electrons are emitted from the surface of a metal illuminated by light of sufficiently short wavelength. The alkali metals are photosensitive to light in the near ultraviolet region of the radiation spectrum. Two of these metals, potassium and cesium, emit photoelectrons when exposed to ordinary visible light. In the case of most metals, the incident light for photoemission corresponds to radiations deep in the ultraviolet region. When a photon of the incident light is absorbed by the metal, its energy is transferred to an electron. If the motion of this electron is toward the surface and its energy at the surface is sufficient to overcome the forces that bind it within the surface of the metal, it is emitted as a photoelectron.

If properly isolated, the metal surface acquires a positive charge as photoelectrons are emitted. As the charge increases, other electrons are prevented from escaping from the metal and the action stops. If, however, the metal is placed in an evacuated tube and made part of a circuit, as in Figure 17-5, it can act as a source of current whenever light is incident upon its surface. The metal thus serves as the electron pump mentioned in Section 17.2. The evacuated tube containing the metallic emitter is called a *photoelectric cell.*

The photoelectric cell shown in Figure 17-5 has a coating of potassium metal deposited on the inner surface of a glass tube, leaving an aperture through which light can enter. A metallic ring near the focus of the emitter surface acts as a collector of photoelectrons. The emitter is connected externally to the negative terminal of a battery, and the collector is connected to the positive terminal. The collector is thus maintained at a positive potential with respect to the emitter. The force of the resulting electric field acts on the emitted electrons, driving them to the collector. The small photoelectron current can thus be maintained in the external circuit as long as light photons are incident on the emitter surface. A *galvanometer,* an electric meter sen-

*The energy supply for the dynamic conversion process comes mainly from burning fossil fuel, from falling water, and from nuclear fission reactions.*

*Review the laws of photoelectric emission in Section 12.7.*

**Figure 17-5** The circuit of a photoelectric cell.

sitive to very feeble currents, can be placed in the circuit to indicate the relative magnitude and direction of the current.

A bright light of effective frequency causes the ejection of many electrons from the surface of the photosensitive metal, while light of the same frequency but lower intensity produces fewer photoelectrons. Thus the current produced by the photoelectric cell is determined by the intensity of the incident light; this is a case in which radiant energy is transformed into electric energy. Some form of photosensitive cell is used in devices that are controlled or operated by light.

*3. Thermoelectric.* Suppose we form a conducting loop circuit that consists of a length of iron wire, a length of copper wire, and a sensitive galvanometer, as shown in Figure 17-6. One copper-iron junction is put in a beaker of ice and water to maintain a low temperature; the other junction is heated by a gas flame. As the second junction is heated, the galvanometer indicates a current in the loop. An electric circuit incorporating such junctions is known as a *thermocouple.* Transducers

The magnitude of the current is related to the nature of the two metals forming the junctions and the temperature difference between the junctions. A thermocouple can be used as a sensitive thermometer designed to measure radiant energy. The iron-copper junction is useful for temperatures up to about 275°C. Junctions of copper and constantan, a copper-nickel alloy, are widely used in lower temperature ranges. Junctions of platinum and rhodium are used to measure temperatures ranging up to 1600°C.

Since heat energy is transformed directly into electric energy, the thermocouple is a thermoelectric source of current. If a sensitive galvanometer is properly calibrated, temperatures can be read directly. The hot junction of the thermocouple can be placed in a remote location where it would be impossible to read an ordinary mercury thermometer.

Recall that the first law of thermodynamics tells us that heat can be converted into other forms of energy, but energy can neither be created nor destroyed. Thus in a closed thermodynamic system no energy will be gained or lost. Thermoelectric converters are fundamentally heat engines and, as for all other heat engines, are limited to the efficiency of the conversion process. The actual efficiency with which heat is converted to electricity is a function of the temperature difference within the operating system.

The heating effect of an electric current in the resistance of a conductor is an irreversible phenomenon. On the other hand, the basic thermoelectric effects discussed in this section are reversible. The best known of these effects is described in this section: when the junctions of two dissimilar metals are subjected to a difference in temperature, a current is set up in the loop. Known as the *Seebeck effect,* it is named after its discoverer

Figure 17-6   A thermocouple.

**(A) Seebeck effect**

**(B) Peltier effect**

**Figure 17-7** The Seebeck and Peltier effects for copper and nickel. One is the inverse of the other.

who first observed the phenomenon in 1821. See Figure 17-7(A).

The *Peltier effect* is produced when a direct current is passed through a junction formed by two dissimilar metals. The junction becomes warmer or cooler depending on the direction of the current. This effect is shown in Figure 17-7(B).

Another thermoelectric effect, called the *Thomson effect,* is observed in certain homogeneous materials. If a single solid is subjected to a temperature gradient between opposite faces, a difference of potential is established across it. This potential difference can be used to supply an electric current in an external circuit connected to the solid.

Certain semiconductor materials show thermoelectric properties and perform the heat-to-electricity conversion more efficiently than metals. In addition to the application of semiconductor converters as electric generators, the Peltier effect makes possible their use as cooling devices.

Thermocouples in which heat from radioactive isotopes is converted to electricity are presently being used in some unmanned satellites. Nuclear heat sources that produce electric current by thermoelectric conversion are used by astronauts on the surface of the moon to provide power for their lunar experiments. These energy converters use plutonium-238 as the heat source.

*4. Piezoelectric.* When certain crystals, such as Rochelle salt and quartz, are subjected to a mechanical stress, the opposite

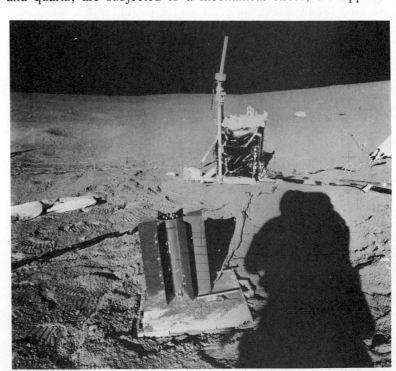

**Figure 17-8** A thermoelectric generator on the surface of the moon. Heat is supplied by nuclear energy. The shadow of an astronaut is seen at the right.

surfaces become electrically charged. The difference of potential between the stressed surfaces is proportional to the amount of stress applied to the crystal. Reversing the stress reverses the charges also.

If the crystal is suitably supported and a conducting circuit is connected between surfaces having a difference of potential, electricity will flow through the circuit. Thus mechanical energy is transformed into electric energy. This transformation is known as the *piezoelectric effect,* and the crystal with its supporting mechanism is called a *piezoelectric cell.*

Crystal microphones use the piezoelectric effect to transform the alternating pressure of sound waves into an electric current that varies as the pressure of the sound waves varies. A crystal phonograph pickup responds in a similar manner to the varying stress caused by the needle riding in the groove of the record.

The piezoelectric effect is reversible; that is, the crystal experiences a mechanical strain when subjected to an electric stress. An alternating difference of potential properly placed across the crystal will cause mechanical vibrations proportional to the variations of the voltage. Crystal headphones use this reciprocal effect.

5. *Chemical.* Certain chemical reactions involve a transfer of electrons from one reactant to the other. The reactions that occur *spontaneously* (that is, of and by themselves) can be used as sources of continuous current. During the chemical reaction, electrons are removed from one reactant. A like number of electrons is added to the other reactant. If the reactants are separated in a conducting environment, the transfer of electrons will take place through an external circuit connecting the reactants. This electron transfer will continue for as long as reactants are available. Such an arrangement is known as an *electrochemical cell.* Chemical energy is transformed into electric energy during the chemical reaction.

Electrochemical cells include primary, storage, and fuel cells. A primary cell, a flashlight cell for example, is ordinarily replaced when its reactants are used up. Storage cells, as in an automobile battery, are reversible. Electric energy is initially stored as chemical energy, and the cell can be repeatedly "recharged" with energy. If the reactants in a primary cell are supplied continuously, the arrangement is called a fuel cell. Fuel cells have been used as the source of electric current in spacecraft.

The essential components of a primary cell are an *electrolyte* and two *electrodes* of unlike materials, one of which reacts chemically with the electrolyte. Let us examine the carbon-zinc dry cell as a common example of the primary cell. A cut-away

## 17.4 The dry cell

**Figure 17-9** The dry cell is a practical source of direct current in the physics laboratory.

*The definitions for electrodes are sometimes based on oxidation-reduction reactions rather than on their electric charge. In that case their names in primary cells become the reverse of those used here.*

**Figure 17-10** A voltaic cell provides electrons of higher potential energy because of chemical action in the cell.

diagram of this cell is shown in Figure 17-9. The electrolyte is a moist paste of ammonium chloride. One electrode is a carbon rod. The other electrode, a zinc cup, is consumed as the cell is used.

When an external circuit is connected across the cell, zinc atoms react with the electrolyte and lose electrons, which remain with the zinc cup. This reaction leaves the zinc electrode *negatively charged*. We shall refer to the negative electrode as the **cathode.** *It is the electron-rich electrode.*

Simultaneously, the electrolyte removes a like number of electrons from the carbon electrode. This reaction leaves the carbon electrode positively charged. We shall call the positive electrode the **anode.** *It is the electron-poor electrode.*

Electrons move through the external circuit from cathode to anode because of the difference in potential between the electrodes. Thus the cell acts as a kind of electron pump. See Figure 17-10. It removes electrons with low potential energy from the anode and supplies electrons with high potential energy to the cathode while current is in the external circuit. Electrons flow through the external circuit from cathode to anode. This unidirectional current is an example of *direct current*, dc.

If we open the circuit and stop the current, the *maximum* potential difference is quickly established across the cell. The magnitude of this *open-circuit* potential difference is dependent solely on the materials that make up the electrodes. For the carbon-zinc cell it is approximately 1.5 volts.

The open circuit potential difference can be referred to as the *emf*, or electromotive force, of the cell. The symbol for emf is *E* and the MKS unit is the *volt* (v). The cell itself must supply a definite amount of energy for each unit of charge that is stored on either electrode; *the **emf** of a source is the energy per unit charge supplied by the source.* Thus the potential difference across the cell on an *open* circuit is equal to the emf of the cell.

$$V_{oc} = E$$

We will see in Section 17.6 that the potential difference, *V*, across a source of emf on a *closed circuit* is less than the emf, *E*.

The carbon-zinc cell has an emf of 1.5 volts, regardless of the size of the cell. However, the larger the electrode surfaces, the larger the current the cell can deliver. The standard No. 6 dry cell is capable of supplying a *momentary* current up to 35 amperes. It should not be required to furnish more than 0.25 ampere of continuous current, however. The internal resistance can vary from less than 0.1 ohm as in the No. 6 cell to over 1 ohm as in small special-purpose cells.

Alkaline-manganese cells can be substituted for carbon-zinc cells in many applications. While more expensive to produce, alkaline cells have lower internal resistance, higher efficiency,

Nickel plated
steel closure
(Negative
electrode)

Sealing
gasket

Contact pin

Manganese
dioxide

Granular zinc
and electrolyte

Porous
separator

Nickel plated
steel closure
(Positive
electrode)

**Figure 17-11** Cross-section of an alkaline-manganese cell. An outer jacket (not shown) and appropriate terminal connections provide the conventional appearance of the carbon-zinc cell.

and the ability to deliver from 50% to 100% more current than their carbon-zinc counterparts.

A sectional view of an alkaline-manganese cell is shown in Figure 17-11. The positive electrode consists of manganese dioxide in conjunction with a steel can that serves as the electrode terminal. The negative electrode is granulated zinc that is mixed with a highly conductive potassium hydroxide electrolyte. The nominal potential difference across the cell is 1.5 volts.

## 17.5 Combinations of cells

Energy-consuming devices that form the loads of electric circuits are designed to draw the proper current for their operation when a specific potential difference exists across their terminals. For example, a lamp designed for use in a 6-volt electric system of an automobile would draw an excessive current and burn out if placed in a 12-volt system. A lamp that is intended for use in a 12-volt system, on the other hand, would not draw sufficient current at 6 volts to function as intended.

Electrochemical cells are sources of emf. Each cell furnishes a certain amount of energy to the circuit for each coulomb of charge that is moved. It is often necessary to combine cells in order to provide either the proper emf or an adequate source of current. Groups of cells can be connected in *series,* in *parallel,* or in *series-parallel* combinations. *Two or more electrochemical cells connected together form a battery.* The emf of a battery depends on the emf of the individual cells and the way in which they are connected.

A *series* combination of cells is shown in Figure 17-12. Observe that the positive terminal of one cell is connected to the

d-c voltmeter

**(A) Pictorial diagram**

**(B) Circuit diagram**

**Figure 17-12** Dry cells connected in series to form a battery. The same quantity of electricity flows through each cell.

external circuit, and the negative terminal is connected to the positive terminal of a second cell. The negative terminal of this cell is connected to the positive terminal of a third cell, and so on. The negative terminal of the last cell in the series is connected to the load to complete the circuit. Thus the cells are joined end to end and *the same quantity of electricity must flow through each cell*.

Suppose we think of the battery as a group of electron pumps connected in *series* (adding). Each electron pump (cell) removes electrons of low potential energy from its anode and supplies electrons of high potential energy to its cathode. The first pump lifts electrons to a certain level of potential energy, the second pump takes them from this level to the next higher level, the third lifts them to a still higher potential energy, and so on. We can readily see that the emfs of the cells are added to give the emf of the battery.

A battery made up of cells connected in *series* has the following characteristics:

*1. The emf of the battery is equal to the sum of the emfs of the individual cells.*

*2. The current in each cell and in the external circuit has the same magnitude throughout.*

*Resistances in series are treated analytically in Section 17.8.*

*3. The internal resistance of the battery is equal to the sum of the internal resistances of the individual cells.*

In a *parallel* combination of cells, all negative terminals are connected together. One side of the external circuit is then connected to any one of these common terminals. The positive terminals are connected together and the other side of the external

**(A) Pictorial diagram**

**(B) Circuit diagram**

**Figure 17-13** Dry cells connected in parallel to form a battery.

circuit can be connected to any one of these common terminals to complete the circuit. See Figure 17-13. This arrangement has the effect of increasing the total cathode and anode surface areas. The battery is then roughly the equivalent of a single cell having greatly enlarged electrodes in contact with the electrolyte and a lower internal resistance. Each cell of a group in parallel merely furnishes its proportionate share of the total circuit current. Of course, cells should not be connected in parallel unless they have equal emfs.

A battery of *identical* cells connected in *parallel* has the following characteristics.

*1. The emf is equal to the emf of each separate cell.*

*2. The total current in the circuit is divided equally among the cells.*

*3. The reciprocal of the internal resistance of the battery is equal to the sum of the reciprocals of the internal resistances of the cells.*

*Resistances in parallel are treated analytically in Section 17.9.*

The lead-acid storage battery for automobiles with 6-volt electric systems consists of three cells connected in series. The emf is approximately 6.6 volts. Six cells are connected in series to make up the battery for 12-volt systems.

As mentioned previously, a No. 6 dry cell should not be required to deliver more than 0.25 ampere of continuous current. Suppose we have an electric device designed to perform with a 0.75-ampere continuous current in a 3-volt circuit. How should the 1.5-volt dry cells be grouped to make up the battery for operating the device?

Certainly, two dry cells in series would provide an emf of 3

**(A) Pictorial diagram**

**Figure 17-14** A circuit using a battery consisting of a series-parallel arrangement of cells.

**(B) Circuit diagram**

volts for the circuit. Three cells in parallel would require no more than 0.25 ampere from each cell. Thus a series-parallel arrangement of dry cells, as shown in Figure 17-14, is appropriate.

# questions

GROUP A

1. What is an electric current?

2. What is the MKS unit of current?

3. Define the unit of current in terms of fundamental MKS units.

4. What is electric resistance?

5. Name five basic sources of continuous current.

6. Name a current-producing device for each of these sources.

7. What are the essential parts of a primary cell?

8. Define an electrolyte.

9. What term is used to identify (a) the negative electrode of an electric cell, (b) the positive electrode?

10. What is the distinguishing characteristic of direct current electricity?

11. Distinguish between the terms "open circuit" and "closed circuit."

12. What is the open-circuit potential difference of a source of current called?

GROUP B

13. What change in the energy of an electron is produced (a) by a source of emf, (b) by a load connected across a source of emf?

14. Both primary and storage cells are sources of emf. What distinguishes one cell from the other?

15. What determines the efficiency with which heat is converted to electricity in thermoelectric converters?

16. Distinguish between potential difference and emf.

17. (a) How would you connect 1.5-volt dry cells to provide a 6-volt battery to supply a continuous current of 0.25 ampere to a load? (b) Draw a circuit diagram of the battery you describe.

18. Does a storage battery store electricity? Justify your answer.

# SERIES AND PARALLEL CIRCUITS

Resistance, *R*, is defined as the opposition to the flow of electric charge. Metallic substances in general are classed as good conductors of electricity. Silver and copper, because of their abundance of free electrons, are excellent conductors; yet even these metals offer some opposition to the current in them. Through its normal range of operating temperatures, every conductor has some inherent resistance. Thus every device or component in an electric circuit offers some resistance to the current in the circuit.

Copper wire is used to connect various circuit components in electric circuits because ordinarily its resistance is low enough to be neglected. Certain metallic alloys offer unusually high resistance to the flow of electricity; *nichrome* and *chromel* are notable examples. Spools wound with wire made from these alloys can be used in an electric circuit to provide either *fixed* amounts of resistance or *variable* resistance in definite amounts.

Carbon granules can be mixed with varying amounts of clay and molded into cylinders having a definite resistance. These devices, known as *carbon resistors*, are commonly used in electronic circuits.

The German physicist Georg Simon Ohm (1787–1854) discovered that *in a closed circuit the ratio of the emf of the source to the current in the circuit is a constant*. This constant is the *resistance* of the circuit. The above statement, known as **Ohm's law of resistance**, describes a basic relationship in the study of current electricity. It can be stated mathematically:

$$\frac{E}{I} = R \quad \text{or} \quad E = IR$$

The MKS units are the volt, ampere, and ohm respectively. The *ohm* ($\Omega$) has the following dimensions:

$$\Omega = \frac{v}{a} = \frac{j/c}{c/s}$$

$$\Omega = \frac{j\,s}{c^2} = \frac{n\,m\,s}{c^2}$$

$$\Omega = \frac{kg\,m^2\,s}{s^2\,c^2} = \frac{kg\,m^2}{c^2\,s}$$

Suppose an emf of 12 v exists in an electric circuit that has 33 $\Omega$ resistance. The current in the circuit is:

$$E = IR \quad \text{so} \quad I = E/R$$

$$I = \frac{12\ v}{33\ \Omega} = 0.36\ a$$

Now suppose the circuit resistance is doubled. In this situation the opposition to the current is doubled but the emf remains the

## 17.6 Ohm's law for d-c circuits

**Figure 17-15** Georg Ohm, the German physicist for whom the unit of resistance is named.

**Figure 17-16** Ohm's law applies equally well to all or any part of an electric circuit.

same, so we should expect the current in the circuit to be reduced to one-half the former value.

$$I = \frac{12 \text{ v}}{66 \text{ } \Omega} = 0.18 \text{ a}$$

The emf, $E$, applied to a circuit equals the drop in potential across the *total* resistance of the circuit, but Ohm's law applies equally well to *any part* of a circuit that does not include a source of emf. Suppose we consider the circuit shown in Figure 17-16. Points **A** and **B** are the terminals of the battery that supplies an emf of 12.0 volts to the circuit. The total resistance of the circuit is 12.0 ohms. Of this total, 0.20 ohm is *internal resistance, r,* of the battery and is conventionally represented as a resistor in series with the battery inside the battery terminals. The remaining 11.8 ohms of resistance consists of a *load resistor, $R_L$,* in the external circuit.

For the entire circuit, the total resistance, $R_T$, is equal to the sum of internal and external resistances.

$$R_T = R_L + r$$

The current in the entire circuit is

$$I = \frac{E}{R_T} = \frac{E}{R_L + r}$$

$$I = \frac{12.0 \text{ v}}{11.8 \text{ } \Omega + 0.20 \text{ } \Omega} = 1.00 \text{ a}$$

When we apply Ohm's law to a part of a circuit that does not include a source of emf, we are concerned with the potential difference, $V$; the current, $I$; and the resistance, $R$, that apply only to that part of the circuit. Thus Ohm's law for a part of the circuit becomes

$$V = IR$$

The drop in potential across the external circuit of Figure 17-16 must be

$$V_L = IR_L$$
$$V_L = 1.00 \text{ a} \times 11.8 \text{ } \Omega = 11.8 \text{ v}$$

The drop in potential across the internal resistance of the battery due to current in the battery can be found by a similar application of Ohm's law.

$$V_r = Ir$$
$$V_r = 1.00 \text{ a} \times 0.20 \text{ } \Omega = 0.20 \text{ v}$$

This is a drop in potential across the battery resistance that removes energy from the electrons. It is, therefore, opposite in sign to the emf of the battery. The potential difference across the battery terminals of a closed circuit with a current $I$ is determined by subtracting this drop in potential from the emf.

$$V = E - Ir$$

The closed-circuit potential difference across the terminals of a source of emf that is applied to the external circuit will always be less than the emf by the amount $Ir$ volts. This is not an important difference for a source of emf of low internal resistance unless an excessive current is in the circuit. (In much of the discussion of Sections 17.8–17.10 the internal resistance of a source of emf will be neglected and the emf will be assumed to be applied to the external circuit.)

A good quality voltmeter is an instrument of very high resistance. When such a voltmeter is connected across the terminals of a source of emf, even a source with low internal resistance, negligible current is drawn from the source. The meter registers an "open circuit" voltage that, for all practical purposes, is the emf of the source. Such a measurement of the emf of a cell or battery provides a convenient method of determining its internal resistance. The following example, based on the circuit shown in Figure 17-17 illustrates this method of determining the internal resistance, $r$, of a dry cell.

## 17.7 Determining internal resistance

Figure 17-17   A circuit for measuring the internal resistance of a cell.

**EXAMPLE**

*A dry cell gives an open-circuit voltmeter reading of 1.5 v with $Sw_1$ closed and $Sw_2$ open. The voltmeter, $V$, is then removed from the circuit by opening switch $Sw_1$, and an external load of 2.8 ohms, $R_L$, is connected across the source of emf by closing switch $Sw_2$. The ammeter, $A$, in the external circuit reads 0.50 a. (a) Find the internal resistance, $r$, of the cell. (b) What would the voltmeter have read if it had been left connected while the current was in the load?*

**SOLUTION**

(a) We are given the following information: the emf of the cell, $E = 1.5$ v; $I = 0.50$ a; and $R_L = 2.8 \, \Omega$. We are asked to find $r$. We know that $E$ is the work done per coulomb of charge moved through the total resistance of the circuit. Thus

$E = IR_T$.    But $R_T = R_L + r$

Substituting for $R_T$:  $E = I(R_L + r)$

Solving for $r$:  $r = \dfrac{E - IR_L}{I}$

$r = \dfrac{1.5 \text{ v} - (0.50 \text{ a} \times 2.8 \, \Omega)}{0.50 \text{ a}} = 0.20 \, \Omega$, the internal resistance

(b) $V = E - Ir = 1.5 \text{ v} - (0.50 \text{ a} \times 0.20 \, \Omega)$
$V = 1.4$ v, the potential difference across the circuit

## 17.8 Resistances in series

*All elements connected in series in a circuit have the same magnitude of current.*

If several electric devices are connected end to end in a circuit, electricity must flow through each in succession. There is a single path for the moving charge. The same current must be in each device or else there would be an accumulation of charge at different points around the conducting circuit. We know that a charge can be accumulated on a conductor only if it is isolated. *An electric circuit with components arranged to provide a single conducting path for current is known as a series circuit.*

Series-circuit operation has several inherent characteristics. If one component of a series circuit fails to provide a conducting path, the circuit is opened. Each component of the circuit offers resistance to the current, and this resistance limits the current in the circuit according to Ohm's law. When components are connected in series, their resistances are cumulative. The greater the number of resistive components, the higher is the total resistance and the smaller is the current in the circuit for a given applied emf. Obviously, since the current must be the same at all points in the circuit, *all devices connected in series must be designed to function at the same current magnitude*.

From Ohm's law, the drop in potential across each component of a series circuit is the product of the current in the circuit and the resistance of the component. Electrons lose energy as they fall through a difference of potential; in a series circuit these losses occur in succession and are therefore cumulative. *The drops in potential across successive components in a series circuit are additive, and their sum is equal to the potential difference across the whole circuit.*

We can summarize these observations by stating three cardinal rules for resistances in series:

*1. The current in all parts of a series circuit has the same magnitude.*

$$I_T = I_1 = I_2 = I_3 = \text{etc.}$$

*2. The sum of all the separate drops in potential around a series circuit is equal to the applied emf.*

$$E = V_1 + V_2 + V_3 + \text{etc.}$$

*3. The total resistance in a series circuit is equal to the sum of all the separate resistances.*

$$R_T = R_1 + R_2 + R_3 + \text{etc.}$$

These rules have been applied to a circuit consisting of several resistors connected in series as shown in Figure 17-18. For simplicity, the internal resistance of the source is assumed to be negligible and is omitted from the circuit diagram. The computations are shown at the right of the circuit. Observe that the "positive" side of $R_1$ is 3.0 volts *positive with respect to the cathode of the battery* and is 9.0 volts *negative with respect to*

$$R_T = R_1 + R_2 + R_3$$
$$R_T = 6.0\,\Omega + 8.0\,\Omega + 10.0\,\Omega$$
$$R_T = 24.0\,\Omega$$
$$I = \frac{E}{R_T} = \frac{12.0\text{ v}}{24.0} = 0.50\text{ a}$$
$$E = V_1 + V_2 + V_3$$
$$E = IR_1 + IR_2 + IR_3$$
$$E = 3.0\text{ v} + 4.0\text{ v} + 5.0\text{ v}$$
$$E = 12.0\text{ v}$$

**Figure 17-18** A series circuit.

*the anode of the battery.* The three voltage drops around the external circuit are in series, and their sum equals the applied emf in magnitude, but their signs are opposite.

Stated in another way, *the algebraic sum of all the changes in potential occurring around the complete circuit is equal to zero.* This is a statement of **Kirchhoff's second law** credited to Gustav Robert Kirchhoff (1824–1887), an eminent German physicist. Since potential difference is an expression of work (or energy) per unit charge involved in transporting a charge around a closed circuit, Kirchhoff's second law can be recognized as an application of the law of *conservation of energy* to electric circuits.

*Kirchhoff's first law is given in Section 17.9.*

## 17.9 Resistances in parallel

Some of the characteristics of series operation of electric devices were mentioned in the preceding section. It would be quite disconcerting to have all the lights go out in your home each time one lamp were turned off. For this reason each lamp is on a separate circuit so that each is operated independently. Such lamps are said to be connected in parallel. *A **parallel circuit** is one in which two or more components are connected across two common points in the circuit to provide separate conducting paths for current.*

Since there can be only one difference of potential between any two points in an electric circuit, *electric devices or appliances connected in parallel should usually be designed to operate at the same voltage.* The currents in the separate branches must vary inversely with their separate resistances since the same potential difference exists across each branch of the parallel circuit.

By Ohm's law, which can be applied to any part of a circuit, the current in each branch is

$$I = \frac{V}{R}$$

But $V$ is constant for all branches in parallel. Then

$$I_{\text{(for each branch)}} \propto \frac{1}{R_{\text{(of that branch)}}}$$

**Figure 17-19** Two resistances in parallel.

*All elements connected in parallel in a circuit have the same voltage across them.*

In Figure 17-19 it is apparent that more electric charge can flow between points **A** and **B** with the two parallel paths $R_1$ and $R_2$ in the circuit than with either path alone. The current $I$ entering junction **A** must be the same as the current $(I_1 + I_2)$ leaving junction **A**. Similarly, the current $(I_1 + I_2)$ entering junction **B** must be the same as the current $I$ leaving junction **B**. Then $I$ must be equal to $I_1 + I_2$.

Let us consider in another way the currents entering and leaving junctions **A** and **B**. Electric current is the rate of transfer of charge, $I = Q/t$. In the steady-state operation of the circuit, the charge of **A** can neither increase nor decrease. Current $I$ carries charge toward this junction and $I_1$ and $I_2$ carry charge away from it. Thus

$$I - I_1 - I_2 = 0$$

Similarly, currents $I_1$ and $I_2$ carry charge toward junction **B** and $I$ carries charge away from it. Using the same sign convention for current direction as before,

$$I_1 + I_2 - I = 0$$

These expressions tell us that *the algebraic sum of the currents at any circuit junction is equal to zero*. This is known as **Kirchhoff's first law**. It states, in effect, a law of *conservation of charge* in electric circuits. Kirchhoff's two laws define the basic principles we must employ in our interpretation of electric circuits: *that energy and charge are conserved*.

In Figure 17-19, assume that $R_1 = 1\bar{0}\ \Omega$, $R_2 = 15\ \Omega$, and $V = 3\bar{0}$ v. From Ohm's law, the current in $R_1$ is

$$I_1 = \frac{V}{R_1} = \frac{3\bar{0}\text{ v}}{1\bar{0}\ \Omega} = 3.0\text{ a}$$

The current in $R_2$ is

$$I_2 = \frac{V}{R_2} = \frac{3\bar{0}\text{ v}}{15\Omega} = 2.0\text{ a}$$

and

$$I = I_1 + I_2 = 5.0\text{ a}$$

According to Ohm's law, the current from **A** to **B**, which is $I$, is the quotient of the potential difference across **A-B** divided by the effective resistance between **A** and **B**. It is convenient to think of the effective resistance due to resistances in parallel as a single *equivalent resistance*, $R_{eq}$, that, if substituted for the parallel resistances, would provide the same current in the circuit.

*An equivalent resistance is shown in Figure 17-19.*

$$I = \frac{V}{R_{eq}}$$

Then

$$R_{eq} = \frac{V}{I} = \frac{30 \text{ v}}{5.0 \text{ a}} = 6.0 \text{ } \Omega$$

The equivalent resistance for the parallel combination of $R_1$ and $R_2$ is *less than* either resistance present. As the current approaching junction **A** *must be larger* than either branch current, clearly the equivalent resistance of the parallel circuit *must be smaller* than the resistance of any branch.

Since

$$I = \frac{V}{R_{eq}} , I_1 = \frac{V}{R_1} , I_2 = \frac{V}{R_2}$$

and

$$I = I_1 + I_2$$

then,

$$\frac{V}{R_{eq}} = \frac{V}{R_1} + \frac{V}{R_2}$$

Dividing by $V$, we get

$$\frac{1}{R_{eq}} = \frac{1}{R_1} + \frac{1}{R_2} \qquad \text{(Equation 1)}$$

Equation 1 shows that the sum of the reciprocals of the resistances in parallel is equal to the reciprocal of their equivalent resistance. Then solving Equation 1 for $R_{eq}$,

$$R_1 R_2 = R_{eq} (R_1 + R_2)$$

and

$$R_{eq} = \frac{R_1 R_2}{R_1 + R_2}$$

$$R_{eq} = \frac{10 \text{ } \Omega \times 15 \text{ } \Omega}{10 \text{ } \Omega + 15 \text{ } \Omega} = \frac{150 \text{ } \Omega^2}{25 \text{ } \Omega}$$

$$R_{eq} = 6.0 \text{ } \Omega$$

Let us summarize these observations by stating three cardinal rules for resistances in parallel.

*1. The total current in a parallel circuit is equal to the sum of the currents in the separate branches.*

$$I_T = I_1 + I_2 + I_3 + \text{ etc.}$$

*2. The potential difference across all branches of a parallel circuit must have the same magnitude.*

$$V = V_1 = V_2 = V_3 = \text{ etc.}$$

*3. The reciprocal of the equivalent resistance is equal to the sum of the reciprocals of the separate resistances in parallel.*

$$\frac{1}{R_{eq}} = \frac{1}{R_1} + \frac{1}{R_2} + \frac{1}{R_3} + \text{ etc.}$$

## 17.10 Resistances in simple networks

**(A) Network**

**(B) Equivalent circuit**

**Figure 17-20** A simple network and its equivalent circuit.

Practical circuits can be quite complex compared to the series and parallel circuits we have considered. There can be resistances in series, other resistances in parallel, and different sources of emf. Such complex circuits are commonly called *networks*.

A simple network is shown in Figure 17-20(A). There is a single source of emf and one resistor in series with the combination of two resistors in parallel. We will use this circuit to demonstrate the steps that can be taken to simplify a network and reduce circuit problems to simple relationships.

We are given the emf and internal resistance of the battery and the resistance of each component resistor in the circuit. The first step is to find the total current in the circuit. Since the emf, $E$, is known, the total resistance, $R_T$, must also be known in order to calculate the total current, $I_T$. To find the total resistance, we must first reduce the parallel resistances to an *equivalent* value.

$$\frac{1}{R_{eq}} = \frac{1}{R_2} + \frac{1}{R_3} \quad \text{and} \quad R_{eq} = \frac{R_2 R_3}{R_2 + R_3}$$

$$R_{eq} = \frac{3.0 \ \Omega \times 6.0 \ \Omega}{3.0 \ \Omega + 6.0 \ \Omega}$$

$$R_{eq} = 2.0 \ \Omega, \text{ the equivalent resistance}$$

A simpler *equivalent* circuit can now be drawn showing this equivalent resistance in series with $R_1$ and $r$. See Figure 17-20(B). The total resistance is now readily seen to be 6.0 ohms.

$$R_T = R_1 + R_{eq} + r = 6.0 \ \Omega$$

And

$$I_T = \frac{E}{R_T} = \frac{6.0 \text{ v}}{6.0 \ \Omega} = 1.0 \text{ a}$$

The drop in potential across $R_1$ is

$$V_1 = I_T R_1 = 1.0 \text{ a} \times 3.5 \ \Omega$$
$$V_1 = 3.5 \text{ v}$$

Since $R_2$ and $R_3$ are in parallel, the same potential drop must appear across each. This is found by considering the total current in the equivalent resistance of the parallel segment.

$$V_{eq} = I_T R_{eq} = 1.0 \text{ a} \times 2.0 \ \Omega$$
$$V_{eq} = 2.0 \text{ v}$$

The potential difference across the terminals of the battery is the difference between the emf and the $I_T r$ drop.

$$V = E - I_T r = 6.0 \text{ v} - (1.0 \text{ a} \times 0.50 \ \Omega)$$
$$V = 5.5 \text{ v}$$

This is verified by the fact that $V$ must equal $V_1 + V_{eq}$.

The current in $R_2$ may be found since the potential difference, $V_{eq}$, is known.

$$I_2 = \frac{V_{eq}}{R_2} = \frac{2.0 \text{ v}}{3.0 \text{ } \Omega}$$

$$I_2 = 0.67 \text{ a}$$

The current in $R_3$ is

$$I_3 = \frac{V_{eq}}{R_3} = \frac{2.0 \text{ v}}{6.0 \text{ } \Omega}$$

$$I_3 = 0.33 \text{ a}$$

This is verified by the fact that $I_3$ must equal $I_T - I_2$.

A more complex network is shown in Figure 17-21(A). The battery is a series-parallel arrangement of similar cells, so the magnitude of the emf will depend on the number of cells in *series*. The total current must be known. The approach is the same as that in our earlier example. First, reduce the segment **F-G** to its equivalent value. We will label this $R_{FG}$. Now $R_{FG}$ is in series with $R_4$, $R_5$, and $R_{10}$ to form one branch of the segment **C-D**. When the two branches of **C-D** are reduced to their equivalent, $R_{CD}$, we can consider $R_1$, $R_{CD}$, and $R_{11}$ to be in series. This reduction provides $R_T$, and $I_T$ may be calculated. See the diagrams in Figure 17-21(B).

(A) Network

(B) Equivalent circuit

**Figure 17-21** A network may be reduced to a simple circuit by the use of equivalent circuit analysis techniques.

Suppose we need to know the magnitude of current in $R_7$ and the drop in potential across this resistor. Now the current in $R_{CD}$ must be $I_T$ and the drop in potential across C-D must be $I_T R_{CD}$, or $V_{CD}$. The current in the branch of C-D containing $R_{FG}$ is the quotient of $V_{CD}$ divided by the sum, $(R_4 + R_5 + R_{FG} + R_{10})$. This current (we will label it $I_{FG}$) is in $R_{FG}$, and the potential drop, $V_{FG}$, across $R_{FG}$ is the product $I_{FG} R_{FG}$.

Since $R_6$ and $R_7$ are in series, the resistance of this branch of F-G is equal to their sum. The current in $R_7$ is $V_{FG}$ divided by $(R_6 + R_7)$. With $I_7$ known, the drop in potential across $R_7$ is the product $I_7 R_7$. You will observe that we have depended on Ohm's law and the six extensions of Ohm's law listed as cardinal rules for series and parallel circuits in Sections 17.8 and 17.9.

## 17.11 The laws of resistance

Various factors affect the resistance of a conductor.

*1. Temperature.* The resistance of all substances changes to some degree with changes in temperature. *In the case of pure metals and most metallic alloys, the resistance increases with a rise in temperature.* On the other hand, carbon, semiconductors, and many electrolytic solutions, show a decrease in resistance as their temperature is raised. A few special alloys, such as constantan and manganin, show very slight changes in resistance over a considerable range of temperatures. For practical purposes, the resistance of these alloys can be considered independent of temperature.

Thermal agitation of the particles composing a metallic conductor increases as the metal is heated. As the temperature is lowered, thermal agitation diminishes. The electric resistance of metals is related to this thermal agitation; their resistance approaches zero as the temperature approaches absolute zero (0°K). The graph of resistance against temperature of a metallic conductor is essentially linear over the normal temperature range of the solid state of a metal. Thus when the electric resistance of a conductor is stated, the temperature of the material at which this resistance applies should be indicated. See Figure 17-22.

*2. Length.* Resistances in series are added to give the total resistance of the series circuit. From this fact we can conclude that 10 meters of a certain conductor should have a resistance 10 times that of 1 meter of the same conductor. Experiments prove this relationship to be true: *The resistance of a uniform conductor is directly proportional to the length of the conductor*

$$R \propto l$$

where $l$ is the length of the conductor.

*3. Cross-sectional area.* If three *equal* resistances are connected in parallel in an electric circuit, the equivalent resistance is

Electrolytic copper
ρ vs. t

(Melts)

Linear region

Resistivity, $10^{-6}$ Ω cm

Temperature, °C

**Figure 17-22** The resistivity of copper as a function of temperature.

one-third the resistance of any one branch. The equal currents in the three branches add to give the total current in the circuit.

Assuming the three resistances to be three similar wires 1 meter in length and each having a cross-sectional area of $0.1$ cm², we can think of the equivalent resistance as a similar wire of the same length but having a cross-sectional area of $0.3$ cm². This deduction is reasonable since a wire carrying a direct current of constant magnitude has a constant current density throughout its cross-sectional area. If the parallel resistances are designated $R_1, R_2,$ and $R_3,$ then

*Current density is the current per unit area of the cross-sectional area of a conductor.*

$$\frac{1}{R_{eq}} = \frac{1}{R_1} + \frac{1}{R_2} + \frac{1}{R_3}$$

But

$$R_1 = R_2 = R_3$$

So

$$\frac{1}{R_{eq}} = \frac{3}{R_1}$$

And

$$R_1 = 3 R_{eq}$$

We can conclude that the resistance of the large wire, $R_{eq}$, is one-third the resistance of the small wire, $R_1$, and experiments prove this conclusion to be true. *The resistance of a uniform conductor is inversely proportional to its cross-sectional area*

$$R \propto \frac{1}{A}$$

where $A$ is the cross-sectional area of the conductor.

4. *Nature of the materials.* A copper wire having the same length and cross-sectional area as an iron wire offers about one-sixth the resistance to an electric current. A similar silver wire presents even less resistance. *The resistance of a given conductor depends on the material of which it is made.*

Taking these four factors into account, several useful conclusions become apparent. For a uniform conductor of a given material and temperature, the resistance is directly proportional to the length and inversely proportional to the cross-sectional area.

$$R \propto \frac{l}{A}$$

Suppose we introduce a proportionality constant, called *resistivity,* represented by the Greek letter $\rho$ (rho). The laws of *resistance* for wire conductors can then be summarized by the following expression:

$$R = \rho \frac{l}{A}$$

Resistivity is dependent only on the material composing the wire and its temperature. See Fig. 17-22. If $R$ is in ohms, $l$ is in centimeters, and $A$ is in centimeters$^2$, then $\rho$ has the dimensions *ohm centimeter.*

$$\rho = \frac{RA}{l}$$

$$\rho = \frac{\Omega \text{ cm}^2}{\text{cm}} = \Omega \text{ cm}$$

*Resistivity,* $\rho$, *is equal to the resistance of a wire 1 cm long and having a uniform cross-sectional area of 1 cm$^2$.* (The resistivities of various materials are listed in Appendix B, Table 20. The wire gauge scale and the dimensions of wire by gauge number are given in Table 21.) If the resistivity of a material is known, the resistance of any other wire composed of the same material can be calculated. See the following example.

| | |
|---|---|
| **EXAMPLE** | *What is the resistance of a copper wire $2\overline{0}$ m long and 0.81 mm in diameter at 20°C? The resistivity of annealed copper at 20°C is 1.72 × 10$^{-6}$ $\Omega$ cm.* |
| **SOLUTION** | We are given the resistivity of copper at 20°C, $\rho = 1.72 \times 10^{-6} \Omega$ cm. The length of wire can be converted to centimeters and expressed as $l = 2.0 \times 10^3$ cm. The diameter of the wire in millimeters can be converted to 0.081 cm. The area, $A$, of a circle with diameter, $d$, = $\frac{\pi d^2}{4}$. |

$$R = \rho \, \frac{l}{A}$$

$$R = 1.72 \times 10^{-6} \, \Omega\,cm \times \frac{2.0 \times 10^3 \, cm}{\dfrac{\pi(0.081 \, cm)^2}{4}}$$

$$R = \frac{1.72 \times 10^{-6} \, \Omega\,cm \times 4 \times 2.0 \times 10^3 \, cm}{\pi \times 6.56 \times 10^{-3} \, cm^2}$$

$R = 0.67 \; \Omega$, the resistance of the wire

The enormous range of resistivities of common materials is shown in Figure 17-23. The resistance of the best insulator can

## 17.12 Range of resistivities

**Figure 17-23** A resistivity spectrum. Observe the enormous range of resistivities between the best conductor and the best insulator.

be greater than that of the best conductor by a factor of approximately $10^{25}$. Insulators and semiconductors can decrease in resistivity with increasing temperature and with increasing potential gradient. We can interpret this latter behavior to mean that these materials do not follow Ohm's law.

A small group of *semiconductors* has assumed considerable importance because of unusual variations in resistance with changes in temperature and potential gradient. Copper oxide *rectifiers* will pass a current when a potential difference is applied in one direction but not in the opposite direction. Silicon and germanium *transistors* are substituted for vacuum tubes in many electronic circuit applications.

At extremely low temperatures, some metals exhibit the unusual property of zero resistance. The production of very low temperatures and the study of the properties of materials at low temperatures is called *cryogenics*. Cryogenic temperatures are generally considered to be those below the boiling point of liquid oxygen which is 80°K (−193°C). Ultra-low temperature research began with the liquefaction of helium in 1908 by the Dutch physicist Heike Kamerlingh Onnes (1853–1926). The boiling point of liquid helium is about 4°K (−269°C).

We have learned that the resistivity of a conductor is a function of its temperature. We would expect that the resistivity would become less and less as the temperature of a conductor drops, until the conductor offers no resistance at all to the passage of electrons. In 1911 Kamerlingh Onnes found that resistivity did indeed continue to drop with falling temperature. However, instead of gradually approaching zero resistivity, some materials had a specific temperature at which the resistivity dropped suddenly to zero. This temperature is called the *transition temperature*. *The condition of zero resistivity below the transition temperature of a material is called* **superconductivity.** Temperatures at which some materials become superconductive are shown in Figure 17-24.

The region of very low temperatures at which superconductivity prevails poses a severe limitation for the utilization of superconductors. Obviously superconductors offer great promise for such applications as power transmission, electric energy storage, and superelectromagnets that operate without power loss. However, the problem of keeping a power line below the transition temperature is a formidable one.

**Figure 17-24** Temperature on the Kelvin scale at which various materials become superconductive.

## 17.13 Measuring resistance

There are several methods of measuring the resistance of a circuit component. Two methods utilizing apparatus normally available in the physics laboratory will be discussed here. These are the *voltmeter-ammeter* method and the *Wheatstone bridge* method.

*1. The voltmeter-ammeter method.* Ohm's law applies equally well to any part of an electric circuit that does not contain a source of emf and to an entire circuit to which an emf is applied.

For a part of a circuit:

$$V = IR \quad \text{and} \quad R = \frac{V}{I}$$

If the potential difference, $V$, across a resistance component is measured with a voltmeter and the current, $I$, in the resistance is measured with an ammeter, the resistance, $R$, can be computed.

Suppose we wish to measure the resistance of $R_1$ in the circuit shown in Figure 17-25. The ammeter is connected in series with the resistance $R_1$ to determine the current in $R_1$. The voltmeter is connected in *parallel* with $R_1$ to determine the potential difference across $R_1$.

If the resistance of $R_1$ is very low, it can have an excessive loading effect on the source of emf, causing an excessive current in the circuit. This difficulty can be avoided by placing a variable resistance, or *rheostat,* in series with $R_1$. The rheostat provides additional series resistance and limits the current in the circuit. The rheostat can be adjusted to provide an appropriate magnitude of current in the circuit. See Figure 17-26. Observe that the voltmeter is connected across that part of the circuit for which resistance is to be determined.

The voltmeter-ammeter method of measuring resistance is convenient but not particularly precise. A voltmeter is a high resistance instrument. However, as it is connected in parallel with the resistance to be measured, there is a small current in it. The ammeter reading is actually the sum of the currents in these two parallel branches. Precision is limited by the extent to which the resistance of $R_1$ exceeds the equivalent resistance of $R_1$ and the voltmeter in parallel.

Of course the ammeter can be placed in the $R_1$ branch in series with $R_1$. In this location the ammeter reading is the current in $R_1$. However, the voltmeter reading is now the sum of the voltage drop across the ammeter and $R_1$ in series.

*2. The Wheatstone bridge method.* A precise means of determining resistance utilizes a simple *bridge* circuit known as the *Wheatstone bridge*. It consists of a source of emf, a galvanometer, and a network of four resistors. If three are of known resistance, the resistance of the fourth can be calculated.

The circuit diagram of a Wheatstone bridge is shown in Figure 17-27, in which an unknown resistance, $R_x$, may be balanced against known resistances $R_1$, $R_2$, and $R_3$. A galvanometer is *bridged* across the parallel branches **ADB** and **ACB**. By adjusting $R_1$, $R_2$, and $R_3$, the bridge circuit can be balanced and the galvanometer will show zero current.

When the bridge is balanced in this manner, there can be no

**Figure 17-25** Determining resistance by the voltmeter-ammeter method.

**Figure 17-26** A rheostat provides a means of limiting the current in a circuit.

**Figure 17-27** The electric circuit of the Wheatstone bridge.

potential difference between **C** and **D**, since the galvanometer indicates zero current. Thus

$$V_{AD} = V_{AC}$$

and

$$V_{DB} = V_{CB}$$

The current in the branch **ACB** is $I_1$, and the current in **ADB** is $I_2$. Then

$$I_2 R_x = I_1 R_1$$

and

$$I_2 R_3 = I_1 R_2$$

Dividing one expression by the other, we have

$$\frac{R_x}{R_3} = \frac{R_1}{R_2}$$

or

$$R_x = R_3 \frac{R_1}{R_2}$$

In the laboratory form of the Wheatstone bridge, resistances $R_1$ and $R_2$ usually consist of a uniform resistance wire, such as constantan, mounted on a meter stick. See Figure 17-28. The length of wire comprising $R_1$ and the length comprising $R_2$ are determined by the position of the contact **C**. If $l_1$ is the length of wire forming $R_1$ and $l_2$ is the length of wire forming $R_2$, it is apparent that

$$\frac{l_1}{l_2} = \frac{R_1}{R_2}$$

**Figure 17-28** The Wheatstone bridge method of measuring resistance.

**Figure 17-29** A plug-type resistance box providing resistance between the terminals from 0.1 ohm to 111 ohms in 0.1-ohm steps. The total resistance across the terminals depends on which plugs are removed.

We do not need to know the resistances of $R_1$ and $R_2$, since the lengths of wire $l_1$ and $l_2$ can be taken directly from the meter stick. Our Wheatstone bridge expression then becomes

$$R_x = R_3 \frac{l_1}{l_2}$$

A precision resistance box of the type shown in Figure 17-29 is often used to provide a suitable known resistance $R_3$ in the bridge circuit. The internal arrangement is shown in the diagram. Resistance coils are wound with manganin or constantan wire to minimize changes in resistance with temperature. The free ends of each resistance coil are soldered to heavy brass blocks that can be electrically connected by inserting brass plugs between them. Each plug in place provides a low-resistance path across a resistance coil and thus effectively removes the coil from the circuit. Each plug removed places a coil in the circuit. The resistance between the terminals of the box is the sum of the resistances of all coils whose plugs are removed.

## summary

Electric current is the rate of flow of charge in a circuit. The charge carriers in metallic conductors are electrons. The current in these conductors is an electron current and its directional sense is from negative to positive. A continuous current requires a source of emf. There are several sources of emf and continuous current, each of which transforms energy of some form to electric energy.

The dry cell is a common source of emf that supplies direct current to a circuit. It is a primary cell that is a form of voltaic cell in which chemical energy is converted to electric energy. Cells can be combined in series, in parallel, or in series-parallel to form batteries of suitable characteristics for a given circuit.

All circuit components offer some resistance to the current in a closed circuit. The relationship between resistance, current, and potential difference is expressed by Ohm's law. Ohm's law applies to an entire circuit or to any part of a circuit.

Resistances can be connected in series, in parallel, or in series-parallel combinations called networks. Networks can be reduced to simple equivalent circuits in which those components in parallel are reduced to their series equivalents. Equivalent circuit problems are solved by the application of Ohm's law for series circuits.

The resistance of a metal conductor depends on the temperature, length, cross-sectional area, and identity of the metal. From a knowledge of these factors, the laws of resistance are formulated and a property of materials called resistivity is defined. Resistivity depends on only the identity of the material and its temperature.

The resistance of a circuit element can be measured directly by the voltmeter-ammeter method or by the Wheatstone bridge method. The voltmeter-ammeter method is rapid, and the Wheatstone bridge method is more precise.

# questions

## GROUP A

1. State Ohm's law (a) verbally, (b) mathematically.
2. What is the mathematical expression for Ohm's law as it applies to a part of a circuit that does not contain a source of emf?
3. What is the identifying characteristic of a series circuit?
4. State the three cardinal rules for circuits in which resistances are in series.
5. Define a parallel circuit.
6. What change occurs in the total resistance of a circuit as additional resistances are added (a) in series, (b) in parallel?
7. State the three cardinal rules for circuits in which resistances are connected in parallel.
8. (a) What is the usual relationship between resistance and temperature of metallic conductors? (b) Is this true of all conducting materials in general?
9. How does the resistance of a conductor vary with its length?
10. What is the relationship between the resistance of a conductor and its cross-sectional area?
11. Define the resistivity constant, rho, that appears in the mathematical expression for the laws of resistance.
12. Demonstrate that resistivity, rho, has the dimensions "ohm-centimeter."

## GROUP B

13. Explain why the fall of potential that appears across the internal resistance of a source of emf when a current is in the circuit is always opposite in sign to the emf of the source.
14. What condition must be assumed in order to determine the emf of a battery by placing a voltmeter across it?
15. Why are lamps in a house-lighting circuit not connected in series?
16. What would happen if a 6-volt lamp and a 120-volt lamp were connected in parallel across a 120-volt circuit?
17. Draw a diagram of an electric circuit that would be classified as a simple network. Include the internal resistance of the source of emf. Assign values to all resistances and to the source of emf, and be prepared to analyze your network for the class.
18. Explain how the voltmeter-ammeter method is used for measuring resistance.
19. Why is the voltmeter-ammeter method not a particularly precise way to measure resistance?
20. In the laboratory form of the Wheatstone bridge, in Figure 17-28, resistors $R_1$ and $R_2$ are lengths of wire. Why can we use the lengths of wire rather than their actual resistances in determining the unknown resistance once the bridge is balanced?
21. Lamps **A**, **B**, and **C** have equal resistances and are connected in series-parallel across an appropriate source of emf, **A** being in series with the parallel combination of **B** and **C**. (a) Draw the circuit diagram. (b) Discuss the relative brightness of the three lamps. (c) If **C** burns out, what change in relative brightness occurs in the remaining lamps? Explain.

# problems

(Refer to Appendix B, Tables 20 and 21)

## GROUP A

1. A resistance of 18 ohms is connected across a 4.5-volt battery. What is the current in the circuit?
2. The load across a 12-volt battery consists of a series combination of three resistances, $R_1$, $R_2$, and $R_3$, that are 15 ohms, 21 ohms, and 24 ohms respectively. (a) Draw the circuit diagram. (b) What is the total resistance of the load? (c) What is the magnitude of the circuit current?
3. What is the potential difference across each of the three resistances of Problem 2?
4. A small lamp is designed to draw 300 ma in a 6.0-v circuit. What is the resistance of the lamp filament?
5. Resistances $R_1$ of 2 ohms and $R_2$ of 4 ohms are connected in series across a combination of 1.5-volt dry cells. An ammeter in the circuit reads 0.5 a. (a) What potential difference is applied across the circuit by the battery? (b) If the continuous current of each cell is limited to 0.25 a, how many cells are used and how are they arranged? (c) Draw the circuit diagram.
6. The resistance of an electric lamp filament is $23\overline{0}$ ohms. The lamp is switched on when the line voltage is 115 volts. What current is in the lamp circuit?
7. If the line voltage of Problem 6 rises to $12\overline{0}$ volts, what current is in the lamp circuit?
8. What would be the filament resistance of a lamp designed to draw the same current as the lamp in Problem 6 but in a 230-volt circuit?

9. Prove algebraically that the equivalent resistance of two resistances, $R_1$ and $R_2$, connected in parallel is:
$$R_{eq} = \frac{R_1 R_2}{R_1 + R_2}$$

10. Two resistances, one 12 ohms and the other 18 ohms, are connected in parallel. What is the equivalent resistance of the parallel combination?

11. Solve the following expression algebraically for $R_{eq}$:
$$\frac{1}{R_{eq}} = \frac{1}{R_1} + \frac{1}{R_2} + \frac{1}{R_3}$$

12. Three resistances of 12 ohms each are connected in parallel. What is the equivalent resistance?

13. (a) What potential difference must be applied across the parallel combination of resistances in Problem 12 to produce a total current of 1.5 amperes? (b) What is the current in each branch?

14. A 3.0-ohm, a 5.0-ohm, and an 8.0-ohm resistance are connected in parallel. What is the equivalent resistance?

15. A 4.0-ohm resistance $R_1$, and a 6.0-ohm resistance $R_2$, are connected in parallel across a 6.0-volt battery. (a) Draw the circuit diagram. (b) What is the total current in the circuit? (c) What is the current in $R_1$? (d) What is the current in $R_2$?

16. A 24-volt lamp has a resistance of 8.0 ohms. What resistance must be placed in series with it if it is to be used on a 117 volt line?

17. At 20°C, 100 m of No. 18 gauge copper wire has a resistance of 2.059 ohms. What is the resistance of 500 m of this wire?

18. The diameter of the copper wire in Problem 17 is 1.024 mm. What is the resistance of 100 m of No. 30 gauge copper wire that has a diameter of 0.2546 mm?

19. What is the resistance of 125 m of No. 20 gauge aluminum wire at 20°C?

20. No. 24 gauge German silver wire has a diameter of 0.511 mm at 20°C. How many centimeters are needed to make a resistance spool of 100 ohms?

GROUP B

21. Three cells of a storage battery, each with a resistance of 0.0100 ohm and an emf of 2.20 volts, are connected in series with a load resistance of 3.27 ohms. (a) Draw the circuit diagram. (b) Determine the current in the circuit. (c) What is the potential difference across the load?

22. Two dry cells connected in series provide an emf of 3.1 volts. When a load of 5.8 ohms is connected across the battery, an ammeter in the external circuit reads 0.50 ampere. Find the internal resistance of each cell.

23. A load connected across a 12.0-volt battery consists of the resistance $R_1$, 40.0 ohms, in series

with the parallel combination of $R_2$ and $R_3$, 30.0 ohms and 60.0 ohms respectively. (a) Draw the circuit diagram. (b) What is the total current in the circuit? (c) What is the potential difference across $R_1$? (d) What is the current in the $R_2$ branch?

24. A 6.0-ohm, a 9.0-ohm, and an 18.0-ohm resistance are connected in parallel and the combination is connected across a battery having an internal resistance of 0.10 ohm and an emf of 6.2 volts. (a) Draw the circuit diagram and the equivalent circuit. (b) Determine the total current in the circuit. (c) What is the potential difference across the load? (d) What is the current in each of the three load resistances?

25. Resistors $R_1$, $R_2$, and $R_3$ have resistances of 15.0 ohms, 9.0 ohms, and 8.0 ohms respectively. $R_1$ and $R_2$ are in series and the combination is in parallel with $R_3$ to form the load across two 6-volt batteries connected in parallel. (a) Draw the circuit diagram. (b) Determine the total current in the circuit. (c) What is the current in the $R_3$ branch? (d) What is the potential drop across $R_2$?

26. A battery with an internal resistance of 1.5 ohms is connected across a load consisting of two resistances, 3.0 ohms and 3.5 ohms, in series. The potential difference across the 3.0-ohm resistance is 9.0 volts. What is the emf of the battery?

27. Two resistances, $R_1$ and $R_2$, of 12.0 ohms and 6.00 ohms are connected in parallel, and this combination is connected in series with a 6.25-ohm resistance, $R_3$, and a battery that has an internal resistance of 0.250 ohm. The current in $R_2$, the 6.00-ohm resistance, is 800 milliamperes. (a) Draw the circuit diagram. (b) Determine the emf of the battery.

28. The resistance of a uniform copper wire 50.0 m long and 1.15 mm in diameter is 0.830 $\Omega$ at 20°C. What is the resistivity of the copper at this temperature?

29. In determining the resistance of a component of an electric circuit by the voltmeter-ammeter method, the voltmeter reads 1.4 volts and the ammeter reads 0.28 ampere. What is the resistance of the component?

30. (a) Reduce the accompanying circuit to its series equivalent circuit. (b) Determine the potential difference across the 1-$\Omega$ resistance.

# lasers

**P**hotonics—the study of laser light—began in 1960 with the construction of the first laser. Since that time laser development has proceeded rapidly, and laser applications are numerous and diversified. Photonics is expected to continue to play a significant role in future technology. Laser light is light of a single wavelength and frequency (coherent) produced by exciting the atoms of certain materials. When coherent light beams are amplified, it is possible to direct them with great precision in space and time. Thus lasers have been used to transmit information and to measure distances to $10^{-6}$ cm. Lasers are used in construction, surveying, and industries involved with fabric cutting, alloy formation, and precision welding. In medicine lasers are used to perform delicate surgery involving the fusion or excision of tissue.

Lasers have important applications in research. Information regarding atomic structure and other properties of matter is obtained by breaking molecular bonds and forming new chemical compounds with lasers. More accurate measurements of the speed of light have been made with lasers. One of the most promising applications is as a power source. Laser temperatures up to 40 trillion watts have been achieved and make the idea of fusion power stations viable.

*Left: A laser can be used in connection with the instrument landing of an airplane.*

*Clockwise, starting at top right:*

*The advent of lasers has provided light sources with enough intensity, sufficiently narrow band widths, and appropriate wavelengths to make the photochemical separation of isotopes practical.*

*The invisible infrared radiation of a $CO_2$ laser is shown drilling a hole into a piece of glass.*

*High-power $CO_2$ lasers are used to cut hard ceramic to the exact shapes required for electronic circuits.*

*Laser light is used here to take high-speed photos. The projectile, traveling at thousands of km/hr, is frozen in flight by a $2 \times 10^{-8}$ s flash.*

*The treatment of a disease of the retina involves aiming a beam of intense light from an argon gas laser into the eye of a patient*

**PHOTO ESSAY**

Top right: In rough terrain a vertical laser beam can be used to facilitate accurate surveying. The technique was originally developed by NASA for use with space vehicles.

Above: A surveyor operates the receiving station of the laser system.

Above: It looks somewhat like a giant whiffle ball, but it's really a laser satellite containing 426 mirrors. Laser beams will be aimed at the satellite from the earth and reflected back. Accurate determinations of the earth's crustal and rotational motions can be made by this laser application.

Left: A scientist uses a laser to measure temperature and detect pollution in a sooting flame. This technique can be applied to gas turbine engines.

Below: A model of a 25-trillion-watt laser that will be used for fusion research at the Department of Energy's Lawrence Livermore Laboratory, CA.

Left: A model of a proposed 10-kilojoule laser for fusion research. Twelve separate lasers are focused on tiny pellets of heavy hydrogen to produce heat energy.

# 18

# Heating and Chemical Effects

## 18.1 Energy of an electric current

*Chemical energy is a form of potential energy.*

**Figure 18-1** The electric energy expended in the lamp filament by the electron charge carriers heats the filament to incandescence; hence the name, "incandescent lamp."

The relationships among objects, time, and space are basic concerns of physics. Work, power, and energy are important physical concepts involved in these relationships. We have described energy as the ability to do work and have measured it in units of work and heat. To maintain an electric current, energy must be supplied by the source of emf. Chemical energy, which can be thought of as the potential energy of chemical bonds, is transformed into electric energy in an electrochemical cell. Thus a charge acquires energy within the cell or other source of emf and expends this energy in the electric circuit.

In Section 16.10 we recognized that one joule of work is done when one coulomb of charge is moved through a potential difference of one volt.

$$W = qV$$

One coulomb of charge transferred in one second constitutes one ampere of current.

$$I = \frac{q}{t} \quad \text{and} \quad q = It$$

Therefore

$$W = VIt \qquad \text{(Equation 1)}$$

Within a source of emf, the charge is moved in opposition to the potential difference and work, *W*, is done on the electrons *by the source of emf*. As the charge moves through the external circuit in response to the potential difference across the circuit,

*W* → heat + light     *W* → heat + motion     *W* → heat + chemical action     *W* → heat

Lamp       Motor       Electrolytic cell       Resistor

$e^-$ of high $E_P$

$E_P$ ← — *W*

$e^-$ of low $E_P$

Source of emf

Switch

work, *W,* is done *by the electrons* on the components of the circuit. It is this electric energy, expended in the external circuit, that is available to perform useful work.

We can observe the work done by an electric current in a variety of ways. If a lamp is in the circuit, part of the work appears as light; if an electric motor is in the circuit, part of the work appears as rotary motion; if an electroplating cell is in the circuit, part of the work promotes chemical action in the cell. In all cases, *part* of the work, *W,* appears as *heat* due to the inherent resistance of the circuit components. If an ordinary resistor comprises the circuit, *all* the work goes to the production of heat since no mechanical work or chemical work is done. See Figure 18-2.

**Figure 18-2** Work is done when a charge is moved through a potential difference.

## 18.2 Energy conversion in resistance

Suppose short lengths of No. 30 gauge copper wire and German silver wire are connected in series and placed in the circuit shown in Figure 18-3. When the switch is closed, the German silver wire may become red hot and melt. The copper wire will become warm but is less likely to melt. The melting point of German silver is about 30C° higher than that of copper, but its resistivity is nearly 20 times higher than that of copper. Since the two wires were in series, the same magnitude of current was in each. We may infer that *a greater quantity of electric energy was converted to heat in the wire having the higher resistance.*

Now suppose a single piece of No. 30 copper wire is connected in the circuit in place of the copper-German silver link. When the switch is closed, the copper wire may warm to a red heat and even melt. Since the resistance of this copper wire is less than that of the copper-German silver link, the current in the circuit is higher. We may infer that *the quantity of electric energy con-*

No. 30 copper       No. 30 German silver

Dry cell       Dry cell

**Figure 18-3** A circuit for studying the heating effect of an electric current.

*verted to heat in the wire is greater when the current is increased.* We may reason also that *the longer the switch is closed* (assuming the wire does not melt), *the greater will be the quantity of electric energy converted to heat.*

From Ohm's law, the potential difference across the resistance of an external circuit is the product of the current in the circuit and the resistance of the circuit.

$$V = IR$$

Substituting this product for $V$ in Equation 1, we have an expression for the energy transferred to the resistance of a circuit.

$$W = I^2Rt \qquad \text{(Equation 2)}$$

## 18.3 Joule's law

*The quantitative study of the relationships between heat and other forms of energy is called thermodynamics.*

James Prescott Joule, the English physicist who first studied the relationship between heat and work, also pioneered the quantitative study of the heating effect of an electric current. From the results of his experiments he formulated the generalization known as **Joule's law**: *The heat developed in a conductor is directly proportional to the resistance of the conductor, the square of the current, and the time the current is maintained.*

Since all of the work done by a current in a resistance appears as heat, the electric energy expended in the resistance is directly proportional to the heat energy that appears.

**Figure 18-4** Electric energy is converted to heat in an electric furnace for the production of special grades of steel.

$$W = JQ \qquad \text{(Equation 3)}$$

where $W$ is the electric energy in joules, $J$ is the proportionality constant we have known previously as the mechanical equivalent of heat (4.19 joules/calorie), and $Q$ is the quantity of heat given up in calories.

Solving Equation 3 for $Q$ we have an expression for Joule's law.

$$Q = \frac{W}{J} \qquad \text{(Equation 4)}$$

By substituting the expression for $W$ in Equation 2 into Equation 4, a useful form of Joule's law evolves from which the quantity of heat developed in the resistance of an electric circuit can be calculated directly.

*Electric power is dissipated in a resistance as heat.*

$$Q = \frac{I^2Rt}{J} \qquad \text{(Equation 5)}$$

Observe that the quantity of heat $Q$ is expressed in kilocalories by introducing the conversion factor kcal/$10^3$ cal.

$$\frac{I^2Rt}{J} = \frac{(\text{a} \times \Omega)(\text{a} \times \text{s})}{\text{j/cal}} \times \frac{\text{kcal}}{\text{cal}}$$

$$= \frac{\text{v} \times \text{c} \times \text{kcal}}{\text{j}} = \frac{\text{j} \times \text{kcal}}{\text{j}}$$

$$= \text{kcal}$$

The following example illustrates an application of Joule's law.

**EXAMPLE**

*The heating element in a percolator has a resistance of 22.0 ohms and is designed for use across a 117-volt circuit. How long will it take to heat 1.00 kg of water at 20.0°C to the boiling point, 100.0°C, assuming no loss of heat to surroundings?*

**SOLUTION**

The problem is concerned basically with the heating effect of an electric current—Joule's law. However, the specific heat of water is a factor in determining the time of the circuit operation. The basic equation is

$$Q = \frac{I^2Rt}{J}$$

The quantity of heat, $Q$, required to warm a given mass of water through a change of temperature, $\Delta T$, is

$$Q = mc\,\Delta T$$

From Ohm's law: $I = \dfrac{V}{R}$

Substituting for $Q$ and $I$ in the basic equation,

$$mc\,\Delta T = \frac{V^2 Rt}{R^2 J} = \frac{V^2 t}{RJ}$$

We now have an expression that makes use of the quantities given in the problem. Since we are solving the problem for time, $t$, our working equation is

$$t = \frac{mc\,\Delta T R J}{V^2}$$

Substituting and solving:

$$t = \frac{1.00 \text{ kg} \times 1 \text{ kcal/kg C}° \times 80.0 \text{ C}° \times 22.0\ \Omega \times 4.19 \text{ j/cal} \times 10^3 \text{ cal/kcal}}{(117 \text{ v})^2}$$

$$t = 538\ \frac{\Omega\,\text{j}}{\text{v}^2} = 538 \text{ s}$$

Dimensional analysis: $\dfrac{\Omega\,\text{j}}{\text{v}^2} = \dfrac{\text{v}}{\text{a}} \times \dfrac{\text{v c}}{\text{v}^2} = \dfrac{\text{c}}{\text{a}} = \dfrac{\text{a s}}{\text{a}} = \text{s}$

## 18.4 Power in electric circuits

*The energy delivered to a circuit element is the product of power and time.*

Power is defined as the rate of doing work. The symbol for power is $P$, and in the MKS system the unit of power is the watt (w). The watt is a rate of one joule of work per second. In electric circuits, it is convenient to think of power as *the rate at which electric energy is delivered to the circuit.*

$$P = \frac{W}{t} \qquad \text{(Equation 6)}$$

Recalling Equation 1 of Section 18.1, $W = VIt$, let us solve this expression for $W/t$.

$$\frac{W}{t} = VI \qquad \text{(Equation 7)}$$

Combining Equations 6 and 7 yields a basic power equation for electric circuits.

$$P = VI \qquad \text{(Equation 8)}$$

If $I$ is in amperes and $V$ is in volts, then $P$ is in watts.

$$P = VI = \frac{\text{joule}}{\text{coulomb}} \times \frac{\text{coulomb}}{\text{second}}$$

$$P = \frac{\text{joule}}{\text{second}} = \text{watt}$$

By Ohm's law, the potential difference across a load resistance in a circuit is equal to the product $IR_L$. Substituting for $V$ in Equation 8,

$$P_L = I \times IR_L$$

or

$$P_L = I^2 R_L \qquad \text{(Equation 9)}$$

*Can you derive Equation 9 from Equations 2 and 6 in just three steps?*

This shows us that *the power expended by a current in a resistance is proportional to the square of the current in the resistance.*

Similarly, the power dissipated in the internal resistance of a source of emf is

$$P_r = I^2 r \qquad \text{(Equation 10)}$$

*Power dissipated in the internal resistance of a source of emf is wasted as heat.*

The total power consumed in a circuit must be the sum of the power dissipated within the source of emf and the power expended in the load of the external circuit.

$$P_T = I_T{}^2 R_T = I_T{}^2 (R_L + r)$$

Recall that

$$E = I_T (R_L + r)$$

Therefore

$$P_T = I_T E \qquad \text{(Equation 11)}$$

There are instances in which the current in a circuit is unknown or of no interest. Power can then be expressed in terms of voltage and resistance since, by Ohm's law,

$$I_T = \frac{E}{R_T}$$

Substituting for $I_T$ in Equation 11, we get

$$P_T = \frac{E^2}{R_T} \qquad \text{(Equation 12)}$$

and for the external circuit,

$$P_L = \frac{V^2}{R_L} \qquad \text{(Equation 13)}$$

---

There are some electric-circuit applications in which the transfer of maximum power to the load is of great importance. One example is the circuit of the starter motor of an automobile engine. To operate the starter, a large amount of electric energy must be supplied by a battery during a short interval of time. Other less familiar examples are the transfer of audio-frequency power from the output stage of a radio to the speaker and the transfer of radio-frequency power from the transmission line to the antenna.

Consider the circuits of Figure 18-5 in order to determine the circumstances under which maximum power from a given source of emf is expended in the load. Observe that the same source of emf is used in all three circuits and loads greater than, less than, and equal to the internal resistance of the source are supplied.

## 18.5 Maximum transfer of power

(A)                    (B)                    (C)

**Figure 18-5** In which circuit is the most power expended in the load?

In each circuit $I_T$, $P_L$, $P_r$, and $P_T$ can be determined by using equations derived in Section 18.4. For comparison these values are listed below.

| Circuit **A** | Circuit **B** | Circuit **C** |
|---|---|---|
| $I_T = 2.0$ a | 5.0 a | 3.0 a |
| $P_L = 4.0$ w | 2.5 w | 4.5 w |
| $P_r = 2.0$ w | 12.5 w | 4.5 w |
| $P_T = 6.0$ w | 15.0 w | 9.0 w |

From such calculations it can be shown that the power expended in the load of circuit **C**, 4.5 w, is the maximum that can be transferred from this source of emf. *Maximum power is transferred to the load when the load resistance is equal to the internal resistance of the source of emf.* The source and the load are said to be *matched*. In circuit **B,** the load resistance is less than the internal resistance of the source and most of the power generated is dissipated as heat in the source itself. This power is wasted. In circuit **A,** the load resistance is greater than the internal resistance of the source and little power is lost in the internal resistance of the source. However, the power expended in the load is not as high as in circuit **C**.

---

## 18.6 Purchasing electric energy

An operating circuit that requires 100 watts of power converts 100 joules of energy per second. Obviously, the longer this circuit continues to operate, the larger will be the total quantity of energy transformed. Since

$$\text{power} = \frac{\text{energy}}{\text{time}}$$

then

$$\text{energy} = \text{power} \times \text{time}$$

In the MKS system, current, potential difference, and resistance are measured in amperes, volts, and ohms respectively; power is expressed in watts and time in seconds. The energy can thus be expressed in *watt seconds* (w s). The watt second is inconveniently small for electric energy sold on a commercial scale. For example, a 100-watt lamp operated for 1 hour transforms $3.6 \times 10^5$ watt seconds of energy. Dividing by $3.6 \times 10^3$ s/hr we can convert this quantity to $1 \times 10^2$ w hr. Dividing again by $1 \times 10^3$ w/kw we have $1 \times 10^{-1}$ kw hr (0.1 kilowatt hour). This is a more practical unit of electric energy. Observe the magnitude of this combined conversion constant:

*Your electric utility statement is based on the number of kilowatt-hours of energy consumed and the cost per kilowatt-hour.*

$$\text{kw hr} \times \frac{10^3 \text{ w}}{\text{kw}} \times \frac{3.6 \times 10^3 \text{ s}}{\text{hr}} = 3.6 \times 10^6 \text{ w s}$$

A kilowatt hour of electric energy usually costs between 1 and 6 cents. The cost of electric energy is calculated in the example that follows.

**EXAMPLE**

*A small electric furnace connected across a 117-v line expends 2.0 kw of power. (a) What current is in the circuit? (b) What is the resistance of the furnace? (c) What is the cost of operation for 24 hr at $0.050 per kw hr? (d) What quantity of heat, in kcal, is developed in 1.0 hr?*

**SOLUTION**

(a) The potential difference across the furnace and the power expended in the furnace are given. We can find the current since

$$P = IV \text{ and, therefore, } I = \frac{P}{V}$$

$$I = \frac{2.0 \text{ kw}}{117 \text{ v}} \times \frac{10^3 \text{ w}}{\text{kw}}$$

$I = 17$ a, the current in the circuit

(b) Knowing both the current in the furnace and the potential drop across it, we can apply Ohm's law to find the resistance.

$$R = \frac{V}{I} = \frac{117 \text{ v}}{17 \text{ a}}$$

$R = 6.9 \ \Omega$, the resistance of the furnace

(c) We are given the power requirement of the furnace, the time of operation, and the cost per kw hr.

$$\text{cost} = \text{kw hr} \times \frac{\text{cost}}{\text{kw hr}} = \frac{2.0 \text{ kw} \times 24 \text{ hr} \times \$0.050}{\text{kw hr}}$$

cost = $2.40, the cost for 24 hr operation

(d) We are given the time of operation, and we have found the current and the resistance.

$$Q = \frac{I^2 R t}{J}$$

$$Q = \frac{(17 \text{ a})^2 \times 6.9 \ \Omega \times 1.0 \text{ hr}}{4.19 \text{ j/cal}} \times \frac{3.6 \times 10^3 \text{ s}}{\text{hr}} \times \frac{\text{kcal}}{10^3 \text{ cal}}$$

$Q = 1.7 \times 10^3$ kcal, the heat in 1 hr

(Proof of answer unit is left to the student.)

# questions

## GROUP A

1. State four ways in which the work done by an electric current in a load may be observed, and name the kind of load responsible in each instance.

2. Equal lengths of silver wire and iron wire having the same diameters are connected in series to form the external circuit across a dry cell. Which wire becomes hotter? Explain.

3. One length of platinum wire is connected across the terminals of a single dry cell. A second platinum wire, identical with the first, is connected across a battery of two dry cells in series. Which wire becomes hotter? Explain.

4. State Joule's law.

5. How may electric power be defined?

6. (a) What change occurs in the heating effect of an electric circuit if the source of emf remains the same but the total resistance is cut in half? (b) Devise a simple circuit problem to prove your answer.

7. If a battery is short-circuited by means of a heavy copper wire, its temperature rises. Explain.

8. Under what circumstance is the power expended in a load the maximum the source is capable of delivering?

9. Suppose you have just paid the electric utility bill for your home. (a) What did you purchase? (b) In what units was it measured?

10. What change occurs in the resistance in the external circuit connected to a source of emf when the load across the source is increased?

## GROUP B

11. Demonstrate that $Q$ in Joule's law can be expressed in kilocalories.

12. Two resistors of equal resistance were originally connected in parallel. By what factor does their combined resistance change when they are connected in series instead?

13. Why is it important that an automobile battery have a very low internal resistance?

14. What special characteristics should a toaster wire have?

15. Express the rate of energy dissipation in a resistance in terms of (a) current and potential difference, (b) current and resistance, (c) potential difference and resistance.

# problems

## GROUP A

1. The current in an electric heater is 7.5 amperes. What quantity of electric charge flows through the heater in 15 minutes?

2. Determine the current in a lamp circuit if 4800 coulombs of electric charge flow through the lamp in 25 minutes.

3. An electric lamp connected across a 117-volt line has a current of 0.52 ampere in it. How much work is done in 12 minutes?

4. What is the approximate wattage rating of the lamp in Problem 3?

5. How many kilocalories of heat are produced by a resistance of 55 ohms connected across a 110-volt line for 10 minutes?

6. A heating coil across a 117-volt line draws 9.00 amperes. How many kilocalories are liberated if the heater operates for 30.0 minutes?

7. The heating element of an electric iron has a resistance of 24 ohms and draws a current of 5.0 amperes. How many kilocalories are developed if the iron is used for 45 minutes?

8. A battery has an emf of 26.4 volts and an internal resistance of 0.300 ohm. A load of 3.00 ohms is connected across the battery. How much power is (a) delivered to the load, (b) dissipated in the battery?

9. (a) To what value would the load resistance of Problem 8 have to be changed in order that maximum power is delivered to the load using the same source of emf? (b) What is the magnitude of the maximum power delivered to this load? (c) What power is now dissipated in the battery?

10. A wire for use in an electric heater has a resistance of 5.25 $\Omega$/m. What length of this wire is needed to make a heating element for a toaster that will draw 8.70 a across a 120-v line?

## GROUP B

11. If electric energy costs 5.0¢ per kw hr, what is the cost of heating 4.6 kg of water from 25°C to the boiling point, assuming no energy is wasted?

12. A percolator with a heating coil of 20.0 ohms resistance is connected across a 120-volt line. (a) What quantity of heat is liberated per second? (b) If it contains 500 g of water at 22.5°C, how much time is required to heat the water to boiling, assuming no loss of heat?

13. An electric iron has a mass of 1.50 kg. The heating element is a 2.00-m length of No. 24 gauge nichrome wire. What time is required for the iron to be heated from 20.0°C to 150°C when connected across a 115-volt line, assuming no loss of heat?

14. An electric hotplate draws 10.0 amperes on a 120-volt circuit. In 7.00 minutes the hotplate can heat 600 g of water at 20.0°C to boiling and boil away 60.0 g of water. What is the efficiency of the hotplate?

15. Each coil of a plug-type resistance box is capable of dissipating heat at the rate of 4.0 watts. What is the maximum voltage that should be applied

across (a) the 2.0-ohm coil, (b) the 20.0-ohm coil?

16. A dial-type rheostat of 10.0 ohms resistance is capable of dissipating heat at the rate of 4.0 watts. (a) What is the maximum current the rheostat can carry? (b) What is the maximum voltage that can be applied across it?

17. How many meters of No. 30 gauge nichrome wire are needed to form the heating element of a 1000-watt electric iron used on a 117-volt line?

18. A lamp operates continuously across a 117-v line dissipating 100 w. How many electrons flow through the lamp per day?

# ELECTROLYSIS

The close relationship between chemical energy and electric energy has already been discussed. Spontaneous reactions that involve the transfer of electrons from one reactant to the other were described in Section 17.3. Such reactions can be sources of emf. In the electrochemical cell chemical energy is converted to electric energy while the spontaneous electron-transfer reaction proceeds. The products of the reaction have less energy than did the reactants.

Similar reactions *that are not spontaneous* can be forced to occur if electric energy is supplied from an external source, as in charging a storage battery. In such forced reactions, the products have more chemical energy than did the reactants. This means that electric energy from the external source of emf is transformed into chemical energy while the reaction proceeds. An arrangement in which a forced electron-transfer reaction occurs is known as an *electrolytic cell*.

The basic requirements for an electrolytic cell are shown in Figure 18-6. The conducting solution contains an electrolyte that furnishes positively and negatively charged ions. Two electrodes are immersed in the electrolytic solution. The negative terminal of a battery or other source of direct current is connected to one electrode to form the *cathode* of the cell; the positive terminal of the source is connected to the other electrode to form the *anode* of the cell.

When the circuit is closed, the cathode becomes negatively charged and the anode positively charged. Positive ions migrate to the cathode where they acquire electrons of high potential energy and are then discharged. Negatively charged ions migrate to the anode and are discharged by giving up electrons of low potential energy to the anode. Note that the electrode reactions occurring in electrochemical cells, presented in Sections 17.3 and 17.4, are just the reverse of those in an electrolytic cell.

## 18.7 Electrolytic cells

**Figure 18-6** The essential components of an electrolytic cell.

*The cathode is the electron-rich electrode.*

*The anode is the electron-poor electrode.*

The loss of electrons by the cathode and the acquisition of a like number of electrons by the anode constitute the conduction of an electric charge through the cell. *The conduction of an electric charge through a solution of an electrolyte or through a fused ionic compound, together with the resulting chemical changes, is called* **electrolysis.**

The end result of electrolysis depends on the nature of the electrolyte, the kinds of electrodes, and to some extent the emf of the source. Electrolytic cells are useful in decomposing compounds, plating metals, and refining metals.

*Chemical reactions in electrochemical cells are spontaneous; those in electrolytic cells are driven.*

## 18.8 Electroplating metals

**Figure 18-7** An electrolytic cell used for copper plating.

An electrolytic cell is set up with a metallic copper anode and positively charged copper(II) ions, $Cu^{++}$, in solution. When a small potential difference is placed across the cell, the $Cu^{++}$ ions acquire electrons from the cathode and form copper atoms. The following chemical equation represents this reaction.

$$Cu^{++} + 2e^- \rightarrow Cu^0 \text{ (Cathode reaction)}$$

These copper atoms plate out on the cathode surface.

Simultaneously, atoms of the copper anode give up electrons to this positively charged anode and form $Cu^{++}$ ions that go into the solution to replace those being plated out as copper atoms. The chemical reaction is

$$Cu^0 \rightarrow Cu^{++} + 2e^- \text{ (Anode reaction)}$$

These $Cu^{++}$ ions pass into the solution from the anode at the same rate as similar $Cu^{++}$ ions leave the solution and form the plate on the cathode. To maintain the concentration of $Cu^{++}$ ions in the electrolytic solution, $Cu^{++}$ ions must continuously pass into the solution from the anode. The result is that the anode is used up in the plating process. A simplified diagram of a copper-plating cell is shown in Figure 18-7.

The reaction at the cathode makes an electrolytic cell useful for the electrolytic deposition, or *electroplating*, of one metal on the surface of another. The object to be plated is used as the cathode of the cell. The plating metal is used as the anode. The conducting solution contains a salt of the metal to be plated out onto the cathode.

Metallic copper of the highest purity is required for electric conductors. Even very small amounts of impurities in copper cause a marked increase in its electric resistance. These impurities can be removed almost completely from the copper by electrolysis. For this purpose an electroplating cell is used in which the anode is composed of impure copper. During electrolysis, refined copper is plated onto the cathode made of pure copper. This electrolytically refined copper metal deposited on the cathode is more than 99.99% pure.

Michael Faraday investigated the distribution of charge on isolated bodies and the nature of electric fields. He also performed experiments on the conduction of electric charge by solutions. Faraday found that a current that deposited a half-penny-weight of silver in ten minutes would deposit one penny-weight of silver in twenty minutes. This discovery suggests an important relationship between the quantity of electric charge that passes through an electrolytic cell and the quantity of a substance liberated by the chemical action.

Suppose we consider the quantitative significance of Faraday's discovery by imagining several cells connected in series and supplied by a source of emf. Each cell has a pair of inert platinum electrodes immersed in a water solution of an electrolyte. See Figure 18-9. Each cell has a different electrolyte: cell No. **1** has sulfuric acid (hydrogen sulfate), cell No. **2** has silver nitrate, cell No. **3** has copper(II) sulfate, and cell No. **4** has aluminum sulfate. Since this is a "thought" experiment we need not be concerned with the possibility of running out of ions in the cells. Since the cells are in series a certain constant current in the circuit for a given time interval signifies that *the same quantity of charge has passed through each cell.*

Hydrogen, silver, copper, and aluminum are liberated at the respective cathodes. The quantity of each liberated substance must be proportional to the quantity of charge that passed through each cell: that is, to the product of the current and the time.

*Faraday's first law: The mass of an element deposited or liberated during electrolysis is proportional to the quantity of charge that passes.*

$$m \propto Q$$

where

$$Q = It$$

## 18.9 Faraday's laws of electrolysis

**Figure 18-8** Michael Faraday, the English scientist who formulated the laws of electrolysis and for whom the unit of electric capacitance is named. His lecture-demonstrations were popular events.

*Recall that there can be only one magnitude of current in a series circuit because there is only one conducting path.*

**Figure 18-9** Electrolytic cells in series must have the same magnitude of current for the same length of time.

Table 18-1

| ELECTROCHEMICAL EQUIVALENTS | | | |
|---|---|---|---|
| Element | g-at wt' (g) | Ionic charge (oxidation state) | z (g/c) |
| aluminum | 27.0 | 3 | 0.0000932 |
| copper | 63.5 | 2 | 0.0003294 |
| hydrogen | 1.01 | 1 | 0.0000104 |
| silver | 108 | 1 | 0.0011179 |

*The number of electrons of an atom of an element participating in a chemical process is sometimes referred to as the valence of the element.*

By varying either current or time interval, we merely vary the quantity of charge passing through each cell. By Faraday's first law, the mass of the element deposited or liberated varies accordingly. It follows that whatever the charge through the cells, the relationship among the quantities of the elements deposited remains *constant*. Such quantities of the elements are said to be *electrochemically equivalent*. The ***electrochemical equivalent,*** z, *of an element is the mass in grams of the element deposited or liberated by 1 coulomb of electric charge.* See Table 18-1. A more extensive table of electrochemical equivalents of common elements is given in Appendix B, Table 19.

Suppose we allow the charge to flow through our cells until 1 g of hydrogen has been liberated in cell No. **1**. We would find 108 g of silver deposited in No. **2**, 31.8 g of copper in No. **3**, and 9 g of aluminum in No. **4**.

The hydrogen ion, $H^+$, and the silver ion, $Ag^+$, are each deficient by 1 electron and carry a net positive charge of 1 unit. The elements hydrogen and silver are said to have an ionic charge of 1, which means they lose 1 electron per atom in a chemical reaction. Similarly the charge of the copper (II) ion, $Cu^{++}$, is 2 and that of the aluminum ion, $Al^{+++}$, is 3.

Using this information and the information previously obtained in the thought experiment, we can make two very interesting and important observations. *First, for a given quantity of charge, the quantity in grams of each element deposited or liberated is proportional to the ratio of its gram-atomic weight (g-at wt) to its ionic charge.* This ratio is known as the ***chemical equivalent*** of an element.

$$\text{chemical equivalent} = \frac{\textbf{g-at wt}}{\textbf{ionic charge}}$$

Thus the chemical equivalents of hydrogen, silver, copper, and aluminum are respectively 1, 108, 31.8, and 9 grams.

*Second, the product of the current in amperes and the time in seconds during which the cells operated to deposit the chemical equivalents of these elements is found to be approximately 96,500 coulombs.* This product is a constant and is called a *faraday:*

$$\textbf{1 faraday} = \textbf{96,500 coulombs}$$

*One* ***faraday***, *96,500 coulombs, is the quantity of electric charge required to deposit one chemical equivalent of an element.* This unit has many significant applications in electrolysis and electrochemistry.

***Faraday's second law:*** *The mass of an element deposited or liberated during electrolysis is proportional to the chemical equivalent of the element.*

$$m \propto \textbf{chemical equivalent}$$

From our definition of the electrochemical equivalent of an element, we can see that

$$z = \frac{\textbf{chemical equivalent}}{\textbf{faraday}}$$

and has the dimensions g/c. The electrochemical equivalent $z$ is a constant for a given element but is different for different elements.

We can combine Faraday's Laws of Electrolysis into the following equation:

$$\boldsymbol{m = zIt}$$

where $m$ is the mass in grams of an element deposited or liberated, $z$ is the electrochemical equivalent in g/c of the element, $I$ is the current in amperes, and $t$ is the time in seconds.

Faraday's laws give us a precise method of measuring the quantity of electric charge flowing through a circuit. If we know the length of time the charge flows, we can determine the average current magnitude as shown in Figure 18-10. A platinum dish is connected with the negative terminal of a source of about 2 volts emf, and then the dish is partly filled with a solution of silver nitrate. A platinum spiral rod is connected to the positive terminal of the source of current and dipped into the silver solution.

**Figure 18-10**   A silver coulombmeter.

One coulomb of charge (one ampere second) flowing through such a silver solution will deposit on the walls of the dish 0.001118 g of silver. If the average current in the circuit is one ampere for one hour, $36\overline{0}0$ coulombs will deposit 4.025 g of silver. From the mass of the silver deposited the number of coulombs of electric charge can be determined with good precision.

# summary

The electric energy expended in a resistance is converted to heat. The relationship among the heat developed in a circuit element, the resistance, and the time the current is maintained is expressed in terms of Joule's law.

Electric power dissipated in the resistance of a circuit is proportional to the square of the circuit current. Power dissipated in the internal resistance of the source of emf is wasted. When it is important to deliver maximum power to the load, the load resistance and that of the source of emf must be matched.

Electrolytic cells are driven by an external source of emf. Electric energy is transformed to chemical energy through electron-transfer reactions at the cell electrodes. The products have higher chemical energy than the reactants. Electrolytic cells are useful in decomposing compounds, plating metals, and refining metals.

Faraday's laws of electrolysis provide an insight into the quantitative significance of energy transformations in chemical reactions. These laws relate the mass of an element deposited during electrolysis to the quantity of charge that passes through the cell and to the chemical equivalent of the element. The silver coulombmeter provides a precise method of measuring the quantity of charge in an electric circuit.

# questions

GROUP A

1. How can electron-transfer reactions that are not spontaneous be forced to occur?

2. What is an electrolytic cell?

3. What may be the effect of the conduction of electric charge through a fused ionic compound?

4. What are the basic requirements for a silver-plating cell?

5. Why is electrolytically refined copper used to make electric conductors?

6. State Faraday's Laws of Electrolysis.

7. What part of a silver coulombmeter is used as the cathode?

GROUP B

8. Distinguish between an electrochemical cell and an electrolytic cell.

9. Compare the cathode and anode reactions in an electrolytic cell with the corresponding electrode reactions in an electrochemical cell.

10. The g-at wt of aluminum is 27, and the g-at wt of gold is 197; both ions have a charge of 3. Which has the higher electrochemical equivalent?

11. Show that the mass of an element deposited according to Faraday's law can be expressed in grams.

12. How could you define the ampere in relation to Faraday's laws and the silver coulombmeter?

# problems

GROUP A

1. How much silver can be deposited in 8.00 minutes by making use of a steady current of 0.500 ampere?

2. An electroplating cell connected across a source of direct current for 15.0 minutes deposits 0.750 g of copper. What is the average current in the cell?

3. How many hours are required for an electrolytic cell to liberate 0.160 g of oxygen using a steady current of 0.300 ampere?

4. A water-decomposition cell is maintained in continuous operation with a constant current of 25.0 ampere. How much hydrogen is recovered per day?

5. How many hours would it take to plate 25.0 g of nickel onto an automobile bumper if the current in the plating bath is 3.40 a?

GROUP B

6. An electrolysis-of-water cell is operated until 1 faraday of electricity has been passed. How many atoms of hydrogen are liberated?

7. (a) What magnitude of electric charge must pass through an electrolysis-of-water cell to liberate one g-at wt of hydrogen? (b) How much oxygen will be liberated during the same time?

8. How long will it take a current of 4.50 a to produce 1.00 liter of hydrogen by the electrolysis of water? Assume STP conditions.

9. Two coulombmeters, one of silver and the other of an unknown metal that forms ions having a +3 charge, are connected in series. A constant current of 2.00 a is maintained in the circuit for 2.00 hr and 2.73 g of the unknown metal are deposited. How much silver is deposited?

10. What is the g-at wt of the unknown metal deposited in Problem 9?

# 19 Magnetic Effects

## MAGNETISM

Today physicists believe that all magnetic phenomena result from forces between electric charges in motion. Vast quantities of electric energy are now generated as a consequence of relative motion between electric conductors and magnetic fields. Electric energy is transformed into mechanical energy by relative motion between electric currents and magnetic fields. The function of many electric measuring instruments depends on the relationship between electricity and magnetism.

The basic theory of electric generators and motors is presented in Chapter 20. Electric measuring instruments are discussed later in this chapter. Before undertaking the study of magnetic effects of electric currents, we shall examine the magnetic properties of substances and learn of the nature of magnetism and magnetic fields.

Deposits of a magnetic iron ore were discovered many centuries ago by the Greeks in a section of Turkey. The region was then known as Magnesia and the ore was called *magnetite*. Deposits of magnetite are found in the Adirondack Mountains of New York and in other regions of the world. Pieces of magnetite are known as *natural magnets*. A suspended piece of magnetite aligns itself with the magnetic field of the earth. These natural magnets, known as lodestones (leading stones), were first used as magnetic compasses during the twelfth century.

A few materials, notably iron and steel, are strongly attracted by magnets: cobalt and nickel are attracted to a lesser degree. These substances are said to have *ferromagnetic* properties. Special alloys such as *permalloy* and *alnico* have extraordinary ferromagnetic properties. Physicists have shown much interest

### 19.1 Magnetic materials

**Figure 19-1** Metal filings attracted to a lodestone give evidence of the field of force surrounding the natural magnet.

*The Latin word for iron is "ferrum," thus the name "ferromagnetic."*

in the structure of materials possessing the property of *ferro-magnetism*.

Today very strong magnets are made from ferromagnetic substances. Alnico magnets may support a weight of over 1000 times that of the magnets themselves. Ferromagnetic substances are commonly referred to simply as "magnetic substances."

*Alnico (Al Ni Co) consists mainly of aluminum, nickel, and cobalt plus iron.*

Materials are commonly classified as magnetic or nonmagnetic. Those that do not demonstrate the strong ferromagnetism of the Iron Family of metals are said to be "nonmagnetic." However, if these materials are placed in the field of a very strong magnet, some are observed to be slightly repelled by the magnet while others are very slightly attracted.

Zinc, bismuth, sodium chloride, gold, and mercury are a few of the substances that are feebly repelled; they are *diamagnetic*. The property of *diamagnetism* is an important concept in the modern theory of magnetism, as we shall see in Section 19.2.

Wood, aluminum, platinum, oxygen, and copper(II) sulfate are examples of substances that are very slightly attracted by a strong magnet. Such materials are *paramagnetic,* and this magnetic behavior is called *paramagnetism*.

## 19.2 The domain theory of magnetism

*The orbiting electron produces a magnetic field because in this motion it constitutes an electric current.*

**Figure 19-2**   Revolving electrons impart a magnetic property to the atom.

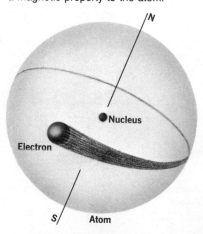

William Gilbert's report on his experiments with natural magnets, published in 1600, probably represents the first scientific study of magnetism. In the years that followed, discoveries by Coulomb, Oersted, and Ampère added to our knowledge of the behavior of magnets and the nature of magnetic forces. Physicists believe, however, that it is only within this century that they have begun to understand the true nature of magnetism. The present view is that the magnetic properties of matter are electric in origin and result from the movements of electrons within the atoms of substances. Since the electron is an electrically charged particle, this theory suggests that *magnetism is a property of a charge in motion*. If so, we can account for the energy associated with magnetic forces by using known laws of physics.

Two kinds of electron motion are important in this modern concept of magnetism. *First, an electron revolving about the nucleus of an atom imparts a magnetic property to the atom structure*. See Figure 19-2. When the atoms of a substance are subjected to the magnetic force of a strong magnet, the force affects this magnetic property, opposing the motion of the electrons. The atoms are thus repelled by the magnet. This is diamagnetism. If the electron's only motion were its movement about the nucleus, all substances would be diamagnetic. Diamagnetic repulsion is quite feeble in its action on the total mass of a substance.

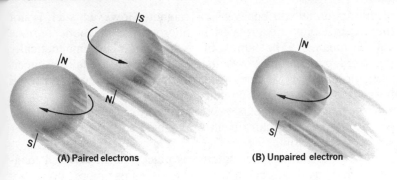

(A) Paired electrons   (B) Unpaired electron

**Figure 19-3** Ferromagnetism in matter stems basically from the spin of electrons.

*The second kind of motion is that of the electron spinning on its own axis. Each spinning electron acts as a tiny permanent magnet.* Opposite spins are designated as + and − spins; electrons spinning in opposite directions tend to form *pairs* and so neutralize their magnetic character. See Figure 19-3. The magnetic character of an atom as a whole may be weak because of the mutual interaction between the electron spins.

Magnetic properties are associated with both kinds of electron motion. The atoms of some substances may possess permanent magnet characteristics because of an imbalance between orbits and spins. These atoms act like tiny magnets, called *dipoles,* and are attracted by strong magnets. Substances in which this attractive effect exceeds the diamagnetism common to all atoms show the property of paramagnetism.

In the atoms of ferromagnetic substances there are unpaired electrons whose spins are oriented in the same way. The common metals iron, cobalt, and nickel and the rare earth elements gadolinium and dysprosium show strong ferromagnetic properties. Some alloys of these and other elements, as well as certain metallic oxides called ferrites, also exhibit strong ferromagnetic properties.

The inner quantum levels, or shells, of the atom structures of most elements contain only paired electrons. The highest quantum level, or outer shell, of each of the noble gases (except helium) consists of a stable octet of electrons made up of four electron pairs. The atoms of other elements achieve this stable configuration by forming chemical bonds. Only in certain transition elements that have incomplete inner shells do unpaired electrons result in ferromagnetic properties. The electron configuration of the iron atom, Figure 19-4, shows four unpaired electrons in the third principal quantum level. The similarly oriented spins of these electrons, enhanced by the influence of nearby atoms in the metallic crystal, account for its strong ferromagnetism.

From the preceding discussion, it would seem that every

*Each iron atom has four unpaired inner-shell electrons.*

**Figure 19-4** The iron atom has strong ferromagnetic properties.

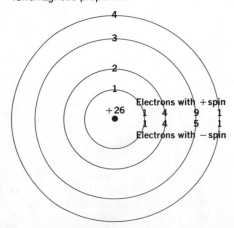

Electrons with +spin

Electrons with −spin

+26

**Figure 19-5** The domains of an un-magnetized ferromagnetic substance are polarized along the crystal axes. Dots and plus signs represent arrows going out of and into the page, respectively.

Table 19-1

| CURIE POINTS OF FERROMAGNETIC ELEMENTS | |
|---|---|
| Element | Curie point |
| iron | 770°C |
| cobalt | 1131°C |
| nickel | 358°C |
| gadolinium | 16°C |

piece of iron should behave as a magnet. However, such is not the case. Atoms are grouped in microscopic magnetic regions called *domains*. The atoms in each domain are magnetically polarized parallel to a crystal axis. In a polycrystalline specimen, ordinarily these axes (and the domains) are oriented in all possible directions. The domains effectively cancel one another and the net magnetism is essentially zero. In Figure 19-5 the polarity of each domain in an unmagnetized material is represented by an arrow.

When a ferromagnetic material is placed in an external magnetic field, two effects occur. The domains more favorably oriented in this magnetic field may increase in size at the expense of less favorably oriented adjacent domains. Other domains may rotate in order to become more favorably oriented with respect to the external field. The material becomes magnetized. If domain boundaries remain extended to some degree after the external magnetizing force is removed, the material is said to be "permanently" magnetized. When the direction of magnetization of a magnetic domain is rotated by an external magnetic field, it must be understood that the *material* of the domain does not change its position in the specimen. It is only its *direction* of magnetization that changes.

When the temperature of a ferromagnetic material is raised above a certain critical value, the domain regions disappear and the material becomes paramagnetic. This temperature is known as the *Curie point*. It is usually lower than the melting point of the substance. The Curie points for some ferromagnetic substances are given in Table 19-1.

When a single crystal of iron is sprinkled with colloidal particles of iron oxide, the microscopic domains become visible. Using this technique, physicists are able to photograph magnetic domains and observe the effects of external magnetic fields on them. Typical photomicrographs of magnetic domains are shown in Figure 19-6.

A recent magnet technology that makes use of a group of ferromagnetic substances known as *ferrites* yields strong hard magnets with unique properties. Ferrites are iron oxides combined with oxides of other metals such as manganese, cobalt,

**Figure 19-6** Photomicrographs of magnetic domains.

IRON                          COBALT

nickel, copper, or magnesium. The combined oxides are powdered, formed into the desired shape under pressure, and fired. The ferrites have very high electric resistance, a property that is extremely important in some applications of ferromagnetic materials. The original lodestone, commonly called magnetic iron oxide, is a material of this type. Chemically it is a combination of iron(II) oxide, FeO, and iron(III) oxide, $Fe_2O_3$. Its formula is considered to be $Fe(FeO_2)_2$.

## 19.3 Force between magnet poles

The fact that iron filings cling mainly to the ends of a bar magnet indicates that the magnetic force acts on the filings primarily in these regions, or *poles*; it does not mean that the middle region of the magnet is unmagnetized. The pole that points toward the north when the magnet is free to swing about a vertical axis is commonly called the *north-seeking pole*, or simply the **N** pole. The opposite pole, which points toward the south, is called the *south-seeking pole*, or **S** pole.

Suppose a bar magnet is suspended as shown in Figure 19-7. When the **N** pole of a second magnet is brought near the **N** pole of the suspended magnet, the two repel each other. A similar action is observed with the two **S** poles. When the **S** pole of one magnet is placed near the **N** pole of the other magnet, they attract each other. Such experiments show that *like poles repel; unlike poles attract*.

Magnets usually have two well-defined poles—one **N** and one **S**. Sometimes long bar magnets acquire more than two poles, and an iron ring may have no poles at all when magnetized. Physicists have long speculated about the existence of single-pole magnetic particles called *monopoles*. Known magnetic poles, however, always come in pairs called *dipoles*. The most elementary magnet has an **S** pole and an **N** pole. If cut in half, each half is found to be dipolar. A magnet has an **S** pole for every **N** pole. An isolated **N** pole of unit strength is sometimes *assumed* in "thought" experiments. *A **unit pole** may be thought of as one that repels an exactly similar pole, placed one centimeter away, with a force of one dyne.* (1 dyne = $10^{-5}$ newton.)

The first quantitative study of the force between two magnetic poles is generally credited to Coulomb. He found this magnetic force to be governed by the same inverse-square relationship that applies to gravitational force and electrostatic force. ***Coulomb's law for magnetism*** *states that the force between two magnetic poles is directly proportional to the product of the strengths of the poles and inversely proportional to the square of the distance between them.* The force is one of repulsion or attraction, depending on whether the magnetic poles are alike or different.

*Like poles repel; unlike poles attract.*

*In 1975 a group of physicists reported experimental evidence of a magnetic monopole. The subsequent lack of any confirming evidence has caused physicists to doubt that a monopole was, in fact, observed.*

**Figure 19-7** Like poles repel. Unlike poles attract.

Like poles repel

## 19.4 Magnetic field of force

**Figure 19-8** The path followed by the floating magnet in this experiment is approximately that of an independent N pole.

**(A)**

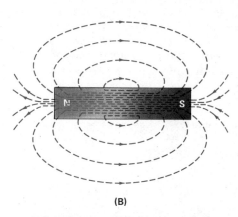

**(B)**

**Figure 19-9** (A) The path taken by an independent N pole in a magnetic field suggests a line of flux. (B) Magnetic flux about a bar magnet.

*Imaginary lines of magnetic flux are useful for mapping magnetic fields.*

In Section 16.9 we described the electric field of force near an electrically charged object. Electric forces are not the only forces that act on charged particles. Sometimes we observe the effect of a force that is both *perpendicular* and proportional to the velocity of a *moving* charge. This force identifies a *magnetic field*. A dipole magnet in such a region of space experiences a torque. We speak of a magnetic field in the space around a bar magnet in the same way we speak of an electric field around a charged rod. Furthermore, *we can represent a magnetic field by lines of flux*, just as we represented an electric field by lines of force.

The behavior of our imaginary independent **N** pole in a magnetic field can be approximated by using a magnetized darning needle as illustrated in Figure 19-8. The needle is supported by cork so that it floats with the **N** pole extended below the surface of the water. The **S** pole is far enough removed to have negligible influence on the movement of the needle. A bar magnet placed under the glass dish with its **N** pole near the needle causes the floating magnet to move along a path that approximates the path an isolated **N** pole would follow.

The path of an independent **N** pole in a magnetic field suggests a *line of flux*. *A **line of flux** is a line so drawn that a tangent to it at any point indicates the direction of the magnetic field*. Flux lines are assumed to emerge from a magnet at the **N** pole and to enter the magnet at the **S** pole. Every flux line is a closed path running from **S** pole to **N** pole within the magnet. See Figure 19-9.

The lines of flux perpendicular to a specified area in the magnetic field are collectively called the magnetic flux, for which the Greek letter Φ (phi) is used. The unit of magnetic flux in the MKS system is the *weber* (wb).

*The **magnetic flux density**, **B**, is the number of flux lines per unit area that permeates the magnetic field*. The flux density $B$ is a vector quantity; the direction of $B$ at any point in the magnetic field is the direction of the field at that point.

$$B = \Phi/A$$

Flux density in the MKS system is expressed in webers per square meter ($wb/m^2$). It determines the *magnetizing force* at any point in the magnetic field. We shall consider how these quantities are measured in Section 19.9.

Flux lines drawn to indicate how tiny magnets would behave when placed at various points in a magnetic field provide a means of *mapping* the field. A line drawn tangent to a flux line at any point indicates the direction a very small magnet would assume if placed there. An arrowhead can be added to the tangent line to indicate the direction in which the **N** pole of the tiny magnet would point, thus giving the direction of the magnetic field, and the $B$ vector, at that point.

Using a suitable scale of flux lines per unit area perpendicular to the field, the flux density, *B,* at any point can be illustrated. Selection of a number of lines to represent a unit of magnetic flux is arbitrary. Usually, one flux line per square meter represents a flux density of 1 wb/m². In this sense, one line of flux is a weber.

The field of a single magnet or a group of magnets is suggested by the pattern formed by iron filings sprinkled on a glass plate laid over the magnet. Photographs of such patterns are shown in Figures 19-10 through 19-12.

**Figure 19-10** Iron filings near a single bar magnet.

**Figure 19-11** Iron filings are shown near unlike poles of two bar magnets in (A) and near their like poles in (B).

(A)                    (B)

**Figure 19-12** (A) Iron filings near the poles of a horseshoe magnet, end view. (B) An idealized drawing of (A) showing lines of flux.

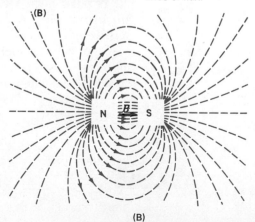

(A)                         (B)

## 19.5 Magnetic permeability

*In a practical sense, all materials except those that are ferromagnetic can be considered magnetically inert. In a magnetic field, they behave just like air.*

In Section 19.4 we described the effect of a magnetic field of force on iron filings and on a magnetized needle as experienced through glass and water. Nonmagnetic materials in general are transparent to magnetic flux; that is, their effect on the lines of flux is not appreciably different than that of air. *The property of a material by which it changes the flux density in a magnetic field from the value in air is called its **permeability**, $\mu$.* Permeability is a ratio of flux densities and is without dimension. The permeability of empty space is taken as unity and that of air as very nearly the same. The permeabilities of diamagnetic substances are slightly less than unity; permeabilities of paramagnetic substances are slightly greater than unity. Permeabilities of ferromagnetic materials are many times that of air.

If a sheet of iron covers a magnet, there is little magnetic field above the sheet. The flux enters the iron and follows a path within the iron itself. Similarly, an iron ring placed between the poles of a magnet provides a better path than air for the magnetic flux. This effect is illustrated in Figure 19-13. The flux density in iron is greater than it is in air; therefore, iron is said to have a high permeability. The permeabilities of other ferromagnetic substances are also very high.

**Figure 19-13** At left, magnetic flux crosses the air gap between the poles of a magnet. At right, magnetic flux follows the soft iron ring, which is more permeable than air.

Suppose a bar of soft iron lies in a magnetic field, as in Figure 19-14. Because of the high permeability of the iron, the field is distorted and the magnetic flux passes through the iron in preference to the air. Under these circumstances the soft iron bar becomes a magnet with end **A** as the **S** pole and end **B** as the **N** pole. Such a bar is said to be magnetized by *induction.* *Magnetism produced in a ferromagnetic substance by the influence of a magnetic field is called **induced magnetism**.*

If the magnetic field is removed by withdrawing the two bar magnets, most of the induced magnetism is lost. Magnets produced by induction are known as temporary magnets. A piece

**Figure 19-14** Magnetizing an iron bar by induction.

of hardened steel is not so strongly magnetized by induction but retains a greater *residual* magnetism when removed from the induction field.

There is no significant difference in the process if the iron bar in Figure 19-14 is brought into contact with one of the magnet poles. The magnetization process is somewhat more efficient due to the reduction of the air gap. See Figure 19-15.

**Figure 19-15** The nail becomes a magnet by induction. Are the tacks also magnets?

Suppose the earth contained a great bar magnet as shown in Figure 19-16. It would produce a magnetic field similar to its actual field. Over most of the earth's populated surface the north-seeking pole of a compass points northward. Although it is the south pole of our fictitious magnet that attracts the **N** pole of the compass, the pole region is conventionally called the *north magnetic pole* because it is located in the northern hemisphere. Similarly, the pole region in the southern hemisphere is called the *south magnetic pole*.

The earth's magnetic axis does not coincide with its polar (geographic) axis, but is inclined to the polar axis at a small angle. The north magnetic pole, at latitude 73°N, longitude 100°W, is about 2000 km (1200 miles) south of the north geographic pole. The south magnetic pole is located in Antarctica near the Ross Sea. Thus from most locations on the earth, the **N** pole of the compass needle does not point to the true geographic north. At any surface location the angle between magnetic north and the true north is called the *declination*, or *variation*. In the region of Los Angeles the compass variation is about 15°E. That is to say a compass needle points about 15° to the east of true north. In the region of Boston the variation is about 15°W. Cincinnati, Ohio, is located very near the line of zero declination. Here the compass needle points to the true north and the variation is 0°.

A compass needle mounted on a horizontal axis and provided with a means of measuring the angle the needle makes with the horizontal plane is called a *dipping* needle. At certain places on the earth's surface, approximately midway between the magnetic poles, the angle of dip is zero and the needle is horizontal. A line drawn through a succession of such points identifies the *magnetic equator*. The angle of dip is 90° at the magnetic pole. The dip, or deviation between the equilibrium position of a dipping needle and the horizontal, is known as the *magnetic inclination*.

In 1600 the English physicist William Gilbert (1540?–1603) published his scientific treatise *De magnete*, which deals with the magnetism of the earth. This is one of the earliest publications on the experimental treatment of a scientific topic. Gilbert inferred that the earth behaved as a large magnet because the

## 19.6 Terrestrial magnetism

**Figure 19-16** The magnetic field of the earth may be produced by electric currents within its fluid core. The field is oriented as though the earth contained a large magnet passing through its center, with the magnetic axis slightly inclined to the axis of the earth.

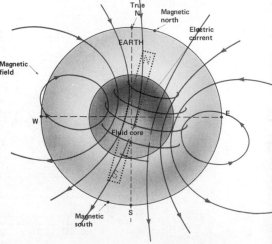

interior consisted of permanently magnetic material. Today scientists believe the core of the earth is too hot to be a permanent magnet and is fluid rather than solid.

The German physicist Karl Friedrich Gauss (1777–1855) showed that the magnetic field of the earth must originate inside the earth. In 1939 the American theoretical physicist Walter M. Elsasser suggested that the earth's magnetic field results from electric currents generated by the flow of matter in the earth's fluid core. See Figure 19-16. Today physicists believe that the magnetic field is due principally to electric currents within the earth, but they have not yet established the origin of these currents.

*Electric current loops inside the earth are responsible for its magnetic field.*

## 19.7 The magnetosphere

Because space vehicles now travel to the outer limits of the earth's atmosphere and beyond, there is a growing interest in a region of the outer atmosphere known as the *magnetosphere*. Located beyond approximately 200 km, the magnetosphere is the region in which the motion of charged particles is governed primarily by the magnetic field of the earth. At lower altitudes, where the density of the atmosphere is much greater, the motion of charged particles is controlled largely by collisions.

The magnetosphere on the side facing the sun extends beyond the earth's surface approximately 57,000 km, or about 10 earth radii. On the side away from the sun, the magnetosphere probably extends outward for hundreds of earth radii. See Figure 19-17. The elongated shape results from the influence of the onrushing *solar wind*, or *solar plasma*. The solar wind,

**Figure 19-17** The magnetosphere of the earth. The overall radiation regions are shown in color. The inner and outer Van Allen belts of intense radiation are the dark regions ranging outward to approximately 4 earth radii.

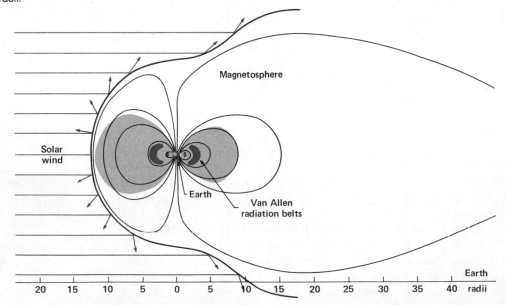

consisting mainly of protons and electrons emitted by the sun, compresses the magnetosphere on the side nearest the sun.

In 1958 regions of intense radiation were discovered within the magnetosphere by a team of physicists headed by Dr. J. A. Van Allen (b. 1914). These regions, now known as the Van Allen radiation belts, contain energetic protons and electrons trapped by the earth's magnetic field. Those trapped in the inner belts probably originate in the earth's atmosphere; those trapped in the outer belts probably have their origin in the sun. When these intense radiation belts were first discovered, scientists were concerned about the serious threat they appeared to present to space travel. Today, astronauts journeying into outer space are able to pass quickly through these regions with adequate protection from the Van Allen radiation.

*Auroral displays over the polar regions are related to the escape of energetic particles from the radiation belts.*

# questions

GROUP A

1. (a) What is a lodestone? (b) Why are lodestones sometimes called natural magnets?
2. What is the distinguishing property of ferromagnetic materials?
3. Distinguish between diamagnetic and paramagnetic materials.
4. What two kinds of electron motion are important in determining the magnetic property of a material?
5. What are electron pairs and what is their significance in regard to magnetic character?
6. (a) What three metals are the most important ferromagnetic materials? (b) What special alloy is often used to make very strong magnets?
7. How can you account for the ferromagnetic properties of the metals of the Iron Family?
8. What are magnetic domains?
9. Describe the condition of a ferromagnetic material in a state of magnetic saturation.
10. State Coulomb's law for magnetism.
11. Under what circumstances will a magnetic force be (a) one of repulsion, (b) one of attraction?
12. Describe a simple way to examine the fields of small magnets.

13. What is the advantage in making a magnet in the shape of a horseshoe?
14. Describe an experiment that illustrates induced magnetism.
15. Distinguish between a north-seeking pole and the north magnetic pole.
16. Why is a declination angle involved in the use of a compass over most of the earth's surface?

GROUP B

17. Explain, on the basis of atomic structure, the property of diamagnetism.
18. Explain paramagnetism on the basis of imbalance between orbits and spins.
19. Assume the dish in Figure 19-8 to be located in the northern hemisphere. Will the magnetized needle be attracted to the north edge of the dish? Explain.
20. How would you prove that a steel bar is magnetized?
21. If a watch mechanism is to be magnetically "insulated," should the case be made of diamagnetic, paramagnetic, or ferromagnetic material? Explain.

## 19.8 The link between an electric current and magnetism

**Figure 19-18** Hans Christian Oersted studied medicine before becoming professor of physics at the University of Copenhagen in 1806. Several years before he performed his famous experiment, he predicted that a link between electricity and magnetism would be found.

It can be easily demonstrated that electrostatic charges and stationary magnets have no effect on one another. However, in 1820 Hans Christian Oersted (*er*-stet) (1777–1851), a Danish physicist and professor of physics at the University of Copenhagen, observed that a small compass needle is deflected when brought near a conductor carrying an electric current. This was the first evidence of a long suspected link between electricity and magnetism. Oersted discovered that forces exist between a magnet and electric charges in motion. His famous experiment is so significant that a brief description of it is in order.

A dry cell, compass, switch, and conducting wire are arranged as shown in Figure 19-19(A). With the switch open, a straight section of the conductor is supported *above* the compass in the vertical plane of the compass needle. In Figure 19-19(B) the dry-cell connection is such that the electron flow will be from north to south. When the switch is closed, the **N** pole of the compass is deflected toward the west. When the dry-cell connections are reversed so electron flow is from south to north, the **N** pole of the compass is deflected to the east, Figure 19-19(C). It is evident that *a magnetic field exists in the region near the conductor when the circuit is closed*. Furthermore, *the direction of the field is dependent on the direction of the current in the conductor*.

If the experiment is repeated with the conductor placed *below* the compass needle, the compass deflection is opposite to that in the first experiment. This suggests, but does not prove, that the magnetic field encircles the conductor.

**Figure 19-19** The Oersted experiment as viewed from above. In each diagram the compass needle is located below the conductor.

$E$    $Sw$    **(A)**

$E$    $Sw$    $e^-$    N    S    $e^-$    **(B)**

$E$    $Sw$    $e^-$    S    N    $e^-$    **(C)**

## 19.9 Magnetic field and a charge in motion

Shortly after Oersted's discovery, the French physicist Ampère determined the shape of the magnetic field about a conductor carrying a current. He had discovered that forces exist between two parallel conductors in an electric circuit. If the two currents are in the same direction the force is one of attraction; the force is one of repulsion if the currents are in opposite directions. See Figure 19-21.

In a quantitative sense, two long, straight, parallel conductors of length $l$ separated by a distance $d$ and carrying currents $I_1$ and $I_2$ will each experience a force $F$ of magnitude

$$F = \frac{2k\,l\,I_1 I_2}{d}$$

The constant $k$ is exactly $10^{-7}$ n/a² in the MKS system. If $I_1$ and $I_2$ are expressed in amperes and $l$ and $d$ in meters, the force $F$ is given in newtons.

Because these attractive and repulsive forces between current-carrying conductors are directly proportional to the currents in the conductors, they provide a precise method of defining the unit of current, the ampere. In this sense, the **ampere** may be defined as *the current in each of two long parallel conductors spaced one meter apart that causes a magnetic force of $2 \times 10^{-7}$ newton per meter length of conductor.*

Following this scheme, the **coulomb** as a quantity of charge (an ampere-second) may be defined as *the quantity of electric charge that passes a given point on a conductor in one second when the conductor carries a constant current of one ampere.*

**Figure 19-20** André Ampère, the French physicist for whom the unit of electric current is named, did fundamental work in electromagnetism.

(A)   (B)

**Figure 19-21** Forces between parallel currents (A) in the same direction and (B) in opposite directions.

Ampère investigated the magnetic fields about conductors to find an explanation of the magnetic forces. Suppose a heavy copper wire passes vertically through the center of a horizontal sheet of stiff cardboard. When the ends of the vertical conductor are connected to a dry cell, iron filings sprinkled over the surface of the cardboard form a pattern of concentric circles around the

**Figure 19-22** The magnetic field encircling a current in a straight conductor.

conductor. See Figure 19-22. If a small compass is placed at successive points around a circle of filings, the needle always comes to rest tangent to the circle and with the same tangential orientation of its **N** pole.

If the direction of current in the vertical conductor is reversed, the compass needle again becomes aligned tangent to the circle of filings, but with its **N**-pole orientation reversed. From these observations we conclude that *a magnetic field encircles an electric charge in motion.* The lines of flux are closed concentric circles in a plane perpendicular to the conductor with the axis of the conductor as their center. The direction of the magnetic field is everywhere tangent to the flux and is dependent on the direction of the current.

*A magnetic field surrounds a moving electric charge.*

Ampère devised a rule, known today as *Ampère's rule,* for determining the direction of the magnetic field around a current in a straight conductor when the direction of the electron flow is known.

*Ampère's rule for a straight conductor:* Grasp the conductor in the left hand with the thumb extended in the direction of the electron current. The fingers then will circle the conductor in the direction of the magnetic flux. See Figure 19-23.

*The left-hand rule for a straight conductor indicates the direction of the magnetic flux surrounding the conductor.*

The flux density, *B,* also called the *magnetic induction,* at any point in the magnetic field of a long straight conductor carrying a current, *I,* is directly proportional to the current in the conductor and inversely proportional to the radial distance, *r,* of the point from the conductor.

$$B = 2k\frac{I}{r}$$

**Figure 19-23** Ampère's rule for a straight conductor.

Left hand

Magnetic field

Current (e⁻)

The constant $k$ again is $10^{-7}$ n/a². When $I$ is given in amperes and $r$ is in meters, $B$ is expressed in newtons per ampere meter, which is equivalent to webers per square meter.

In Section 19.4 flux density is defined in terms of the lines of flux per unit area that permeate the magnetic field. In this sense the expression for flux density is $B = \Phi/A$. Thus

$$\Phi = BA$$

When $B$ is expressed in newtons per ampere meter, the MKS unit for $\Phi$, the weber, can be shown to be 1 newton meter per ampere. Dimensionally

$$\mathbf{wb} = \frac{\mathbf{n}}{\mathbf{a\ m}} \times \mathbf{m^2} = \frac{\mathbf{n\ m}}{\mathbf{a}}$$

Whether $\Phi$ is expressed in webers or newton meters per ampere and $B$ is expressed in webers per square meter or newtons per ampere meter is a matter of convenience in each situation.

Observe that the definition of $B$ given in Section 19.4 is based on the force exerted on an isolated unit pole. An isolated pole exists only in the fiction of a thought experiment; consequently, measurements based on this definition lack precision. The more practical definition given above involves quantities that can be measured precisely and is therefore generally preferred.

$B = \dfrac{2\mu_0 n I}{r}$ *coil*

---

Keeping Ampère's rule in mind, let us consider a loop in a conductor carrying a current. The magnetic flux from all segments of the loop must pass through the inside of the loop in the same direction; that is, *the face of the loop must show polarity.* See Figure 19-24.

This loop magnet can be made stronger if the flux density is increased. Because the magnetic field around a conductor varies with the current, the flux density can be increased by increasing the magnitude of the current in the conducting loop, by forming additional loops in the conductor, or by both.

## 19.10 Magnetic field and a current loop

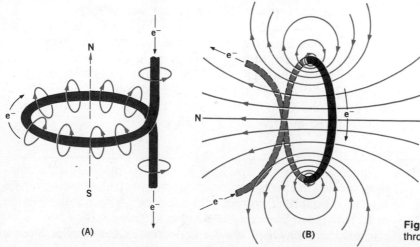

(A)      (B)

**Figure 19-24** The magnetic field through a current loop.

**Figure 19-25** Magnetic field about a solenoid.

*A magnetic tube is an imaginary tube bounded by magnetic lines. It always links the current that produces the field.*

**Figure 19-26** Ampère's rule for a solenoid.

A linear coil of such conducting loops takes the form of a helix, and is called a *solenoid*. The cylindrical column of air inside the loops, extending the length of the coil, is called the *core*. When a current is in a solenoid, the core of each *turn* (loop) becomes a magnet; the core of the solenoid is a magnetic tube through which practically all the magnetic flux passes. See Figure 19-25.

Since a solenoid carrying a current acts like a bar magnet, we may determine its polarity by means of a compass. However, the magnetic flux in the core of the solenoid is derived from the magnetic field of each turn of the conductor. Thus we shall modify Ampère's rule to fit this special case.

*Ampère's rule for a solenoid:* Grasp the coil in the left hand with the fingers circling the coil in the direction of the electron current. The extended thumb will point in the direction of the **N** pole of the core. See Figure 19-26.

## 19.11 The electromagnet

A solenoid with a core of air, wood, or some other nonmagnetic material does not produce a very strong electromagnet because the permeability of all nonmagnetic substances is essentially equal to that of air—unity. Substitution of such materials for air does not appreciably change the flux density.

Soft iron, on the other hand, has a high permeability. If an iron rod is substituted for air as the core material, the flux density is greatly increased. Strong electromagnets therefore have ferromagnetic cores with high permeability. For a given core material, the strength of the electromagnet depends on the magnitude of the current and the number of turns. In other words, its strength is determined by *the number of ampere-turns*.

## 19.12 The galvanometer

Suppose we form a wire loop in a vertical plane, place a compass needle (free to rotate in a horizontal plane) in the center of it, and introduce a current into the loop. The needle will be deflected. If we increase the number of turns sufficiently, even a feeble current will produce a deflection of the needle. Such a

**Figure 19-27** A super-conducting electromagnet. In operation, the eight-foot cylinder is immersed in liquid helium (-232°C). At this temperature the niobium-titanium strips imbedded in the copper coils lose all electric resistance and the magnet produces a force field up to 5000 times greater than that of the earth.

device, called a *galvanoscope,* may be used to detect the presence of an electric current or to determine its direction. A simple galvanoscope is shown in Figure 19-28.

A more versatile instrument for detecting feeble currents is the *galvanometer,* the essential parts of which are shown in Figure 19-29. A coil of wire wound on a soft iron core is pivoted

**Figure 19-28 (left)** A simple galvanoscope.

Galvanometer

**Figure 19-29 (right)** The basic components of a moving-coil galvanometer.

on jeweled bearings between the poles of a permanent horse-shoe magnet. The coil becomes a magnet when current is in it. The instrument then has two magnets: a permanent horseshoe magnet in a fixed position and an electromagnet free to turn on its axis. Electric connections to the coil are made through two control springs (not shown), one above and one below the coil. These coiled springs also restrain the rotational motion of the coil so that the attached pointer returns to the zero scale position when no current is present in the coil. This zero position is often located at the midpoint of the scale, as in Figure 19-29.

When there is a current in the movable coil, its core is magnetized. The poles of the core are then attracted and repelled by the poles of the permanent magnet. A torque acts upon the coil and the coil rotates in an attempt to align its plane perpendicular to the line joining the poles of the permanent magnet. As the coil rotates, however, it does work against the two control springs. Its final position is reached when the torque acting on it is just neutralized by the reaction of the springs. Since the permanent field flux is constant, the torque on the coil is proportional to the current in it. We may assume, for small movements of the coil, that the reaction of the springs is proportional to the deflection angle. When the coil reaches its equilibrium position, these two opposing torques are equal, and the deflection angle of the coil is therefore proportional to the current in it.

*Because a magnetic field exerts forces on moving charges, it exerts torques on current-carrying coils.*

The scale of the galvanometer is marked at intervals on either side of the zero center. Readings are made on this scale by means of a small, lightweight pointer attached to the coil. For a coil current in one direction, the needle deflection is to the left. If the current direction is reversed, the needle is deflected to the right.

The galvanometer is a sensitive instrument for detecting feeble currents of the order of microamperes. For translation of a reading into absolute current values, the *current sensitivity* of the specific instrument must be known. Current sensitivity is usually expressed in *microamperes per scale division*.

The pointer deflection, $d$, of a galvanometer is proportional to the current, $I_M$, in the coil

$$I_M \propto d$$

or

$$I_M = kd$$

and

$$k = \frac{I_M}{d}$$

where $k$ is the current sensitivity in microamperes per scale division.

The moving coil of the galvanometer has resistance. By

Ohm's law, a potential difference appears across the resistance of the meter when a current is in the coil. We can express the *voltage sensitivity* of the instrument since it must be equal to the product of the meter resistance and the current per scale division.

$$\text{Voltage sensitivity} = kR_M = \frac{I_M}{\text{div}} \times R_M$$

where $R_M$ is the resistance of the meter movement. Voltage sensitivity is given in microvolts per scale division.

If provision is made to prevent excessive currents from entering the coil, the galvanometer can be adapted for service as either a d-c ammeter or d-c voltmeter.

The following examples illustrate calculations involving the galvanometer.

**Figure 19-30** Sensitive galvanometers use a mirror to indicate the position of a suspended coil by producing an image of a scale viewed through a telescope or by reflecting a beam of light onto a scale.

**EXAMPLE**

*What current is required for full-scale deflection of a galvanometer having a current sensitivity of 50.0 μu per scale division? The meter has exactly 50 divisions on either side of the mid-scale index.*

**SOLUTION**

We are given the current sensitivity, $k = 50.0$ μa/div, and the number of divisions on either side of mid-scale (zero) position, $d = 50$ div.

$$I_M = kd = \frac{50.0 \text{ μa}}{\text{div}} \times 50 \text{ div}$$

$I_M = 25\overline{0}0$ μa, or $2.50 \times 10^{-3}$ a, the required current

**EXAMPLE**

*What potential difference appears across the galvanometer described in the previous example when the pointer is fully deflected? The meter resistance is 10.0 Ω.*

**SOLUTION**

We are given the current sensitivity, $k = 50.0$ μa/div, the resistance of the meter, $R_M = 10.0$ Ω, and the number of divisions of deflection, $d = 50$ div.

$$V_M = I_M R_M$$

But

$$I_M = kd$$

Then

$$V_M = kdR_M = \frac{50.0 \text{ μa}}{\text{div}} \times 50 \text{ div} \times 10.0 \text{ Ω}$$

$V_M = 2.50 \times 10^4$ μv, or $2.50 \times 10^{-2}$ v, the potential difference across the meter.

## 19.13  The d-c voltmeter

d-c voltmeter

Pointer

Coiled control
spring

Permanent
magnet

Movable coil on
magnetic core

Coils of high
resistance wire

Electrons which flow through the
voltmeter pass through the rear
coiled control spring and into the
windings on the movable coil

N          S

Electrons from the movable coil
windings pass through the front
control spring, and through the
high resistance coils to the
positive terminal

The high resistance coils permit only a few electrons
to flow through the movable coil of a voltmeter

**Figure 19-31** The construction of a d-c voltmeter, showing the high resistance in series with the windings of the movable coil.

**Figure 19-32** Converting a galvanometer to a voltmeter.

Galvanometer
movable coil

Series resistor

$R_S$

$R_M = 10.0 \ \Omega$
$I_M = 0.00250 \ a$

The potential difference across a galvanometer is quite small even when the needle is fully deflected. If a galvanometer is to be used to measure voltages of ordinary magnitudes, we must convert it to a high-resistance instrument. The essential parts of a d-c voltmeter are shown in Figure 19-31.

If a high resistance is added in series with the moving coil, most of the potential drop appears across this series resistor or *multiplier*. Since *a voltmeter is connected in parallel* with the part of a circuit across which the potential difference is to be measured, a high resistance prevents an appreciable loading effect. By the proper choice of resistance, the meter can be calibrated to read any desired voltage.

Suppose we convert the galvanometer used in the examples in Section 19.12 to a voltmeter reading 15.0 volts on full-scale deflection. The current required for full deflection has been found to be $2.50 \times 10^{-3}$ ampere, and the resistance of the meter coil is 10.0 ohms. We must determine the value of the resistor $R_S$ to be placed in series with the moving coil. Figure 19-32 illustrates this problem.

Since $R_M$ and $R_S$ (of Figure 19-32) are in series,

$$V = I_M R_M + I_M R_S$$

Then

$$R_S = \frac{V}{I_M} - R_M$$

$$R_S = \frac{15.0 \text{ v}}{2.50 \times 10^{-3} \text{ a}} - 10.0 \ \Omega$$

$R_S = 5990 \ \Omega$, value of the series resistor

Observe that the total resistance between the terminals of the meter is 6000 ohms.

The voltmeter sensitivity is frequently expressed in terms of *ohms per volt*. When the ohms-per-volt sensitivity of a voltmeter is known, we can quickly estimate the loading effect it will have when placed across a known resistance component of a circuit. For example, at 400 ohms per volt, our meter, which reads from 0 to 15 volts, has 6000 ohms between the terminals. If it were placed across resistances greater than about 600 ohms, the loading effect would result in serious meter errors.

## 19.14 The d-c ammeter

We could use the basic galvanometer in Section 19.12 as a microammeter by calibrating the graduated scale to read directly in microamperes. However, the meter would not be useful in circuits in which the current exceeded 2500 microamperes. Current in the resistance of a galvanometer coil produces $I^2R$ heating, and an excessive current would burn out the meter.

**Figure 19-33** The construction of a d-c ammeter, showing the low resistance in parallel with the windings of the movable coil.

Figure 19-34 Converting a galvanometer to an ammeter.

To convert the galvanometer to read larger currents, an alternate (parallel) low-resistance path for current, called a *shunt,* must be provided across the terminals. By the proper choice of shunt resistance, we can calibrate the meter to read over the required range of current magnitudes. See Figure 19-33.

Suppose we wish to convert the same galvanometer to an ammeter reading 10.0 amperes full scale. As before, the current required for the full deflection of the moving coil is $2.50 \times 10^{-3}$ ampere and the resistance is $10.0\ \Omega$. We must determine the resistance of the shunt to be used across the coil. Figure 19-34 applies.

Since $R_M$ and $R_S$ are in parallel,

$$I_M R_M = I_S R_S$$

But

$$I_S = I_T - I_M$$

Then

$$R_S = \frac{I_M R_M}{I_T - I_M}$$

$$R_S = \frac{2.50 \times 10^{-3}\ a \times 10.0\ \Omega}{10.0\ a - 0.00250\ a}$$

$$R_S = 0.00250\ \Omega, \text{ the value for the shunt resistor}$$

The total resistance of the ammeter is the equivalent value for 10.0 ohms and 0.00250 ohm in parallel; it will be less than 0.00250 ohm. This exercise demonstrates clearly why *an ammeter must be connected in series* in a circuit, and why it does not materially alter the magnitude of current in the circuit.

## 19.15 The ohmmeter

An ohmmeter provides a convenient means of measuring the resistance of a circuit component. A basic ohmmeter circuit is shown in Figure 19-35. Its accuracy limitation is approximately the same as that of the voltmeter-ammeter method of measuring resistance; actually, it is a modified version of this method. The ohmmeter must be used only on a completely de-energized circuit.

The ohmmeter circuit of Figure 19-35 shows a milliammeter requiring 1 ma for full-scale deflection. With an emf of 4.5 volts, by Ohm's law, 4500 ohms of resistance will provide 1 ma of current when terminals **A-B** are short-circuited. A fixed resistor, $R_2$, of 4000 ohms and a rheostat, $R_1$, of 0-1000 ohms are provided.

To use this ohmmeter, **A** and **B** are short-circuited and $R_1$ is adjusted to give full deflection. If the emf is 4.5 v, $R_1$ will be set at 500 ohms. The pointer position at full-scale deflection is now marked as zero ohm (0 $\Omega$). The rest position of the pointer

Figure 19-35 A simple ohmmeter circuit.

is the open-circuit position with infinite resistance between **A** and **B**. This position is marked as $\infty\ \Omega$. Other resistance calibrations may be made from Ohm's law applications. For example, 4500 ohms between **A** and **B** will mean a total of 9000 ohms in the circuit and 0.5 ma of current. This mid-scale position of the pointer can be marked 4500 $\Omega$. The meter, when recalibrated, will read the resistance between terminals **A-B**.

Each time the ohmmeter is used, it is first shorted across **A-B** and $R_1$ is adjusted to "zero" the meter. This operation calibrates the meter and accommodates any decrease in the terminal voltage of the battery with age. The resistance $R_1$ allows the ohmmeter to be used until $E$ drops below 4.0 volts.

**Figure 19-36** An ohmmeter being used to measure the resistance of a non-operating circuit.

## summary

Magnetite, a magnetic iron ore, is a natural magnet. Metals of the Iron Family and special metallic alloys and oxides are strongly attracted by magnets; they have ferromagnetic properties. Very strong magnets are made from ferromagnetic substances. Materials that are not ferromagnetic are commonly said to be nonmagnetic. Ferromagnetic materials have high permeabilities. Nonmagnetic materials in general are transparent to magnetic flux. These materials may be very feebly diamagnetic or paramagnetic. Magnetism is explained by the domain theory.

Coulomb's law for magnetism is a quantitative expression for the force acting between two magnetic poles. A magnetic field, and its influence on a fictitious N pole, shows similarities to an electric field and its influence on a positive test charge.

A charge in motion is surrounded by a magnetic field. The core of a coil carrying an electric current becomes a magnet. Strong electromagnets are produced by winding a conducting coil around a ferromagnetic core. The strength of an electromagnet depends on the number of turns of coil and the magnitude of the current in the coil.

The galvanometer is the basic meter for d-c measurements. The galvanometer can be calibrated as a voltmeter by placing a high resistance in series with the galvanometer coil. It can be calibrated as an ammeter by placing a very low resistance shunt across the galvanometer coil. An ohmmeter requires a source of emf, an adjustable resistance, and a sensitive ammeter. It is essentially a voltmeter-ammeter method of measuring resistance.

## questions

GROUP A

1. What important discovery was made by Oersted?

2. A conductor carrying a current is arranged so that electrons flow in one segment from north to south. If a compass is held over this segment of the wire, in what direction is the needle deflected?

3. Describe a simple experiment to show the nature of the magnetic field about a straight conductor carrying a current.

4. Suppose an electron flow in a conductor passing perpendicularly through this page is represented by a dot inside a small circle when the direction of flow is up out of the page. What is the direction of the magnetic flux about this current?

5. Upon what factors does the strength of an electromagnet depend?

6. What prevents the movable coil of a galvanometer from aligning its magnetic field parallel to that of the permanent magnet each time a current is in the coil?

7. (a) Why is it necessary that an ammeter be a low-resistance instrument? (b) Why must a voltmeter be a high-resistance instrument?

GROUP B
8. A solenoid with ends marked **A** and **B** is suspended by a thread so that the core can rotate in the horizontal plane. A current is maintained in the coil such that the electron flow is clockwise when viewed from end **A** toward end **B**. How will the coil align itself in the earth's magnetic field?

9. A stream of electrons is projected horizontally to the right. A straight conductor carrying a current is supported parallel to the electron stream and above it. (a) What is the effect on the electron stream if the direction of the current in the conductor is from left to right, (b) if the current is reversed?

10. Suppose the conductor in Question 9 is replaced by a magnet that produces a magnetic field directed downward. What is the effect on the electron stream? Explain.

11. Why might the potential difference indicated by a voltmeter placed across a circuit load be different from the potential difference with the meter removed?

12. Suppose the resistance of a high-resistance load is to be determined using the voltmeter-ammeter method. Considering the design characteristics of ammeters and voltmeters, how would you arrange the meters in the circuit to reduce the error to a minimum? Draw your circuit diagram and justify your arrangement.

13. Suppose the resistance of a low-resistance load is to be determined using the voltmeter-ammeter method. How would you arrange the meters in this circuit to reduce the error to a minimum? Draw your circuit diagram and justify your arrangement.

# problems

GROUP B
1. Two parallel conductors 2.0 m long and 1.0 m apart and carrying equal currents experience a total force of $1.6 \times 10^{-6}$ n. What magnitude of current is in each conductor?

2. An ammeter that has a resistance of 0.01 ohm is connected in a circuit and indicates a current of 10 amperes. A shunt having a resistance of 0.001 ohm is then connected across the meter terminals. What is the new reading on the meter? Assume the introduction of the shunt does not affect the total circuit current.

3. A galvanometer has a zero-center scale with 20.0 divisions on each side of zero. The pointer deflects 15.0 scale divisions when a current of 375 $\mu$a is in the movable coil. (a) What is the current sensitivity of the meter? (b) What current will produce a full-scale deflection?

4. A galvanometer has a resistance of 50.0 $\Omega$ and requires 75.0 ma to produce a full-scale deflection. What resistance must be connected in series with the galvanometer in order to use it as a voltmeter for measuring a maximum of 300.0 v?

5. A galvanometer movement has a resistance of 2.5 ohms and when fully deflected has a potential difference of $5\overline{0}$ millivolts across it. What shunting resistance is required to enable the instrument to be used as an ammeter reading 7.5 amperes full scale?

6. A repulsive force of $9.6 \times 10^{-4}$ n is experienced by each of two parallel conductors 5.0 m long when a current of 3.2 a is in each conductor. By what distance are they separated?

# 20 Electromagnetic Induction

*[handwritten notes:]* instantaneous volt. & current / Inductance — calc. for series & para
counter emf — induced field — like a magnetism test
motor- generator, a little
3 phase- single phase

## INDUCED CURRENTS

In Section 19.8 we discussed Oersted's discovery of the link between magnetism and electricity. Soon after Oersted's work, other scientists attempted to find out whether an electric current could be produced by the action of a magnetic field. In 1831 Michael Faraday discovered that *an emf is set up in a closed electric circuit located in a magnetic field whenever the total magnetic flux linking the circuit is changing.* The American physicist Joseph Henry (1797–1878) made a similar discovery at about the same time. This phenomenon is called *electromagnetic induction.* The emf is called an *induced emf,* and the resulting current in the closed conducting loop is called an *induced current.*

The production and distribution of ample electric energy are essential functions of a modern technological economy. The invention of electric generators and transformers has made it possible to provide these essential services. The discoveries of Faraday and Henry represent the initial step in the development of the broad knowledge base in electromagnetic induction that makes such inventions possible.

We shall examine some of Faraday's experiments in order to understand their significance. Suppose we connect a sensitive galvanometer in a closed conducting loop as shown in Figure 20-1. A segment of the conductor is poised in the field flux of a strong magnet. In Figure 20-1(A) as the conductor is moved down between the poles of the magnet, there is a momentary deflection of the galvanometer needle, indicating an induced current. The

### 20.1 Discovery of induced current

*Magnetic lines of flux always* link *the current loop that sets up the magnetic field. Review Section 19.9.*

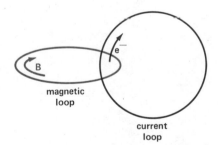

magnetic loop

current loop

### 20.2 Faraday's induction experiments

**(A)**                                                                                    **(B)**

**Figure 20-1** A current is induced in a closed conducting loop when the magnetic flux linked through the circuit is changing.

needle shows no deflection when the conductor is stationary in the magnetic flux. This leads to the observation that *the induced current is related to the motion of the conductor in the magnetic flux.*

Raising the conductor between the poles of the magnet, as in Figure 20-1(B), results in another momentary deflection of the galvanometer; this time in the opposite direction. This leads to the observation that *the direction of the induced current in the conductor is related to the direction of motion of the conductor in the field.* The emf induced in the conductor is of opposite polarity to that in the first experiment.

Faraday found that he could induce an emf in a conductor either by moving the conductor through a stationary field or by moving the magnetic field near a stationary conductor. He observed that the direction of the induced current in the conducting loop is reversed with a change in either the direction of motion or the direction of the magnetic field.

Supporting the conducting loop of Figure 20-1 in a fixed position and lifting the magnet result in a deflection similar to that of Figure 20-1(A). When the magnet is lowered, the galvanometer needle is momentarily deflected as in Figure 20-1(B). The relative motion between the conductor and the magnetic flux is the same whether the conductor is raised through the stationary field or the field is lowered past the stationary conductor.

So far we have considered the relative motion of the conductor to be essentially *perpendicular* to the magnetic flux. If the

**Induced emf** +

**S**

**N**

−

**Motion**

**No induced emf**

**S**

**N**

**Motion**

**(A) Change in flux linkage**

**(B) No change in flux linkage**

**Figure 20-2** An emf is induced in a conductor when there is a change of flux linked by the conductor.

conductor is moved in the magnetic field *parallel* to the flux lines, no emf is induced and no deflection is observed on the galvanometer. *When a conductor cuts across lines of flux, the magnetic flux linking the conducting loop changes;* a conductor moving parallel to the flux experiences no change in flux linkage. See Figure 20-2. This leads to the observation that *relative motion between a conductor and a magnetic field that produces a change of magnetic flux linked by the conductor results in an induced emf in the conductor.*

Suppose the conductor is looped so that several turns are poised in the magnetic field, as in Figure 20-3. When the coil is moved down between the poles of the magnet as before, there is a greater deflection on the galvanometer. By increasing the rate of motion of the coil across the magnetic flux or by substituting a stronger magnetic field, greater deflections are produced. In each of these cases the effect is to increase the number of flux lines "cut" by turns of the conductor in a given length of time. We can then state that *the magnitude of the induced emf, or of the induced current in a closed loop, is related to the rate at which the flux linked by the conductor changes.*

*The conducting segment of Figure 20-2 is part of a conducting loop that includes a galvanometer as shown in Figure 20-1.*

*Recall that magnetic flux lines are imaginary lines devised to help describe the properties of magnetic fields.*

**Conductor**

e⁻

**S**     **N**

**Motion**

e⁻

**Galvanometer**

**Figure 20-3** A greater change in flux linkage occurs when several turns of a conductor cut through the magnetic flux.

## 20.3 Factors affecting induced emf

Faraday found that an emf is induced in a conductor whenever any change occurs in the magnetic flux (lines of induction) linking the conductor. Very careful experiments have shown that *the emf induced in each turn of a coiled conductor is proportional to the time rate of change of magnetic flux linking each turn of the coil.*

The total magnetic flux linking the coil is designated by the Greek letter $\Phi$. If we let $\Delta\Phi$ represent the *change* in magnetic flux linking the coil during the time interval $\Delta t$, the emf, $E$, induced in a single turn of the coil can be expressed as

$$E \propto -\frac{\Delta\Phi}{\Delta t}$$

By introducing a proportionality constant $k$, the value of which depends on the system of units used, the expression can be written as

$$E = -k\frac{\Delta\Phi}{\Delta t}$$

In the MKS system where $E$ is measured in volts and $\Phi$ in webers, the numerical value of $k$ is unity and the equation becomes

$$E = -\frac{\Delta\Phi}{\Delta t}$$

This is to say that a change in the magnetic flux linking a coil occurring at the rate of 1 weber/second will induce an emf of 1 volt in a single turn of the coil.

A coil consists of turns of wire that are, in effect, connected in series. Thus the emf induced in the coil is simply the sum of the emfs induced in the individual turns. A coil of **N** turns has **N** times the emf of the separate turns. This can be written as

$$E = -N\frac{\Delta\Phi}{\Delta t}$$

The negative sign merely indicates the relative polarity of the induced voltage. It expresses the fact that the induced emf is of such polarity as to oppose the change that induced it. This is a basic energy conservation principle, which is discussed in detail in Section 20.6.

To illustrate this concept, suppose a coil of 150 turns linking the flux of a magnetic field uniformly is moved perpendicular to the flux and a change in flux linkage of $3.0 \times 10^{-5}$ weber occurs in 0.010 second. The induced emf is then

$$E = -N\frac{\Delta\Phi}{\Delta t}$$

$$E = -150 \times \frac{3.0 \times 10^{-5}\,\mathbf{wb}}{1.0 \times 10^{-2}\,\mathbf{s}}$$

$$E = -0.45\,\mathbf{v}$$

$$\left(\frac{\mathbf{wb}}{\mathbf{s}} = \frac{\mathbf{n\ m/a}}{\mathbf{s}} = \frac{\mathbf{j}}{\mathbf{c}} = \mathbf{v}\right)$$

A length of conductor moving in a magnetic field has an emf induced across it that is proportional to the rate of change of flux linkage. However, an induced current persists *only* if the conductor is a part of a closed circuit. In order to understand the cause of an induced emf, we shall make use of several facts that have already been established.

A length of copper wire poised in a magnetic field, as shown in Figure 20-4, contains many free electrons, and these moving charges constitute an electric current. In Section 19.12 we recognized that a force acts on the movable coil of a galvanometer in a magnetic field when a current is in the coil. This force, in effect, acts on the moving charges themselves. We shall call this force a *magnetic force* to distinguish it from the force exerted on free electrons by the electrostatic field of a stationary charge.

Suppose the copper wire of Figure 20-4, at right angles to the uniform magnetic field, is pushed downward (into the page) with a velocity $v$ through the magnetic field of flux density $B$. As a consequence of the motion of the wire, the free electrons of the copper conductor may be considered to move perpendicular to the flux with the speed, $v$. A magnetic force, $F$, acts on them in a direction perpendicular to both $B$ and $v$. In response to the magnetic force, these electrons move toward end **a** and away from end **b**. Because the two ends of the conductor are not connected in a circuit that would provide a closed path for the induced electron flow, end **a** acquires a growing negative charge while a residual positive charge builds up on end **b**. Thus a difference of potential is established across the conductor with **a** the negative end and **b** the positive end. If either the motion of the wire or the magnetic field is reversed, the direction of $F$ in Figure 20-4 is reversed and an emf is induced so that end **a** is positive and end **b** is negative.

The growing accumulations of charges at the ends of the conductor establish an electric field that increasingly opposes

## 20.4 The cause of an induced emf

**Figure 20-4**   A force acts on a moving charge in a magnetic field.

Copper wire

$a$

$F$

$l$

$e^-$

$N$      $B$      $S$

$v$

$b$

$+$

the movement of electrons through the conductor. The force of this electric field acting on the electrons from **a** toward **b** soon balances the magnetic force arising from the motion of the conductor, and the flow of electrons ceases.

*The movement of electrons through the open conductor of Figure 20-4 comprises a "transient" induced current of extremely short duration.*

*The equilibrium potential difference across the open conductor is numerically equal to the induced emf* and depends on the length, $l$, of wire linking the magnetic flux; the flux density, $B$, of the field; and the speed, $v$, with which the conductor is moved through the field.

$$E = Blv$$

When $B$ is in newtons/ampere meter (or webers/meter$^2$), $l$ in meters, and $v$ in meters/second, $E$ is given in volts.

*Flux density, B, is also called the magnetic induction.*

Assume that the length of conductor linking the magnetic field in Figure 20-4 is 0.075 m and the flux density is 0.040 n/a m. If the conductor is moved down through the flux with a velocity of 1.5 m/s, the induced emf is

> **$E = Blv$**
> **$E = $ 0.040 n/a m $\times$ 0.075 m $\times$ 1.5 m/s**
> **$E = $ 0.0045 v or 4.5 mv**

In Figure 20-4 a magnetic force equal but opposite to $F$ will act on the positively charged protons in the copper nuclei. Since these are in the bound parts of the copper atoms, they will not move in response to this force. However, positively charged ions in a liquid or gas would move.

*To compare the response of a moving electric charge to an electric force and to a magnetic force, see Figures 16-11 and 20-5.*

The vectors $B$, $v$, and $F$ are all mutually perpendicular as shown in Figure 20-5. If a charge $Q$ moves with a velocity $v$ through a magnetic field of flux density $B$, the force, $F$, acting on the charge becomes

$$F = QvB$$

*Verify that if B is expressed in n/a m, $\Phi$ can be expressed in n m/a.*

In the MKS system $F$ is in newtons, $Q$ is in coulombs, $v$ is in meters/second, and $B$ is in newtons/ampere meter (or webers/meter$^2$).

**Figure 20-5** The magnetic force acting on a charge moving in a magnetic field. (A) The charge is positive and the force is directed out of the page. (B) The charge is negative and the force is directed into the page.

Now consider that a length of conductor is used outside the magnetic flux to connect ends **a** and **b** of the copper wire in Figure 20-4, thus providing a closed-loop path for electron current. We shall call the length of wire linked with magnetic flux the *internal circuit* and the rest of the conducting path the *external circuit*.

When the straight conductor is pushed downward, as in Figure 20-4, electrons move from the negative end **a** through the external circuit to the positive end **b** and through the internal circuit from end **b** to end **a**. Over the external path from **a** to **b**, electrons transform the potential energy acquired in the internal circuit into kinetic energy that they expend in the external circuit. In the internal path, the electric force acting on the electrons from **a** to **b** is reduced below its equilibrium value because of the partial depletion of accumulated charges at **a** and **b**. A net magnetic force pumps electrons from **b** to **a** maintaining a potential difference across the internal circuit. The value of this potential difference is less than the open-circuit potential difference which, you will recall, was numerically equal to the induced emf.

## 20.5 The direction of induced current

The downward motion of the copper wire in Figure 20-4 is maintained by exerting a force on it in the direction of *v*. This force may be thought of as the action that generates the induced electron current in the closed circuit.

The relationship between the direction of an induced current and the action inducing it was recognized in 1834 by the German physicist Heinrich Friedrich Lenz (1804–1865). His discovery, now referred to as *Lenz's law,* is true of all induced currents. Because Lenz's law refers to induced currents, it applies only to closed circuits. **Lenz's law** states that *an induced current is in such a direction that it opposes the change that produced it.* Accordingly, the magnetic effect of the induced current in Figure 20-4 must be such that it opposes the downward force (the pushing action) applied to the conductor segment in the external field of the magnet.

We can readily visualize what this effect must be. A cross-sectional view of a conductor poised in a magnetic field is shown in Figure 20-6(A). The conductor corresponds to end **b** of the

## 20.6 Lenz's law

*Faraday discovered how to determine the direction of an induced current also, but he did not express it as clearly as Lenz.*

**Figure 20-6** Two interacting magnetic fields. The separate magnetic lines of the fields of the magnet and of the induced current (into the page) are shown in (A). The lines of the resultant field are shown in (B).

Motion

(A) Electron current in

Motion

(B) Electron current in

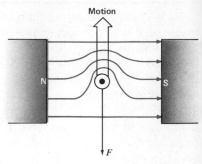

(A) Electron current out                          (B) Electron current out

**Figure 20-7** Two interacting magnetic fields. The separate magnetic lines of the fields of the magnet and of the induced current (out of the page) are shown in (A). The lines of the resultant field are shown in (B).

*See Section 19.9 for Ampère's rule.*

wire in Figure 20-4. It is part of a closed circuit that cannot be seen in this cross-sectional diagram. As the wire is pushed downward through the magnetic field, the induced electron current is directed into the page as indicated by the × symbol (tail of the arrow). By Ampère's rule for a straight conductor, the magnetic field of this induced current encircles the current in the counterclockwise sense. Similar diagrams in Figure 20-7 represent the effects of the wire being pulled up through the magnetic field. Here the induced electron current is directed out of the page as indicated by the · symbol (head of the arrow). The composite, or resultant, fields are shown in Figures 20-6(B) and 20-7(B). They suggest that the agent moving the conductor always experiences an opposing force.

The fact that an induced current always opposes the motion that induces it illustrates the conservation-of-energy principle. Work must be done to induce a current in a closed circuit. The energy expended comes from outside the system and is a result of work done by the external force required to keep the conductor segment moving. The induced current can produce heat or do mechanical or chemical work in the external circuit as electrons of high potential energy fall through a difference of potential.

# questions

GROUP A

1. What is the essential condition under which an emf is induced in a conductor?

2. What determines the magnitude of the emf induced in a length of conductor moving in a magnetic field?

3. In what two ways may the rate of change of magnetic flux linking a conductor be increased?

4. Distinguish between an induced emf and an induced current.

5. What is the source of the energy expended as work is done in a load by an induced current resulting from the movement of the conductor in a magnetic field?

6. State Lenz's law.

7. What is the meaning of the negative sign in the expression $E = -N\Delta\Phi/\Delta t$?

GROUP B

8. If a bar magnet is held in a vertical position with the **N** pole down and is dropped through a closed-loop coil whose plane is horizontal, what is the direction of the induced current as the **N** pole approaches the loop?

9. What is the direction of the force acting on the loop in Question 8 as the **N** pole approaches?

10. What physical quantities are measured in (a) webers, (b) webers per meter², (c) webers per second, (d) joules per coulomb?

11. Explain how Lenz's law illustrates conservation of energy.

12. Demonstrate that the product *Blv* is properly expressed in volts.

13. Demonstrate that the product *QvB* is properly expressed in newtons.

14. The **S** pole of a bar magnet is entering a solenoid. What is the direction of the flux lines of the induced current inside the solenoid?

15. A permanent magnet is moved away from a stationary coil as shown in the accompanying diagram. (a) What is the direction of the induced current in the coil? (Indicate direction of electron flow in the straight section of conductor below the coil.) (b) What magnetic polarity is produced across the coil by the induced current? (c) Justify your answers to (a) and (b).

Stationary coil     Motion

N     S

Permanent magnet

a     b

# problems

GROUP A

1. A coil of 325 turns moving perpendicular to the flux in a uniform magnetic field experiences a change in flux linkage of $1.15 \times 10^{-5}$ weber in 0.00100 s. What is the induced emf?

2. How many turns are required to produce an induced emf of 0.25 volt for a coil that experiences a change in flux linkage at the rate of $5.0 \times 10^{-3}$ weber per s?

3. A straight conductor $1\bar{0}$ cm long is moved through a magnetic field perpendicular to the flux at a velocity of 75 cm/s. If the flux density is 0.025 weber/m², what emf is induced in the conductor?

4. A coil of 75 turns and an area of 4.0 cm² is removed from the gap between the poles of a magnet having a uniform flux density of 1.5 wb/m² in 0.025 s. What voltage is induced across the coil?

5. A rod 15 cm long is perpendicular to a magnetic field of $4.5 \times 10^{-1}$ n/a m and is moved at right angles to the flux at the rate of $3\bar{0}$ cm/s. Find the emf induced in the rod.

# GENERATORS AND MOTORS

An emf is induced in a conductor whenever the conductor experiences a change in flux linkage. When the conductor is part of a closed circuit, an induced current can be detected in the circuit. By Lenz's law, work must be done to induce a current in a conducting circuit. Accordingly, this is a practical source of electric energy.

Moving a conductor up and down in a magnetic field is not a convenient method of inducing a current. A more practical way is to shape the conductor into a loop, the ends of which are connected to the external circuit by means of *slip rings,* and rotate it in the magnetic field. See Figure 20-8.

Such an arrangement is a simple *generator.* The loop across which an emf is induced is called the *armature.* The ends of the loop are connected to slip rings that rotate as the armature is turned. A graphite *brush* rides on each slip ring, connecting the armature to the external circuit. *An **electric generator** converts mechanical energy into electrical energy.* The essential compo-

## 20.7 The generator principle

**Figure 20-8**   A simple electric generator.

**Figure 20-9**   The left-hand generator rule.

nents of a generator are a *field magnet, an armature,* and *slip rings and brushes.*

The induced emf across the armature and the induced current in the closed circuit result from relative motion between the armature and the magnetic flux that effects a change in the flux linkage. Thus either the armature or the magnetic field may be rotated. In some commercial generators the field magnet is rotated and the armature is the stationary element.

According to Lenz's law, an induced current will appear in such a direction that the magnetic force on the electrons comprising the induced current opposes the motion producing it. The direction of induced current in the armature loop of a generator can be easily determined by use of a *left-hand rule* known as the *generator rule*. This rule takes into account Lenz's law and the fact that an electric current in a metal conductor consists of a flow of electrons. See Figure 20-9.

*The generator rule:* Extend the thumb, forefinger, and the middle finger of the left hand at right angles to each other. Let the forefinger point in the direction of the magnetic flux and the thumb in the direction the conductor is moving; the middle finger points in the direction of the induced electron current.

The two sides of the conducting loop in Figure 20-8 move through the magnetic flux in opposite directions when the armature is rotated. By applying the generator rule to each side of the loop, the direction of the induced current is shown to be toward one slip ring and away from the other. Thus a single-direction current loop is established in the closed circuit. As the direction of each side of the loop changes with respect to the flux, the direction of the induced current is reversed. As the armature rotates through a complete cycle, there are two such reversals in direction of the induced current.

In Figure 20-10 one side of a conducting loop rotating in a magnetic field is shown cross-sectionally in color while the other side is shown in black. In (A) the colored side of the loop is shown moving down and cutting through the flux. By the generator rule, the induced current is directed into the page. (The white × represents the tail of the arrow.) The motion of the black side of the loop induces a current directed out of the page. (The white dot represents the head of the arrow.)

An emf is induced in a conductor as a result of a change in the flux linking the conductor. In (B) both sides of the loop are moving parallel to the flux and there is no change in linkage. Therefore, no emf is induced across the loop and no current is in the closed circuit.

In (C) the black side of the loop is moving down and cutting through the flux so that the induced current is directed into the page. The colored side is moving up through the flux, thus the induced current is directed out of the page. The direction of the current in the circuit is the reverse of that in (A). A quarter cycle later, the emf again drops to zero and there is no current in the circuit. The emf induced across the conducting loop reaches a maximum value when the sides of the loop are moving perpendicular to the magnetic flux. See Section 20.2.

It is not difficult to see from Figure 20-10 that the magnitude of the induced emf across the conducting loop must vary from zero through a maximum and back to zero during a half cycle of rotation. The emf must then vary in magnitude in a similar manner, from zero through the same magnitude maximum and back to zero, during the second half cycle. However, polarity across

## 20.8 The simple a-c generator

**Figure 20-10** An emf is induced only when there is a change in the flux linking a conductor.

(A)                    (B)                    (C)

**Figure 20-11**  One cycle of operation of an a-c generator.

the loop is opposite. The emf across the loop thus *alternates* in polarity.

Similarly, the current in a circuit connected to the rotating armature by way of the slip rings alternates in direction: electrons flowing in one direction during one half cycle and in the opposite direction during the other half cycle. *A current that has one direction during part of a generating cycle and the opposite direction during the remainder of the cycle is called an* **alternating current,** *ac*. A generator that produces an alternating current must, of course, produce an alternating emf. See Figure 20-11.

Commercial electric power is usually supplied by the generation of alternating currents and voltages. Such power is referred to as *a-c power*. The expressions *a-c* and *d-c* are commonly used as prefixes to distinguish between alternating-current and direct-current properties: a-c voltage, d-c current are two examples.

## 20.9 Instantaneous current and voltage

The open-circuit voltage across a battery has a constant magnitude characteristic of the chemical makeup of the battery. The voltage across an armature rotating in a magnetic field, however, has no constant magnitude. It varies from zero through a maximum in one direction and back to zero during one half cycle. It then rises to a maximum in the opposite direction and falls back to zero during the other half cycle of armature rotation. At successive instants of time, different magnitudes of induced voltage exist across the rotating armature. *The magnitude of a varying voltage at any instant of time is called the* **instantaneous voltage,** *e*.

The maximum voltage, $E_{max}$, is obtained when the conductor is moving perpendicular to the magnetic flux because the rate of change of flux linking the conductor is maximum during this time. *If the armature is rotating at a constant rate in a magnetic field of uniform flux density, the magnitude of the induced voltage varies sinusoidally (as a sine wave) with respect to time.*

In Figure 20-12 a single loop is rotating in a uniform magnetic field. When the plane of the loop is perpendicular to the flux (**MN** of Figure 20-12), the conductors are moving parallel to the flux lines; the displacement angle of the loop is said to be zero. We shall refer to this angle between the plane of the loop and the perpendicular to the magnetic flux as $\theta$ (theta). When $\theta = 0°$ and $180°$, $e = 0$ v. When $\theta = 90°$, $e = E_{max}$; and when $\theta = 270°$, $e = -E_{max}$. These relationships are apparent from Figure 20-11. In general, the instantaneous voltage, $e$, varies with the sine of the displacement angle of the loop.

$$e = E_{max} \sin \theta$$

The current in the external circuit of a simple generator consisting of pure resistance will vary in a similar way; the *maximum current*, $I_{max}$, occurs when the induced voltage is maximum. From Ohm's law

$$I_{max} = \frac{E_{max}}{R}$$

The *instantaneous current*, $i$, is accordingly

$$i = \frac{e}{R}$$

but

$$e = E_{max} \sin \theta$$

so

$$i = \frac{E_{max}}{R} \sin \theta$$

and

$$i = I_{max} \sin \theta$$

**Figure 20-12** The instantaneous value of an induced voltage varies with the sine of the displacement angle of tho loop in the magnetic field.

---

The simple generator consists of a coil rotating in the magnetic field of a permanent magnet. Any small generator employing a permanent magnet is commonly called a *magneto*. Magnetos are often used in the ignition systems of gasoline engines for lawn mowers, motor-bikes, and boats.

The generator output is increased in a practical generator by increasing the number of turns on the armature or increasing the field strength. The field magnets of large generators are strong electromagnets; in a-c generators they are supplied with direct current from an auxiliary d-c generator called an *exciter*. See Figure 20-13.

The performance of large a-c generators is generally more satisfactory if the armature is stationary and the field rotates inside

**20.10 Practical a-c generators**

**Figure 20-13** The field of an alternating-current generator is produced by an electromagnet.

the armature. Such stationary armatures are referred to as *stators* and the rotating field magnets as *rotors*. Circuit current is taken from the stator at the high generated voltage without the use of slip rings and brushes. The exciter voltage, which is much lower than the armature voltage, is applied to the rotor through slip rings and brushes.

In a simple two-pole generator one cycle of operation produces one cycle or two alternations of induced emf, as shown in Figure 20-14. If the armature (or the field) rotates at the rate of 60 cycles per second, the frequency, *f,* of the generated voltage sine wave is 60 hertz and the period, *T*, is ¹/₆₀ second.

*The **frequency** of an alternating current or voltage is the number of cycles of current or voltage per second.* If the generator has a 4-pole field magnet, 2 cycles of emf are generated during 1 revolution of the armature or field. Such a generator turning at 30 rps would generate a 60 hz voltage. In general

$$f = \text{No. of pairs of poles} \times \text{revolution rate}$$

**Figure 20-14** A sine curve representing current or voltage generated by a single-loop armature rotating at a constant rate in a uniform magnetic field. Positions 0 through 12 on the graph correspond to positions of the rotating armature in the magnetic field, as shown to the left.

(A) Three-phase generator    (B) Voltage output    (C) Voltage vector diagram

**Figure 20-15** The principle of the three-phase alternator. Armature coils schematically diagrammed in (A) are spaced 120° apart generating peak voltage output in three phases as shown in (B). Part (C) shows this output as a vector diagram.

Practically all commercial power is generated by *three-phase* generators having three armature coils spaced symmetrically and producing emfs spaced 120° apart. The coils are usually connected so that the currents are carried by three conductors.

It is evident from Figure 20-15(B) that three-phase power is smoother than the single-phase power of Figure 20-14. Electric power is transmitted by a three-phase circuit but is commonly supplied to the consumer by a single phase circuit.

The output of an a-c generator is not suitable for circuits that require a direct current. However, the a-c generator can be made to supply a *unidirectional* current to the external circuit by connecting the armature loops to a *commutator* instead of slip rings. *A **commutator** is a split ring, each segment of which is connected to an end of a corresponding armature loop.*

The current and voltage generated in the armature are alternating, as we would expect. By means of the commutator, the connections to the external circuit are reversed at the same instant that the direction of the induced emf reverses in the loop. See Figure 20-16. The alternating current in the armature appears as a *pulsating* direct current in the external circuit, and a pulsating d-c voltage appears across the load. A graph of the instan-

## 20.11 The d-c generator

**Figure 20-16 (left)** A split-ring commutator of two segments.

**Figure 20-17 (right)** The variation of current or voltage with time in the external circuit of a simple generator with a two-segment commutator.

taneous values of the pulsating current from a generator with a two-segment commutator plotted as a function of time is shown in Figure 20-17. A graph of the voltage across a resistance load would have a similar form. Compare this pulsating d-c output to the a-c output of the generator shown in Figure 20-14.

To secure from a d-c generator a more constant voltage and one having an instantaneous value that approaches the average value of the emf induced in the entire armature, many coils are wound on the armature. Each coil is connected to a different pair of commutator segments. The two brushes of each commutator segment are positioned so that they are in contact with successive pairs of commutator segments at the time when the induced emf in their respective coils is in the $E_{max}$ region. See Figure 20-18.

**Figure 20-18** The output of a d-c generator having three armature coils and a six-segment commutator is fairly constant.

## 20.12 Field excitation

Most d-c generators use part of the induced power to energize their field magnets and are said to be *self-exciting*. The field magnets may be connected in series with the armature loops so that all of the generator current passes through the coil windings. In the *series-wound* generator an increase in the load increases the magnetic field and consequently the induced emf. See Figure 20-19.

**(A) Pictorial diagram**          **(B) Circuit diagram**

**Figure 20-19** A series-wound d-c generator.

The field magnets may also be connected in parallel with the armature so that only a portion of the generated current is used to excite the field. In this *shunt-wound* generator, Figure 20-20, an increase in load results in a decrease in the field and hence a decrease in the induced emf.

By using a combination of both series and shunt windings to excite the field magnets, the potential difference across the external circuit of a d-c generator may be maintained fairly constant; an increase in load causes an increase in current in the series windings and a decrease in current in the parallel windings.

(A) Pictorial diagram

(B) Circuit diagram

**Figure 20-20** A shunt-wound d-c generator.

With the proper number of turns of each type of winding, a constant flux density can be maintained under varying loads. A compound-wound generator is shown in Figure 20-21.

(A) Pictorial diagram

(B) Circuit diagram

**Figure 20-21** A compound-wound d-c generator.

We can think of the armature turns as the source of emf in the d-c generator circuit. If the field magnet were separately excited, this emf would appear across the armature terminals on open-circuit operation since there would be no induced armature current.

However in a self-excited generator the armature circuit is completed through the field windings. The resistance of the armature turns, $r_a$, is in this current loop, and a situation analogous to that of a battery with internal resistance furnishing current to an external circuit results. A potential drop, $I_a r_a$, of opposite polarity to the induced emf, must appear across the armature. The armature potential difference, $V$, is

$$V = E - I_a r_a$$

**20.13 Ohm's law and generator circuits**

**Figure 20-22** The resistance circuit of a series-wound d-c generator.

The resistance circuit of the series-wound generator is shown in Figure 20-22. The resistance of the field windings, $R_f$, is in series with the internal resistance of the armature and the load resistance so that the armature current is in all three resistances.

In Figure 20-20, the resistance of the shunt windings is in parallel with the load. The resistance circuit of a shunt-wound generator is diagrammed in Figure 20-23, with the resistance of the shunt windings shown as $R_f$. The total current of the circuit, $I_a$, must be in $r_a$, producing an $I_a r_a$ drop across the armature. The potential difference, $V$, which has been shown to be $E - I_a r_a$, then appears across the network consisting of $R_f$ and $R_L$ in parallel. The following Ohm's law relationships hold:

$$I_f = \frac{V}{R_f}$$

$$I_L = \frac{V}{R_L}$$

**Figure 20-23** The resistance circuit of a shunt-wound d-c generator.

and

$$I_a = I_f + I_L$$

The total electric power in the generator circuit, $P_T$, derived from the mechanical energy source that turns the armature, is the product of the armature current, $I_a$, and the induced emf, $E$.

$$P_T = E I_a$$

Some of this power is dissipated as heat in the armature resistance, and some is dissipated in the field windings; the remaining power is delivered to the load.

$$P_T = P_a + P_f + P_L$$

or

$$E I_a = I_a{}^2 r_a + I_f{}^2 R_f + I_L{}^2 R_L$$

The application of these relationships to the d-c shunt-wound generator is illustrated in the example that follows.

Figure 20-24 shows the resistance circuit of a compound-wound generator. Observe the similarity between this circuit and the resistance network shown in Figure 17-20, Section 17.10. How would you proceed to analyze this resistance circuit of the compound-wound d-c generator?

**Figure 20-24** The resistance circuit of a compound-wound d-c generator.

**EXAMPLE** | *The armature resistance of a shunt-wound generator is 0.50 ohm, the resistance of the shunt winding is 60.0 ohms, and 0.960 kilowatt is delivered to a 15.0-ohm load. (a) What is the potential difference across the load? (b) What is the magnitude of the armature current? (c) What is the emf of the generator?*

SOLUTION | The circuit of Figure 20-23 applies.

(a) $P_L = I_L^2 R_L = \dfrac{V_L^2}{R_L}$

$V_L = \sqrt{P_L R_L} = \sqrt{960 \text{ w}} \times 15.0 \ \Omega$

$V_L = 120 \text{ v}$

(b) $I_a = I_f + I_L$

$I_f = \dfrac{V_f}{R_f}$ and $I_L = \dfrac{V_L}{R_L}$

But $V_L = V_f = V$

$I_a = \dfrac{V}{R_f} + \dfrac{V}{R_L} = \dfrac{120 \text{ v}}{60.0 \ \Omega} + \dfrac{120 \text{ v}}{15.0 \ \Omega}$

$I_a = 2.00 \text{ a} + 8.00 \text{ a} = 10.00 \text{ a}$

(c) $V = E - I_a r_a$

$E = V + I_a r_a = 120 \text{ v} + (10.00 \text{ a} \times 0.50 \ \Omega)$

$E = 125 \text{ v}$

---

We have learned that a current is induced in a conducting loop when the conductor is moving in a magnetic field so that the magnetic flux linking the loop is changing. This is the generator principle. By Lenz's law, we have seen that work must be done against a magnetic force as an induced current is generated in the conducting loop. Recall that an induced current always produces a magnetic force that opposes the force causing the motion by which the current is induced.

Instead of employing a mechanical effort to move a conductor poised in the magnetic field, suppose a current is *supplied* to the conductor from an external source. The magnetic field is distorted, as discussed in Section 20.6, and the resulting magnetic force tends to expel the conductor from the magnetic field. This action is known as the *motor effect,* and it is illustrated in Figure 20-25.

## 20.14 The motor effect

**Figure 20-25** A visual representation of the motor effect.

Expulsion force

N   X   S

(A) Electron current in

N   •   S

Expulsion force

(B) Electron current out

**Figure 20-26** The resultant magnetic field of a current loop in the external field of a magnet gives a visual suggestion of the forces acting on the loop.

**Figure 20-27** The torque on a current loop in a magnetic field is proportional to the perpendicular distance between the forces acting on the conductors.

**Figure 20-28** The right-hand motor rule.

If a current is supplied to an armature loop poised in a uniform magnetic field, as in Figure 20-26, the field around each conductor is distorted. A force acts on each side of the loop proportional to the flux density and the current in the armature loop. These two forces, equal in magnitude but opposite in direction, constitute a *couple* and produce a torque, *T,* that causes the armature loop to rotate about its axis. The magnitude of this torque is equal to the product of the force and the *perpendicular* distance between the two forces.

It is evident from Figure 20-26 that the perpendicular distance between the torque-producing forces is maximum when the conductors are moving perpendicular to the magnetic flux. This distance is equal to the width of the armature loop. When the loop is in any other position with respect to the flux lines, the perpendicular distance between the forces is less than the width of the loop, and consequently the resulting torque must be less than the maximum value. See Figure 20-27.

We shall refer to the angle between the plane of the loop and the magnetic flux as angle $\alpha$ (alpha). When the angle is zero, the plane of the loop is parallel to the flux lines and the torque is maximum.

$$T_{\max} = Fw$$

where $F$ is the magnetic force acting on either conductor and $w$ is the width of the conducting loop.

As the armature turns, the angle $\alpha$ approaches $90°$ and the torque diminishes since the perpendicular distance between the couple approaches zero. In general, the perpendicular distance between the forces acting on the two conductors is equal to $w \cos \alpha$, as shown in Figure 20-27. Hence

$$T = Fw \cos \alpha$$

When the plane of the loop is perpendicular to the magnetic flux, angle $\alpha$ is $90°$, the cosine of $90° = 0$, and the torque is zero. As the inertia of the conductor carries it beyond this point, a torque develops that reverses the motion of the conductor and returns it to the zero-torque position. In order to prevent this action, the direction of the current in the armature loop must be reversed at the proper instant. To reverse the current when the neutral position is reached, the conducting loop terminates in a commutator.

An electric motor performs the reverse function of a generator. *Electric energy is converted to mechanical energy* using the same electromagnetic principles employed in the generator. We can determine the direction of the motion of the conductor on a motor armature by use of a *right-hand rule* known as the *motor rule*. It is illustrated in Figure 20-28.

*The motor rule:* Extend the thumb, forefinger, and middle finger of the right hand at right angles to each other. Let the forefinger point in the direction of the magnetic flux and the middle finger in the direction of the electron current; the thumb points in the direction of the motion of the conductor.

---

## 20.15 Back emf in a motor

The simple d-c motor does not differ essentially from a generator; it has a field magnet, an armature, and a commutator ring. In fact, *the operating motor also acts as a generator.* As the conducting loop of the armature rotates in a magnetic field, an emf is induced across the armature turn. The magnitude of this emf depends on the speed of rotation of the armature.

Suppose an incandescent lamp and an ammeter are connected in series with the armature of a small battery-driven motor, as shown in Figure 20-29. If the motor armature is held so that it cannot rotate as the circuit is closed, the lamp glows and the circuit current is indicated on the meter. Releasing the armature allows the motor to gain speed, and the lamp dims; the ammeter indicates a smaller current.

According to Lenz's law, the induced emf must oppose the motion inducing it. The emf induced by the generator action of a motor consequently opposes the voltage applied to the armature. *Such an induced emf is called the **back emf** of the motor.*

**Figure 20-29** Demonstrating the back emf of a motor.

**(A) Motor stalled**

**(B) Motor running**

The difference between the applied voltage and the back emf determines the current in the motor circuit.

A motor running at full speed under no load generates a back emf nearly equal to the applied voltage; thus a small current is required in the circuit. The more slowly the armature turns, the smaller is the back emf and consequently the larger is the voltage difference and the circuit current. A motor starting under a full load has a large initial current that decreases due to the generation of a back emf as the motor gains speed.

The induced emf in a generator is equal to the terminal voltage *plus* the voltage drop across the armature resistance.

$$E = V + I_a r_a$$

In the motor, the induced emf is equal to the terminal voltage *minus* the voltage drop across the armature resistance.

$$E = V - I_a r_a$$

Hence, the back emf in a motor must always be less than the voltage impressed across the armature terminals.

## 20.16 Practical d-c motors

A simple motor with a single armature coil would be impractical for many purposes because it has neutral positions and a pulsating torque. In practical motors a large number of coils is used in the armature; in fact there is little difference in the construction of motor and generator armatures. Multiple-pole field coils can be used to aid in the production of a uniform torque. The amount of torque produced in any given motor is proportional to the armature current and to the flux density.

Depending on the method used to excite the field magnets, practical d-c motors are of three general types. These are *series*, *shunt*, and *compound* motors. The excitation methods are similar to those of the d-c generators discussed in Section 20.12.

## 20.17 Practical a-c motors

Nearly all commercial distributors of electric power supply alternating-current power. Except for certain specialized applications, a-c motors are far more common than d-c motors. Much of the theory and technology of a-c motors is complex. We will briefly summarize the general characteristics of three common types of a-c motors: *the universal motor, the induction motor,* and *the synchronous motor*.

*1. The universal motor.* Any small d-c series motor can be operated from an a-c source. When this is done, the currents in the field windings and armature reverse direction simultaneously, maintaining torque in the same direction throughout the operating cycle. Heat losses in the field windings are extensive, however, unless certain design changes are incorporated into the motor. With laminated pole pieces and special field windings, small series motors operate satisfactorily on either a-c or d-c power. They are known as *universal* motors.

2. *The induction motor.* Induction motors are the most widely used a-c motors. This is because they are rugged, simple to build, and well adapted to constant speed requirements. They have two essential parts—a stator of field coils and a rotor. The rotor is usually built of copper bars laid in slotted, laminated iron cores. The ends of the copper bars are shorted by a copper ring to form a cylindrical cage; this common type is known as a *squirrel-cage* rotor.

By using three pairs of poles and a three-phase current, the magnetic field of the stator is made to rotate electrically and currents are induced in the rotor. In accordance with Lenz's law, the rotor will then turn so as to follow the rotating field. Since induction requires relative motion between the conductor and the field, the rotor must *slip* or lag behind the field in order for a torque to be developed. An increase in the load causes a greater slip, a greater induced current, and consequently a greater torque.

For its operation, an induction motor depends on a rotating magnetic field. Thus a single-phase induction motor is not self-starting because the magnetic field of its stator merely reverses periodically and does not rotate electrically. Single-phase induction motors can be made self-starting by a *split-phase winding,* a *capacitor,* a *shading coil,* or a *repulsion winding.* The name of the motor usually indicates the auxiliary method used for starting it.

3. *The synchronous motor.* We can illustrate the principle of synchronism by placing a thoroughly magnetized compass needle in a rotating magnetic field. The magnetized needle aligns itself with the magnetic field and rotates in synchronization with the rotating field.

The synchronous motor is a constant speed motor, running in synchronism with the a-c generator that supplies the stator current. However, it is not self-starting; the rotor must be brought up to synchronous speed by auxiliary means.

Electric clocks are operated by small single-phase synchronous motors that start automatically as a form of induction motor. Once synchronism is attained, they run as synchronous motors. Electric power companies maintain very accurate control of the 60-hz frequency of commercial power now that electric clocks are in general use.

Large industrial synchronous motors use an electromagnetic rotor supplied with d-c power, and a stator supplied with three-phase a-c power. The synchronous motors are used where the speed requirements are very exacting.

**Figure 20-30** A cut-away view of an induction motor.

# questions

GROUP A

1. What are the essential components of an electric generator?
2. State the rule that helps us determine the direction of the induced current in the armature loops of a generator.
3. Distinguish between a direct current and an alternating current.
4. Under what circumstances does a simple generator produce a sine-wave variation of induced voltage?
5. What does the term $\theta$ (theta) represent in the expression $e = E_{max} \sin \theta$?
6. (a) What is a magneto? (b) For what is it used?
7. What is the function of an *exciter* in the generation of a-c power?
8. (a) What is meant by the frequency of an alternating current? (b) Under what circumstances will the frequency of a generated current be the same as the rps of the armature?
9. How can a generator be made to supply a direct current to its external circuit?
10. In what way is the output of a d-c generator different from the d-c output of a battery?
11. (a) What methods are used to energize the field magnets of d-c generators? (b) Draw a circuit diagram of each method.
12. What are the three power-consuming parts of a d-c generator circuit?
13. What is meant by the term $\alpha$ (alpha) in the torque expression $T = Fw \cos \alpha$?

14. State the rule that helps us determine the direction of motion of the armature loops of a motor.
15. (a) What is meant by back emf? (b) How is it induced in an electric motor?
16. What two quantities influence the amount of torque produced in a motor?
17. What are the three common types of a-c motors?

GROUP B

18. What is the advantage of having a 4- or 6-pole field magnet in a generator producing a 60-hz output?
19. How does an increase in the load on a series-wound d-c generator affect the induced emf? Explain.
20. How does an increase in the load on a shunt-wound d-c generator affect the induced emf? Explain.
21. How is torque produced on the armature loops of a motor?
22. Why is it true that an operating motor is also a generator?
23. The torque in a series motor increases as the load increases. Explain.
24. Explain why a single-phase induction motor is not self-starting.
25. Why are synchronous motors used in electric clocks?
26. Two conducting loops, identical except that one is silver and the other aluminum, are rotated in a magnetic field. In which case is the larger torque required to turn the loop?

# problems

GROUP A

1. A series-wound d-c generator turning at its rated speed develops an emf of 28 volts. The current in the external circuit is 16 amperes and the armature resistance is 0.25 ohm. What is the potential drop across the external circuit?
2. A d-c generator delivers $15\bar{0}$ amperes at $22\bar{0}$ volts when operating at normal speed connected to a resistance load. The total losses are $32\bar{0}0$ watts. Determine the efficiency of the generator.
3. A shunt-wound generator has an armature resistance of 0.15 ohm and a shunt winding of 75.0-ohms resistance. It delivers 18.0 kw at $24\bar{0}$ v to a load. (a) Draw the circuit diagram. (b) What is the generator emf? (c) What is the total power developed by the armature?

4. A magnetic force of 3.5 n acts on one conductor of a conducting loop in a magnetic field. A second force of equal magnitude but opposite direction acts on the opposite conductor of the loop. The conducting loop is 15 cm wide. Find the torque acting on the conducting loop (a) when the plane of the loop is parallel to the magnetic flux, (b) after the loop has rotated through 30°.
5. The maximum torque that acts on the armature loop of a motor is 10 m n. At what positions of the loop with respect to the magnetic flux will the torque be 5 m n?
6. A shunt-wound motor connected across a 117-v line generates a back emf of 112 v when the armature current is $1\bar{0}$ a. What is the armature resistance?

# INDUCTANCE

An emf is induced across a conductor in a magnetic field when there is a change in the flux linking the conductor. In our study of the generator we observed that an induced emf appears across the armature loop whether the conductors move across a stationary field or the magnetic flux moves across stationary conductors. *In either action there is relative motion between conductors and magnetic flux.*

This relative motion can be produced in another way. By connecting a battery to a solenoid through a contact key, an electromagnet is produced that has a magnetic field similar to that of a bar magnet. When the key is open, there is no magnetic field. As the key is closed, the magnetic field builds up from zero to some steady value determined by the number of ampere-turns. The magnetic flux spreads out and permeates the region about the coil. *An expanding magnetic field is a field in motion.* When the key in the solenoid circuit is opened, the magnetic flux collapses to zero. *A collapsing magnetic field is also a field in motion.* Its motion, however, is in the opposite sense to that of the expanding field.

Suppose the solenoid is inserted into a second coil whose terminals are connected to a galvanometer as in Figure 20-32. The coil connected to a current source is called the *primary;* the coil connected to the load is called the *secondary.* At the instant the contact key is closed, a deflection shows on the galvanometer. There is no deflection, however, while the key remains closed. When the key is opened, a galvanometer deflection again occurs, but in the opposite direction. An emf is induced across the secondary turns whenever the flux linking the secondary is increasing or decreasing.

The relative motion between conductors and flux is in one direction when the field expands and in the opposite direction when the field collapses. Thus the emf induced across the secondary as the key is closed is of opposite polarity to that induced as the key is opened. The more rapid this relative motion, the greater the magnitude of the induced emf; the greater the number of turns in the secondary, the greater the magnitude of the induced emf. A soft iron core placed in the primary greatly increases the flux density and the induced emf.

Two circuits arranged so that a change in magnitude of current in one causes an emf to be induced in the other show *mutual inductance. The **mutual inductance**, M, of two circuits is the ratio of the induced emf in one circuit to the rate of change of current in the other circuit.*

The unit of mutual inductance in the MKS system is called the *henry,* h, after the American physicist Joseph Henry. The mutual inductance of two circuits is *one henry* if *one volt of emf*

## 20.18 Mutual inductance

**Figure 20-31**  The 12-volt induction coil of an automobile shown out of its housing. The primary, secondary, and soft iron core are visible.

**Figure 20-32**  Varying the current in the primary induces an emf in the secondary.

**Figure 20-33** Joseph Henry, the American physicist for whom the unit of inductance is named.

is induced in the secondary when the current in the primary changes at a rate of *one ampere per second*.

$$M = \frac{-E_S}{\Delta I_P / \Delta t}$$

Here $M$ is the mutual inductance of the two circuits in henrys, $E_S$ is the average induced emf across the secondary in volts, and $\Delta I_P / \Delta t$ is the time rate of change of current in the primary in amperes per second. The minus sign indicates that the induced voltage opposes the change in current according to Lenz's law. From this equation the emf induced in the secondary becomes

$$E_S = -M \frac{\Delta I_P}{\Delta t}$$

See the following example.

**EXAMPLE**

*Two coils have a mutual inductance of 1.25 henrys. Find the average emf induced in the secondary if the current in the primary builds up to 10.0 amperes in 0.0250 second after the switch is closed.*

**SOLUTION**

The primary current must build up from zero to 10.0 amperes during 0.0250 s, so

$$\frac{\Delta I_P}{\Delta t} = \frac{10.0 \text{ a}}{0.0250 \text{ s}}$$

The mutual inductance is given as 1.25 h

$$E_S = -M \frac{\Delta I_P}{\Delta t} = -1.25 \text{ h} \times \frac{10.0 \text{ a}}{0.0250 \text{ s}}$$

$E_S = -50\overline{0}$ v, the emf induced in the secondary

Observe that since $h = \dfrac{v}{a/s}$, the units $h \times \dfrac{a}{s} = \dfrac{v \times s \times a}{a \times s} = v$

---

**20.19 Self-inductance**

Suppose a coil is formed by winding many turns of insulated copper wire on an iron core and connected in a circuit to a 6-volt battery, a neon lamp, and a switch. See Figure 20-34. Since the neon lamp requires about 85v-dc to conduct, it acts initially as an open switch in a 6-volt circuit.

When the switch is closed, a conducting path is completed through the coil; the fact that the lamp does not light is evidence that it is not in the conducting circuit. If now the switch is quickly opened, the neon lamp conducts for an instant, producing a flash of light. This means that the lamp is subjected to a potential difference considerably higher than that of the battery. What is the source of this higher voltage?

Any change in the magnitude of current in a conductor causes a change in the magnetic flux about the conductor. If the conductor is formed into a coil, a changing magnetic flux about one turn cuts across adjacent turns and induces a voltage across them. According to Lenz's law, the polarity of this induced voltage acts to oppose the motion of the flux inducing it. The sum of the induced voltages of all the turns constitutes a *counter* emf across the coil.

If a rise in current with its expanding magnetic flux is responsible for the counter emf, this rise in current will be opposed. Therefore, the counter emf is opposite in polarity to the applied voltage. When the switch in Figure 20-34 was closed, the rise in current from zero to the steady-state magnitude was opposed by the counter emf induced across the coil. Once the current reached a steady value, the magnetic field ceased to expand and the opposing voltage fell to zero.

If a fall in current with its collapsing flux is responsible for the induced voltage across the coil, the fall in current is opposed. In this case the induced emf has the same polarity as the applied voltage and tends to sustain the current in the circuit. A very rapid collapse of the magnetic field may induce a very high voltage. *It is the change in current, not the current itself, that is opposed by the induced emf.* It follows, then, that the greater the rate of change of current in a circuit containing a coil, the greater is the magnitude of the induced emf across the coil that opposes this change of current.

The property of a coil that causes a counter emf to be induced across it by the change in current in it is known as *self-inductance*, or simply *inductance*. The **self-inductance**, L, of a coil is the *ratio of the induced emf across the coil to the rate of change of current in the coil.*

The unit of self-inductance in the MKS system is the *henry*, the same unit used for mutual inductance. Self-inductance is *one henry* if *one volt of emf* is induced across the coil when the current in the circuit changes at the rate of *one ampere per second*.

$$L = \frac{-E}{\Delta I / \Delta t}$$

Here $L$ is the inductance in henrys, $E$ is the emf induced in volts, and $\Delta I / \Delta t$ is the rate of change of current in amperes per second. The minus sign merely shows that the induced voltage is in opposition to the change of current. From this expression the induced emf is given by

$$E = -L \frac{\Delta I}{\Delta t}$$

**Figure 20-34** A circuit to demonstrate self-inductance.

The equation for inductance, $L$, is analogous to the defining equation for capacitance, $C$, as expressed in Section 16.14.

$$C = \frac{Q}{V}$$

The presence of a magnetic field in a coil conducting an electric current corresponds to the presence of an electric field in a charged capacitor.

Once a coil has been wound, its inductance is a constant property that depends on *the number of turns, the diameter of the coil, the length of coil,* and *the nature of the core.* Because of its property of inductance, a coil is commonly called an *inductor*.

Inductance in electricity is analogous to inertia in mechanics: the property of matter that opposes a *change* of velocity. If a mass is at rest, its inertia opposes a change that imparts a velocity; if the mass has a velocity, its inertia opposes a change that brings it to rest. The flywheel in mechanics illustrates the property of inertia. We know that energy is stored in a flywheel as its angular velocity is increased and is removed as its angular velocity is decreased.

In an electric circuit inductance has no effect as long as the current is steady. An inductance does, however, oppose any change in the circuit current. An increase in current is opposed by the inductance; energy is stored in its magnetic field since work is done by the source against the counter emf induced. A decrease in current is opposed by the inductance; energy is removed from its field, tending to sustain the current. *We can think of inductance as imparting a flywheel effect in a circuit having a varying current.* This concept is very important in alternating-current circuit considerations.

## 20.20 Inductors in series and parallel

The total inductance of a circuit consisting of inductors in series or parallel can be calculated in the same manner as total resistance. When inductors are connected in series the total inductance, $L_T$, is equal to the sum of the individual inductances, providing there is no mutual inductance between them.

$$L_T = L_1 + L_2 + L_3 + \text{etc.}$$

However, when two inductors are in series and arranged so that the magnetic flux of each links the turns of the other, the total inductance is

$$L_T = L_1 + L_2 \pm 2M$$

The $\pm$ sign is necessary in the general expression because the counter emf induced in one coil by the flux of the other may either aid or oppose the counter emf of self-induction. The two coils can be connected either in series "aiding" or series "opposing," depending on the manner in which their turns are wound.

Inductors connected in parallel so that each is unaffected by the magnetic field of another provide a total inductance according to the following general expression:

$$\frac{1}{L_T} = \frac{1}{L_1} + \frac{1}{L_2} + \frac{1}{L_3} + \text{etc.}$$

See Figure 20-35 for schematic representation of these series and parallel connections for inductors.

**Figure 20-35** Inductors in series (A) and in parallel (B).

## 20.21 The transformer

In principle the transformer consists of two coils, a primary and a secondary, electrically insulated from each other and wound on the same ferromagnetic core. Electric energy is transferred from the primary to the secondary by means of the magnetic flux in the core. A transformer is shown in its simplest form in Figure 20-36.

Refer to Figure 20-14, in which the current sine wave produced by the a-c generator is given. The current is changing at its maximum rate as it passes through zero. Consequently, the emf induced across the secondary winding of a transformer is maximum as the primary current passes through zero. The polarity of the secondary emf reverses each time the primary current passes through a positive or negative maximum, since at these instants the current is changing at its minimum rate.

In a power transformer, a *closed* core is used to provide a continuous path for the magnetic flux, ensuring that practically all the primary flux links secondary turns. Since the same flux

**(A) Step-up transformer**

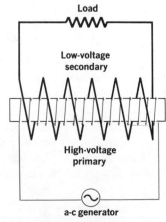

**(B) Step-down transformer**

**Figure 20-36** The transformer in its simplest forms.

links both primary and secondary turns, the same emf per turn is induced in each and the ratio of secondary to primary emf is equal to the ratio of secondary to primary turns. Neglecting losses, we may assume the terminal voltages to be equal to the corresponding emfs. Thus

$$\frac{V_S}{V_P} = \frac{N_S}{N_P}$$

where $V_S$ and $V_P$ are the secondary and primary terminal voltages and $N_S$ and $N_P$ are the number of turns in the secondary and primary windings respectively.

If there are 20 turns in the secondary winding for every turn of the primary, the transformer is said to have a *turns ratio* of 20.

$$\textbf{Turns ratio} = \frac{N_S}{N_P} = \frac{20}{1} = 20$$

If the primary voltage is 110 volts, the secondary terminal voltage is 2200 volts and the transformer is called a *step-up transformer*. If the connections are reversed and the coil with the larger number of turns is made the primary, the transformer becomes a *step-down transformer*. The same primary voltage now produces a voltage across the secondary of 5.5 volts.

It can be shown that when power is delivered to a load in the secondary circuit, the product of the secondary current and secondary turns is essentially equal to the product of the primary current and primary turns.

$$I_S N_S = I_P N_P$$

or

$$\frac{I_S}{I_P} = \frac{N_P}{N_S}$$

Thus when the voltage is stepped up, the current is stepped down; there is no power gain as a result of transformer action. Ideally primary and secondary power are equal, but actually there are power losses as in any machine.

The efficiencies of practical transformers are high and constant over a wide power range. Transformer efficiencies above 95% are common. Efficiency can be expressed as the ratio of the power dissipated in the secondary circuit to the power used in the primary.

$$\textbf{Efficiency} = \frac{P_S}{P_P} \times 100\%$$

**Figure 20-37**  External view, low-voltage side of a power transformer.

While transformer efficiencies are high, the transfer of energy from the primary circuit to the secondary circuit does not occur without some loss. We shall consider two types: *copper losses* and *eddy-current losses*. They represent wasted energy and appear as heat.

*1. Copper losses.* These losses result from the resistance of the copper wires in the primary and secondary turns. Copper losses are $I^2R$ heat losses. They cannot be avoided.

*2. Eddy-current losses.* When a mass of conducting metal is moved in a magnetic field or is subjected to a changing magnetic flux, induced currents circulate in the mass. These closed loops of induced current circulating in planes perpendicular to the magnetic flux are known as *eddy currents*.

Eddy currents in motor and generator armatures and transformer cores produce heat due to the $I^2R$ losses in the resistance of the iron. They are induced currents that do no useful work, and they waste energy by opposing the change that induces them according to Lenz's law. Eddy-current losses are reduced by *laminating* the armature frames and cores. Thin sheets of metal with insulated surfaces are used to build up the armatures and cores. The laminations are set in planes parallel to the magnetic flux so that the eddy-current loops are confined to the width of the individual laminations. The high resistance associated with the narrow width of the individual laminations effectively reduces the induced currents and thus the $I^2R$ heating losses.

## 20.22 Transformer losses

*Recall that resistance is inversely proportional to cross-sectional area.*

# summary

An emf is induced in a conductor when relative motion between the conductor and a magnetic field produces a change in the flux linkage. The greater the rate of relative motion, the greater is the magnitude of the induced emf. If the conductor is part of a closed circuit, an electron current is induced in the circuit. The direction of an induced current is always in accord with Lenz's law.

An electric generator converts mechanical energy into electric energy. The direction of induced electron current in the armature turns is determined by use of the left-hand generator rule. The generator induces a sinusoidal emf across the armature turns. The current in the armature circuit alternates. The frequency of the generated current is expressed in hertz; one hertz is equivalent to one cycle per second. An a-c generator may be modified for a pulsating d-c output. The d-c generator is self-excited.

The electric motor converts electric energy into mechanical energy. The motor effect is the result of an electric current in a magnetic field; it is the reverse of the generator effect. The direction of motion of the armature turns is determined by the use of the right-hand motor rule. An electric motor produces a back emf that subtracts from the applied voltage. Practical d-c motors are of three types: series, shunt, and compound wound. Three common types of a-c motors are the universal motor, the induction motor, and the synchronous motor. Of these, the induction motor is most widely used.

If a change in current in one circuit induces an emf in a second circuit, the two have a property of mutual inductance. An emf is induced across a coil by a change of current in the coil; this property is known as self-inductance. The unit of inductance is the henry. The induced emf across a given inductance depends on the time rate of change of current in the inductance. The property of inductance is described as a kind of electric inertia.

Transformers are alternating-current devices. Primary and secondary windings have a common core. For a given primary voltage, the turns ratio determines the secondary voltage. The transformer may either step up or step down the a-c voltage of the primary circuit. Efficient and economical distribution of a-c power is possible through the use of the transformer principle.

# questions

GROUP A

1. Define (a) mutual inductance, (b) self-inductance.
2. What types of losses occur in a transformer?
3. What is the effect on the inductance of a coil when an iron core is inserted?
4. Why is a closed core used in a power transformer?
5. If an ideal transformer triples the voltage, how does the secondary current compare with the primary current?

GROUP B

6. Why is an inductor in an electric circuit said to impart a flywheel effect?
7. Why is a transformer considered to be an a-c circuit device?

8. The primary of a step-up transformer with negligible losses is connected to a source of emf and the secondary is connected to a resistance load. What is the relationship between primary and secondary (a) current, (b) power, and (c) number of turns?
9. Explain why the galvanometer in Figure 20-32 indicates a current in the secondary at the time the key in the primary circuit is closed or opened but not while it remains closed.
10. The voltage induced across the secondary of an ideal transformer is ten times the voltage applied across the primary. Explain why there is no power gain in the secondary circuit.

# problems

GROUP B

1. A step-up transformer is used on a 120-volt line to provide a potential difference of 2400 volts. If the primary has 75 turns, how many turns must the secondary have (neglecting losses)?
2. An initial rise in current in a coil occurs at the rate of 7.5 a/s at the instant a potential difference of 16.5 v is applied across it. (a) What is the self-inductance of the coil? (b) At the same instant a potential difference of $5\overline{0}$ v is induced across an adjacent coil. Find the mutual inductance of the two coils.
3. A coil with an inductance of 1.2 h and a resistance of 65 ohms is connected across an $8\overline{0}$-v d-c line. What is the rate of current rise at the instant it is connected to the line? (Suggestion: Consider the inductance and resistance of the coil to be in series.)
4. A coil with an inductance of 0.42 h and a resistance of 25 ohms is connected across a 110-v d-c line. What is the rate of current rise (a) at the instant the switch is closed, (b) at the instant the current reaches 85% of its steady-state value?

5. A 5:1 step-down transformer with negligible losses is connected to a $12\overline{0}$-v a-c source. The secondary circuit has a resistance of 15.0 ohms. (a) What is the potential difference across the secondary? (b) What is the secondary current? (c) How much power is dissipated in the secondary resistance? (d) What is the primary current?
6. Assume that the transformer of Problem 5 is replaced by one having an efficiency of 92.5%. What is the primary current?
7. A transformer with a primary of $40\overline{0}$ turns is connected across a 120-v a-c line. The secondary circuit has a potential difference of $300\overline{0}$ v. The secondary current is 60.0 ma and the primary current is 1.85 a. (a) How many turns are in the secondary winding? (b) What is the transformer efficiency?
8. A $27\overline{0}$-ohm resistor, a 2.50-h coil, and a switch are connected in series across a 12.0-v battery. At a certain instant after the switch is closed the current is 20.0 ma. What is the potential difference (a) across the resistor? (b) across the inductor? (c) What is the rate of change of current at this instant?

# Alternating-Current Circuits

## a-c MEASUREMENTS

A single conducting loop rotating at a constant speed in a uniform magnetic field generates an alternating emf. The magnitude of the emf varies with the sine of the angle that the plane of the loop makes with the perpendicular to the magnetic flux. The instantaneous value of the emf is

$$e = E_{\max} \sin \theta$$

The instantaneous current in a pure resistance load comprising the external circuit of the generator is similarly expressed as

$$i = I_{\max} \sin \theta$$

This current is a consequence of the alternating voltages impressed across the load, and its maxima and minima occur at the same instants as the voltage maxima and minima. The alter-

### 21.1 Power in an a-c circuit

*Review Section 20.9 and Figures 20-11 and 20-12.*

**Figure 21-1** Thomas A. Edison and Charles P. Steinmetz in Steinmetz's laboratory in Schenectady, N.Y., in 1922. Steinmetz was a brilliant mathematician and electrical engineer. He developed the mathematical analysis of alternating-current circuits and provided the firm mathematical base of electrical engineering.

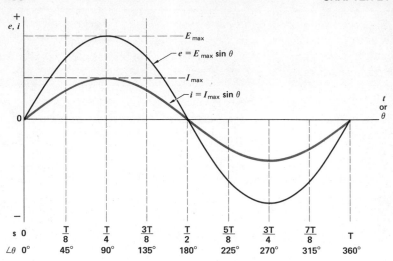

**Figure 21-2** One cycle of alternating current and voltage in phase.

nating current and voltage are said to be *in phase*. This in-phase relationship is characteristic of a resistance load across which an alternating voltage is applied. Sine curves of in-phase alternating current and voltage are shown in Figure 21-2.

In a d-c circuit, electric power, $P$, is the product $E \times I$. In an a-c circuit, the instantaneous power, $p$, is the product $e \times i$. These relationships are shown in Figure 21-3.

The voltage and current in Figure 21-3(B) are shown in phase as they are in a resistive load. The instantaneous power curve varies between some positive maximum and zero and has an average value $P$. Observe that the instantaneous power curve, $p$, has a frequency twice that of $e$ and $i$. The ordinates of this power curve are always positive since $e$ and $i$ are in phase. During the first half-cycle, both $e$ and $i$ are positive, so their product is positive. During the second half-cycle, both $e$ and $i$ are negative, but their product is positive.

**Figure 21-3** A comparison of d-c and a-c power.

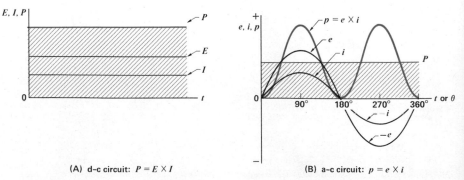

(A) d-c circuit: $P = E \times I$          (B) a-c circuit: $p = e \times i$

If a zero-centered d-c ammeter were placed in an a-c circuit, the pointer would tend to swing alternately in the positive and negative directions. At all but the very lowest frequencies, the inertia of the meter movement would cause the pointer to remain at zero. This, in effect, averages out the sine-wave variations. The same would be true of an a-c voltage measurement. *The average value of a sine curve of alternating current or voltage is zero.* This is true regardless of the magnitude of the maximum values attained.

The most useful value of an alternating current is based on its heating effect in an electric circuit and is commonly referred to as the *effective value*. The **effective value** *of an alternating current is the number of amperes that, in a given resistance, produces heat at the same average rate as that number of amperes of steady direct current.*

Let us assume that a resistance element is immersed in water in a calorimeter and that a steady direct current of 1 ampere in the circuit raises the temperature of the water 25 C° in 10 minutes. An alternating current in the same resistance that would raise the temperature the same amount in the same time is said to have an effective value of 1 ampere. The symbol for the effective value of an alternating current is $I$, the same as that for steady direct current. When the magnitudes of alternating currents are given in amperes, they are understood to be effective values unless other values are clearly stated.

From Joule's law, $Q = I^2Rt/J$, we know that the heating effect of an electric current is proportional to $I^2$. The average rate of heat production by an alternating current is proportional to the mean (average) of the instantaneous values of current squared. From Figure 21-4 it is evident that the mean value of $I^2$ is $\frac{1}{2}I_{max}^2$ because the square of the instantaneous values of the alternating current of frequency $f$ gives a curve of frequency $2f$ that varies between $I_{max}^2$ and zero. Thus

$$I^2 = \frac{I_{max}^2}{2}$$

and

$$I = \sqrt{\frac{I_{max}^2}{2}} = \frac{I_{max}}{\sqrt{2}}$$

$$I = 0.707\, I_{max}$$

Then

$$I_{max} = 1.414\, I$$

A sine curve of alternating current having a maximum value of 10.0 amperes is plotted in Figure 21-4. *The effective value is*

## 21.2 Effective values of current and voltage

*a-c meters indicate effective values of current and voltage, except in special applications.*

**Figure 21-4.** Current and current squared curves showing the effective value of an alternating current.

the square root of the mean of the instantaneous values squared and is frequently called the *root-mean-square*, rms, value. In the example shown, the rms, or effective value, of current is

$$I = \sqrt{\frac{I_{max}^2}{2}} = \sqrt{\frac{10\overline{0}\ a^2}{2}} = \sqrt{50.0\ a^2} = 7.07\ a$$

The rms, or effective value, of an a-c emf is expressed similarly.

$$E = 0.707\ E_{max}$$

*In special applications a-c meters can be calibrated to indicate maximum values.*

Then

$$E_{max} = 1.414\ E$$

For a potential difference that does not include a source of emf, these expressions become

$$V = 0.707\ V_{max}$$

and

$$V_{max} = 1.414\ V$$

Thus a house-lighting circuit rated at 120 volts (effective) varies between $+170$ volts and $-170$ volts during each cycle. An appliance that draws 10.00 amperes (effective) when connected across this circuit has a current that varies between $+14.14$ amperes and $-14.14$ amperes. The meters used for measurements in a-c circuits are usually designed to indicate effective values rather than maximum values. Representative a-c meter movements are shown in Figure 21-5, (A, B, C, D).

**Figure 21-5(A)** Moving iron-vane meter. When a magnetizing current is in the actuating coil, a repelling force develops between the fixed and movable iron vanes. The moving vane exerts a force against the restoring spring, and the final pointer position is a measure of the current in the coil. The moving-vane mechanism is used in inexpensive a-c ammeters and voltmeters.

**Figure 21-5(B)** Hot-wire meter. When a current is in the meter circuit, the temperature of the platinum-alloy resistance wire **AB** rises because of $I^2R$ heating. The resulting expansion reduces the tension on wire **CD** and allows the spring to pull thread **EF** to the left. The pulley rotates and moves the pointer slowly to the final deflection. The hot-wire mechanism is sensitive to temperature variations. A low-resistance shunt is added for ammeter functions. A high resistance is added in series with wire **AB** for voltmeter functions.

If the load in an a-c circuit is a pure resistance, the current and voltage are in phase and the average power consumed is

$$P = I^2R = VI$$
$$P = 120 \text{ v} \times 10.00 \text{ a}$$
$$P = 1200 \text{ w}$$
$$(\text{v} \times \text{a} = \text{j/c} \times \text{c/s} = \text{j/s} = \text{w})$$

If, however, the current and voltage are not in phase, *the average power of the circuit is not a simple product of the effective values of voltage and current*. The products $I^2R$ and $VI$ are no longer the same; $I^2R$ gives the *actual* power dissipation and $VI$ gives the *apparent* power. This is a basic difference between d-c and a-c circuits, and it stems from the fact that phase differences between current and voltage may be produced by capacitance and inductance in an a-c circuit. These effects add a new dimension to alternating-current circuits known as *impedance*, which is considered in Section 21.6.

*The galvanometer shown in Figure 19-29 provides the basic movement for d-c meters. At ordinary frequencies the inertia of the moving coil prevents it from following the alternations in an a-c circuit. If the galvanometer were placed in an a-c circuit, the pointer would simply vibrate about its zero position and the meter would probably self-destruct.*

**Figure 21-5(C)** Electrodynamometer. The electrodynamometer is similar to the galvanometer movement of d-c meters except that it does not include a permanent magnet. The moving coil rotates in the magnetic field of a pair of fixed coils carrying magnetizing current. As a current in the fixed coils produces magnetic flux **B,** a current in the moving coil produces a flux along its axis, and the coil tends to align the two magnetic fields. This torque produces a pointer deflection related to the product of the two coil currents. The dynamometer mechanism is used in quality ammeters, voltmeters, and watt meters.

**Figure 21-5(D)** Induction watt-hour meter. The induction watt-hour meter, used to record electric energy consumption, is essentially a small single-phase induction motor that turns at a rate proportional to the power being used. A coil **V** is connected in parallel with the circuit load and acts as a voltage winding. The coils **$C_1$** and **$C_2$** are connected in series with the load and act as current windings. An aluminum disk **A** turns as an induction-motor armature to follow the sweeping flux set up by the combination of coils. Permanent magnets **M** induce eddy currents in the rotating disk that oppose the motion of the disk and produce the slippage required for the induction-motor operation.

## 21.3 Inductance in an a-c circuit

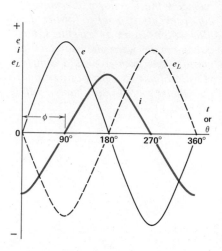

**Figure 21-6** Current and voltages in an a-c circuit containing pure inductance.

**Figure 21-7** Phase relation of an a-c current and voltage in pure resistance and pure inductance circuits.

In Section 20.19 inductance was described as an inertia-like property that opposes any *change* in current in a coil and causes a counter emf proportional to the rate of change of current to be induced across the coil. Figure 21-6 shows the waveforms characteristic of a circuit consisting of pure inductance to which an alternating voltage is applied. The instant the current is passing through zero in a positive direction, it is changing at its maximum rate. Thus the counter emf induced across the coil at this instant must be at its negative maximum value. When the current reaches the positive maximum, the rate of change of current is zero and the induced emf is zero. Again 90° later, the current is changing in a negative direction at its maximum rate and the counter emf is at its positive maximum.

The counter emf follows behind the current inducing it by 90° and is opposite in polarity to the applied voltage, as shown in Figure 21-6. The current in the circuit must then *lag behind* the applied voltage by 90°. It is just as appropriate to consider that the voltage leads the current by 90°; the *difference in phase* is 90°.

We can think of alternating currents and voltages in terms of rotors, or *phasors*, rotating counterclockwise as spokes of a wheel. *A **phasor** is a representation of the concepts of magnitude and direction in a reference plane.* Phasors are used in

**(A) e and i in pure resistance**

Phase diagram

**(B) e and i in pure inductance**

Phase diagram

I HAVE TO KILL MY IMAGINATION!

Figure 21-7 to show the phase relation between current and voltage in a pure resistance (A) and in a pure inductance (B). Phasors usually represent effective values of current and voltage in *phase* diagrams such as those shown at the right in Figure 21-7.

The phase angle between voltage and current is commonly referred to as the angle $\phi$ (the lower case Greek letter phi). This relation in an a-c circuit can be expressed as follows:

$$i = I_{max} \sin \theta$$
$$e = E_{max} \sin (\theta + \phi)$$

The phase angle, $\phi$, of a leading voltage is *positive*, and it indicates that the voltage is ahead of the current in phase. Suppose the effective value of voltage represented in Figure 21-7(B) is 10.0 volts. When the displacement angle, $\theta$, is 30°, the instantaneous value $e$ will be

$$e = E_{max} \sin (\theta + \phi)$$
$$e = E_{max} \sin (30° + 90°)$$
$$e = E_{max} \sin 120°$$

But

$$E_{max} = 1.414\ E = 1.414 \times 10.0\ v$$
$$E_{max} = 14.1\ v$$

Then

$$e = 14.1\ v \times \sin 120°$$
$$\sin 120° = \sin 60° = 0.866$$
$$e = 14.1\ v \times 0.866$$
$$e = 12.2\ v$$

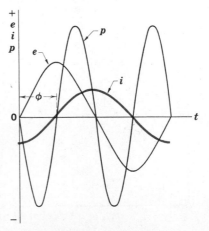

**Figure 21-8** Power curve in a pure inductance.

Plotted as a function of time, the products of the instantaneous values of voltage and current in a pure inductance yield an instantaneous power curve as shown in Figure 21-8. Observe that the average power is zero. While the current is changing from zero to a positive maximum, energy is taken from the source and stored in the magnetic field of the inductor. These portions of the power curve are positive. When the current is changing from a positive maximum to zero, all the energy stored in the magnetic field is returned to the source. These portions of the power curve are negative. Therefore, the net energy removed from the source during a cycle by a pure inductance is zero; the product of the rms voltage and current can indicate only an *apparent power*.

## 21.4 Inductance and resistance

An inductor cannot be entirely without resistance since it is not possible to have pure inductance in a circuit. The ordinary resistance of the conductor is an inherent property of any coil. We can treat the resistance of an inductive circuit as a lumped value in series with a pure inductance. This arrangement is shown in Figure 21-9(A).

The same current must be present in all parts of a series circuit. The circuit current is thus used as a reference to show the phase relation between current and voltages in the resistance and inductance. The voltage across the resistance is in phase with the circuit current; this in-phase relation is shown in Figure 21-9(B). The voltage across the inductance leads the circuit current by 90°, as shown in Figure 21-9(C). The voltage across the series combination of $R$ and $L$ then leads the circuit current by some angle between 0° and 90°.

**Figure 21-9** An **L-R** circuit showing the phase relations between voltage and current in the resistance and in the inductance.

**(A) Series circuit**

**(B) Voltage and current in phase**

**(C) Voltage and current 90° out of phase**

*Vector addition is geometric except for phase angles of 0° and 180°.*

**Figure 21-10** A phase diagram showing the addition of voltage phasors in a series circuit containing inductance and resistance.

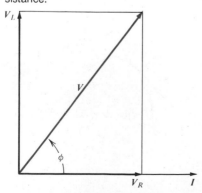

With the circuit current of Figure 21-9 as a reference, it is apparent that $V_R$ and $V_L$ have a phase difference of 90°. These two voltages in series cannot be added algebraically but must be added vectorially to give the circuit voltage, $V$. This voltage $V$ across the external circuit is the *resultant*, or vector sum, of voltages $V_R$ and $V_L$ shown in the phase diagram, Figure 21-10. The phase angle, $\phi$, has a positive value less than 90°.

No power is dissipated in the inductance. The average power dissipated in the resistance is equal to the product of the effective values of the circuit current and the voltage across the resistance.

$$P_R = V_R I$$

From the voltage diagram shown in Figure 21-10 it is apparent that

$$V_R = V \cos \phi$$

Thus the actual power consumed in the external circuit is

$$P = VI \cos \phi$$

The total power consumed in the internal and external circuits is, of course,

$$P_T = EI \cos \phi$$

When the phase angle, $\phi$, is *zero* (a pure resistive load), then $\cos \phi = 1$ and the product $VI \cos \phi = VI$. When the phase angle, $\phi$, is $+90°$ (a pure inductive load), $\cos \phi = 0$ and the product $VI \cos \phi = 0$ (Figure 21-8). The cosine of $\phi$ is known as the *power factor*, pf, of an a-c circuit. See Figure 21-11.

$$\mathbf{pf} = \cos \phi = \frac{V_R}{V}$$

Electric power companies strive to maintain a power factor near unity in their distribution lines. Why?

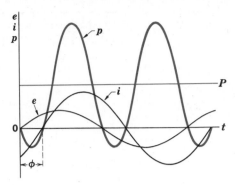

**Figure 21-11** Power in an a-c circuit containing resistance and inductance.

If $\phi = 0°$, $VI = I^2R$ in an a-c circuit.

*Inductance   Henry milli   micro*

---

## 21.5 Inductive reactance

The potential drop across the resistance in the circuit of Figure 21-9 is represented by the phasor $V_R$ in Figure 21-10. This potential difference is equal to the product $IR$, where $R$ is the common resistance to current in the external circuit. As a consequence of its nonresistive opposition to the current in the circuit, the inductance has a potential difference across it. This opposition is *nonresistive* because no power is dissipated in the inductance and is called *reactance*, $X$. Reactance is expressed in *ohms*. When reactance is due to inductance, it is referred to as *inductive reactance*, $X_L$. **Inductive reactance**, $X_L$, *is the ratio of the effective value of inductive potential, $V_L$, to the effective value of current, $I$.*

$$X_L = \frac{V_L}{I}$$

Thus the voltage $V_L$ of Figure 21-10 is equal to the product $IX_L$.

The inductive reactance of a coil is directly proportional to the inductance and to the frequency of the current in the circuit. This is true because the rate of change of a given current increases with frequency. The larger the inductance, the greater is the opposition to the change in current at a given frequency.

$$X_L = 2\pi fL$$

When $f$ is in hertz and $L$ is in henrys, $X_L$ is expressed in ohms of inductive reactance; $2\pi$ is a proportionality constant.

## 21.6 Impedance

The vector sum of $IX_L$ and $IR$ is equal to the voltage, $V$, applied to the external circuit, as in Figure 21-10. This potential difference is the product of the circuit current, $I$, and the combined effect of the inductive reactance, $X_L$, and the resistance, $R$, in the load. The joint effect of reactance and resistance in an a-c circuit is called *impedance*, $Z$. It is expressed in ohms. Thus $V$ is equal to the product $IZ$. See Figure 21-12(A). If each voltage is divided by the current $I$, $IX_L$ yields inductive reactance $X_L$, $IR$ yields resistance $R$, and $IZ$ yields impedance $Z$. This is illustrated in the *impedance diagram* shown in Figure 21-12(B).

*If reactance is inductive, the phase angle is positive.*

The tangent of the phase angle $\phi$ is defined by the ratio of the side opposite $\phi$ to the side adjacent to $\phi$. In the impedance diagram these are the sides $X$ and $R$, respectively, of the right triangle. Therefore

$$\frac{X}{R} = \tan \phi$$

This equation gives $X/R$ as a *function* of $\phi$. It also enables us to determine $\phi$ as a function of $X/R$; that is, $\phi$ *is an angle* whose tangent is $X/R$. This expression gives the *inverse function* of the above equation and is commonly written as

$$\phi = \arctan \frac{X}{R}$$

*Relate $Z = \sqrt{R^2 + X^2}$ to the Pythagorean theorem of geometry.*

The impedance, $Z$, has a magnitude equal to $\sqrt{R^2 + X^2}$ and a direction angle $\phi$ (with respect to $R$) whose tangent is $X/R$. It can be written in the polar form $Z\lfloor\phi$ as

$$Z = \sqrt{R^2 + X^2} \, \lfloor\arctan X/R$$

When the reactance is inductive, $X = X_L$ and $\phi$ is a positive angle whose tangent is $X_L/R$.

We can now rewrite the Ohm's-law expression for d-c circuits in a form that applies to a-c circuits. For the entire circuit:

$$E = IZ$$

For the external circuit:

$$V = IZ$$

(A)  Voltage diagram

(B)  Impedance diagram

**Figure 21-12** The derivation of an impedance diagram of an **L-R** series circuit.

EXAMPLE

*A coil with a resistance of $3\bar{0}$ ohms and an inductance of 0.12 henry is connected across a 120-volt, $6\bar{0}$-hertz source. (a) What is the magnitude of the circuit current? (b) What is the phase angle? (c) What power is expended in the external circuit?*

SOLUTION

The circuit shown in Figure 21-9 and the phasor diagram shown in Figure 21-10 apply to this problem.

(a) The magnitude of $Z$ will be determined since only the magnitude of the circuit current is required in part ($a$).

By Ohm's law, $I = \dfrac{V}{Z}$

where the magnitude of $Z = \sqrt{R^2 + X_L^2}$ and $X_L = 2\pi fL$

So, $Z = \sqrt{R^2 + (2\pi fL)^2}$

Thus, $I = \dfrac{V}{\sqrt{R^2 + (2\pi fl)^2}} = \dfrac{120 \text{ v}}{\sqrt{(3\bar{0}\ \Omega)^2 + (2\pi \times 6\bar{0}/s \times 0.12\ \text{h})^2}}$

$I = \dfrac{120 \text{ v}}{54\ \Omega} = 2.2$ a, the circuit current

(b) $\phi = \arctan \dfrac{X_L}{R} = \arctan \dfrac{45\ \Omega}{3\bar{0}\ \Omega} = \arctan 1.5$

From Appendix B, Table 6, $\phi = 56°$, indicating a leading voltage.

(c) $P = VI \times \text{pf} = VI \cos \phi = 120 \text{ v} \times 2.2 \text{ a} \times \cos 56° = 120 \text{ v} \times 2.2 \text{ a} \times 0.56$
$P = 150$ w

---

## 21.7 Capacitance in an a-c circuit

A capacitor in a d-c circuit charges to the applied voltage and effectively opens the circuit. The potential difference across a capacitor can change only as the charge on the capacitor changes. Since $Q = CV$, the charge $Q$, in coulombs, is directly proportional to the potential difference $V$, in volts, for a given capacitor. Thus we can refer to the charge in terms of the voltage across the capacitor.

An uncharged capacitor offers no opposition to a charging current from a source of emf. However, as a charge builds up on the capacitor plates, a voltage develops across the capacitor that opposes the charging current. When the charge is such that the voltage across the capacitor is equal to the applied voltage, the charging current must be zero. Why? These two conditions are illustrated in Figure 21-13. We can conclude that *the current in a capacitor circuit is maximum when the voltage across the capacitor is zero and is zero when the capacitor voltage is maximum*.

*Because $Q \propto V$, we describe the charge on a capacitor in terms of its voltage.*

(A) $C$ uncharged              (B) $C$ fully charged

**Figure 21-13** As a capacitor is charged, a voltage develops across it that opposes the charging current.

Let us examine the effect of pure capacitance in an a-c circuit. When the initial charging current is a positive maximum, the voltage across the capacitor plates is zero. As the capacitor charges, the potential difference builds up and the current decays; the charging current reaches zero when the capacitor voltage is maximum.

As the charging current reverses direction and increases toward a negative maximum, electrons flow from the negative plate of the capacitor through the circuit to the positive plate, thereby removing the charge. The capacitor then charges in the opposite sense, and the potential difference reaches a maximum with opposite polarity as the current returns to zero. Thus *the voltage across the capacitor lags the circuit current by 90°*. See Figure 21-14.

The phase angle, $\phi$, in an a-c circuit with a pure capacitance load is −90°, and the circuit has a *lagging* voltage. The phase relationship is expressed as

$$i = I_{max} \sin \theta \qquad \text{and} \qquad e = E_{max} \sin (\theta + \phi)$$

These expressions are similar to those given for $i$ and $e$ in Section 21.3. However, the phase angle of a lagging voltage is *negative*. Hence the sign of the phase angle, $\phi$, must always be introduced properly.

**Figure 21-14** Pure capacitance in an a-c circuit.

(A) Circuit                    (B) $e_C$ and $i$ vs. time

Suppose the effective value of voltage across a capacitor is 10.0 volts. When the displacement angle, $\theta$, is 30°, the instantaneous value of $e$ is

$$e = E_{max} \sin (\theta + \phi)$$
$$e = E_{max} \sin [30° + (-90°)]$$
$$e = E_{max} \sin (-60°)$$

Now

$$E_{max} = 1.414 \, E = 1.414 \times 10.0 \text{ v}$$
$$e = 14.1 \text{ v} \times \sin (-60°)$$

and

$$\sin (-60°) = -0.866$$

Therefore

$$e = 14.1 \text{ v} \times (-0.866)$$
$$e = -12.2 \text{ v}$$

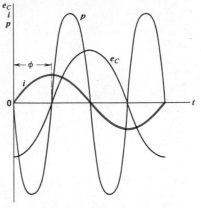

**Figure 21-15**  Power curve in a circuit of pure capacitance.

Compare this result with the similar computation in Section 21.3.

Plotted as a function of time, the product of the instantaneous values of current and voltage in a circuit of pure capacitance results in the instantaneous power curve shown in Figure 21-15. Similar to a circuit with pure inductance, the average power is zero. As the current changes from each maximum to zero, energy is taken from the source of emf and stored in the electric field between the capacitor plates. All this energy is returned to the source as the current rises from zero to either maximum. Thus the product of the effective values of current and voltage indicates an *apparent power*. The phase angle of $-90°$ yields a power factor equal to zero [$\cos (-90°) = 0$], and so the *actual power* dissipated must be zero.

## 21.8 Capacitance and resistance

*If reactance is capacitive, the phase angle is negative.*

In an a-c circuit the opposition to the current due to capacitance is *nonresistive* since no power is dissipated in the capacitor. This nonresistive opposition is called *capacitive reactance*. The symbol for capacitive reactance is $X_C$ and the unit is the *ohm*.

The inherent resistance in any practical circuit containing capacitance can be represented in series with $X_C$. An $R$-$C$ series circuit is shown in Figure 21-16. The potential difference, $V$, across the external circuit is the vector sum of $V_C$ and $V_R$; the series current is used as the reference. There is, of course, no electron flow through the capacitor; it is alternately charged, first in one sense and then in the other, as the charging current

**Figure 21-16** An **R-C** series circuit showing the phase relations of the different voltages to the circuit current.

(A) Circuit diagram          (B) Voltage diagram

alternates. The phase angle, $\phi$, is negative, which is characteristic of a lagging voltage.

The corresponding impedance diagram can be produced by dividing each voltage phasor by the circuit current. See Figure 21-17. Just as $V_C$ is negative with respect to $V_L$ in Figure 21-12(B), so $X_C$ is plotted in the opposite direction to $X_L$.

Because $V_C = Q/C$, the larger the capacitance, the lower the potential difference developed across it for a given charge. *Thus the reactance to a circuit current is inversely proportional to the capacitance in the circuit.* As the frequency of a charging current is increased, a shorter time is available during each current cycle for the capacitor to charge and discharge. Smaller changes in voltage occur across the capacitor. *Hence the capacitive reactance to the circuit current is inversely proportional to the current frequency.*

$$X_C = \frac{1}{2\pi fC}$$

**Figure 21-17** The derivation of an impedance diagram of an **R-C** series circuit.

(A) Voltage diagram          (B) Impedance diagram

When $f$ is in hertz and $C$ is in farads, the capacitive reactance, $X_C$, is expressed in ohms.

The impedance of a circuit containing capacitance and resistance in series has a magnitude equal to $\sqrt{R^2 + X^2}$ and a phase angle, $\phi$, whose tangent is $-X_C/R$. The impedance, in its general polar form $Z\underline{|\phi}$, is expressed as $\sqrt{R^2 + X^2}\underline{|arctan\ X/R}$, where $X = X_C$. See the following example.

EXAMPLE

*A capacitance of 20.0 μf and a resistance of $10\overline{0}$ Ω are connected in series across a $12\overline{0}$-v, 60.0-hertz source. (a) Find the impedance of the circuit. (b) What is the circuit current? (c) What is the potential difference across the capacitor?*

SOLUTION

(a) The circuit and diagrams shown in Figure 21-16 and Figure 21-17 apply.

$$Z = \sqrt{R^2 + X^2}\ \underline{|arctan\ X/R}$$

But

$$X = X_C = \frac{1}{2\pi fC} = \left(\frac{1}{2\pi \times 60.0 \times 20.0 \times 10^{-6}}\right)\ \text{ohms}$$

$$X_C = 133\ \Omega$$

Magnitude of $Z$

$$Z = \sqrt{(10\overline{0}\ \Omega)^2 + (133\ \Omega)^2}$$

$$Z = 166\ \Omega$$

Phase angle

$$\phi = \arctan \frac{-X_C}{R} = \arctan \frac{-133\ \Omega}{10\overline{0}\ \Omega}$$

$$\phi = \arctan -1.33$$
$$\phi = -53°, \text{ the phase angle of a lagging voltage}$$

Therefore the impedance can be expressed as
$$Z = 166\ \Omega\ \underline{|-53°}$$

(b) $I = \dfrac{V}{Z} = \dfrac{12\overline{0}\ \text{v}}{166\ \Omega}$

$I = 0.723$ a, the circuit current

(c) $V_C = IX_C = 0.723$ a $\times 133\ \Omega$
$V_C = 96.2$ v, the potential difference across $C$

## 21.9 L, R, and C in series

*If reactance is zero, the phase angle is zero.*

Inductance produces a leading voltage and a positive phase angle in an a-c circuit. Capacitance produces a lagging voltage and a negative phase angle. Of course, the voltage across a resistance must be in phase with the current in the resistance.

Suppose values of $L, R,$ and $C$ are connected in series across an a-c source of emf as in Figure 21-18(A). The *total reactance* of the circuit is

$$X = X_L - X_C$$

since $X_L$ and $X_C$ are 180° apart.

The impedance has the general form $Z\underline{|\phi}$.

$$Z = \sqrt{R^2 + X^2} \underline{\;|\text{arctan } X/R}$$

However, $X$ can be either positive or negative ($X^2$ is always positive) since

$$X = X_L - X_C = 2\pi f L - \frac{1}{2\pi f C}$$

Therefore the magnitude of the impedance can be expressed as

$$Z = \sqrt{R^2 + (X_L - X_C)^2}$$

$$Z = \sqrt{R^2 + \left(2\pi f L - \frac{1}{2\pi f C}\right)^2}$$

*The calculation of $X_L$ is shown in Section 21.5.*

*The calculation of $X_C$ is shown in Section 21.8.*

Suppose the resistance $R$ in Figure 21-18(A) is 16.0 Ω and the a-c source is a 60.0-hz generator that applies a potential difference of $10\overline{0}$ v across the external circuit. At this frequency, $X_L$ is determined to be 22.0 Ω and $X_C$ to be 10.0 Ω. The impedance, $Z$, of the circuit is calculated from these known values of $R, X_L,$ and $X_C$ as illustrated in the following example.

$$Z = \sqrt{R^2 + X^2} \underline{\;|\text{arctan } X/R}$$

**Figure 21-18** An **L-R-C** series circuit with voltage and impedance diagrams.

(A) L–R–C series circuit      (B) Voltage diagram      (C) Impedance diagram

But

$$X = X_L - X_C = 22.0 \ \Omega - 10.0 \ \Omega = 12.0 \ \Omega$$

$$Z = \sqrt{(16.0 \ \Omega)^2 + (12.0 \ \Omega)^2} \ \underline{|\text{arctan } 12.0 \ \Omega/16.0 \ \Omega}$$

$$Z = 20.0 \ \Omega \ \underline{|37.0°}$$

By calculating $Z\underline{|\phi}$ we found that the magnitude of the impedance is 20.0 $\Omega$ and its direction angle, $\phi$, is 37.0° positive with respect to $R$. The impedance diagram is shown in Figure 21-18(C). This angle $\phi$ is positive because $X_L$ is larger than $X_C$. Thus the voltage across the external circuit must *lead* the circuit current, $I$, by an angle of 37.0°. This voltage was given as $10\overline{0}$ v. Therefore the magnitude of the current is

$$I = \frac{V}{Z} = \frac{10\overline{0} \text{ v}}{20.0 \ \Omega} = 5.00 \text{ a}$$

Knowing the circuit current, we can determine the magnitudes of the voltages across $L, R$, and $C$.

$$V_L = IX_L = 11\overline{0} \text{ v}$$
$$V_R = IR = 80.0 \text{ v}$$
$$V_C = IX_C = 50.0 \text{ v}$$

Observe that the vector sum of $V_L$, $V_R$, and $V_C$ must be equal to $V$.

From the voltage diagram of Figure 21-18(B) it is evident that the magnitude of the voltage $V$ across the external circuit is

$$V = \sqrt{V_R^2 + V_X^2}$$

where

$$V_X = V_L - V_C$$

Then

$$V = \sqrt{(80.0 \text{ v})^2 + (60.0 \text{ v})^2}$$
$$V = 10\overline{0} \text{ v}$$

This result is in agreement with the value of the external circuit voltage $V$ assumed at the beginning of this circuit-computation exercise. The direction angle of $V$ must be 37.0° since this is the phase angle, $\phi$, using $I$ as the reference. This example of a series *L-R-C* circuit illustrates the fact that the magnitude of the voltage across a reactance in an a-c circuit can exceed the magnitude of the applied voltage across the entire external circuit.

Resistive and reactive components may also be connected in parallel in practical a-c circuits. The analysis of their parallel impedance networks is beyond the scope of this book.

# questions

1. What is the significant relationship between an alternating current and alternating voltage that are in phase?
2. In a-c circuits what type of load has a current in phase with the voltage across it?
3. What is meant by instantaneous power?
4. Upon what property of an alternating current is its effective value based?
5. Define the effective value of an alternating current.
6. What is the phase relation between (a) the current in a pure inductance and the applied voltage, (b) the current and the induced voltage, (c) the applied voltage and the induced voltage?
7. Express power factor (a) in terms of the phase angle, (b) in terms of $V$ and $V_R$. (c) What is the significance of the power factor pertaining to an a-c circuit?
8. Why is reactance described as being non-resistive?
9. (a) Define impedance. (b) Draw an impedance diagram for an inductor with reactance $X_L$ and resistance $R$. (c) Draw an impedance diagram for a capacitor with reactance $X_C$ and resistance $R$.
10. Describe the difference in the performance of a capacitor in a d-c circuit and in an a-c circuit.
11. What is the power factor of an a-c circuit containing (a) pure inductance, (b) pure resistance, (c) pure capacitance?
12. Express Ohm's law for an a-c circuit (a) that includes a source of emf, (b) that does not include a source of emf.

13. Explain why the instantaneous power curve for current in a resistive load varies between some positive maximum value and zero.
14. Demonstrate algebraically that the heating effect of an electric current is proportional to the effective value of current squared.
15. (a) Plot the current and current squared curves for an alternating current having a maximum value of 5.7 amperes. Use cross-section paper and a suitable scale for the coordinate axes to produce a graph similar to Figure 21-4. (b) Show that the rms value of the current is 4.0 amperes.
16. If an a-c circuit has a pure inductance load, the average power delivered to the load is zero. Does this mean that there is no energy transfer between the source and the load? Explain.
17. (a) Considering the expression for $X_L$ in terms of frequency and inductance, draw a rough graph of $X_L$ as a function of frequency for a given inductance. (b) What is the nature of the curve? (c) What is the significance of the fact that $X_L$ is zero when $f$ is zero, regardless of the value of $L$?
18. Considering the expression for $X_C$ in terms of frequency and capacitance, what is the significance of the fact that when the frequency is zero, $X_C$ is infinitely high for any given capacitance?
19. (a) In an $L$-$R$-$C$ series circuit operating at a certain frequency, what determines whether the load is inductive or capacitive? (b) Suggest a circumstance in which the load would be resistive.
20. What is the significance of the negative portions of the power curve shown in Figure 21-15?

# problems

*Note:* Compute angles to the nearest 0.5 degree.

1. A current in an a-c circuit measures 5.5 amperes. What is the maximum instantaneous magnitude of this current?
2. A capacitor has a voltage rating of $45\bar{0}$ v maximum. What is the highest rms voltage that can be impressed across it without danger of dielectric puncture?
3. The emf of an a-c source has an effective value of 122.0 volts. What is the instantaneous value when the displacement angle, $\theta$, is 50.0°?
4. An alternating current in a 25.0-ohm resistance produces heat at the rate of $25\bar{0}$ watts. What is the effective value (a) of current in the resistance, (b) of voltage across the resistance?

5. An inductor has an inductance of 2.20 henrys and a resistance of $22\bar{0}$ ohms. (a) What is the reactance if the a-c frequency is 25.0 hz? (b) Draw the impedance diagram and determine graphically the magnitude and phase angle of the impedance.
6. A 2.00-$\mu$f capacitor is connected across a 60.0-hertz line and a current of 167 milliamperes is indicated. (a) What is the reactance of the circuit? (b) What is the voltage across the line?
7. A capacitance of 2.65 $\mu$f is connected across a 120-volt line and is found to draw $12\bar{0}$ milliamperes. What is the frequency of the source?
8. When a resistance of 4.0 ohms and an inductor of negligible resistance are connected in series across a 110-volt, $6\bar{0}$-hertz line, the current is $2\bar{0}$ amperes. What is the inductance of the coil?

GROUP B

9. A 0.50-$\mu$f capacitor and a 3$\bar{0}$-ohm resistor are connected in series across a source of emf whose frequency is $8.0 \times 10^3$ hz. (a) Draw the circuit diagram. (b) Find the capacitive reactance. (c) Draw the impedance diagram and determine the magnitude and phase angle of the impedance.

10. The current in the circuit of Problem 9 is found to be 5$\bar{0}$ milliamperes. (a) What is the magnitude of the voltage across the series circuit? (b) What is the phase relation of this voltage to the circuit current? (c) What is the voltage across the capacitor? (d) What is the voltage across the resistor?

11. A 60.0-hertz circuit has a load consisting of resistance and inductance in series. A voltmeter, ammeter, and wattmeter, properly connected in the circuit, read respectively 117 v, 4.75 a, and 40$\bar{0}$ w. (a) Determine the power factor. (b) What is the phase angle? (c) What is the resistance of the load? (d) What is the inductive reactance of the load? (e) Determine the voltage across the resistance. (f) Determine the voltage across the inductance. (g) Draw the voltage diagram with the circuit current as the reference phasor. What is the applied voltage as found graphically? Express in polar form.

12. A coil has a resistance of 9$\bar{0}$ ohms and an inductance of 0.019 henry. (a) What is the impedance (complex) at a frequency of $1.0 \times 10^3$ hz? (b) What is the magnitude of the current when a potential difference of 6.0 volts at this frequency is applied across it? (c) How much power is delivered to the coil?

13. A capacitance of 5$\bar{0}$ $\mu$f and a resistance of 6$\bar{0}$ ohms are connected in series across a 120-volt, 6$\bar{0}$-hertz line. (a) What is the magnitude of current in the circuit? (b) What power is dissipated? (c) What is the power factor? (d) Determine the voltage across the resistance. (e) Determine the voltage across the capacitance. (f) Draw the voltage diagram with the circuit current as the reference phasor. What is the applied voltage found graphically? Express in polar form.

14. An inductance of 4.8 millihenrys, a capacitance of 8.0 $\mu$f, and a resistance of 1$\bar{0}$ ohms are connected in series, and a 6.0-volt, $1.0 \times 10^3$-hertz signal is applied across the combination. (a) What is the magnitude of the impedance of the series circuit? (b) What is the phase angle? (c) Determine the magnitude of the current in the circuit. (d) Find the potential drop across each component of the load, and draw the voltage diagram.

15. An inductor, a resistance, and a capacitor are connected in series across an a-c circuit. A voltmeter reads 9$\bar{0}$ volts when connected across the inductor, 16 volts across the resistor, and 120 volts across the capacitor. (a) What will the voltmeter read when placed across the series circuit? (b) Draw the voltage diagram, and graphically verify your answer to (a). (c) Compute the power factor.

# RESONANCE

An inductor in a d-c circuit has no effect on the steady, direct current except for that due to the ordinary resistance of the wire forming the coil. A steady, direct current can be thought of as an alternating current having a frequency of zero hz. Since $X_L = 2\pi fL$, inductive reactance in the d-c circuit must be zero.

An alternating current changes from its positive maximum to its negative maximum in a time equal to one-half the period, $T$;

## 21.10 Inductive reactance vs. frequency

**Figure 21-19** Current changes at a higher rate when the frequency is higher.

(A) dc, $f-0$          (B) ac, $f-n$          (C) ac, $f=2n$

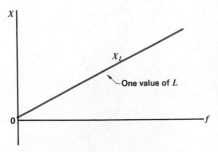

**Figure 21-20** The reactance of a given inductor plotted as a function of frequency.

if the frequency of this current is increased, the time rate of change of current is increased accordingly. See Figure 21-19. The inductive reactance presented to the current in an a-c circuit by an inductor increases as the frequency of this current is increased.

Consider the reactance of a certain inductance over a range of frequencies. A plot of the values of inductive reactance as ordinates against frequencies as abscissas produces the linear curve shown in Figure 21-20. Any value of inductance yields a reactance curve that starts at the origin of the coordinate axes; the larger the value of inductance, the greater is the slope of the curve.

## 21.11 Capacitive reactance vs. frequency

*Think of the source of emf for a d-c circuit as having zero frequency.*

*$X_C$ for a given capacitor varies inversely with frequency.*

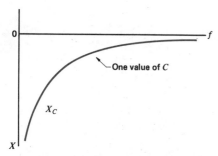

**Figure 21-21** The reactance of a given capacitor plotted as a function of frequency. $X_c$ is plotted as $-1/(2\pi fC)$ for comparison with $X_L$ in Figure 21-20.

When a capacitor in a d-c circuit is charged to the applied voltage, it acts as an open switch and the current in the circuit is zero. While the capacitor remains in this fully charged state, the capacitive reactance in the circuit is infinitely high regardless of the value of $C$.

A capacitor in an a-c circuit has a very different effect on the alternating current and voltage. Electrons flow in one direction during one half-cycle, charging the capacitor in one sense. The electrons flow in the opposite direction during the other half-cycle, reversing the charge on the capacitor.

If the current has a very low frequency, the capacitive reactance is very large since $X_C = 1/(2\pi fC)$. This large reactance effectively limits the circuit current. At higher frequencies, less change occurs in the charge on the capacitor during each half-cycle and the reactive opposition to the circuit current is lower. At extremely high frequencies, the change in capacitor charge becomes negligible and the capacitive reactance in the circuit becomes a negligible factor in limiting the circuit current. The larger the capacitor in the circuit, the more rapidly the capacitive reactance decreases with increasing frequency. Observe that in the above equation for $X_C$, the magnitude of $X_C$ varies inversely with frequency $f$, with capacitance $C$, and with their product $fC$.

In Figure 21-21 values of reactance for a given capacitor are plotted as a function of frequency. The slope of the curve is hyperbolic, which is typical of the inverse relation between capacitive reactance, $X_C$, and frequency, $f$. A larger capacitor will yield a reactance-frequency curve with a greater slope than that shown.

## 21.12 Series resonance

In Section 21.9 it was stated that the voltages across an inductance and a capacitance in a series circuit are of opposite polarity. If $X_L$ is larger than $X_C$, the circuit is inductive and the voltage across the circuit leads the current. If $X_C$ is the larger reactance, the circuit is capacitive and the circuit voltage lags behind the current. In either instance the impedance, $Z$, has a magnitude $\sqrt{R^2 + (X_L - X_C)^2}$ and a phase angle, $\phi$, whose tangent is $(X_L - X_C)/R$.

The frequency of an a-c voltage applied to a series circuit with fixed values of $L, R$, and $C$ determines the reactance of the circuit. If Figures 21-20 and 21-21 are combined, they will show that the reactance of the circuit is inductive over a range of high frequencies and capacitive over a range of low frequencies. At some intermediate frequency, the inductive and capacitive reactances are equal; the reactance of the circuit, $X_L - X_C$, equals zero. At this frequency the impedance, $Z$, is at its minimum value for the series circuit. It is equal to the inherent circuit resistance, $R$. As is true of all circuits with pure ohmic resistance, the voltage across the circuit and the current in the circuit are in phase. This special circuit condition is known as *series resonance*. The frequency at which resonance occurs is called the *resonant frequency, $f_r$*. **Series resonance is a condition in which the impedance of an L-R-C series circuit is equal to the circuit resistance, and the voltage across the circuit is in phase with the circuit current.**

Suppose an inductor of $1\bar{0}$ millihenrys inductance and 25 ohms resistance is placed in series with an ammeter and a capacitor of 1.0 microfarad capacitance. A signal of $1\bar{0}$ volts rms from a variable frequency source, such as an audio signal generator, is applied. The circuit is shown in Figure 21-22. When the frequency of the applied signal is varied through the audio range, a distinct rise in the current occurs as the frequency approaches 1600 hz. The current magnitude quickly falls away as the frequency of the signal increases beyond this value. We can conclude that the series circuit is resonant at 1600 hz.

**Figure 21-22** An **L-R-C** series circuit that has a resonant frequency of 1600 hz.

(A) Circuit diagram

(B) Voltage diagram

At resonance, $X_L = X_C$ and the value of each is found as follows:

$$X_L = 2\pi f_r L$$

$$X_L = (2\pi \times 1.6 \times 10^3 \times 1.0 \times 10^{-2})\ \Omega$$

$$X_L = 1.0 \times 10^2\ \Omega$$

$$X_C = \frac{1}{2\pi f_r C}$$

$$X_C = \left(\frac{1}{2\pi \times 1.6 \times 10^3 \times 1.0 \times 10^{-6}}\right)\ \Omega$$

$$X_C = 1.0 \times 10^2\ \Omega$$

The impedance at resonance is

$$Z = \sqrt{R^2 + X^2}\ \underline{|\ \text{arctan}\ X/R}$$

But

$$X = X_L - X_C = 0\ \Omega$$

and the phase angle

$$\phi = \text{arctan}\ \frac{X}{R} = 0°$$

Thus

$$Z = R = 25\ \Omega$$

The impedance, $Z$, of the series resonant circuit is the minimum value and is equal to $R$. The current, $I$, is the maximum value and is equal to $V/R$.

$$I_r = \frac{V}{R} = \frac{1\bar{0}\ \text{v}}{25\ \Omega} = 0.40\ \text{a}$$

$$V_L = I_r X_L = 0.40\ \text{a} \times 1.0 \times 10^2\ \Omega$$

$$V_L = 4\bar{0}\ \text{v}$$

$$V_C = I_r X_C = 0.40\ \text{a} \times 1.0 \times 10^2\ \Omega$$

$$V_C = 4\bar{0}\ \text{v}$$

$$I_r X_L - I_r X_C = 4\bar{0}\ \text{v} - 4\bar{0}\ \text{v} = 0\ \text{v}$$

$$V_R = I_r \times R = 0.40\ \text{a} \times 25\ \Omega = 1\bar{0}\ \text{v}$$

The phase angle, $\phi$, at resonance is $0°$ and the power factor of the circuit, which is the cosine of $\phi$, is 1. The series resonant circuit has unity power factor. Thus maximum power, $P$, is dissipated in the circuit at resonance.

$pf = cos\ \phi = cos\ 0° = 1$

$$P = VI_r\ \text{cos}\ \phi = VI_r$$

The frequency at which a series circuit resonates is determined by the combination of $L$ and $C$ used. For a particular combination, there is one resonant frequency, $f_r$. At series resonance

$$X_L = X_C$$

$$2\pi f_r L = \frac{1}{2\pi f_r C}$$

Solving for $f_r$

$$f_r^2 = \frac{1}{4\pi^2 LC}$$

$$f_r = \frac{1}{2\pi\sqrt{LC}}$$

**Figure 21-23** The reactance characteristic of an **L-R-C** series circuit on either side of the resonant frequency.

When $L$ is in henrys and $C$ is in farads, $f_r$ is expressed in hertz.

At frequencies below the resonance point, the series circuit is capacitive, performing as one with an $X_C$ and $R$ in series. At the resonant frequency, $f_r$, the circuit performs as one containing pure resistance. Above the resonant frequency, it is inductive. These characteristics of the $L$-$R$-$C$ series circuit are shown by the reactance curve $X$ in Figure 21-23.

A resonant circuit responds to impressed voltages of different frequencies in a very selective manner. The circuit presents a high impedance to a signal voltage of a frequency above or below the resonant frequency of the circuit. The resulting current is correspondingly small. This same circuit presents a low impedance, consisting of the circuit resistance, to a signal voltage at the resonant frequency. The current is correspondingly large.

A tuned circuit thus *discriminates* among signal voltages of different frequencies. This property of signal discrimination is known as the circuit's *selectivity*. The lower the resistance of the series circuit, the higher is the resonant current and the more sharply selective is the circuit. The family of current-resonance curves shown in Figure 21-24 illustrates the influence of circuit resistance on selectivity. Curves are shown for three different values of circuit resistance.

The usual series-resonant circuit consists of an inductor and a capacitor. The only resistance is that inherent in the circuit, which is almost entirely the resistance of the coil. The characteristics of the series-resonant circuit depend primarily on the ratio of the inductive reactance to the circuit resistance, $X_L/R$. This ratio is called the $Q$, quality factor, of the circuit. It is essentially a design characteristic of the inductor. The higher the $Q$, the more sharply selective is the series-resonant circuit.

## 21.13 Selectivity in series resonance

**Figure 21-24** The magnitude of current in a series-resonant circuit plotted as a function of frequency.

Resonant circuits can be tuned over a range of frequencies by making either the inductance or the capacitance variable. The position of a powdered-iron core in a coil can be varied to change the coil's inductance. A capacitor can be made variable by providing a means of changing its plate area or its plate separation. A variable capacitor of the type used in the tuning circuits of small radios is shown in Figure 21-25. Resonance is particularly important in communication circuits.

**Figure 21-25** A two-gang variable capacitor of the type used in the tuning circuits of radio receivers. Each capacitor section has a set of stator plates and a set of rotor plates. The rotor plates are attached to the shaft. The capacitances are varied simultaneously by rotating the shaft and thus varying the amounts of effective plate areas in the capacitor.

## summary

The power expended in the load of an a-c circuit is determined by the average of the instantaneous values over the period of one cycle. Instantaneous power is the product of the instantaneous current and the instantaneous voltage. In a resistive load, the average power is the product of the effective values of current and voltage. In either a pure inductive load or a pure capacitive load, the average power is zero. Power in an a-c circuit is equal to the product of the effective value of the current, the effective value of the voltage, and the cosine of the phase angle.

An a-c circuit containing both inductance and resistance produces a current that lags behind the voltage. Such a load presents an impedance to the source. This impedance is the vector sum of the resistance and the inductive reactance in the circuit. The phase angle is the angle at which the current lags the voltage.

Capacitance and resistance in an a-c circuit produce an impedance equal to the vector sum of the capacitive reactance and resistance in the circuit. The phase angle in this case is due to a lagging voltage. When both inductance and capacitance are present, the phase angle is determined by the relative magnitudes of the two reactances. Inductive reactance is directly proportional to both frequency and inductance. Capacitive reactance is inversely proportional to both frequency and capacitance.

Series circuits containing inductance, capacitance, and resistance can be analyzed by the application of Ohm's law for a-c circuits.

At zero frequency the reactance of an inductor is zero, with a linear increase as the frequency increases. The reactance of a capacitor is infinitely large at zero frequency and decreases nonlinearly with increasing frequency. The resonant frequency of the circuit is the frequency at which the inductive and capacitive reactances of a circuit are equal.

At the resonant frequency the impedance of a series-resonant circuit is minimum and is equal to the circuit resistance. The resonant current is the maximum current possible in the series circuit and is in phase with the applied voltage. If the $Q$ of the circuit is high, the resonant current is very large compared with the average circuit current over a range of frequencies. The current curve is sharply peaked. The selectivity of such a resonant circuit is high.

## questions

GROUP A

1. Select three different values of inductance, and determine the reactance of each at four different frequencies. Plot a curve of inductive reactance as a function of frequency for each using the same coordinate axes. (a) What is the shape of each curve? (b) Which curve has the greatest slope? (c) Why should each curve start at the origin of the coordinate axes?

2. Define series resonance.

3. What is the relation between the voltage across a series L-R-C circuit and the current in the circuit at a frequency below the resonant frequency? Explain.

4. What is the relation between the voltage across a series L-R-C circuit and the circuit current at a frequency above the resonant frequency? Explain.

5. What factor largely determines the sharpness of the rise of current near the resonance frequency in a series-resonant circuit?

6. What is the advantage of a resonant circuit having a high $Q$?

7. How is the $Q$ of a resonant circuit affected by an increase in (a) resistance, (b) inductance, (c) frequency?

GROUP B

8. How can the resonant frequency of an L-R-C circuit be varied?

9. What would be the effect of having an inductor connected in series with a lamp in an a-c circuit? Explain.

10. A variable capacitor is connected in series in the circuit of Question 9 and when adjusted, the lamp glows normally. Explain.

11. A series L-R-C circuit is connected across an a-c signal source of variable frequency. Draw a curve to show the way in which the circuit current varies with the frequency of the source.

12. An a-c circuit has a low power factor because of an inductive load. (a) What is the effect of this low power factor on the circuit current? (b) Suggest a way to raise the power factor closer to unity.

# problems

GROUP B

1. A resonant circuit has an inductance of 320 $\mu$h and a capacitance of $8\bar{0}$ pf. What is the resonant frequency?

2. Assume that the frequency of the signal voltage applied to the resonant circuit of Problem 1 is varied from a value of 25 khz below the resonant frequency to 25 khz above. (a) Obtain values of inductive reactance for every 5 khz over this range of frequencies. Plot a curve showing inductive reactance as a function of frequency, using the frequency as the reference abscissa. (b) Obtain values of ca-

pacitive reactance for every 5 khz, and plot a curve showing capacitive reactance as a function of frequency, using the same reference abscissa. (c) Determine the resonant frequency graphically from your curves by plotting the values for $(X_L - X_C)$.

3. The variable capacitor used to tune a broadcast receiver has a maximum capacitance of 350 pf. The lowest frequency to which we wish to tune the receiver is 550 khz. What value of inductance should be used in the resonant circuit?

4. The minimum capacitance of the variable capacitor of Problem 3 is 15 pf. What is the highest resonant frequency that may be obtained from the circuit?

# 22 Electronic Devices

## 22.1 Vacuum-tube applications

The development of vacuum tubes marked the beginning of the engineering art called *electronics*. Through electronics vacuum tubes have been used in ways that have had a profound impact on our lives and our standard of living. Vacuum tubes made possible the development of radio, long distance communications, sound motion pictures, public address systems, television, radar, electronic computers, and industrial automation. Vacuum tubes have been designed to perform many different functions:

1. As *rectifiers*, they convert alternating current to direct current.

2. As *mixers*, they combine separate signals to produce a different signal.

3. As *detectors*, they separate the useful component from a complex signal.

4. As *amplifiers*, they increase the strength of a signal.

5. As *oscillators*, they convert a direct current to an alternating current of a desired frequency.

6. As *wave-shapers*, they change a voltage waveform into a desired shape for a special use.

A vacuum tube usually contains a *cathode* as a source of electrons, an *anode*, commonly called a *plate*, that attracts electrons from the cathode, and one or more *grids* for controlling the flow of electrons between cathode and plate. These electrodes are enclosed in a highly evacuated, gas-tight envelope. Modified forms of the vacuum tube may contain only a cathode and a plate, or two independent sets of electrodes in a single

**Figure 22-1** Modern vacuum tubes are designed to perform a variety of highly specialized functions. Shown here is a magnetron that serves as the radiation source in a microwave oven. More powerful magnetrons serve as transmitter tubes in pulsed radar systems.

envelope. In some tubes, a small amount of a particular gas is introduced to obtain special operating characteristics.

Common tubes are classified as *diodes*, *triodes*, *tetrodes*, and *pentodes*, according to the number of electrodes. High-vacuum tubes are known as *hard* tubes and those containing a gas under very low pressure are known as *soft* tubes. Special tubes have special names. For example, the cathode-ray tube is a visual-indicating tube used in cathode-ray oscilloscopes. It serves also as the picture tube in television sets, the indicator tube in radar equipment, and the visual-display tube in computers.

## 22.2 Vacuum tube development

*1. The Edison effect.* While experimenting with the first electric lamp in 1883, Thomas Edison (1847–1931) was plagued by the frequent burning out of the carbon filament and the accompanying black deposit inside the bulb. In an effort to correct this difficulty Edison sealed a metal plate inside the lamp near the filament and connected it through a galvanometer to the filament battery, as shown in Figure 22-2. He observed a deflection on the galvanometer when the plate was connected to the positive terminal of the battery, but no deflection when the plate was connected to the negative terminal. Edison recorded these observations and continued his lamp experiments without attempting to explain the phenomenon.

Several years later the English physicist Sir Joseph Thomson (1856–1940) discovered the electron and provided the explanation for the *Edison effect*. When the plate in Figure 22-2 was made positive, electrons escaping from the heated carbon filament were attracted through the evacuated space to the plate. The resulting electron current in the galvanometer circuit produced the meter deflection that Edison had observed. When the plate was made negative, on the other hand, the escaping electrons were repelled from the plate and there was no electron current in the galvanometer circuit.

*2. The Fleming valve.* Near the end of 1901 "wireless telegraphy," the forerunner of modern radio communications, was successfully used to transmit radio signals over long distances. In these early days of radio, crystals of semiconductor materials were used as receivers to *detect*, or recover, the message from the transmitted signals. These crystals were unsatisfactory in many ways. A better method of detection was clearly needed.

In 1904 the English physicist J. A. Fleming (1849–1945) patented the first *diode*, called the *Fleming valve*. He used the Edison effect to develop a crude detector for radio signals. Fleming's valve was so insensitive that it found little immediate application, and yet it was an important link in the evolution of the vacuum tube.

Figure 22-2   The Edison effect.

**Figure 22-3** Lee De Forest was one of the pioneers of the development of wireless telegraphy in America. Among his many inventions was the triode, known as the audion, which made long-distance telephone and radio broadcasting possible. De Forest also invented a system for recording sound on film, which made sound motion pictures possible.

**Figure 22-4** De Forest's three-element vacuum tube, the triode.

*3. The De Forest triode.* In 1906 the American inventor Lee De Forest (1873–1961) developed a vacuum tube that could amplify feeble radio signals that neither the Fleming valve nor the crystal detector was sensitive enough to detect.

De Forest placed a third electrode, consisting of a *grid* of fine wire between the filament and plate of the diode, as shown in Figure 22-4. He found that a small variation in voltage applied to the grid produced a large variation of current in the plate circuit of the tube. Thus the feeble radio signals from an antenna could be amplified by De Forest's *triode*. The amplified signals could then be successfully detected by the Fleming valve to provide the varying d-c signal necessary to operate headphones. The success of the De Forest triode led to the development of modern vacuum tubes.

## 22.3 Thermionic emission

Electric conduction involves a transfer of some kind of charged particles. Metallic substances conduct electricity because they have many free electrons. In a tube containing a gas under low pressure, ionized gas molecules are responsible for conduction. The number of gas particles in a highly evacuated tube is so small, however, that conduction by gas ionization is insignificant. Conduction in a high vacuum involves the introduction of charged particles into the electric field in the evacuated space between two electrodes. The charged particles released into the electric field are electrons. These electrons are released from a metallic surface by a process known as *thermionic emission*.

The free electrons of a metallic conductor are in continuous motion with speeds that increase with temperature. To escape from the surface of a conductor, an electron must do work to overcome the attractive forces at the surface of a material. At ordinary temperatures, the kinetic energies of electrons are not large enough to exceed the work function of the surface; the electrons cannot escape.

At a *high* temperature the average kinetic energy of the free electrons is large and a relatively large number will have enough energy to escape through the surface of the material. ***Thermionic emission** is the emission of electrons from a hot surface*. It is analogous to the evaporation of molecules from the surface of water.

The rate at which electrons escape from an emitting surface increases as the temperature of the emitter is raised. In the photoelectric effect, photons of light supply the energy required to eject electrons through the surface barrier of the photosensitive material. In thermionic emission, it is thermal energy that produces this same effect.

The high temperatures needed for satisfactory thermionic emission in vacuum tubes limit the number of suitable emitters to such substances as *tungsten*, *thoriated tungsten*, and certain *oxide-coated metals*. Tungsten and thoriated tungsten operate at very high temperatures and are connected directly to a source of filament current. These *directly heated cathodes* are known as *filament cathodes*, or simply *filaments*. They are used as electron emitters in large transmitting tubes.

Oxide-coated emitters consist of a metal such as nickel coated with a mixture of barium and strontium oxides, which in turn are covered with a surface layer of metallic barium and strontium. The electrons are emitted from this metallic surface layer. Such emitters can be heated to operating temperature either directly as a filament cathode or indirectly by radiation from an incandescent tungsten filament. *Indirectly heated cathodes* are commonly called *heater cathodes*, or simply *cathodes*. See Figure 22-6. Since practically all receiving tubes in use today have oxide-coated emitters, we shall concern ourselves principally with vacuum tubes of this type.

*Work function is explained in Section 12.7 in connection with photoelectric effect.*

**Figure 22-5** Vacuum tubes vary widely in their appearance because different designs are manufactured for different circuit requirements. This vacuum tube, designed for high-power applications, has radiation fins to dissipate heat.

(A) Directly heated cathode    (B) Indirectly heated cathode    (C) Heater symbol omitted

**Figure 22-6** Circuit symbols for directly and indirectly heated cathodes.

The simplest vacuum tubes are diodes that contain two elements—a cathode and a plate. Diode circuit symbols are shown in Figure 22-7. If the plate is made positive with respect to the cathode, the diode conducts because electrons flow from the cathode to the plate inside the tube and from the plate through the plate circuit to the cathode outside the tube. If the plate is negative with respect to the cathode, the diode does not conduct and there is no plate current in the external circuit. Thus a diode acts as a one-way valve for electrons; it allows electrons to flow in one direction through the circuit, but not in the other.

As electrons are emitted from the hot cathode, the space

## 22.4 Diode characteristics

(A)               (B)

**Figure 22-7** Circuit symbols for diodes with indirectly heated cathode (A) and directly heated cathode (B).

*When the plate charge is positive, electrons are accelerated toward the plate by the intervening electric field.*

about the cathode becomes negatively charged. This negatively charged space, called the *space charge*, opposes the escape of additional electrons from the cathode. The extent of electron emission depends on the temperature of the cathode.

At low positive plate voltages only those electrons near the plate are attracted to it, so a small plate current is produced. As the plate voltage is increased, greater numbers of electrons are attracted and the plate current is increased while the space charge is reduced.

In an ordinary circuit resistance the proportionality of current to voltage is described by Ohm's law. The resistor is said to be a linear, or *ohmic*, element in the circuit. In the case of the diode, the plate current is not proportional to the plate voltage. The diode and other such devices are said to be nonlinear, or nonohmic, elements in the circuit.

A diode circuit from which we can determine the plate current, $I_P$, as a function of plate voltage, $E_P$, for different filament temperatures is shown in Figure 22-8(A). The family of $I_P$ vs. $E_P$ curves is shown in Figure 22-8(B).

**Figure 22-8** A dioide circuit and characteristic curves showing the plate current as a function of plate voltage at different filament temperatures.

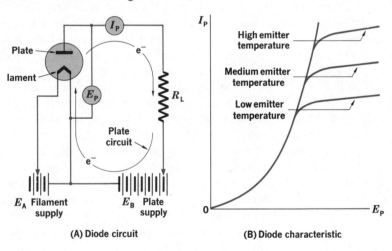

(A) Diode circuit              (B) Diode characteristic

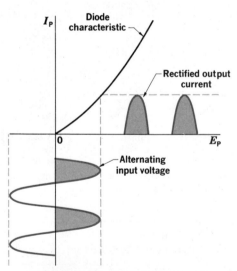

**Figure 22-9** A diode characteristic used to show the rectifying action of a power diode.

Diode tubes can be classified as *power* diodes or *signal* diodes. The difference is primarily one of size and power-handling capabilities. Power diodes are used as rectifiers in power-supply circuits and must be large enough to dissipate the heat generated during their operation. Signal diodes are small and handle signals of negligible power. They are used principally as detectors and wave-shapers. See Figure 22-9. They are frequently enclosed in the same envelope with triodes and pentodes.

## 22.5 The triode amplifier

De Forest perfected the first *triode* amplifier by inserting a third electrode between the cathode and plate of a diode. This electrode consists of an open spiral of fine wire that presents a neg-

Grid wires

(A)                    (B)

**Figure 22-10** Sketch of the electrode configuration of a triode (A) and the triode circuit symbol (B).

ligible physical barrier to electrons flowing from cathode to plate. However, a small potential difference between this electrode and the cathode has an important controlling effect on the flow of electrons from cathode to plate, and thus on the current in the plate circuit. For this reason the third electrode is called a *control grid*. We may think of a triode as an adjustable electron valve. The electrode configuration of a triode and the triode circuit symbol are shown in Figure 22-10.

If the control grid is made sufficiently negative with respect to the cathode, all electrons are repelled toward the cathode. In this condition the plate current is zero and the triode is said to be *cut off*. The grid-to-cathode voltage is called the *grid bias*. *The smallest negative grid voltage for a given plate voltage that causes the tube to cease to conduct is the **cut-off bias***. This design characteristic of vacuum tubes containing control grids is important in the circuit applications of these tubes.

The effects of different grid-bias voltages on the plate current of a triode are shown in Figure 22-11. If a negative grid bias less than the cut-off value is used, some electrons pass through the grid and reach the plate to provide some magnitude of plate current. As the negative grid bias is reduced toward zero, the plate current increases accordingly. At zero bias, the plate current is fairly large and depends primarily on the plate voltage. The performance of the triode is now essentially the same as that of a diode of similar construction.

**Figure 22-11** The effects of control-grid bias on the plate current of a triode.

**(A) High negative bias**

**(B) Low negative bias**

**(C) Zero bias**

**(D) Low positive bias**

**Figure 22-12** A basic triode amplifier circuit.

*There is no d-c current in the grid circuit because the grid bias is negative with respect to the cathode. See Figure 22-11(B).*

*The sum of the potential drops around a series circuit must equal the applied emf.*

If, on the other hand, the grid is made positive with respect to the cathode, it no longer repels the electrons of the space charge but accelerates them in the direction of the plate. The plate current is increased by this action; however, *some electrons are attracted to the grid and produce an appreciable current in the grid circuit*. Grid current causes power dissipation in the grid circuit, which represents a waste of power. Thus the grid is normally maintained at some negative potential with respect to that of the cathode.

A basic triode amplifier circuit is shown in Figure 22-12. Small variations in grid potential cause larger variations in plate current than those caused by similar variations in plate potential. Thus voltage amplification across the circuit is possible. A small a-c voltage across the input circuit can produce an amplified a-c voltage across the output circuit.

With batteries $E_B$ and $E_C$ in the circuit of Figure 22-12, a d-c current is in the plate circuit of the triode. Observe that the d-c plate circuit consists of the plate-supply battery $E_B$, the cathode-to-plate resistance in the triode (an inherent value characteristic of the triode used), and the plate-load resistance $R_L$.

The plate current $I_P$ produces a drop in potential $I_P R_L$ across the load resistance. Consequently, the d-c plate potential $E_P$ is less than $E_B$ by the magnitude of $I_P R_L$.

$$E_P = E_B - I_P R_L$$

In Figure 22-12, $E_B$ is $25\overline{0}$ v, $E_C$ is $-5.0$ v, and $R_L$ is 10.0 kΩ. With no a-c signal on the grid, typical d-c operating conditions of the amplifier circuit can be established by assuming a d-c plate current $I_P$ of 10.0 ma.

A d-c current of 10.0 ma in $R_L$ produces a drop in potential across $R_L$ of $10\overline{0}$ v.

$$I_P R_L = 10.0 \text{ ma} \times 10.0 \text{ k}\Omega = 10\overline{0} \text{ v}$$

The d-c plate potential $E_P$ is therefore $15\overline{0}$ v.

$$E_P = E_B - I_P R_L = 25\overline{0} \text{ v} - 10\overline{0} \text{ v} = 15\overline{0} \text{ v}$$

These circuit values of $I_P$, $E_P$, and $I_P R_L$ represent the steady-state (d-c) operating conditions of the amplifier circuit. These steady-state values are shown in Figure 22-13.

Suppose we now apply an a-c signal of $\pm 1.0$ v across the grid circuit of Figure 22-12. This a-c voltage is imposed on the steady-state grid bias of $-5.0$ v. It gives an a-c component $e_G$ that varies between $-4.0$ v and $-6.0$ v *at the frequency of the a-c signal*.

When the input signal is $+1.0$ v, $e_G$ will be $-4.0$ v ($-5.0$ v $+ 1.0$ v $= -4.0$ v) and the plate current will increase because the grid bias is *less negative*. Assuming that the plate current increases to 15.0 ma, $i_P R_L$ will *increase* to $15\overline{0}$ v (15.0 ma ×

10.0 kΩ = 15$\bar{0}$ v). Therefore $e_P$ will *decrease* to 10$\bar{0}$ v. (Note that 25$\bar{0}$ v − 15$\bar{0}$ v = 10$\bar{0}$ v.) See the first half-period $e_G$, $i_P$, and $e_P$ waveforms in Figure 22-13.

*Note that a +1.0-v signal raises $e_G$ in the positive sense, raises $i_P$, and lowers $e_P$.*

(A) $e_G$ vs. $t$

(B) $i_P$ vs. $t$

(C) $e_P$ vs. $t$

**Figure 22-13** Grid voltage, plate current, and plate voltage variations of a vacuum triode amplifer showing phase inversion between $e_G$ and $e_P$.

When the input signal is $-1.0$ v, $e_G$ will be $-6.0$ v [$-5.0$ v $+$ $(-1.0$ v$) = -6.0$ v] and the plate current will *decrease* because the grid bias is *more negative*. If $i_P$ decreases to 5.0 ma, $i_PR_L$ will *decrease* to $5\bar{0}$ v ($5.0$ ma $\times$ $10.0$ k$\Omega$ = $5\bar{0}$ v). As a result, $e_P$ will *increase* to $20\bar{0}$ v. (Again, $25\bar{0}$ v $- 5\bar{0}$ v $= 20\bar{0}$ v.)

*Note that a $-1.0$-v signal lowers $e_G$ in a negative sense, lowers $i_P$, and raises $e_P$.*

Figure 22-13 shows that a variation of $\pm 1.0$ v at the grid produces a variation of $\pm 5\bar{0}$ v at the plate; voltage amplification or "gain" across the amplifier circuit is $5\bar{0}$. Note that a change in grid voltage in a positive sense results in a change in plate voltage in a negative sense. The output voltage is opposite in *phase* to that of the input voltage. The a-c voltage gain across the amplifier circuit is accompanied by a voltage phase inversion.

## 22.6 The cathode-ray tube

The cathode-ray tube is a special kind of vacuum tube used in test equipment, radar, television receivers, and computers to present a visual display of information. Electrons are emitted from a cathode, accelerated to a high velocity, and brought to focus on a fluorescent screen. This screen is a translucent coating on the inside surface of the glass face of the tube. It *fluoresces*, emitting visible light at the point where the electron beam strikes.

When bombarded by electrons, fluorescent substances emit light of characteristic colors. All fluorescent substances have some *phosphorescence*, or after-glow, the persistence of which depends on the material and the energy of the bombarding electrons. Cathode-ray tubes used in test equipment such as the oscilloscope have short-persistence screens that emit predominantly green light. The picture tubes of television receivers have long-persistence screens.

The electron beam is moved over the fluorescent screen in response to the information signals being presented. This means that the information, in the form of electric signals, must be used to deflect the beam from its quiescent path within the tube.

An electron has negligible inertia since its mass is approximately $10^{-27}$ gram. Thus a beam of electrons can be deflected back and forth across the screen of a cathode-ray tube at very high speeds in response to weak signals. In a television receiver, for example, the electron beam sweeps across the face of the picture tube 15,750 times each second at a speed of the order of 24,000 km per hour.

There are two general methods of deflecting the electron beam in cathode-ray tubes: *electrostatic deflection* and *electromagnetic deflection*.

*1. Electrostatic deflection systems.* A cathode-ray tube employing electrostatic deflection is shown in Figure 22-14. The electrode arrangement that produces a focused beam of electrons is called the *electron gun*. It consists of an indirectly heated *cathode* capable of high emission, a *control grid* that regulates the intensity of the electron beam, a *focusing anode*, and an *accelerating anode*. The two anodes are maintained at high positive potentials with respect to the cathode. They produce an electric field that acts as an *electrostatic lens* to converge the electron paths at a point on the screen.

Deflection of the beam is accomplished by two pairs of *deflecting plates* set at right angles to each other. Signal voltages applied to these plates establish electrostatic fields through which the electrons move. The electron beam is subjected to deflecting forces in both the horizontal and vertical planes. Since electrons have negligible inertia, their response to these forces is practically instantaneous in the direction of the resultant force. Electrostatic deflection is generally used in the small cathode-ray tubes of test equipment.

2. *Electromagnetic deflection*. Large cathode-ray tubes have electromagnetic deflection systems. The beam can be focused either electrostatically, as shown in Figure 22-14, or magnetically by means of an external focusing coil. Beam control is accomplished with coils formed into a deflection yoke placed on the neck of the tube.

**Figure 22-14** The construction of a cathode-ray tube using electrostatic deflection.

The most common color picture tubes have three electron guns, one for each primary-color phosphor. These color phosphors are on a tricolor, phosphor-dot screen. The electron beams scan the screen to produce the primary colors of light on the face of the tube. The structure of a typical color television tube is shown in Figure 22-15. Cathode-ray tubes with more than three electron guns have been developed for use in highly specialized electronic equipment.

**Figure 22-15** A cutaway view of a color-TV picture tube.

## 22.7 Photomultiplier tube

**Figure 22-16** Photomultiplier tube with six stages of secondary emission.

Secondary emission, the liberation of electrons from a metal surface by the impact of a high-speed electron, can be used in conjunction with the photoelectric effect to detect light of very low intensity. This special form of photoelectric cell is known as a *photomultiplier tube*.

A diagram of a photomultiplier tube is shown in Figure 22-16. The number of photoelectrons emitted by the light-sensitive cathode in a given time is proportional to the intensity of the incident light. These photoelectrons are attracted to the first secondary-emission electrode, which is 100 volts positive with respect to the emitter cathode. On impact, additional electrons are released by secondary emission.

Successive secondary-emission electrodes, each more positive (less negative) than the one preceding it, contribute additional electrons as the electron stream progresses toward the collector anode. Thus a meager photoemission from a faint incident light can develop into an avalanche of electrons by the time it arrives at the collector plate. If each electron impact produces **n** secondary electrons, a photomultiplier tube with **x** secondary-emission electrodes will supply **n**$^x$ electrons to the collector plate for each photoelectron emitted.

Suppose a faint light incident on the photoemission cathode of the tube shown in Figure 22-16 will produce *five* photoelectrons per millisecond. Also suppose that each electron impact will produce *four* secondary electrons. Since the tube has *six* secondary-emission stages, the number of electrons arriving at the collector plate will be of the order of $2 \times 10^4$ per millisecond.

$$5n^x = 5 \times 4^6 = 2 \times 10^4$$

This equation suggests the extraordinary gain that can be achieved with a photomultiplier tube compared to that of a regular photoelectric cell.

# questions

GROUP A

1. What device is primarily responsible for the development of electronics as a branch of engineering?

2. What discovery by J. J. Thomson provided the explanation for the Edison effect?

3. What significant advantage was realized with De Forest's triode that had not been possible with previously developed diodes?

4. (a) Define thermionic emission. (b) What type of emitter is commonly used in receiving tubes?

5. Why is the grid of a triode called a control grid?

6. What is meant when a vacuum tube is said to be cut off?

7. Why is the control grid of a vacuum tube normally maintained at some negative potential with respect to the cathode?

GROUP B

8. Suggest two possible reasons why Edison did not offer an explanation for the phenomenon known as the Edison effect.

9. Explain voltage inversion between the control grid and plate in a vacuum-tube circuit.

10. What is the electron gun of a cathode-ray tube?

11. What is the basic difference between the electrostatic and electromagnetic deflecting systems used in cathode-ray tubes?

12. (a) Explain why the first secondary-emission electrode of a photomultiplier tube is maintained at a positive (less negative) potential with respect to the photoemission electrode. (b) Why is each successive secondary-emission electrode at a positive potential with respect to the preceding electrode?

# TRANSISTORS

Metals are good *conductors* of electric currents. Many nonmetallic materials are classed as *insulators* because their resistivities are enormous compared with those of metals. For most practical purposes they are considered to be *nonconductors*. Some elements, including germanium, silicon, and selenium, and certain compounds, such as copper oxide, lead sulfide, and zinc oxide, are in a class of crystals called *semiconductors*. These substances have resistivities that fall between those of conductors and insulators.

One of the devices from the early days of radio that is found in modern electronic circuits is the *crystal diode*. The rectifying property of silicon or galena (lead sulfide) crystals was used in early receivers before the development of the diode tube. During World War II, improved crystal diodes were developed for use in radar receivers. They are now used extensively in many types of circuits to perform a variety of specialized functions. They have the advantage of small size, and they require no heater or filament power.

A modern crystal diode can consist of a tiny wafer of silicon or germanium and a platinum *catwhisker*, all contained in a sealed

## 22.8 Crystal diodes

*Refer to the resistivity spectrum of Figure 17-23.*

Case — | Metal base | Marks cathode end | Plate | Cathode

Plate lead | Catwhisker | Germanium wafer | Cathode lead

**(A) Crystal diode**

**(B) Circuit symbol**

**Figure 22-17** A crystal diode and its circuit symbol.

capsule. See Figure 22-17. The crystal acts as the cathode of the diode and the catwhisker acts as the anode. The diode characteristic depends on the unique property of a semiconductor that permits a relatively large flow of electrons in the *forward* direction with a small applied voltage, and only a very small flow of electrons in the *reverse* direction, even at a much larger applied voltage.

## 22.9 Transistor development

After nearly a decade of basic research in the physics of semiconductors, physicists discovered how to produce a semiconductor device that could amplify. This device, known as a *transistor*, was developed by a team of physicists at the Bell Telephone Laboratories in 1948. Transistors are tiny, rugged structures that require very little power. The development of a family of transistors that can perform the functions of vacuum tubes has made possible the miniaturization of electronic circuits. See Figure 22-18.

The first transistors were known as *point-contact* transistors. These devices have been replaced by *junction* transistors. Junction transistors can be further classified into several broad categories depending on the forming process and performance characteristics. Another addition to the semiconductor family is the *field-effect* transistor.

As the physicist's knowledge of semiconductor materials expands, new transistor configurations with improved frequency response and power-handling capabilities continue to appear. The key to the transistor effect is the introduction of specific impurities into silicon and germanium crystals to form **P**- and **N**-type semiconductor materials. The process is referred to as *doping*.

**Figure 22-18** Semiconductor components are produced for a variety of circuit designs. The coin (dime) suggests component size.

## 22.10 P- and N-type semiconductors

Silicon and germanium are quite similar in their structure and chemical behavior. The atoms of both elements have *four* valence electrons bound in the same way in their respective crystals. In its transistor functions, germanium is the more versatile semiconductor. It has a diamond cubic crystal lattice

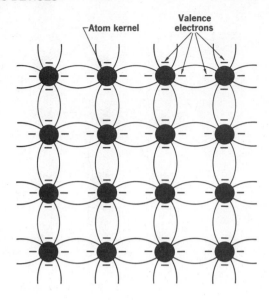

**Atom kernel**

**Valence electrons**

**Figure 22-19** Electron-paired bonds in a pure germanium crystal.

in which each atom is bonded to four neighboring atoms through shared electrons, as illustrated in Figure 22-19. This arrangement binds the four valence electrons of each atom so that pure germanium would appear to be a nonconductor. *Germanium acquires the diode property of rectification and the transistor property of amplification through the presence of trace quantities of certain impurities in the crystal structure*. Two types of impurities are important: one is known as a *donor*, the other as an *acceptor*.

Antimony, arsenic, and phosphorus are typical donor elements. The atoms of each have *five* valence electrons. When minute traces of phosphorus are added to germanium, each phosphorus atom joins the crystal lattice by *donating* one electron to the crystal structure. Four of the five valence electrons are paired, but the fifth electron is relatively free to wander through the lattice like the free electrons of a metallic conductor. The detached electron leaves behind a phosphorus atom with a unit positive charge bound into the crystal lattice. Germanium with this kind of crystal structure is known as *N-type*, or *electron-rich* germanium, because most of its conductivity results from *negative* charge carriers. *N-type germanium consists of germanium to which are added equal numbers of free electrons and bound positive charges so that the net charge is zero*. The added negative charge carriers (the free electrons) greatly increase conductivity over that of the pure semiconductor. An **N**-type semiconductor crystal is illustrated in Figure 22-20(A).

Atoms with *three* valence electrons, such as those of aluminum, boron, and gallium, will act as acceptors. When minute traces

*The controlled addition of donor or acceptor atoms to a semiconductor material during crystal growth is referred to as "doping" the semiconductor.*

*In N-type semiconductors the charge carriers are negatively charged electrons.*

(A)   N-type semiconductor

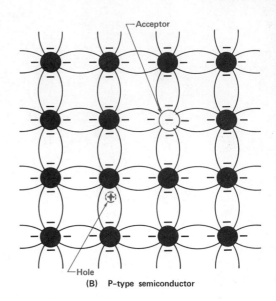

(B)   P-type semiconductor

**Figure 22-20** The **N**-type germanium crystal illustrated in (A) has donor atoms and free electrons in equal numbers. The **P**-type germanium crystal in (B) has acceptor atoms and free (positive) holes in equal numbers.

of aluminum are added to germanium, each aluminum atom joins the crystal lattice by *accepting* a single electron from a neighboring germanium atom. This leaves a *hole* in the electron-pair bond from which the electron is acquired.

We can think of this hole as the equivalent of a *positive charge* since it acts as a trap into which an electron can fall. As an electron fills the hole, it leaves another hole behind, into which another electron can fall. *In effect* then, the hole (positive charge) detaches itself and becomes free to move in the opposite sense to that of the electron, leaving behind the aluminum atom with a unit negative charge bound into the crystal lattice. Germanium with this crystal structure is called *P-type*, or *hole-rich* germanium, because most of the conductivity results from *positive* charge carriers. ***P-type germanium** consists of germanium to which are added equal numbers of free positive holes and bound negative charges so that the net charge is zero*. The added positive charge carriers (the holes) greatly increase conductivity over that of the pure semiconductor. A **P**-type semiconductor crystal is illustrated in Figure 22-20(B).

*In P-type semiconductors the charge carriers are, in effect, positively charged holes.*

## 22.11 The P-N junction

*Review electric fields in Sections 16.9 and 16.16.*

As a germanium crystal is formed, donor and acceptor atoms can be added in such a way that a definite boundary is created between **P**-type and **N**-type regions of the crystal. At this boundary some free electrons from the **N** region drift into the **P** region and a corresponding number of holes from the **P** region drift into the **N** region. An electric field, $\mathscr{E}$, is established across the bound-

**Figure 22-21** The electric barrier of the **P-N** junction.

ary layer as it becomes devoid of electron carriers on the **N** side and of hole carriers on the **P** side. In the resulting equilibrium state the boundary layer becomes a kind of electric barrier. It is called the *P-N junction*. The electric barrier of the **P-N** junction is illustrated in Figure 22-21.

The crystal as a whole has properties of a diode and is called a *P-N junction diode*. The hole-charge carriers of the **P** region cannot pass through the electric barrier of the **P-N** junction to reach the **N** region. The electron-charge carriers of the **N** region cannot pass through the electric barrier to reach the **P** region.

A small potential difference impressed across the diode, as in Figure 22-22(A), enables the free electrons to cross the junction and pass into the **P** crystal. A corresponding number of holes cross into the **N** crystal. Recall that the apparent movement of holes is in the opposite sense to the actual movement of electrons that fall in the holes of the **P**-type crystal. Thus an electron current is established across the **P-N** junction and in the external circuit.

*The P-N junction is the meeting zone of oppositely doped regions of a semiconductor crystal.*

**Figure 22-22** The **P-N** junction is the rectifying element of semiconductor crystals.

(A)          (B)

If the battery connections are reversed, as in Figure 22-22(B), the free electrons in the **N** crystal and the free holes of the **P** crystal are attracted away from the **P-N** junction. The junction region is left without current carriers; consequently, there is no conduction across the junction and no current in the circuit.

The junction has the diode characteristic of permitting unidirectional electron flow with ease when a small voltage is applied in the proper sense. Thus the **P-N** junction is the rectifying element of semiconductor crystals.

### 22.12 Two types of junction transistors

Junction transistors consist of two **P-N** junctions back to back with a thin **P**-type or **N**-type region formed between them. If the center region is composed of **P**-type material, the transistor is designated **N-P-N**. The physical diagram of an **N-P-N** transistor and its circuit symbol are illustrated in Figure 22-23(A).

Physical diagram    (A) N-P-N transistor

**Figure 22-23** A comparison of **N-P-N** and **P-N-P** junction transistors.

Physical diagram    (B) P-N-P transistor

The **N**-type material shown at the left of the **P**-type center is the *emitter*. It is normally biased negatively with respect to the **P**-region, which is called the *base*. The **N**-type material on the right of the base is the *collector*. It is biased positively with respect to the base. The basic circuit of the **N-P-N** transistor is shown in Figure 22-24(A).

Transistors in which the center region is composed of **N**-type semiconductor material are designated **P-N-P**. A diagram of a **P-N-P** transistor and its circuit symbol are shown in Figure 22-23(B).

**Figure 22-24** Basic **N-P-N** and **P-N-P** junction transistor circuits. Compare these circuits with that of the vacuum triode circuit of Figure 22-12.

(A) N-P-N circuit          (B) P-N-P circuit

The basic circuit of **P-N-P** transistors is given in Figure 22-24(B). Observe that it is the same as that for **N-P-N** transistors except that the battery connections are reversed.

In either **N-P-N** or **P-N-P** transistors, the emitter is biased to supply charges—electrons or holes—to be acquired by the collector through the two junctions of the base. An **N**-type emitter is biased negatively with respect to the base to supply electrons to its **N-P** junction and then to the **P**-type base. A **P**-type emitter is biased positively to withdraw electrons from its **P-N** junction and thus from the **N**-type base. This statement is equivalent to saying that the **P**-type emitter supplies holes to its **P-N** junction and then to the **N**-type base. Both emitter types are said to have *forward* bias. The emitter circuits of Figure 22-24(A) and Figure 22-24(B) have forward-bias voltages applied by batteries $E_E$.

In the transistor circuit symbol, the arrowhead at the emitter is conventionally drawn to indicate the direction of the positive hole current. *Electron current is in the opposite direction*. This arrowhead in the transistor circuit symbol provides a way of showing which type of transistor is represented in a circuit diagram. In the **P-N-P** circuit symbol, note that the arrowhead at the emitter *points toward the base*. It points *away from the base* in the **N-P-N** circuit symbol.

An **N**-type collector is biased positively with respect to the base to attract electrons from its **N-P** junction and from the **P**-type base. A **P**-type collector is biased negatively to transfer electrons to its **P-N** junction and into the **N**-type base. Again, this is equivalent to saying it attracts holes from its **P-N** junction and thus from the **N**-type base. Both collector types are said to have *reverse* bias. The collector circuits of Figure 22-24(A) and Figure 22-24(B) have reverse-bias voltages applied by batteries $E_C$.

The forward bias on emitters and the reverse bias on collectors have the effect of producing an electron current in the **N-P-N** transistor from emitter to base in the emitter circuit and from base to collector in the collector circuit. Forward emitter bias and reverse collector bias in the **P-N-P** transistor produce an electron current from collector to base and from base to emitter.

The base section serves to isolate the emitter input circuit from the collector output circuit of a transistor. This isolation results from the barrier voltages established at the two junctions. The barrier polarities at these two junctions are reversed because the base has an **N-P** junction at one side and a **P-N** junction at the other.

Forward bias at the emitter junction overcomes the barrier voltage and enables the emitter to supply charge to the base. The reversed polarity of the barrier voltage at the collector junction, augmented by the reverse collector bias, aids the transfer of charge through the junction to the collector. Transistor performance is achieved when the collector current is controlled by the emitter current in the base.

### 22.13 Transistor amplification

The transistor circuits shown in Figure 22-24 are *common-base* amplifiers. Small signals introduced into the emitter circuit are supplemented by energy from the collector battery and larger signals are transferred from the collector circuit. This effect is accomplished in spite of the fact that the collector current is slightly smaller than the emitter current.

Amplification in the common-base transistor amplifier is due to the ratio of output impedance to input impedance, which may be of the order of 1000:1. Low emitter impedance is obtained by the *forward* biasing of the emitter junction, that is, the junction between the emitter section and the base section. As stated in Section 22.12, the effect is to reduce the electric field across the emitter junction. High collector impedance is obtained by the *reverse* biasing of the junction between the collector section and the base section. This effect is to increase the electric field across the collector junction.

Only 1% to 5% of the emitter current passes through the base leg of the circuit. The remaining 99% to 95% passes through the collector circuit. This current can pass through the collector circuit because of the thinness of the base section and the consequent ease with which positive holes from the emitter diffuse across it to be collected.

A typical **P-N-P** common-base amplifier circuit is shown in Figure 22-25. A small signal current $i_E$ in the emitter circuit results in a low input power $i_E^2 Z_E$ because the input impedance $Z_E$ is low. The slightly smaller collector current $(i_C = i_E - i_B)$ yields a higher output power $i_C^2 Z_C$ because of the high output impedance $Z_C$. The *power gain* of the circuit is the ratio of the output power to the input power.

$$P_{\text{gain}} = \frac{P_{\text{out}}}{P_{\text{in}}}$$

**Figure 22-25** A **P-N-P** common-base amplifier.

Suppose the input impedance of the amplifier is $5\overline{0}$ Ω, the a-c emitter current is 2.0 ma, the collector current is 1.9 ma, and the output impedance is $1\overline{0}$ kΩ.

The power input is

$$P_{in} = i_E{}^2 Z_E = (2.0 \text{ ma})^2 \times 5\overline{0} \text{ Ω}$$
$$P_{in} = 0.20 \text{ w}$$

The power output is

$$P_{out} = i_C{}^2 Z_C = (1.9 \text{ ma})^2 \times 1\overline{0} \text{ kΩ}$$
$$P_{out} = 36 \text{ w}$$

The power gain is

$$P_{gain} = \frac{P_{out}}{P_{in}} = \frac{36 \text{ w}}{0.20 \text{ w}} = 180$$

A **P-N-P** transistor is used in Figure 22-25. An **N-P-N** transistor would serve just as well with the bias-voltage polarities reversed. In some circuits the two types of junction transistors are equivalent. In other circuits one type of junction transistor may have small advantages over the other.

The common-base transistor circuit that we have been considering is one of three general circuit configurations for junction transistors. Others are the common-emitter and the common-collector configurations. These configurations for both **N-P-N** and **P-N-P** transistors are shown in Figure 22-26. Observe that in all circuits the emitters have forward bias to provide low impedance and the collectors have reverse bias to provide high impedance.

(A) Common–base          (B) Common–emitter          (C) Common–collector

**Figure 22-26** Circuit configurations for N-P-N and P-N-P junction transistors.

The amplifier output signal in Figure 22-25 is *in phase* with the input signal. The common-base amplifier *does not* produce phase inversion. On the other hand, the common-emitter amplifier *does* produce a phase shift, as does a vacuum-tube amplifier.

The amplifying property of a transistor is the result of current changes that occur in the different regions of the structure when proper voltages are applied. Consequently, the transistor is often referred to as a current amplifier. More precisely, it is a *current-operated device* in much the same way that a vacuum triode is a voltage-operated device. A transistor amplifier can produce a voltage gain, a current gain, or a power gain, depending on the circuit configuration.

When the operation of a transistor is compared with that of a vacuum triode, the emitter is equivalent to the cathode, the base to the control grid, and the collector to the plate. These relationships are illustrated in Figure 22-27. The emitter and base form the signal input circuit for a transistor amplifier in the same way that the grid and cathode form the input circuit of the vacuum-triode amplifier. The collector is the output section of the transistor just as the plate is the output of the vacuum triode.

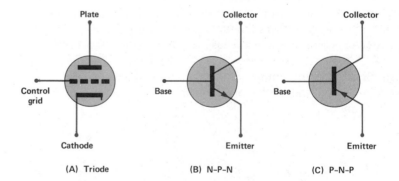

**Figure 22-27** Transistor elements compared with those of a vacuum triode. (A) Triode, (B) **N-P-N** transistor, (C) **P-N-P** transistor.

---

## 22.14 Transistor characteristics

A small signal applied to the input circuit of a transistor can be amplified because the magnitude of collector current in its output circuit is controlled by the current in its input circuit. The performance of a transistor is indicated by its family of characteristic curves. These curves describe the behavior of the transistor in a specific circuit configuration.

Typical output characteristics for an **N-P-N** transistor in a common-base configuration are shown in Figure 22-28. Each curve shows how the collector current $I_C$ varies with the output voltage $V_{CB}$, measured between the collector and base terminals, for a given value of emitter current $I_E$. The family of curves is produced by using different values of emitter current.

**Figure 22-28** Typical common base output characteristic curves for an **N-P-N** transistor. (A) Common-base test circuit, (B) $I_C - V_{CB}$ characteristics.

These curves show that the collector current is independent of the collector voltage but is dependent on the magnitude of emitter current. Variations in $I_E$ produce variations in $I_C$. At a constant value of $V_{CB}$, the ratio of a change in $I_C$ to a change in $I_E$ expresses the *current gain* of the common-base circuit. It is expressed as a positive number without dimension and is denoted by the Greek letter $\alpha$ (alpha).

$$\alpha = \frac{\Delta I_C}{\Delta I_E} \ (V_{CB} \ \textbf{constant})$$

Referring to Figure 22-28(B), suppose the emitter current $I_E$ is varied from 2.0 ma to 4.0 ma (a change of 2.0 ma) while the voltage $V_{CB}$ is held constant at 15 v. Reading from the collector current axis, $I_C$ will be found to vary from 1.9 ma to 3.8 ma (a change of 1.9 ma). The current gain can be determined from these data as follows:

$$\alpha = \frac{\Delta I_C}{\Delta I_E} = \frac{\textbf{1.9 ma}}{\textbf{2.0 ma}} = \textbf{0.95}$$

The forward current gain, or alpha characteristic, of a common-base circuit is always slightly less than unity. Typical values of $\alpha$ range from 0.95 to 0.99. The closer $\alpha$ is to unity, the better the quality of the transistor.

Figure 22-29 shows a typical family of characteristic curves of transistor performance in a common-emitter configuration. Collector current $I_C$ is plotted as a function of output voltage $V_{CE}$, measured between collector and emitter, for each value of base current $I_B$.

Base currents are very small compared to emitter and collector currents. In the common-emitter circuit, small changes in $I_B$ produce large variations in $I_C$. At a constant value of $V_{CE}$, the ratio of a change in $I_C$ to a change in $I_B$ expresses the *current*

**Figure 22-29** Typical common-emitter output characteristic curves for a **P-N-P** transistor. (A) Common-emitter test circuit, (B) $I_C - V_{CE}$ characteristics.

(A)                                                        (B)

*gain* for the common-emitter circuit. This current-gain factor is denoted by the Greek letter $\beta$ (beta).

$$\beta = \frac{\Delta I_C}{\Delta I_B} \quad (V_{CE} \text{ constant})$$

Using the typical curves of Figure 22-29(B), we will assume that the base current $I_B$ is varied from $2\overline{0}$ $\mu$a to $4\overline{0}$ $\mu$a (a change of $2\overline{0}$ $\mu$a) while $V_{CE}$ is held constant at $2\overline{0}$ v. Projecting to the collector current axis, we find that $I_C$ will vary from 1.0 ma to 2.3 ma (a change of 1.3 ma). The current gain, or $\beta$ characteristic, of this common-emitter circuit will be

$$\beta = \frac{\Delta I_C}{\Delta I_B} = \frac{1.3 \times 10^{-3}\text{a}}{2.0 \times 10^{-5}\text{a}} = 65$$

Typical values of $\beta$ range from 20 to 200. Either the common-base or the common-emitter transistor circuit will provide amplification of an input signal. With a low impedance load, where high *current gain* is desired, the common-emitter circuit is preferred. With a high impedance load, where large *power gain* is desired, the common-base circuit will serve as well and is even preferable.

The common-collector circuit is essentially the reverse of the common-emitter circuit. This configuration can be recognized in Figure 22-26. The common-collector circuit has a high input impedance and a low output impedance and a voltage gain of less than unity. Thus it has little value as an amplifier but can be used for impedance-matching between a high impedance source and a low impedance load.

## 22.15 The photovoltaic effect

Several energy-conversion processes are described in Section 17.3 as sources of electric currents. For example, heat is the source of electric current in thermoelectric action. Mechanical stress is the source of current in piezoelectric action. Chemical reactions are the source of current in fuel-cell action. These processes are characterized by a capability for *direct* conversion of thermal, mechanical, or chemical energy to electric energy.

Semiconductor materials can provide the direct conversion of radiant energy to electric energy under suitable conditions. The process is known as the *photovoltaic effect*. If a semiconductor **P-N** junction is designed to absorb incident light, a potential difference can be developed across the junction as a consequence of photovoltaic action. This potential difference can generate an electron current in a load resistance connected across the junction. Thus the **P-N** junction can act as a source of emf while exposed to light radiations.

The silicon *solar cell* is a photovoltaic converter of considerable interest. The components of a solar-cell photovoltaic circuit are shown schematically in Figure 22-30. The cell consists of a thin base layer of **P**-type silicon crystal over which a very thin (about 0.5 $\mu$m) **N**-type layer is formed. The **P-N** junction is a barrier layer with its electric field situated where the **P**- and **N**-type materials are joined. The external circuit of the cell consists of the resistance load $R_L$ connected across the **P-N** junction at terminals in contact with the **P** and **N** surfaces.

Photons of light radiations with energies corresponding to wavelengths shorter than approximately $10^{-6}$ m can dislodge electrons from silicon atoms in the crystal lattice of the solar cell. Reference to the radiation spectrum of Figure 12-8 shows that this minimum energy radiation ($\lambda = 10^{-6}$ m) lies in the near infrared region of the electromagnetic spectrum. Figure 12-8 also suggests that roughly half of the sun's radiation, including the visible and ultraviolet regions, has photon energies that can be converted to electric energy by the silicon solar cell.

When light is incident on the exposed surface of the solar cell, most of the photons pass through the very thin **N** layer and are absorbed by atoms of the crystal lattice in the vicinity of the **P-N** junction. The energy $hf$ of an absorbed photon is trans-

*The P- and N-type semiconductor sections of a photovoltaic cell can just as well be the reverse of the arrangement shown in Figure 22-30.*

*Review the formation of the P-N junction in Section 22.11.*

*$\lambda = 10^{-6}$ m = 1 $\mu$m (1 micron) = $10^4$ Å identifies radiation in the near infrared region of the solar spectrum.*

**Figure 22-30** Photovoltaic action in a silicon solar cell.

ferred to an electron which is then ejected from the atom, leaving behind a positive hole. In this way, light photons generate *electron-hole pairs* in the region of the junction layer. The electric field of the **P-N** junction forces electrons that have not recombined into the **N** layer and a corresponding number of holes into the **P** layer. These electrons are excess negative charge carriers in the **N** layer and flow through the external circuit from the **N** terminal to the **P** terminal. They then combine with the excess holes in the **P** layer. Thus the illuminated solar cell acts as a source of emf and of electron current in its external circuit.

Batteries of solar cells provide electric energy for space vehicles. Earth-bound solar batteries serve many purposes; for example, they supply energy for telephone lines and recharge storage batteries that replace the solar batteries during hours of darkness. The silicon solar cell has an important role in the ongoing search for practical and efficient ways to harness solar energy.

*The photoelectric effect is described in Section 12.6.*

A photovoltaic cell of the type usually used in photographic exposure meters consists of a junction formed by a film of copper oxide deposited on metallic copper, or of a film of selenium deposited on metallic iron. Incident light photons pass through the selenium film to the iron. Electrons are moved from the iron into the selenium layer and an emf is generated across the junction. The iron becomes the positive electrode and the selenium the negative electrode of the photovoltaic cell. If a sensitive galvanometer is connected across these electrodes, the emf produces an electron current in the meter that is proportional to the illumination on the cell. By calibrating the galvanometer in light values, proper exposure conditions can be indicated directly by the meter.

*A photoelectric circuit is shown in Figure 17-5.*

Photovoltaic action is a type of photoelectric effect in the sense that electron ejection from a parent atom is initiated by a light photon. The distinction between photoelectric action and photovoltaic action is that the former requires a vacuum environment and an external source of emf in the photoemission circuit. The latter does not require a vacuum environment, and it generates its own emf. Both types of cells are commonly referred to as *photocells*.

## summary

High-vacuum tubes are identified as diodes, triodes, tetrodes, and pentodes based on the number of electrodes present. Low-vacuum tubes contain a gas under reduced pressure. Diodes are used as detectors for radio signals and as rectifiers for converting alternating current to direct current. They are classed as signal or power diodes.

Electrons are emitted from the cathode of a vacuum tube by a process of thermionic emission. Electron emission is a function of emitter temperature. Emitters can be either directly or indirectly heated.

Voltage and power amplification are possible in triode circuits because a small signal on the grid circuit is capable of controlling a large current in the plate circuit. Conduction in a vacuum tube results from the thermionic emission of electrons from the cathode and the attraction of the electrons to the positively charged plate. The tube bias voltage between the control grid and the cathode establishes the operating condition of the tube. Bias voltages are produced by three methods. The a-c voltage gain across a vacuum-tube amplifier is accompanied by a voltage phase inversion.

P- and N-type semiconductors are formed by doping with trace quantities of acceptor and donor atoms respectively. N-type semiconductors are electron-rich materials. The free electrons are the negative charge carriers. P-type semiconductors are hole-rich materials. The holes act as positive charge carriers. The P-N junction acts as an electric barrier in the meeting zone of oppositely doped regions of a semiconductor crystal. The direction of the electric field across the junction is from the N side to the P side.

Junction transistors consist of two P-N junctions back to back with thin P or N regions in between. They are designated N-P-N and P-N-P. Transistor elements correspond functionally to the elements of a vacuum triode. In transistor circuits the emitter has a forward-bias voltage and the collector has a reverse-bias voltage. Three circuit configurations are used: common base, common emitter, and common collector.

The transistor is a current-operated device. The amplifying property is the result of current changes that occur in the different transistor regions when proper voltages are applied to the transistor elements. The performance of a transistor is indicated by its family of characteristic curves. The forward current gain of a common-base configuration is called its alpha characteristic. It is the ratio of the change in collector current to the change in emitter current for a constant collector-to-base voltage. The current gain of a common-emitter configuration is called its beta characteristic. It is the ratio of the change in collector current to the change in base current for a constant collector-to-emitter voltage.

The photovoltaic effect can provide the direct conversion of radiant energy to electric energy. Photovoltaic action is a type of photoelectric effect. The solar cell is a semiconductor diode in which the semiconductor crystal is doped in a special way. The construction and P-N junction provide the energy conversion effect when light strikes the cell's surface.

# questions

GROUP A

1. What is the property of a semiconductor crystal known as the diode characteristic?
2. Why is **N**-type germanium referred to as electron-rich germanium?
3. Why is **P**-type germanium referred to as hole-rich germanium?
4. What is the **P-N** junction of a semiconductor?
5. How are the two types of junction transistors designated?
6. Draw the circuit symbol for an **N-P-N** transistor. Label the emitter, base, and collector.
7. Draw the circuit symbol for a **P-N-P** transistor. Label the emitter, base, and collector.
8. What is the significance of the arrowhead at the emitter in a transistor circuit symbol?
9. Which sections of a junction transistor are equivalent to the cathode, control grid, and plate of a vacuum triode?
10. What are the different circuit configurations used for transistor service?

GROUP B

11. Distinguish between a germanium diode and a germanium transistor.

12. Distinguish between a **P-N-P** transistor and an **N-P-N** transistor.
13. The emitter of an **N-P-N** transistor is biased negatively and the emitter of a **P-N-P** transistor is biased positively with respect to the base. In both cases they are described as forward bias. Explain.
14. What is the alpha characteristic of a transistor and to what transistor configuration does it apply?
15. Why must the current gain in a common-base transistor circuit always be less than unity?
16. Which transistor circuit configuration most closely resembles the basic vacuum triode circuit? Explain why.
17. To what does the beta characteristic of a transistor refer?
18. How can you account for amplification in a common-base transistor circuit when the collector current in the output circuit can never be as large as the emitter current in the input circuit?
19. Photovoltaic action is a type of photoelectric effect. How do the two actions differ?
20. Suggest a reason for the exposed layer of a solar cell being so thin that most of the incident photons will penetrate the layer and be absorbed by atoms in or very near the **P-N** junction layer.

# computers

In the early 1800s, the English mathematician Charles Babbage realized that if a machine capable of remembering numbers and recognizing simple arithmetic situations could be built, it could be programmed to do complex calculations automatically. His "Difference Engine" and "Analytic Engine" were the first steps toward a true computer. Computer technology has come a long way since then; vacuum tubes and semiconductors have given rise to integrated circuits. Computer applications have grown to include fields as diverse as astronomy, medicine, and athletics!

*Left: The formation of a silicon chip begins with the growth of huge silicon crystals. Very precise temperature and a 12-hr growing period are required.*

*Bottom left: Razor-thin slices of silicon floating on an air cushion are processed to become advanced memory chips. The tubelike optical sensor loops control the movement of the wafers.*

*Bottom right: Using closed-circuit TV, an operator aligns a silicon wafer with a circuit mask during fabrication of integrated circuits. Special lighting and contamination-free conditions are essential.*

## PHOTO ESSAY

*Left: An electron-beam system interconnects up to 704 logic circuits on 4.6-mm² bipolar logic chips for circuits in high-speed computers.*

*Below left: Vacuum needles in this chip-placement machine precisely place individual silicon chips onto ½-inch-square ceramic circuit modules.*

*Bottom left: The finished product—the new dense, high-performance bipolar logic circuit. This chip contains up to 704 logic circuits with a nominal speed of 3 nanoseconds ($3 \times 10^{-9}$) per circuit.*

*In an attempt to further increase circuit density, scientists are experimenting with magnetic bubbles. This microcircuit chip contains all the elements needed to read, write, and store information.*

Top left: The transparent screen pinpoints 130 buildings whose lights, heat, airconditioning, and fire management are environmentally controlled by computer.

Top right: The time between the drawing board and production line can be greatly reduced by utilizing computer graphics in automobile design.

Bottom right: A computer that reads and talks allows this blind telephone operator to perform efficiently and effectively.

Above: Computer-assisted instruction (CAI) enables students to receive individualized instruction. Here students converse with a computer by means of a video display during a vector-learning activity.

One of the more exciting computer applications has been made in the field of astronomy. In an attempt to explain the peculiar forms of certain galaxies as a result of tidal distortions, computer simulations re-create events that took place millions of years ago. Alar Toomre, a pioneer in this endeavor, has produced the sequence of computer drawings shown here. Separated by 100 million years or more, these frames re-create the close passage of two identical model galaxies and their encounter that produced two tidal tails similar to the tails in the photograph of NGC 2623 in Cancer (top). The two central masses approach each other in elliptical orbits (1). Prior to and during the instant of closest approach (2), they feel a severe pull from the other central mass and the effects of tidal forces are evident. These forces cause the material from the far side of each disk to stretch into an ever-lengthening tail of debris (3). The arching tails appear to be crossed and the bodies of the galaxies to be overlapping toward the end of the encounter (4). The computer can further rotate the model in one dimension to reveal the unprecedented sight of how a couple of galaxies would look from a perspective other than the earth.

# 23

# Atomic Structure

### 23.1 Subatomic particles

Toward the end of the 19th century, evidence indicating that atoms were not the ultimate particles of the universe began to appear. A simple way of demonstrating the existence of subatomic particles is shown in Figure 23-1. In each picture, the glass tube contains hydrogen gas under low pressure. The conductor leading to the center of the tube is connected to the negative terminal of a direct-current source of electricity. The conductor at the top of the right bulb in each picture is connected to the positive terminal. When a high voltage is impressed across the tubes, two beams shoot out in opposite directions from the hollow electrode in the center. The two beams have different colors.

Since the tubes contain only hydrogen atoms, the differently colored beams indicate that the hydrogen atom has at least two different parts. The fact that the beams flow in opposite directions shows that the two parts of the hydrogen atom have opposite electric charges. One beam is negatively charged since it passes into the part of the tube where the positive electrode is located. The other beam is positively charged since it is attracted through the negative electrode at the center and into the left side of the tube.

The magnets in the pictures tell still more about the parts of the hydrogen atom. In the top picture, the magnet is held near the positive beam. The effect on the beam is not very pronounced. In the bottom picture, the magnet is held near the negative beam. This time the bending effect is more noticeable. This suggests that the particles composing the two beams have differences in addition to that of opposite charge. Further studies show that the main reason for the difference in the way the beams react

**Figure 23-1** Evidence of subatomic particles. The dumbell-shaped apparatus contains hydrogen gas. With a d-c voltage, hydrogen atoms separate into streams of oppositely charged particles. These photos show that hydrogen atoms are composed of at least two different parts.

to magnetism is that the positive particles have much larger masses than do the negative particles.

Starting from evidence of this kind, scientists have developed a comprehensive theory of atomic structure. Various parts of this theory will be presented in this and later chapters. It is important to remember, however, that all these discussions are based on the best current knowledge of atomic structure. Revisions will frequently become necessary as new investigations and new interpretations are made. What sort of picture of the atom will finally emerge from this research no one can fully predict. It is certain that the atom is made up of a number of still smaller particles that are arranged in various complex ways. These subatomic particles interact with each other and compose different atoms.

*The different colors in the tube also indicate that the electrons of the hydrogen atoms have been excited to different energy levels. Refer to Section 12.11.*

The first subatomic particle to be identified and studied by scientists was the electron. Actually, the discovery of this particle was a by-product of other investigations. Toward the end of the 19th century physicists were using tubes similar to the one previously described to study the conduction of electricity through various gases. When such a tube was filled with air (at atmospheric pressure), electricity would not flow between the electrodes, even under high voltages. When some of the air was removed, however, electricity began to flow from one electrode to the other through the rarefied air. The air in the tube glowed with a purplish light. When still more air was pumped from the tube, the purplish light faded and the glass walls of the tube glowed with a greenish fluorescence.

Further work with evacuated tubes showed that the greenish glow on the glass walls was produced by particles emitted from the cathode, the negative electrode. Figure 23-2(A) shows how

## 23.2 Discovery of the electron

*mass - helmholts apparatus*

**Figure 23-2** Properties of cathode rays. The shadow cast by the cross in (A) shows that cathode rays travel in straight lines. The coated screen in (B) shows the ability of cathode rays to produce fluorescence. In (C) the negative charge of cathode rays is determined by means of a magnet.

(A)

(B)

(C)

this was deduced. With the electrodes placed as shown in the figure, the walls of the tube glowed everywhere except where the cross inside the tube cast a shadow on the face of the tube. The shadow is in a direct line with the cross and the cathode. This means that the green glow is produced by something coming from the cathode in straight lines. These so-called *cathode rays* are invisible to the eye unless they produce a visible effect on some other substance, such as a glow on the glass walls of the tube. In addition, these cathode rays can be stopped by substances like the cross inside the tube.

In 1895, the French scientist Jean Perrin (1870–1942) discovered another property of cathode rays. He arranged an evacuated tube as shown in Figure 23-2(B). The slit in the tube forms a broad beam of cathode rays that strikes the fluorescent screen and causes it to glow. The screen is placed at an angle so that the beam is visible along the entire length of the screen. Ordinarily, the beam would trace a straight horizontal path on the screen. But when Perrin placed a magnet in the position shown in Figure 23-2(C), the beam was deflected downward. When he reversed the poles of the magnet, the beam was deflected upward. Since light beams are not deflected by magnets, Perrin concluded that cathode rays were really streams of negative electricity coming from the cathode.

The modern television picture tube makes use of many of the principles discovered many years ago by scientists working with cathode rays. The face of the picture tube glows when cathode rays strike it. In color television, different chemicals are used on the face of the tube so that multicolored glows are produced. The position of the picture on the tube is adjusted by magnets surrounding the neck of the tube inside the set.

Other scientists continued the investigation of cathode rays begun by Perrin. Among these were the English physicists Sir William Crookes (1832–1919) and Sir Joseph Thomson. Thomson was able to show that cathode-ray particles are much lighter than atoms and are present in all forms of matter. He arrived at this latter conclusion by observing that the nature of the particles did not change when he changed the composition of the cathode or of the gas in his tubes. Thus Thomson was the first to discover a subatomic particle—the ***electron***.

*The electron is named after a Greek word meaning beaming sun.*

## 23.3 Measuring the mass of the electron

It is obviously impossible to use a laboratory balance to determine the mass of something as small as an electron. Even if you could pile as many as $10^{13}$ electrons on the balance, the total mass would still amount to only $10^{-17}$ kg. An indirect method must therefore be used. Thomson developed such a method in a famous series of experiments in 1897. The basic parts of this experiment are shown in Figure 23-3. The cathode rays (electrons) emanating from the electrode at the left are accelerated and focused by the positively charged disk that has a small hole in its center. The potential difference, $V$, between the cathode and the disk determines the kinetic energy of each electron since $eV = \frac{1}{2}mv^2$, where $e$ is the electric charge on a single electron. A second disk further narrows the electron beam.

The beam then passes between two oppositely charged plates on its way to a fluorescent screen. These two oppositely charged plates produce an electric field. Surrounding the neck of the tube is a magnetic field that is set at right angles to the electric field. In the arrangement of Figure 23-3, the electron beam is under the influence of a downward force due to the electric field and an upward force due to the magnetic field. Both forces depend on the charge of the electrons, but the force due to the magnetic field also depends on the speed of the electrons. By varying these forces until they exactly balance each other, the speed of the electrons, $v$, can be determined and used in $eV = \frac{1}{2}mv^2$. Two unknowns, $e$ and $m$, still remain. Though neither $e$ nor $m$ can be determined individually by this method, their ratio $e/m$ can be calculated from the measured values of the potential difference, the electric field, and the magnetic field. In other words, Thomson was able to calculate the quantity of electric charge per unit mass of electrons. This quantity is expressed in coulombs per kilogram of electrons. The presently accepted value for the ratio is $1.7588047 \times 10^{11}$ c/kg.

This measurement is a step in the right direction, but it still does not tell us the mass of an electron. If the charge on a single electron could be measured, then the charge-to-mass ratio could be used to calculate the mass. Similarly, if the mass could be determined, the ratio would tell us the charge. In 1912, the American physicist Robert A. Millikan succeeded in measuring the charge on the electron; the problem was solved. His experiment will be described in the next section. Now we shall take a look at a completely different way of measuring the electron's mass.

As mentioned in Chapter 1, Einstein's equation, $E = mc^2$, states the relationship between mass and energy. Consequently, if an electron could be converted into energy, Einstein's equation could be used to calculate the original mass of the electron from the resulting energy. Conversely, if a form of energy such as a beam of X rays could be converted into an electron, the mass could again be calculated from the known energy of the X rays. Figure 23-4 shows the results of such an experiment. As the diagram to the right of the photograph indicates, X rays entered from the left and then changed into a pair of electrons, one with a positive charge, called a positron, and one with a negative charge. The bubble chamber in which the photograph was taken was in a magnetic field that caused the two particles

**Figure 23-3** The Thomson experiment. By means of an evacuated tube such as this, Thomson found that cathode radiation particles are subatomic in mass and are present in all forms of matter.

*helmholts ?*

*Millikan's work with photoelectric emissions is described in Section 12.7.*

**Figure 23-4** Pair production, as photographed in a bubble chamber. X rays entering from the left were converted into a positron-electron pair.

to spiral off in opposite directions after their formation; the positron spiraled away from the camera while the electron spiraled toward it.

Repeated experiments have shown that in order to produce an electron pair, X rays must have an energy value of $1.64 \times 10^{-13}$ joule. Since X rays with this energy produce two particles (a single electron is never produced), and since we assume that the two particles have equal masses, the mass of each particle is equivalent to half of this energy, or $8.2 \times 10^{-14}$ joule. Solving Einstein's equation for $m$ and substituting

$$m = \frac{E}{c^2} = \frac{8.2 \times 10^{-14} \text{ j}}{(3.0 \times 10^8 \text{ m/s})^2}$$
$$m = 9.1 \times 10^{-31} \text{ kg}$$

In Section 1.14 it was mentioned that the mass of an object varies with its velocity. In the case of the positron and electron in Figure 23-4, the two particles have velocities so low that they can be considered almost at rest. Thus the mass computed above is called the *rest mass*. In terms of atomic mass units, this amounts to 0.00054858026 $u$ or $\frac{1}{1837}$ of the mass of an atom of hydrogen. Obviously electrons do not account for a very large share of the mass of substances. Other subatomic particles must be responsible for most of the mass. Later in this chapter we shall see how these particles are identified.

The determination of the charge on the electron by Millikan is one of the classic experiments of physics. A diagram of the apparatus is shown in Figure 23-6. Charged capacitor plates were placed inside a metal box in which temperature and pressure conditions could be held constant. The top plate had a small hole in the center. The plates were connected to a source of high electric potential that could be varied at will. The plates were parallel and the distance between them was carefully measured. From the voltage and the plate spacing, the electric field could be computed. The space between the plates was illuminated by a spotlight. Through a telemicroscope, a combination of two instruments used for viewing small objects at intermediate distances, this illuminated space could be viewed.

A mist of light oil was sprayed into the region above the plates. Eventually a single oil drop fell through the opening in the top capacitor plate. The spray was then turned off so that this single drop could be studied as it fell between the plates. When the plates were uncharged, the drop fell through the field of view with a constant terminal velocity that was dependent on the drop's weight. By means of crosshairs in the eyepiece of the telemicroscope, this velocity could be accurately measured. When the voltage was turned on, however, the behavior of the oil drop changed. The drop slowed its descent, stopped in midair, or even began to rise. These variations in behavior depended upon the weight of the drop, the amount of charge it acquired in the oil-spraying process, and the strength of the electric field between the capacitor plates.

Consider the case of a drop that was suspended motionless between the two plates. The force of gravity on the drop was exactly balanced by the force of the electric field between the two plates. In order for this to happen there had to be an elec-

## 23.4 The electronic charge

Figure 23-5 Hobert Millikan, the American physicist who was the first to measure the charge on the electron.

Figure 23-6 Millikan's oil drop experiment. When the oil drop is stationary, the upward force of attraction of the charged plates equals the downward force of gravitation.

Mist of oil droplets

Window

Telemicroscope

To 10,000 volt battery

Oil droplet being observed (enlarged)

Capacitor plates

tric charge on the oil drop upon which the electric field could exert a force. Hence the field strength between the capacitor plates needed to suspend the drop was a measure of the electric charge on the drop. This observation did not tell how many charged particles were on the drop, and so the value of the unit charge was still unknown.

Millikan studied the behavior of thousands of oil drops in the apparatus. By firing X rays at the drops, he was able to change the charge on a drop in midair as a result of the photoelectric effect. Finally he was able to arrive at two important conclusions:

1. Even though the equipment was capable of detecting much smaller values, the charges on the oil drops never fell below a certain minimum value.

2. All charges were integral multiples of the minimum charge.

Millikan correctly concluded that the minimum charge he had measured was the electronic charge—the charge on a single electron. This important fundamental unit of physics has the presently accepted value of $1.6021892 \times 10^{-19}$ c. The mass of the electron could now be computed by dividing the charge by the charge-to-mass ratio found by Thomson.

*See Section 23.3 for the value of e/m.*

$$m = \frac{e}{e/m} = \frac{1.6021892 \times 10^{-19} \text{ c}}{1.7588047 \times 10^{11} \text{ c/kg}}$$
$$m = 9.109534 \times 10^{-31} \text{ kg}$$

This result agrees with the mass of the electron as determined by the bubble chamber method described earlier. It is, however, much more precise.

## 23.5 Size of the electron

Measuring the size of the electron presents a problem that is not encountered in the determination of mass and charge. Mass and charge can be determined without "seeing" the electron in any way, by the methods just described. The electron is far too small to be seen with visible light. Its size can only be measured in some indirect way.

*The sizes of various atoms are given in Section 7.3.*

Since the electron is a subatomic particle, it must be smaller than the smallest atom, which is only about 1 Å in diameter. Suppose a narrow beam of electrons is fired through a thin metal foil and then allowed to strike a fluorescent screen. The interatomic distances in the foil can be quite accurately measured by X rays. If the electrons are very small, they can be expected to pass straight through the space between the foil atoms and to produce a bright narrow spot on the screen. Some of the electrons will come close enough to an atom in the foil to be partly deflected (scattered) by the atom, producing a fuzziness around the spot on the screen. A few may even come so close to atom centers as to be strongly scattered, still further broadening the spot on the screen. Careful measurements of such scattering could be used to estimate the size of the electron. The actual result of such experiments, however, is not a broad fuzzy spot on the screen but a series of rings. Figure 23-7 is a photograph of the image produced in such an experiment. It is obviously different from what might be expected. The central spot is understandable, but where do the concentric rings come from? In Chapter 15 we saw that a diffraction grating produces several discrete images of the incident light. The grating was a one-dimensional array of equally spaced lines. In a similar sense, the metal foil is a three-dimensional array of regularly spaced atoms. This should produce a set of discrete images that are symmetrical around a center spot. Indeed this is the case when X rays, which are short wavelength photons, pass through a crystal. When X rays pass through a metal foil, the pattern will appear very much like Figure 23-7. In other words, the attempt to measure the size of the electron produced the unexpected evidence that the electron has wave properties!

Further experiments with electron patterns have shown that the patterns vary not only with the type of metal foil through which the electrons are fired but also with the momentum of the electron beam. If a description of the electron is given in terms of its wavelength, and if this wavelength is computed from the changing ring patterns, we must conclude that the size of the electron varies with its momentum.

In the measurements of Thomson and Millikan the electron behaved as a charged particle in an electric or magnetic field. Now we see that it behaves as a wave. Does this mean that an electron is sometimes a particle and sometimes a wave? No. It means that *an electron sometimes exhibits particle characteristics and sometimes wave characteristics, depending upon the nature of the experiment and the measuring instruments used.* Thus an electron may at times be described as a wave and at times as a particle. Actually, it is neither a particle nor a wave —it is an electron.

**Figure 23-7** An electron diffraction pattern made with an electron microscope of a gold film about 40 Å thick. The pattern shows the rings characteristic of a crystalline substance.

*This is a form of the wave-particle duality of matter that was mentioned in Section 1.14.*

---

Figures 23-8 and 23-9 are typical representations of hydrogen and carbon atoms. It is important to note that the electrons are not shown as either particles or waves; they are shown as being in a certain location around the center of each atom. Electrons are negatively charged. Hence a neutral atom must have an equal positive charge in its nucleus. If the electrons were not in motion, the force of attraction between these opposite charges would immediately produce a collapse of the atom. Our knowledge of atomic and nuclear sizes, and of chemical and nuclear reactions precludes the possibility of the existence of collapsed atoms. The

## 23.6 Motions of the electron

**Figure 23-8 (left)** A hydrogen atom has a nucleus consisting of one proton. One electron moves about this nucleus in the K shell. Electron paths are not as definite as these diagrams show.

**Figure 23-9 (right)** A carbon atom has a nucleus consisting of 6 protons and 6 neutrons. Two electrons are in the K shell and 4 electrons are in the L shell.

force of attraction between the electron and the nucleus provides a centripetal force sufficient to hold the electron in its orbit.

The wave-particle duality of the electron makes it difficult to describe its path around the nucleus. Each electron has a definite amount of energy that determines the *orbital* in which it moves. An orbital is not an orbit or path in the sense that the orbit of a planet is. An orbital is a probable pattern of movement characteristic of the energy of the electron. Groups of orbitals in an atom are usually called *shells*. Shells are frequently designated by letters of the alphabet beginning with K and running sequentially to Q in the most complex elements. They also may be given numbers from 1 to 7. The number of orbitals in a shell is the square of the shell number (1st shell, 1 orbital; 2nd shell, 4 orbitals; 3rd shell, 9 orbitals, etc.). The maximum number of electrons that can occupy an orbital is 2; thus the maximum number of electrons that can occupy a shell is two times the number of orbitals in the shell.

The aggregate of electrons is referred to as the *electron cloud*. The characteristics of the electron cloud about an atom give the atom its volume and prevent the interpenetration of one atom by another under ordinary conditions.

*The evidence and consequence of electron spin were mentioned in Section 19.2 and will be further discussed in Section 25.14.*

Experiments have not only justified the use of an atomic model in which the electron orbits the nucleus but also one in which the electron spins on its own axis.

# questions

GROUP A

1. (a) Why are cathode rays so called? (b) What is the relationship between cathode rays and electrons?

2. (a) Who is credited with the discovery of the electron? (b) Explain his experiments and conclusions.

3. (a) What are two ways in which the mass of the electron can be determined? (b) Which way is more precise?

4. In what two ways was the charge placed on the oil drops in Millikan's experiment?

5. What difficulties are encountered in measuring the size of the electron?

6. Is an electron a particle or a wave? Explain your answer.

7. What is the relationship between the orbital of an electron and an electron shell?

8. (a) How does the mass of an electron compare with the total mass of a hydrogen atom? (b) What does this signify?

# THE NUCLEUS

It has already been noted that in order to be electrically neutral, an atom must contain a positive charge of the same magnitude as the total negative charge of its electrons. But what is the exact location of the positive charge? At the time of the discovery of the electron, there were a number of theories about this. Some scientists suggested that the atom has a uniform structure in which the electrons are distributed evenly throughout a positively charged mass: something like the fruit in a fruitcake. Others thought that the positive charge was concentrated at the center and that the electrons surrounded this positive core.

To test the validity of these theories, in 1911 the English physicist Ernest Rutherford conducted a series of experiments with particles emitted by radioactive materials. As will be explained more fully in Chapter 24, certain elements emit rays and particles that can be studied and identified as being subatomic in nature. One of these particles, called an *alpha particle*, was found to be the same as an atom of helium with its electrons missing. In other words, an alpha particle is a subatomic particle with a positive charge.

In his experiment, Rutherford used alpha particles that were emitted by a piece of radioactive polonium contained in a lead box, as shown in Figure 23-10. These alpha particles have a velocity of $1.60 \times 10^7$ m/s. This gave Rutherford subatomic "bullets" of known mass, charge, and velocity with which to explore the structure of other atoms.

Rutherford directed the alpha particles at thin metal foils of various kinds. First he used gold because it can be hammered into extremely thin sheets. The thickness of the foil was about

## 23.7 Discovery of the atomic nucleus

*An alpha particle is a helium nucleus.*

**Figure 23-10** Rutherford's alpha scattering experiment. Fluorescent screens show whether the alpha particles from a sample of polonium are deflected as they strike a metal foil.

Beam of
alpha particles

A few alpha particles
are greatly deflected

Fluorescent screen

Polonium

Lead block

Fluorescent screen

Thin metal foil

Most alpha particles
pass straight through

**Figure 23-11** Alpha particle tracks in a sample of chlorine gas. Most of the particles are not scattered, but occasionally a particle is deflected through a large angle.

*Astronomers call a star that consists only of atomic nuclei a "black hole" because not even light can escape from its concentrated gravitational field.*

$10^{-7}$ m, equivalent to only a few hundred layers of gold atoms. Most of the alpha particles passed straight through the foil. This indicated that the metal foil was very porous to the alpha particles even though the atoms of the metal were tightly packed into many layers. Some of the alpha particles were deflected from their paths, however, at angles ranging from a very slight deflection to a direct rebound. The large deflections were a surprise. Could a massive alpha particle be deflected up to 180° by electrons of much smaller masses found inside the atom or by a positive charge spread out uniformly within the atom? In Rutherford's words: "It was about as credible as if you fired a 15-inch shell at a piece of tissue paper and it came back and hit you."

The answer must be that the positive charge within the atom is not uniformly distributed as had been thought by some scientists. Instead, it is concentrated in a dense *atomic nucleus* that is able to deflect alpha particles the way a brick wall would deflect a tennis ball. Furthermore, the number of alpha particles rebounding compared with the number passing through the foil provided a clue to the size of the atomic nucleus compared with the size of the entire atom. Rutherford's students sat for hours in a darkened room to count and measure the deflections on a fluorescent screen. They found that about one out of every 8000 alpha particles was deflected by more than 90°.

From this and subsequent evidence, scientists have been able to determine the radius of the largest atomic nucleus at about $10^{-14}$ m or $10^{-4}$ Å. This is less than 1/10,000th of the diameter of the smallest atom, and less than 1/1,000,000,000,000th of its volume. No wonder that alpha particles, which are themselves atomic nuclei, are able to pass through the atomic structure of metal foils with only an occasional collision! This situation is like shooting at widely separated peas with an air rifle from the opposite side of a large football stadium.

Yet this tiny nucleus accounts for more than 99.95% of the mass of the entire atom. Thus the density of the atomic nucleus is extremely high: about $10^{13}$ times the density of lead. One cubic centimeter of closely packed atomic nuclei would have a mass of 10,000,000 metric tons! Astrophysicists believe that some stars are made of very concentrated nuclei, and the electrons of the composite atoms have been forced into the nuclei by intense pressures.

## 23.8 The proton

The existence of positive charges in the atom was known even before the time of Rutherford's experiments. If a perforated disk is used as a cathode in a discharge tube, luminous rays are seen coming through the hole on the side opposite the anode, as in Figure 23-1. In 1895, Perrin tested this radiation with magnets and with electrically charged plates and showed that it consists of particles with a positive charge. In 1907, Thomson named them *positive rays*.

It was found that the properties of the positive rays, unlike those of cathode rays, depend on the nature of the gas in the tube. The charge-to-mass ratio of the particles composing positive rays indicated that they are charged particles formed from atoms of the gas in the tube. No positive particles with a charge-to-mass ratio similar to that of the electron were found. The lightest particle found in positive rays has the mass of a hydrogen atom and carries a charge equal in magnitude but opposite in sign to that carried by the electron. This positive particle was assumed to be a hydrogen atom from which one electron had been removed.

The measurement of the amount of positive charge in the nuclei of various elements was also the work of Rutherford and his colleagues. They developed equations stating that the scattering of alpha particles depends on three factors: the thickness of the metal foil, the velocity of the alpha particles, and the amount of positive charge in the atomic nuclei. Experiments soon showed that the first two of these relationships agreed remarkably with the results as predicted by the equations. So it could be assumed that the third relationship, scattering vs. relative nuclear charge, was also true. Tests were made with many different elements, and it was found that *the nuclear charge of the atoms of a given element is always the same and is characteristic of that element*.

The smallest nuclear charge is that of the hydrogen nucleus. In 1920, the name **proton** was given to the nuclear particle carrying this unit positive charge. The number of protons, and therefore the amount of positive charge (measured in units of electron charge), is called the **atomic number**. Atomic numbers range from 1 for hydrogen to over 100 for the most massive elements. The positive charge of a proton has the same magnitude as the negative charge of an electron. Consequently the atomic number of an element also gives the number of electrons surrounding the nucleus of neutral atoms.

*The atomic number of an element is the number of protons in its nucleus.*

The mass of the proton has been found to be $1.6726485 \times 10^{-27}$ kg or $1.007276470$ $u$ on the atomic mass scale. This is $\frac{1836}{1837}$ of the mass of a hydrogen atom. Thus the mass of a hydrogen atom is contained almost entirely in its nucleus.

## 23.9 The neutron

If an atom consisted entirely of electrons and protons and if the mass of the atom were almost entirely contained in its protons, then it should be possible to predict the atomic mass of an element from its atomic number. For example, since the atomic number of oxygen is 8, the atomic mass of oxygen should be eight times the atomic mass of hydrogen, which consists of a single proton and single electron. Similarly, the atomic mass of uranium ought to be 92. But this is not the case. The atomic mass of the most abundant form of oxygen is about 16 and that of the most common form of uranium is about 238. The same discrepancy shows up in all the elements except ordinary hydrogen. What explanation can resolve this discrepancy?

One possibility is that the excess mass is due to protons whose positive charge is neutralized by electrons located within the nucleus. However, such an arrangement presents a number of complex problems that rule it out as a possible solution. For instance, the spin of such nuclear electrons would produce effects that disagree with observed nuclear behavior.

The answer was provided by the English physicist James Chadwick (1891–1974). In 1930 physicists found that when certain elements, such as beryllium or boron, are bombarded with alpha particles from the radioactive element polonium, a radiation with very high penetrating power is obtained. Two years later Chadwick discovered that this highly penetrating radiation is able to knock protons out of a block of paraffin, a compound containing carbon and hydrogen atoms. Figure 23-12 is a schematic diagram of Chadwick's experiment. The radiation that produces this proton emission is not a beam of X rays because it can be shown that X rays would require unusually high energies to expel protons from paraffin. Chadwick reasoned that the radiation is a stream of neutral particles. Calculations showed that the particles have masses similar to that of the proton.

Additional experiments indicated that the same neutral particles can be released from a great variety of elements. This means that the neutral particles are regular components of atomic nuclei. Chadwick called these particles **neutrons**. They have a

**Figure 23-12** Chadwick's neutron experiment. Particles ejected from beryllium were in turn able to knock protons out of a sample of paraffin. The intermediate particles were found to have no charge but have a mass similar to that of the proton. Chadwick called them neutrons.

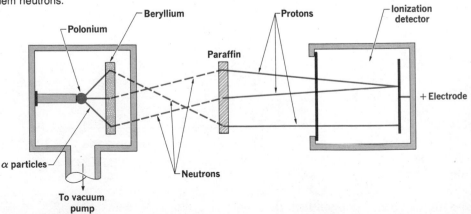

mass of $1.674943 \times 10^{-27}$ kg (very slightly higher than that of the proton) or $1.008665012$ $u$ on the atomic mass scale. The two particles are also quite similar in size.

An interesting result of recent research with neutrons is shown in Figure 23-13. The bottom photo, which was made with the help of neutrons, shows more inner detail in the opaque toy locomotive than does the X-ray photo in the center. The neutrograph is made by passing high-intensity neutrons through the locomotive to a metallic converter, where they release the rays that expose the photographic film. Industrial and medical applications of neutron radiography are being developed.

PHOTOGRAPH
HO SCALE LOCOMOTIVE

X-RAY RADIOGRAPH

NEUTROGRAPH

**Figure 23-13**  Neutrons can be used to take pictures of opaque objects, revealing more inner detail than is obtainable with X rays.

Experiments have shown that the chemical properties of an element are related to its atomic number, $Z$. For hydrogen $Z = 1$, for carbon $Z = 6$, and for uranium $Z = 92$. The total number of protons and neutrons in the nucleus of an atom is equal to the mass number, $A$. Using the symbol $N$ to represent the number of neutrons,

$$A = Z + N$$

Protons and neutrons are referred to collectively as *nucleons*. Thus in the formula above, $A$ equals the number of nucleons.

All atoms of an element have the same chemical properties, but their masses may be different. The number of neutrons in the atomic nucleus of a given element may vary. Atoms of a given element that have different masses are called *isotopes*. *Isotopes of an element contain the same number of protons but a different number of neutrons. Each different variety of atom as determined by the composition of its nucleus is called a nuclide.* Nuclides having the same atomic number are isotopes. There are three isotopes of hydrogen: *protium* (ordinary hydrogen), 1 proton, no neutrons; *deuterium*, 1 proton, 1 neutron; and *tritium*, 1 proton, 2 neutrons. Isotopes of all chemical elements either occur naturally or have been produced artificially.

In general, nuclei with odd atomic numbers exist naturally in only one or two isotopic forms. Those with even atomic numbers exist in several isotopic forms; some elements have as many as eleven variations. Figure 23-14 is a graph of the nuclei of the naturally occurring light nuclides in which $Z$ is plotted as the abscissa and $N$ as the ordinate. Notice that $Z$ and $N$ are equal in many of the lightest nuclides, but that the neutrons outnumber the protons as the mass number increases. This fact is reflected in the properties of the elements, some of which will be discussed in the next chapter.

## 23.10 Isotopes

*Refer to Section 7.3 for a definition of mass number.*

**Figure 23-14**  Nuclei of the stable isotopes of the light elements. Note that the lightest nuclides have equal numbers of neutrons and protons, but in the heavier nuclides there are more neutrons than protons.

Naturally occurring elements are mixtures of isotopes in quite definite proportions. Hydrogen consists of 99.985% protium, 0.015% deuterium, and less than 0.001% tritium. *The* **atomic weight** *of an element is the average atomic mass of the atoms of the element, based on a large number of samples found in nature*. The atomic weight scale is based on the carbon isotope that has a mass number of 12. This isotope is assigned the atomic mass of exactly 12 *u*. On this scale, naturally occurring carbon has an atomic weight of 12.01115 *u* and hydrogen has an atomic weight of 1.00797 *u*. Similarly, the atomic weights of all naturally occurring elements are mixed numbers.

*The atomic weight of an element is the average of the atomic masses of the natural isotopes of the element, based on their abundance.*

## 23.11 The mass spectrograph

The masses of ionized atoms can be measured with great precision in a device called a *mass spectrograph*. There are many different types of mass spectrographs, but in all types the operation depends on the slight difference in mass between isotopes. One type of spectrograph is shown in Figure 23-15.

A beam of ions enters from the ion gun and passes into a region of crossed electric and magnetic fields that allows only the ions with a specific velocity to pass through the slit **S**. The velocity of the ions is inversely proportional to their masses. (Ions with other velocities are deflected and blocked by the chamber wall around the slit.) As the ions enter the upper chamber they are influenced by another magnetic field perpendicular to the plane of the page. This magnetic field causes the ions to move in a circular path. If the ions have the same mass-charge ratio, they will all describe the same arc and will strike the photographic plate at the same place. However, if the beam entering the slit contains ions of various masses, the less massive ions will be deflected to a greater extent than the more massive ones and will strike the photographic plate at different places. If the photographic plate is replaced by collecting vessels, the mass spectrograph can be used to separate isotopes.

**Figure 23-15** Diagram of a mass spectrograph. The magnetic field deflects the less massive ions more than the more massive ones.

## 23.12 Nuclear binding

A very strong force holds protons and neutrons together in the nucleus. This force is not electrostatic because the similarly charged protons would then repel each other. The force cannot be gravitational either because calculations show that it would be much too weak. It is a completely unique force that acts only within the extremely small distances between nucleons. Experiments have shown that this *nuclear binding force* is effective to a distance of $2.0 \times 10^{-15}$ m or $2.0 \times 10^{-5}$ Å. This is less than the diameter of a proton, which is $2.6 \times 10^{-5}$ Å.

The magnitude of the nuclear binding force has been investigated in several ways. One way is to study the scattering pattern that results when nucleons are fired at each other, very much like the scattering experiments of Rutherford and Chadwick. Another way is to compare the mass of a nucleus with the sum of the masses of the uncombined nucleons that make up the nucleus. In each case, the magnitude of the nuclear force is derived from measurements of the energy involved.

Careful measurements have shown that *the mass of a nucleus is always less than the sum of the uncombined masses of its constituent particles. This difference in mass is called the* **nuclear mass defect**. The reason for the nuclear mass defect is found in Einstein's equation $E = mc^2$. When a nucleus is formed, energy is released. This is similar to the energy release that occurs when atoms combine to form a molecule. Einstein's equation states that a decrease in energy must be accompanied by a corresponding decrease in mass since the two quantities are directly proportional. This decrease in mass is the nuclear mass defect.

*The nuclear mass defect of a nucleus is the difference between its mass and the sum of the masses of its uncombined constituent particles.*

The nuclear mass defect can be used to compute the total *nuclear binding energy*. Binding energy is equivalent to the energy released during the formation of a nucleus and is the energy that must be applied to the nucleus in order to break it apart. Let us consider the formation of a helium nucleus (alpha particle) as an example. It contains 2 protons and 2 neutrons. Each proton has a mass of 1.007277 $u$, and each neutron has a mass of 1.008665 $u$. The mass of a helium nucleus is 4.001509 $u$. The nuclear mass defect can now be computed as follows:

$$\begin{aligned}
\textbf{2 protons} &= 2 \times \textbf{1.007277 } u = \textbf{2.014554 } u \\
\textbf{2 neutrons} &= 2 \times \textbf{1.008665 } u = \underline{\textbf{2.017330 } u} \\
&\qquad\qquad\qquad\qquad\quad \textbf{4.031884 } u \\
\textbf{helium nucleus} &= \underline{\textbf{4.001509 } u} \\
\textbf{nuclear mass defect} &= \textbf{0.030375 } u
\end{aligned}$$

In nuclear physics, nuclear binding energy is expressed in electron volts (ev). *An* **electron volt** *is the energy required to move an electron between two points that have a potential difference of one volt.* The mega electron volt (Mev) is also used. A single atomic mass unit is the equivalent of 931 Mev. Hence the binding energy of the helium nucleus is

*One atomic mass unit has a nuclear binding energy equivalent to 931 mega electron volts.*

$$\textbf{0.030375 } u \times \textbf{931 Mev}/u = \textbf{28.3 Mev}$$

If the nuclear binding energy is divided by the number of nucleons, the binding energy per nucleon is obtained. For helium, this is 28.3 Mev/4 = 7.1 Mev/nucleon. The graph in Figure 23-16 shows the variation of binding energy per nucleon with the mass number. Note that elements of low or high mass number have lower binding energies per nucleon than those of intermediate mass number. The binding energy per nucleon is low for the lightest nuclei because the nucleons are all on the surface of the nucleus and are not held on all sides by other

**Figure 23-16** Graph showing the relationship between mass number and binding energy per nucleon.

*The disintegration of a nucleus is a form of nuclear reaction. This is the topic of the next chapter.*

nucleons. This geometry reduces the binding energy per nucleon. As the number of nucleons increases, more and more of them are completely surrounded and the binding energy per nucleon increases. Beyond the maximum of 8.7 Mev/nucleon, the repelling force between the protons begins to cancel the binding force. Finally a point is reached at which the nucleus begins to fall apart.

# summary

The electron was the first subatomic particle to be identified by scientists. It was found to have a mass of $9.1 \times 10^{-31}$ kg and a negative charge of $1.6 \times 10^{-19}$ c. The electron exhibits both particle and wave characteristics. It orbits the nucleus of the atom in a path determined by its energy.

Almost all the mass of an atom is contained in its nucleus, which takes up only a very small percentage of the space occupied by an atom. The positive charge of the nucleus is due to protons. The magnitude of the charge of a proton is the same as that of an electron. The number of protons in a neutral atom is equal to the number of orbiting electrons. This number is known as the atomic number.

The atomic nucleus also contains uncharged particles called neutrons. The mass of a neutron is slightly greater than the mass of a proton. Protons and neu-

trons are collectively called nucleons, and their total number is the mass number of the atom. Isotopes are atoms with the same atomic number but different mass numbers. Each variety of an atom as determined by its nuclear composition is a nuclide. The atomic weight of an element is the average atomic mass of naturally occurring samples of an element. The atomic weight scale is based on the carbon-12 isotope. Nuclides can be separated with a mass spectrograph.

The mass of a nucleus is always less than the combined mass of its constituent particles by an amount called the nuclear mass defect. The nuclear mass defect is equivalent to the nuclear binding energy. Binding energies are expressed in mega electron volts. Elements with intermediate mass numbers have higher binding energies per nucleon than do elements with low or high mass numbers.

# questions

## GROUP A

1. Compare the relative masses, charges, and sizes of the following particles: molecule, atom, electron, proton, neutron, nucleus.

2. Distinguish between atomic mass and atomic weight.

3. (a) What do the isotopes of an element have in common? (b) How do they differ?

4. Define the following: (a) $A$, (b) Å, (c) $Z$, (d) $N$, (e) $u$, (f) Mev.

5. What is the standard for the system of atomic weights?

6. Copy and complete the following table on a separate sheet of paper.

| Nuclide | $Z$ | $A$ | $N$ | Binding energy/nucleon ($Mev/A$) |
|---------|-----|-----|-----|-------------------------------|
| deuterium | 1 | | | |
| carbon-14 | 6 | | | |
| oxygen-18 | 8 | | | |
| sodium-23 | 11 | | | |
| sulfur-32 | 16 | | | |
| argon-40 | 18 | | | |
| uranium-235 | 92 | | | |
| uranium-238 | 92 | | | |

## GROUP B

7. (a) How did Rutherford obtain alpha particles? (b) How did he detect them after they had passed through the metal foils?

8. (a) What did the experiments of Perrin and Rutherford have in common? (b) Of Rutherford and Chadwick?

9. How did Rutherford know that the alpha particles did not rebound from the electrons in the metal foils?

10. What is the general relationship between the atomic number of an atom and the number of its isotopes?

11. (a) What is meant by nuclear mass defect? (b) What is nuclear binding energy? (c) How are they related?

12. What element has the highest Mev/nucleon?

# problems

(Note: Consult Appendix B, Table 23, for the atomic masses of nuclides.)

## GROUP A

1. (a) Calculate the mass in grams of an atom of an isotope of iron that has an atomic mass of 55.9349. (b) What is the mass number of this isotope?

2. The mass of an atom of an unstable isotope of neon is $3.818 \times 10^{-23}$ g. (a) What is its atomic mass? (b) Its mass number?

3. A calcium ion has 20 protons, 20 neutrons, and 18 electrons. What is the magnitude of its charge in coulombs?

4. (a) What is the atomic number of a zinc atom composed of 30 protons, 34 neutrons, and 30 electrons? (b) What is the mass number of the atom?

5. What particles, and how many of each, make up an atom of silver (atomic number 47, mass number 109)?

## GROUP B

6. Calculate the binding energy per nucleon in Mev for carbon-12. This nuclide consists of 6 protons, 6 neutrons, and 6 electrons. Its atomic mass is 12.00000.

7. Calculate the binding energy per nucleon in Mev for sulfur-32 that consists of 16 protons, 16 neutrons, and 16 electrons.

8. Calculate the atomic weight for chlorine if naturally occurring chlorine consists of 75.4% Cl-35 and 24.6% Cl-37.

9. Naturally occurring magnesium consists of 78.6% Mg-24, 10.1% Mg-25, and 11.3% Mg-26. Calculate the atomic weight.

10. An electron pair is produced from X rays with a total energy of 1.5 Mev. If the positron and electron each receive half of the extra energy, calculate what the resulting velocity of each particle would be if we could disregard relativity.

# 24 Nuclear Reactions

## TYPES OF NUCLEAR REACTIONS

### 24.1 Discovery of radioactivity

*Thomson's work with cathode rays is described in Section 23.2.*

*In 1903 Becquerel and the Curies received the Nobel Prize in Physics for their work in radioactivity.*

**Figure 24-1** Henri Becquerel, the French physicist who discovered radioactivity.

At the time that Thomson was conducting his experiments with cathode rays, other scientists were accumulating evidence that the atom could be subdivided. Some of this new evidence showed that certain atoms disintegrate by themselves. In 1896 Henri Becquerel (1852–1908) discovered this phenomenon while investigating the properties of *fluorescent* minerals. Fluorescent minerals glow after they have been exposed to strong light. Becquerel used photographic plates to record this fluorescence.

One of the minerals Becquerel worked with was a uranium compound. During a day when it was too cloudy to expose his mineral samples to direct sunlight, Becquerel stored some of the compound in the same drawer with the photographic plates. When he later developed these same plates for use in his experiments, he discovered that they were fogged. What could have produced this fogging? The plates were wrapped tightly before being used, so the fogging could not be due to stray light. Also, only the plates that were in the drawer with the uranium compound were fogged. Becquerel reasoned that the uranium compound must give off a type of radiation that could penetrate heavy paper and affect photographic film.

Elements that emit such radiation are said to be *radioactive* and possess the property of *radioactivity*. ***Radioactivity** is the spontaneous breakdown of an unstable atomic nucleus with the emission of particles and rays.* At the suggestion of Becquerel, Pierre (1859–1906) and Marie (1867–1934) Curie investigated uranium and its various ores. They found that all uranium ores were radioactive. However, one of them, pitch-blende, was four times as radioactive as might be expected from the amount of uranium in it. Further studies showed that this extra radiation was actually due to the presence of two previously unknown elements, *polonium* and *radium*, both of which were intensely radioactive. The elements polonium and radium were discovered and named by the Curies.

Several more radioactive elements have since been discovered and isolated. All of the naturally occurring elements with atomic numbers greater than 83 are radioactive. A few naturally radioactive isotopes of elements with atomic numbers smaller than 83 are also known. Many artificial radioactive nuclides have been produced and put to use in different ways, as we shall see later in this chapter.

**Figure 24-2**   Marie and Pierre Curie discovered the highly radioactive elements, radium and polonium.

All radioactive nuclides have certain common characteristics.

*1. Their radiations affect the emulsion on a photographic film.* Even though photographic film is wrapped in heavy black paper and kept in the dark, some of the radiations from radioactive nuclides penetrate the wrapping and affect the film. When the film is developed, a black spot can be seen where the invisible radiations struck the film. Some of the radiations penetrate paper, wood, flesh, *thin* sheets of metal, and, as shown in Figure 24-3, even thick sheets of glass.

*2. Their radiations ionize the surrounding air molecules.* The radiations from radioactive nuclides knock out electrons from the atoms of the gas molecules in the air surrounding the radioactive material. This leaves the gas molecules with a positive charge. An atom or a group of atoms having an electric charge is called an ion. The production of ions is termed ionization. An electroscope can detect the ionization of gas molecules in the air.

*3. Their radiations make certain compounds fluoresce.* Radiations from radioactive nuclides produce bright flashes of light when they strike certain compounds. The combined effect of these flashes is a fluorescence, or glow, given off by the affected material. For example, radium compounds added to zinc sulfide cause the zinc sulfide to glow. Since the glow is visible in the dark, the mixture is useful as an ingredient in luminous paint.

*4. Their radiations have special physiological effects.* Radiations from natural radioactive sources can destroy the germinating power of plant seeds, kill bacteria, and even injure and kill large animals. Burns from radioactive materials heal with great difficulty and may sometimes be fatal.

*5. They undergo radioactive decay.* The atoms of all radioactive elements continually decay into simpler atoms and simultaneously emit radiations. However, it is not possible to predict

## 24.2 Nature of radioactivity

**Figure 24-3**   Rectangular blocks containing 70,000 curies of $^{137}CsCl$. The only source of illumination for this time exposure, which was taken through a 3-foot-thick heavy-glass window, was the natural radioactivity of the cesium-137.

when a specific atom will decay. The rate of decay may be described by a rule that states how long it will take for half of the atoms in a given sample to decay. The accuracy of the rule is greater for larger samples. The time associated with radioactive decays of a certain type is called the *half-life* of the nuclide. *Half-life is the length of time during which, on the average, half of a given number of atoms of a radioactive nuclide decays*. For example, the half-life of radium-226 is 1620 years. This means that one-half of a given sample of radium-226 atoms can be expected to decay into simpler atoms in 1620 years.

## 24.3 Types of natural radioactivity

*Rutherford's alpha-scattering experiments are described in Section 23.7.*

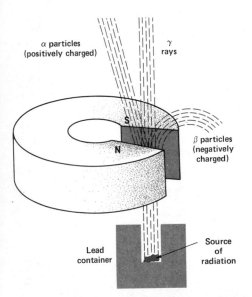

**Figure 24-4** Types of radioactivity. Alpha and beta particles are deflected by a magnet, but gamma rays are not.

*Electrons are described in Sections 23.2–23.6.*

*Photons are described in Sections 12.9–12.13.*

In the course of his alpha-scattering experiments, Rutherford discovered that the radiations from radioactive materials could be separated into three distinct types by means of a strong magnet. A diagram of this separation is shown in Figure 24-4.

*1. α (alpha) particles.* These are composed of two protons and two neutrons; hence they are helium nuclei. This conclusion can be proved by collecting large quantities of alpha particles in a partially evacuated tube and passing an electric discharge through the tube. The alpha particles acquire electrons from the residual air molecules in the tube. This spectrum of the resulting substance is identical with the spectrum of helium. Alpha particles have two positive electric charges, speeds about one-tenth the speed of light, and masses about four times that of the hydrogen atom. Hence they are deflected only slightly by the field of a magnet. Their penetrating power is not very great. They can be stopped by a thin piece of aluminum foil or by a thin sheet of paper.

*2. β (beta) particles.* These are electrons, just like cathode rays. They have single negative charges and may travel with nearly the speed of light. Their mass is only a small fraction of the mass of alpha particles. Hence, even though they have only half as much charge, they are deflected significantly more by a magnetic field and in the opposite direction. The high speed of beta particles makes them much more penetrating than alpha particles. It was the beta particles from the uranium compound that fogged Becquerel's photographic plates.

*3. γ (gamma) rays.* These are high energy photons. They are the same kind of radiation as visible light, but of much shorter wavelength and thus higher frequency. Gamma rays are produced by energy transitions in the nucleus that do not change the composition of the nuclide. They are the most penetrating radiations given off by radioactive elements. They are not electrically charged and are not deflected by a magnetic field.

Changes in matter can be classified into three types: *physical, chemical,* and *nuclear.* When a physical change occurs, the identity of the substance is not lost. When water freezes and forms ice, the composition of its molecules is not changed; if we heat the ice it changes back into water. When sugar dissolves in water it undergoes a physical change; if the water evaporates, the sugar remains behind. *In a physical change the composition of the substance is not changed.* The substance consists of the same molecules, atoms, or ions that it did before the change occurred.

When a chemical change occurs, new substances are formed from the atoms or ions of the original substances. These new substances have their own distinct chemical and physical properties. The rusting of iron and the souring of milk are examples of chemical changes. *In a chemical change the composition of the substance is changed, and new substances with new properties are produced.* The type and number of atoms or ions remain the same, but the atoms or ions are rearranged to form new substances. A chemical change does not involve the nuclei of the interacting atoms.

A nuclear change is similar to a chemical change in that new substances with new properties are formed. However, *in a nuclear change the new materials are formed by changes in the identity of the atoms themselves.* The radioactive decay of radium is a nuclear change, as are all forms of alpha, beta, and gamma emission.

Both chemical and nuclear changes are usually represented by equations. In equations, symbols or formulas are used to represent the particles that enter into a reaction and that are produced by it. You are probably familiar with the symbols of many of the chemical elements. In working with nuclear equations, you must know how to use the symbols for some of the subatomic particles and radiations. The most basic of these are given in Table 24-1.

Except for the gamma-ray symbol, all the symbols in the table have subscripts and superscripts. The subscript designates the electric charge of the particle. The superscript denotes the number of nucleons in the particle. These charge and nucleon designations are also used with the symbols of all other atomic nuclei presented in nuclear equations.

In a chemical equation, the same atoms appear on both sides of the equation in equal numbers. This is true because the identity of the atoms is not changed. In a nuclear equation, however, the same atomic symbols do not necessarily appear on both sides. The factors that remain constant in a nuclear equation are the total number of nucleons and the arithmetic sum of the electric charges on each side.

## 24.4 Nuclear symbols and equations

*In a nuclear change the atomic number of the nucleus is changed.*

*The symbols of other subatomic particles are given in Chapter 25.*

Table 24-1

| SYMBOLS FOR SUBATOMIC PARTICLES | |
| --- | --- |
| Symbol | Particle |
| $^1_0n$ | neutron |
| $^1_1H$ | proton (hydrogen nucleus) |
| $^0_{-1}e$ | electron (beta particle) |
| $^0_{+1}e$ | positron (positive electron) |
| $^4_2He$ | alpha particle (helium nucleus) |
| $\gamma$ | gamma ray |

Note: In the case of the proton and the alpha particle the atomic symbols for hydrogen and helium are used to designate the nuclei only.

The following example will illustrate this.

$$^{14}_{7}N + ^{4}_{2}He \rightarrow ^{17}_{8}O + ^{1}_{1}H$$

In this equation, a nitrogen nucleus (charge, 7; nucleons, 14) reacts with an alpha particle (charge, 2; nucleons, 4) to form an oxygen nucleus (charge, 8; nucleons, 17) and a proton (charge, 1; nucleon, 1). There is a total of 9 electric charges and 18 nucleons on each side of the equation.

## 24.5 Radioactive decay

It was noted in Section 24.1 that the atoms of all naturally occurring elements with atomic numbers greater than 83 are unstable and decay spontaneously into lighter particles. This is also true of several naturally occurring nuclides and a great many artificially made nuclides with atomic numbers below 83. As a general rule, an atomic nucleus is stable only if the ratio of its neutrons to its protons is about 1 for the light elements and about $1\frac{1}{2}$ for the heavier elements. When there are more neutrons than

*The fact that natural radioactivity stops with lead makes that element a good shielding material for radioactive experiments.*

this, a *nuclear transformation* will probably take place.

Figure 24-5 shows a series of nuclear transformations beginning with uranium-238 and ending with lead-206. Each step of the series can be represented by a nuclear equation in which nucleons and charge are conserved. For instance the equation for the first step in the chart may be written as

$$^{238}_{92}U \rightarrow ^{234}_{90}Th + ^{4}_{2}He$$

**Figure 24-5**  The uranium disintegration series.

This reaction is called *alpha decay* because an alpha particle is emitted.

The next two steps in the series are examples of *beta decay*. In the first step, a neutron in the thorium nucleus ejects a beta particle and becomes a proton. This transformation increases the nuclear charge by one, and the nucleus becomes a protactinium nucleus.

$$^{234}_{90}\text{Th} \rightarrow\ ^{234}_{91}\text{Pa} +\ ^{0}_{-1}\text{e}$$

The chart also shows the half-life of each nuclide in the decay series. You will notice that there is a wide variation in these values, from small fractions of a second to millions of years. In each case the exact length of the half-life is related to the energy change that accompanies the transformation. As a rule, the shorter the half-life of the nuclide, the greater is the kinetic energy of the alpha or beta particle it emits.

From the definition of half-life it is obvious that the radio-activity of a substance depends on the total number of nuclei present. The ratio between the number of nuclei decaying per unit time and the total number of original nuclei is known as the *decay constant*. If the half-life of a nuclide is known, its decay constant can be calculated by the following equation:

$$\lambda = \frac{0.693}{T_{1/2}}$$

In this equation $\lambda$ (the Greek letter lambda) designates the decay constant in reciprocal seconds, $1/s$ or $s^{-1}$, if the half-life $T_{1/2}$ is given in seconds. For example, for $^{226}_{88}\text{Ra}$, $T_{1/2} = 1620$ years and

$$\lambda = \frac{0.693}{1620 \text{ yr} \times 365 \text{ da/yr} \times 86,400 \text{ s/da}}$$

$$\lambda = 1.36 \times 10^{-11} \text{ s}^{-1}$$

In 1.000 kg of radium there are $2.665 \times 10^{24}$ nuclei. Consequently, the number of radium nuclei decaying per second is $2.665 \times 10^{24}$ nuclei $\times\ 1.36 \times 10^{-11}\ s^{-1} = 3.62 \times 10^{13}$ nuclei $s^{-1}$. Observe that this equation does not indicate when a particular nucleus will decay. Instead it says that in a certain amount of time a definite proportion of nuclei will decay. A relationship of this kind represents the statistical behavior of a very large number of individual situations. It uses the mathematical methods of statistics or the theory of probability. The half-life

**Figure 24-6** Half-life curve of a radio-active nuclide with a half-life of three hours and an original strength of 40,000 disintegrations per second.

*In 1901 Roentgen received the first Nobel Prize in Physics for his discovery of X rays.*

probability law is shown in the form of a graph in Figure 24-6. The *average life* of any nuclide is 1.44 times its half-life.

The unit used for measuring radioactivity is the *curie*. *One **curie** is the quantity of any radioactive nuclide that undergoes $3.7 \times 10^{10}$ disintegrations per second.* This rate of radioactivity is very close to that of one gram of radium. Since the curie is a very large unit, the millicurie ($10^{-3}$ curie) and microcurie ($10^{-6}$ curie) are frequently used. For example a source with a strength of 4 microcuries emits $1.48 \times 10^5$ particles per second.

The unit used to measure exposure to radiation is the *roentgen*. It is named after the German physicist Wilhelm Roentgen (1845–1923) who discovered X rays. *A **roentgen** is the amount of gamma radiation that will produce $1.61 \times 10^{12}$ pairs of ions when it is absorbed in one gram of air.*

The *rad* is the unit used to measure the amount of radiation absorbed by a person, such as a patient who undergoes cancer treatment or a worker who is exposed to radioactive substances. *One **rad** is equal to the absorption of 0.01 joule of radioactive energy per kilogram of absorbing matter.* Occupational exposure to radiation is also measured in *rems* (for *r*adiation *e*quivalent *m*an). For X rays, gamma rays, and electrons, a rem is equivalent to a rad. In fact for most radiation exposure, 1 roentgen = 1 rad = 1 rem.

In the 1950s the United States government adopted a standard of 5 rems per year as a safe limit for federal workers who are exposed to radiation. This is the equivalent of more than 150 normal chest X rays. In light of recent cancer research, however, it has been recommended that the safety standard be reduced to as low as 0.5 rem per year.

## 24.6 Nuclear bombardment

**Figure 24-7** Rutherford's transformation experiment. Bombardments from the radioactive sample ejected protons from the nitrogen gas in the chamber. The protons produced scintillations on a fluorescent screen.

The study of radioactive decay led scientists to believe that transformations that would produce a different element could be achieved by adding protons to the nucleus. The first successful transformation of this kind was carried out by Rutherford in 1919. A diagram of his apparatus is shown in Figure 24-7. The container was filled with nitrogen gas. A radioactive source emitted alpha particles. A silver foil thick enough to absorb any alpha particles not absorbed by the nitrogen gas was used. A zinc sulfide screen recorded the scintillations of any particles with enough energy to pass through the silver foil. These scintillations could be observed through the microscope.

Rutherford observed scintillations on the screen when the chamber was filled with nitrogen and other light gases. However, there were no scintillations when he used oxygen and other heavy gases such as carbon dioxide. He concluded that low density gases were changed by the alpha-particle bombardment with the accompanying emission of a high-energy particle such as a proton. The nuclear equation in Section 24.4 represents the transformation produced by the alpha bombardment of nitrogen. The detection of oxygen gas in the container after the alpha bombardment of pure nitrogen helps to verify the validity of the equation.

The alpha bombardment of nitrogen results in the emission of protons. Other bombardments produce other subatomic particles. In 1932 J. D. Cockcroft and E. T. S. Walton bombarded lithium with high-speed protons.

$$^{7}_{3}\text{Li} + ^{1}_{1}\text{H} \rightarrow ^{4}_{2}\text{He} + ^{4}_{2}\text{He} + \text{energy}$$

In this case all the products have lower mass numbers than the original target material. In addition there is the release of a considerable amount of binding energy. Actually, adjustments in binding energy are involved in all nuclear reactions. Cockcroft

*The method of computing binding energy is described in Section 23.12.*

and Walton found that the measured energy in their experiments agreed closely with the theoretical value as derived from Einstein's equation, $E = mc^2$.

Another nuclear bombardment, also carried out in 1932, led to the discovery of the neutron. The nuclear equation for Chadwick's experiment is

$$_4^9\text{Be} + {}_2^4\text{He} \rightarrow {}_6^{12}\text{C} + {}_0^1\text{n} + \textbf{energy}$$

*Neutrons are described in Section 23.9. In 1935 Chadwick received the Nobel Prize in Physics for his discovery of the neutron.*

Many similar bombardments have since been found to produce neutrons. Since the neutron is not electrically charged, it penetrates atomic nuclei more easily than do charged particles like the proton or the alpha particle. Hence the neutron has become an important nuclear "bullet." In fact one of the main problems in neutron bombardment is to get the neutrons to move *slowly* enough to produce a transformation. The problem is quite the opposite with charged particles. The equation for a typical neutron absorption is

$$_5^{10}\text{B} + {}_0^1\text{n} \rightarrow {}_3^7\text{Li} + {}_2^4\text{He} + \textbf{energy}$$

Bombardment reactions are usually designated by the symbols for the incident and emitted subatomic particles. For example, the preceding equation is called a (n, $\alpha$) reaction. In bombardment reactions, the mass number of the target nucleus is increased or decreased by several units. Sometimes, however, a nucleus will split into two large segments when struck by a neutron moving at just the right speed. This reaction is extremely important in nuclear physics and is the topic of the next section.

## 24.7 Fission

As has already been mentioned, fast-moving neutrons are not effective for nuclear bombardment. Neutrons with energies of about 1 Mev will usually pass right through the nucleus of an atom without causing much change in it. On the other hand, slow neutrons with energies of the order of 10 ev are frequently trapped by a nucleus. This makes the nucleus unstable. Fast neutrons may be slowed down by passage through materials called *moderators*, composed of elements of low atomic weight. Deuterium oxide or graphite are useful moderators.

When a slow neutron is captured by $_{92}^{238}\text{U}$, the following reaction takes place:

$$_{92}^{238}\text{U} + {}_0^1\text{n} \rightarrow {}_{92}^{239}\text{U}$$

This new isotope of uranium is unstable, and so it emits a beta particle.

$$_{92}^{239}\text{U} \rightarrow {}_{93}^{239}\text{Np} + {}_{-1}^0\text{e}$$

$^{239}_{93}$Np has a half-life of 2.3 days and decays by emitting another beta particle.

$$^{239}_{93}\text{Np} \rightarrow \,^{239}_{94}\text{Pu} + \,^{0}_{-1}\text{e}$$

Neptunium and plutonium were the first two artificial *transuranium* elements. *A transuranium element is one with an atomic number greater than 92, the atomic number of uranium.* At the time of this printing, fourteen artificial transuranium elements have been confirmed. All of them are radioactive, and some of them exist for only a small fraction of a second.

Uranium-238 accounts for 99.3% of naturally occurring uranium. 0.7% is uranium-235. There are also traces of uranium-234. When $^{235}_{92}$U absorbs a slow neutron, the reaction is quite different from that described above for $^{238}_{92}$U. Instead of emitting alpha or beta particles, the $^{235}_{92}$U may split into segments of intermediate mass. *The splitting of a heavy nucleus into nuclei of intermediate mass is called* **fission**. During the process of fission, neutrons are emitted and a large amount of energy is released. One equation for the fission of $^{235}_{92}$U is

$$^{235}_{92}\text{U} + \,^{1}_{0}\text{n} \rightarrow \,^{138}_{56}\text{Ba} + \,^{95}_{36}\text{Kr} + 3\,^{1}_{0}\text{n} + \textbf{energy}$$

The energy involved in this reaction can be computed from the atomic masses of the particles as given in Appendix B, Table 23.

*The slow-neutron fission of U-235 yields products having atomic numbers from 30 to 65 and mass numbers from 72 to 161. See Figure 24-8. Fission into two equal fragments is not the most probable. The highest yield is of particles with mass numbers 95 and 138.*

$$^{235}_{92}\text{U} = 235.0439 \quad u$$

$$^{1}_{0}\text{n} = \underline{\quad 1.008665 \; u}$$

$$236.0526 \quad u$$

$$^{138}_{56}\text{Ba} = 137.9050 \quad u$$

$$^{95}_{36}\text{Kr} = \;\; 94.9 \qquad u$$

$$3 \times \,^{1}_{0}\text{n} = \underline{\;\; 3.025995 \; u}$$

$$235.8 \qquad u$$

**nuclear mass defect = 236.0526 $u$ − 235.8 $u$ = 0.3 $u$**

**binding energy released = 0.3 $u$ × 931 Mev/$u$ = 300 Mev**

The above calculation was simplified by using the masses of the neutral atoms given in the table, rather than the masses of the nuclei by themselves. No error is introduced in this case because the masses of the electrons cancel out. When a beta particle or a positron is emitted, however, the masses of the nuclei must be used in the calculation.

Note that the atomic mass of $^{95}_{36}$Kr is not known with the same precision as the masses of the other particles in this reaction. This uncertainty is due to the fact that the atoms of the nuclide are so unstable that it is very difficult to measure their mass. Since the mass of krypton-95 is given in three significant fig-

**Figure 24-8** This graph shows the yield of various nuclides that are produced by the slow-neutron fission of uranium-235. The products vary in mass number from 72 to 161. The most probable products have mass numbers of 95 and 138. Observe the low probability of fission products of nearly equal mass numbers.

ures, the mass defect and binding energy can be computed with a precision of only one significant figure.

The first successful fission reaction was carried out in 1939. It was later discovered that the element plutonium also undergoes fission and produces more neutrons when bombarded with slow neutrons.

## 24.8 Fusion

The graph of binding energy per nucleon in Section 23.12 suggests that a great deal of binding energy could be released by combining nuclei of the light elements into nuclei of medium mass. In fact, we could expect energies of about 7 Mev/nucleon as compared with about 1 Mev/nucleon for fission reactions. *A reaction in which light nuclei combine to form a nucleus with a larger mass number is called fusion.* Because fusion can take place only under extremely high temperature conditions, the process is also called a *thermonuclear reaction*.

One of the first fusion reactions to be accomplished was the combination of two deuterons (nuclei of the isotope of hydrogen, deuterium).

$$\ _{1}^{2}\text{H} + \ _{1}^{2}\text{H} \rightarrow \ _{2}^{3}\text{He} + \ _{0}^{1}\text{n} + 3.3 \text{ Mev}$$

The total energy released in this reaction is less than that of uranium fission, but the energy per nucleon is much greater. In other words, less material is required to produce the energy. In 1938 the American astrophysicist Hans Bethe (b. 1906) suggested that the tremendous and long-lasting rate of energy production of the sun and other stars is due to nuclear fusion. The sufficiently high temperatures and pressures of a star bring about the fusion of hydrogen nuclei to form nuclei of helium, with the accompanying release of energy. The net result of such a reaction is

$$4\ _{1}^{1}\text{H} \rightarrow \ _{2}^{4}\text{He} + 2\ _{+1}^{0}\text{e} + 25.7 \text{ Mev}$$

The intermediate steps that take place in the thermonuclear reactions in the stars are not completely understood. Some scientists believe that the reaction is somewhat different in different parts of the interior of a star. But it is almost certain that several other atomic nuclei, especially those of oxygen and nitrogen, play an important role. Both oxygen and nitrogen have been identified in the sun and other stars.

Estimates of the sun's energy output indicate that about $6 \times 10^{11}$ kg of hydrogen are converted into helium *every second*, with a mass defect of $4 \times 10^{9}$ kg *every second*. It is comforting to know that the sun has a mass of $2 \times 10^{30}$ kg, and so there is no immediate danger that its mass will disappear.

A thermonuclear bomb, sometimes called a hydrogen bomb

or H-bomb, produces energy by a fusion reaction. The formation of alpha particles and tremendous amounts of energy from a compound of lithium and deuterium, $^{6}_{3}Li^{2}_{1}H$, is one possible reaction in a hydrogen bomb. This reaction is started by subjecting the compound to extremely high temperature and pressure and using a fission reaction as a detonator.

$$^{6}_{3}Li^{2}_{1}H \rightarrow 2^{4}_{2}He + 22.4 \text{ Mev}$$

This reaction results in 22.4 Mev for 8 nucleons, or 2.80 Mev/nucleon, as compared with 186 Mev for 236 nucleons in uranium fission, or only 0.788 Mev/nucleon. In addition a thermonuclear bomb is theoretically unlimited in possible size.

The problem of releasing fusion energy in controlled amounts has not yet been solved. One approach under study is the containment of hydrogen and deuterium in a strong magnetic field while the temperature of the mixture is raised to the extremely high level required for a fusion reaction. Temperatures of 60,000,000° C—four times hotter than the sun's interior—have been attained briefly by this method. The apparatus for this experiment is shown in Figure 24-9.

High temperature is only one of the requirements for obtaining power from nuclear fusion. The other requirements are fuel-confinement time and fuel density. To obtain sustained power, the product of the three requirements, when expressed in C°, seconds, and particles/cm², must exceed $10^{14}$!

**Figure 24-9** The Princeton Large Torus, which is shown here, has been used to produce temperatures of 60,000,000°C. Physicists hope to achieve controlled nuclear fusion with this kind of research.

**24.9 Cosmic rays**     When a charged electroscope is exposed to the air, it will slowly discharge, even though no radioactive material is present. This indicates that there are always some ions in the atmosphere. Experiments have shown that most of this ionization is caused by particles coming into the atmosphere at great speeds from outer space. *Particles whose high energy suggests that they come from beyond the solar system are called **cosmic rays**.*

Cosmic rays have great penetrating power. Their intensity varies with latitude, indicating that they are charged and are affected by the earth's magnetic field. Scientists believe that cosmic rays consist largely of the nuclei of elements of low atomic weight, protons (hydrogen nuclei) being the most abundant type. Other nuclei, ranging up to those as heavy as iron and beyond, have also been detected in the upper atmosphere. A few of these particles from outer space reach the surface of the earth, but most of them collide with the gas particles in the upper atmosphere and produce showers of secondary particles. In effect, cosmic rays are furnishing the nuclear physicist with a constant supply of bombarding nuclei that would otherwise not be available for study.

Scientists believe that gigantic magnetic fields in space, in galaxies, and near certain stars may be influential in producing cosmic rays. Some cosmic radiation is also thought to originate from highly energetic explosions on certain stars, including the flares that erupt from our own sun.

# questions

## GROUP A

1. (a) How was radioactivity discovered? (b) By whom was it discovered?
2. (a) Define radioactivity. (b) Which elements are naturally radioactive?
3. List four effects of radioactive radiation.
4. Give another name for (a) alpha particles, (b) beta particles, (c) gamma rays.
5. In a nuclear equation, (a) what do the letter symbols represent, (b) what do the subscripts indicate, (c) what do the superscripts indicate?
6. (a) What is a nuclear transformation? (b) Describe two ways in which it can occur.
7. (a) Define half-life. (b) How is half-life used to find the decay constant of a radioactive nuclide? (c) Define the various units associated with radioactivity.
8. What important conclusion was drawn from the experimental work of Cockcroft and Walton?

9. Why are neutrons more effective than other particles for bombarding nuclei?
10. (a) What is the purpose of a moderator? (b) List two substances that are used as moderators.
11. (a) How many chemical elements are known today? (b) How many of them occur naturally?
12. (a) Write the equation for the reaction that is believed to be responsible for the energy of the stars. (b) How is this reaction used on earth? (c) What problems are associated with its use?
13. What quantities are balanced in a balanced nuclear equation?
14. (a) What are cosmic rays? (b) What is known about their source?

## GROUP B
15. How can a magnet be used to identify the radiations from a radioactive substance?
16. List three differences between gamma rays and other radioactive emissions.

17. (a) What is the source of the energy released in a nuclear reaction? (b) Give a specific example.

18. How does the stability of a nucleus vary with (a) mass, (b) the proton-neutron ratio?

19. (a) What is the difference between the average life of a radioactive nuclide and its half-life? (b) What is the relationship between the average life of a nuclide and its half-life?

20. (a) Suggest a way in which $^{200}_{80}Hg$ (mercury) might be changed into $^{196}_{79}Au$ (gold). (b) Write nuclear equations for the reactions that are required.

21. Write the nuclear equations for the alpha decay of (a) $^{234}_{90}Th$, (b) $^{234}_{92}U$, (c) $^{214}_{83}Bi$, (d) $^{210}_{84}Po$.

22. Write nuclear equations showing the preparation of $^{239}_{94}Pu$ from $^{238}_{92}U$.

23. (a) Which nuclides have the smallest binding energy per nucleon? (b) Which have the largest binding energy per nucleon? (c) How does the binding energy per nucleon affect the stability of a nucleus?

24. Describe the difference in the results when $^{235}_{92}U$ and $^{238}_{92}U$ absorb neutrons.

25. Explain, using a specific example, whether the half-life of an element tells when its nucleus will disintegrate.

26. When a radioactive nucleus disintegrates, the products have kinetic energy even though the original nucleus was at rest. What is the source of this energy?

# problems

GROUP A
(Note: Consult Appendix B, Table 23 for the atomic masses of nuclides.)

1. How much energy in Mev is evolved in the decay of a $^{222}_{86}Rn$ nucleus?

2. Calculate the energy evolved when a $^{214}_{82}Pb$ nucleus decays.

3. What is the decay constant of $^{222}_{86}Rn$ that has a half-life of 3.82 da?

4. Determine the decay constant of $^{238}_{92}U$ if its half-life is $4.49 \times 10^9$ years.

GROUP B

5. (a) What is the radioactivity in millicuries of $10\bar{0}$ g of pure $^{232}_{90}Th$? Its half-life is $1.4 \times 10^{10}$ yr, and it decays to $^{228}_{88}Ra$. (b) What is the rate of energy evolution?

6. (a) Calculate the radioactivity of $5.00 \times 10^{-3}$ g of $^{222}_{86}Rn$. (b) What is the rate of energy evolution?

7. In which of the following reactions is a greater proportion of the fuel elements converted into energy: $^{239}_{94}Pu + ^{1}_{0}n \rightarrow ^{137}_{52}Te + ^{100}_{42}Mo + 3^{1}_{0}n + energy$, $2^{2}_{1}H \rightarrow ^{4}_{2}He + energy$?

8. If the sun continues producing energy at its present rate, what fraction of the sun's mass would disappear in the next 1000 years?

9. The earth receives $3 \times 10^{22}$ joules of energy from the sun per day. If this energy is expressed as mass, what is the proportional increase in the earth's mass in one year? (The mass of the earth is presently $6 \times 10^{24}$ kg.)

10. Compute the mass defect and binding energy per nucleon of $^{13}_{6}C$.

11. (a) Compute the mass defect and binding energy per nucleon of $^{14}_{7}N$. (b) Compare the stability of $^{13}_{6}C$ and $^{14}_{7}N$.

# USES OF NUCLEAR ENERGY

In a fission reaction the target nucleus may break up in a great many different ways. The reaction involving uranium-235 in Section 24.7, for example, is only one of the ways in which this nucleus may react under neutron bombardment. In most cases, however, two or three neutrons are emitted in the process. This is an example of a *chain reaction*. *In a **chain reaction** the material or energy that starts a reaction is also one of the products and can cause similar reactions*. The neutrons emitted during

**24.10 Chain reactions**

Figure 24-10 A chain reaction. Neutrons from the fission of a U-235 nucleus, when slowed down by a moderator, can cause fission in other U-235 nuclei. Fission products other than barium and krypton are also produced.

*In 1938 Fermi received the Nobel Prize in Physics for his work in neutron bombardment.*

fission are moving too fast to be absorbed by other fissionable nuclei. Hence the neutrons must be slowed down by a suitable moderator. Figure 24-10 shows the sequence of events in a typical chain reaction involving uranium-235. The first controlled chain reaction was carried out at the University of Chicago in 1942 under the direction of the Italian physicist Enrico Fermi (1901–1954).

If the material surrounding a fission reaction has the right dimensions and characteristics, the reaction is self-sustaining. *The amount of a particular fissionable material required to make a fission reaction self-sustaining is called the* **critical mass**. If the critical mass is exceeded and if the emitted neutrons are not absorbed by nonfissionable material, the reaction runs out of control and a nuclear explosion results. For example, suppose that two neutrons from each fission are able to produce further fission reactions and that $10^{-8}$ second elapses between successive reactions. In one millionth of a second, 100 successive reactions can take place. The total energy released is 200 Mev/nucleus $\times 2^{100}$ reactions, or $4 \times 10^{19}$ j. This is an enormous amount of energy.

Actually, the chain reaction continues until all the fissionable nuclei have split or until the neutrons no longer strike the fissionable material. This is what happens in an uncontrolled chain reaction such as the explosion of a nuclear warhead. Two subcritical masses are placed a short distance from each other inside the warhead. To detonate it, the two masses are brought together quickly by means of explosive charges. The resulting mass exceeds the critical mass and an uncontrolled chain reaction takes place.

## 24.11 Nuclear reactors

*A* **nuclear reactor** *is a device in which the controlled fission of certain substances is used to produce new substances and energy.* One of the earliest reactors using natural uranium as a fuel was built in 1943 at Oak Ridge, Tennessee. It had a lattice-type construction with blocks of graphite forming the framework and acting as a moderator. Rods of uranium were placed between the blocks of graphite. Control rods of neutron-absorbing boron steel were inserted in the lattice to regulate the number of free neutrons. The reactor contained a critical mass of uranium. A typical nuclear reactor is shown in Figure 24-11.

Two types of reactions occur in this kind of reactor. Neutrons cause $^{235}_{92}$U nuclei to undergo fission. Fast neutrons from this fission are slowed down by passage through the graphite. Some neutrons strike other $^{235}_{92}$U nuclei and continue the chain reaction. Other neutrons strike $^{238}_{92}$U nuclei and initiate the changes that produce plutonium. Because great quantities of heat energy are liberated, the reactor is cooled continuously by air blown through tubes in the lattice. The rate of the nuclear reactions is controlled by insertion or removal of the control rods.

*A **breeder reactor** is one in which a fissionable material is produced at a greater rate than the fuel is consumed.* The fuel is a mixture of $^{238}_{92}$U and $^{239}_{04}$Pu. Neutrons from the fission of $^{239}_{94}$Pu strike the $^{238}_{92}$U nuclei and convert them to $^{239}_{92}$U. These nuclei decay to $^{239}_{94}$Pu by double beta decay, as described in Section 24.7. Thus $^{239}_{94}$Pu is produced at the same time that it is being consumed.

Breeder reactors can extract more than sixty times as much energy from natural uranium as can be obtained through regular reactors. Unlike their conventional counterparts, breeder reactors have a heat exchanger, usually liquid sodium, that is not pressurized; this ensures greater reactor safety.

*The nuclear equations for these changes are given in Section 24.7.*

**Figure 24-11** A nuclear reactor. The workman in the front is inserting a sample into the pile for neutron bombardment while the other technician is monitoring the level of radioactivity in the area.

## 24.12 Nuclear power

A kilogram of uranium has a volume of only about 52 cm³. Yet when completely utilized in fission reactions, it has about the same fuel value as 3,000,000 kg of coal or 12,000,000 kg of oil burned in the conventional way. Obviously, nuclear power is an important substitute for the world's dwindling supplies of fossil fuels. The challenge is to produce it safely and economically.

Contrary to what many people imagine, there is not much difference between a nuclear power plant and an ordinary power plant. As Figure 24-13 shows, the basic difference is in the way in which the steam that turns the turbines is produced. In an ordinary plant, the steam comes from a boiler fired with coal, oil, or gas. In a nuclear plant, the steam is generated by the heat released during the fission process in the reactor.

The reactor in a nuclear power plant must be able to sustain a chain reaction. Several factors determine whether a chain re-

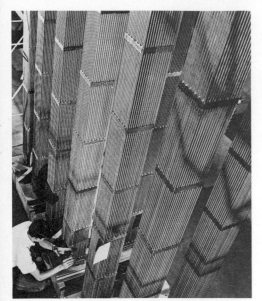

**Figure 24-12** Bundles of uranium fuel elements being inspected before insertion in a nuclear power reactor.

Table 24-2

| NEUTRONS IN A REACTOR | |
| --- | --- |
| Number of neutrons | History |
| 100 | produce new fissions |
| 90 | captured by U-238 |
| 20 | captured by U-235 |
| 30 | absorbed by moderator |
| 5 | absorbed by housing |
| 9 | escape from reactor |
| 2 | absorbed by control rods |
| 256 | |

**Figure 24-13** A nuclear power plant differs from other power plants only in the way in which steam is generated for the turbines.

action will continue. The relationship among these factors is described by the following equation:

$$k = \frac{P}{A + L}$$

In this equation $k$ is known as the *multiplication factor*, $P$ is the rate of production of neutrons in the reactor, $A$ is the rate of absorption, and $L$ is the rate of leakage. When $k = 1$, the reactor is said to be *critical* and the reaction is self-sustaining.

The power production of a nuclear reactor depends largely on the rate of neutron production. Neutron production, in turn, reduces the amount of fissionable material in the reactor. Hence, to keep the reactor critical it is necessary to reduce the rate of absorption, $A$, or to increase the production of neutrons, $P$. The former is accomplished by gradually withdrawing the control rods, while the latter requires the addition of fissionable material.

Natural uranium contains only about 0.7% of the fissionable isotope U-235. Consequently, when natural uranium is used as a reactor fuel, the rate of neutron leakage, $L$, is so high that the reactor can never become critical. $L$ can be reduced, however, by using a moderator to slow down the neutrons so that they are more likely to strike U-235 nuclei. Another way to make the reactor critical is to use fuel that has been processed to increase the concentration of U-235.

A typical "neutron history" in a nuclear reactor is given in Table 24-2. It shows the relative number of neutrons involved in other events for every 100 neutrons that produce new fissions. Thus of a total of 256 neutrons, only the two that are absorbed by the control rods are available for increasing the power of the reactor. When the control rods are withdrawn, of course, these two neutrons will raise the multiplication factor of the reactor.

The first nonexplosive application of nuclear power was in the American submarine *Nautilus*, which was launched in 1954. Two years later, the first large scale nuclear power plant was placed in operation in Shippingport, Pennsylvania. It had an output of 60,000 kilowatts of electric power. Today there are many similar plants in operation or under construction through-

**Figure 24-14** Browns Ferry Nuclear Plant in northern Alabama. Research on the effect of heated water from the plant on aquatic life is carried out in the six long channels in the foreground.

out the country. The largest of these, with a capacity of nearly 3,500,000 kw, is shown in Figure 24-14.

A nuclear plant under construction in Tennessee has a projected capacity of over 5,000,000 kw. This is more than the combined capacity of all twenty-nine hydroelectric power plants operated by the Tennessee Valley Authority. Six European countries are jointly financing the construction in France of a breeder reactor with an output of 1,200,000 kw. The Soviet Union presently operates the world's largest nuclear reactor. It has an output of 2,455,000 kw. By the year 2000, the Soviets plan to meet one-third of their power requirements through nuclear reactors.

As we saw in Figure 1-1, less than 1% of the energy consumed in the United States is presently obtained from nuclear plants. This figure is expected to rise to about 20% by 1990.

## 24.13 Radioisotopes

*A **radioisotope** is a radioactive isotope of an element.* Some radioisotopes are the products of natural radioactive decay, as in the case of the uranium decay series in Section 24.5. Since the advent of the nuclear reactor, however, a far greater number of radioisotopes has been prepared artificially. The reactor produces radioisotopes during the fission process. In addition, radioisotopes can be prepared by inserting elements into the reactor while it is operating. Radioisotopes of all the elements have been prepared in this way.

One way in which an element becomes radioactive in a re-actor is by absorbing a neutron. For example, $^{13}_{6}C$ will turn into $^{14}_{6}C$, which is a radioisotope. In other cases, elements will absorb a neutron and immediately emit a proton. This process lowers the atomic number of the element but does not change its mass number. For example, natural sulfur may change into radio-phosphorus.

$$^{32}_{16}S + ^{1}_{0}n \rightarrow ^{32}_{15}P + ^{1}_{1}H$$

A large reactor can release neutrons at the rate of $10^{14}$ neutrons/$cm^2$ s. When the reactor is used to produce radioisotopes, it must be run at a rate that is somewhat higher than the rate needed for a chain reaction by itself. The extra neutrons are then available for radioisotope production. Special control and shielding arrangements make it possible to insert and remove substances without shutting down the reactor. Figure 24-15 is a diagram of a typical reactor in which radioisotopes are produced.

It is often desirable to incorporate radioisotopes into specific compounds before they are used. This can be done by chemically combining the radioisotope with other elements. The *radiocompound* that results is said to be tagged, or *labeled*. Complex compounds that cannot be tagged by direct combination can sometimes be labeled through the biological processes of plants and animals. Radioisotopes are injected into or fed to an animal and then removed from the blood or tissue in the form of radiocompounds. Similar procedures can be used with plants.

**Figure 24-15** Cutaway view of a ura-nium reactor used for the preparation of radioisotopes. Note the thick concrete shield used to protect the technicians from radiation.

Concrete shield

Graphite moderator

Boron steel control rod

Removing aluminum tubes containing radioisotopes

Aluminum tubes containing uranium

Protective lead shield

Elevator

Second floor

Holes for aluminum tubes

Long graphite holders

First floor

The many uses of radioisotopes can be divided into three categories:

1. Effects of radioisotope radiations on materials.
2. Effects of materials on radioisotope radiations.
3. Tracing materials with radioisotope radiations.

In the first of these categories, the radioisotope is used as a source of radiation, just as X rays and radium are used. The target material consists of the substance that is to be changed or destroyed by the radiation. In this way cancer can be treated and food and drugs can be sterilized to prevent deterioration. Plastic can be irradiated to change its properties, static electricity can be reduced or eliminated by irradiating the air surrounding the source of the static electricity, and special paints can be made to luminesce by incorporating radioisotopes.

In the second category of radioisotope utilization, the effect of the material on the radiation yields information about the material. Radiation is beamed at a target and the amount that is transmitted or reflected is recorded on photographic film or with some other detection device. Radiations from radioisotopes that are given to a patient can be used to trace or diagnose physiological processes. This method can also be used to measure the thickness of a moving sheet of metal or other material, to analyze the internal structure of a metal casting, to measure the level of a liquid inside a closed container, and even to sort out materials on a moving conveyor.

The third category of radioisotope utilization is perhaps the most widely used. In this method, a carefully selected radioisotope acts as a *tracer* that makes it possible to follow the course of some complicated chemical or biological process. The target and the radioisotope are intimately mixed or combined. The radioisotope then serves as the label that indicates the whereabouts of the successive compounds or materials with which the radioisotope becomes associated. Detection instruments or photographic film again serve as measuring devices. The material that is labeled and traced may be food that is consumed by a human being, feed that is converted into milk inside the body of a cow, water that is running out of an undiscovered underground leak, atoms that are rearranged to form a complex molecule, wax that is worn away from the hood of a polished car, or any one of a great many other research materials or industrial products. Figure 24-16 shows how tracers are used to study the performance of piston rings in an automobile engine.

An interesting use of a natural radioisotope is the process known as *carbon-14 dating*, which was developed by the American chemist W. F. Libby (b. 1908) in 1952. $^{14}_{7}N$ atoms in the atmosphere are constantly being bombarded by radiations from outer space and converted into the radioisotope $^{14}_{6}C$. In the process of photosynthesis, living plants absorb $^{14}_{6}C$ (as carbon dioxide)

Figure 24-16 A tracer experiment. Radioactive iron (Fe-59) in the piston rings is transferred to the oil through friction while the motor is running. As little as 0.0003 gram of iron in the oil can be detected by the counter at the right.

*In 1960 Libby received the Nobel Prize in Chemistry for his work with carbon-14 dating.*

along with the more common and nonradioactive $^{12}_6C$. When the plant dies, it no longer replaces the carbon atoms in its cells with carbon atoms from the atmosphere and the intake of $^{14}_6C$ stops. The amount of radioactivity in the plant gradually decreases due to the fact that the half-life of $^{14}_6C$ is 5600 years. Measurements show that a gram of carbon from a living plant has an activity of 16 disintegrations/min. Consequently, a sample showing an activity of 8 disintegrations/g min is assumed to be 5600 years old. A sample with 4 disintegrations/g min is 11,200 years old, etc. See Figure 24-17. The precision of carbon-14 dating falls off rapidly after several half-life periods, although objects up to about 30,000 years old have been dated in this way.

Other nuclear dating methods are used to learn the age of rocks on the earth and the moon. Moon rocks as old as 4.5 billion years have been dated. It is believed that the solar system itself is not much older than this.

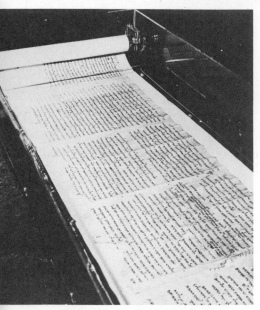

**Figure 24-17** Carbon-14 dating. The age of organic compounds can be determined by measuring the remaining amount of radioactive carbon (right). The relative error is between 5% and 10%. The Dead Sea Scrolls, a portion of which is pictured above, were dated in this manner.

## summary

Radioactivity is the spontaneous decay of atomic nuclei with the emission of particles and rays. It is a property of all elements with atomic numbers greater than 83. Radioactive elements have these characteristics in common: effect on photographic film, ionization of air, production of fluorescence in certain compounds, special physiological effects, and radioactive decay.

The radiations from radioactive elements consist of alpha particles (helium nuclei), beta particles (high-speed electrons), and gamma rays (high-energy photons). In a nuclear change, new materials are formed by changes in the identity of the atoms themselves.

There are four types of energy-producing nuclear reactions: radioactive decay, nuclear bombardment, fission, and fusion. The rate at which a radioactive nuclide decays is called its half-life. Radioactivity is also described in terms of curies, roentgens, rems, and rads. In nuclear bombardment, a nuclide breaks into a large and a small fragment. In fission, two large fragments are produced. In fusion, two small fragments combine to form a larger one. More energy is produced from equal masses of fuel by fusion reactions than by fission reactions.

A chain reaction yields as a product the material or energy that started the reaction. The amount of material required to sustain a fission reaction is called the critical mass. The isotopes U-235 and Pu-239 capture slow neutrons and undergo fission, thereby producing neutrons to continue the chain reaction.

Nuclear reactors produce heat energy for power plants, new fissionable materials, and radioisotopes. The effects of radioisotopes on certain materials and the effects of certain materials on radioisotopes are used in research. Radioisotopes are also used to trace materials in chemical or biological processes. Carbon-14 dating is an example of a use of a natural radioisotope.

# questions

GROUP A

1. (a) What conditions are necessary for a chain reaction? (b) What is meant by critical mass?

2. Describe the two types of reactions in a nuclear
   reactor.

3. (a) How does a nuclear reaction produce electric
   power? (b) What is meant by a critical reactor? (c)
   How can natural uranium be used in a critical
   reactor?

4. How does a breeder reactor differ from conventional reactors?

5. What are the similarities and differences between
   a nuclear power plant and a fossil-fuel plant?

6. What is the status of nuclear power generation in
   your locality?

7. (a) What are radioisotopes? (b) How are they made?

8. How could radioisotopes be used to determine the
   effectiveness of a fertilizer?

9. Estimate the age of a carbon sample showing an
   activity of 3 disintegrations/g min.

# High-Energy Physics

## 25.1 The uncertainty principle

As we saw in Section 12.9, the quantum theory states that light exhibits particle-like properties in addition to its wave-like properties. This means that light energy is transferred in discrete quantities, or photons. Applying this idea to the atom, Bohr concluded that the electron is not free to assume any orbit whatever; rather, the size and shape of the electron orbit are governed by the quantum theory. An electron cannot move into a lower orbit unless it loses enough energy to emit a photon; an electron cannot move into a higher orbit unless it gains enough energy. An electron must stay in its orbit unless sufficient energy is gained or lost so that an abrupt orbital transition can take place. This process can occur spontaneously.

Bohr's model was remarkably successful in explaining the spectral lines of low-atomic-numbered elements. But the model ran into trouble when it was used to explain the behavior of helium atoms or atoms with large atomic numbers. Then, too, small but important differences were found between the predictions of the Bohr model regarding atomic spectra and the results of experiments based on the predictions. Attempts were made to account for these differences by suggesting that electron orbits are elliptical rather than circular and by using relativistic mass (a method that was successful in solving a similar problem with the orbit of the planet Mercury). These explanations resolved only some of the discrepancies.

There were other problems with the Bohr atom. The effect of the spin of the electron (Sections 19.2 and 23.6) on its orbital motion had not been taken into account by Bohr. Such spinning sets up electromagnetic forces that must be considered in computing the total energy of the orbiting electron.

The most serious blow to the Bohr model of the atom came in 1927 with the announcement of the *uncertainty principle* by the German physicist Werner Heisenberg (1901–1976). The *uncertainty principle* states that *it is impossible to specify simultaneously the exact position of an object and its momentum*. Other pairs of physical quantities related to the motion of an object, such as time and energy, are also subject to the uncertainty principle. For bodies of ordinary mass, the inherent uncertainty in any such simultaneous determination is smaller than errors in measurement, so the uncertainty effect is not observed. With electrons, however, the effect is pronounced. This principle means that it is possible to determine where an electron is, but it is not possible to determine its exact speed or direction *simultaneously*. The reason is that the method used to determine the position of the electron, short wavelength radiation, changes the electron's momentum. Likewise, to determine an electron's momentum, an instrument that changes the electron's direction of motion is used; the determination of the electron's position is prevented.

**Figure 25-1** Werner Heisenberg, the German physicist, formulated the uncertainty principle which provides a basis for quantum mechanics.

*In 1932 Heisenberg received the Nobel Prize for Physics for his work in quantum mechanics.*

## 25.2 Quantum numbers

To understand the description of the atom according to the quantum theory, it is necessary to be familiar with the idea of *quantum numbers*. As used in atomic physics, a **quantum number** *is a number that describes the allowable value of certain physical quantities*. For example, quantum numbers are used in special equations to compute the energy of a particle, such as the electron. *The branch of physics that deals with the behavior of particles whose specific properties are given by quantum numbers is called* **quantum mechanics**.

The quantum-theory model of the atom is three-dimensional. The motion of the electron is not restricted to a single plane, as in the Bohr atom. Within the limits prescribed by its quantum numbers, the electron describes an orbit that completely encloses the nucleus.

The first quantum number for the electron describes the radius of its orbit. It is called the *principal quantum number* and is designated by the letter $n$. The principal quantum number may have the integral values 1, 2, 3, 4, etc., which correspond to the similarly numbered energy levels of the Bohr atom. For example, an electron with a principal quantum number 1 is in the first energy level, an electron with the number 2 is in the second level, and so on.

The equation for finding the energy of an electron from its principal quantum number is

$$E = -\frac{me^4}{8\,\epsilon_0^2 h^2 n^2}$$

where $E$ is the energy of the electron, $m$ is its mass, $e$ is the electronic charge, $\epsilon_0$ (the Greek letter epsilon) is a constant with the value $8.854 \times 10^{-12}$ c$^2$/n m$^2$, $h$ is Planck's constant, and $n$ is the principal quantum number. The energy is expressed as a negative quantity to show that the electron is held by the nucleus.

Thus far the use of the principal quantum number yields exactly the same results for the orbits of electrons that Bohr obtained for his atomic model. But here the similarity ends. A second quantum number, called the *angular momentum quantum number* or *secondary quantum number*, describes the magnitude of the angular momentum of the orbiting electron. This quantum number is designated by the letter $l$. Unlike energy, which is a scalar quantity, angular momentum is a vector with both magnitude and direction. The equation for the magnitude of the angular momentum is

$$L = \sqrt{l(l+1)}\,\frac{h}{2\pi}$$

where $L$ is the angular momentum, $l$ is the angular momentum quantum number, and $h$ is Planck's constant. $l$ may have integral values ranging from zero to $n-1$ and is therefore limited by the principal quantum number. In effect, a high value of $l$ means that the electron's orbit is circular. The lower the value of $l$, the more elliptical the orbit is.

The magnitude of the angular momentum in a magnetic field is described by a third quantum number, the *magnetic quantum number*. It is designated as $m_l$ and can have integral values ranging from $-l$ through zero to $+l$. The equation using $m_l$ is

$$L_z = m_l\,\frac{h}{2\pi}$$

in which $L_z$ is the component of the angular momentum that is parallel to the magnetic field.

Since $m_l$ can have several values for all values of $n$ except $n=1$, the energy levels of an atom are split into two or more sublevels when the atom is subjected to a magnetic field. This effect is called the *Zeeman effect,* after the Dutch physicist Pieter Zeeman (1865–1943). The Zeeman effect can be detected in the spectra of excited atoms, as is shown in the photo of Figure 25-2.

In the 1920s it was discovered that many pairs of spectral lines could be described in terms of a model in which electrons

**Figure 25-2** The Zeeman effect. The single line at the top is the 3779-Å line of the element curium. At the bottom is the spectrum of the same line in a powerful magnetic field.

spin on their axes. This electron spin model also harmonizes with the relativistic explanation of the behavior of matter. The spin of the electron is designated by the *spin quantum number, s*, which has the value $\frac{1}{2}$. The equation for the magnitude of spin angular momentum is

$$L_s = \sqrt{s(s+1)}\,\frac{h}{2\pi}$$

The component of spin angular momentum that is parallel to a magnetic field is given by the equation

$$L_s = m_s \frac{h}{2\pi}$$

where $m_s$ is the *spin magnetic quantum number* and can have the values $+\frac{1}{2}$ and $-\frac{1}{2}$. The + and − signs indicate that the electrons are spinning in opposite directions.

The assignment of four quantum numbers to each electron leads to the logical question of how the quantum numbers of any one electron compare with the numbers of other electrons. Does it ever happen that two electrons have the same set of numbers? The answer to this question is provided by the *exclusion principle* of the Austrian physicist Wolfgang Pauli (1900–1958).

**Figure 25-3** Wolfgang Pauli, the Austrian-born physicist, developed the exclusion principle which states that no two electrons in an atom can have the same set of quantum numbers.

*In 1945 Pauli received the Nobel Prize for Physics for his discovery of the exclusion principle.*

The **exclusion principle** states that *no two electrons in an atom can have the same set of quantum numbers*. The number of different energy levels that could be computed if there were no restrictions on the quantum numbers associated with each electron is far greater than those revealed by spectral evidence.

With the help of the four quantum numbers and the exclusion principle, it is possible to determine the electron configuration of any particular atom. Electron configurations for several elements are given in Table 25-1. In each case, the number of elec-

Table 25-1

| | | | ELECTRON CONFIGURATION OF THE LIGHT ELEMENTS | | | | | | |
|---|---|---|---|---|---|---|---|---|---|
| Atomic number | Symbol | Element | Electron configuration of atom | | | | | | |
| | | | $n = 1$ | $n = 2$ | | $n = 3$ | | | $n = 4$ | |
| | | | $l = 0$ | $l = 0, l = 1$ | | $l = 0, l = 1, l = 2$ | | | $l = 0, l = 1$ | |
| 1 | H | hydrogen | 1 | | | | | | | |
| 2 | He | helium | 2 | | | | | | | |
| 3 | Li | lithium | 2 | 1 | | | | | | |
| 4 | Be | beryllium | 2 | 2 | | | | | | |
| 5 | B | boron | 2 | 2 | 1 | | | | | |
| 6 | C | carbon | 2 | 2 | 2 | | | | | |
| 7 | N | nitrogen | 2 | 2 | 3 | | | | | |
| 8 | O | oxygen | 2 | 2 | 4 | | | | | |
| 9 | F | fluorine | 2 | 2 | 5 | | | | | |
| 10 | Ne | neon | 2 | 2 | 6 | | | | | |
| 11 | Na | sodium | 2 | 2 | 6 | 1 | | | | |
| 12 | Mg | magnesium | 2 | 2 | 6 | 2 | | | | |
| 13 | Al | aluminum | 2 | 2 | 6 | 2 | 1 | | | |
| 14 | Si | silicon | 2 | 2 | 6 | 2 | 2 | | | |
| 15 | P | phosphorus | 2 | 2 | 6 | 2 | 3 | | | |
| 16 | S | sulfur | 2 | 2 | 6 | 2 | 4 | | | |
| 17 | Cl | chlorine | 2 | 2 | 6 | 2 | 5 | | | |
| 18 | Ar | argon | 2 | 2 | 6 | 2 | 6 | | | |
| 19 | K | potassium | 2 | 2 | 6 | 2 | 6 | | 1 | |
| 20 | Ca | calcium | 2 | 2 | 6 | 2 | 6 | | 2 | |
| 21 | Sc | scandium | 2 | 2 | 6 | 2 | 6 | 1 | 2 | |
| 22 | Ti | titanium | 2 | 2 | 6 | 2 | 6 | 2 | 2 | |
| 23 | V | vanadium | 2 | 2 | 6 | 2 | 6 | 3 | 2 | |
| 24 | Cr | chromium | 2 | 2 | 6 | 2 | 6 | 5 | 1 | |
| 25 | Mn | manganese | 2 | 2 | 6 | 2 | 6 | 5 | 2 | |
| 26 | Fe | iron | 2 | 2 | 6 | 2 | 6 | 6 | 2 | |
| 27 | Co | cobalt | 2 | 2 | 6 | 2 | 6 | 7 | 2 | |
| 28 | Ni | nickel | 2 | 2 | 6 | 2 | 6 | 8 | 2 | |
| 29 | Cu | copper | 2 | 2 | 6 | 2 | 6 | 10 | 1 | |
| 30 | Zn | zinc | 2 | 2 | 6 | 2 | 6 | 10 | 2 | |
| 31 | Ga | gallium | 2 | 2 | 6 | 2 | 6 | 10 | 2 | 1 |
| 32 | Ge | germanium | 2 | 2 | 6 | 2 | 6 | 10 | 2 | 2 |
| 33 | As | arsenic | 2 | 2 | 6 | 2 | 6 | 10 | 2 | 3 |
| 34 | Se | selenium | 2 | 2 | 6 | 2 | 6 | 10 | 2 | 4 |
| 35 | Br | bromine | 2 | 2 | 6 | 2 | 6 | 10 | 2 | 5 |
| 36 | Kr | krypton | 2 | 2 | 6 | 2 | 6 | 10 | 2 | 6 |

trons in a particular sublevel is found by using the permissible values of each quantum number. For example, aluminum has 13 electrons. When $n = 1$, $l$ equals 0, $m_l$ equals 0, and $m_s$ can have values of $+\frac{1}{2}$ and $-\frac{1}{2}$. In other words, two electrons can be listed in the column headed $n = 1$. When $n = 2$, $l$ can be 0 or 1. When $l = 0$, $m_l$ equals 0 and $m_s$ can be $+\frac{1}{2}$ and $-\frac{1}{2}$, as before. Hence two electrons are listed under $l = 0$ in this column. When $l = 1$, $m_l$ can be $+1$ or 0 or $-1$. For each of these three values of $m_l$, there are again two values of $m_s$. In other words, there are six possible combinations of quantum numbers when $l = 1$. When $n = 3$ and $l = 0$, two values of $m_s$ are again possible. This tally leaves only one more electron to account for in the aluminum atom; this final electron is listed under $l = 1$. All atoms can be analyzed in this manner.

Quantum mechanics allows only a definite number of orbiting electrons for each value of the principal quantum number. For $n = 1$, it is 2 electrons, for $n = 2$, it is 8 electrons, and so on. When an atom has the maximum number of electrons for a particular electron shell (or subshell for heavy atoms), it is said to have a *complete shell*. In most cases, atoms are stable when they have complete shells.

The stability of an atom is described in terms of *ionization energy*. **Ionization energy** *is the energy required to remove an electron from an atom.* Obviously, the ionization energy must be equal to the energy of the electron as described by its quantum numbers, and it must also have the same sign. As $n$ increases, the energy of the electron decreases. Consequently, the outermost electrons are usually the easiest to remove from an atom. Figure 25-4 illustrates the transfer of electrons in the formation of sodium chloride.

Chlorine molecules

Sodium

Sodium chloride

**Figure 25-4** When sodium reacts with chlorine to form common salt, an electron is transferred from the outer shell of each sodium atom to the outer shell of each chlorine atom. The particles composing the salt are sodium ions and chloride ions.

---

A final word of explanation about the equations of the quantum theory is necessary at this point. You will notice that Planck's constant, $h$, is used in each of the equations. In Section 12.11,

**25.3 Matter waves**

**Figure 25-5** Louis de Broglie, the French physicist who proposed the wave nature of matter.

*In 1929 de Broglie received the Nobel Prize for Physics for his discovery of the wave nature of electrons.*

we saw that *h* is associated with wave motion. The use of this same constant in describing the behavior of subatomic particles suggests that the particles have wave-like characteristics. This wave-particle duality was mentioned in the very first chapter and in the discussion of light. Now it is important to emphasize it once more. About 1924 the French physicist Louis de Broglie suggested that *all* matter possesses wave characteristics, and that these matter waves become longer as the momentum of a particle of matter decreases.

In Section 12.11, the wavelength of a matter wave was given by the equation

$$\lambda = \frac{h}{mv}$$

where $\lambda$ is the wavelength, *h* is Planck's constant, *m* is the mass of the particle, and *v* is its velocity. Since *h* has a very small value $(6.62 \times 10^{-34}$ j s), it can be seen from the equation that *m* likewise must be extremely small before $\lambda$ can become large enough to be detectable. This is why the wave properties of, let us say, a moving baseball are completely undetectable, while the wavelength of the electron is long enough to consider in the modern view of the atom.

It must not be assumed, however, that a de Broglie wave is like the physical disturbance of the water in a ripple tank. A de Broglie wave is not a motion, but rather a property of matter. Matter waves can exist in a vacuum in the same way that light waves can. They permeate space in the way a gravitational or magnetic field influences the area surrounding a mass or a magnet. In the final analysis, it is not possible to construct an analogy for matter waves. Furthermore, it should be recognized that de Broglie waves, like so many other descriptions in science, represent a particular model of the universe. As with all models in the history of science, this one can also be modified and improved as our understanding of the universe keeps growing.

# questions

**GROUP A**

1. (a) Why is it impossible to determine simultaneously the position and velocity of an electron? (b) What is the name of this principle? (c) Who first postulated it?

2. (a) What is quantum mechanics? (b) How is it used to explain atomic structure?

3. (a) Define the four quantum numbers of an electron. (b) What quantum number always has only two values? (c) Why?

4. (a) What is the Zeeman effect? (b) How can spectra be used to tell whether a specific example of the Zeeman effect is the result of the angular momentum of an electron or of electron spin?

5. (a) What is meant by the exclusion principle? (b) Who postulated it? (c) What led him to this conclusion?

6. How does the ionization energy of an electron affect the stability of an atom?

7. Why is the wavelength of a moving baseball undetectable while that of a much smaller and less massive electron is noticeable?

8. (a) How do matter waves differ from water waves? (b) Describe an analogy for de Broglie waves.

# problems

1. List the quantum numbers for each electron in the following atoms: (a) helium, (b) sodium, (c) argon, (d) magnesium.

2. (a) Compute the energy of an electron with a principal quantum number of 3. Use MKS units. The mass and charge of the electron and the value of Planck's constant are given in Appendix B, Table 4. (b) Convert this energy to electron volts, and compare it with the ionization energy of the outer electron of the neutral sodium atom.

3. (a) Find the wavelength of a baseball with a mass of 0.15 kg and a velocity of 26 m/s. (b) Compare this wavelength with that of an electron moving at $5.5 \times 10^6$ m/s.

4. Show that the number of electrons that can exist in a particular shell is given by the expression $2n^2$, in which $n$ is the principal quantum number.

# PARTICLE ACCELERATORS

As we saw in Chapter 24, nuclear reactions can be caused by particles and radiations from naturally radioactive substances. But the subatomic research that can be conducted in this way is limited by the energy of the radioactive emissions. To provide nuclear "bullets" that have greater penetrating power, it is necessary to accelerate them. In the following sections of this chapter, we shall describe several particle accelerators, among which are the largest and most powerful scientific devices ever built.

**25.4 Providing high-energy particles**

One of the first particle accelerators was developed in 1931 by the American physicist R. J. Van de Graaff (1901–1967). As Figure 25-6 illustrates, a Van de Graaff generator projects electrons onto an insulated moving belt as a result of repulsion from a strongly negative electrode. The electrons ride on the belt to the other end of the generator, where they are picked off by a collector and transferred to a metal sphere. Since an electric charge always resides on the *outside* of a hollow conductor, the inside of the sphere is able to receive more charges. Thus a large negative charge is built up on the sphere.

Conversely, a large positive charge may be built up on the sphere by removing electrons from the belt by use of a strongly positive electrode. The large difference of electric potential thus obtained can be used to accelerate electrons or ions. Since the high charge on a Van de Graaff generator leaks off into the atmosphere if the air is humid, such generators are sometimes built under a large, pear-shaped shell that is filled with dry air under pressure to keep the charge on the sphere. Also, to avoid the necessity of tall buildings, many large Van de Graaff generators are installed horizontally.

To provide maximum energy to particles, Van de Graaff

**25.5 Van de Graaff generators**

**Figure 25-6** Schematic diagram of a Van de Graaff generator.

generators are sometimes used in series with linear accelerators. The world's most powerful Van de Graaff installation is a pair of horizontal generators in series located at the Brookhaven National Laboratory in New York. This installation is capable of accelerating hydrogen ions to an energy of 30 Mev. Although this is not as high as the energies produced in other types of large accelerators, the Van de Graaff machines have certain other advantages. For example, the particle beam can be more precisely focused, energy variations are more easily controlled, and a wide range of particles can be employed.

## 25.6 Circular accelerators

Shortly after the development of the Van de Graaff generator, it was found that charged particles can be accelerated to very high velocities by driving them in a circular path with the aid of electromagnets. A variety of such accelerators has since been built.

*1. The betatron.* As its name implies, the betatron is used to accelerate beta particles (electrons). The betatron uses the principle of the transformer; the primary is a huge electromagnet

**Figure 25-7** The inventor of the betatron, Donald Kerst, is shown with his original accelerator, a 2.5-Mev model built in 1940. In the background is the world's biggest betatron, a 340-Mev instrument used at the University of Illinois.

and the secondary is the stream of electrons that are being accelerated. The electrons are enclosed in a circular, evacuated tube called the *doughnut*. After the electrons have acquired maximum energy, they are directed toward a metal plate. The impact of the electrons on the metal plate produces high-energy X rays that are used for nuclear studies and for industrial and medical applications. In effect, the betatron is a large X-ray machine, producing energies up to about 300 Mev. See Figure 25-7. Beyond this range, electrons rapidly lose energy by electromagnetic radiation.

2. *Cyclotrons*. In 1932 the American physicist E. O. Lawrence (1901–1958) developed a circular accelerator in which various kinds of charged particles could be used. He called it a *cyclotron*. It consists of a large cylindrical box placed between the poles of an electromagnet, as shown in Figure 25-8. The box is exhausted until a very high vacuum exists inside. Charged particles, such as protons or deuterons, are fed into the center of the box. Inside the box are two hollow, D-shaped electrodes called *dees* that are connected to a source of high-voltage electricity.

When the cyclotron is in operation, the electric charge on the dees is reversed very rapidly by an oscillator. The action of the field of the electromagnet causes the charged particles inside the cylindrical box to move in a semicircle in a fixed period of time. The potential applied to the dees is adjusted to reverse itself in the same time period. Thus at each transit across the

**Figure 25-8** Schematic diagram of a cyclotron.

*In 1939 Lawrence received the Nobel Prize for Physics for his invention of the cyclotron.*

*The relationship between mass and velocity is described in Section 1.14.*

**Figure 25-9** Sections of the world's most powerful particle accelerator. The voltage multiplier at the far left supplies an initial acceleration of protons to 750 kev. Second from left is a view of the linear accelerator that drives the protons up to 200 Mev. At the top right is part of the magnet ring of the booster accelerator that raises the energy to 8 Gev. The main accelerator tunnel, a section of which is shown at the bottom right, is 6.6 km long. Protons emerge from this final stage of the accelerator with energies of more than 500 Gev.

gap between the dees, the ions gain energy from the electric field. While the ions are inside the dees, their velocity is constant because there is no electric field on the inside. But at each transit, the ions move faster and approach the outside of the box. When they reach the outer rim of the box, they are deflected toward the target.

The energy of particles accelerated in a conventional cyclotron may reach 15 Mev. To obtain higher values, it is necessary to modify the accelerator to deal with the relativistic increase in mass of the particles as their velocity increases. This increased mass keeps the particles from gaining enough speed to reach the end of the dees by the time the oscillating voltage reverses. To overcome this difficulty, it is necessary to vary the oscillating frequency. Then as the mass of the particles increases and their acceleration decreases, the frequency of the oscillator can be reduced. The changes in voltage of the field are timed to coincide with the slower acceleration of the more massive particles. This type of accelerator is called a *synchrocyclotron*. It can boost the energy of particles to about 800 Mev.

*3. Synchrotrons.* A newer type of particle accelerator is the *synchrotron*. Like the cyclotron, it operates on the principle of accelerating particles by making them move with increasing velocity in a circular path. However, the path of the particle is confined to a doughnut (as in the betatron) by varying both the oscillating voltage and the magnetic field.

The energies attainable in a synchrotron are theoretically unlimited. At the present time, the installation at the Fermi National Accelerator Laboratory in Batavia, Illinois, is the world's most powerful accelerator. It consists of four different kinds of accelerators in series. See Figure 25-9. The circular path of the synchrotron in the final stage is 6.6 km long! Scientists plan to use superconducting magnets with this synchrotron and to obtain proton energies of 1000 Gev (1 Tev) and velocities greater than 99.999% of the velocity of light. High-energy synchrotrons are also called *bevatrons* or *cosmotrons*.

*4. Intersecting storage rings.* The circular accelerators mentioned thus far produce particles by the collision of beams of high-energy particles with stationary targets. The disadvantage of this arrangement is that most of the beam's energy is dissipated in pushing against the target material; only a small amount of the energy is available for nuclear reactions.

In the intersecting storage accelerator, particles are made to collide with each other head-on as they move in opposite directions. To increase the number of collisions, the two beams are first concentrated in *storage rings*. When the density of particles in the storage rings is sufficiently high, the beams are allowed to collide.

Large intersecting storage accelerators are located in Hamburg, West Germany; Geneva, Switzerland; and at Stanford University in California. ISABELLE, another intersecting storage accelerator, is under construction at the Brookhaven National Laboratory in New York. Scheduled for completion in 1985, ISABELLE will contain storage rings that intersect in six places. See Figure 25-10. More than 1000 superconducting

**Figure 25-10** Schematic diagram of the intersecting storage accelerator under construction at the Brookhaven National Laboratory. Almost all the energy of the proton beams is converted into particle production in the head-on collisions in this accelerator.

Protons collide at six stations where rings intersect

1219 meters

Beams from smaller accelerator enter storage rings and accelerate in opposite directions

Underground tunnel

Proton collision is monitored and recorded

Supercooled magnets direct proton beams

Evacuated tubes carry beams

*The first three letters of ISABELLE stand for Intersecting Storage Accelerator. BELLE means "beauty," which describes the concept of the instrument and the information that it is hoped it will provide.*

magnets will guide the beams inside the rings. Designed to study collisions between protons, ISABELLE will set a new record for accelerator energies—over 800 Bev. Because of the efficiency of intersecting accelerators, this is thirteen times greater than the available energy of the most powerful non-intersecting accelerator in operation today.

Since intersecting storage rings are best used with protons, however, and since the total number of collisions per second is not very large compared to that in other accelerators, intersecting storage accelerators cannot be used for all experiments.

## 25.7 Linear accelerators

**Figure 25-11** Schematic diagram of a linear accelerator. Charged particles accelerate as they are attracted by the alternately charged drift tubes.

A linear accelerator is a device that moves charged particles to high velocities along a straight path, in contrast to the circular arrangements in cyclotrons and synchrotrons. Linear accelerators are used both individually and in conjunction with other accelerators.

A simplified diagram of a linear accelerator is shown in Figure 25-11. A series of hollow *drift tubes* is mounted in a long, evacuated chamber. Charged particles are fed into one end of this arrangement and are accelerated by means of a high-frequency alternating voltage applied to the drift tubes. At any given instant, successive tubes have opposite charges. The alternating voltage is timed in such a way that the particle is repelled by the tube it is leaving and attracted by the tube it is approaching. In this way, the particle is accelerated every time it crosses the gap between two tubes. Because of this acceleration, the drift tubes are successively longer so that the particles will always be in a gap when the voltage is reversed.

A 3.3-km-long linear accelerator is located near Palo Alto, California. It is pictured in Figure 25-12. Inside a copper tube in a concrete tunnel buried 7.6 m underground, electrons are accelerated to 40 Gev. As mentioned previously, some circu-

**Figure 25-12** The world's largest linear accelerator. Electrons are injected at the far end of the 3.3-km-long structure (upper right). Particle production and analysis take place in the two buildings at the lower left.

lar accelerators are limited in their ability to accelerate electrons because of electromagnetic radiation losses. This difficulty is not encountered in linear accelerators. In addition, the beam of particles can be more easily controlled in a linear accelerator than in a circular one. A linear accelerator is also more accessible than a circular one, and it can provide a higher frequency of impacts on the target material.

# questions

GROUP A

1. (a) How does a Van de Graaff generator accelerate particles? (b) What type of particles can it *not* accelerate? (c) Why not?

2. (a) In what units is a particle accelerator rated? (b) Define the unit. (c) Give the ratings of a large Van de Graaff generator, a large cyclotron, and a large synchrotron.

3. Distinguish between a cyclotron and a synchrotron.

4. (a) What is the function of a drift tube in a linear accelerator? (b) Why are drift tubes made successively longer inside the accelerator?

5. One particle accelerator can accelerate electrons to a speed of 99.9% of the speed of light. Another machine can bring protons up to a speed of 10% of the speed of light. In terms of particle mass, which machine requires more energy?

6. (a) How does a cyclotron accelerate a proton? (b) How does it keep the proton inside the machine? (c) Why is it impossible for a cyclotron to accelerate neutrons?

7. (a) Why is an intersecting storage accelerator more efficient than a single-beam accelerator? (b) In what ways is the single-beam accelerator better?

8. Why are magnets unnecessary in a linear accelerator?

# DETECTION INSTRUMENTS

**25.8 Types of detectors**

Subatomic particles are far too small to be observed and measured directly. Most of these particles have extremely short half-lives. This, together with the high speed at which they usually travel, means that the time available to study them is very short. As is true of the construction of high-energy accelerators, the development of instruments capable of detecting such elusive targets is one of the most impressive accomplishments of modern technology. Some particle detectors are able to photograph the effects of subatomic particles that spend as little as $10^{-11}$ second in the instruments!

In the following sections we will describe several low-energy detection instruments that have been available to physicists for many years. Then we shall examine three commonly used high-energy detectors: the bubble chamber, the spark chamber, and the solid-state detector.

**25.9 Low-energy detectors**

*1. The electroscope.* One of the first instruments to be used to detect and measure radioactivity is the electroscope, shown in Figure 25-13. A negatively charged electroscope becomes

**Figure 25-13** A gold leaf electroscope. Radioactive materials are placed in the hinged drawer at the bottom.

**Figure 25-14** An ionization chamber. The passage of a subatomic particle (represented by the arrow) separates the gas in the chamber into charged particles. The negatively charged particles are then attracted to the anode on the right side of the chamber.

discharged when ions in the air take electrons from the electroscope. Similarly, a positively charged electroscope becomes discharged as it takes electrons from ions in the air. Thus the rate at which an electroscope is discharged is a measure of the number of ions in the air near the electroscope.

Madame Curie used the electroscope to study the radioactivity of uranium ore. She found that some ores discharged the electroscope more rapidly than others. This finding suggested the presence of an undiscovered, highly radioactive element in some of the ores and led to the isolation of radium.

*2. The spinthariscope.* The spinthariscope (derived from the Greek word meaning "spark") is another instrument that was used in early studies of radioactivity. In this device, alpha and beta particles from radioactive materials or nuclear collisions strike a zinc sulfide screen. Where they strike the screen, they produce a momentary flash of light that can be observed through a magnifier. By counting the number of flashes in a given period of time, the intensity of the radiation can be determined.

*3. The scintillation counter.* As its name implies, the scintillation counter registers the flashes of light produced when subatomic particles hit a fluorescent screen. In this respect the scintillation counter is similar to both the spinthariscope and a television picture tube. However, the scintillation counter also provides information about the energy, and thus the identity, of the particles it detects. This is done by having the screen of the counter coupled with a photomultiplier tube. (See Section 22.7.)

*4. The ionization chamber.* The ionization chamber, shown in Figure 25-14, contains fixed electrodes. When the gas in the chamber becomes ionized due to the passage of a high-speed particle or ray, the electrons and ions drift to the electrodes. The electrons drift to the positive plate while the positively charged ions drift to the negative plate.

The charge produced by a single passing particle is much too small to activate the circuit in an ionization chamber, so an amplifier is used in conjunction with the instrument. The resulting impulse can then be used to trigger a light or some other recording device.

*5. The Geiger tube.* The principle of the ionization chamber is also used in the Geiger tube, which is named after the German physicist Hans Geiger (1882–1945). A hollow cylinder acts as the negative electrode and a thin wire down the center is the positive electrode. The tube is filled with a gas at low pressure, and a potential difference of about 1000 volts is applied to the electrodes. This potential difference is slightly less than the voltage required to ionize the gas and enable it to conduct an electric current between the electrodes.

When a charged particle or gamma ray enters the Geiger tube, it releases electrons from the atoms in its path and produces ions, as shown in Figure 25-15. These electrons are then attracted to the positively charged wire. As they move toward the wire, they collide with more gas atoms to produce additional free electrons and positive ions. Eventually, the surge of electrons toward the positive electrode is large enough to register as a detectable current flowing through the tube. Thus the Geiger tube acts as its own amplifier for the detection of nuclear events. The Geiger tube is generally used in conjunction with external circuits to activate flashing lights, a loudspeaker, or a counting device.

6. *The cloud chamber*. A device that makes the paths of ionizing particles clearly visible is the cloud chamber. It was invented by the British physicist C. T. R. Wilson (1869–1959) in 1911. Its principle of operation is quite simple, and an operating cloud chamber can be assembled with a minimum of material and effort. Figure 25-16 shows a simple, homemade cloud chamber.

The chamber is a plastic or glass container. It is resting on a block of dry ice. A piece of dark cloth is saturated with alcohol and placed around the inside of the container near the top. A radioactive source is placed in the eye of a needle that is suspended from a cork placed on the lid of the container. A photo of alpha-particle tracks in such a cloud chamber is shown in Figure 25-17.

In the chamber, alcohol evaporates from the cloth and condenses again as it reaches the cold region at the bottom of the chamber. Just above the floor of the chamber there is a region where the alcohol vapor does not condense unless there are "seeds" around which drops of alcohol can form. (The situation is similar to a cloud that can be made to form rain by "seeding" it with a powdered chemical.) If there is no dust in the chamber,

**Figure 25-15** A Geiger tube. The ions produced by the subatomic particle (arrow) permit the passage of a flow of electrons between the cathode and the anode.

*In 1927 Wilson received the Nobel Prize for Physics for his work with cloud chambers.*

**Figure 25-16** A simple cloud chamber. The radioactive source is placed in the eye of the needle that is suspended from the cork.

**Figure 25-17** Tracks of alpha particles in a simple cloud chamber.

the only seeds available are ions produced by the passage of charged particles or rays. The resulting trail of alcohol droplets is then visible against the black bottom of the chamber and can be photographed.

The device we have just described is called a *diffusion cloud chamber*. Others, including the chamber developed by Wilson, rely on pressure changes instead of low temperatures to produce condensation. It is possible to use many other liquid-vapor arrangements to produce the tracks. In all cloud chambers, it is the ionizing effect of high-speed particles that makes a visible trail possible.

## 25.10 The bubble chamber

In a cloud chamber, nuclear events are visible because of the condensation of a substance like alcohol. In a bubble chamber, exactly the opposite principle is used. A container is filled with a liquid, and the tracks of particles become visible as a series of bubbles when the liquid boils.

One substance used in bubble chambers is liquid hydrogen. As long as the temperature and pressure conditions are right, the hydrogen stays in liquid form. If the pressure is suddenly lowered, however, the hydrogen boils violently. If high-speed charged particles are allowed to pass through the hydrogen at this same instant, ions are formed. The hydrogen boils a few thousandths of a second sooner around these ions than in the rest of the chamber. Carefully timed photos, such as the one in Figure 25-18, are used to record the resulting bubble trails.

The advantage of the bubble chamber over the cloud chamber is that more nuclear collisions take place in the dense liquid of the bubble chamber. This difference makes it possible to study particles and rays having speeds that are much higher than those that produce recordable events in a cloud chamber.

**Figure 25-18** This photograph shows tracks of subatomic particles in a liquid hydrogen bubble chamber resulting from its bombardment by a beam of 2.85 Gev protons from the synchrotron at Brookhaven National Laboratory, Upton, Long Island, NY. Two charged particles arise from the collision shown at the left. One of these undergoes an additional collision at lower left center. The straight tracks show that many protons travel through the hydrogen without interaction. Some protons collide with electrons of the hydrogen atoms in the chamber. These electrons move in spiral paths under the influence of the powerful magnetic field that is acting on the bubble chamber.

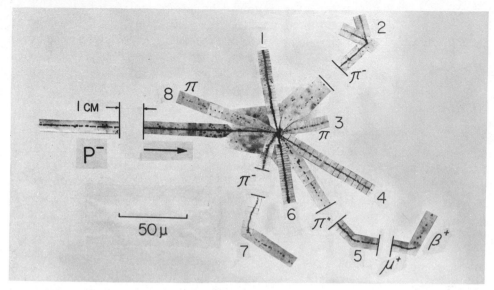

In addition to its use with detection instruments, photographic film can be used directly to record the passage of subatomic particles. When charged particles or gamma rays strike photographic film, they change the chemicals in the emulsion in much the same way that a ray of light changes them. When the film is developed, the passage of the particle or ray is recorded as a spot. If a stack of photographic plates is exposed to a nuclear event, the event is recorded as a series of streaks through the emulsions, as shown in Figure 25-19. The proper development and alignment of these plates require considerable skill, but the result is one of the most direct and most useful detection techniques in particle physics.

**Figure 25-19** Impressions of subatomic particles on photographic film. An antiproton (p⁻) entered from the left and produced a shower of eight other particles when it collided with a proton. This is the first photo of the reaction between a proton and its antiparticle. Other particles are identified by their Greek symbols.

*It was the fogging of a photographic plate that led to the discovery of radioactivity by Becquerel, as described in Section 24.1.*

The passage of subatomic particles can be made visible through an arrangement like the one shown in Figure 25-20. Positive and negative electrodes are placed in series in this device. When a particle triggers a current, its path becomes visible as a series of sparks. These sparks can be easily photographed. An image amplifier may also be used to increase the visibility of the sparks.

A spark chamber is faster than a bubble chamber. The "recycling" time between successive photos is shorter with the spark chamber, and so fewer tracks are recorded on a photo taken with the spark chamber than on a photo taken with a bubble chamber. Also, the charge on the electrodes of a spark chamber can be adjusted so that only the particles with energies above a given value will be recorded. A disadvantage of the spark

## 25.11 The spark chamber

**Figure 25-20** A spark chamber. When voltage is applied to the electrodes, sparks are produced along the ionized trail of the subatomic particle (arrow).

chamber, however, is that it is not able to record the paths of particles that move parallel to the electrodes.

A bubble chamber serves as both the target and the analyzer for subatomic experiments. Spark chambers usually serve as analyzers only. Bubble chambers are for general use. Spark chambers are usually designed for specific experiments.

## 25.12 Solid-state detectors

When certain nonconducting solids are exposed to charged nuclear particles, tracks that can be seen with an electron microscope are produced in the solids. The tracks are regions of distortion of the crystal lattices of the solids. Etching the solids with acid makes the tracks more permanent and more readily visible.

Cosmic rays and various radioactive decay products have left tracks in naturally occurring solids since the origin of the solar system. See Figure 25-21. Through the etching technique just described, scientists have examined these fossil tracks in rocks, in ancient artifacts, in meteorites, and in lava from the ocean floor. Important clues about the history of the earth have been gathered from these studies. The same technique was used on lunar samples.

One of the first solid-state detectors made was a thin sheet of mica used by two British scientists in 1959 in connection with a fission experiment. Glass and certain plastics have also been used as detectors. Plastics are particularly sensitive to slow protons and alpha particles.

Each solid used as a solid-state detector has a threshold below which no tracks are produced. This property makes the detector particularly suited for the study of high-energy particles; the dense background of light-particle tracks that is present in other types of detectors is eliminated by the threshold property of the solid-state detector. It was with the help of glass detectors that Russian scientists first studied the production of element No. 104, khurchatovium, from the bombardment of plutonium with high-energy neon atoms.

Another type of solid-state detector, the *junction detector*, is based on the transistor principle. See Figure 25-22. An applied bias removes all free carriers from the detector. When charged particles enter the device, ionization is produced in the base and an output signal results. In essence, the junction detector is a solid-state ionization chamber. However, the junction detector is smaller in size, requires less power, has a faster response, is completely insensitive to magnetic fields, and produces an output signal that is directly proportional to the energy of the incident particle.

**Figure 25-21** By etching fragments of lunar rocks collected by American astronauts, scientists have discovered that the rocks are marked with tracks left by cosmic rays. The arrow points to a typical cosmic-ray track.

**Figure 25-22** A junction detector. The passage of a charged particle (represented by the arrow) ionizes a region of the P-type base and produces an output signal.

# questions

1. (a) Which detection instrument was the first to record the effects of nuclear radiation? (b) Describe the event.
2. (a) What is the derivation of the term "spinthariscope"? (b) How does this instrument detect subatomic particles?
3. Distinguish between a scintillation counter and a spinthariscope.
4. List one similarity and one difference between a Geiger tube and an electroscope.
5. Describe the construction of a simple cloud chamber.
6. (a) What substance is commonly used in a bubble chamber? (b) Why?
7. Evaluate the statement: "It is possible to see subatomic particles with a bubble chamber."
8. List two advantages of a spark chamber over a bubble chamber.
9. Explain the property of solid-state detectors that makes them particularly suited for the study of high-energy particles.

# SUBATOMIC REACTIONS

Through the use of the detection devices and particle accelerators just described, physicists have liberated or produced more than two hundred different subatomic particles. Almost all these particles are unstable, and many of them have extremely short half-lives. Nevertheless, these fleeting fragments of matter are essential pieces in the puzzle of nuclear structure. The puzzle is far from solved, but great strides have been made during the past thirty years. In the remainder of this chapter, we shall look at the picture of the atom that is emerging from these investigations.

More than one hundred years ago, scientists recognized relationships among the chemical elements that made it possible to arrange them in groups according to their properties. This arrangement is called the *periodic table of the chemical elements*. As more and more subatomic particles were discovered, it became evident that a similar grouping could be made of the subatomic particles. In 1957 such a table was proposed by the American physicist Murray Gell-Mann (b. 1929). Working independently, the Japanese scientist Nishijima (b. 1912) also proposed such a table.

Table 25-2 shows the main features of the Gell-Mann/Nishijima table of subatomic particles. Although all known particles in each category are not listed, enough of them are shown so that the purpose of the classification is clear.

The names and symbols of subatomic particles are taken from Greek words and letters. The names refer to the masses: *baryon* (*berry*-on) means heavy, *meson* (*mez*-on) means medium, and *lepton* (*lep*-ton) means small. Baryons and mesons are also called *hadrons* (*had*-rons); hadron comes from a Greek word meaning bulky. *Bosons* (*boz*-ons) are named after the Indian physicist Satyendranath Bose (b. 1894). The four major divisions

## 25.13 Classification of subatomic particles

*The first useful periodic table of the chemical elements was devised by the Russian chemist Dmitri Mendeleyev (1834–1907).*

*In 1969 Gell-Mann received the Nobel Prize for Physics for his work with subatomic particles.*

Table 25-2

## SUBATOMIC PARTICLES

| Category | Name | Symbol | Antiparticle | Mass (Mev) | Baryon number | Lepton number | Hypercharge | Half-life (s) |
|---|---|---|---|---|---|---|---|---|
| baryons | omega hyperon | $\Omega^-$ | $\Omega^+$ | 1672 | +1 | 0 | -2 | $1.3 \times 10^{-10}$ |
| | xi hyperon | $\Xi^-$ | $\overline{\Xi}^-$ | 1321 | +1 | 0 | -1 | $1.2 \times 10^{-10}$ |
| | | $\Xi^0$ | $\overline{\Xi}^0$ | 1315 | +1 | 0 | -1 | $2.1 \times 10^{-10}$ |
| | sigma hyperon | $\Sigma^-$ | $\overline{\Sigma}^-$ | 1197 | +1 | 0 | 0 | $1.0 \times 10^{-10}$ |
| | | $\Sigma^0$ | $\overline{\Sigma}^0$ | 1192 | +1 | 0 | 0 | $\sim 10^{-20}$ |
| | | $\Sigma^+$ | $\overline{\Sigma}^+$ | 1189 | +1 | 0 | 0 | $5.5 \times 10^{-11}$ |
| | lambda hyperon | $\Lambda^0$ | $\overline{\Lambda}^0$ | 1116 | +1 | 0 | 0 | $1.8 \times 10^{-10}$ |
| | neutron | $n$ | $\overline{n}$ | 940 | +1 | 0 | +1 | 700 |
| | proton | $p$ | $\overline{p}$ | 938 | +1 | 0 | +1 | stable |
| mesons | eta meson | $\eta^0$ | $\overline{\eta}^0$ | 549 | 0 | 0 | 0 | $\sim 10^{-20}$ |
| | kaon (kappa meson) | $K^0$ | $\overline{K}^0$ | 498 | 0 | 0 | +1 | $8.5 \times 10^{-7}$ |
| | | $K^+$ | $\overline{K}^+$ | 494 | 0 | 0 | +1 | $6.4 \times 10^{-9}$ |
| | | | | | | | | $3.5 \times 10^{-8}$ |
| | pion (pi meson) | $\pi^+$ | $\pi^-$ | 140 | 0 | 0 | 0 | $1.0 \times 10^{-8}$ |
| | | $\pi^0$ | $\overline{\pi}^0$ | 135 | 0 | 0 | 0 | $0.6 \times 10^{-16}$ |
| leptons | muon (mu meson) | $\mu^-$ | $\mu^+$ | 105.6 | 0 | +1 | 0 | $1.5 \times 10^{-6}$ |
| | electron | $e^-$ | $e^+$ | 0.5 | 0 | +1 | 0 | stable |
| | mu neutrino | $\nu_\mu$ | $\overline{\nu}_\mu$ | 0 | 0 | +1 | 0 | stable |
| | e-neutrino | $\nu_e$ | $\overline{\nu}_e$ | 0 | 0 | +1 | 0 | stable |
| bosons | photon | $\gamma$ | $\gamma$ | 0 | 0 | 0 | 0 | stable |
| | graviton | $g$ | $g$ | 0 | 0 | 0 | 0 | stable |

Note: The baryon, lepton, and hypercharge values are those of the particle named at the left. In each case, the antiparticle has values with the same magnitude but with opposite sign. The half-life is that of the particle at the left.

of the table were first based largely on mass. However, this distinction could not be strictly applied as new particles were discovered. Today, instead of mass alone, "baryon number" and "lepton number" are used for the classification.

The masses of the subatomic particles are given as the energy equivalents (in Mev) of the rest masses. Neutrinos, photons, and gravitons are given a mass of zero because they do not exist as stationary entities.

*Baryon numbers, lepton numbers, and hypercharge will be explained in Section 25.15.*

The main reasons for the construction of ever-larger particle accelerators are to study the interrelationships between nuclear particles and to explore the possibility that they are, in turn, composed of still simpler particles. Discoveries made with high-energy accelerators often require the revision of existing theories about the structure of matter. These studies of the building blocks of the universe are often referred to as "modern physics."

For many years, nuclear physicists have speculated on the interesting idea that every particle in the universe has a mirror-image counterpart. The table of subatomic particles suggests this idea by listing an antiparticle for each particle. When a particle and its antiparticle are put together, all physical quantities associated with the particle or antiparticle (mass, charge, etc.) disappear and pure energy is left.

*The electron-positron pair discussed in Section 23.3 is an example of a particle and its antiparticle.*

*A substance composed of antiparticles is called **antimatter**.* The collision of a particle with its antiparticle, or of matter with antimatter, results in the annihilation of matter. Such a collision illustrates the interchangeability of matter and energy. Scientists believe that large quantities of antimatter may exist in the universe in the form of stars or even entire galaxies (or antistars and antigalaxies, to be more exact).

As we saw in Section 4.1, a force produces a change in the state of motion of an object. In quantum mechanics, the broader concept of "interaction" replaces the Newtonian concept of force. *An **interaction** is any change in the amount or quantum numbers of particles that are near each other.* For example, an interaction occurs when an electron and a positron collide and change into two photons. An interaction is not merely another word for force. In an interaction, the identity of the particles that are colliding is changed as new particles are created and annihilated. The intermediate particles of an interaction are sometimes called "carriers."

**25.14 Particle interactions**

*1. Strong interactions.* The nature of the strong interaction was discussed in Section 23.12. The strong interaction holds the particles of the nucleus together against the electromagnetic repulsion of the nucleus' similarly charged particles. The strong interaction is independent of charge. In other words, the attrac-

**Figure 25-23** The American physicists Richard Feynman (left) and Murray Gell-Mann both won the Nobel Prize in Physics in 1965 and 1969, respectively, for their work with subatomic particles.

*In 1949 Yukawa received the Nobel Prize for Physics for his prediction of mesons.*

**Figure 25-24** A Feynman diagram. In this interaction, a neutral pi meson is exchanged during the close approach of a proton and a neutron. The energy transferred by the carrier meson changes the momenta of the two baryons.

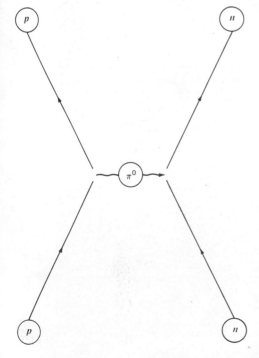

tion between two neutrons is the same as that between a proton and a neutron or between two protons.

Although the strong interaction is the strongest of all interactions, it has a very limited range. It is not effective beyond a distance of $2.0 \times 10^{-5}$ Å. The carrier of the strong interaction is believed to be the meson; there is a constant exchange of mesons among the baryons of a stable nucleus. When the baryons are separated by the intervention of a high-energy particle from an accelerator, the carrier mesons are released.

The production and exchange of particles during an interaction is usually represented by a *Feynman diagram*, named after the American physicist Richard Feynman (b. 1918). In Figure 25-24, a Feynman diagram illustrates the reaction that takes place during the close approach of a proton and a neutron; the reaction in which a meson is emitted and absorbed. This carrier meson transfers the energy that is responsible for the change in momentum of the two baryons. The explanation of the strong "force" by meson exchange is the main reason the process is now called an interaction. In 1935 the Japanese physicist Hideki Yukawa (b. 1907) proposed the theory of the existence of energy-carrying mesons to explain the strong interaction. But mesons were not actually detected until 1947.

*2. Electromagnetic interactions.* These interactions differ from other interactions in several ways. (*1*) Electromagnetic interactions can either attract or repel the objects on which they are acting. The other three interactions are attractive only. (*2*) Electromagnetic interactions can act in directions other than along a straight line between objects. (*3*) The electromagnetic interactions depend on the relative velocities of particles. This is not true of other interactions. The carrier of the electromagnetic interaction is the photon.

Electromagnetism keeps electrons in orbit around the nucleus. The same interaction is responsible for the bonding between atoms to form molecules and between molecules to form larger substances. Nevertheless, the electromagnetic interaction is less than $10^{-2}$ as strong as the strong interaction.

*3. Weak interactions.* This is the most mysterious of the known interactions between particles. As the study of the nucleus progressed and the number of subatomic particles grew, a "strange" principle was discovered. Some particles were always produced in pairs, such as a lambda hyperon and K meson, and these particles had much longer half-lives than was expected.

To explain the behavior of these so-called "strange particles," the "weak interaction" was postulated. Its ratio to the strong interaction is about $10^{-13}$ to 1, so it affects only leptons. Beta decay is an example of a weak interaction.

The theoretical carrier for weak interactions is the $W^{\pm}$ particle. ($W$ stands for weak, and the $\pm$ is the charge of the particle and its antiparticle.) The $W^{\pm}$ particle is also called the intermediate vector boson. It has not yet been detected.

*4. Gravitational interactions.* Gravitation was the first of the interactions to be studied, yet it is the weakest of them all. Its ratio to the strong interaction is only $10^{-38}$ to 1. Gravitation has no known distance limitations, so its effects are easily observed in the behavior of large objects on the earth and in the motions of celestial bodies. Within the atomic nucleus, the effect of gravitational interactions is negligible in comparison with the other interactions that are present.

The carrier for the gravitational interaction has been named the *graviton*. Like the photon, its rest mass is thought to be zero. Because they are very weak, gravity waves are difficult to detect. Scientists at the University of Maryland used 1000-kg aluminum cylinders as receivers for gravity waves from certain massive stars, but the results were inconclusive. In 1978, astrophysicists from the University of Massachusetts announced that they had verified the existence of gravity waves after four years of observations with a large radio telescope in Puerto Rico. See Figure 25-25. Aimed at a pair of massive stars that are orbiting each other, the telescope recorded a cumulative delay of $4 \times 10^{-4}$ s in the orbital period, which is exactly the amount predicted by the theory of relativity if gravity waves are draining energy from the two stars.

**Figure 25-25** This 305-meter receiver near Arecibo, Puerto Rico, is the world's largest radio telescope. It was used to confirm the existence of gravity waves in an experiment that extended over a 4-year period.

## 25.15 Conservation of subatomic properties

Repeatedly in your study of physics, the importance of the conservation principles has been emphasized. The conservation of mass-energy, the conservation of linear and angular momentum, the conservation of electric charge—these laws are basic to an understanding of all reactions above the atomic scale. Similar laws hold true in subatomic interactions. We have already seen in Section 24.4, for example, that both mass-energy and electric charge are conserved in nuclear reactions. As other subatomic particles were discovered, additional conservation laws were formulated.

*1. Conservation of baryons.* When a baryon decays or reacts with another particle, the number of baryons is the same on both sides of the equation. For example, if a neutron is left by itself it will decay as follows:

$$n^0 \rightarrow p + e^- + \bar{\nu}$$
$$\text{Baryon No.} = +1 = +1 \quad +0 \quad +0$$

The neutron and proton are both baryons, while the electron and antineutrino have baryon numbers of zero. Consequently, the baryon number of the equation is $+1$ on each side.

The conservation of baryons keeps the universe from deteriorating into mesons and leptons. If such a deterioration could happen, atoms as we know them would no longer exist and matter would become a rather homogeneous mixture of a few kinds of low-mass particles.

*2. Conservation of leptons.* The decay of the neutron illustrates another nuclear conservation principle. The lepton number of the neutron and proton is zero. The lepton number of the electron is $+1$. The lepton number of the antineutrino is $-1$, since it is an antiparticle. Consequently, the arithmetic sum of the lepton numbers is the same on each side of the equation. This principle holds true for every interaction in which leptons are involved.

$$n^0 \rightarrow p + e^- + \bar{\nu}$$
$$\text{Lepton No.} = 0 = 0 \quad +1 \quad -1$$

Lepton conservation explains the necessity of pair production, which was considered "strange" when it was first discovered. When a lepton is created in an interaction, a particle with the opposite lepton number must also be created in order to conserve the lepton value of the reaction. Similarly, a lepton can be annihilated only by interacting with a particle of opposite lepton value.

The conservation of baryons and leptons does not prevent the change of a particle to another particle within the same category, however. In neutron decay, one kind of baryon (the neutron) changed into another kind (the proton). The decay of the antimuon is another example:

$$\mu^+ \rightarrow e^+ + \nu - \bar{\nu}$$
$$\textbf{Lepton No.} = -1 = -1 \quad +1 \quad -1$$

*3. Conservation of hypercharge.* Some baryons and some mesons have a property called *hypercharge*. Hypercharge can be either positive or negative. The hypercharge sign of a particle is the opposite of the hypercharge sign of its antiparticle. Hypercharge is conserved in strong and electromagnetic interactions, but it is not conserved in weak interactions.

Consider the following interaction involving hypercharge:

$$\pi^+ + p \rightarrow K^+ + \Lambda^0$$
$$\textbf{Hypercharge} = 0 \quad +1 = +1 \quad +0$$

The identity of the original particles has changed completely, but the sum of the hypercharges is +1 on each side of the reaction. (The sum of the baryon numbers is also +1 on each side.)

*4. Conservation of parity.* The distribution of matter in space is often described in terms of *parity*. **The *law of parity*** states *that for every process in nature there is a mirror-image process that is indistinguishable from the original process.* Another way to state this law is to say that there is no absolute and independent way of describing right and left, clockwise and counterclockwise, in the universe. Any experiment devised to establish one of these directions is matched by an equally probable event in the opposite direction.

Parity experiments deal largely with the spin of nuclear particles. Spin is also responsible for the direction in which particles are emitted in subatomic interactions. The conservation of parity stipulates that particles will be emitted in opposite directions in equal numbers since nature shows no preference for spin direction. But in 1956 a series of experiments based on predictions by the Chinese physicists Tsung-Dao Lee (b. 1926) and Chen Ning Yang (b. 1922) showed that this was not the case. In the case of weak interactions involving beta decay, parity was not conserved!

Experiments were specifically designed to test the conservation of parity in other interactions. The question was whether parity is still conserved in a larger sense when particles are replaced by their antiparticles in subatomic interactions. In 1966 physicists at the Brookhaven National Laboratory in New York discovered a violation of parity with antiparticles as well. So perhaps there is an absolute sense of direction in the universe after all.

In 1974 evidence suggested that the subatomic conservation laws are not completely inviolate at high energies. At 300 Gev, collisions of electrons and positrons were found to produce

*In 1957 Lee and Yang jointly received the Nobel Prize for Physics for their discovery of violations of the parity principle.*

hadrons and vice versa. This suggests that the weak interaction is not a constant and that under certain conditions it may become stronger than the electromagnetic interaction.

One explanation of this phenomenon suggests that colliding leptons exchange a so-called Z particle. This interaction is known as a *neutral weak current* (since there is no change in the charges of the colliding particles). The discovery of neutral weak currents is an important step toward a *unified field theory*, a theory in which all forces in the universe are part of a single concept.

In 1974 two subnuclear particles that do not fit into present classifications were discovered. Both particles have unusually large masses and long half-lives. They have been named psi 3100 and psi 3700 (representing their masses in Mev units) by scientists at the Stanford Linear Accelerator Center. Scientists at Brookhaven National Laboratory have called the particles J-1 and J-2 (since J is one of the few unused letters in nuclear terminology).

## 25.16 The quark theory

*The word "quark" does not have a specific meaning. It appears in the novel* Finnegans Wake *by James Joyce.*

*The "color" and "flavor" of quarks are analogous to the quantum numbers of electrons. These terms do not refer to the senses of sight and taste.*

Rather than simplify the problem, the discovery of large numbers of subatomic particles has complicated the search for the fundamental units of matter. That is why physicists have suggested that hadrons are made up of smaller particles called *quarks*. The quark theory was first proposed in 1963 by Gell-Mann and the American physicist George Zweig (b. 1937). The discovery of J/psi particles helped to advance the quark theory.

Quarks and antiquarks are thought to have charges of $\pm\frac{1}{3}$ or $\pm\frac{2}{3}$. According to the theory, baryons are composed of three quarks each, and mesons are composed of two quarks each. To avoid possible violations of the exclusion principle, quarks are also thought to possess properties called "color" and "flavor." It has also been suggested that quarks may differ in rest mass. More massive quarks are said to be "charmed." In 1974 and 1976 baryons and mesons that may consist of charmed quarks and charmed antiquarks were discovered.

Quarks are said to be held together by a force that increases, rather than decreases, with distance. Perhaps this is why present accelerators have not been able to isolate quarks for identification. The carrier for the quark force is called the "gluon." Evidence of the existence of gluons was announced in 1979.

The profusion of quarks, even before their discovery, shows that the search for simplicity in the subatomic world is not succeeding. No one really knows what the ultimate model of matter will be or if such a model will ever emerge. Perhaps it is even misleading to look for fundamental *particles*. Perhaps the basic units of matter will turn out to be some other entity. Perhaps all interactions will be found to be special cases of a more fundamental interaction. The search for such new knowledge requires a close correlation between theory and technology. The pursuit of new knowledge has already taken physics to frontiers that were totally unknown a generation ago.

# summary

Modern atomic models take into account the uncertainty principle, which states that the exact position and momentum of an object cannot be simultaneously specified. The allowable values of physical quantities in modern atomic theory are given in terms of quantum numbers. The first quantum number for the electron describes its orbital radius. The second quantum number gives its angular momentum. The third quantum number specifies its direction in terms of a magnetic field. The fourth quantum number designates the spin of the electron. The exclusion principle states that no two electrons in an atom may have the same set of quantum numbers.

The stability of an electron is described in terms of ionization energy, which is the energy required to remove an electron from its orbit. All the equations for quantum numbers include Planck's constant. This indicates that all matter has wave characteristics.

Particle accelerators fall into three main categories: Van de Graaff accelerators, circular accelerators, and linear accelerators. In Van de Graaff generators, energies of up to 20 Mev may be produced. Betatrons, cyclotrons, synchrotrons, and intersecting storage rings are types of circular accelerators. The world's largest accelerator is a synchrotron, in which proton energies of 1000 Gev are achieved after several preliminary stages of acceleration in other devices. Intersecting storage accelerators are more efficient than

other types of circular accelerators. Linear accelerators avoid the radiation losses encountered in circular accelerators.

Subatomic particles can be detected and studied because they are able to ionize certain substances or to produce visible paths. Low-energy detectors include the electroscope, the spinthariscope, the scintillation counter, the ionization chamber, the Geiger tube, and the cloud chamber.

The bubble chamber detects high-energy particles by producing momentary trails of hydrogen or helium gas, which are then photographed. The spark chamber is faster than the bubble chamber and is usually designed for a specific experiment. Solid-state detectors are also more selective than bubble chambers. Some solid-state detectors work on the transistor principle.

The number of identified subatomic particles now exceeds two hundred. They can be classified into baryons, mesons, and leptons. Baryons and mesons are also called hadrons. Each particle has an antiparticle with opposite charge.

The four known subatomic interactions are strong, electromagnetic, weak, and gravitational. In strong interactions, the number of baryons and leptons remains constant. Hypercharge and parity are not conserved in weak interactions.

Hadrons are thought to consist of quarks. Quarks with color, flavor, and charm have been postulated, but none has yet been detected and isolated.

# questions

GROUP A

1. (a) Who proposed the table of subatomic particles? (b) What other scientific table does it resemble?

2. Define: (a) baryon, (b) meson, (c) lepton, (d) hadron, (e) boson.

3. (a) What is antimatter? (b) What happens when a particle collides with its antiparticle?

4. (a) List the four types of interactions in the universe in order of their increasing magnitude. (b) Name the carrier of each interaction. (c) Which of these interactions are effective only within the size range of the atomic nucleus?

5. Distinguish between a Newtonian force and a subatomic interaction.

6. (a) What are Feynman diagrams? (b) How are they used to describe subatomic interactions?

7. (a) List four kinds of conservation in subatomic interactions. (b) List two properties of matter that are not always conserved on the subatomic scale.

8. How does the conservation of baryons prevent the collapse of matter?

9. What is the relationship between symmetry and parity?

10. What is meant by a unified field theory?

11. Discuss the quark theory with regard to why, when, and by whom it was proposed.

12. Describe a quark.

13. How does the quark theory avoid violations of the exclusion principle?

# Mathematics Refresher

## 1. Introduction.

The topics selected for this Mathematics Refresher are those which sometimes trouble physics students. You may want to study this section before working on certain types of physics problems. The presentation here is not so detailed as that given in mathematics textbooks, but there is sufficient review to help you perform certain types of mathematical operations.

The following references are given for your convenience in reviewing these topics:

Section 2.3 defines *significant figures* and gives rules for their notation.

Section 2.4 explains the *scientific notation* system.

Section 2.7 describes the *orderly procedure* you should use *in problem solving*, and the proper method of handling units in computations.

## 2. Conversion of a fraction to a decimal.

Divide the numerator by the denominator, carrying the answer to the required number of significant figures.

*Example*

Convert $\frac{45}{85}$ to a decimal.

*Solution*

Dividing 45 by 85, we find the equivalent decimal to be 0.53, rounded to two significant figures.

$$
\begin{array}{r}
0.529 \\
85\overline{)45.000} \\
42\ 5 \\
\hline
2\ 50 \\
1\ 70 \\
\hline
800 \\
765 \\
\hline
\end{array}
$$

## 3. Calculation of percentage.

Uncertainty always exists in measurements of physical phenomena. Uncertainty exists because measuring instruments have limited precision. The instruments you use in laboratory experiments generally have less precision than those used by the physicists who obtained the "best known values" you find in tables. *The precision of any measurement is limited to the measurement detail which the instrument used is capable of providing.* In physics, an error is defined as the difference between experimentally obtained data and the accepted values for these data. In experimental work, the *relative error* (percentage error) is usually more significant than the *absolute error* (the actual difference between an observed value and its accepted value). Hence, as a physics student you must be able to calculate percentages and percentage errors, and convert fractions to percentages and percentages to decimals.

*Example*
What percentage of 19 is 13?

*Solution*
We divide 13 by 19, and multiply the quotient by 100%. A multiplication by 100% does not change the value of the quotient, since 100% actually has a value of 1. When we multiply by 100%, we multiply the number by 100, and affix the % sign to the product: $\frac{13}{19} \times 100\% = 68\%$ rounded to two significant figures.

## 4. Calculation of relative error.

$$\text{Relative Error} = \frac{\text{Absolute Error}}{\text{Accepted Value}} \times 100\%$$

where the *absolute error* is the difference between the *observed value* and the *accepted value*.

*Example*
In a laboratory experiment carried out at 20.0°C, a student found the speed of sound in air to be 329.8 m/s. The accepted value at this temperature is 343.5 m/s. What was the relative error?

*Solution*
$$\text{Absolute Error} = 343.5 \text{ m/s} - 329.8 \text{ m/s}$$
$$= 13.7 \text{ m/s}$$
$$\text{Relative Error} = \frac{13.7 \text{ m/s}}{343.5 \text{ m/s}} \times 100\% = 3.99\%$$

## 5. Conversion of fractions to percentages.

To convert a fraction to a percentage, divide the numerator by the denominator and multiply the quotient by 100%.

*Example*
Express $\frac{11}{13}$ as a percentage.

*Solution*
$\frac{11}{13} \times 100\% = 85\%$, rounded to two significant figures.

## 6. Conversion of percentages to decimals.

To convert a percentage to a decimal, move the decimal point two places to the left, and remove the percent sign.

*Example*
Convert 62.5% to a decimal.

*Solution*
If we express 62.5% as a fraction, it becomes 62.5/100. If we actually perform

the indicated division, we obtain 0.625 as the decimal equivalent. Observe that the only changes have been to move the decimal point two places to the left, and remove the percent sign.

## 7. *Proportions.*

Many physics problems involving temperature, pressure, and volume relationships of gases may be solved by using proportions.

*Example*

Solve the proportion $\dfrac{x}{225 \text{ mL}} = \dfrac{273°}{298°}$ for $x$.

*Solution*

Multiply both sides of the equation by 225 mL, the denominator of $x$, giving $x = \dfrac{225 \text{ mL} \times 273°}{298°}$. Solving, $x = 206 \text{ mL}$.

## 8. *Fractional Equations.*

The equations for certain problems involving lenses, mirrors, and electric resistances produce fractional equations where the unknown is in the denominator. To solve such equations, clear them of fractions by multiplying each term by the lowest common denominator. Then isolate the unknown and complete the solution.

*Example*

Solve $\dfrac{1}{d_o} + \dfrac{1}{d_i} = \dfrac{1}{f}$ for $f$.

*Solution*

The lowest common denominator of $d_o$, $d_i$, and $f$ is $d_o d_i f$. Multiplying the fractional equation by this product, we obtain

$$\frac{d_o d_i f}{d_o} + \frac{d_o d_i f}{d_i} = \frac{d_o d_i f}{f} \qquad \text{or} \qquad d_i f + d_o f = d_o d_i$$

Thus, $f(d_o + d_i) = d_o d_i$ and $f = \dfrac{d_o d_i}{d_o + d_i}$

## 9. *Equations.*

When a known equation is employed in solving a problem and the unknown quantity is not the one usually isolated, the equation should be solved algebraically to isolate the unknown quantity of the particular problem. Then the values (with units) of the known quantities can be substituted and the indicated operations performed.

*Example*

From the equation for potential energy, $E_p = mgh$, we are to calculate $h$.

*Solution*

Before substituting known values for $E_p$, $m$, and $g$, the unknown term $h$ is isolated and expressed in terms of $E_p$, $m$, and $g$. This is accomplished by dividing both sides of the basic equation by $mg$.

$$\frac{E_p}{mg} = \frac{mgh}{mg} \qquad \text{or} \qquad h = \frac{E_p}{mg}$$

If $E_p$ is given in joules, $m$ in kilograms, and $g$ in meters/second$^2$, the unit of $h$ is

$$h = \frac{j}{kg \ m/s^2} = \frac{kg \ m^2/s^2}{kg \ m/s^2} = m \qquad \text{Thus } h \text{ is expressed in meters.}$$

### 10. Laws of exponents.

Operations involving exponents may be expressed in general fashion as $a^m \times a^n = a^{m+n}$; $a^m \div a^n = a^{m-n}$; $(a^m)^n = a^{mn}$; $\sqrt[n]{a^m} = a^{m/n}$. For example:

$$x^2 \times x^3 = x^5 \quad 10^5 \div 10^{-3} = 10^8 \qquad (t^2)^3 = t^6 \quad \sqrt[4]{4^2} = 4^{2/4} = 4^{1/2} = 2$$

### 11. Quadratic formula.

The two roots of the quadratic equation $ax^2 + bx + c = 0$ in which $a$ does not equal zero are given by the quadratic formula

$$x = \frac{-b \pm \sqrt{b^2 - 4ac}}{2a}$$

### 12. Triangles.

In physics some facts about triangles are used to solve problems about forces and velocities.

1. *30°—60°—90° right triangle.* It is useful to remember that the hypotenuse of such a triangle is twice as long as the side opposite the 30° angle. The length of the side opposite the 60° angle is $l\sqrt{3}$, where $l$ is the length of the side opposite the 30° angle.

2. *45°—45°—90° right triangle.* The sides opposite the 45° angles are equal. The length of the hypotenuse is $l\sqrt{2}$, where $l$ is the length of a side.

3. *Trigonometric functions.* Trigonometric functions are ratios of the lengths of sides of a right triangle and depend on the magnitude of one of its acute angles. Using right triangle **ABC**, below, we define the following trigonometric functions of $\angle$ **A**:

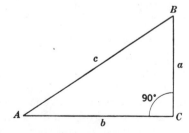

$$\text{sine } \angle \mathbf{A} = \frac{\mathbf{a}}{\mathbf{c}}$$

$$\text{cosine } \angle \mathbf{A} = \frac{\mathbf{b}}{\mathbf{c}}$$

$$\text{tangent } \angle \mathbf{A} = \frac{\mathbf{a}}{\mathbf{b}}$$

These functions are usually abbreviated as sin **A**, cos **A**, and tan **A**. Appendix B, Table 6, gives values of trigonometric functions.

*Example*

In a right triangle one side is 25.3 and the hypotenuse is 37.6. Find the angle between these two sides.

*Solution*

Using the designations in the triangle shown above, $b = 25.3$ and $c = 37.6$. You are to find $\angle A$. Hence you will use the trigonometric function $\cos A = b/c$, or cos $A = 25.3/37.6 = 0.673$. From Appendix B, Table 6, the cosine of $47.5°$ is $0.676$ and the cosine of $48.0°$ is $0.669$. The required angle is $3/7 \times 0.5°$, or $0.2°$, greater than $47.5°$. Thus $\angle A = 47.7°$.

*Example*

In a right triangle, one angle is $23.8°$ and the adjacent side (not the hypotenuse) is $43.2$. Find the other side.

*Solution*

Again using the designations in the above triangle, $\angle A = 23.8°$ and $b = 43.2$. The function involving these values and the unknown side, $a$, is $\tan A = a/b$. Solving for $a$: $a = b \tan A$. From Appendix B, Table 6, $\tan 23.8° = 0.441$. Thus $a = 43.2 \times 0.441 = 19.1$.

*4. Sine law and cosine law.* For any triangle **ABC**, below, the sine law and the cosine law enable us to calculate the magnitudes of the remaining sides and angles if the magnitudes of one side and of any other two parts are given.

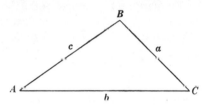

Sine law: $\dfrac{a}{\sin A} = \dfrac{b}{\sin B} = \dfrac{c}{\sin C}$

Cosine law: $a = \sqrt{b^2 + c^2 - 2bc \cos A}$

$b = \sqrt{c^2 + a^2 - 2ca \cos B}$

$c = \sqrt{a^2 + b^2 - 2ab \cos C}$

## 13. Circles.

The circumference of a circle is $c = \pi d$, where $d$ is the diameter.
The area of a circle is $A = \pi r^2$, where $r$ is the radius.

## 14. Cylinders.

The volume of a circular cylinder is $V = \pi r^2 h$, where $r$ is the radius of the base and $h$ is the height.

## 15. Spheres.

The surface area of a sphere is $A = 4\pi r^2$, where $r$ is the radius.
The volume of a sphere is $V = \frac{4}{3}\pi r^3$, where $r$ is the radius.

## 16. Logarithms.

The common logarithm of a number is the exponent or the power to which 10 must be raised in order to obtain the given number. A logarithm is composed of two parts: the *characteristic*, or integral part; and the *mantissa*, or decimal part. The characteristic of the logarithm *of any whole or mixed number* is one less than the number of digits to the left of its decimal point. The characteristic of the logarithm *of a decimal fraction* is always negative and is numerically one greater than the number of zeros immediately to the right of the decimal point. Mantissas are always positive and are read from tables such as Appendix B, Table 24. Proportional parts are used when numbers having four significant figures are involved. In determining the mantissa, the decimal point in the original number is ignored since its position is indicated by the characteristic.

Logarithms are exponents and follow the laws of exponents:

Logarithm of a product = sum of the logarithms of the factors

Logarithm of a quotient = logarithm of the dividend minus logarithm of the divisor

To find the number whose logarithm is given, determine the digits in the number from the table of mantissas. The characteristic indicates the position of the decimal point.

*Example*

Find the logarithm of 35.76.

*Solution*

There are two digits to the left of the decimal point. Therefore the characteristic of the logarithm of 35.76 is one less than two, or 1. To find the mantissa, ignore the decimal point and look up 3576 in Appendix B, Table 24. Read down the *n* column to 35. Follow this row across to the 7 column, where you will find 5527. This is the mantissa of 3570. Similarly, the mantissa for 3580 is 5539. To calculate the mantissa for 3576, take 6/10 of the difference between 5527 and 5539, or 7, and add it to 5527. Thus, the required mantissa is 5534, and the complete logarithm of 35.76 is 1.5534.

*Example*

Find the logarithm of 0.4692.

*Solution*

There are no zeros immediately to the right of the decimal point, hence the characteristic of the logarithm of 0.4692 is $-1$. However, only the characteristic is negative; the mantissa is positive and is found from Appendix B, Table 24, to be 6714. The complete logarithm of 0.4692 may be written as $\overline{1}.6714$, or $0.6714 - 1$, or $9.6714 - 10$.

*Example*

Find the logarithm of (1) 357,600,000        (2) 0.0000003576

*Solution*

(1)  $357,600,000 = 3.576 \times 10^8$        $\log = 8.5534$

(2)  $0.0000003576 = 3.576 \times 10^{-7}$    $\log = \overline{7}.5534$, or $0.5534 - 7$, or $3.5534 - 10$

# Appendix A—Equations

*(The number indicates the section in which the equation is introduced.)*

## 1.9 Mass Density

$$\text{mass density} = \frac{\text{mass}}{\text{volume}}$$

## 1.14 Mass-Energy Relationship

$$E = mc^2$$

$E$ is energy; $m$ is mass; $c$ is speed of light.

## 2.3 Relative Error

$$E_r = \frac{E_a}{A} \times 100\%$$

$E_r$ is relative error; $E_a$ is absolute error; $A$ is accepted value.

## 3.2 Speed

$$\text{Average Speed} = \frac{\text{total path length}}{\text{elapsed time}}$$

## 3.3 Velocity

$$v_{av} = \frac{d_f - d_i}{t_f - t_i} = \frac{\Delta d}{\Delta t}$$

$v_{av}$ is average velocity; $d_i$ is initial position at time $t_i$; $d_f$ is final position at time $t_f$; $\Delta d$ is displacement; $\Delta t$ is time interval.

## 3.5 Acceleration

$$a_{av} = \frac{v_f - v_i}{t_f = t_i} = \frac{\Delta v}{\Delta t}$$

$a_{av}$ is average acceleration; $v_i$ is initial velocity at time $t_i$; $v_f$ is final velocity at time $t_f$; $\Delta v$ is change in velocity; $\Delta t$ is time interval.

## 3.6 Uniformly Accelerated Motion

$$v_f = v_i + a\Delta t \quad \text{or} \quad v_f = v_i + g\Delta t$$

$v_f$ is final velocity; $v_i$ is initial velocity; $a$ is acceleration or $g$ is free-fall acceleration; $\Delta t$ is elapsed time.

## 3.6 Accelerated Motion

$$\Delta d = v_i\Delta t + \tfrac{1}{2}a\Delta t^2 \quad \text{or} \quad \Delta d = v_i\Delta t + \tfrac{1}{2}g\Delta t^2$$

$\Delta d$ is displacement; $v_i$ is initial velocity; $\Delta t$ is elapsed time; $a$ is acceleration or $g$ is free-fall acceleration.

## 3.6 Accelerated Motion

$$v_f = \sqrt{v_i^2 + 2a\Delta d} \quad \text{or} \quad v_f = \sqrt{v_i^2 + 2g\Delta d}$$

$v_f$ is final velocity; $v_i$ is initial velocity; $a$ is acceleration or $g$ is free-fall acceleration; $\Delta d$ is displacement.

## 3.9 Newton's Second Law of Motion

$$F = ma$$

$F$ is force; $m$ is mass; $a$ is acceleration.

## 3.9 Force and Acceleration on Bodies of Known Weight

$$F = \frac{F_w a}{g}$$

$F$ is force; $F_w$ is weight; $a$ is acceleration; $g$ is free-fall acceleration.

## 3.9 Weight and Mass

$$F_w = mg$$

$F_w$ is weight; $m$ is mass; $g$ is free-fall acceleration.

## 3.11 Law of Universal Gravitation

$$F = \frac{G\, m_1 m_2}{d^2}$$

$F$ is force of attraction; $G$ is gravitational constant; $m_1$ and $m_2$ are masses of bodies; $d$ is distance between their centers of mass.

## 3.12 Acceleration of Gravity

$$g = \frac{Gm_e}{d^2}$$

$g$ is free-fall acceleration; $G$ is gravitational constant; $m_e$ is mass of earth; $d$ is distance from center of earth.

## 4.5 Composition of Forces – The resultant of two forces acting at an angle of between 0° and 180° upon a given point is equal to the diagonal of a parallelogram of which the two force vectors are sides. The equilibrant force has a magnitude equal to that of the resultant of the separate forces, but it acts in the opposite direction.

## 4.8 Coefficient of Friction

$$\mu = \frac{F_f}{F_N}$$

$\mu$ is coefficient of friction; $F_f$ is force of friction; $F_N$ is force normal to surface.

## 5.2 Centripetal Force

$$\text{Centripetal Force} = \frac{mv^2}{r}$$

$m$ is mass; $v$ is velocity; $r$ is radius of path.

## 5.3 Motion in Vertical Circle

$$v_{min} = \sqrt{rg}$$

$v_{min}$ is critical velocity; $r$ is radius of vertical circle; $g$ is free fall acceleration.

## 5.6 Angular Velocity

$$\omega = \frac{\Delta\theta}{\Delta t}$$

$\omega$ is angular velocity; $\Delta\theta$ is angular displacement; $\Delta t$ is time.

## 5.7 Angular Acceleration

$$\alpha = \frac{\Delta\omega}{\Delta t}$$

$\alpha$ is angular acceleration; $\Delta\omega$ is angular velocity; $\Delta t$ is time.

## 5.7 Accelerated Rotary Motion

$$\omega_f = \omega_i + \alpha\Delta t$$
$$\Delta\theta = \omega_i\Delta t + \tfrac{1}{2}\alpha\Delta t^2$$
$$\omega_f = \sqrt{\omega_i^2 + 2\alpha\theta}$$

$\omega_f$ is final angular velocity; $\omega_i$ is initial angular velocity; $\alpha$ is angular acceleration; $\Delta t$ is time; $\Delta\theta$ is angular displacement.

## 5.8 Rotational Inertia

$$T = I\alpha$$

$T$ is torque; $I$ is rotational inertia; $\alpha$ is angular acceleration.

## 5.8 Torque

$$T = Fr$$

$T$ is torque; $F$ is tangential force; $r$ is distance from pivot point to point of application of force.

## 5.12 Pendulum

$$T:T' = \sqrt{l}:\sqrt{l'}$$

$T$ is period of first pendulum; $T'$ is period of second pendulum; $l$ is length of first pendulum; $l'$ is length of second pendulum.

## 5.12 Pendulum

$$T = 2\pi\sqrt{\frac{l}{g}}$$

$T$ is period; $l$ is length; $g$ is free-fall acceleration.

## 6.1 Work

$$W = F\Delta d$$

$W$ is work; $F$ is force; $\Delta d$ is displacement.

## 6.3 Work (Rotary Motion)

$$W = T\Delta\theta$$

$W$ is work; $T$ is torque; $\Delta\theta$ is angular displacement.

## 6.4 Efficiency

$$\text{Efficiency} = \frac{W_{out}}{W_{in}}$$

$W_{out}$ is work output; $W_{in}$ is work input.

### 6.5 Power

$$P = \frac{F \Delta d}{\Delta t}$$

$P$ is power; $F$ is force; $\Delta d$ is displacement; $\Delta t$ is time.

### 6.6 Power (Rotary Motion)

$$P = T\omega$$

$P$ is power; $T$ is torque; $\omega$ is angular velocity.

### 6.7 Gravitational Potential Energy

$$E_p = mg\Delta h$$

$E_p$ is gravitational potential energy; $m$ is mass; $g$ is free-fall acceleration; $\Delta h$ is vertical distance.

### 6.8 Kinetic Energy

$$E_K = \tfrac{1}{2}mv^2$$

$E_K$ is kinetic energy; $m$ is mass; $v$ is velocity.

### 6.9 Kinetic Energy (Rotary Motion)

$$E_K = \tfrac{1}{2}I\omega^2$$

$E_K$ is kinetic energy; $I$ is rotational inertia; $\omega$ is angular velocity.

### 6.10 Potential Energy (Elastic)

$$E_p = \tfrac{1}{2}k(\Delta d)^2$$

$E_p$ is potential energy; $k$ is elastic constant; $\Delta d$ is displacement.

### 6.12 Impulse and Change of Momentum

$$F \Delta t = m \Delta v$$

$F$ is force; $\Delta t$ is elapsed time; the product $F\Delta t$ is impulse; $m$ is mass; $\Delta v$ is change of velocity; the product $m\Delta v$ is the change of momentum.

### 6.14 Elastic Collisions in One Dimension

$$mv_i + m'v_i' = mv_f + m'v_f'$$

$m$ is mass of first body, $v_i$ its initial velocity, $v_f$ its final velocity; $m'$ is mass of second body, $v_i'$ its initial velocity, $v_f'$ its final velocity.

### 6.15 Angular Impulse and Change of Angular Momentum

$$T\Delta t = I\omega_f - I\omega_i$$

$T$ is torque; $\Delta t$ is elapsed time; the product $T\Delta t$ is angular impulse; $I$ is moment of inertia; $\omega_f$ is final angular velocity; $\omega_i$ is initial angular velocity; the product $I\omega$ is angular momentum.

### 7.11 Hooke's Law

$$Y = \frac{Fl}{\Delta lA}$$

$Y$ is Young's modulus; $F$ is distorting force; $l$ is original length; $\Delta l$ is change in length; $A$ is cross-sectional area.

### 8.2 Kelvin Temperature

$$°K = °C + 273°$$

$°K$ is Kelvin temperature; $°C$ is Celsius temperature.

### 8.4 Linear Expansion

$$\Delta l = \alpha l \Delta T$$

$\Delta l$ is change in length; $\alpha$ is coefficient of linear expansion; $l$ is original length; $\Delta T$ is change in temperature.

### 8.5 Volume Expansion

$$\Delta V = \beta V \Delta T$$

$\Delta V$ is change in volume; $\beta$ is coefficient of volume expansion; $V$ is original volume; $\Delta T$ is change in temperature.

### 8.7 Charles' Law

$$\frac{V}{T_K} = \frac{V'}{T_K'}$$

$V$ is original volume; $T_K$ is original Kelvin temperature; $V'$ is new volume; $T_K'$ is new Kelvin temperature; provided pressure is constant.

### 8.8 Boyle's Law

$$pV = p'V'$$

$p$ is original pressure; $V$ is original volume; $p'$ is new pressure; $V'$ is new volume; provided temperature is constant.

### 8.8 Variation of Gas Density with Pressure

$$\frac{D}{D'} = \frac{p}{p'}$$

$D$ is gas density at pressure $p$; $D'$ is gas density at pressure $p'$.

## 8.9 Boyle's and Charles' Laws Combined

$$\frac{pV}{T_\text{K}} = \frac{p'V'}{T_\text{K}'}$$

$p$, $V$, and $T_\text{K}$ are original pressure, volume, and Kelvin temperature, respectively; $p'$, $V'$, and $T_\text{K}'$ are new pressure, volume, and Kelvin temperature, respectively.

## 8.10 Ideal Gas Equation

$$pV = nRT_\text{K}$$

$p$ is pressure; $V$ is volume; $n$ is number of moles; $R$ is universal gas constant; $T_\text{K}$ is Kelvin temperature.

## 8.11 Heat Capacity

$$\text{heat capacity} = Q/\Delta T$$

$Q$ is quantity of heat; $\Delta T$ is change in temperature.

## 8.12 Specific Heat

$$c = \frac{Q}{m\,\Delta T}$$

$c$ is specific heat; $Q$ is quantity of heat; $m$ is mass of material; $\Delta T$ is change in temperature.

## 8.13 Heat Exchange

$$Q_1 = Q_\text{g}$$

$Q_1$ is heat lost; $Q_\text{g}$ is heat gained.

## 9.1 Mechanical Equivalent of Heat

$$W = JQ$$

$W$ is work; $J$ is mechanical equivalent of heat; $Q$ is quantity of heat.

## 9.6 Ideal Heat Engine Efficiency

$$\text{Efficiency} = \frac{T_1 - T_2}{T_1} \times 100\%$$

$T_1$ is input Kelvin temperature; $T_2$ is exhaust Kelvin temperature.

## 9.7 Change in Entropy

$$\Delta S = \Delta Q/T$$

$\Delta S$ is change in entropy; $\Delta Q$ is heat added or removed; $T$ is Kelvin temperature.

## 10.6 Wave Formula

$$v = f\lambda$$

$v$ is wave speed; $f$ is frequency; $\lambda$ is wavelength.

## 11.7 Intensity Level

$$\beta = 10 \log\frac{I}{I_0}$$

$\beta$ is intensity level in db; $I$ is intensity of sound; $I_0$ is intensity of threshold of hearing.

## 11.9 Doppler effect

*1. Source moving toward stationary listener.*

$$f_\text{LF} = f_\text{s}\frac{v}{v - v_\text{s}}$$

*2. Source moving away from stationary listener.*

$$f_\text{LB} = f_\text{s}\frac{v}{v + v_\text{s}}$$

*3. Listener moving toward stationary source.*

$$f_\text{LC} = f_\text{s}\frac{v + v_\text{LC}}{v}$$

*4. Listener moving away from stationary source.*

$$f_\text{LO} = f_\text{s}\frac{v - v_\text{LO}}{v}$$

$f_\text{LF}$, $f_\text{LB}$, $f_\text{LC}$, $f_\text{LO}$ represent frequency of sound reaching the listener in the different listener-source conditions stated; $f_\text{s}$ is the frequency of the source; $v$ is the velocity of sound in the medium; $v_\text{s}$ is the velocity of the source; $v_\text{LC}$ is the closing velocity of the listener; $v_\text{LO}$ is the opening velocity of the listener.

## 11.13 Laws of Strings

*1. Law of Lengths*

$$\frac{f}{f'} = \frac{l'}{l}$$

$f$ and $f'$ are frequencies corresponding to lengths $l$ and $l'$.

*2. Law of Diameters*

$$\frac{f}{f'} = \frac{d'}{d}$$

$f$ and $f'$ are frequencies corresponding to diameters $d$ and $d'$.

*3. Law of Tensions*

$$\frac{f}{f'} = \frac{\sqrt{F}}{\sqrt{F'}}$$

$f$ and $f'$ are frequencies corresponding to tensions $F$ and $F'$.

*4. Law of Densities*

$$\frac{f}{f'} = \frac{\sqrt{D'}}{\sqrt{D}}$$

$f$ and $f'$ are frequencies corresponding to densities $D$ and $D'$.

## 11.15  Resonance in Tubes

*1. Closed Tube*

$$\lambda = 4(l + 0.4d)$$

$\lambda$ is wavelength; $l$ is length of tube; $d$ is diameter of tube.

*2. Open Tube*

$$\lambda = 2(l + 0.8d)$$

$\lambda$ is wavelength; $l$ is length of tube; $d$ is diameter of tube.

## 11.16  Beats

$$f_{av} = \tfrac{1}{2}(f_1 + f_h)$$

$f_{av}$ is difference frequency; $f_1$ is lower frequency; $f_h$ is higher frequency.

## 12.9  Photon Energy

$$E = hf$$

$E$ is energy; $h$ is Planck's constant ($6.63 \times 10^{-34}$ joule sec); $f$ is frequency.

## 12.10  Photoelectric Equation

$$\tfrac{1}{2}mv^2{}_{max} = hf - w$$

$\tfrac{1}{2}mv^2{}_{max}$ is maximum kinetic energy of photoelectrons; $h$ is Planck's constant; $f$ is frequency of impinging radiation; $w$ is work function of emitting material.

## 12.11  Photon Wavelength

$$\lambda = \frac{h}{mc}$$

$\lambda$ is photon wavelength; $h$ is Planck's constant; $c$ is velocity of light; $mc$ is photon momentum.

## 12.11  Wavelength of Particle Having a Velocity $v$

$$\lambda = \frac{h}{mv}$$

$\lambda$ is particle wavelength; $h$ is Planck's constant; $m$ is mass of particle; $v$ is velocity; ($mv$ is particle momentum).

## 12.17  Illumination

*1. Uniformly Illuminated Surface*

$$E = \frac{\Phi}{A}$$

$E$ is illumination; $\Phi$ is luminous flux; $A$ is area uniformly illuminated.

*2. Surface Perpendicular to Luminous Flux*

$$E - \frac{I}{r^2}$$

$E$ is illumination; $I$ is intensity of source; $r$ is the distance from source to surface perpendicular to the beam.

*3. Surface at Any Angle to Luminous Flux*

$$E = \frac{I \cos \theta}{r^2}$$

$E$ is illumination; $I$ is intensity of source; $\theta$ is the angle which the light beam makes with the normal to the illuminated surface; $r$ is the distance from source to surface.

## 13.12  Images in Mirrors and Lenses

$$\frac{h_i}{h_o} = \frac{d_i}{d_o}$$

$h_o$ is object size; $h_i$ is image size; $d_o$ is object distance; $d_i$ is image distance.

## 13.12  Focal Length of Mirrors and Lenses

$$\frac{1}{f} = \frac{1}{d_o} + \frac{1}{d_i}$$

$f$ is focal length; $d_o$ is object distance; $d_i$ is image distance.

### 14.3 Snell's Law

$$n = \frac{\sin i}{\sin r}$$

$n$ is index of refraction; $i$ is the angle of incidence; $r$ is the angle of refraction.

### 14.12 Simple Magnifier

$$M = \frac{25 \text{ cm}}{f} \text{ (approx.)}$$

$f$ is focal length of lens in cm.

### 14.13 Compound Microscope

$$M = \frac{25 \text{ cm} \times l}{f_e \times f_o} \text{ (approx.)}$$

$l$ is length of tube; $f_e$ is focal length of eyepiece lens; $f_o$ is focal length of objective lens in cm.

### 14.14 Refracting Telescope

$$M = \frac{f_o}{f_e}$$

$f_o$ is focal length of objective lens; $f_e$ is focal length of eyepiece lens.

### 15.4 Diffraction Grating Equation

$$\lambda = \frac{d \sin \theta_n}{n}$$

$\lambda$ is wavelength; $d$ is grating constant; $\theta$ is diffraction angle; $n$ is the order of image.

### 16.8 Coulomb's Law of Electrostatics

$$F = k\frac{Q_1 Q_2}{d^2}$$

$F$ is force between two point charges; $k$ is a proportionality constant; $Q_1$ and $Q_2$ are the two charges; $d$ is distance separating the charges.

### 16.9 Electric field intensity

$$\mathscr{E} = \frac{F}{q}$$

$\mathscr{E}$ is the electric field intensity; $F$ is force acting on a charge; $q$ is quantity of charge.

### 16.10 Potential Difference

$$V = \frac{W}{q}$$

$V$ is potential difference; $W$ is work done in moving a charge; $q$ is quantity of charge moved.

### 16.14 Capacitance of a Capacitor

$$C = \frac{Q}{V}$$

$C$ is capacitance of a capacitor; $Q$ is charge on either plate; $V$ is potential difference between the plates.

### 16.17 Capacitors in Parallel

$$C_T = C_1 + C_2 + C_3 + \text{etc.}$$

$C_T$ is total capacitance; $C_1, C_2, C_3$, etc. are separate capacitances connected in parallel.

### 16.17 Capacitors in Series

$$\frac{1}{C_T} = \frac{1}{C_1} + \frac{1}{C_2} + \frac{1}{C_3} + \text{etc.}$$

$C_T$ is total capacitance; $C_1, C_2, C_3$, etc. are separate capacitances connected in series.

### 17.1 Electric Current

$$I = \frac{Q}{t}$$

$I$ is current; $Q$ is quantity of charge; $t$ is time.

### 17.6 Ohm's Law of Resistance

*1. Entire Circuit Including a Source of emf*

$$E = IR \quad \text{or} \quad E = IZ$$

$E$ is emf of source; $I$ is current in the circuit; $R$ is resistance of the circuit; $Z$ is impedance of a-c circuit.

*2. Any Part of a Circuit That Does Not Include a Source of emf*

$$V = IR \quad \text{or} \quad V = IZ$$

$V$ is potential difference across a part of the circuit; $I$ is the current in that part of the circuit;

$R$ is the resistance of that part of the circuit; $Z$ is the impedance of that part of an a-c circuit.

## 17.8 Resistances in Series

$$R_T = R_1 + R_2 + R_3 + \text{etc.}$$

$R_T$ is the total resistance; $R_1$, $R_2$, $R_3$, etc. are separate resistances connected in series.

## 17.9 Resistances in Parallel

$$\frac{1}{R_{eq}} = \frac{1}{R_1} + \frac{1}{R_2} + \frac{1}{R_3} + \text{etc.}$$

$R_{eq}$ is equivalent resistance; $R_1$, $R_2$, $R_3$, etc. are separate resistances connected in parallel.

## 17.11 Law of Resistance

$$R = \rho \frac{l}{A}$$

$R$ is resistance; $\rho$ is resistivity, a proportionality constant; $l$ is length; $A$ is cross-sectional area.

## 18.3 Joule's Law

$$Q = \frac{I^2 R t}{J}$$

$Q$ is quantity of heat energy; $I$ is current; $R$ is resistance; $t$ is time; $J$ is the mechanical equivalent of heat.

## 18.4 Electric Power

*1. Total Power Consumed in a Circuit*

$$P_T = I_T^2 R_T \quad \text{or} \quad P_T = EI \cos \phi$$

$P_T$ is total power; $I_T$ is total current; $R_T$ is total resistance; $E$ is emf; $\phi$ is phase angle between current and voltage in an a-c circuit.

*2. Power Expended in the Circuit Load*

$$P_L = I^2 R_L \quad \text{or} \quad P_L = I^2 Z_L$$

$P_L$ is load power; $I$ is current; $R_L$ is load resistance; $Z_L$ is load impedance of an a-c circuit.

*3. Power Dissipated in a Source of emf*

$$P_r = I^2 r$$

$P_r$ is power dissipated in the internal resistance of source; $I$ is current; $r$ is internal resistance of source.

## 18.9 Faraday's Laws of Electrolysis

$$m = zIt$$

$m$ is mass; $z$ is the electrochemical equivalent; $I$ is current; $t$ is time.

## 19.4 Magnetic Flux Density

$$B = \Phi/A$$

$B$ is magnetic flux density; $\Phi$ is magnetic flux; $A$ is area.

## 20.3 Induced emf *(Coil in a Magnetic Field)*

$$E = -N \frac{\Delta \Phi}{\Delta t}$$

$E$ is induced emf; $N$ is number of turns; $\Delta \Phi/\Delta t$ is the change in flux linkage in a given interval of time.

## 20.4 Induced emf *(Conductor in a Magnetic Field)*

$$E = Blv$$

$E$ is induced emf; $B$ is flux density of the magnetic field; $l$ is length of conductor; $v$ is velocity of conductor across magnetic field.

## 20.9 Instantaneous Voltage

$$e = E_{max} \sin \theta$$

$e$ is instantaneous voltage; $E_{max}$ is maximum voltage; $\theta$ is displacement angle, the angle between the plane of the conducting loop and the perpendicular to the magnetic flux.

## 20.9 Instantaneous Current

$$i = I_{max} \sin \theta$$

$i$ is instantaneous current; $I_{max}$ is maximum current; $\theta$ is displacement angle, the angle between the plane of the conducting loop and the perpendicular to the magnetic flux.

## 20.14 The Motor Effect

$$\text{Torque} = Fw \cos \alpha$$

$F$ is magnetic force acting on either conductor of loop; $w$ is width of conducting loop; $\alpha$ is the angle between the plane of the loop and the magnetic flux.

## 20.18 Mutual Inductance

$$M = \frac{-E_S}{\Delta I_P / \Delta t}$$

$M$ is mutual inductance; $E_S$ is average induced emf across the secondary; $\Delta I_P / \Delta t$ is time rate of change of current in the primary.

## 20.19 Self-inductance

$$L = \frac{-E}{\Delta I / \Delta t}$$

$L$ is self-inductance; $E$ is the average emf induced across the coil; $\Delta I / \Delta t$ is time rate of change of current in the coil.

## 20.20 Inductors in Series

*1. No Mutual Inductance Between Inductors*

$$L_T = L_1 + L_2 + L_3 + \text{etc.}$$

$L_T$ is total inductance; $L_1$, $L_2$, $L_3$, etc. are separate inductances connected in series.

*2. Mutual Inductance Between Two Inductors*

$$L_T = L_1 + L_2 \pm 2M$$

$L_T$ is total inductance; $L_1$ and $L_2$ are inductances connected in series; $M$ is mutual inductance between them.

## 20.20 Inductors in Parallel

$$\frac{1}{L_T} = \frac{1}{L_1} + \frac{1}{L_2} + \frac{1}{L_3} + \text{etc.}$$

$L_T$ is total inductance; $L_1, L_2, L_3$, etc. are separate inductances connected in parallel so that each is unaffected by the magnetic field of the other.

## 20.21 Transformer

*1. Voltage Ratio*

$$\frac{V_S}{V_P} = \frac{N_S}{N_P}$$

$V_S$ and $V_P$ are secondary and primary terminal voltages; $N_S / N_P$ is the turns ratio, secondary to primary.

*2. Current Ratio*

$$\frac{I_P}{I_S} = \frac{N_S}{N_P}$$

$I_P$ and $I_S$ are primary and secondary currents; $N_S / N_P$ is the turns ratio, secondary to primary.

## 21.4 Power Factor

$$\text{pf} = \cos \phi$$

pf is power factor; $\phi$ is phase angle between voltage and current.

## 21.5 Inductive Reactance

$$X_L = 2\pi f L$$

$X_L$ is inductive reactance; $f$ is frequency; $L$ is inductance.

## 21.8 Capacitive Reactance

$$X_C = \frac{1}{2\pi f C}$$

$X_C$ is capacitive reactance; $f$ is frequency; $C$ is capacitance.

## 21.9 Impedance

$$Z = \sqrt{R^2 + X^2} \; \underline{|\arctan X/R}$$

$Z$ is impedance; $R$ is resistance; $X$ is reactance ($X_L - X_C$).

## 21.12 Resonance

$$f_r = \frac{1}{2\pi \sqrt{LC}}$$

$f_r$ is resonant frequency; $L$ is inductance; $C$ is capacitance.

## 22.14 Transistor Characteristics

*1. Current gain, common-base circuit*

$$\alpha = \frac{\Delta I_C}{\Delta I_E} \; (V_{CB} \text{ constant})$$

$\alpha$ is current gain; $\Delta I_C$ is change in collector current; $\Delta I_E$ is change in emitter current.

*2. Current gain, common-emitter circuit*

$$\beta = \frac{\Delta I_C}{\Delta I_B} \ (V_{CE} \text{ constant})$$

$\beta$ is current gain; $\Delta I_C$ is change in collector current; $\Delta I_B$ is change in base current.

## 23.10 Mass Number

$$A = Z + N$$

$A$ is mass number of an atom; $Z$ is atomic number; $N$ is number of neutrons.

## 24.5 Decay Constant

$$\lambda = \frac{0.693}{T_{1/2}}$$

$\lambda$ is decay constant; $T_{1/2}$ is half-life.

## 25.2 Quantum Mechanics

*1. Energy of Electron*

$$E = -\frac{me^4}{8\epsilon_0^2 h^2 n^2}$$

$E$ is energy; $m$ is mass; $e$ is electronic charge; $\epsilon_0$ is a constant; $h$ is Planck's constant; $n$ is principal quantum number.

*2. Angular Momentum of Electron*

$$L = \sqrt{l(l+1)}\,\frac{h}{2\pi}$$

$L$ is angular momentum; $l$ is angular momentum quantum number; $h$ is Planck's constant.

# Appendix B—Tables

## Contents

## Table 1  PREFIXES OF THE METRIC SYSTEM

| Factor | Prefix | Symbol |
|--------|--------|--------|
| $10^{12}$ | tera | T |
| $10^{9}$ | giga | G |
| $10^{6}$ | mega | M |
| $10^{3}$ | kilo | k |
| $10^{2}$ | hecto | h |
| 10 | deka | da |
| $10^{-1}$ | deci | d |
| $10^{-2}$ | centi | c |
| $10^{-3}$ | milli | m |
| $10^{-6}$ | micro | $\mu$ |
| $10^{-9}$ | nano | n |
| $10^{-12}$ | pico | p |
| $10^{-15}$ | femto | f |
| $10^{-18}$ | atto | a |

## Table 2  GREEK ALPHABET

| Greek letter | | Greek name | English equivalent | Greek letter | | Greek name | English equivalent |
|--------------|--|-----------|--------------------|--------------|--|-----------|--------------------|
| A | $\alpha$ | alpha | ä | N | $\nu$ | nu | n |
| B | $\beta$ | beta | b | Ξ | $\xi$ | xi | ks |
| Γ | $\gamma$ | gamma | g | O | o | omicron | o |
| Δ | $\delta$ | delta | d | Π | $\pi$ | pi | p |
| E | $\epsilon$ | epsilon | e | P | $\rho$ | rho | r |
| Z | $\zeta$ | zeta | z | Σ | $\sigma$ | sigma | s |
| H | $\eta$ | eta | ā | T | $\tau$ | tau | t |
| Θ | $\theta$ | theta | th | Y | $\upsilon$ | upsilon | ü, ōō |
| I | $\iota$ | iota | ē | Φ | $\phi$ | phi | f |
| K | $\kappa$ | kappa | k | X | $\chi$ | chi | h |
| Λ | $\lambda$ | lambda | l | Ψ | $\psi$ | psi | ps |
| M | $\mu$ | mu | m | Ω | $\omega$ | omega | ō |

## Table 3  SELECTED PHYSICAL QUANTITIES AND MEASUREMENT UNITS

| Physical quantity | Quantity symbol | Measurement unit | Unit symbol | Unit dimensions |
|-------------------|-----------------|------------------|-------------|-----------------|
| | | *Fundamental Units* | | |
| length | $l$ | meter | m | m |
| mass | $m$ | kilogram | kg | kg |
| time | $t$ | second | s | s |
| electric charge | $Q$ | coulomb | c | c |
| temperature | $T$ | degree Kelvin | °K | °K |
| luminous intensity | $I$ | candle | cd | cd |
| | | *Derived Units* | | |
| acceleration | $a$ | meter per second per second | m/s² | m/s² |
| area | $A$ | square meter | m² | m² |
| capacitance | $C$ | farad | f | c² s²/kg m² |
| density | $D$ | kilogram per cubic meter | kg/m³ | kg/m³ |
| electric current | $I$ | ampere | a | c/s |
| electric field intensity | $\mathscr{E}$ | newton per coulomb | n/c | kg m/c s² |
| electric resistance | $R$ | ohm | Ω | kg m²/c² s |
| emf | $E$ | volt | v | kg m²/c s² |
| energy | $E$ | joule | j | kg m²/s² |
| force | $F$ | newton | n | kg m/s² |
| frequency | $f$ | hertz | hz | s⁻¹ |
| heat | $Q$ | joule | j | kg m²/s² |
| illumination | $E$ | lumen per square meter | lm/m² | cd/m² |
| inductance | $L$ | henry | h | kg m²/c² |

(Cont. on next page)

**Table 3  SELECTED PHYSICAL QUANTITIES AND MEASUREMENT UNITS (Cont'd)**

| Physical quantity | Quantity symbol | Measurement unit | Unit symbol | Unit dimensions |
|---|---|---|---|---|
| luminous flux | $\Phi$ | lumen | lm | cd |
| magnetic flux | $\Phi$ | weber | wb | kg m$^2$/c s |
| magnetic flux density | $B$ | weber per square meter | wb/m$^2$ | kg/c s |
| potential difference | $V$ | volt | v | kg m$^2$/c s$^2$ |
| power | $P$ | watt | w | kg m$^2$/s$^3$ |
| pressure | $p$ | newton per square meter | n/m$^2$ | kg/m s$^2$ |
| velocity | $v$ | meter per second | m/s | m/s |
| volume | $V$ | cubic meter | m$^3$ | m$^3$ |
| work | $W$ | joule | j | kg m$^2$/s$^2$ |

**Table 4  PHYSICAL CONSTANTS**

| Quantity | Symbol | Value |
|---|---|---|
| atmospheric pressure, normal | atm | $1.01325 \times 10^5$ n/m$^2$ |
| atomic mass unit, unified | $u$ | $1.6605655 \times 10^{-27}$ kg |
| Avogadro number | $N_A$ | $6.022094 \times 10^{23}$/mole |
| charge to mass ratio for electron | $e/m_e$ | $1.7588047 \times 10^{11}$ c/kg |
| electron rest mass | $m_e$ | $9.109534 \times 10^{-31}$ kg |
| | | $5.4858026 \times 10^{-4}$ $u$ |
| electron volt | ev | $1.60210 \times 10^{-19}$ j |
| electrostatic constant | $k$ | $8.987 \times 10^9$ n m$^2$/c$^2$ |
| elementary charge | $e$ | $1.6021892 \times 10^{-19}$ c |
| faraday | $f$ | $9.648456 \times 10^4$ c/mole |
| gas constant, universal | $R$ | $6.236 \times 10^4$ mm cm$^3$/mole °K |
| | | $8.20568 \times 10^{-2}$ L atm/mole °K |
| | | $8.3143 \times 10^0$ j/mole °K |
| gravitational acceleration, standard | $g$ | $9.80665 \times 10^0$ m/s$^2$ |
| mechanical equivalent of heat | $J$ | $4.1868 \times 10^0$ j/cal |
| molar volume of ideal gas at STP | $V_m$ | $2.241383 \times 10^1$ L/mole |
| neutron rest mass | $m_n$ | $1.6749543 \times 10^{-27}$ kg |
| | | $1.008665012 \times 10^0$ $u$ |
| Planck's constant | $h$ | $6.626176 \times 10^{-34}$ j s |
| proton rest mass | $m_p$ | $1.6726485 \times 10^{-27}$ kg |
| | | $1.007276470 \times 10^0$ $u$ |
| speed of light in a vacuum | $c$ | $2.99792458 \times 10^8$ m/s |
| speed of sound in air at STP | $v$ | $3.3145 \times 10^2$ m/s |
| universal gravitational constant | $G$ | $6.6720 \times 10^{-11}$ n m$^2$/kg$^2$ |

**Table 5  CONVERSION FACTORS**

**Length**

$1 \text{ m} = 10^{-3} \text{ km} = 10^2 \text{ cm} = 10^3 \text{ mm} = 10^6 \ \mu\text{m} = 10^9 \text{ nm} = 10^{10} \text{ Å}$

$1 \ \mu = 1 \ \mu\text{m} = 10^{-6} \text{ m} = 10^{-4} \text{ cm} = 10^{-3} \text{ mm} = 10^3 \text{ m}\mu = 10^3 \text{ nm} = 10^4 \text{ Å}$

$1 \text{ m}\mu = 1 \text{ nm} = 10^{-9} \text{ m} = 10^{-7} \text{ cm} = 10^{-6} \text{ mm} = 10 \text{ Å}$

$1 \text{ Å} = 10^{-10} \text{ m} = 10^{-8} \text{ cm} = 10^{-4} \ \mu = 10^{-1} \text{ m}\mu = 10^{-1} \text{ nm}$

**Area**

$1 \text{ m}^2 = 10^{-6} \text{ km}^2 = 10^4 \text{ cm}^2 = 10^6 \text{ mm}^2$

**Volume**

$1 \text{ m}^3 = 10^{-9} \text{ km}^3 = 10^3 \text{ L} = 10^6 \text{ cm}^3$

$1 \text{ L} = 10^3 \text{ mL} = 10^3 \text{ cm}^3 = 10^{-3} \text{ m}^3$

**Angular**

$1° = 1.74 \times 10^{-2} \text{ radian} = 2.78 \times 10^{-3} \text{ revolution}$

$1 \text{ radian} = 57.3° = 1.59 \times 10^{-1} \text{ revolution}$

$1 \text{ revolution} = 360° = 6.28 \text{ radians}$

**Mass**

$1 \text{ kg} = 10^3 \text{ g} = 10^6 \text{ mg} = 6.02 \times 10^{26} \ u$

$1 \text{ g} = 10^{-3} \text{ kg} = 10^3 \text{ mg} = 6.02 \times 10^{23} \ u$

$1 \ u = 1.66 \times 10^{-24} \text{ g} = 1.66 \times 10^{-21} \text{ mg} = 1.66 \times 10^{-27} \text{ kg}$

**Time**

$1 \text{ hr} = 60 \text{ min} = 3.6 \times 10^3 \text{ s}$

$1 \text{ min} = 60 \text{ s} = 1.67 \times 10^{-2} \text{ hr}$

$1 \text{ s} = 1.67 \times 10^{-2} \text{ min} = 2.78 \times 10^{-4} \text{ hr}$

**Velocity**

$1 \text{ km/hr} = 10^3 \text{ m/hr} = 16.7 \text{ m/min} = 2.78 \times 10^{-1} \text{ m/s}$

$1 \text{ m/min} = 10^2 \text{ cm/min} = 1.67 \times 10^{-2} \text{ m/s} = 1.67 \text{ cm/s}$

$1 \text{ m/s} = 10^{-3} \text{ km/s} = 3.6 \text{ km/hr} = 10^2 \text{ cm/s}$

**Acceleration**

$1 \text{ cm/s}^2 = 10^{-2} \text{ m/s}^2 = 10^{-5} \text{ km/s}^2$

$1 \text{ m/s}^2 = 10^2 \text{ cm/s}^2 = 10^{-3} \text{ km/s}^2$

$1 \text{ km/hr/s} = 10^3 \text{ m/hr/s} = 2.78 \times 10^{-1} \text{ m/s}^2 = 2.78 \times 10^1 \text{ cm/s}^2 = 2.78 \times 10^2 \text{ mm/s}^2$

**Force**

$1 \text{ n} = 10^5 \text{ dynes}$

$1 \text{ dyne} = 10^{-5} \text{ n}$

**Pressure**

$1 \text{ atm} = 760.00 \text{ mm Hg} = 1.013 \times 10^5 \text{ n/m}^2 = 1.013 \times 10^6 \text{ dynes/cm}^2$

$1 \text{ n/m}^2 = 10 \text{ dynes/cm}^2 = 9.87 \times 10^{-6} \text{ atm}$

**Energy**

$1 \text{ j} = 10^7 \text{ ergs} = 2.39 \times 10^{-1} \text{ cal} = 2.39 \times 10^{-4} \text{ kcal} = 2.78 \times 10^{-7} \text{ kw hr} = 6.25 \times 10^{18} \text{ ev}$

$1 \text{ cal} = 10^{-3} \text{ kcal} = 4.19 \text{ j} = 1.16 \times 10^{-6} \text{ kw hr}$

$1 \text{ kcal} = 10^3 \text{ cal} = 4.19 \times 10^3 \text{ j} = 1.16 \times 10^{-3} \text{ kw hr}$

$1 \text{ ev} = 10^{-6} \text{ Mev} = 1.60 \times 10^{-12} \text{ erg} = 1.60 \times 10^{-19} \text{ j}$

$1 \text{ kw hr} = 10^3 \text{ w hr} = 3.6 \times 10^3 \text{ kw s} = 3.6 \times 10^6 \text{ w s} = 8.6 \times 10^5 \text{ cal}$

$1 \text{ w s} = 2.78 \times 10^{-4} \text{ w hr} = 2.78 \times 10^{-7} \text{ kw hr}$

**Mass-Energy**

$1 \text{ j} = 1.11 \times 10^{-17} \text{ kg} = 1.11 \times 10^{-14} \text{ g} = 6.69 \times 10^9 \ u$

$1 \text{ ev} = 1.07 \times 10^{-9} \ u = 1.78 \times 10^{-33} \text{ g}$

$1 u = 1.49 \times 10^{-3} \text{ erg} = 1.49 \times 10^{-10} \text{ j} = 931 \text{ Mev} = 9.31 \times 10^8 \text{ ev}$

$1 \text{ kg} = 9.00 \times 10^{16} \text{ j} = 9.00 \times 10^{23} \text{ ergs}$

### Table 6  NATURAL TRIGONOMETRIC FUNCTIONS

| Angle (°) | Sine | Cosine | Tangent | Angle (°) | Sine | Cosine | Tangent |
|---|---|---|---|---|---|---|---|
| 0.0 | 0.000 | 1.000 | 0.000 | | | | |
| 0.5 | 0.009 | 1.000 | 0.009 | 23.0 | 0.391 | 0.921 | 0.424 |
| 1.0 | 0.017 | 1.000 | 0.017 | 23.5 | 0.399 | 0.917 | 0.435 |
| 1.5 | 0.026 | 1.000 | 0.026 | 24.0 | 0.407 | 0.914 | 0.445 |
| 2.0 | 0.035 | 0.999 | 0.035 | 24.5 | 0.415 | 0.910 | 0.456 |
| 2.5 | 0.044 | 0.999 | 0.044 | 25.0 | 0.423 | 0.906 | 0.466 |
| 3.0 | 0.052 | 0.999 | 0.052 | 25.5 | 0.431 | 0.903 | 0.477 |
| 3.5 | 0.061 | 0.998 | 0.061 | 26.0 | 0.438 | 0.899 | 0.488 |
| 4.0 | 0.070 | 0.998 | 0.070 | 26.5 | 0.446 | 0.895 | 0.499 |
| 4.5 | 0.078 | 0.997 | 0.079 | 27.0 | 0.454 | 0.891 | 0.510 |
| 5.0 | 0.087 | 0.996 | 0.087 | 27.5 | 0.462 | 0.887 | 0.521 |
| 5.5 | 0.096 | 0.995 | 0.096 | 28.0 | 0.470 | 0.883 | 0.532 |
| 6.0 | 0.104 | 0.995 | 0.105 | 28.5 | 0.477 | 0.879 | 0.543 |
| 6.5 | 0.113 | 0.994 | 0.114 | 29.0 | 0.485 | 0.875 | 0.554 |
| 7.0 | 0.122 | 0.992 | 0.123 | 29.5 | 0.492 | 0.870 | 0.566 |
| 7.5 | 0.131 | 0.991 | 0.132 | 30.0 | 0.500 | 0.866 | 0.577 |
| 8.0 | 0.139 | 0.990 | 0.141 | 30.5 | 0.508 | 0.862 | 0.589 |
| 8.5 | 0.148 | 0.989 | 0.149 | 31.0 | 0.515 | 0.857 | 0.601 |
| 9.0 | 0.156 | 0.988 | 0.158 | 31.5 | 0.522 | 0.853 | 0.613 |
| 9.5 | 0.165 | 0.986 | 0.167 | 32.0 | 0.530 | 0.848 | 0.625 |
| 10.0 | 0.174 | 0.985 | 0.176 | 32.5 | 0.537 | 0.843 | 0.637 |
| 10.5 | 0.182 | 0.983 | 0.185 | 33.0 | 0.545 | 0.839 | 0.649 |
| 11.0 | 0.191 | 0.982 | 0.194 | 33.5 | 0.552 | 0.834 | 0.662 |
| 11.5 | 0.199 | 0.980 | 0.204 | 34.0 | 0.559 | 0.829 | 0.674 |
| 12.0 | 0.208 | 0.978 | 0.213 | 34.5 | 0.566 | 0.824 | 0.687 |
| 12.5 | 0.216 | 0.976 | 0.222 | 35.0 | 0.574 | 0.819 | 0.700 |
| 13.0 | 0.225 | 0.974 | 0.231 | 35.5 | 0.581 | 0.814 | 0.713 |
| 13.5 | 0.233 | 0.972 | 0.240 | 36.0 | 0.588 | 0.809 | 0.726 |
| 14.0 | 0.242 | 0.970 | 0.249 | 36.5 | 0.595 | 0.804 | 0.740 |
| 14.5 | 0.250 | 0.968 | 0.259 | 37.0 | 0.602 | 0.799 | 0.754 |
| 15.0 | 0.259 | 0.966 | 0.268 | 37.5 | 0.609 | 0.793 | 0.767 |
| 15.5 | 0.267 | 0.964 | 0.277 | 38.0 | 0.616 | 0.788 | 0.781 |
| 16.0 | 0.276 | 0.961 | 0.287 | 38.5 | 0.622 | 0.783 | 0.795 |
| 16.5 | 0.284 | 0.959 | 0.296 | 39.0 | 0.629 | 0.777 | 0.810 |
| 17.0 | 0.292 | 0.956 | 0.306 | 39.5 | 0.636 | 0.772 | 0.824 |
| 17.5 | 0.301 | 0.954 | 0.315 | 40.0 | 0.643 | 0.766 | 0.839 |
| 18.0 | 0.309 | 0.951 | 0.325 | 40.5 | 0.649 | 0.760 | 0.854 |
| 18.5 | 0.317 | 0.948 | 0.335 | 41.0 | 0.656 | 0.755 | 0.869 |
| 19.0 | 0.326 | 0.946 | 0.344 | 41.5 | 0.663 | 0.749 | 0.885 |
| 19.5 | 0.334 | 0.943 | 0.354 | 42.0 | 0.669 | 0.743 | 0.900 |
| 20.0 | 0.342 | 0.940 | 0.364 | 42.5 | 0.676 | 0.737 | 0.916 |
| 20.5 | 0.350 | 0.937 | 0.374 | 43.0 | 0.682 | 0.731 | 0.932 |
| 21.0 | 0.358 | 0.934 | 0.384 | 43.5 | 0.688 | 0.725 | 0.949 |
| 21.5 | 0.366 | 0.930 | 0.394 | 44.0 | 0.695 | 0.719 | 0.966 |
| 22.0 | 0.375 | 0.927 | 0.404 | 44.5 | 0.701 | 0.713 | 0.983 |
| 22.5 | 0.383 | 0.924 | 0.414 | 45.0 | 0.707 | 0.707 | 1.000 |

### Table 6 NATURAL TRIGONOMETRIC FUNCTIONS (cont'd)

| Angle (°) | Sine | Cosine | Tangent | Angle (°) | Sine | Cosine | Tangent |
|---|---|---|---|---|---|---|---|
| 45.5 | 0.713 | 0.701 | 1.018 | 68.0 | 0.927 | 0.375 | 2.475 |
| 46.0 | 0.719 | 0.695 | 1.036 | 68.5 | 0.930 | 0.366 | 2.539 |
| 46.5 | 0.725 | 0.688 | 1.054 | 69.0 | 0.934 | 0.358 | 2.605 |
| 47.0 | 0.731 | 0.682 | 1.072 | 69.5 | 0.937 | 0.350 | 2.675 |
| 47.5 | 0.737 | 0.676 | 1.091 | 70.0 | 0.940 | 0.342 | 2.747 |
| 48.0 | 0.743 | 0.669 | 1.111 | 70.5 | 0.943 | 0.334 | 2.824 |
| 48.5 | 0.749 | 0.663 | 1.130 | 71.0 | 0.946 | 0.326 | 2.904 |
| 49.0 | 0.755 | 0.656 | 1.150 | 71.5 | 0.948 | 0.317 | 2.983 |
| 49.5 | 0.760 | 0.649 | 1.171 | 72.0 | 0.951 | 0.309 | 3.078 |
| 50.0 | 0.766 | 0.643 | 1.192 | 72.5 | 0.954 | 0.301 | 3.172 |
| 50.5 | 0.772 | 0.636 | 1.213 | 73.0 | 0.956 | 0.292 | 3.271 |
| 51.0 | 0.777 | 0.629 | 1.235 | 73.5 | 0.959 | 0.284 | 3.376 |
| 51.5 | 0.783 | 0.622 | 1.257 | 74.0 | 0.961 | 0.276 | 3.487 |
| 52.0 | 0.788 | 0.616 | 1.280 | 74.5 | 0.964 | 0.267 | 3.606 |
| 52.5 | 0.793 | 0.609 | 1.303 | 75.0 | 0.966 | 0.259 | 3.732 |
| 53.0 | 0.799 | 0.602 | 1.327 | 75.5 | 0.968 | 0.250 | 3.867 |
| 53.5 | 0.804 | 0.595 | 1.351 | 76.0 | 0.970 | 0.242 | 4.011 |
| 54.0 | 0.809 | 0.588 | 1.376 | 76.5 | 0.972 | 0.233 | 4.165 |
| 54.5 | 0.814 | 0.581 | 1.402 | 77.0 | 0.974 | 0.225 | 4.331 |
| 55.0 | 0.819 | 0.574 | 1.428 | 77.5 | 0.976 | 0.216 | 4.511 |
| 55.5 | 0.824 | 0.566 | 1.455 | 78.0 | 0.978 | 0.208 | 4.705 |
| 56.0 | 0.829 | 0.559 | 1.483 | 78.5 | 0.980 | 0.199 | 4.915 |
| 56.5 | 0.834 | 0.552 | 1.511 | 79.0 | 0.982 | 0.191 | 5.145 |
| 57.0 | 0.839 | 0.545 | 1.540 | 79.5 | 0.983 | 0.182 | 5.396 |
| 57.5 | 0.843 | 0.537 | 1.570 | 80.0 | 0.985 | 0.174 | 5.671 |
| 58.0 | 0.848 | 0.530 | 1.600 | 80.5 | 0.986 | 0.165 | 5.976 |
| 58.5 | 0.853 | 0.522 | 1.632 | 81.0 | 0.988 | 0.156 | 6.314 |
| 59.0 | 0.857 | 0.515 | 1.664 | 81.5 | 0.989 | 0.148 | 6.691 |
| 59.5 | 0.862 | 0.508 | 1.698 | 82.0 | 0.990 | 0.139 | 7.115 |
| 60.0 | 0.866 | 0.500 | 1.732 | 82.5 | 0.991 | 0.131 | 7.596 |
| 60.5 | 0.870 | 0.492 | 1.767 | 83.0 | 0.992 | 0.122 | 8.144 |
| 61.0 | 0.875 | 0.485 | 1.804 | 83.5 | 0.994 | 0.113 | 8.777 |
| 61.5 | 0.879 | 0.477 | 1.842 | 84.0 | 0.994 | 0.104 | 9.514 |
| 62.0 | 0.883 | 0.470 | 1.881 | 84.5 | 0.995 | 0.096 | 10.38 |
| 62.5 | 0.887 | 0.462 | 1.921 | 85.0 | 0.996 | 0.087 | 11.43 |
| 63.0 | 0.891 | 0.454 | 1.963 | 85.5 | 0.997 | 0.078 | 12.71 |
| 63.5 | 0.895 | 0.446 | 2.006 | 86.0 | 0.998 | 0.070 | 14.30 |
| 64.0 | 0.899 | 0.438 | 2.050 | 86.5 | 0.998 | 0.061 | 16.35 |
| 64.5 | 0.903 | 0.431 | 2.097 | 87.0 | 0.999 | 0.052 | 19.08 |
| 65.0 | 0.906 | 0.423 | 2.145 | 87.5 | 0.999 | 0.044 | 22.90 |
| 65.5 | 0.910 | 0.415 | 2.194 | 88.0 | 0.999 | 0.035 | 28.64 |
| 66.0 | 0.914 | 0.407 | 2.246 | 88.5 | 1.000 | 0.026 | 38.19 |
| 66.5 | 0.917 | 0.399 | 2.300 | 89.0 | 1.000 | 0.017 | 57.29 |
| 67.0 | 0.921 | 0.391 | 2.356 | 89.5 | 1.000 | 0.009 | 114.1 |
| 67.5 | 0.924 | 0.383 | 2.414 | 90.0 | 1.000 | 0.000 | . . . |

#### Table 7   TENSILE STRENGTH OF METALS

| Metal | Tensile strength ($n/m^2$) |
|---|---|
| aluminum wire | $2.4 \times 10^8$ |
| copper wire, hard drawn | $4.8 \times 10^8$ |
| iron wire, annealed | $3.8 \times 10^8$ |
| iron wire, hard drawn | $6.9 \times 10^8$ |
| lead, cast or drawn | $2.1 \times 10^8$ |
| platinum wire | $3.5 \times 10^8$ |
| silver wire | $2.9 \times 10^8$ |
| steel (minimum) | $2.8 \times 10^8$ |
| steel wire (maximum) | $32 \ \ \times 10^8$ |

#### Table 8   YOUNG'S MODULUS

| Metal | Elastic modulus ($n/m^2$) |
|---|---|
| aluminum, 99.3%, rolled | $6.96 \times 10^{10}$ |
| brass | $9.02 \times 10^{10}$ |
| copper, wire, hard drawn | $11.6 \times 10^{10}$ |
| gold, pure, hard drawn | $7.85 \times 10^{10}$ |
| iron, cast | $9.1 \ \times 10^{10}$ |
| iron, wrought | $19.3 \ \times 10^{10}$ |
| lead, rolled | $1.57 \times 10^{10}$ |
| platinum, pure, drawn | $16.7 \ \times 10^{10}$ |
| silver, hard drawn | $7.75 \times 10^{10}$ |
| steel, 0.38% C, annealed | $20.0 \ \times 10^{10}$ |
| tungsten, drawn | $35.5 \ \times 10^{10}$ |

#### Table 9   RELATIVE DENSITY AND VOLUME OF WATER

The mass of one $cm^3$ of water at 4°C is taken as unity.
The values given are numerically equal to the absolute density in g/mL.

| T (°C) | D ($g/cm^3$) | V ($cm^3/g$) | T (°C) | D ($g/cm^3$) | V ($cm^3/g$) |
|---|---|---|---|---|---|
| −10 | 0.99815 | 1.00186 | 45 | 0.99025 | 1.00985 |
| −5 | 0.99930 | 1.00070 | 50 | 0.98807 | 1.01207 |
| 0 | 0.99987 | 1.00013 | 55 | 0.98573 | 1.01448 |
| +1 | 0.99993 | 1.00007 | 60 | 0.98324 | 1.01705 |
| 2 | 0.99997 | 1.00003 | 65 | 0.98059 | 1.01979 |
| 3 | 0.99999 | 1.00001 | 70 | 0.97781 | 1.02270 |
| 4 | 1.00000 | 1.00000 | 75 | 0.97489 | 1.02576 |
| 5 | 0.99999 | 1.00001 | 80 | 0.97183 | 1.02899 |
| +10 | 0.99973 | 1.00027 | 85 | 0.96865 | 1.03237 |
| 15 | 0.99913 | 1.00087 | 90 | 0.96534 | 1.03590 |
| 20 | 0.99823 | 1.00177 | 95 | 0.96192 | 1.03959 |
| 25 | 0.99707 | 1.00294 | 100 | 0.95838 | 1.04343 |
| 30 | 0.99567 | 1.00435 | 110 | 0.9510 | 1.0515 |
| 35 | 0.99406 | 1.00598 | 120 | 0.9434 | 1.0601 |
| 40 | 0.99224 | 1.00782 | 150 | 0.9173 | 1.0902 |

## Table 10   SURFACE TENSION OF VARIOUS LIQUIDS

| Liquid | In contact with | Temp. (°C) | Surface tension (n/m) |
|---|---|---|---|
| carbon disulfide | vapor | 20 | $3.233 \times 10^{-2}$ |
| carbon tetrachloride | vapor | 20 | $2.695 \times 10^{-2}$ |
| ethyl alcohol | air | 0 | $2.405 \times 10^{-2}$ |
| ethyl alcohol | vapor | 20 | $2.275 \times 10^{-2}$ |
| water | air | 20 | $7.275 \times 10^{-2}$ |

## Table 11   MASS DENSITY OF GASES

| Gas | (T = 0°C; p = 760 mm Hg) Formula | Density (g/L) |
|---|---|---|
| acetylene | $C_2H_2$ | 1.17910 |
| air, dry, $CO_2$ free | | 1.29284 |
| ammonia | $NH_3$ | 0.77120 |
| argon | Ar | 1.78364 |
| chlorine | $Cl_2$ | 3.214 |
| carbon dioxide | $CO_2$ | 1.9769 |
| carbon monoxide | CO | 1.25004 |
| ethane | $C_2H_6$ | 1.3562 |
| helium | He | 0.17846 |
| hydrogen | $H_2$ | 0.08988 |
| hydrogen chloride | HCl | 1.6392 |
| methane | $CH_4$ | 0.7168 |
| neon | Ne | 0.89990 |
| nitrogen | $N_2$ | 1.25036 |
| oxygen | $O_2$ | 1.42896 |
| sulfur dioxide | $SO_2$ | 2.9262 |

## Table 12   EQUILIBRIUM VAPOR PRESSURE OF WATER

| Temp. (°C) | Pressure (mm Hg) | Temp. (°C) | Pressure (mm Hg) | Temp. (°C) | Pressure (mm Hg) |
|---|---|---|---|---|---|
| 0 | 4.6 | 25 | 23.8 | 90 | 525.8 |
| 5 | 6.5 | 26 | 25.2 | 95 | 633.9 |
| 10 | 9.2 | 27 | 26.7 | 96 | 657.6 |
| 15 | 12.8 | 28 | 28.3 | 97 | 682.1 |
| 16 | 13.6 | 29 | 30.0 | 98 | 707.3 |
| 17 | 14.5 | 30 | 31.8 | 99 | 733.2 |
| 18 | 15.5 | 35 | 42.2 | 100 | 760.0 |
| 19 | 16.5 | 40 | 55.3 | 101 | 787.5 |
| 20 | 17.5 | 50 | 92.5 | 103 | 845.1 |
| 21 | 18.7 | 60 | 149.4 | 105 | 906.1 |
| 22 | 19.8 | 70 | 233.7 | 110 | 1074.6 |
| 23 | 21.1 | 80 | 355.1 | 120 | 1489.1 |
| 24 | 22.4 | 85 | 433.6 | 150 | 3570.5 |

## Table 13  HEAT CONSTANTS

| Material | Specific heat (cal/g C°) | Melting point (°C) | Boiling point (°C) | Heat of fusion (cal/g) | Heat of vaporization (cal/g) |
|---|---|---|---|---|---|
| alcohol, ethyl | 0.581 (25°) | −115 | 78.5 | 24.9 | 204 |
| aluminum | 0.214 (20°) | 660.2 | 2467 | 94 | 2520 |
|  | 0.217 (0–100°) |  |  |  |  |
|  | 0.220 (20–100°) |  |  |  |  |
|  | 0.225 (100°) |  |  |  |  |
| ammonia, liquid | 1.047 (−60°) | −77.7 | −33.35 | 108.1 | 327.1 |
| liquid | 1.125 (20°) |  |  |  |  |
| gas | 0.523 (20°) |  |  |  |  |
| brass (40% Zn) | 0.0917 | 900 |  |  |  |
| copper | 0.0924 | 1083 | 2595 | 49.0 | 1150 |
| glass, crown | 0.161 |  |  |  |  |
| iron | 0.1075 | 1535 | 3000 | 7.89 | 1600 |
| lead | 0.0305 | 327.5 | 1744 | 5.47 | 207 |
| mercury | 0.0333 | −38.87 | 356.58 | 2.82 | 70.613 |
| platinum | 0.0317 | 1769 | 3827 ± 100 | 27.2 |  |
| silver | 0.0562 | 960.8 | 2212 | 26.0 | 565 |
| tungsten | 0.0322 | 3410 ± 10 | 5927 | 43 |  |
| water | 1.00 |  | 100.00 |  | 538.7 |
| ice | 0.530 | 0.00 |  | 79.71 |  |
| steam | 0.481 |  |  |  |  |
| zinc | 0.0922 | 419.4 | 907 | 23.0 | 420 |

## Table 14  COEFFICIENT OF LINEAR EXPANSION

**(Increase in length per unit length per Celsius degree)**

| Material | Coefficient (Δl/l C°) | Temperature (°C) | Material | Coefficient (Δl/l C°) | Temperature (°C) |
|---|---|---|---|---|---|
| aluminum | 23.8 $\times 10^{-6}$ | 20–100 | invar (nickel steel) | 0.9 $\times 10^{-6}$ | 20 |
| brass | 19.30 $\times 10^{-6}$ | 0–100 | lead | 29.40 $\times 10^{-6}$ | 18–100 |
| copper | 16.8 $\times 10^{-6}$ | 25–100 | magnesium | 26.08 $\times 10^{-6}$ | 18–100 |
| glass, tube | 8.33 $\times 10^{-6}$ | 0–100 | platinum | 8.99 $\times 10^{-6}$ | 40 |
| crown | 8.97 $\times 10^{-6}$ | 0–100 | rubber, hard | 8\bar{0} $\times 10^{-6}$ | 20–60 |
| Pyrex | 3.3 $\times 10^{-6}$ | 20–300 | quartz, fused | 0.546 $\times 10^{-6}$ | 0–800 |
| gold | 14.3 $\times 10^{-6}$ | 16–100 | silver | 18.8 $\times 10^{-6}$ | 20 |
| ice | 50.7 $\times 10^{-6}$ | −10–0 | tin | 26.92 $\times 10^{-6}$ | 18–100 |
| iron, soft | 12.10 $\times 10^{-6}$ | 40 | zinc | 26.28 $\times 10^{-6}$ | 10–100 |
| steel | 10.5 $\times 10^{-6}$ | 0–100 |  |  |  |

**The coefficient of cubical expansion may be taken as three times the linear coefficient.**

## Table 15  COEFFICIENT OF VOLUME EXPANSION

(Increase in volume per unit volume per C° at 20° C)

| Liquid | Coefficient ($\Delta V/V$ C°) |
|---|---|
| acetone | $14.87 \times 10^{-4}$ |
| alcohol, ethyl | $11.2 \ \times 10^{-4}$ |
| benzene | $12.37 \times 10^{-4}$ |
| carbon disulfide | $12.18 \times 10^{-4}$ |
| carbon tetrachloride | $12.36 \times 10^{-4}$ |
| chloroform | $12.73 \times 10^{-4}$ |
| ether | $16.56 \times 10^{-4}$ |
| glycerol | $5.05 \times 10^{-4}$ |
| mercury | $1.82 \times 10^{-4}$ |
| petroleum | $9.55 \times 10^{-4}$ |
| turpentine | $9.73 \times 10^{-4}$ |
| water | $2.07 \times 10^{-4}$ |

## Table 16  HEAT OF VAPORIZATION OF SATURATED STEAM

| Temp. (°C) | Pressure (mm Hg) | Heat of vaporization (cal/g) |
|---|---|---|
| 95 | 634.0 | 541.9 |
| 96 | 657.7 | 541.2 |
| 97 | 682.1 | 540.6 |
| 98 | 707.3 | 539.9 |
| 99 | 733.3 | 539.3 |
| 100 | 760.0 | 538.7 |
| 101 | 787.5 | 538.1 |
| 102 | 815.9 | 537.4 |
| 103 | 845.1 | 536.8 |
| 104 | 875.1 | 536.2 |
| 105 | 906.1 | 535.6 |
| 106 | 937.9 | 534.9 |

## Table 17  SPEED OF SOUND

| Substance | Density (g/L) | Velocity (m/s) | $\Delta v/\Delta t$ (m/s C°) |
|---|---|---|---|
| *GASES* (STP) | | | |
| air, dry | 1.293 | 331.45 | 0.59 |
| carbon dioxide | 1.977 | 259 | 0.4 |
| helium | 0.178 | 965 | 0.8 |
| hydrogen | 0.0899 | 1284 | 2.2 |
| nitrogen | 1.251 | 334 | 0.6 |
| oxygen | 1.429 | 316 | 0.56 |
| *LIQUIDS* (25°C) | (g/cm³) | | |
| acetone | 0.79 | 1174 | |
| alcohol, ethyl | 0.79 | 1207 | |
| carbon tetrachloride | 1.595 | 926 | |
| glycerol | 1.26 | 1904 | |
| kerosene | 0.81 | 1324 | |
| water, distilled | 0.998 | 1497 | |
| water, sea | 1.025 | 1531 | |
| *SOLIDS* (thin rods) | | | |
| aluminum | 2.7 | 5000 | |
| brass | 8.6 | 3480 | |
| brick | 1.8 | 3650 | |
| copper | 8.93 | 3810 | |
| cork | 0.25 | 500 | |
| glass, crown | 2.24 | 4540 | |
| iron | 7.85 | 5200 | |
| lucite | 1.18 | 1840 | |
| maple (along grain) | 0.69 | 4110 | |
| pine (along grain) | 0.43 | 3320 | |
| steel | 7.85 | 5200 | |

## Table 18  INDEX OF REFRACTION

(λ = 5893 Å; Temperature = 20°C except as noted)

| Material | Refractive index |
|---|---|
| air, dry (STP) | 1.00029 |
| alcohol, ethyl | 1.360 |
| benzene | 1.501 |
| calcite | 1.6583 |
|  | 1.4864 |
| canada balsam | 1.530 |
| carbon dioxide (STP) | 1.00045 |
| carbon disulfide | 1.625 |
| carbon tetrachloride | 1.459 |
| diamond | 2.4195 |
| glass, crown | 1.5172 |
| flint | 1.6270 |
| glycerol | 1.475 |
| ice | 1.310 |
| lucite | 1.50 |
| quartz | 1.544 |
|  | 1.553 |
| quartz, fused | 1.45845 |
| sapphire ($Al_2O_3$) | 1.7686 |
|  | 1.7604 |
| water, distilled | 1.333 |
| water vapor (STP) | 1.00025 |

## Table 19  ELECTROCHEMICAL EQUIVALENTS

| Element | g-at wt (g) | Valence (+ ionic charge) | z (g/c) |
|---|---|---|---|
| aluminum | 27.0 | 3 | 0.0000932 |
| cadmium | 112 | 2 | 0.0005824 |
| calcium | 40.1 | 2 | 0.0002077 |
| chlorine | 35.5 | 1 | 0.0003674 |
| chromium | 52.0 | 6 | 0.0000898 |
| chromium | 52.0 | 3 | 0.0001797 |
| copper | 63.5 | 2 | 0.0003294 |
| copper | 63.5 | 1 | 0.0006558 |
| gold | 197 | 3 | 0.0006812 |
| gold | 197 | 1 | 0.0020435 |
| hydrogen | 1.01 | 1 | 0.0000104 |
| lead | 207 | 4 | 0.0005368 |
| lead | 207 | 2 | 0.0006150 |
| magnesium | 24.3 | 2 | 0.0001260 |
| nickel | 58.7 | 2 | 0.0003041 |
| oxygen | 16.0 | 2 | 0.0000829 |
| potassium | 39.1 | 1 | 0.0004051 |
| silver | 108 | 1 | 0.0011179 |
| sodium | 23.0 | 1 | 0.0002383 |
| tin | 119 | 4 | 0.0003075 |
| tin | 119 | 2 | 0.0006150 |
| zinc | 65.4 | 2 | 0.0003388 |

## Table 20  RESISTIVITY

(Temperature = 20° C)

| Material | Resistivity (Ω cm) | Melting point (°C) |
|---|---|---|
| advance | 48 × $10^{-6}$ | 1190 |
| aluminum | 2.824 × $10^{-6}$ | 660 |
| brass | 7.00 × $10^{-6}$ | 900 |
| climax | 87 × $10^{-6}$ | 1250 |
| constantan (Cu 60, Ni 40) | 49 × $10^{-6}$ | 1190 |
| copper | 1.724 × $10^{-6}$ | 1083 |
| german silver (Cu 55, Zn 25, Ni 20) | 33 × $10^{-6}$ | 1100 |
| gold | 2.44 × $10^{-6}$ | 1063 |
| iron | 1$\bar{0}$ × $10^{-6}$ | 1535 |
| magnesium | 4.6 × $10^{-6}$ | 651 |
| manganin (Cu 84, Mn 12, Ni 4) | 44 × $10^{-6}$ | 910 |
| mercury | 95.783 × $10^{-6}$ | −39 |
| monel metal | 42 × $10^{-6}$ | 1300 |
| nichrome | 115 × $10^{-6}$ | 1500 |
| nickel | 7.8 × $10^{-6}$ | 1452 |
| nickel silver (Cu 57, Ni 43) | 49 × $10^{-6}$ | 1190 |
| platinum | 1$\bar{0}$ × $10^{-6}$ | 1769 |
| silver | 1.59 × $10^{-6}$ | 961 |
| tungsten | 5.6 × $10^{-6}$ | 3410 |

## Table 21  PROPERTIES OF COPPER WIRE

| American Wire Gauge (B&S)—for any metal | | (Temperature, 20°C) | for copper only | |
|---|---|---|---|---|
| Gauge number | Diameter | Cross section | Resistance | |
| | (mm) | (mm²) | (Ω/km) | (m/Ω) |
| 0000 | 11.68 | 107.2 | 0.1608 | 6219 |
| 000 | 10.40 | 85.03 | 0.2028 | 4932 |
| 00 | 9.266 | 67.43 | 0.2557 | 3911 |
| 0 | 8.252 | 53.48 | 0.3224 | 3102 |
| 1 | 7.348 | 42.41 | 0.4066 | 2460 |
| 2 | 6.544 | 33.63 | 0.5027 | 1951 |
| 3 | 5.827 | 26.67 | 0.6465 | 1547 |
| 4 | 5.189 | 21.15 | 0.8152 | 1227 |
| 5 | 4.621 | 16.77 | 1.028 | 972.9 |
| 6 | 4.115 | 13.30 | 1.296 | 771.5 |
| 7 | 3.665 | 10.55 | 1.634 | 611.8 |
| 8 | 3.264 | 8.366 | 2.061 | 485.2 |
| 9 | 2.906 | 6.634 | 2.599 | 384.8 |
| 10 | 2.588 | 5.261 | 3.277 | 305.1 |
| 11 | 2.305 | 4.172 | 4.132 | 242.0 |
| 12 | 2.053 | 3.309 | 5.211 | 191.9 |
| 13 | 1.828 | 2.624 | 6.571 | 152.2 |
| 14 | 1.628 | 2.081 | 8.258 | 120.7 |
| 15 | 1.450 | 1.650 | 10.45 | 95.71 |
| 16 | 1.291 | 1.309 | 13.17 | 75.90 |
| 17 | 1.150 | 1.038 | 16.61 | 60.20 |
| 18 | 1.024 | 0.8231 | 20.95 | 47.74 |
| 19 | 0.9116 | 0.6527 | 26.42 | 37.86 |
| 20 | 0.8118 | 0.5176 | 33.31 | 30.02 |
| 21 | 0.7230 | 0.4105 | 42.00 | 23.81 |
| 22 | 0.6438 | 0.3255 | 52.96 | 18.88 |
| 23 | 0.5733 | 0.2582 | 66.79 | 14.97 |
| 24 | 0.5106 | 0.2047 | 84.21 | 11.87 |
| 25 | 0.4547 | 0.1624 | 106.2 | 9.415 |
| 26 | 0.4049 | 0.1288 | 133.9 | 7.486 |
| 27 | 0.3606 | 0.1021 | 168.9 | 5.922 |
| 28 | 0.3211 | 0.08098 | 212.9 | 4.697 |
| 29 | 0.2859 | 0.06422 | 268.5 | 3.725 |
| 30 | 0.2546 | 0.05093 | 338.6 | 2.954 |
| 31 | 0.2268 | 0.04039 | 426.9 | 2.342 |
| 32 | 0.2019 | 0.03203 | 538.3 | 1.858 |
| 33 | 0.1798 | 0.02540 | 678.8 | 1.473 |
| 34 | 0.1601 | 0.02014 | 856.0 | 1.168 |
| 35 | 0.1426 | 0.01597 | 1079 | 0.9265 |
| 36 | 0.1270 | 0.01267 | 1361 | 0.7347 |
| 37 | 0.1131 | 0.01005 | 1716 | 0.5827 |
| 38 | 0.1007 | 0.007967 | 2164 | 0.4621 |
| 39 | 0.08969 | 0.006318 | 2729 | 0.3664 |
| 40 | 0.07987 | 0.005010 | 3441 | 0.2906 |

## Table 22  THE CHEMICAL ELEMENTS

| Name of element | Symbol | Atomic number | Atomic weight | Name of element | Symbol | Atomic number | Atomic weight |
|---|---|---|---|---|---|---|---|
| actinium | Ac | 89 | [227] | lawrencium | Lr | 103 | [257] |
| aluminum | Al | 13 | 26.9815 | lead | Pb | 82 | 207.2 |
| americium | Am | 95 | [243] | lithium | Li | 3 | 6.941 |
| antimony | Sb | 51 | 121.75 | lutetium | Lu | 71 | 174.97 |
| argon | Ar | 18 | 39.948 | magnesium | Mg | 12 | 24.305 |
| arsenic | As | 33 | 74.9216 | manganese | Mn | 25 | 54.9380 |
| astatine | At | 85 | [210] | mendelevium | Md | 101 | [256] |
| barium | Ba | 56 | 137.34 | mercury | Hg | 80 | 200.59 |
| berkelium | Bk | 97 | [247] | molybdenum | Mo | 42 | 95.94 |
| beryllium | Be | 4 | 9.01218 | neodymium | Nd | 60 | 144.24 |
| bismuth | Bi | 83 | 208.9806 | neon | Ne | 10 | 20.179 |
| boron | B | 5 | 10.81 | neptunium | Np | 93 | 237.0482 |
| bromine | Br | 35 | 79.904 | nickel | Ni | 28 | 58.71 |
| cadmium | Cd | 48 | 112.40 | niobium | Nb | 41 | 92.9064 |
| calcium | Ca | 20 | 40.08 | nitrogen | N | 7 | 14.0067 |
| californium | Cf | 98 | [249] | nobelium | No | 102 | [254] |
| carbon | C | 6 | 12.011 | osmium | Os | 76 | 190.2 |
| cerium | Ce | 58 | 140.12 | oxygen | O | 8 | 15.9994 |
| cesium | Cs | 55 | 132.9055 | palladium | Pd | 46 | 106.4 |
| chlorine | Cl | 17 | 35.453 | phosphorus | P | 15 | 30.9738 |
| chromium | Cr | 24 | 51.996 | platinum | Pt | 78 | 195.09 |
| cobalt | Co | 27 | 58.9332 | plutonium | Pu | 94 | [244] |
| copper | Cu | 29 | 63.546 | polonium | Po | 84 | [210] |
| curium | Cm | 96 | [245] | potassium | K | 19 | 39.102 |
| dysprosium | Dy | 66 | 162.50 | praseodymium | Pr | 59 | 140.097 |
| einsteinium | Es | 99 | [254] | promethium | Pm | 61 | [147] |
| erbium | Er | 68 | 167.26 | protactinium | Pa | 91 | 231.0359 |
| europium | Eu | 63 | 151.96 | radium | Ra | 88 | 226.0254 |
| fermium | Fm | 100 | [255] | radon | Rn | 86 | [222] |
| fluorine | F | 9 | 18.9984 | rhenium | Re | 75 | 186.2 |
| francium | Fr | 87 | [223] | rhodium | Rh | 45 | 102.9055 |
| gadolinium | Gd | 64 | 157.25 | rubidium | Rb | 37 | 85.4678 |
| gallium | Ga | 31 | 69.72 | ruthenium | Ru | 44 | 101.07 |
| germanium | Ge | 32 | 72.59 | rutherfordium | Rf | 104 | [261] |
| gold | Au | 79 | 196.9665 | samarium | Sm | 62 | 150.4 |
| hafnium | Hf | 72 | 178.49 | scandium | Sc | 21 | 44.9559 |
| hahnium | Ha | 105 | [260] | selenium | Se | 34 | 78.96 |
| helium | He | 2 | 4.00260 | silicon | Si | 14 | 28.086 |
| holmium | Ho | 67 | 164.9303 | silver | Ag | 47 | 107.868 |
| hydrogen | H | 1 | 1.0080 | sodium | Na | 11 | 22.9898 |
| indium | In | 49 | 114.82 | strontium | Sr | 38 | 87.62 |
| iodine | I | 53 | 126.9045 | sulfur | S | 16 | 32.06 |
| iridium | Ir | 77 | 192.22 | tantalum | Ta | 73 | 180.9479 |
| iron | Fe | 26 | 55.847 | technetium | Tc | 43 | 98.9062 |
| krypton | Kr | 36 | 83.80 | tellurium | Te | 52 | 127.60 |
| kurchatovium | Ku | 104 | [261] | terbium | Tb | 65 | 158.9254 |
| lanthanum | La | 57 | 138.9005 | thallium | Tl | 81 | 204.37 |

Table 22  THE CHEMICAL ELEMENTS (cont'd)

| Name of element | Symbol | Atomic number | Atomic weight | Name of element | Symbol | Atomic number | Atomic weight |
|---|---|---|---|---|---|---|---|
| thorium | Th | 90 | 232.0381 | vanadium | V | 23 | 50.9414 |
| thulium | Tm | 69 | 168.9342 | xenon | Xe | 54 | 131.30 |
| tin | Sn | 50 | 118.69 | ytterbium | Yb | 70 | 173.04 |
| titanium | Ti | 22 | 47.90 | yttrium | Y | 39 | 88.9059 |
| tungsten | W | 74 | 183.85 | zinc | Zn | 30 | 65.37 |
| uranium | U | 92 | 238.029 | zirconium | Zr | 40 | 91.22 |

A value given in brackets denotes the mass number of the isotope of longest known half-life. The atomic weights of most of these elements are believed to have no error greater than ±1 of the last digit given.

Table 23  MASSES OF SOME NUCLIDES

| Element | Symbol | Atomic mass* (u)** | Element | Symbol | Atomic mass* (u)** |
|---|---|---|---|---|---|
| hydrogen | $^{1}_{1}H$ | 1.007825 | sodium | $^{23}_{11}Na$ | 22.9898 |
| deuterium | $^{2}_{1}H$ | 2.0140 | magnesium | $^{24}_{12}Mg$ | 23.98504 |
| helium | $^{3}_{2}He$ | 3.01603 | | $^{25}_{12}Mg$ | 24.98584 |
| | $^{4}_{2}He$ | 4.00260 | | $^{26}_{12}Mg$ | 25.98259 |
| lithium | $^{6}_{3}Li$ | 6.01512 | sulfur | $^{32}_{16}S$ | 31.97207 |
| | $^{7}_{3}Li$ | 7.01600 | chlorine | $^{35}_{17}Cl$ | 34.96885 |
| beryllium | $^{6}_{4}Be$ | 6.0197 | | $^{37}_{17}Cl$ | 36.96590 |
| | $^{8}_{4}Be$ | 8.0053 | potassium | $^{39}_{19}K$ | 38.96371 |
| | $^{9}_{4}Be$ | 9.01218 | | $^{41}_{19}K$ | 40.96184 |
| boron | $^{10}_{5}B$ | 10.0129 | krypton | $^{95}_{36}Kr$ | 94.9 |
| | $^{11}_{5}B$ | 11.00931 | molybdenum | $^{100}_{42}Mo$ | 99.9076 |
| carbon | $^{12}_{6}C$ | 12.00000 | silver | $^{107}_{47}Ag$ | 106.90509 |
| | $^{13}_{6}C$ | 13.00335 | | $^{109}_{47}Ag$ | 108.9047 |
| nitrogen | $^{12}_{7}N$ | 12.0188 | tellurium | $^{137}_{52}Te$ | 136.91 |
| | $^{14}_{7}N$ | 14.00307 | barium | $^{138}_{56}Ba$ | 137.9050 |
| | $^{15}_{7}N$ | 15.00011 | lead | $^{214}_{82}Pb$ | 213.9982 |
| oxygen | $^{16}_{8}O$ | 15.99491 | bismuth | $^{214}_{83}Bi$ | 213.9972 |
| | $^{17}_{8}O$ | 16.99914 | polonium | $^{218}_{84}Po$ | 218.0089 |
| | $^{18}_{8}O$ | 17.99916 | radon | $^{222}_{86}Rn$ | 222.0175 |
| fluorine | $^{19}_{9}F$ | 18.99840 | radium | $^{228}_{88}Ra$ | 228.0303 |
| neon | $^{20}_{10}Ne$ | 19.99244 | thorium | $^{232}_{90}Th$ | 232.0382 |
| | $^{22}_{10}Ne$ | 21.99138 | uranium | $^{235}_{92}U$ | 235.0439 |
| | | | | $^{238}_{92}U$ | 238.0508 |
| | | | plutonium | $^{239}_{94}Pu$ | 239.0522 |

*Atomic mass of neutral atom is given.

**1 atomic mass unit (u) = $1.6605655 \times 10^{-27}$ kg.

### Table 24 FOUR-PLACE LOGARITHMS

| n | 0 | 1 | 2 | 3 | 4 | 5 | 6 | 7 | 8 | 9 |
|---|---|---|---|---|---|---|---|---|---|---|
| 10 | 0000 | 0043 | 0086 | 0128 | 0170 | 0212 | 0253 | 0294 | 0334 | 0374 |
| 11 | 0414 | 0453 | 0492 | 0531 | 0569 | 0607 | 0645 | 0682 | 0719 | 0755 |
| 12 | 0792 | 0828 | 0864 | 0899 | 0934 | 0969 | 1004 | 1038 | 1072 | 1106 |
| 13 | 1139 | 1173 | 1206 | 1239 | 1271 | 1303 | 1335 | 1367 | 1399 | 1430 |
| 14 | 1461 | 1492 | 1523 | 1553 | 1584 | 1614 | 1644 | 1673 | 1703 | 1732 |
| 15 | 1761 | 1790 | 1818 | 1847 | 1875 | 1903 | 1931 | 1959 | 1987 | 2014 |
| 16 | 2041 | 2068 | 2095 | 2122 | 2148 | 2175 | 2201 | 2227 | 2253 | 2279 |
| 17 | 2304 | 2330 | 2355 | 2380 | 2405 | 2430 | 2455. | 2480 | 2504 | 2529 |
| 18 | 2553 | 2577 | 2601 | 2625 | 2648 | 2672 | 2695 | 2718 | 2742 | 2765 |
| 19 | 2788 | 2810 | 2833 | 2856 | 2878 | 2900 | 2923 | 2945 | 2967 | 2989 |
| 20 | 3010 | 3032 | 3054 | 3075 | 3096 | 3118 | 3139 | 3160 | 3181 | 3201 |
| 21 | 3222 | 3243 | 3263 | 3284 | 3304 | 3324 | 3345 | 3365 | 3385 | 3404 |
| 22 | 3424 | 3444 | 3464 | 3483 | 3502 | 3522 | 3541 | 3560 | 3579 | 3598 |
| 23 | 3617 | 3636 | 3655 | 3674 | 3692 | 3711 | 3729 | 3747 | 3766 | 3784 |
| 24 | 3802 | 3820 | 3838 | 3856 | 3874 | 3892 | 3909 | 3927 | 3945 | 3962 |
| 25 | 3979 | 3997 | 4014 | 4031 | 4048 | 4065 | 4082 | 4099 | 4116 | 4133 |
| 26 | 4150 | 4166 | 4183 | 4200 | 4216 | 4232 | 4249 | 4265 | 4281 | 4298 |
| 27 | 4314 | 4330 | 4346 | 4362 | 4378 | 4393 | 4409 | 4425 | 4440 | 4456 |
| 28 | 4472 | 4487 | 4502 | 4518 | 4533 | 4548 | 4564 | 4579 | 4594 | 4609 |
| 29 | 4624 | 4639 | 4654 | 4669 | 4683 | 4698 | 4713 | 4728 | 4742 | 4757 |
| 30 | 4771 | 4786 | 4800 | 4814 | 4829 | 4843 | 4857 | 4871 | 4886 | 4900 |
| 31 | 4914 | 4928 | 4942 | 4955 | 4969 | 4983 | 4997 | 5011 | 5024 | 5038 |
| 32 | 5051 | 5065 | 5079 | 5092 | 5105 | 5119 | 5132 | 5145 | 5159 | 5172 |
| 33 | 5185 | 5198 | 5211 | 5224 | 5237 | 5250 | 5263 | 5276 | 5289 | 5302 |
| 34 | 5315 | 5328 | 5340 | 5353 | 5366 | 5378 | 5391 | 5403 | 5416 | 5428 |
| 35 | 5441 | 5453 | 5465 | 5478 | 5490 | 5502 | 5514 | 5527 | 5539 | 5551 |
| 36 | 5563 | 5575 | 5587 | 5599 | 5611 | 5623 | 5635 | 5647 | 5658 | 5670 |
| 37 | 5682 | 5694 | 5705 | 5717 | 5729 | 5740 | 5752 | 5763 | 5775 | 5786 |
| 38 | 5798 | 5809 | 5821 | 5832 | 5843 | 5855 | 5866 | 5877 | 5888 | 5899 |
| 39 | 5911 | 5922 | 5933 | 5944 | 5955 | 5966 | 5977 | 5988 | 5999 | 6010 |
| 40 | 6021 | 6031 | 6042 | 6053 | 6064 | 6075 | 6085 | 6096 | 6107 | 6117 |
| 41 | 6128 | 6138 | 6149 | 6160 | 6170 | 6180 | 6191 | 6201 | 6212 | 6222 |
| 42 | 6232 | 6243 | 6253 | 6263 | 6274 | 6284 | 6294 | 6304 | 6314 | 6325 |
| 43 | 6335 | 6345 | 6355 | 6365 | 6375 | 6385 | 6395 | 6405 | 6415 | 6425 |
| 44 | 6435 | 6444 | 6454 | 6464 | 6474 | 6484 | 6493 | 6503 | 6513 | 6522 |
| 45 | 6532 | 6542 | 6551 | 6561 | 6571 | 6580 | 6590 | 6599 | 6609 | 6618 |
| 46 | 6628 | 6637 | 6646 | 6656 | 6665 | 6675 | 6684 | 6693 | 6702 | 6712 |
| 47 | 6721 | 6730 | 6739 | 6749 | 6758 | 6767 | 6776 | 6785 | 6794 | 6803 |
| 48 | 6812 | 6821 | 6830 | 6839 | 6848 | 6857 | 6866 | 6875 | 6884 | 6893 |
| 49 | 6902 | 6911 | 6920 | 6928 | 6937 | 6946 | 6955 | 6964 | 6972 | 6981 |
| 50 | 6990 | 6998 | 7007 | 7016 | 7024 | 7033 | 7042 | 7050 | 7059 | 7067 |
| 51 | 7076 | 7084 | 7093 | 7101 | 7110 | 7118 | 7126 | 7135 | 7143 | 7152 |
| 52 | 7160 | 7168 | 7177 | 7185 | 7193 | 7202 | 7210 | 7218 | 7226 | 7235 |
| 53 | 7243 | 7251 | 7259 | 7267 | 7275 | 7284 | 7292 | 7300 | 7308 | 7316 |
| 54 | 7324 | 7332 | 7340 | 7348 | 7356 | 7364 | 7372 | 7380 | 7388 | 7396 |

Table 24   FOUR-PLACE LOGARITHMS (cont'd)

| n | 0 | 1 | 2 | 3 | 4 | 5 | 6 | 7 | 8 | 9 |
|---|---|---|---|---|---|---|---|---|---|---|
| **55** | 7404 | 7412 | 7419 | 7427 | 7435 | 7443 | 7451 | 7459 | 7466 | 7474 |
| 56 | 7482 | 7490 | 7497 | 7505 | 7513 | 7520 | 7528 | 7536 | 7543 | 7551 |
| 57 | 7559 | 7566 | 7574 | 7582 | 7589 | 7597 | 7604 | 7612 | 7619 | 7627 |
| 58 | 7634 | 7642 | 7649 | 7657 | 7664 | 7672 | 7679 | 7686 | 7694 | 7701 |
| 59 | 7709 | 7716 | 7723 | 7731 | 7738 | 7745 | 7752 | 7760 | 7767 | 7774 |
| **60** | 7782 | 7789 | 7796 | 7803 | 7810 | 7818 | 7825 | 7832 | 7839 | 7846 |
| 61 | 7853 | 7860 | 7868 | 7875 | 7882 | 7889 | 7896 | 7903 | 7910 | 7917 |
| 62 | 7924 | 7931 | 7938 | 7945 | 7952 | 7959 | 7966 | 7973 | 7980 | 7987 |
| 63 | 7993 | 8000 | 8007 | 8014 | 8021 | 8028 | 8035 | 8041 | 8048 | 8055 |
| 64 | 8062 | 8069 | 8075 | 8082 | 8089 | 8096 | 8102 | 8109 | 8116 | 8122 |
| **65** | 8129 | 8136 | 8142 | 8149 | 8156 | 8162 | 8169 | 8176 | 8182 | 8189 |
| 66 | 8195 | 8202 | 8209 | 8215 | 8222 | 8228 | 8235 | 8241 | 8248 | 8254 |
| 67 | 8261 | 8267 | 8274 | 8280 | 8287 | 8293 | 8299 | 8306 | 8312 | 8319 |
| 68 | 8325 | 8331 | 8338 | 8344 | 8351 | 8357 | 8363 | 8370 | 8376 | 8382 |
| 69 | 8388 | 8395 | 8401 | 8407 | 8414 | 8420 | 8426 | 8432 | 8439 | 8445 |
| **70** | 8451 | 8457 | 8463 | 8470 | 8476 | 8482 | 8488 | 8494 | 8500 | 8506 |
| 71 | 8513 | 8519 | 8525 | 8531 | 8537 | 8543 | 8549 | 8555 | 8561 | 8567 |
| 72 | 8573 | 8579 | 8585 | 8591 | 8597 | 8603 | 8609 | 8615 | 8621 | 8627 |
| 73 | 8633 | 8639 | 8645 | 8651 | 8657 | 8663 | 8669 | 8675 | 8681 | 8686 |
| 74 | 8692 | 8698 | 8704 | 8710 | 8716 | 8722 | 8727 | 8733 | 8739 | 8745 |
| **75** | 8751 | 8756 | 8762 | 8768 | 8774 | 8779 | 8785 | 8791 | 8797 | 8802 |
| 76 | 8808 | 8811 | 8820 | 8825 | 8831 | 8837 | 8842 | 8848 | 8854 | 8859 |
| 77 | 8865 | 8871 | 8876 | 8882 | 8887 | 8893 | 8899 | 8904 | 8910 | 8915 |
| 78 | 8921 | 8927 | 8932 | 8938 | 8943 | 8949 | 8954 | 8960 | 8965 | 8971 |
| 79 | 8976 | 8982 | 8987 | 8993 | 8998 | 9004 | 9009 | 9015 | 9020 | 9025 |
| **80** | 9031 | 9036 | 9042 | 9047 | 9053 | 9058 | 9063 | 9069 | 9074 | 9079 |
| 81 | 9085 | 9090 | 9096 | 9101 | 9106 | 9112 | 9117 | 9122 | 9128 | 9133 |
| 82 | 9138 | 9143 | 9149 | 9154 | 9159 | 9165 | 9170 | 9175 | 9180 | 9186 |
| 83 | 9191 | 9196 | 9201 | 9206 | 9212 | 9217 | 9222 | 9227 | 9232 | 9238 |
| 84 | 9243 | 9248 | 9253 | 9258 | 9263 | 9269 | 9274 | 9279 | 9284 | 9289 |
| **85** | 9294 | 9299 | 9304 | 9309 | 9315 | 9320 | 9325 | 9330 | 9335 | 9340 |
| 86 | 9345 | 9350 | 9355 | 9360 | 9365 | 9370 | 9375 | 9380 | 9385 | 9390 |
| 87 | 9395 | 9400 | 9405 | 9410 | 9415 | 9420 | 9425 | 9430 | 9435 | 9440 |
| 88 | 9445 | 9450 | 9455 | 9460 | 9465 | 9469 | 9474 | 9479 | 9484 | 9489 |
| 89 | 9494 | 9499 | 9504 | 9509 | 9513 | 9518 | 9523 | 9528 | 9533 | 9538 |
| **90** | 9542 | 9547 | 9552 | 9557 | 9562 | 9566 | 9571 | 9576 | 9581 | 9586 |
| 91 | 9590 | 9595 | 9600 | 9605 | 9609 | 9614 | 9619 | 9624 | 9628 | 9633 |
| 92 | 9638 | 9643 | 9647 | 9652 | 9657 | 9661 | 9666 | 9671 | 9675 | 9680 |
| 93 | 9685 | 9689 | 9694 | 9699 | 9703 | 9708 | 9713 | 9717 | 9722 | 9727 |
| 94 | 9731 | 9736 | 9741 | 9745 | 9750 | 9754 | 9759 | 9763 | 9768 | 9773 |
| **95** | 9777 | 9782 | 9786 | 9791 | 9795 | 9800 | 9805 | 9809 | 9814 | 9818 |
| 96 | 9823 | 9827 | 9832 | 9836 | 9841 | 9845 | 9850 | 9854 | 9859 | 9863 |
| 97 | 9868 | 9872 | 9877 | 9881 | 9886 | 9890 | 9894 | 9899 | 9903 | 9908 |
| 98 | 9912 | 9917 | 9921 | 9926 | 9930 | 9934 | 9939 | 9943 | 9948 | 9952 |
| 99 | 9956 | 9961 | 9965 | 9969 | 9974 | 9978 | 9983 | 9987 | 9991 | 9996 |

# Glossary

**abscissa.** The value corresponding to the horizontal distance of a point on a graph from the Y axis. The X coordinate.

**absolute deviation.** See *deviation, absolute.*

**absolute error.** See *error, absolute.*

**absolute zero.** The temperature of a body at which the kinetic energy of its molecules is at a minimum; 0°K or −273.15°C.

**absorption spectrum.** A continuous spectrum interrupted by dark lines or bands that are characteristic of the medium through which the radiation has passed.

**acceleration.** Time rate of change of velocity.

**acceleration, angular.** Time rate of change of angular velocity.

**acceleration, centripetal.** Acceleration directed toward the center of a circular path.

**acceptor.** An element with three valence electrons per atom which when added to a semiconductor crystal provides electron "holes" in the lattice structure of the crystal.

**accuracy.** Closeness of a measurement to the accepted value for a specific physical quantity; expressed in terms of error.

**adhesion.** The force of attraction between unlike molecules.

**adiabatic process.** A thermal process in which no heat is added to or removed from a system.

**alpha (α) particle.** A helium-4 nucleus, especially when emitted from the nucleus of a radioactive atom.

**alternating current.** An electric current that has one direction during one part of a generating cycle and the opposite direction during the remainder of the cycle.

**ammeter.** An electric meter designed to measure current.

**ampere.** The unit of current in the MKS system; one coulomb per second.

**amplifier.** A device consisting of one or more vacuum tubes (or transistors) and associated circuits, used to increase the strength of a signal.

**amplitude.** The maximum displacement of a vibrating particle from its equilibrium position.

**angle of incidence.** The angle between the incident ray and the normal drawn to the point of incidence.

**angle of reflection.** See *reflection, angle of.*

**angle of refraction.** See *refraction, angle of.*

**Ångstrom.** A unit of linear measure equal to $10^{-10}$ m.

**angular acceleration.** See *acceleration, angular.*

**angular impulse.** See *impulse, angular.*

**angular momentum.** See *momentum, angular.*

**angular velocity.** See *velocity, angular.*

**anode.** (1) The positive electrode of an electric cell. (2) The positive electrode or plate of an electronic tube. (3) The electron-poor electrode.

**antimatter.** A substance composed of antiparticles.

**antiparticle.** A counterpart of a subatomic particle having opposite properties (except for equal masses).

**aperture.** Any opening through which radiation may pass. The diameter of an opening that admits light to a lens or mirror.

**apparent power.** See *power, apparent.*

**armature.** A coil of wire formed around an iron or steel core that rotates in the magnetic field of a generator or motor.

**atom.** The smallest particle of an element that can exist either alone or in combination with other atoms of the same or other elements.

**atomic mass unit.** One-twelfth of the mass of carbon-12, or $1.6605655 \times 10^{-27}$ kg.

**atomic number.** The number of protons in the nucleus of an atom.

**atomic weight.** See *weight, atomic*.

**audio signal.** The alternating voltage proportional to the sound pressure produced in an electric circuit.

**average velocity.** See *velocity, average*.

**back emf.** An induced emf in the armature of a motor that opposes the applied voltage.

**band spectrum.** An emission spectrum consisting of fluted bands of color. The spectrum of a substance in the molecular state.

**barometer.** A device used to measure the pressure of the atmosphere.

**baryon.** A subatomic particle with a large rest mass, e.g., the proton.

**basic equation.** See *equation, basic*.

**beam.** Several parallel rays of light considered collectively.

**beat.** The interference effect resulting from the superposition of two waves of slightly different frequencies propagating in the same direction. The amplitude of the resultant wave varies with time.

**beta (β) particle.** An electron emitted from the nucleus of a radioactive atom.

**betatron.** A device that accelerates electrons by means of the transformer principle.

**bevatron.** A high-energy synchrotron.

**binding energy.** See *energy, binding*.

**boiling point.** The temperature at which the vapor pressure of a liquid equals the pressure of the atmosphere.

**boson.** A subatomic particle with zero charge and rest mass, e.g., the photon.

**Boyle's law.** See *law, Boyle's*.

**breeder reactor.** A nuclear reactor in which a fissionable material is produced at a greater rate than the fuel is consumed.

**Brownian movement.** The irregular and random movement of small particles suspended in a fluid, known to be a consequence of the thermal motion of fluid molecules.

**bubble chamber.** Instrument used for making the paths of ionizing particles visible as a trail of tiny bubbles in a liquid.

**calorie.** The quantity of heat equal to 4.19 joules.

**calorimeter.** Nested metal cups separated by an air space, used in heat experiments.

**candle.** The unit of luminous intensity of a light source.

**capacitance.** The ratio of the charge on either plate of a capacitor to the potential difference between the plates.

**capacitive reactance.** See *reactance, capacitive*.

**capacitor.** A combination of conducting plates separated by layers of a dielectric that is used to store an electric charge.

**capillarity.** The elevation or depression of liquids in small diameter tubes.

**cathode.** (1) The negative electrode of an electric cell. (2) The electron-emitting electrode of an electronic tube. (3) The electron-rich electrode.

**cathode rays.** Particles emanating from a cathode; electrons.

**Celsius scale.** The temperature scale using the ice point as 0° and the steam point as 100°, with 100 equal divisions or degrees between; formerly the centigrade scale.

**center of curvature.** The center of the sphere of which the mirror or lens surface forms a part.

**center of gravity.** See *gravity, center of*.

**centrifugal force.** See *force, centrifugal*.

**centripetal acceleration.** See *acceleration, centripetal*.

**centripetal force.** See *force, centripetal*.

**chain reaction.** A reaction in which the material or energy that starts the reaction is also one of the products and can cause similar reactions.

**Charles' law.** See *law, Charles'*.

**chemical change.** A change in which new substances with new properties are formed.

**chemical equivalent.** The quantity of an element, expressed in grams, equal to the ratio of its atomic weight to its valence.

**chromatic aberration.** The nonfocusing of light of different colors.

**circular motion.** See *motion, circular*.

**cloud chamber.** A device used to detect the passage of charged subatomic particles by the trails of liquid droplets they form in a special chamber.

**coefficient of area expansion.** The change in area per unit area of a solid per degree change in temperature.

**coefficient of cubic expansion.** The change in volume per unit volume of a solid or liquid per degree change in temperature.

**coefficient of linear expansion.** The change in length per unit length of a solid per degree change in temperature.

**coefficient of sliding friction.** See *friction, coefficient of sliding.*

**coherence.** The property of two wave trains with identical wavelengths and a constant phase relationship.

**cohesion.** The force of attraction between like molecules.

**collision, elastic.** A collision in which objects rebound from each other without a loss of kinetic energy.

**collision, inelastic.** A collision in which the colliding objects stick together after impact.

**color.** A description of a sensation received through our eyes.

**commutator.** A split ring in a d-c generator, each segment of which is connected to an end of a corresponding armature loop.

**complementary colors.** Two colors that combine to form white light.

**complete vibration.** See *vibration, complete.*

**component.** One of the several vectors that can be combined geometrically to yield a resultant vector.

**composition of forces.** The combining of two or more component forces into a single resultant force.

**compression.** The region of a longitudinal wave in which the vibrating particles are closer than their equilibrium distance.

**concave.** Surface with center of curvature on the same side as the observer.

**concave lens.** A lens that diverges parallel light rays (assuming the outside refractive index to be smaller).

**concave mirror.** A mirror that converges parallel light rays incident on its surface.

**conceptual unit.** See *unit, conceptual.*

**concurrent forces.** See *forces, concurrent.*

**condensation.** The change of phase from a gas or vapor to a liquid.

**conductance.** The reciprocal of the ohmic resistance.

**conductor.** A material through which an electric charge is readily transferred.

**conservation of baryons, law of.** When a baryon decays or reacts with another particle, the number of baryons is the same on both sides of the equation.

**conservation of energy, law of.** The total amount of energy of all kinds in a given situation is a constant.

**conservation of hypercharge, law of.** Hypercharge is conserved in strong and electromagnetic interactions, but not in weak interactions.

**conservation of leptons, law of.** In a reaction involving leptons, the arithmetic sum of the lepton numbers is the same on each side of the equation.

**conservation of mechanical energy, law of.** The sum of the potential and kinetic energy of an ideal energy system is constant.

**conservation of momentum, law of.** When no net external forces are acting on an object, the total vector momentum of the object remains constant.

**conservative forces.** See *forces, conservative.*

**continuous spectrum.** A spectrum without dark lines or bands or in which there is an uninterrupted change from one color to another.

**converging lens.** A lens that is thicker in the middle than it is at the edge and bends incident parallel rays toward a common point.

**convex.** Surface with center of curvature on the opposite side from the observer.

**convex lens.** A lens that converges parallel light rays (assuming the outside refractive index to be smaller).

**convex mirror.** A mirror that diverges parallel light rays incident on its surface.

**cosmic rays.** High-energy particles, apparently originating from beyond our solar system.

**cosmotron.** A high-energy synchrotron.

**coulomb.** The quantity of electricity equal to the charge on $6.25 \times 10^{18}$ electrons.

**Coulomb's law for magnetism.** The force between two magnetic poles is directly proportional to the strengths of the poles and inversely proportional to the square of their distance apart.

**Coulomb's law of electrostatics.** See *electrostatics, Coulomb's law of*.

**couple.** Two forces of equal magnitude acting in opposite directions in the same plane, but not along the same line.

**crest.** A region of upward displacement in a transverse wave.

**critical angle.** That limiting angle of incidence in the optically denser medium that results in an angle of refraction of 90°.

**critical mass.** The amount of a particular fissionable material required to make a fission reaction self-sustaining.

**critical point.** The upper limit of the temperature-pressure curve of a substance.

**critical pressure.** See *pressure, critical*.

**critical temperature.** See *temperature, critical*.

**critical velocity.** See *velocity, critical*.

**curie.** The quantity of any radioactive nuclide that undergoes $3.7 \times 10^{10}$ disintegrations per second.

**current sensitivity.** Current per unit scale division of an electric meter.

**curvilinear motion.** See *motion, curvilinear*.

**cut-off bias.** The smallest negative grid voltage, for a given plate voltage, that causes a vacuum tube to cease to conduct.

**cut-off frequency.** See *frequency, cut-off*.

**cut-off potential.** A negative potential on the collector of a photoelectric cell that reduces the photoelectric current to zero.

**cycle.** A series of changes produced in sequence resulting in the system returning periodically to its initial condition.

**cyclotron.** A device for accelerating charged atomic particles by means of D-shaped electrodes.

**damping.** The reduction in amplitude of a wave due to the dissipation of wave energy.

**decay constant.** The ratio between the number of nuclei decaying per second and the total number of nuclei.

**decibel.** A unit of sound intensity level. The smallest change of sound intensity that the normal human ear can detect.

**declination.** The angle between magnetic north and the true north from any surface location.

**dees.** The electrodes in a cyclotron.

**density.** See *mass density*.

**deviation, absolute.** Difference between single measured value and average of several measurements made in same way.

**deviation, relative.** Percentage average deviation of a set of measurements.

**dew point.** The temperature at which a given amount of water vapor will exert equilibrium vapor pressure.

**diamagnetism.** The property of a substance whereby it is feebly repelled by a strong magnet.

**dichroism.** A property of certain crystalline substances in which one polarized component of incident light is absorbed and the other is transmitted.

**dielectric.** An electric insulator. A nonconducting medium.

**dielectric constant.** The ratio of the capacitance with a particular material separating the plates of a capacitor to the capacitance with a vacuum between the plates.

**diffraction.** The spreading of a wave disturbance into a region behind an obstruction.

**diffraction angle.** The angle that a diffracted wavefront forms with the grating plane.

**diffraction grating.** An optical surface, either transmitting or reflecting, with several thousand equally spaced and parallel grooves ruled in it.

**diffusion.** (1) The penetration of one type of particle into a mass of a second type of particle. (2) The scattering of light by irregular reflection.

**diode.** A two-terminal device that will conduct electric current more easily in one direction than in the other.

**direct current.** An essentially constant-value current in which the movement of charge is in only one direction.

**dispersion.** The process of separating polychromatic light into its component wavelengths.

**displacement.** (1) A change of position in a particular direction. (2) Distance of a vibrating particle from the midpoint of its vibration.

**dissipative forces.** See *forces, dissipative*.

**distillation.** The evaporation of volatile materials from a liquid or solid mixture and their condensation in a separate vessel.

**distillation, fractional.** The process of separating the components of a liquid mixture through differences in their boiling points.

**diverging lens.** A lens that is thicker at the edge than it is in the middle and bends incident parallel rays so that they appear to come from a common point.

**domain.** A microscopic magnetic region composed of a group of atoms whose magnetic fields are aligned in a common direction.

**donor.** A substance with five valence electrons per atom which when added to a semiconductor crystal provides free electrons in the lattice structure of the crystal.

**Doppler effect.** The change observed in the frequency with which a wave from a given source reaches an observer when the source and the observer are in relative motion.

**double refraction.** See *refraction, double*.

**drift tubes.** Charged cylinders used to accelerate charged subatomic particles in a linear accelerator.

**ductility.** The property of a metal that enables it to be drawn through a die to produce a wire.

**eddy currents.** Closed loops of induced current set up in a piece of metal when there is relative motion between the metal and a magnetic field. Eddy currents are in such direction that the resulting magnetic forces oppose the relative motion.

**Edison effect.** The emission of electrons from a heated metal in a vacuum.

**effective value of current.** The magnitude of an alternating current that in a given resistance produces heat at the same average rate as that magnitude of steady direct current.

**efficiency.** The ratio of the useful work output of a machine to total work input.

**elastic collision.** See *collision, elastic*.

**elastic limit.** The condition in which a substance is on the verge of becoming permanently deformed.

**elastic potential energy.** See *energy, elastic potential*.

**elasticity.** The ability of an object to return to its original size or shape when the external forces producing distortion are removed.

**electric current.** The rate of flow of charge past a given point in an electric circuit.

**electric field.** The region in which a force acts on an electric charge brought into the region.

**electric field intensity.** See *intensity, electric field*.

**electrification.** The process of charging a body by adding or removing electrons.

**electrochemical cell.** A cell in which chemical energy is converted to electric energy by a spontaneous electron-transfer reaction.

**electrochemical equivalent.** The mass of an element, in grams, deposited by one coulomb of electric charge.

**electrode.** A conducting element in an electric cell, electronic tube, or semiconductor device.

**electrolysis.** The conduction of electricity through a solution of an electrolyte or through a fused ionic compound, together with the resulting chemical changes.

**electrolyte.** A substance whose solution conducts an electric current.

**electrolytic cell.** A cell in which electric energy is converted to chemical energy by means of an electron-transfer reaction.

**electromagnetic induction.** See *induction, electromagnetic*.

**electromagnetic interaction.** See *interaction, electromagnetic.*

**electromagnetic waves.** Transverse waves having an electric component and a magnetic component, each being perpendicular to the other and both perpendicular to the direction of propagation.

**electromotive force.** See *emf.*

**electron.** A negatively charged subatomic particle, having a rest mass of $9.109534 \times 10^{-31}$ kg and a charge of $1.6021892 \times 10^{-19}$ c.

**electron cloud.** The aggregate of electrons about the nucleus of an atom.

**electron shell.** A region about the nucleus of an atom in which electrons move: made up of electron orbitals.

**electron volt.** See *volt, electron.*

**electronics.** The branch of physics concerned with the emission, behavior, and effects of electrons.

**electroscope.** A device used to observe the presence of an electrostatic charge.

**electrostatics, basic law of.** Objects that are similarly charged repel each other; those with unlike charges attract each other.

**electrostatics, Coulomb's law of.** The force between two point charges is directly proportional to the product of their magnitudes and inversely proportional to the square of the distance between them.

**elementary colors.** The six regions of color in the solar spectrum observed by the dispersion of sunlight: red, orange, yellow, green, blue, and violet.

**elongation strain.** The ratio of the increase in length to the unstretched length.

**emf.** The energy per unit charge supplied by a source of electric current.

**emission spectrum.** A spectrum formed by the dispersion of light from an incandescent solid, liquid, and gas.

**endothermic.** Referring to a process that absorbs energy.

**energy.** A physical quantity that has the capacity for doing work.

**energy, binding.** Energy that must be applied to a nucleus to break it up.

**energy, elastic potential.** The potential energy in a stretched or compressed elastic object.

**energy, gravitational potential.** Potential energy acquired by an object when work is done on it against gravity.

**energy, internal.** Total potential and kinetic energy of the molecules and atomic particles of a substance.

**energy, kinetic.** The energy due to the motion of an object.

**energy, nuclear binding.** The energy required to break a nucleus apart.

**energy, potential.** Energy that is due to the position of an object.

**energy, thermal.** The total potential and kinetic energy associated with the random motions of the particles of a material.

**energy level.** One of a series of discrete energy values that characterize a physical system governed by quantum rules.

**entropy.** (1) The internal energy of a system that cannot be converted to mechanical work. (2) The property that describes the disorder of a system.

**entropy, law of.** A natural process always takes place in such a direction as to increase the entropy of the universe.

**equation, basic.** An equation that expresses the required quantity of a problem in terms of its usual defining quantities.

**equation, working.** An equation that expresses the solution to a problem in terms of the known quantities given.

**equilibrant force.** See *force, equilibrant.*

**equilibrium.** The state of a body in which there is no change in its motion.

**equilibrium, rotational.** The state of a body in which the sum of all the clockwise torques in a given plane equals the sum of all the counterclockwise torques about a pivot point.

**equilibrium, translational.** The state of a body in which there are no unbalanced forces acting on it.

**equilibrium position.** Midpoint of the path of an object describing simple harmonic motion.

**equilibrium vapor pressure.** See *pressure, equilibrium vapor.*

**error, absolute.** Actual difference between a measured value and its accepted value.

**error, relative.** Percentage absolute error of a set of measurements.

**evaporation.** The change of phase from a liquid to a gas or vapor.

**exclusion principle.** No two electrons in an atom can have the same set of quantum numbers.

**exothermic.** Referring to a process that liberates energy.

**expansion, cubic, coefficient of.** See *coefficient of cubic expansion.*

**expansion, linear, coefficient of.** See *coefficient of linear expansion.*

**"f" number.** The ratio of the focal length of a lens to the effective aperture.

**farad.** The MKS unit of capacitance; one coulomb per volt.

**faraday.** The quantity of electricity (96,500 coulombs) required to deposit one chemical equivalent of an element.

**Faraday's first law.** See *law, Faraday's first.*

**Faraday's second law.** See *law, Faraday's second.*

**ferromagnetism.** The property of a substance by which it is strongly attracted by a magnet.

**Feynman diagram.** A diagram showing the production and exchange of particles during a subatomic interaction.

**field, gravitational.** Region of space in which each point is associated with the value of gravitational acceleration at that point.

**field intensity.** See *intensity, electric field, magnetic field.*

**fission.** The splitting of a heavy nucleus into nuclei of medium mass.

**flash tube.** The ionization tube that emits the light in a chemical laser.

**Fleming valve.** First vacuum tube diode.

**fluorescence.** The emission of light during the absorption of radiation from another source.

**flux.** Flow.

**flux, line of.** See *line of flux.*

**focal length.** The distance between the principal focus of a lens or mirror and its optical center or vertex.

**focal plane.** The plane perpendicular to the principal axis of a converging lens or mirror that contains the principal focus.

**focus.** A point at which light rays meet or from which rays of light diverge.

**focus, principal.** A point to which rays parallel to the principal axis converge or from which they diverge after reflection or refraction.

**force.** A measure of the momentum gained per second by an accelerating body. A physical quantity that can affect the motion of an object.

**force, centrifugal.** Force that tends to move the particles of a rotating object away from the center of rotation.

**force, centripetal.** The force that produces centripetal acceleration.

**force, equilibrant.** The force that produces equilibrium.

**force, gravitational.** The mutual force of attraction between particles of matter.

**force, magnetic.** A force associated with the motion of electric charges.

**force, nuclear binding.** The force that acts within the small distances between nucleons.

**force, resultant.** The single force that has the same effect as two or more forces applied simultaneously at the same point.

**force of gravity.** See *gravity.*

**forced vibration.** Vibration that is due to the application of a periodic force, and not to the natural vibrations of the system.

**forces, concurrent.** Forces with lines of action that pass through the same point.

**forces, conservative.** Forces for which the law of conservation of mechanical energy holds true; gravitational forces and elastic forces.

**forces, dissipative.** Forces for which the law of conservation of mechanical energy does not hold true; frictional forces.

**forward bias.** Voltage applied to a semiconductor P-N junction that increases the electron current across the junction.

**fractional distillation.** See *distillation, fractional.*

**frame of reference.** Any system for specifying the precise location of objects in space.

**frame of reference, inertial.** A nonaccelerating frame of reference in which Newton's first law holds true.

**frame of reference, noninertial.** An accelerating frame of reference in which Newton's first law does not hold true.

**freezing point.** The temperature at which a liquid changes to a solid.

**frequency.** Number of vibrations, oscillations, or cycles per unit time.

**frequency, cut-off.** A characteristic threshold frequency of incident light below which, for a given material, the photoelectric emission of electrons ceases.

**friction.** A force that resists the relative motion of objects that are in contact with each other.

**friction, coefficient of sliding.** The ratio of the force needed to overcome sliding friction to the normal force pressing the surfaces together.

**fuel cell.** An electrochemical cell in which the chemical energy of continuously supplied fuel is converted into electric energy.

**fundamental.** The lowest frequency produced by a musical tone source. The harmonic component of a wave that has the lowest frequency.

**fusion.** (1) The change of phase from a solid to a liquid; melting. (2) A reaction in which light nuclei combine to form a nucleus with a larger mass number.

**fusion, heat of.** The heat required per unit mass to change a substance from solid to liquid at its melting point.

**galvanometer.** An instrument used to measure minute electric currents.

**gamma (γ) ray.** See *ray, gamma (γ).*

**gas, ideal.** A theoretical gas consisting of infinitely small molecules that exert no forces on each other.

**gas constant, universal.** Constant of proportionality, $R$, in the ideal gas equation.

**Geiger tube.** Instrument used for the detection of subatomic particles through ionization.

**general gas law.** See *law, general gas.*

**gravitational field.** See *field, gravitational.*

**gravitational force.** See *force, gravitational.*

**gravitational interaction.** See *interaction, gravitational.*

**gravitational potential energy.** See *energy, gravitational potential.*

**graviton.** The carrier for the gravitational interaction.

**gravity.** The force of gravitation on an object on or near the surface of a celestial body.

**gravity, center of.** The point at which all of the weight of a body may be considered to be concentrated.

**grid.** An element of an electronic tube. An electrode used to control the flow of electrons from the cathode to the plate.

**grid bias.** The grid to cathode voltage.

**ground, electric.** (1) A conductor connected with the earth to establish zero (ground) potential. (2) A common return to an arbitrary zero potential.

**half-life.** The length of time during which, on the average, half of a large number of radioactive nuclides decay.

**harmonics.** The fundamental and the tones whose frequencies are whole number multiples of the fundamental.

**heat.** Thermal energy in the process of being added to, or removed from, a substance.

**heat, mechanical equivalent of.** The conversion factor that relates heat units to work units. 4.19 j/cal.

**heat, specific.** The heat capacity of a material per unit mass.

**heat capacity.** The quantity of heat needed to raise the temperature of a body one degree.

**heat exchange, law of.** In any heat transfer system, the heat lost by hot materials equals the heat gained by cold materials.

**heat of fusion.** See *fusion, heat of.*

**heat pump.** A device that absorbs heat from a cool environment and gives it off to a region of higher temperature.

**heat sink.** A reservoir that absorbs heat without a significant increase in temperature.

**heat of vaporization.** See *vaporization, heat of.*

**henry.** The MKS unit of inductance; one henry of inductance is present in a circuit when a change in the current of 1 ampere per second induces an emf of 1 volt.

**Hooke's law.** See *law, Hooke's.*

**hyperbola.** Graph of an inverse proportion.

**hypercharge.** A property of some baryons and leptons that is conserved in strong and electromagnetic interactions but not in weak interactions.

**hypothesis.** A plausible solution to a problem.

**ice point.** The melting point of ice when in equilibrium with water saturated with air at standard atmospheric pressure.

**ideal gas.** See *gas, ideal.*

**illumination.** The luminous flux per unit area of a surface.

**image.** The optical counterpart of an object formed by lenses or mirrors.

**image, real.** An image that is formed by actual rays of light.

**image, virtual.** An image that only appears to be formed by rays of light.

**impedance.** (1) The ratio of applied wave-producing force to resulting displacement velocity of a wave-transmitting medium. (2) The ratio of sound pressure to volume displacement at a given surface in a sound-transmitting medium. (3) The ratio of the effective voltage to the effective current in an a-c circuit.

**impedance matching.** A technique used to ensure maximum transfer of energy from the output of one circuit to the input of another.

**impulse.** The product of a force and the time interval during which it acts.

**impulse, angular.** The product of a torque and the time interval during which it acts.

**index of refraction.** See *refraction, index of.*

**induced magnetism.** Magnetism produced in a ferromagnetic substance by the influence of a magnetic field. Magnetization.

**inductance.** The property of an electric circuit by which a varying current induces a back emf in that circuit or a neighboring circuit.

**inductance, mutual.** The ratio of the induced emf in one circuit to the rate of change of current in the other.

**inductance, self.** The ratio of the induced emf across a coil to the rate of change of current in the coil.

**induction.** The process of charging one body by bringing it into the electric field of another charged body.

**induction, electromagnetic.** The process by which an emf is set up in a conducting circuit by a changing magnetic flux linked by the circuit.

**inductive reactance.** See *reactance, inductive.*

**inelastic collision.** See *collision, inelastic.*

**inertia.** The property of matter that opposes any change in its state of motion.

**inertia, rotational.** The property of an object that resists changes in its angular momentum when the object is rotating.

**inertial frame of reference.** See *frame of reference, inertial.*

**infrared light.** See *light, infrared.*

**infrasonic range.** Vibrations in matter below 20 cycles/second.

**instantaneous current.** The magnitude of a varying current at any instant of time.

**instantaneous speed.** See *speed, instantaneous.*

**instantaneous velocity.** See *velocity, instantaneous.*

**instantaneous voltage.** The magnitude of a varying voltage at any instant of time.

**insulator.** A material through which an electric charge is not readily transferred.

**intensity, electric field.** The force per unit positive charge at a given point in an electric field.

**intensity, magnetic field.** The force exerted by a magnetic field on a unit N pole situated in the field.

**intensity, sound.** The rate at which sound energy flows through a unit area.

**intensity level.** The logarithm of the ratio of the intensity of a sound to the intensity of the threshold of hearing.

**interaction.** Any change in the amount or quantum numbers of particles that are near each other.

**interaction, electromagnetic.** The interaction that keeps electrons in orbit and forms bonds between atoms and molecules.

**interaction, gravitational.** The interaction that has no known distance limitations, but is the weakest interaction of all.

**interaction, strong.** The interaction that holds the particles of the nucleus together and is independent of charge.

**interaction, weak.** The interaction that produces pairs of particles that have unusually long half-lives.

**interface.** A surface that forms the boundary between two phases or systems.

**interference.** (1) The superposing of one wave on another. (2) The mutual effect of two beams of light, resulting in a reduction of energy in certain areas and an increase of energy in others.

**internal energy.** See *energy, internal.*

**intersecting storage ring.** See *storage ring, intersecting.*

**inverse photoelectric effect.** See *photoelectric effect, inverse.*

**inverse proportion.** The relation between two quantities whose product is a constant.

**ion.** An atom or a group of atoms having an electric charge.

**ionization chamber.** A device used to detect the passage of charged rays or particles by their ionizing effect on a gas.

**ionization energy.** The energy required to remove an electron from an atom.

**isothermal process.** A thermal process that takes place at constant temperature.

**isotopes.** Atoms whose nuclei contain the same number of protons but different numbers of neutrons.

**joule.** The MKS unit of work; the product of a force of one newton acting through a distance of one meter.

**Joule's law.** See *law, Joule's.*

**Kelvin scale.** The scale of temperature having a single fixed point, the temperature of the triple point of water, which is assigned the value $273.16°$ K.

**kilocalorie.** Heat energy equal to $4.19 \times 10^3$ joules; $10^3$ calories.

**kilowatt hour.** A unit of electric energy equal to $3.6 \times 10^6$ w s.

**kinetic energy.** See *energy, kinetic.*

**kinetic theory.** See *theory, kinetic.*

**Kirchhoff's first law.** See *law, Kirchhoff's first.*

**Kirchhoff's second law.** See *law, Kirchhoff's second.*

**laser.** An acronym for light amplification by stimulated emission of radiation.

**law.** A statement that describes a natural phenomenon; a principle.

**law, Boyle's.** The volume of a dry gas varies inversely with the pressure exerted upon it, provided the temperature is constant.

**law, Charles'.** The volume of a dry gas is directly proportional to its Kelvin temperature, providing the pressure is constant.

**law, Faraday's first.** The mass of an element deposited during electrolysis is proportional to the quantity of charge that passes through the electrolytic cell.

**law, Faraday's second.** The mass of an element deposited during electrolysis is proportional to the chemical equivalent of the element.

**law, general gas.** Equation that combines Boyle's and Charles' laws.

**law, Hooke's.** Within the limits of perfect elasticity, strain is directly proportional to stress.

**law, Joule's.** The heat developed in a conductor is directly proportional to the resistance of the conductor, the square of the current, and the time the current is maintained.

**law, Kirchhoff's first.** The algebraic sum of the currents at any circuit junction is equal to zero.

**law, Kirchhoff's second.** The algebraic sum

of all the changes in potential occurring around any loop in a circuit equals zero.

**law, Lenz's.** An induced current is in such direction that its magnetic property opposes the change by which the current is induced.

**law, Ohm's.** The ratio of the emf applied to a closed circuit to the current in the circuit is a constant.

**law of conservation of baryons.** See *conservation of baryons, law of.*

**law of conservation of energy.** See *conservation of energy, law of.*

**law of conservation of hypercharge.** See *conservation of hypercharge, law of.*

**law of conservation of leptons.** See *conservation of leptons, law of.*

**law of conservation of mechanical energy.** See *conservation of mechanical energy, law of.*

**law of conservation of momentum.** See *conservation of momentum, law of.*

**law of electrostatics, Coulomb's.** See *electrostatics, Coulomb's law of.*

**law of electrostatics, basic.** See *electrostatics, basic law of.*

**law of entropy.** See *entropy, law of.*

**law of heat exchange.** See *heat exchange, law of.*

**law for magnetism, Coulomb's.** See *Coulomb's law for magnetism.*

**law of universal gravitation, Newton's.** See *universal gravitation, Newton's law of.*

**laws of motion, Newton's.** See *motion, Newton's first, second, third laws of.*

**laws of photoelectric emission.** See *photoelectric emission, first, second, third laws of.*

**laws of thermodynamics.** See *thermodynamics, first, second laws of.*

**lepton.** A subatomic particle with a small rest mass, e.g., the electron.

**light, infrared.** Electromagnetic waves longer than visible light but shorter than radio waves.

**light, monochromatic.** Light consisting of only one color.

**light, polarized.** Light with vibrations in a single plane perpendicular to the ray.

**light, polychromatic.** Light composed of several colors.

**light, ultraviolet.** Electromagnetic radiations of shorter wavelength than visible light but longer than X rays.

**line of flux.** A line so drawn that a tangent to it at any point indicates the direction of the magnetic field.

**line of force.** A line so drawn that a tangent to it at any point indicates the direction of the electric field.

**line spectrum.** A spectrum consisting of monochromatic slit images having wavelengths characteristic of the atoms present in the source.

**linear accelerator.** A device for accelerating particles in a straight line through many stages of small potential difference.

**longitudinal wave.** A wave in which the vibrations are parallel to the direction of propagation of the wave.

**loop.** A midpoint of a vibrating segment of a standing wave.

**loudness.** The sensation that depends principally on the intensity of sound waves reaching the ear.

**lumen.** The unit of luminous flux; the luminous flux on a unit surface all points of which are at unit distance from a point source of one candle.

**luminous.** Visible because of the light emitted by its oscillating particles.

**luminous flux.** The part of the total energy radiated per unit of time from a luminous source that is capable of producing the sensation of sight.

**machine.** A device that multiplies force at the expense of distance or that multiplies distance at the expense of force.

**magnetic field.** A region in which a magnetic force can be detected.

**magnetic flux.** Lines of flux through a region of a magnetic field, considered collectively.

**magnetic flux density.** The magnetic flux through a unit area normal to the magnetic field.

**magnetic force.** See *force, magnetic.*

**magnetosphere.** A region of the upper atmosphere in which the motion of charged particles is governed primarily by the magnetic field of the earth.

**magnification.** The ratio of the image distance to the object distance; the ratio of the image size to the object size.

**malleability.** The property of a metal that enables it to be hammered or rolled into sheets.

**mass.** A measure of the quantity of matter; a fundamental physical quantity.

**mass, relativistic.** The mass of an object in motion with respect to the observer.

**mass, rest.** The mass of an object at rest with respect to the observer.

**mass defect, nuclear.** The arithmetic difference between the mass of a nucleus and the larger sum of its uncombined constituent particles.

**mass density.** Mass per unit volume of a substance.

**mass number.** (1) The sum of the number of protons and neutrons in the nucleus of an atom. (2) The integer nearest to the atomic mass.

**mass spectrograph.** Instrument used to determine the mass of ionized particles.

**mass unit, atomic.** See *atomic mass unit.*

**matter.** Anything that has the properties of mass and inertia.

**mechanical equivalent of heat.** See *heat, mechanical equivalent of.*

**mechanical wave.** A wave that originates in the displacement of a portion of an elastic medium from its normal position, causing it to oscillate about an equilibrium position.

**medium.** Any region through which a wave disturbance propagates. Mechanical waves require a matter medium. Electromagnetic waves propagate through a vacuum and various matter media.

**melting point.** The temperature at which a solid changes to a liquid.

**meniscus.** The crescent-shaped surface of a liquid column.

**meson.** A subatomic particle with a rest mass intermediate between that of a lepton and a baryon; the carrier of the strong interaction.

**meter.** A unit of length in the metric system: equivalent to 1,650,763.73 wavelengths of the orange-red light emitted by krypton-86.

**micron.** A metric unit of length; $10^{-6}$ meter.

**moderator.** A material that slows neutrons.

**mole.** Amount of substance containing the Avogadro number of particles such as atoms, molecules, ions, electrons, etc.

**molecule.** The smallest particle of an element or compound capable of stable independent existence.

**momentum.** The product of the mass and velocity of a moving body.

**momentum, angular.** The product of the rotational inertia of a body and its angular velocity.

**monochromatic light.** See *light, monochromatic.*

**motion, circular.** Motion of a body along a circular path.

**motion, curvilinear.** Motion of a body along a curved path.

**motion, Newton's first law of.** If there is no net force acting on a body, it will continue in its state of rest, or will continue moving along a straight line with uniform speed.

**motion, Newton's second law of.** The acceleration of a body is directly proportional to the net force exerted on the body, is inversely proportional to the mass of the body, and is in the same direction as the force.

**motion, Newton's third law of.** Whenever one body exerts a force on another, the second body exerts on the first a force of equal magnitude in the opposite direction.

**motion, periodic.** Motion repeated in each of a succession of equal time intervals.

**motion, rotary.** Motion of a body about an axis.

**motion, simple harmonic.** Motion in which the force exerted on the particle and the resulting acceleration are directly proportional to the displacement from the equilibrium position and in which the force and acceleration are directed toward the equilibrium position.

**mutual inductance.** See *inductance, mutual.*

**neutral weak current.** A subatomic reaction in which leptons collide without a change in the charges of the colliding particles.

**neutron.** A neutral subatomic particle having a mass of $1.674943 \times 10^{-27}$ kg.

**newton.** The unit of force in the MKS system; the force required to accelerate one kilogram of mass at the rate of one meter per second each second.

**Newton's law of universal gravitation.** See *universal gravitation, Newton's law of.*

**Newton's laws of motion.** See *motion, Newton's first, second, third laws of.*

**node.** A point of no disturbance of a standing wave.

**noise.** Sound produced by irregular vibrations in matter which is unpleasant to the listener.

**noninertial frame of reference.** See *frame of reference, noninertial.*

**normal.** A line drawn perpendicular to a line or surface.

**N-type germanium.** "Electron-rich" germanium consisting of equal numbers of free electrons and bound positive charges so that the net charge is zero.

**nuclear binding force.** See *force, nuclear binding.*

**nuclear change.** A change in the identity of atomic nuclei.

**nuclear mass defect.** See *mass defect, nuclear.*

**nuclear reactor.** A device in which the controlled fission of certain substances is used to produce new substances and energy.

**nucleon.** A proton or neutron in the nucleus of an atom.

**nucleus.** The positively charged dense central part of an atom.

**nuclide.** An atom of a particular mass and of a particular element.

**octave.** The interval between a given musical tone and one with double or half the frequency.

**ohm.** The unit of electrical resistance in the MKS system, one volt per ampere.

**Ohm's law.** See *law, Ohm's.*

**optical center.** The point in a thin lens through which the secondary axes pass.

**optical density.** A property of a transparent material that is a measure of the speed of light through it.

**orbital.** The probability pattern of position of an electron about the nucleus of an atom.

**order of magnitude.** A numerical approximation to the nearest power of ten.

**ordinate.** The value corresponding to the vertical distance of a point on a graph from the X axis. The Y coordinate.

**oscilloscope.** A cathode-ray tube with associated electronic circuits that enable external voltages to deflect the electron beam of the cathode-ray tube simultaneously along both horizontal and vertical axes.

**parallel circuit.** An electric circuit in which two or more components are connected across two common points in the circuit so as to provide separate conducting paths for the current.

**paramagnetism.** The property of a substance by which it is feebly attracted by a strong magnet.

**parity, principle of.** The principle that for every process in nature there is a mirror-image process which is indistinguishable from the original process.

**pendulum.** A body suspended so that it can swing back and forth about an axis.

**penumbra.** The partially illuminated part of a shadow.

**period.** (1) The time for one complete cycle, vibration, revolution, or oscillation. (2) The time required for a single wavelength to pass a given point.

**periodic motion.** See *motion, periodic.*

**permeability.** The property of a material by which it changes the flux density in a magnetic field from the value in air.

**phase.** (1) A condition of matter. (2) In any periodic phenomenon, a number that describes a specific stage within each oscillation. (3) The angular relationship between current and voltage in an a-c circuit. (4) The number of separate voltage waves in a commercial a-c supply.

**phase angle.** (1) Of any periodic function, the angle obtained by multiplying the phase by 360 if the angle is to be expressed in degrees, or by $2\pi$ if in radians. (2) The angle between the voltage and current vectors.

**phasor.** A representation of the concepts of magnitude and direction in a reference plane; a rotating vector.

**photoelastic.** Pertaining to certain materials that become double refracting when strained.

**photoelectric effect.** The emission of electrons by a substance when illuminated by electromagnetic radiation of sufficiently short wavelength.

**photoelectric effect, inverse.** The emission of photons of radiation due to the bombardment of a material with high-speed electrons.

**photoelectric emission, first law of.** The rate of emission of photoelectrons is directly proportional to the intensity of the incident light.

**photoelectric emission, second law of.** The kinetic energy of photoelectrons is independent of the intensity of the incident light.

**photoelectric emission, third law of.** Within the region of effective frequencies, the maximum kinetic energy of photoelectrons varies directly with the difference between the frequency of the incident light and the cut-off frequency.

**photoelectrons.** Electrons emitted from a light-sensitive material when it is illuminated with light of sufficiently short wavelength.

**photometer.** An instrument used for comparing the intensity of a light source with that of a standard source.

**photometry.** The quantitative measurement of visible radiation from light sources.

**photon.** A quantum of light energy; the carrier of the electromagnetic interaction.

**photovoltaic effect.** The generation of a potential difference across a P-N junction as a consequence of the absorption of incident light of appropriate frequency.

**physical change.** A change in which the composition and identifying properties of a substance remain unchanged.

**piezoelectric effect.** The property of certain natural and synthetic crystals to develop a potential difference between opposite surfaces when subjected to a mechanical stress, and conversely.

**pitch.** The identification of a certain sound with a definite tone; depends on the frequency which the ear receives.

**pivot point.** The point from which the lengths of all torque arms are measured.

**Planck's constant.** A fundamental constant in nature that determines what values are allowed for physical quantities in quantum mechanics; $h = 6.63 \times 10^{-34}$ J s.

**plate.** The anode of an electronic tube.

**P-N junction.** The boundary between P- and N-type materials in a semiconductor crystal.

**polarized light.** See *light, polarized.*

**polarizing angle.** A particular angle of incidence at which polarization of reflected light is complete.

**polychromatic light.** See *light, polychromatic.*

**positive rays.** Rays coming through holes in a cathode on the side opposite the anode in a discharge tube. Positively charged ions.

**potential difference.** The work done per unit charge as a charge is moved between two points in an electric field.

**potential energy.** See *energy, potential.*

**potential gradient.** The change in potential per unit distance.

**power.** The time rate of doing work.

**power, apparent.** The product of the effective values of alternating voltage and current.

**power factor.** The cosine of the phase angle between current and voltage in an a-c circuit.

**precession.** The motion that results from the application of a torque that tends to displace the axis of rotation of a rotating object.

**precision.** Agreement among several measurements made in the same way, expressed in terms of deviation.

**pressure.** Force per unit area.

**pressure, critical.** The pressure needed to liquefy a gas at its critical temperature.

**pressure, equilibrium vapor.** The pressure exerted by vapor molecules in equilibrium with liquid.

**pressure, standard.** The pressure exerted by exactly 760 mm of mercury at 0°C under standard gravitational acceleration $g$.

**primary.** A transformer winding that carries current and normally induces a current in one or more secondary windings.

**primary cell.** An electrochemical cell in which the reacting materials must be replaced after a given amount of energy has been supplied to the external circuit.

**primary colors.** Colors in terms of which all other colors may be described or from which all other colors may be evolved by mixtures.

**primary pigments.** The complements of the primary colors.

**principal axis.** (1) A line drawn through the center of curvature and the vertex of a curved mirror. (2) A line drawn through the center of curvature and the optical center of a lens.

**principal focus.** See *focus, principal.*

**principle.** See *law.*

**principle of parity.** See *parity, principle of.*

**property.** A measurable aspect of matter, e.g., mass and inertia.

**proton.** A positively charged subatomic particle, having a mass of $1.6726485 \times 10^{-27}$ kg and a charge equal and opposite to that of the electron.

**P-type germanium.** "Hole-rich" germanium consisting of equal numbers of free positive holes and bound negative charges so that the net charge is zero.

**pulse.** A single nonrepeated disturbance.

**quality.** The property of sound waves that depends on the number of harmonics and their prominence.

**quantum.** An elemental unit of energy; a photon of energy $hf$.

**quantum mechanics.** The branch of physics that deals with the behavior of particles whose specific properties are given by quantum numbers.

**quantum number.** One of a set of notations used to characterize a discrete value that a quantized variable is allowed to assume.

**quantum theory.** See *theory, quantum.*

**quark.** A hypothetical subatomic particle of which all other subatomic particles are composed.

**quiescent.** A steady-state condition. The operating condition of an electronic circuit when no input signal is applied.

**rad.** A unit of measurement of absorption of radiation; the absorption of 0.01 joule of radioactive energy per kilogram of absorbing matter.

**radian.** A unit of angular measurement; the angle that, when placed with its vertex at the center of a circle, subtends on the circumference an arc equal in length to the radius of the circle; 57.3° approximately.

**radio waves.** Also called Hertzian waves. Electromagnetic radiations produced by rapid reverses of current in a conductor.

**radioactivity.** The spontaneous breakdown of an atomic nucleus with the emission of particles and rays.

**radioisotope.** An isotope of an element that is radioactive.

**rarefaction.** The region of a longitudinal wave in which the vibrating particles are farther apart than their equilibrium distance.

**ray, light.** A directed line showing the direction of propagation of light.

**ray, gamma ($\gamma$).** High-energy photon emitted from the nucleus of a radioactive atom.

**reactance.** The nonresistive opposition to current in an a-c circuit.

**reactance, capacitive.** Reactance in an a-c circuit due to capacitance that produces a lagging voltage.

**reactance, inductive.** Reactance in an a-c circuit due to inductance that produces a lagging current.

**reaction motor.** A heat engine whose acceleration is produced by the thrust of exhaust gases.

**real image.** See *image, real.*

**rectifier.** A device for changing alternating current to direct current.

**rectilinear propagation.** Traveling in a straight line.

**reflectance.** The ratio of the light reflected from a surface to the light falling on it, expressed in percentage.

**reflection.** The return of a wave from the boundary of a medium.

**reflection, angle of.** The angle between the reflected ray and the normal drawn to the point of incidence.

**reflection, irregular.** Scattering. Reflection in many different directions from an irregular surface.

**reflection, regular.** Reflection from a polished surface in which scattering effects are negligible.

**reflection, total.** The reflection of light at the boundary of two transparent media when the angle of incidence exceeds the critical angle.

**refraction.** The bending of a wave disturbance as it passes obliquely from one medium into another in which the disturbance has a different velocity.

**refraction, angle of.** The angle between the refracted ray and the normal drawn to the point of refraction.

**refraction, double.** The separation of a beam of unpolarized light into two refracted plane-polarized beams by certain crystals such as quartz and calcite.

**refraction, index of.** The ratio of the speed of light in a vacuum to its speed in a given substance.

**regelation.** The melting of a substance under pressure and the refreezing after the pressure is released.

**relative deviation.** See *deviation, relative.*

**relative error.** See *error, relative.*

**relative humidity.** The ratio of the water vapor pressure in the atmosphere to the equilibrium vapor pressure at a given temperature.

**rem.** A unit of measurement of occupational exposure to radiation (radiation equivalent man); the equivalent of one rad or one roentgen.

**residual magnetism.** Magnetism retained in magnet after the magnetizing field has been removed.

**resistance.** The ratio of the potential difference across a conductor to the magnitude of current in it.

**resistivity.** A proportionality constant that relates the length and cross-sectional area of a given electric conductor to its resistance, at a given temperature.

**resolution of forces.** The resolving of a single force into component forces acting in given directons on the same point.

**resonance.** (1) The inducing of vibrations of a natural rate by a vibrating source having the same frequency. (2) The condition in an a-c circuit in which the inductive reactance and capacitive reactance are equal.

**resonance, series.** A condition in which the impedance of a series circuit containing resistance, inductance, and capacitance is equal to the resistance of the circuit, and the voltage across the circuit is in phase with the current.

**resultant.** A vector representing the geometric sum of several components.

**resultant force.** See *force, resultant.*

**reverse bias.** Voltage applied to a semiconductor P-N junction that reduces the electron current across the junction.

**rheostat.** A variable resistance.

**roentgen.** A unit of measurement of exposure to radioactivity; the amount of gamma radiation that will produce $1.61 \times 10^{12}$ pairs of ions when absorbed in one gram of air.

**root-mean-square (rms) current.** The effective value of an alternating current; the square root of the mean of the instantaneous values squared.

**rotary motion.** See *motion, rotary.*

**rotational equilibrium.** See *equilibrium, rotational*.

**rotational inertia.** See *inertia, rotational*.

**scalar quantity.** A quantity that is completely specified by a magnitude.

**scientific notation.** A positive number expressed in the form of $M \times 10^n$ in which M is a number between 1 and 10 and n is an integral power of 10.

**scintillation counter.** A device that counts the impacts of charged subatomic particles on a fluorescent screen by means of a photomultiplier tube.

**second.** A unit of time; equivalent to 9,192,631,770 vibrations of cesium-133.

**secondary.** A transformer output winding in which the current is due to inductive coupling with another winding called the primary.

**secondary axis.** Any line other than the principal axis drawn through the center of curvature of a mirror or the optical center of a lens.

**secondary emission.** Emission of electrons as a result of the bombardment of an electrode by high-velocity electrons.

**selectivity.** The property of a tuned circuit that discriminates between signal voltages of different frequencies.

**self-inductance.** See *inductance, self*.

**series circuit.** An electric circuit in which the components are arranged to provide a single conducting path for current.

**series resonance.** See *resonance, series*.

**short circuit.** An electric circuit through a negligible resistance that usually shunts a normal load and overloads the circuit.

**significant figures.** Those digits in a number that are known with certainty plus the first digit that is uncertain.

**simple harmonic motion.** See *motion, simple harmonic*.

**solar spectrum.** The band of colors produced when sunlight is dispersed by a prism.

**solenoid.** A long helically wound coil of insulated wire.

**solid state detector.** A device used to detect the passage of charged subatomic particles by their crystal-distorting or ionizing effects on a nonconducting or semiconducting solid.

**solidification.** The change of phase from a liquid to a solid.

**sonometer.** A device, consisting of two or more wires or strings stretched over a sounding board, used for testing the frequency of strings and for showing how they vibrate.

**sound.** The series of disturbances in matter to which the human ear is sensitive. Also similar disturbances in matter above and below the normal range of human hearing.

**space charge.** The negative charge in the interelectrode space between the cathode and plate of a vacuum tube.

**spark chamber.** A device used to detect the passage of charged subatomic particles by the light flashes they trigger.

**specific heat.** See *heat, specific*.

**spectroscope.** Optical instrument used for the study of spectra.

**speed.** Time rate of motion.

**spherical aberration.** The failure of parallel rays to meet at a single point after reflection or refraction on a spherical surface.

**spinthariscope.** A device used to detect subatomic particles by the light flashes they produce on a zinc sulfide screen.

**standard pressure.** See *pressure, standard*.

**standard temperature.** See *temperature, standard*.

**standard unit.** See *unit, standard*.

**standing wave.** The resultant of two wave trains of the same wavelength, frequency, and amplitude traveling in opposite directions through the same medium.

**static electricity.** Electricity at rest.

**steam point.** The boiling point of water at standard atmospheric pressure.

**steradian.** The ratio of the intercepted surface area of a sphere to the square of the radius. A unit of solid angle.

**storage cell.** An electrochemical cell in which the reacting materials are renewed by the use of a reverse current from an external source.

**storage ring, intersecting.** An accelerator in which particles collide as they move in opposite directions.

**strain.** The relative amount of distortion produced in a body under stress.

**stress.** The distorting force per unit area.

**strong interaction.** See *interaction, strong.*

**sublimation.** The change of a solid to a gaseous phase followed by condensation to the solid phase, without passing through the liquid phase.

**superconductivity.** The condition of zero resistivity below the transition temperature of a substance.

**supercooling.** The process of cooling a substance below its normal phase-change point without a change of phase.

**superposition.** Combining the displacements of two or more waves vectorially to produce a resultant displacement.

**surface tension.** The tendency of a liquid surface to contract; the measure of this tendency in newtons per meter.

**sympathetic vibration.** See *resonance.*

**synchrotron.** A particle accelerator in which the oscillating frequency varies.

**temperature.** The physical quantity that is proportional to the average kinetic energy of translation of particles in matter.

**temperature, critical.** The temperature to which a gas must be cooled before it can be liquefied by pressure.

**temperature, standard.** $0°C$; $273.15°K$.

**temporary magnet.** A magnet produced by induction.

**tensile strength.** The force required to break a rod or wire of unit cross-sectional area.

**theory.** A plausible explanation for observed phenomena in terms of a simple model that has familiar properties.

**theory, kinetic.** A theory that the molecules of matter are in constant motion and that collisions between molecules are perfectly elastic.

**theory, quantum.** A unifying theory based on

the concept of the subdivision of radiant energy into discrete quanta (photons) and applied in the studies of structure at the atomic and molecular levels.

**thermal energy.** See *energy, thermal.*

**thermionic emission.** The liberation of electrons from the surface of a hot body.

**thermocouple.** An electric circuit composed of two dissimilar metals whose junctions are maintained at different temperatures.

**thermodynamics.** Study of quantitative relationships between heat and other forms of energy.

**thermodynamics, first law of.** When heat is converted to another form of energy or when other forms of energy are converted into heat, there is no loss of energy.

**thermodynamics, second law of.** It is impossible for an engine to transfer heat from one body to another at a higher temperature unless work is done on the engine.

**thermoelectric effect.** The production of an electron current in a closed circuit consisting of two dissimilar metals as a result of the emf developed when the two junctions are maintained at different temperatures.

**thermonuclear reaction.** Nuclear fusion.

**threshold of hearing.** The intensity of the faintest sound audible to the average human ear, $10^{-16}$ w/cm$^2$ at $10^3$ hz.

**threshold of pain.** For audible frequencies of sound, an intensity level above which pain results in the average human ear.

**tolerance.** Degree of precision obtainable with a measuring instrument.

**torque.** Product of a force and the effective length of its torque arm.

**torque arm.** The perpendicular distance between the line of action of the torque producing force and the axis of rotation.

**total reflection.** See *reflection, total.*

**transformer.** A device for changing an alternating voltage from one potential to another.

**transistor.** A semiconductor device used as a substitute for vacuum tubes in electronic applications.

**translational equilibrium.** See *equilibrium, translational.*

**transuranium elements.** Elements with atomic number greater than 92.

**transverse wave.** A wave in which the vibrations are at right angles to the direction of propagation of the wave.

**triode.** Vacuum tube consisting of a plate, grid, and cathode.

**triple point.** The single condition of temperature and pressure at which the solid, liquid, and vapor phases of a substance can coexist in stable equilibrium.

**trough.** A region of downward displacement in a transverse wave.

**tuning fork.** A metal two-prong fork that produces a sound of a definite pitch.

**ultrasonic range.** Vibrations in matter above 20,000 vibrations/second.

**ultraviolet light.** See *light, ultraviolet.*

**umbra.** The part of a shadow from which all light rays are excluded.

**uncertainty principle.** It is impossible to specify simultaneously both the position of an object and its momentum.

**unified field theory.** The principle that all forces in the universe are part of a single concept.

**unit, conceptual.** A standard of measurement based on a natural phenomenon.

**unit, standard.** An arbitrary standard of measurement.

**unit magnetic pole.** One that repels an exactly similar pole placed one centimeter away with a force of one dyne.

**universal gas constant.** See *gas constant, universal.*

**universal gravitation, Newton's law of.** The force of attraction between two objects is directly proportional to the product of their masses and inversely proportional to the square of the distance between their centers of mass.

**universal gravitational constant.** Constant of proportionality in Newton's law of universal gravitation; $G = 6.67 \times 10^{-11}$ nm²/kg².

**Van de Graaff generator.** A particle accelerator that transfers a charge from an electron source to an insulated sphere by means of a moving belt composed of an insulating material.

**vapor.** The gaseous phase of a substance that exists as a liquid or solid under normal conditions.

**vaporization.** The change in phase from a solid or a liquid to a gas.

**vaporization, heat of.** The heat required per unit mass to change a substance from liquid to vapor at its boiling point.

**variation.** See *declination.*

**vector quantity.** A quantity that is completely specified by a magnitude and a direction.

**velocity.** Speed in a particular direction.

**velocity, angular.** The time rate of angular displacement.

**velocity, average.** Total displacement divided by elapsed time.

**velocity, critical.** Velocity below which an object moving in a vertical circle will not describe a circular path.

**velocity, instantaneous.** Short displacement divided by elapsed time. Slope of the line that is tangent to a velocity graph at a given point.

**vertex.** The center of a curved mirror.

**vibration, complete.** Back and forth motion of an object describing simple harmonic motion.

**virtual image.** See *image, virtual.*

**volt.** The MKS unit of potential difference; the potential difference between two points in an electric field such that one joule of work moves a charge of one coulomb between these points.

**volt, electron.** The energy required to move an electron between two points that have a potential difference of one volt.

**voltage sensitivity.** Voltage per unit scale division of an electric instrument.

**voltaic cell.** A device that changes chemical into electric energy by the action of two dissimilar metals immersed in an electrolyte.

**voltmeter.** An instrument used to measure

the difference of potential between two points in an electric circuit.

**$W^{\pm}$ particle.** The theoretical carrier for weak subatomic interactions.

**watt.** The MKS unit of power; one joule per second.

**wavelength.** In a periodic wave, the distance between consecutive points of corresponding phase.

**weak interaction.** See *interaction, weak.*

**weber.** The unit of magnetic flux in the MKS system.

**weight.** The measure of the gravitational force acting on a substance.

**weight, atomic.** The weighted average of the atomic masses of isotopes based on their relative abundance.

**Wheatstone bridge.** Instrument used for the measurement of electric resistance.

**work.** The product of a displacement and the force in the direction of the displacement.

**work function.** The minimum energy required to remove an electron from the surface of a material and send it into field-free space.

**working equation.** See *equation, working.*

**X rays.** Invisible electromagnetic radiations of great penetrating power.

**Young's modulus.** (For a rod or wire.) The ratio of the tensile stress to the associated linear strain.

**Zeeman effect.** The splitting of atomic energy levels into two or more sublevels by means of a magnetic field as seen in spectral lines under these conditions.

# Index

# Picture Credits

p. xx   Photo Courtesy Department of Energy

*Chapter 1*   p.2 IBM; p.3(both) General Electric Company; p.5 National Laboratory, Oak Ridge, Tennessee; p.7 National Bureau of Standards; p.8(both) Alex Mulligan; p.9(both) Sargent-Welch Scientific Company; p.12 John G. Zimmerman; p.13 Deutsches Museum, Munich; p.14 Wide World

*Photo Essay: ENERGY*   p.18(t) Vermont Castings, Inc., (b,l) Gulf Oil Corporation, photo courtesy Lois M. Weissflog, (b,r) American Petroleum Institute; p.19(t,l) Bruce Roberts/Photo Researchers, (t,r) Davis-Gilette/Photo Researchers, (b,l) Richard Dibon-Smith/Photo Researchers, (b,r) Sandia Laboratories; p.20(t,l&b,r) UPI, (m,l) Tom McHugh/Photo Researchers, (m,r) Lockheed Missiles & Space Co., Inc., photo courtesy Department of Energy, (b,l) Hempstead Resources Recovery Corporation; p.21(l) Pacific Gas & Electric Company, (r) Georg Gerster/Photo Researchers

*Chapter 2*   p.22(l) Ken Chen, (r) Metric Commission, Canada, (b) Cincinnati Reds, Inc.; p.24 National Bureau of Standards; p.25 Dr. Harold E. Edgerton, Massachusetts Institute of Technology; p.26 Alex Mulligan; p.27 Cenco; p.30 Mount Wilson and Palomar Observatories

*Chapter 3*   pp.40&48 *Project Physics,* HRW; p.49 The Bettmann Archive; p.53 Dave Waterman/ Woodfin Camp; p.55 The New York Public Library; p.56(both) Loomis Dean, *Life* magazine © 1954 Time Inc.; pp.63&66 NASA

*Chapter 4*   p.68 Bucyrus-Erie Company; p.80 Austrian Press and Information Service

*Chapter 5*   p.90 *PSSC Physics,* D. C. Heath and Company; p.95 Department of the Navy

*Chapter 6*   p.115 The New York Public Library; p.124 Dr. Harold E. Edgerton, Massachusetts Institute of Technology; p.125 Ken Chen; p.126 The Ealing Corporation; p.129(both) Henry Hirschfeld; p.131 *PSSC Physics,* D. C. Heath and Company

*Photo Essay: CAREERS*   p.132(t) IBM, (b) UPI; p.133(t) Lawrence Livermore Laboratory, photo courtesy Department of Energy, (m) Bruce Roberts /Photo Researchers, (b,l) Betty Medsger, (b,c) Brookhaven National Laboratory, (b,r) Argonne National Laboratory, photo courtesy Department of Energy; p.134(t&b,l) NASA, (b,r) Betty Medsger; p.135(l) Lawrence Livermore Laboratory, photo courtesy Department of Energy, (r) Fermi National Accelerator Laboratory

*Chapter 7*   p.138 M. Isaacson, M. Utlaut, M. Ohtsuki, A. Crewe, The University of Chicago; p.141 United States Steel Corporation; pp.147& 148 Ken Chen; p.149 Steve Koch; p.151 John King; p.152 Dick Saunders, *Ebony Magazine;* p.157 M. Woodbridge Williams, National Park Service

*Chapter 8*   p.161 National Bureau of Standards; p.167 Alex Mulligan; p.189 Carrier Corporation

*Chapter 9*   p.192 The Bettmann Archive; p.196 General Electric Company; p.201 The Granger Collection

*Chapter 10*   p.206 Verna R. Johnston/ Photo Researchers; p.213 Jack Zehrt/ FPG; p.215 Fundamental Photographs from The Granger Collection; p.216(l) *PSSC Physics,* D. C. Heath and Company, (r) Education Development Center; p.217 *PSSC Physics,* D. C. Heath and Company; p.218(t) Education Development Center, (b) *PSSC Physics,* D. C. Heath and Company; p.221(both) *PSSC Physics,* D.C. Heath and Company; p.223(all) Fundamental Photographs from The Granger Collection; p.226 Education Development Center

*Chapter 11*   p.231 *College Physics,* HRW; p.234 Bell Telephone Laboratories; p.242 Education Devel-

The cover design of MODERN PHYSICS 1980 is a photograph of an experimental magnetic bubble lattice device. The storage area of this fully operational microcircuit chip appears as a parallelogram. The area contains 1024 information-bearing bubbles arranged in a lattice. The 5-micrometer diameter bubbles store information at a density of over 800,000 bits per cm². Information is represented by controllable differences in the magnetic structure of the bubble walls. Gold conductors that serve as an access channel for feeding individual bubbles into and out of the array form a pattern across the parallelogram. Isolated bubbles are generated and encoded in the "write station," the rectangular area below the lattice. Information contained in the bubbles is detected in the "read station," the rectangle above the lattice.